HOW JOYCE WROTE
Finnegans Wake

Irish Studies in Literature and Culture

MICHAEL PATRICK GILLESPIE
Series Editor

HOW JOYCE WROTE *Finnegans Wake*

A Chapter-by-chapter Genetic Guide

Edited by

LUCA CRISPI and SAM SLOTE

THE UNIVERSITY OF WISCONSIN PRESS

The University of Wisconsin Press
1930 Monroe Street, 3rd floor
Madison, Wisconsin 53711-2059

www.wisc.edu/wisconsinpress/

3 Henrietta Street
London WC2E 8LU, England

5 4 3 2

Printed in the United States of America

Library of Congress Cataloging-in-Publication Data
How Joyce wrote Finnegans wake : a chapter-by-chapter genetic guide /
edited by Luca Crispi and Sam Slote.
p. cm.—(Irish studies in literature and culture)
Includes bibliographical references and index.
ISBN 0-299-21860-0 (cloth : alk. paper)
1. Joyce, James, 1882–1941. Finnegans wake—Criticism, Textual.
I. Crispi, Luca. II. Slote, Sam. III. Series.
PR6019.09F59353 2007
823′.912—dc22 2006008621

ISBN 0-299-21864-3 (pbk. : alk. paper)

Contents

Preface

MICHAEL GRODEN

In one of the richest pages of *Ulysses* Stephen, on the sea shore, communing with himself and tentatively building with words, calls for his tablets. These should have been library slips, acquired by the impecunious and ingenious poet from the library counter. . . . [T]he portrait was still like, only in Zürich Joyce was never without them. And they were not library slips, but little writing blocks specially made for the waistcoat pocket. At intervals, alone or in conversation, seated or walking, one of these tablets was produced, and a word or two scribbled on it at lightning speed as ear or memory served his turn. No one knew how all this material was given place in the completed pattern of his work, but from time to time in Joyce's flat one caught glimpses of a few of those big orange-coloured envelopes that are one of the glories of Switzerland, and these I always took to be storehouses of building material. The method of making a multitude of criss-cross notes in pencil was a strange one for a man whose sight was never good. A necessary adjunct to the method was a huge oblong magnifying glass.

—FRANK BUDGEN, *James Joyce and the Making of "Ulysses"*

every person, place and thing in the chaosmos of Alle anyway connected with the gobblydumped turkery was moving and changing every part of the time: the travelling inkhorn (possibly pot), the hare and turtle pen and paper, the continually more and less intermisunderstanding minds of the anticollaborators, the as time went on as it will variously inflected, differently pronounced, otherwise spelled, changeably meaning vocable scriptsigns. No, so holp me Petault, it is not a miseffectual whyacinthinous riot of blots and blurs and bars and balls and hoops and wriggles and juxtaposed jottings linked by spurts of speed: it only looks as like it as damn it; [. . .] and look at this prepronominal *funferal*, engraved and retouched and edgewiped and puddenpadded, very like a whale's egg farced with pemmican, as were it sentenced to be nuzzled over a full trillion times for ever and a night till his noddle sink or swim by that ideal reader suffering from an ideal insomnia: all those red raddled obeli cayennepeppercast over the text, calling unnecessary attention to errors, omissions, repetitions and misalignments.

—*Finnegans Wake*, 118.21–31, 120.09–16

To a certain kind of critic "genetic criticism" is a misprint for "generic criticism." To some practitioners of French *critique génétique* it is a critical movement that began in Paris in the 1970s. But genetic criticism (properly so dubbed)—an investigation of the processes through which a work came into being—has been an active part of Joyce studies for over fifty years now. With *critique génétique* providing a solid theoretical foundation and also becoming more widely known to English-reading critics and scholars, genetic criticism is flourishing in a new wave. It offers an increasingly sophisticated and fascinating way of looking at Joyce's works, especially *Ulysses* and *Finnegans Wake.*[1]

Genetic studies start with Joyce himself. He presented versions of the artist at work and of the text's multivalent manuscripts in both *Ulysses* and *Finnegans Wake,* and with his envelopes of notes for *Ulysses* he inspired Frank Budgen to introduce readers to Joyce's writing processes, even if briefly, in a book from the same year that *Ulysses* itself was first legally published in the United States. Partly because the manuscripts quickly became available, partly because any approach to works as bewildering as *Ulysses* and *Finnegans Wake* seemed worth pursuing, the manuscript materials provide the basis for some of the earliest lasting scholarship on Joyce. By the late 1970s many aspects of Joyce's once totally mysterious writing methods had been clarified to a large extent, and Hans Walter Gabler's genetically based edition of *Ulysses* in 1984 in many ways culminated the first era of Joycean genetic scholarship.[2]

In *"Ulysses" in Progress* I argued that reading Joyce's book through its prepublication materials is an important and valuable approach because Joyce "retained the results of each stage he passed through, even after he had progressed into the next, so that he presented *Ulysses* as a palimpsest of his development from 1914 to 1922."[3] An episode such as "Aeolus" is especially fascinating in this light, since several early states of the text survive that lack the newspaper heads Joyce later added to the text, and a reader can extract an earlier state from the published version. In an episode that praises a journalist for communicating forbidden information about a Dublin murder to a New York newspaper by doing something like superimposing a map of Dublin onto a coffee ad, Joyce's decision to present *Ulysses* as a superimposition of later states of the text onto earlier ones gives thematic as well as archival relevance to materials that René Wellek and Austin Warren once described as "not, finally, necessary to an understanding of the finished work."[4]

These materials are, if anything, even more important for *Finnegans*

Wake. Containing explicit and lengthy accounts of writing processes and physical documents such as the one I've quoted as an epigraph, Joyce's last work was published in several early versions during its seventeen-year period of development, and its provisional title of "Work in Progress" signaled its state as a text that was "moving and changing every part of the time." Very soon after the book was published as *Finnegans Wake* Harriet Shaw Weaver gave the British Museum (now the British Library) a huge collection of drafts, manuscripts, typescripts, and proofs, and the Poetry Collection at the University at Buffalo, State University of New York, acquired an enormous collection of notebooks for the *Wake.* These documents inspired early studies and editions of documents by scholars such as Walton Litz, Fred Higginson, and (despite his book's flaws) Thomas Connolly as well as many of the articles and notes in *A Wake Newslitter,* and in 1963 David Hayman produced *A First-Draft Version of "Finnegans Wake,"* providing an alternate text of the work, a composite first draft stitched together from the earliest versions of each phrase and passage in the book. When, in the late 1970s, *The James Joyce Archive* included the British Library documents, along with manuscript materials from other libraries, in twenty of its volumes and the Buffalo notebooks in sixteen (printing two notebook pages per *Archive* page), the "blots and blurs and bars and balls and hoops and wriggles and juxtaposed jottings" became available for the scholarly public to see and study. In the post-*Archive* years the manuscript materials formed the bases for books such as David Hayman's *The "Wake" in Transit* and Danis Rose's *The Textual Diaries of James Joyce* and articles in the journal *A "Finnegans Wake" Circular* and the essay collections *Probes: Genetic Studies in Joyce* and *Genitricksling Joyce.* The ongoing *"Finnegans Wake" Notebooks at Buffalo* project presents reproductions of the notebooks along with transcriptions and identifications of the sources and Joyce's uses of the notes in subsequent drafts of *Work in Progress,* and, by the time the project is completed, scholars will have much more convenient and usable versions of the notes to work with than Joyce's undigested and notoriously difficult-to-read handwritten pages.

"Now, patience; and remember patience is the great thing, and above all things else we must avoid anything like being or becoming out of patience," Joyce wrote in the *Wake* (FW: 108.08–10). Every scholar who approaches Joyce's or any other writer's manuscripts knows the pertinence of this advice. It takes time and endurance to read and decipher the manuscripts, to work out the relationships among them and to identify sources, to determine what critical approach(es) or theoretical model(s) might be appropriate, and maybe to reach some conclusions. The goal might be to show how the published text came into being or to demonstrate how the earlier documents can illuminate the published text, or it might be more a matter of studying the writing process in itself. There are many kinds of genetic criticism. Louis Hay has written that "it is high time we learned to make [manuscripts] speak," and, as scholars have learned and the contributors to this collection will show, manuscripts invited to speak have many different things to say.[5]

Other books on *Finnegans Wake* have offered chapter-by-chapter analysis, and one—the *Conceptual Guide to "Finnegans Wake"* from 1974—presented an essay by a different critic on each chapter. Now is an especially appropriate time for a new generation of *Wake* scholars to provide a chapter-by-chapter guide, and, as the essays that follow will demonstrate, approaching the chapters from different genetic perspectives is particularly rewarding. Louis Hay describes the process of writing as "always virtually present in the background, a kind of third dimension of the written work," and the editors of a special of issue of *Yale French Studies* claim that "genetic criticism attempts to reinscribe the work in the series of its variations, in the space of its possibilities."[6] These essays will show just how varied is the space of *Finnegans Wake*'s possibilities and how much can be gained by recognizing and investigating its third dimension.

Notes

1. For more on *critique génétique* see the translated essays in Jed Deppman, Daniel Ferrer, and Michael Groden, eds., *Genetic Criticism: Texts and Avant-Textes* (Philadelphia: University of Pennsylvania Press, 2004).

2. Among many other smaller and more specialized studies, this first wave of genetic work on *Ulysses* includes A. Walton Litz, *The Art of James Joyce* (New York: Oxford University Press, 1961); Joseph Prescott, *Exploring James Joyce* (Carbondale: Southern Illinois University Press, 1964); James Van Dyck Card, *An Anatomy of "Penelope"* (Rutherford: Fairleigh Dickinson University Press, 1984); Phillip F. Herring, ed., *Joyce's "Ulysses" Notesheets in the British Museum* (Charlottesville: University Press of Virginia, 1972) and *Joyce's Notes and Early Drafts for "Ulysses": Selections from the Buffalo Collection* (Charlottesville: University Press of Virginia, 1977); Michael Groden, *"Ulysses" in Progress* (Princeton: Princeton University Press, 1977); and Rodney Wilson Owen, *James Joyce and the Beginnings of "Ulysses"* (Ann Arbor: UMI Research Press, 1983). It was facilitated by John J. Slocum and Herbert Cahoon, comps., *A Bibliography of James Joyce: 1882–1941* (New Haven: Yale University Press, 1953); Robert E. Scholes, comp., *The Cornell*

Joyce Collection: A Catalogue (Ithaca: Cornell University Press, 1961); and Peter Spielberg, comp., *James Joyce's Manuscripts and Letters at the University of Buffalo: A Catalogue* (Buffalo: University of Buffalo, 1962). The work moved into a different realm when first the Rosenbach Manuscript appeared in facsimile (*Ulysses: A Facsimile of the Manuscript,* 3 vols. [Philadelphia: Philip H. and A. S. W. Rosenbach Foundation, 1975]) and then so did the other extant drafts, manuscripts, typescripts, and proofs in *The James Joyce Archive.*

3. Groden 1977, 23.

4. René Wellek and Austin Warren, *Theory of Literature,* 3rd ed. (New York: Harcourt, Brace and World, 1962), 91.

5. Louis Hay, "History or Genesis?" trans. Ingrid Wassenaar, *Drafts, Yale French Studies* 89, ed. Michel Contat, Denis Hollier, and Jacques Neefs (1996): 191–207, 207.

6. Louis Hay, "Does 'Text' Exist?" trans. Matthew Jocelyn and Hans Walter Gabler, *Studies in Bibliography* 41 (1988): 64–76, 75; Michel Contat, Denis Hollier, and Jacques Neefs, "Editors' Preface," trans. Alyson Waters, Contat, Hollier, and Neefs 1996, 1–5, 2.

Acknowledgments

We are grateful to the Estate of James Joyce for allowing us to reproduce text and, exceptionally, images from Joyce's œuvre. © the Estate of James Joyce.

We are also grateful to the British Library for allowing us to reproduce manuscripts from their collection.

We would like to express our gratitude to the Poetry Collection, University Libraries, University at Buffalo, for their initial support of this work while we were Joyce Scholars in Residence (Luca Crispi, 1996–2003; Sam Slote, 1999–2005).

We would like to thank Ronan Crowley for compiling the index to this volume.

Editions and Abbreviations

We have adopted the following editions of Joyce's works as our standards:

D	James Joyce, *"Dubliners": Text, Criticism, and Notes,* ed. Robert Scholes and A. Walton Litz (New York: Viking Press, 1969)
E	James Joyce, *Exiles* (Harmondsworth: Penguin, 1973)
FDV	James Joyce, *A First-Draft Version of "Finnegans Wake,"* ed. David Hayman (Austin: University of Texas Press, 1963)
FW	plus page and line number. James Joyce, *Finnegans Wake* (London: Faber and Faber, 1975)
GJ	James Joyce, *Giacomo Joyce,* ed. Richard Ellmann (New York: Viking Press, 1968; London: Faber and Faber, 1968)
JJA	plus volume and page number. *The James Joyce Archive,* ed. Michael Groden et al. (New York: Garland Publishing, 1978–79)
JJ/PL	*The James Joyce–Paul Léon Papers in the National Library of Ireland,* comp. Catherine Fahy (Dublin: National Library of Ireland, 1992)
JJ/SB	*James Joyce's Letters to Sylvia Beach,* ed. Melissa Banta and Oscar A. Silverman (Bloomington: Indiana University Press, 1987)

LI, LII, & LIII	James Joyce, *Letters of James Joyce,* vol. I, ed. Stuart Gilbert (New York: Viking Press, 1957; reissued with corrections, 1966), vols. II and III, ed. Richard Ellmann (New York: Viking Press, 1966)
P	James Joyce, *"A Portrait of the Artist as a Young Man": Text, Criticism, and Notes,* ed. Chester G. Anderson (New York: Viking Press, 1968)
PSW	James Joyce, *Poems and Shorter Writings,* ed. Richard Ellmann, A. Walton Litz, and John Whittier-Ferguson (London: Faber and Faber, 1991)
SH	James Joyce, *Stephen Hero,* ed. Theodore Spencer, John J. Slocum, and Herbert Cahoon (New York: New Directions, 1963)
SL	James Joyce, *Selected Letters of James Joyce,* ed. Richard Ellmann (New York: Viking Press, 1975)
U	plus episode and line number. James Joyce, *Ulysses,* ed. Hans Walter Gabler et al. (New York: Garland Publishing, 1984, 1986), in paperback by Garland, Random House, Bodley Head, and Penguin

We have adopted the following editions of Joyce criticism as our standards:

Buffalo VI.B.	plus notebook number. *The "Finnegans Wake" Notebooks at Buffalo,* ed. Vincent Deane, Daniel Ferrer, and Geert Lernout (Turnhout: Brepols, 2001–)
Geni	*Genitricksling Joyce,* ed. Sam Slote and Wim Van Mierlo (Amsterdam: Rodopi, 1999)
JJII	Richard Ellmann, *James Joyce,* rev. ed. (Oxford and New York: Oxford University Press, 1982)
McHugh	Roland McHugh, *Annotations to "Finnegans Wake,"* rev. ed. (Baltimore: Johns Hopkins University Press, 1991)
Probes	*Probes: Genetic Studies in Joyce,* ed. David Hayman and Sam Slote (Amsterdam: Rodopi, 1995)
TDJJ	Danis Rose, *The Textual Diaries of James Joyce* (Dublin: Lilliput, 1995)

UFW	Danis Rose and John O'Hanlon, *Understanding "Finnegans Wake"* (New York: Garland, 1982)
WiT	David Hayman, *The "Wake" in Transit* (Ithaca: Cornell University Press, 1990)

The following abbreviations are used for journals:

AFWC	*A "Finnegans Wake" Circular*
AWN	*A Wake Newslitter*
JJQ	*James Joyce Quarterly*
JSA	*Joyce Studies Annual*

Due to the focus of this present volume on genetic matters, the following conventions have been used:

Notebooks are cited by notebook number (as cataloged by the Poetry Collection, University at Buffalo, State University of New York) and page number. When available, references will also be given to *The "Finnegans Wake" Notebooks at Buffalo.*

In notebook transcriptions line breaks are indicated by a slash (/) and page breaks by a double slash (//).

Notebook cancellations are indicated by a superscript letter designating the color of the cancellation; a terminal superscript is used only if the cancellation ends within the range of the cited text. The color codes are bl = blue; bk = black; br = brown; g = green; o = orange; r = red; y = yellow. For example: "^{bl}this / is a notebook entry^{bl} / as is this." In this example the first two lines are crossed through in blue, and the third line is uncrossed.

Drafts and manuscripts are cited by their holding institution and catalog number:

BL	British Library
Buffalo	The Poetry Collection, University at Buffalo, State University of New York
Cornell	Department of Rare Books, Cornell University

NLI	National Library of Ireland
Princeton	Firestone Library, Princeton University
Stanford	Special Collections, Stanford University
Texas	Harry Ransom Humanities Research Center, University of Texas at Austin
Tulsa	Special Collections, McFarlin Library, University of Tulsa
Yale	Beinecke Rare Book and Manuscript Library, Yale University

They are also cited by both the volume and page number as they appear in *The James Joyce Archive* (JJA). When relevant, page references to *A First-Draft Version of "Finnegans Wake"* (FDV) and *Finnegans Wake* (FW) will also be given. For example: "BL 47477 f. 2; JJA 51: 6; FDV: 130; FW: 220.01."

Deletions on drafts are indicated as strike-throughs. For example: "This is ~~deleted~~."

Additions are within carets flanked by a superscript indicating the level of addition. Example: ^^{1}word^{1}^ indicates that "word" is a first-level addition; ^^{2}phrase^{2}^ indicates that "phrase" is a second-level addition.

Substitutions are indicated as deletion plus addition.

All editorial interpolations, including ellipses, into Joyce's works are enclosed in square brackets.

Instances of overwriting in a word will be designated as follows: <b^l^>etter. This means Joyce originally wrote "better," then replaced the b with an l to make "letter."

Wherever possible, transcriptions will be simplified to avoid unnecessary confusion. In these cases it will be indicated if the transcription is simplified.

Sigla

While writing *Finnegans Wake* Joyce developed a system of signs (traditionally referred to as "sigla") in his notebooks to designate the different characters of his work in progress. These will be discussed further in the introduction and in some of the essays. The following are the most common sigla:

ᗰ ∃ E Ш	HCE, in various manifestations
Δ	ALP
⊏	Shem
Λ	Shaun
/⊏	Shem and Shaun
⊣ ⊢ ⊥ I	Issy (or Isolde), in various manifestations
T	Tristan
X	Mamalujo (or the Four Masters)
≲	Snake
P	Patrick
K	Kevin or Kate
O	The Twelve
⬭	The Maggies (or Rainbow Girls)
□	The Book

The sigla font used in this book was designed by Sam Slote.

HOW JOYCE WROTE
Finnegans Wake

Introduction

LUCA CRISPI, SAM SLOTE, and DIRK VAN HULLE

Overview

Contrary to popular belief, the final words of *Finnegans Wake* are not "A way a lone a last a loved a long the"; instead they are "PARIS, / 1922–1939." This epigraph, a familiar formula to Joyce since *A Portrait,* testifies to the span of time he spent on his work. In order to read the *Wake* as a neat Vichian loop from "the" to "riverrun" one must "jump over" this witness to the text's composition. The goal of this volume is to show what might be gained from recognition of what is implied in this epigraph, that is, from reading *Finnegans Wake* in the context of its prepublication manuscripts. Since the final text of *Finnegans Wake* so self-consciously refers to its own production as a "Work in Progress," such an approach would have obvious benefits. The editors and the contributors believe that readings of *Finnegans Wake* can only benefit from a solid critical awareness of the archive of the *Wake*'s composition. It is with this belief that we set about assembling this volume as an introduction to *Finnegans Wake* from the perspective of its composition. This volume, thus, serves as an introduction to *Finnegans Wake* from the perspective of how it was written and as an introduction to genetic criticism in general.

A compelling argument for presenting such an approach now is that the manuscripts for *Finnegans Wake* are no longer a vast and daunting uncharted landscape. Over the last decade many—but hardly all—issues regarding the nature and interrelationship of Joyce's drafts and notes have been interrogated, thereby changing or modifying many earlier assumptions that still persist among Joyceans. Furthermore, a complete edition of

Joyce's *Wake* notebooks, annotated with sources and draft insertion data, edited by Vincent Deane, Daniel Ferrer, and Geert Lernout, is well under way. For the first time one can now approach the *Wake*'s manuscripts from a position of at least *some* certainty. Furthermore, the discovery of new *Wake* manuscripts in 2006 makes this a very lively time in genetic studies. We hope to present here the fruits of the past decade's consolidation of *Wakean* genetic studies in the hopes of stimulating and encouraging further work.

To be sure, there is no such thing as a consensus as to how genetic methodologies should be employed with *Finnegans Wake*. Indeed, the contributors to this volume do not necessarily share the same views about the purpose and practice of genetic criticism.[1] Another goal of this volume is to help arrive at an overall understanding of genetic criticism by providing examples of the different ways Joyce's manuscripts can be investigated. To this end, it seems propitious to divide the book into its constituent chapters, with each chapter being covered by an individual scholar who will explain that chapter from his or her own specific genetic perspective. Such an approach, convenient for an introductory volume, immediately presents a problem from a genetic overview, since *Finnegans Wake* was not written chapter by chapter, and so a straightforward synchronic approach to the *Wake*'s composition obscures, at least partially, some crucial facets of its evolution. But the editors believe that since no account of the *Wake*'s writing can be absolutely comprehensive, this compromise is acceptable in light of the possible merits our format allows. By presenting *Finnegans Wake* on the basis of how each chapter was written, we hope to produce a better-informed climate for understanding *Finnegans Wake* in general, and not just in the field of genetic criticism. To help contextualize the essays in this volume we will, in this introduction, provide a brief overview of the chronological composition of *Finnegans Wake,* a survey of the manuscripts, as well as a general introduction to genetic criticism. We should also note that two sets of chapters, I.2–4 and III.1–2, will be covered as groups in this volume and not individually, since they were both initially composed as units. Furthermore, in the interests of providing a suitable *ricorso,* this volume will end with a second essay on the first chapter of *Finnegans Wake,* thereby ending at the beginning again.

While we believe that a genetically informed approach to reading and understanding *Finnegans Wake* can be important, we realize that genetic criticism is not a privileged perspective for understanding Joyce's final work. In the first book-length genetic study of *Ulysses* and *Finnegans Wake, The Art of James Joyce,* A. Walton Litz wrote that, contrary to his initial expectations, his study of the manuscripts yielded no definitive key to unlock the *Wake.*[2] Genetic criticism may not provide the answers, but, rather, it should help make the questions more interesting, no matter what overall critical orientation one ultimately brings to bear on Joyce's "sindbook" (FW: 229.32).

LC & SS

A Compositional History of *Finnegans Wake*

Returning to the *Wake*'s epigraph of composition, the odd thing about the dates Joyce provides is that they appear to exaggerate the amount of time he spent writing *Finnegans Wake.* The inception date for the *Wake* is usually seen as being in early 1923. At the end of a letter to Harriet Shaw Weaver, dated 11 March 1923, Joyce writes, almost as an afterthought, "Yesterday I wrote two pages—the first I have written since the final *Yes* of *Ulysses*" (LI: 202). These pages are the first draft of the "Roderick O'Conor" sketch, which was only in 1938 incorporated as the conclusion to chapter 3 of Book II (FW: 380.07–382.30).[3]

Although Joyce may have begun writing drafts in 1923, he had not been completely idle in the months immediately after the publication of *Ulysses.* Almost immediately, he set to work on preparing a list of errata for *Ulysses.* On 3 November 1922, while he was staying in Nice, Joyce sent Weaver a list of corrections for *Ulysses* up to page 258, although he claimed that the list extended to page 290 (LI: 192).[4] The remaining corrections can be found in a small stenographer's notebook that also contains entries that were eventually used in the early drafts for *Finnegans Wake.* This notebook—designated VI.B.10—can be dated from late October 1922, while Joyce was in Nice, and is thus the earliest surviving record of *Finnegans Wake.*[5]

The first surviving page of VI.B.10 reads:

282 l 7 ff I dare him / and I doubledare him
284 l 8 freely⊂freckled
l 9 ruddyfaced,
285 l 5 Michelangelo,
286 l 5 Jude's √,[6]
288 l 7 say√s[7]
Polyphemous is Ul's shadow
[bl]clipper ship
dead horse
crimps

Una
Every W in I sh$^{\underline{d}}$ down tools
^{bl}ladies foursome tournament
face fungus golf
Royal beaver (baffi e barba) [Italian for "moustache and beard"]
^{bl}walrus
King Beaver redwhiskered / policeman on a / green bicycle (VI.B.10: 1; *Buffalo VI.B.10,* 18–20)[8]

The development of the notes on this page is striking. Joyce begins by sequentially recording corrections to the "Cyclops" episode of *Ulysses,* continuing the work he had sent to Weaver. After the sixth entry he abruptly changes track and writes the curious line "Polyphemous is Ul[ysses]'s shadow." Obviously, this line was prompted by the episode of *Ulysses* he was correcting, but it is hardly an emendation. It is as if he is taking a step back to think about an aspect of the text he had just written and its relationship with its Homeric background. This may well be an overstatement, but it seems that with this line Joyce has begun the process of leaving *Ulysses* behind. (There are several additional references to *Ulysses* in this notebook, but none of these are corrections.)

The remainder of the notes on this page are of a qualitatively different nature. They are taken from the 20 October 1922 edition of the *Irish Times* and combine words from various sections of that paper.[9] Instead of continuing his list of corrections for *Ulysses,* Joyce has begun to record words that strike his fancy, for whatever reason, for some later, as yet undetermined use. Most of the remaining pages in this notebook are filled with similar notes derived mostly from journals.[10]

A great deal of the *Wake's* verbiage derives from notes taken from a variety of sources (newspapers, books, overheard conversations, etc.). In some cases, especially with the later notebooks, Joyce took the notes for specific purposes, and in others he merely jotted down random words that were then subsequently used because they struck his fancy a second time, when he was going over his notebooks and preparing drafts. It appears that Joyce was amassing a heterogeneous stockpile of phrases in order to litter his work with all sorts of echoes of the world around him (of course, these echoes are almost impossible to identify without recourse to the notebooks). In this regard, Joyce really was "a scissors and paste man," as he admitted in 1931 to George Antheil (LI: 297).

There is a curious cluster of notes a few pages into VI.B.10:

Tristan— Binyon
Tennyson
Wagner
Michael Field
Swinburne
Arnold
Debussy
Gordon Bottomly
write it in love

O la musique
Avec les soldiques

Isolde of —Pen[elope]
Britt[any] Calyp[so]
— — white hands
(VI.B.10: 15; *Buffalo VI.B.10,* 31)

The first series of notes derives from a two-part article on modern versions of the Tristan and Isolde legend by Thomas Sturge Moore that was published in T. S. Eliot's *Criterion* (October 1922 and January 1923).[11] All the writers mentioned here had written versions of Tristan and Isolde, and all had, in Sturge Moore's opinion, failed miserably. Sturge Moore unfavorably compares these modern writers with Shakespeare, and he seems to constantly bemoan the fact that Shakespeare never took up the story of Tristan and Isolde.[12] On the one hand, Joyce may well have been amused by Sturge Moore's relentlessly unironic championing of this hypothetical Shakespearean Tristan and Isolde; on the other hand, perhaps Joyce decided that he would take up the challenge of giving Tristan and Isolde "the treatment due to the subject."[13]

The notes taken after the list of unfortunately un-Shakespearean writers from Sturge Moore's piece are provocative. Joyce makes a parallel between Isolde, Penelope, and Calypso. David Hayman has suggested that this note can be regarded as Joyce "contemplating using the Tristan tale much as he had the *Odyssey,* as a template for his new novel" (WiT: 58).[14] It is entirely possible that this is Joyce's first note toward conceptualizing the work that would occupy him after *Ulysses.*[15]

Joyce had been thinking of Tristan and Isolde before he read Sturge Moore's article. Georges Borach recalls that Joyce had claimed in 1918 that "there are indeed hardly more than a dozen original themes in world literature. Then there is an enormous number of combinations of these themes. *Tristan und Isolde* is an example of an original theme."[16]

After VI.B.10 the next extant notebook is VI.B.3.[17] Unlike those in VI.B.10, the notes in VI.B.3 are somewhat coherent (see *Buffalo VI.B.3,* 4–13). This notebook has many entries involving Tristan, Isolde, and (King) Mark. Joyce manipulates these characters in novel and unusual combinations. His notes never exploit the mythic or heroic resonances of the Tristan and Isolde story. Indeed, many of his notes treat the characters in a trivial manner; for example, "Is[olde]—they haven't / the heart to make / a cup of tay (Bretonnes)" (VI.B.3: 8). In some cases he interpolates the notes with material taken from other, seemingly unrelated source texts. For example, the entry "[r]Isolde—ornaments / her father's calligraphy / Vere Foster"[18] (VI.B.3: 10) derives from the following passage in J. M. Flood's book *Ireland: Its Saints and Scholars:* "Christian Art in Ireland attained its highest excellence in four branches: the writing and ornamentation of manuscripts, metal-work, stone carving, and building . . . the excellence of the Irish school of calligraphy."[19]

In the elaboration of Tristan and Isolde Joyce took a curious turn. On page 61 he writes: "[o]Is's Pop and Mop / (Pa and Ma)." By working through Tristan and Isolde Joyce arrives at a new character altogether, Isolde's father, here christened "Pop." At this stage Mop—or Mom, Pop's wife—is a very weakly established presence. In what survives of this notebook Joyce starts to broaden and expand the terrain for this Pop, and he slowly begins to make him into a kind of universal father figure. Pop becomes a crucial element of *Finnegans Wake,* and he began as one of many experimental developments of the Tristan and Isolde story in VI.B.3.[20] As Hayman has persuasively argued, Pop is the ur-HCE (WiT: 105–16). The note "[r]Tris like Pop / he boasts (Is)" (VI.B.3: 140) clearly places Pop in the context of the Tristan and Isolde story as the aged suitor who faces a young rival (WiT: 113). The notes for Pop in VI.B.3 emphasize his ridiculousness and also, slowly, start to intimate some sexual indiscretion. In some instances this indiscretion involves Isolde, in others it is independent of her.

Here is a sampling of Pop-related notes in VI.B.3:

Pop gave wh[ore] bob for / job & 3p tip (VI.B.3: 34)
Papa Is[olde] goes to bed in socks (VI.B.3: 49)

Pop—after dinner / he blew his nose (VI.B.3: 79)
Pop composed / extempore verse (VI.B.3: 93)[21]
Pop made † [sign of cross] / whenever saw éclair (VI.B.3: 98)
Is's Mum copies Pop's curses (VI.B.3: 111)
[r]Pop has Waterbury watch (VI.B.3: 130)
Pop in shirtsleeves / makes political / lovespeech (VI.B.3: 131)
[r]It is not true that / Pop was homosexual / he had been arrested / at the request of some / nursemaids to whom / he had temporarily / exposed himself / in the Temple gardens (VI.B.3: 153)

The last note is important both because it is a logical extension of the more sordid elements of Pop's personality from earlier notes and because it seems like the earliest direct draft of HCE's indiscretion in the park in I.2 (FW: 033.14–034.29). The note derives from the 1918 edition of Frank Harris's biography of Oscar Wilde. In an appendix Harris refutes the accusation that Horatio Lloyd, Wilde's father-in-law, had been suspected of homosexuality and writes: "The charge against Horatio Lloyd was of a normal kind. It was for exposing himself to nursemaids in the gardens of the Temple."[22] Although he was perhaps generated through King Mark from Tristan and Isolde, Pop is informed by a variety of other sources, such as Lloyd, and he quickly starts to take on a referential life of his own.

In VI.B.3 Joyce also uses the name Earwicker, the name Pop assumes once he becomes more fully evolved into HCE (i.e., Humphrey Chimpden Earwicker): "Earwicker's bath / [r]Is[olde]'s piss liquid sunshine" (VI.B.3: 38). In this one note Joyce combines Earwicker, Isolde, and a suggestion of sexual impropriety. Earwicker (pronounced "Erricker") is the name of an old family in Sidlesham, Sussex, that Joyce might have heard of during his trip to nearby Bognor in the middle of 1923.[23] This notebook also contains what may be a premonition of *Finnegans Wake,* which develops directly from the Tristan and Isolde theme: "Is[olde] dream of last day / vision of T— / Setting—a wake <!^?^>" (VI.B.3: 131; WiT: 31–32, 113).

Another notebook from this era is VI.A, otherwise known as Scribbledehobble (as that is the first word found in this notebook). All agree that Scribbledehobble is an exceptional notebook, if only because of its size and format. Until Rose and O'Hanlon positively dated VI.B.10 as having been begun in October 1922, Scribbledehobble was widely assumed to be the earliest notebook for *Finnegans Wake.* It seems that the notes in ink in Scribbledehobble are a collection and rationalization of notes from other early notebooks.[24]

Perhaps the most interesting notes in Scribbledehobble fall under the *Exiles* and *Ulysses* episode headings. The notes under *Exiles* contain a good deal of material related to Joseph Bédier's *Roman de Tristan et Iseult* of 1900, presumably because of the comment Joyce made in the notes to his play linking Bertha with Isolde.[25] Both Scribbledehobble and VI.B.3 contain notes from Bédier's attempt to reconstruct an ur-narrative for Tristan and Isolde. Scribbledehobble also contains a lot of what Hayman calls "epiphanoids": these are notebook entries that record simple and brief quotidian matters for possible reconfiguration. Hayman suggests that by the time Joyce was jotting down entries for the *Finnegans Wake* notebooks, he no longer believed in the "spirituality" of the epiphanic experience (as described in *A Portrait*) but instead continued his earlier habit of recording odd moments of experience for possible use in his new work.[26]

The sketches involve themes that are medieval, Irish, and hagiographic. They directly descend from the early notebooks. The facts that are certain can be summarized as follows:

10 March: Joyce writes the first draft of "Roderick O'Conor" (LI: 202).

Mid-March: Joyce suffers an eye attack but, bedridden, nevertheless manages to compose a new sketch, which he dictates to Nora (unpublished letter dictated to Giorgio Joyce, BL 57347 f. 89). This letter refers to the first draft of the "St Kevin" sketch, which is on pages 42–45 of notebook VI.B.3 (see *Buffalo VI.B.3,* 46–48).

28 March: Once the spell of conjunctivitis has ended, Joyce writes at least one other sketch "by using a charcoal pencil (*fusain*) which broke every three minutes and a large sheet of paper" (LIII: 73).

The announcement by the National Library of Ireland in March 2006 of previously unknown drafts of the several sketches changes our understanding of the earliest genesis of *Finnegans Wake.* However, even with these new documents it is clear that we still do not have the full inventory of drafts from 1923. It now seems likely that the late-March sketch (the one written in charcoal pencil) is the first version of "Tristan and Isolde."[27] In this draft, Tristan is called "Smiling Johnny" and regales Isolde with a list of his earlier lovers, most of whom were French, preparatory to propositioning her. None of the material on this draft was directly picked up on the subsequent drafts of the "Tristan and Isolde" sketch.

This draft is on the first of the new NLI sheets and continues directly onto a page in the British Library collection (BL 47480 f. 267v; JJA 56: 7). The other side of this British Library sheet contains the earliest extant draft of "Roderick O'Conor." Until the discovery of the NLI sheet, the "Tristan" side of the British Library page was difficult to understand since it contains a heavily revised text that begins in mid-sentence.[28] Along with the continuation of "Tristan and Isolde," this page includes an early draft of the poem "Nightpiece," which is based on a scene recorded in *Giacomo Joyce* (GJ: 10) and was later published in *Pomes Penyeach* in 1927 with the epigraph "Trieste, 1915" to emphasize its earlier provenance and to obviate any connection to the *Wake* (PSW: 59).[29]

The second new NLI draft is a previously unknown sketch about St Dympna, who also functions as a young Isolde. This draft was likely composed at the same time as the first version of the "Tristan and Isolde" sketch since it is written with the same charcoal pencil on a similar sheet of paper (there are some marginal additions in Nora's hand). Although unelaborated in this draft, there is a thematic contiguity between Isolde and St Dympna in that both were pursued by older men, in Dympna's case, her father. Thematically and stylistically, as the story of a precociously pious child, this sketch matches "St Kevin" (who is mentioned in an addition). The sketch begins with Dympna's lessons and includes her Paternoster, called "Isolde's nightprayer," which was initially drafted in VI.B.3 (VI.B.3: 58–59).[30] This portion of the sketch could be construed as a rough predecessor to what became the "night lessons" in II.2 although none of the material here was ever directly incorporated into the *Wake*. The latter part of the sketch includes a scene where Dympna encounters a beggar-girl in a park and gives her her petticoat (the name Dympna occurs in this sketch only during this incident and the syntax is such that it refers to the beggar-girl as well as to Young Isolde; such ambiguity is possibly deliberate). This scene could be construed as an anticipation of either Issy's bifurcated nature or HCE's encounter in the park with the cad.

The third new NLI draft is on both sides of two sheets of paper in Nora's hand, with revisions by Joyce. Most likely these sheets were written in mid-April, shortly after Joyce's conjunctivitis attack (JJII: 543). This draft is a retelling of "Tristan and Isolde" through the perspective of blind narrators called the "Four Waves of Erin." This fourfold narrator is the earliest extant indication of what will become Mamalujo (named after the arch-chroniclers of Christianity, Matthew, Mark, Luke, and John). The blind narrators reflect Joyce's status as a blind writer. Temporarily crippled as a writer, and blind bard (or muse) to Nora his amanuensis, Joyce conceived the crippled chroniclers who eventually provide the major narrative voice for the *Wake.* Subsequent to this draft, Joyce split Mamalujo out of "Tristan and Isolde" to create a separate sketch. We know that by October 1923, at the latest, Joyce had written a distinct "Mamalujo" sketch (LI: 203 and SL: 296–97). Prior to the discovery of this draft, it had been assumed that initially "Mamalujo" had been composed separately from "Tristan and Isolde."

This document also contains a draft of the poem "Tutto è Sciolto," which is sung in celebration of Tristan and Isolde's first kiss. Like "Nightpiece," this poem is based on a scene from *Giacomo Joyce* (GJ: 2–3) that was ultimately published in *Pomes Penyeach* (PSW: 55).

Joyce spent the summer of 1923 in Bognor, where he reworked the early sketches (JJII: 553–55). In early August he returned to Paris and sent out revised drafts to Weaver for typing. On 2 August Joyce sent Weaver "a piece describing the conversion of S. Patrick by Ireland" (LIII: 79). The earliest extant draft of "St Patrick" is from July, although there was likely an earlier draft, perhaps contemporaneous with the other sketches (Patrick is briefly mentioned in the composite "Tristan"/"Mamalujo" sketch). On 12 August Joyce sent Weaver a copy of "Tristan and Isolde" (BL 57347 f. 89). These sketches all underwent heavy and concerted revision in the months that followed. As with *Ulysses, Finnegans Wake* emerged through constant revision, rewriting, and textual accumulation and distortion. Joyce tended to fill all available space on the page with revisions. He would continually add passages in the margins and tag them for insertion with a variety of addition marks until the page was a dense, scrawled web of writing and revision. The language of the earliest passages does not show the linguistic complexity of the final text. For these early passages the brazenly eccentric language was added cumulatively on subsequent drafts. The early drafts, "however basically English" (FW: 116.26), are not without linguistic distortion in terms of rhythm, pace, syntax, and diction.[31]

In late August Joyce began work on a new sketch, "Here Comes Everybody": "Of course I have broken my promise and have begun drafting other parts in spite of the heat, noise, confusion and suffocation" (LIII: 80). Thematically, this sketch is a departure from its predecessors: it deals with HCE and with how he acquired his most curious agnomen. In the notebook contemporaneous with the drafting of this sketch, VI.B.2, Pop has almost completely given way to HCE. The first appearance of the initials HCE in this and perhaps in any notebook is interesting: "Trist weeps to pa / T & I constantly alter faces / [bl]HCE capable of any / crime (E[zra] P[ound])" (VI.B.2: 3). Here, characteristics for the father figure emerge through Tristan and Isolde, in this case the polymorphous criminality of HCE. Many of Joyce's notes in Scribbledehobble—especially those dealing with Tristan and Isolde—derive from Pound's *Instigations* (WiT: 79–87), and so perhaps HCE's protean criminality derives from something Pound had said about King Mark.

In November 1923 Joyce expanded the "Here Comes Everybody" sketch into a full-scale, albeit episodic, narrative of a carnivalesque HCE and his possible sexual malfeasance (both recognizably evolved from Pop in the notebooks) and the gradual, farcical destruction of his reputation by malicious slander. The extension to "Here Comes Everybody" was composed in a large red-backed copybook (BL 47471b). In "Here Comes Everybody" HCE acquires his agnomen and in the extension he loses it. This section forms what Bill Cadbury calls the "kernel draft" of chapters 2–4 in Book I of *Finnegans Wake*.[32]

After Joyce expanded "Here Comes Everybody" into I.2–4, he began work on a new episode, "The Revered Letter." The earliest indication for it is found in VI.B.3: "[r]Mum—letterwriter" (VI.B.3: 123). Another key element of the "Letter" follows from the *Exiles I* section of Scribbledehobble: "[r]on the N.E. slope of the dunghill the slanteyed hen of the Grogans scrutinised a clayed p.c. [postcard] from Boston (Mass) of the 12th of the 4th to dearest Elly from her loving sister with 4 1/2 kisses" (VI.A: 271).[33] This episode possesses a strong narrative connection with I.2–4. HCE comes to be accused of a crime (following from the earliest Pop notes in VI.B.3), and there is some letter by Mum, his consort, that purports to defend him from those accusations, but that letter has since been hidden or obscured until its possible retrieval by a hen. The role of HCE's consort, Mum, thus emerges through her function as the writer of the letter. After having drafted the "Letter," Joyce planned on writing an entire chapter to follow the I.2–4 suite in which it would be placed. However, in the course of writing I.5 Joyce decided to leave the "Letter" out. In a sense, the context (i.e., the apparatus for the presentation of the letter) discarded the text. The "Letter" languished for many years until it was finally incorporated into the last chapter of the *Wake*.[34]

Joyce also wrote a three-page treatment of the circuitous delivery of the letter by an errant mailman named Shaun the Post: "And congruously enough the confusion of its composition as fitly capped by the zigzaggery of its delivery" (BL 47471b f. 35v, simplified; JJA 46: 292; FDV: 90).

Presumably, this episode was also intended for I.5, but, like the "Letter" itself, it moved around until ultimately it became the inspiration for Book III. Unlike the "Letter," the "Delivery" was never directly incorporated into the text.

By late 1923 Joyce had written various sketches in various combinations and had begun working on the direct expansion of one of them into a suite of chapters. Joyce's own explanation of how he perceived their function is interesting in this regard:

> The construction is quite different from *Ulysses* where at least the ports of call were known beforehand.
>
> I am sorry that Patrick and Berkeley are unsuccessful in explaining themselves. The answer, I suppose, is that given by Paddy Dignam's apparition: metempsychosis. Or perhaps the theory of history so well set forth (after Hegel and Giambattista Vico) by the four eminent annalists who are even now treading the typepress in sorrow will explain part of my meaning. I work as much as I can because *these are not fragments but active elements and when they are more and a little older they will begin to fuse themselves.* (LI: 204, 9 October 1923, emphasis added)

In *Ulysses* Joyce had a clear enough template to work from: Homer's *Odyssey* and certain events in Dublin on 16 June 1904 through the perspective of three clearly defined characters. In a very broad sense the narrative of *Ulysses* progressively emerges from these two fields. (There are, of course, others—we are simplifying the question of narrative in *Ulysses* for the sake of comparison with *Finnegans Wake.*) In distinction, from its beginning *Finnegans Wake* lacked such clear points of contact. It would seem that with the sketches Joyce created his own points of resonance. Rather than work as an intertextual echo of Homer (and others), the *Wake* works as a concatenated series of *intratextual* echoes that proceed from the sketches. In order to get the *Wake* going Joyce needed to set up an initial chain of discrete textual events, the sketches, that would then, "when they are more and a little older," start to generate further swaths of text that would in turn generate more verbiage, and so on, and so on. Joyce had experimented with a similar kind of textual concatenation in *Ulysses,* but there the intratextual echoes (or motifs) were suspended within discernible if not always blatant referential points of contact (such as Homer and Dublin). In distinction, in the *Wake* the scaffolding is generated internally. Hayman calls this procedure "nodality": the sketches function as nodes around which other passages coalesce in varying degrees. The text is built up of an almost fugal concatenation of these textual echoes. Instead of proceeding from a story or from a single theme, the text proceeds from the *interactions* of various discrete passages.[35] This would be why Joyce was, from the very beginning, collecting seemingly random bits of text for his work: he needed to amass the raw components he later would need to fill in the avenues suggested by the interminglings of his text. This would also help explain why Joyce made various analogies between his authorship of the *Wake* and a mechanic: "I have taken this up because I am really one of the greatest engineers, if not the greatest" (LI: 251). In a sense, the sketches were but the initiating spark for a perpetual motion text machine.[36]

Once "Here Comes Everybody" started to generate a series of chapters, the work of nodality had begun in earnest. A freestanding piece of text began to grow of itself and build into a larger textual unit. This unit in turn inspired other units, such as the "Letter," which, as described above, led to the development of a chapter, I.5, that ultimately spurned its initial inspiration. Therefore, by late 1923 work on the *Wake* had begun in earnest. Joyce had enough basic text assembled that it could then lead him further on. The text built its own "ports of call" as it grew. Indeed, Joyce used one single copybook (BL 47471b) for the initial drafts and redrafts of all the material that directly exfoliated from "Here Comes Everybody": I.2–5, 7–8, the "Letter," and the "Delivery."

Danis Rose has proposed a different narrative of the sketches and of their role in *Finnegans Wake.* He denies that the sketches were integrally woven into the warp of the *Wake*'s growth and instead suggests that their relationship to the final text is roughly analogous to that of *Stephen Hero* to *A Portrait.* That is, the sketches comprise Joyce's *first* idea for his post-*Ulysses* book: an independent series of short stories based on Irish and mythological themes that was to be called *Finn's Hotel.*[37] In late 1923, according to Rose, once the sketches that formed *Finn's Hotel* were drafted, Joyce discarded this plan completely because one of them, "Here Comes Everybody," opened up a different path altogether, one that would lead ultimately to *Finnegans Wake.* Therefore, Joyce abandoned these sketches in favor of the "new" work that emerged from "Here Comes Everybody" (TDJJ: 20–23, 46–61, passim).

Rose's argument that the sketches form a separate, independent, and coherent work rests on their thematic congruity and on the fact that they were only incorporated into the text of the *Wake* in 1938 (TDJJ: 130–31). Rose's proposal concerning the title *Finn's Hotel* comes from a different direction:

the large number of references to the name "Finn's Hotel" in the notebooks and the paucity of references to "Finnegans Wake." Rose claims that Joyce planned on retaining the title *Finn's Hotel* after he had abandoned the sketches in favor of the work generated by "Here Comes Everybody" (TDJJ: 55). In other words, the title *Finn's Hotel* outlived the aborted book *Finn's Hotel.* He states that the title *Finnegans Wake* could not have predated the composition of I.1 in 1926, and he even suggests, in what he admits is a "rather extreme" interpretation, that this title was not even chosen until 1938.[38] The theory of the title, however, does little to corroborate the idea that the sketches formed a separate and independent work. According to Rose, *Finnegans Wake* (even if it was then called something else) was born in late 1923/early 1924 with the expansion of "Here Comes Everybody" into I.2–4, although the title *Finnegans Wake* came at least two years later. Hayman more or less agrees with the idea that *Finnegans Wake,* as such, began with the development of I.2–4, but he sees this as the result of textual evolution and not as a drastic change of direction.

Rose and Hayman agree that in early 1923 Joyce's initial plans were far from isomorphic with the book he would eventually write. Hayman's position is that Joyce's initial uncertainties slowly but steadily gave way to a measure of coherence as the text began to grow. Rose, on the other hand, gives the early sketches a very strong degree of independence from the text they generated and, ultimately, were subsumed within. He claims that the project of the sketches differs enough from *Finnegans Wake* that they should be considered as separate yet not absolutely unrelated entities.[39] The discovery of the new NLI drafts undermines Rose's theory since these documents show that Joyce considered these sketches to be interchangeable and malleable rather than as discrete units to be published in short story form. Indeed, these new manuscripts seem to corroborate Hayman's view that the *Wake* gradually emerged from Joyce's writing experiments in both the notebooks and sketches of the first half of 1923. Unsure of where he was going with his writing, Joyce apparently experimented with all sorts of configurations until he found something he could engage with (the "story" of HCE and a Mamalujan narrative voice). The problems with Rose's *Finn's Hotel* theory do not undermine the strengths of his *Textual Diaries,* which offers a strong and thorough account of the history of the development of *Finnegans Wake.* (In particular, Rose's dating of the notebooks is very convincing.)

An important development in the *Wake*'s genesis occurred in October 1923 in Ezra Pound's Paris flat. Ford Madox Ford persuaded Joyce to contribute something to a new journal that he was editing, the *transatlantic review* (JJII: 558–59). Joyce's decision ultimately had profound effects, since *Finnegans Wake,* much more so than *Ulysses,* was very much directly shaped by the tangled history of its serial publication. The piece Joyce submitted to Ford was "Mamalujo." In February 1924 he received the first round of proofs and was dismayed by how the printer, not surprisingly, had been unable to deal with Joyce's labyrinthine network of additions. On 29 February he complained about this to Robert McAlmon: "The T.R. sent me round a proof. O, my goodness! And I will not send it back to the printer as I do not trust his brains. So I wrote for Ford's secretary to come round. No reply. It is grotesque, I think" (LI: 212). The corrections and further additions delayed the publication of this piece until the fourth issue of the *transatlantic review* in April. It appeared under the title "Work in Progress," a term that was also applied to works by Ernest Hemingway and Tristan Tzara in that issue. Joyce kept on using this anonymous title to refer to his work until its final publication as *Finnegans Wake* in 1939.

In VI.B.6 (December 1923–February 1924) Joyce begins using a series of signs, or sigla, to designate the names of the characters of *Work in Progress,* who have, by this time, evolved into a complicated family.[40] In this notebook he also amplifies the role and nature of Mom, now unequivocally and frequently designated by the siglum Δ. The initials HCE are used interchangeably with the siglum ᗰ. These two parents are joined by Tristan and Isolde as well as by the pair ∧ and ⊏ and the mysterious ⋝. On page 101 Joyce lists these sigla together in the first surviving example of many such lists he will make in the notebooks: "ᗰ Δ T I ⋝ ⊏ ∧." Later, Joyce would use the siglum ⊥ to designate Isolde: this siglum illustrates her relationship to Tristan as his partner and/or inverted reflection. The siglum ⊥ thus takes on an iconic value that was amplified even as the importance of Tristan waned.

Joyce explained the sigla to Weaver in a letter he wrote on 24 March 1924 once they had settled down to a fairly stable network. "In making notes I used signs for the chief characters" (LI: 213).[41] The sigla thus emerged as a kind of shorthand more abstract than just using initials, as had been Joyce's norm until late 1923.[42] The list Joyce gives in his letter to Weaver is interesting:

ᗰ (Earwicker, HCE by moving letter around)
Δ Anna Livia

⊏ Shem-Cain
∧ Shaun
≲ Snake
P S. Patrick
T Tristan
⊥ Isolde
X Mamalujo
□ This stands for the title but I do not wish to say it yet until the book has written more of itself. (LI: 213)

Already in VI.B.2 Joyce had begun linking his father and mother characters to Adam and Eve, the prototypical ur-father-and-mother: "Heva (Living) / A-dam (Pa & Ma) / breath = spirit / spirits of beasts man" (VI.B.2: 13). By extension, this would make HCE's crime somehow analogous to original sin. In turn, this would require some figure to tempt the hapless pair, hence ≲, the snake. This in turn raised the question of the pair's brood, the squabbling brothers, who take the names Shem and Shaun. As Joyce's letter suggests, Shem is also a Cain figure, and this would make Shaun Abel. Vincent Deane has observed that the Shem and Shaun sigla, ⊏ and ∧, suggest a stylized C and A, Cain and Abel (TDJJ: 57 and 57 n. 1). Ingeborg Landuyt has confirmed this supposition with her discovery that many of Joyce's notes on Shem and Shaun in VI.B.6 derive from a Catholic commentary on the book of Genesis.[43] At the time Joyce made the first brief list in VI.B.6, Shaun was not developed at all beyond being the necessary fraternal complement to Shem.

In early 1924 Joyce announced to Weaver his plans for the book after I.2–5. Two sections originally intended for I.5, the "Letter" and the "Delivery," were to be relocated: "Between the words 'penman' and 'Revered' are three further passages, a description of Shem-Ham-Cain-Esau[44] etc and his penmanship, Anna Livia's visits and collaboration and delivery of the memorial by Shawn the post" (LI: 208). The word "penman" was at the end of I.5§4, which Joyce had just drafted, and "Revered" is the first word of the "Letter." Therefore, Joyce at this point was planning on interpolating three chapters between I.5 and the "Letter," thereby shunting the "Letter" away from the chapter that describes its genesis and contents. These chapters would be on Shem the Penman, on ALP, and on Shaun—the latter presumably being an expansion of the "Delivery" episode. It seems that at this point the "Delivery" episode was conceived of as being only a single chapter rather than an entire suite of chapters. The initial drafts of both I.7 and

I.8 proceeded comparatively smoothly. A draft of I.7 was sent to Weaver in February (LI: 210) and one of I.8 in March (LI: 212–13). Joyce seems to have enjoyed writing the Shem chapter, as it is, in part, a satire of himself (SL: 282). Details of their composition will be addressed in fuller detail in their respective chapters in this volume.

As mentioned earlier, Shaun's first foray into the text was in the aborted "Delivery" episode. However, Joyce stopped work on this, probably dissatisfied with how it was turning out. Wim Van Mierlo explains in his essay on III.1–2 that the turning point for Shaun, and indeed for *Finnegans Wake,* came when Joyce read a book by Léon Metchnikoff, *La Civilisation et les grands fleuves historiques.*[45] Metchnikoff describes Giambattista Vico's cyclical theories of *corsi* and *ricorsi* as the underlying dynamic for historical progress. Joyce had already been interested in Vico, but this book seemed to have energized his thoughts on the matter and especially on how he could deal with Shaun. The delivery of the letter is no longer a single episode in the saga of HCE but rather a repetition and recapitulation, "by a commodious vicus of recirculation" (FW: 003.02), of that saga into a different register. Shaun's delivery of the letter replays HCE's downfall, which is what is recorded, somehow, in the letter itself. The discovery of Shaun's role could thus be seen as the final nail in the coffin of *Wakean* narrative as "goahead plot" (LIII: 146). With Book III *Wakean* narrative turns back on itself to repeat "the seim anew" (FW: 215.23). If Book I could be said to move forward in the explication of HCE's fate, then Book III moves backward. As Joyce explained to Weaver, the first part of Book III "is a description of a postman travelling backwards in the night through events already narrated. It is written in the form of a *via crucis* of 14 stations but is actually only a barrel rolling down the river Liffey" (LI: 214). What Joyce had been experimenting with at the local level with the textual reverberations emanating from the sketches (what Hayman calls nodality) has now, with the invention of Shaun, become the organizing structural principle for the work as a whole.

Another element Joyce derived from Metchnikoff's book is a quotation from the French philosopher of history Edgar Quinet's book *Introduction à la philosophie de l'histoire de l'humanité* (Joyce copied it from Metchnikoff into VI.B.1: 84–85). It is clear that Joyce derived the quote from Metchnikoff, since he reproduces Metchnikoff's errors.[46] The sentence describes the effects of temporal change, and Joyce described it as "beautiful"

(LI: 295). The sentence was ultimately to take on a kind of nodal resonance as it wound up being incorporated into the text six times with varying degrees of *Wakean* distortion.

The composition of Book III was not as straightforward as the early history of Book I. Joyce frequently used the Shaun siglum to designate the four chapters of Book III. As he correctly predicted to Weaver in March 1924, "Shaun is going to give me a very great deal of trouble" (LI: 213). Through early 1926 Joyce kept working on and slowly expanding Book III. The initial drafts elaborate on Shaun's delivery of the letter and include "a long absurd and rather incestuous Lenten lecture to Izzy, his sister" (LI: 216). Shaun has begun to usurp at least part of Tristan's role as Isolde's suitor. By the end of 1924 Joyce had so augmented and reconfigured this new chapter that he split it into two, thereby making the first two watches of Shaun (LI: 224).

Ultimately, III.3 grew into one of the *Wake*'s longest chapters. It was composed as a series of discrete units that Joyce revised before moving further. It deals with the ultimate dissolution of Shaun under examination by Mamalujo. In a sense, in his disappearance Shaun comes to mimic the trajectory of HCE in Book I. Indeed, when he finally disappears, he becomes a vessel through which the quest for HCE is pursued. This final part of the chapter rapidly evolved into a set-piece monologue later published under the title *Haveth Childers Everywhere.*

On 16 August 1924 Joyce wrote to Weaver that he was unsure as to how he would link the two parts of *Work in Progress* thus far composed. "But it is true that I have been thinking and thinking how and how and how can I and can it—all about the fusion of two parts of the book—while my one bedazzled eye searched the sea like Cain-Shem-Tristan-Patrick from his lighthouse in Boulogne. I hope the solution will presently appear" (LI: 220). The solution, though, would take its time.

While he was revising earlier chapters for print in various publications, Joyce began work on Λd, the fourth chapter of Book III and Shaun's last watch. "I know that Λd ought to be about roads, all about dawn and roads, and go along repeating that to myself all day as I stumble along the roads hoping it will dawn on me how to show up them roads so as everybody'll know as how roads etc" (LI: 232). The initial draft of this chapter is very complex: it was composed in one copybook (BL 47482a) as a series of rapidly written and revised subunits that were later rearranged and integrated in the fair copy (see FDV: 37–38). Shaun's role in this chapter is minimal in comparison to the rest of Book III: he is reduced to being a child within a somewhat fractious household that also includes the infants Shem and Issy. As he wrote III.4 Joyce revised the other chapters in Book III and expected their publication in the near future.

The following year, 1926, saw major advances and small but not insignificant setbacks. By May Joyce announced to Weaver that his earlier problem of how to mesh the HCE-ALP sequence with the Shaun sequence had been resolved, at least conceptually: "I have the book now fairly well planned out in my head. I am as yet uncertain whether I shall start on the twilight games of ⊏, Λ and ⊣ which will follow immediately after Δ or on K's orisons, to follow Λd" (LI: 241).[47] Joyce would add an entirely new section in which he would focus on the childhood antics of Shem, Shaun, and Issy. This idea directly followed from his work on the dysfunctional household of III.4.[48]

A few weeks later Joyce announced his decision: "Between the close of Δ at nightfall and Λa there are three or four other episodes, the children's games, night studies, a scene in the 'public' and a 'lights out in the village'" (LI: 241). The new section is not just a single chapter of twilight games but an entirely new book interpolated between ALP (I.8) and Λa (III.1). Joyce's own compositional pattern of *Work in Progress* has here taken a Vichian zigzag. By June he had written a one-page plan for Book II organized around the sigla (BL 47482a f. 2; JJA 51: 3).[49]

The first part of this new Book to be undertaken was a section of the night studies, II.2, "⊏ coaching Λ how to do Euclid Bk I,1" (LI: 242). This section of II.2 was initially called "The Triangle," and Joyce assigned it the siglum Δ2 (LIII: 142). It was drafted in a notebook (BL 47482a) immediately after the "Dave the Dancekerl" passage in III.3. In August Joyce went to Belgium, where he continued taking notes for II.2. His Flemish idyll was interrupted by the rejection of Λabcd by the *Dial*. This was to be the first of several major setbacks that year. To Weaver he lamented, "I am sorry the *Dial* has rejected the pieces as I wanted them to appear slowly and regularly in a prominent place" (LI: 245).[50]

In this same letter Joyce made a curious request to Weaver. "A rather funny idea struck me that you might 'order' a piece and I would do it" (LI: 245). A week later Weaver obliged and sent Joyce a description of a giant's grave at Saint Andrew's in Penrith (JJII: 582). This "commission" meshed neatly with what Joyce was already planning for the introduction to *Work in Progress*, chapter I.1. Work on this chapter forced "The Triangle," and Book II, aside.[51]

It is clear that by this time—once the conundrum of meshing Λabcd and HCE and ALP through the connective tissue of Book II had been solved—Joyce had the overall itinerary of his book finally mapped out. The overall structure of the book was to be Vichian, as he explained to Weaver: "The book really has no beginning or end. (Trade secret, registered at Stationers Hall.) It ends in the middle of a sentence and begins in the middle of the same sentence" (LI: 246).[52] To accomplish this scheme he would write a short fourth book, a Vichian *ricorso* that would "rearrive" at the beginning. In the letter he then went on to explain how the pieces already written would fit into this circular scheme. With the plan set Joyce could undertake the first chapter, the chapter that would lay out the basic themes and patterns of the work as a whole. He finally had his roadmap on the circular Vico Road (Dalkey) that "goes round and round" (FW: 452.21). Joyce was later to tell his friend Padraic Colum that "I use [Vico's] cycles as a trellis."[53] In any case, it was a more-than-convenient trellis for Joyce's enmeshed *Work in Progress.*

By this time Joyce had reached a perhaps perverse proficiency in his distorted and distended "nat language" (FW: 083.12) and was now able to compose new passages directly into his "ersebest idiom" (FW: 253.01) of translinguistic portmanteaux. As a result, the first drafts from this point on are more complex than the essentially English first drafts from a few years before.

By late 1926 Joyce was going to get his wish of having *Work in Progress* "appear slowly and regularly in a prominent place." On 12 December, through Sylvia Beach, Joyce met Eugene Jolas. Along with his colleague Elliot Paul, Jolas was planning to start a new journal, to be called *transition,* and he was eager to have Joyce as a contributor (JJII: 588–89). As I.1 was virtually ready when Joyce met Jolas and Paul, that piece was promised for the first issue of *transition.* For most of 1927 Joyce worked to revise the other chapters in Book I for publication there. The publication schedule of *transition* more or less revolved around the availability of Joyce's chapters. The early issues appeared very regularly, almost monthly, since the chapters for Book I had already been drafted. Once the cache of available chapters had been exhausted, subsequent issues of *transition* appeared more infrequently.

In 1927 the pace of Joyce's writing slowed down. On 16 April 1927 he declared to Weaver that, in writing the *Work in Progress,* he is perhaps the greatest engineer (LI: 251). Almost a month later he claims that the engine can proceed without him: "I lay down my pen anyhow and if I knew anyone who I thought had the patience and the wish and the power to write Part II on the lines indicated I think I would leave the chair too and come back in a few years to indicate briefly how Part IV should be done. But who is the person? There is no such absurd person as could replace me except the incorrigible god of sleep and no waster quite so wasteful though there is one much more so" (LI: 252). A week later Joyce announced to Weaver that he believes that James Stephens would be an ideal replacement: "Of course he would never take a fraction of the time or pains I take but so much the better for him and me and possibly for the book itself. If he consented to maintain three or four points which I consider essential and I showed him the threads he could finish the design. JJ and S (the colloquial Irish for John Jameson and Son's Dublin whisky) would be a nice lettering under the title" (LI: 253–54).

Joyce did not approach Stephens until sometime around the end of 1927 (JJII: 592), and only in July 1929 did he finally propose to Stephens that he take over *Work in Progress.* Stephens tentatively agreed and voiced his admiration for Joyce's writing (LI: 282).[54] Joyce persisted in courting Stephens to replace him, and by late 1929 he wrote Weaver that he had "explained to him all about the book, at least a great deal, and he promised me that if I found it was madness to continue, in my condition, and saw no other way out, that he would devote himself heart and soul to the completion of it, that is the second part and the epilogue or fourth. I was very glad to speak with him and we will leave it at that for the moment" (LI: 288).

What special knowledge Joyce imparted to Stephens regarding *Work in Progress,* if any, remains undocumented. Although Joyce never did relinquish *Work in Progress* to Stephens, they remained close through the 1930s. While it is difficult to ascertain just how serious Joyce was with this possible "abdication," this episode reveals both Joyce's increasing despondency with his work as well as his faith that he had established a work that could progress by itself. His "vicociclometer" (FW: 614.27) thus no longer requires the direct initiative of its creator, who, like Stephen Dedalus's ideal artist, can remain "within or behind or beyond or above his handiwork, invisible, refined out of existence, indifferent, paring his fingernails" (P: 215). Unfortunately for Joyce (and perhaps fortunately for Stephens), the machine was not quite as *automatic* as he had hoped and claimed.

Although Joyce was already considering abandoning *Work in Progress* in May 1927, he was still writing. On 26 July he announced to Weaver, "I am working night and day at a piece I have to insert between the last [chapter published in *transition,* I.5] and ⊏ [I.7]. It must be ready by Friday evening.

I never worked against time before. It is very racking" (LIII: 163). Jolas later described some of the effects of Joyce's frantic composition for this chapter for *transition* 6 (September 1927):

> [Joyce's] meticulousness in the correction of proofs—not to mention the fact that correction, in his case, meant inevitably amplification and refinement of minutiae—made the editorial task an unusually hectic one. . . . I recall, among numerous similar happenings, one particular case, when a four-page addition had to be made after the first four hundred copies of the review had already been stitched. Everything was held up. The addition that had been announced by telephone came by the early mail and was rushed to the composing room. During the day the completed copies were ripped apart, and by evening a sufficiently clean proof of the new text had been obtained for us to feel we could call it a day. For the second time the *bon à tirer* [ready to print] was given. Just as we rolled slowly out of the printer's street, there arrived a telegraph messenger with a few more corrections.[55]

This four-page addition was the fable of "The Mookse and the Gripes," one of two fables in which Joyce directly counters and reconfigures Wyndham Lewis's charge that he is a time-centric writer.[56] In this fable Lewis's position is taken up by the Shaunish Mookse. At the end of the second fable, "The Ondt and the Gracehoper" (first drafted in March 1928 for insertion in III.1 [SL: 329–32]), the Gracehoper asks the Ondt, "*But, Holy Saltmartin, why can't you beat time?*" (FW: 419.09). Thanks to Jolas's dedication, Joyce was able to beat time and get "The Mookse and the Gripes" included in *transition.*

This new chapter, I.6, completes the sequence of Book I. This chapter is organized as a kind of catechism around the sigla: there are twelve questions, each of which, in the preliminary drafts, are flagged by sigla (BL 47473 f. 150v; JJA 47: 2; and BL 47473 f. 132v; JJA 47: 28). In this way this chapter grew out of the sigla lists Joyce had assembled in the notebooks several years earlier. Essentially, it functions as a kind of dramatis personae of the *Wake.*[57] He admitted that this chapter, with its emphasis on Shaun in the eleventh question, works "as ballast and the whole piece is to balance Λabcd more accurately" (LI: 258). The four chapters of Book III would be offset by eight chapters in Book I. Rather than linearity, Joyce was trying to effect symmetry. However, each attempt to set the balance right seemed to create a further imbalance that would then need to be rectified. If I.6 was to help balance Book I against Book III, then the fable of "The Mookse and the Gripes" in I.6 had to be balanced by a new fable in Book III, that of "The Ondt and the Gracehoper," written the following year.

After a two-issue hiatus publication of *Work in Progress* resumed in *transition* with the appearance of a heavily revised "The Triangle," now renamed "The Muddest Thick," in *transition* 11 (February 1928). Joyce then began concerted work on revising Book III for *transition.* III.1 appeared in number 12 (March 1928) and III.2 in number 13 (July). He worked on III.3 through January 1929, and it finally appeared in *transition* 15 (Winter 1929). In October he revised III.4 for *transition* 18 (November 1929). With its appearance, all of Book III had been published.

In May 1930 Joyce began preliminary work on Book II, the first new composition he had undertaken in several years, and that autumn he set about writing II.1. He wrote Weaver: "I enclose the final sheet of the first draft of about two thirds of the first section of Part II (2,200 words) which came out like drops of blood. Excuse me for not having written but I have had a dreadful amount of worry all this last month. . . . I think the piece I sent you is the gayest and lightest thing I have done in spite of the circumstances" (LI: 295). Over the next few months Joyce wrote out most of II.1. This chapter deals with the children's games played by Shem, Shaun, and Issy, who seems to blur out into becoming a group of twenty-nine girls.[58] By January 1931 Joyce had drafted the core of II.1; after that he did not touch this chapter again for almost a year and a half.

Joyce began work on revising Book I for final publication in the autumn of 1931; this, of course, further delayed any progress on II.1. On 27 October he wrote Weaver: "I finished pulling together the first 8 episodes [i.e., Book I]. . . . To my great relief I find that much more of the book is done than I had hoped for" (LIII: 232). At the time he wrote this letter he had received but temporarily mislaid sample proof pages (see LIII: 232, 235) made by Faber and Faber's printer, R. MacLehose and Company (Glasgow), from randomly selected pages.

In preparing Book I Joyce gathered together pages from *transition* augmented by the two portions of Book I that had appeared separately and thus had received additional draftings ("Anna Livia Plurabelle" and "The Mookse and the Gripes"). In practice, the revisions wound up being made somewhat chaotically across a series of multiple copies of the various previously printed installments. Although Joyce may have tentatively started this work in late 1931, he probably did not begin concerted revisions until late 1933 (JJA 61: x), and even then it took him several more years to complete it, no doubt through further intermittent labors.

On 28 August 1932 Joyce wrote Paul Léon that he was getting II.1 ready for publication in the October issue of *transition* (JJ/PL: 5). As it turned out, II.1 did not appear until February 1933, in *transition* 22. Part of the delay was due to a manuscript that went missing, thereby forcing Joyce to re-create certain passages from memory and his notes (LI: 326–27). During his revisions of that chapter Joyce added both an introduction and a conclusion.

In late 1933 Joyce hired Mme France Raphaël as his amanuensis (JJII: 671–72). She worked for him off and on until late 1936. Her primary job was to transfer unused notes from Joyce's previous notebooks (i.e., the notes not already crossed out) into new notebooks in a larger, more legible handwriting so that Joyce might be able to use them. Understandably, she made a good number of mistakes. The transference of older notes into a new context in a new hand did have some strange effects on the composition of later portions of *Work in Progress.*[59]

Mme Raphaël also helped with the revisions of Books I and III for final publication. At this time Joyce continued the work on Book I he had started two years before. He also began work on Book III. Mme Raphaël copied out some unused portions of Joyce's earlier notebooks as well as some extradraft notes for Joyce's use during the revision of Book III. Since some of the material in these extradraft notes was used in II.2, these can be dated to 1933–34. The process of preparing Books I and III continued intermittently over a period of many years.

In June 1934 Joyce returned to II.2 after more than a year of dealing with other matters. He took some but not all of the extraneous passages he had drafted earlier and reconfigured them into a new format replete with marginalia and footnotes. These passages comprised both the beginning and the end of II.2. This excerpt was published, after further revision, in *transition* 23 in July 1935. The chapter had thus changed its contours drastically. In addition to the new and unusual format, the "Scribbledehobbles" section, originally planned as the chapter's introduction, had now been shunted closer to the center. This section, in addition to "The Muddest Thick" (which had already been published), as well as some other extraneous sections drafted by Joyce during the first round of composition, were all to be withheld from publication until the final text of *Finnegans Wake* appeared in 1939.[60]

Starting in 1935 Joyce's nine-year period of stagnation would slowly come to an end. Since he had settled on the overall design for his book in 1926 he had written only three new chapters (I.6, II.1, and II.2) and had revised Books I and III. In early 1935 he began preparatory work on II.3, which would turn out to be the longest chapter in his book. As he had told Weaver in his early plan for Book II back in 1926, this would be a "scene in the 'public,'" that is, a scene in a bar, a public house. The focus of Book II thus shifts from the children to their beleaguered father, a publican or "pilsener had the baar" (FW: 313.14–15). Joyce started by taking notes in VI.B.40, VI.B.38, and VI.B.37. The first of these notebooks contains entries relating to the story of "The Norwegian Captain and the Tailor," although there are references to this story in earlier notebooks. This farcical story, dealing with a misshapen captain who orders a suit from a Dublin tailor, was a favorite of Joyce's father (JJII: 23). Joyce began writing this section in 1935, but, after a few drafts, he turned to completing his revisions of the *transition* pages for Book I and Book III, a task he had started almost five years earlier (JJ/PL: 178). These revisions were finished by 11 July 1936; this was the date he marked on the cover of one of the revised sets of *transition* (BL 47486a 70; JJA 61: 3).[61] By December 1936 Joyce had sent off typescripts of "The Norwegian Captain" to Weaver and to Jolas for publication in *transition* 26 in May 1937.

The final years of Joyce's *Work in Progress* involved piecing the book together out of a jigsaw puzzle–like state. Books I and III were in fairly advanced stages, and, once their manuscripts had been assembled, all that remained for them was the revision of galley proofs (which proved to be, in some cases, considerable). However, the rest of the book was not as well developed at this time. Only one other chapter, II.1, could be considered complete. All the pieces for II.2 existed, but they had not yet been assembled. II.3 was still being written piecemeal. II.4 and IV did not even exist yet, although they would eventually be built from some of the sketches that had been written back in 1923. Over the next few years Joyce found himself shuttling between final revisions on advanced drafts and work on relatively new material.

In late 1936 Joyce began extending II.3. One of these continuations, the "Butt and Taff" skit, was based on another of John Joyce's tales, "How Buckley Shot the Russian General." Joyce had been interested in using this story since *Ulysses.* He made reference to it four times on the *Ulysses* notesheets.[62] Notes referring to this story also appear in VI.B.3 (80–83) and Scribbledehobble.[63]

Faber and Faber had a set of galleys for Book I ready by 12 March 1937, and these were soon followed by galleys for Book III. Joyce worked hard on revising these during the next few months. On 6 August he wrote his close friend Constantine Curran, "I am trying to finish my *Work in Progress* (I work about 16 hours a day, it seems to me)" (LI: 395; see also LI: 392 and LIII: 402, 407). Faber and Faber sent Joyce multiple copies of the galleys, which he revised individually.

Starting in the middle of 1937 and continuing through the rest of the year, Joyce began preparing the more advanced portions of Book II for Faber and Faber (JJ/PL: 70). II.3 was sent to the printers piecemeal as various passages became available. This first round of disjointed revisions to Book II was finished by 18 December (LIII: 409). Joyce was still hoping for final publication in 1938, preferably in time for his birthday, but T. S. Eliot disabused him of this idea, since the text was still not in final form, and, even if it was, the printers would still need more time (JJ/PL: 180–81).

At this late stage of composition Joyce finally started to work in the sketches he had drafted back in 1923. With the exception of "Here Comes Everybody," the sketches all remained unmodified since 1923 and unincorporated into *Work in Progress.* "Mamalujo" had appeared in Ford's *transatlantic review* in 1924, but none of the others, again with the exception of "Here Comes Everybody," had been published. As noted above, Rose claims that Joyce had simply forgotten these sketches, since they had been intended for *Finn's Hotel,* a work Joyce supposedly abandoned when he started developing "Here Comes Everybody" into what would become *Finnegans Wake.*[64] However, it seems unlikely that Joyce forgot about the sketches. Throughout the composition of *Work in Progress* he made many references to the sketches both in letters and in drafts. Although the sketches were not assimilated into *Work in Progress* until the very end, they were still very much a part of it throughout its evolution through the accumulation of references, allusions, and echoes.

The first sketch to be worked in was "St Kevin." In late 1937 Joyce began writing what would become the start of Book IV, the *ricorso,* and by early 1938 he had prepared a manuscript that linked the introduction of Book IV to a newly revised version of the 1923 "St Kevin" sketch.[65] Work began on Book IV during the time when Joyce would be revising almost every section of *Work in Progress* virtually simultaneously.

Faber and Faber sent Joyce the first round of galleys for both II.1 and "The Norwegian Captain" in January 1938. At the end of that month he announced to Frank Budgen that he had finished his revisions of the Book

III galleys (LIII: 413). The Book I galleys were done in two batches, the first of which was finished by February and the second by May. Some additional work on these books continued past these dates. On 9 February Joyce groused to Pound of retinal congestion in his left eye because of months of "allnight work in finishing W i P" (LIII: 415). Also in February Joyce sent to the printer the rest of II.2 along with instructions on how it would fit together. It was only at this late stage that II.2 as a whole came into being. The galleys for all of II.2 were sent back to Joyce in March. At this time Joyce was also working on preparing "Butt and Taff" for publication in *transition.* This was the last part of *Work in Progress* to come out in serial form, and it appeared in the final issue of *transition,* number 27 (April–May 1938). In June he quickly began the process of marking up the *transition* pages of "Butt and Taff" for Faber and Faber. Also in June he finished revising the galleys for II.1, and shortly thereafter he revised the II.2 galleys.

In late July Joyce began his work of transforming "Mamalujo" and "Tristan and Isolde" into II.4 (JJ/PL: 71). He began by marking up the *transatlantic review* pages of "Mamalujo" from 1924. From these pages a fresh typescript was made upon which Joyce made a significant number of revisions, including the addition of large chunks of the "Tristan and Isolde" sketch newly "translated" into *Wakese.* The Tristan and Isolde story, which had been inaugural for the *Wake,* was now, finally, finding its place in the text. As Jed Deppman describes in his essay on this chapter, Joyce pulverized and recombined the two sketches in a very complex manner. As the new NLI manuscripts reveal, in 1923 "Mamalujo" emerged from an early draft of "Tristan and Isolde," whereas in 1938, as Deppman demonstrates, "Tristan and Isolde" was grafted into "Mamalujo" to become II.4. At this time Joyce also continued work on Book IV. He reworked the "St Patrick" sketch and retrieved the "Letter," which had been discarded from I.5 many years before. He also began work on ALP's "Soft morning city" monologue as the book's conclusion. In September Joyce returned to "Roderick O'Conor"—the first text he wrote after *Ulysses*—and integrated it carefully into II.3. While the sketch itself was relatively unchanged, Joyce appended a new section and meticulously worked out a linking section to the rest of II.3.[66] The various elements of Book IV and II.4 as well as the final segment of II.3 were all sent individually to Faber and Faber in the autumn of 1938. By this point Joyce also began the process of revising page proofs for the first half of his book.[67]

By the end of 1938 the only work that remained was cleaning up the more recently composed passages. Joyce received page proofs for Books II and IV as they became available. By the middle of November Joyce began to pronounce the book finished.[68] This jubilation proved to be premature, since Joyce still had further proofs to deal with. The page proofs for II.4 were sent out by Faber and Faber in December and those for Book IV the following January. Joyce finished revising them by month's end (JJ/PL: 74). Just in time for his birthday on 2 February, Joyce received an advance copy of *Finnegans Wake.* And so, with its publication, *Work in Progress* finally became *Finnegans Wake.* Indeed, Harriet Weaver did not even know the final title until she saw it on the page proofs of the title page (JJ/PL: 74). Joyce still had some remaining revisions to attend to before the edition was ready for official publication on 4 May (JJ/PL: 74).

In July Joyce began complaining about mistakes in the edition (JJ/PL: 189), and shortly thereafter he started to mark up corrections in the margins of an unbound copy of the book (JJ/PL: 32). He primarily focused on rectifying errors perpetrated on the late additions to the text, that is, those made on the galley or page proofs. These corrections were subsequently collated and transcribed. The errata list was not published until 1945, when it appeared as a pamphlet tipped into the book. Subsequent printings incorporated the corrections into the text.[69]

As he had done in 1922 with VI.B.10, Joyce did not stop taking notes once his latest book was published. The habit of note taking seems to have been too firmly entrenched in his mind. In the second half of 1939 he filled up a small black imitation snakeskin notebook, VI.B.48, with mostly arbitrary jottings.[70] In their random style these entries resemble VI.B.10, but none of them are crossed out, since none of them were ever used. If Joyce was contemplating writing a new work that would be—as he told George Pelorson in April 1939—"very simple and very short" (JJII: 731), this notebook gives no indication as to what that work might have been. One curious note, presumably a reflection on his newly completed book, reads "ᗰ sur J.J." (VI.B.48: 25).

In early 1942, a year after Joyce died, Ezra Pound and Stanislaus Joyce shared a brief correspondence. Stanislaus sent Pound a copy of his memoir of Joyce from the Florentine magazine *Letteratura.*[71] Pound, very much agreeing with Stanislaus's criticisms of *Finnegans Wake* (as it was now called), wrote back: "Since I took to referring to the late Finnigan [*sic*] as a work in regress, his Eminence desisted after a time from sending me the subsequent hunks, so there is a pair of us haven't read it. I suppose the book may be all right, but it was his earwigs and fleas that made it a nuissance by their clatter. It was a sad day we set him up on a platform; but he might have had a harder life otherwise. . . . Its a damn nuissance his dyin'."[72]

With Joyce dead two Shauns write and post letters to each other, their inveterate criticisms tinged by loss. In their own ways these two people, who demurred from having "lovesoftfun at Finnegan's Wake" (FW: 607.16), contributed more than a little to Joyce's "warping process" (FW: 497.03).

SS

The *Finnegans Wake* Manuscripts

More than 25,000 pages survive of the textual record of *Finnegans Wake,* a book of just 628 pages.[73] This remarkable phenomenon in the history of literature affords an unparalleled opportunity for the critical study of its author's creative processes. These varied manuscripts document Joyce's almost-eighteen-year struggle to create and continually emend this patchwork text. They provide an almost daily account of this arduous labor from 1 November 1922 to 28 August 1940, spanning his corrections to *Ulysses* and *Finnegans Wake.* Well over fourteen thousand pages of notes, the text's lexical building blocks, are in the Poetry Collection at the University at Buffalo, State University of New York, and almost nine thousand draft manuscript pages are in the British Library alone.[74] Although these are the primary two repositories of *Finnegans Wake* manuscripts, at least another two thousand pages are in several other holding libraries and private collections.[75] Although the reproduction of all the then-known notebooks and manuscripts in *The James Joyce Archive* has fostered their study around the world, much work still needs to be done.[76] When reproduced in the *Archive,* the *Wake* manuscripts alone comprise thirty-five of its sixty-three volumes.[77] Even when usually published four to a volume, the *Wake* notebooks alone comprise a quarter of the series' volumes.

Examples of every stage of the work's complex material evolution abound. Besides the sheer quantity of the *Finnegans Wake* manuscripts, other factors explain why they have so far remained intimidating to most readers and scholars. The difficulty of Joyce's handwriting is only the most obvious cause deterring their further exploration. He wrote in at least three distinct hands, a fact that had little or nothing to do with the persistent difficulties he had with his eyesight. The first was an exceedingly neat and precise letter-writing hand that one encounters in thousands of his letters. Another was a scrupulous fair hand that he employed to recopy previous drafts as well as correct, revise, and emend any manuscript that would be typed or set in print. His eyesight and other physical factors permitting, Joyce wrote as clearly as he could whenever he expected anyone else to read his handwriting. Nonetheless, he also had a script that was reserved for his eyes only that he used to compile his notebooks and write early drafts.[78] Furthermore, the quality of the paper, pencils, inks, and crayons Joyce used varied considerably because, like so many authors, he rarely took an interest in them beyond their utilitarian value. He usually used whatever writing materials were most readily available.

Throughout his life Joyce had little interest creatively or practically in his own manuscripts after they were no longer his working documents. Fortunately, he recognized their heuristic value, at the very least, and consigned them to his collaborators and friends, several of whom played vital roles in the preservation of these documents. For both sentimental and practical reasons Joyce entrusted all the *Finnegans Wake* manuscripts he found to Harriet Shaw Weaver, his publisher, patron, and confidante in London. Given Joyce's unsettled lifestyle while in Paris, it is unlikely that even a fraction of these manuscripts would have survived otherwise. As early as 19 July 1923, while traveling in Bognor, Sussex, Joyce availed himself of Weaver as *Finnegans Wake*'s first reader and typist: "*Pour commencer* may I have recourse to your offered aid and ask you to type the enclosed [the fair copy of the "Roderick O'Conor" sketch] (2 copies)? I shall send you the original sheet (now quite illegible) when I have transcribed what is on the back of it. I think it would give me pleasure to see the first page of type. I hope it is legible. I wrote it as well as I could" (LI: 203). The very next day Weaver also became the *Wake*'s first archivist when Joyce wrote asking: "May I trouble you to make three copies of this at your leisure? Please keep one yourself for in moving today I have lost one of your sheets and I should like to have a complete set of these scattered passages when needed" (LIII: 79). This informal pact continued virtually uninterrupted until 17 August 1939, three months after *Finnegans Wake* was first published, when Paul Léon sent Weaver some further pages of the work's corrected typescript that he had only recently found (JJ/PL: 77).[79] Weaver's task as the work's first bibliographer and geneticist began in earnest in 1948. She wrote of it to David Hayman on 15 April 1959:

> All I know is that Mr. Joyce used to send [the manuscripts] as and when he had finished with them, saying once, I remember: 'I send you a little waste paper to get it out of the way.' They came in no particular order and often were sent by anyone helping with the typing, chiefly Mr. Paul Léon, sometimes

> Mrs. Jolas or Mr. Stuart Gilbert. And sometimes at the end, disconnected loose pages would be included, that had been forgotten or mislaid. So that altogether the sorting of them was not easy. There was no arrangement what ever between Mr. Joyce and myself about this. He just took to sending them and I kept safely whatever reached me. (FDV: 4)

Weaver painstakingly preserved and ordered everything Joyce sent her: letters, manuscripts, and books as well as thousands of newspaper clippings on Joyce and his work. As Jane Lidderdale and Mary Nicholson have written, Weaver felt that "[Joyce's] incomparable gift to her must be passed on in good order."[80] In 1951 Weaver donated her unparalleled collection to the British Library, and, together with the library's archivists, George Painter and T. J. Brown, she arranged the manuscripts, typescripts, and proofs according to their eventual publication in the work: all the manuscripts were bound in eighteen volumes. Although the manuscripts themselves were not rearranged, their ordering was significantly revised first by Hayman during his work on *A First-Draft Version* and then again by Danis Rose, with the assistance of John O'Hanlon, for *The James Joyce Archive.*[81] Virtually every tangible stage of the creative work in progress of *Finnegans Wake* can be identified and mapped. Even those stages and documents that have not survived (or have not yet come to light) can be inferred from a comparison of those that have.[82]

Joyce's draft manuscripts can be generally categorized as early drafts (the most basic drafts); several stages of later drafts (each usually more legible than its predecessor); fair copies (more legible manuscripts produced from his drafts, most often so that they could be typed); typescripts (usually prepared for printers); galley and page proofs for serial and deluxe publication; printed texts that Joyce further revised for another publication; and the galley and page proofs for *Finnegans Wake* itself.[83]

The drafts of all the various texts, from 1923 through 1938, are replete with additions, and they resemble one another in their complexity and density. Joyce would then recopy these early drafts in a larger and almost always more legible hand, usually in pencil. As was already his practice when writing *Ulysses,* Joyce purposefully wrote the central text with an ever-increasing left margin on the page and usually reserved the other sides (versos of the preceding pages) for additional words, phrases, sentences, and larger blocks of texts that he would then integrate in the next copy of the draft. Compared with the central, fair-copied text, the material Joyce added interlinearly and in the margins on all sides tended to be in a smaller hand, in various directions, often both in pencil and ink, and barely legible. He relied on a complex system of tags and a tangled web of lines covering the page to remind him where to insert all of these supplementary texts. Subsequently, Joyce would cross through blocks of text with large crayon exxes once he had recopied them to another draft, and, because he was both author and scribe, he would often further revise the text as he transcribed it. The result is a page so crowded that it is difficult for almost any reader, including its author, to unravel and decipher. These drafts document in space and time the creative bursts of the text's sporadic but deliberate elaboration. Although the central text of subsequent drafts became progressively more legible, the marginal and interlinear additions continued to overwhelm the text.

From March through early October 1923 Joyce wrote the first drafts of his earliest sketches on whatever paper he had at hand, mostly large sheets of paper, filling both sides; he even resorted to restaurant stationery. Like so many of the early drafts that followed over the years, Joyce filled almost all the available space in the margins of his "jigsaw puzzle sketches" (LI: 206). But in mid-November 1923, when the work began to coalesce around HCE as its focal point, he reverted to writing his drafts in bound copybooks, just as he had in the later stages of writing *Ulysses.*[84] From 1923 through mid-1927 Joyce wrote his first and second drafts (as well as his earliest fair copies) in four bound copybooks.[85] After he had composed all the chapters of Books I and III and the first section of Book II in these copybooks Joyce wrote the remaining early drafts of Book II and what remained to be written of Book IV on loose sheets of paper.

When he fair-copied his drafts so a typescript could be prepared, Joyce usually turned these loose sheets and filled them lengthwise, again leaving spacious left margins for further revision. Several typists were employed over the years, both friends and professionals. Given the difficulty of his text and the complex and multiple levels of revisions they were asked to incorporate, Joyce was usually as attentive as he could be to the errors the typists inevitably introduced but he rarely checked this newer text against his own previous version, rather he emended the text before him as it had been typed or set in proofs. Nonetheless, once a clean typescript was prepared, Joyce compulsively revised it, sometimes for a further typescript or yet another fair copy but ultimately for a printer.

Work in Progress, as such, was inaugurated with the publication of Ford's *transatlantic review* in April 1924, and with it began the tremendous work of correcting and revising proofs that continued until January 1939.[86]

Printers usually sent Joyce multiple copies of several sets of each stage of proofs in preparation for publication. Unlike most authors, Joyce did not use these occasions simply to verify a correct setting of the text; instead (as with the typescripts), he used the clean copy to further emend it at virtually every opportunity.[87] The shocked reaction of the *transition* printers was quite common among Joyce's printers.[88] Several thousand pages of proofs are testimony to the continuing accretion of the text at these relatively late stages of the production. Then, after twelve issues of *transition* and several other publications of *Work in Progress* had appeared, the first deluxe edition, *Anna Livia Plurabelle* (Crosby Gaige), was published at the end of October 1928. Seven further deluxe editions and various other magazine publications followed, and at almost each stage Joyce revised and augmented his text. This process of writing and amplification continued from August 1931, with the first Faber and Faber specimen proof pages, to 16 January 1939, with the final page proofs of *Finnegans Wake.*

Another of Joyce's friends and collaborators, Paul Léon, his lawyer and assistant, played a heroic role in the preservation of Joyce's manuscripts, books, and family belongings. Disregarding personal danger, Léon returned to Joyce's apartment several times in 1939, salvaging what he believed were the most important documents, including all of the *Finnegans Wake* notebooks.[89] These notebooks are predraft manuscripts; that is, Joyce most often compiled them before he wrote the particular draft stage in which they would be used.[90] He almost always took these notes verbatim from printed sources and occasionally noted snatches of conversations (and some of his thoughts as well). Joyce relied on these notebooks to compose or revise every stage of the writing of *Finnegans Wake,* crossing through the notes he had used in crayon.[91]

The vast majority of the extant *Finnegans Wake* notebooks are part of the Wickser Joyce Collection at Buffalo. Peter Spielberg sorted these manuscripts into four basic groups, A through D. (All are prefixed with the Roman numeral VI, denoting the *Finnegans Wake* manuscripts at Buffalo.) He arranged the notebooks chronologically based on a comparison with the appearance of the words in pre–*Finnegans Wake* publications. His ordering is now known to be inaccurate and has been revised, first by Roland McHugh and, more recently and conclusively, by Danis Rose in his *Textual Diaries.*[92]

Notebook VI.A (Scribbledehobble, as it has come to be known) is unique among Joyce's notebooks for several reasons: it differs from the others because of its large size (1,008 pages) and its superior quality. It is also exceptional because of the fact that it is primarily filled with notes Joyce transferred from his other notebooks rather than directly from the sources. Unlike VI.A, notebooks VI.B.1–48 are all primarily in Joyce's hand. They too vary significantly in kind and quality, because it appears he purchased whatever notebook was readily available at the stationer's, anything from pulp paper tablets and quite common, inexpensive accounting ledgers to leather-bound journals with better-quality paper. Not only did Joyce use his notebooks at his desk, but, depending on their size, he would carry them around, jotting down fleeting notes as the need or opportunity arose. From October 1922 through April 1924 the first notebooks Joyce used were all similar stenographer's tablets, with horizontal spines. When opened, Joyce treated these pages as one long sheet, filling them with long lists of words and phrases.[93] Although well suited for note taking, these notebooks were presumably too awkward or too fragile to use when Joyce harvested material from them for his drafts. From mid-1924 on he alternated between different kinds of notebooks.[94] They too vary considerably in durability, size, and bulk, and the paper was variously ruled and lined or neither and even graph paper.

Notebooks VI.C.1–18, on the other hand, are completely in the hand of an amanuensis, Mme France Raphaël, whom Joyce employed from 1933 to 1936 solely to transcribe the by-then unused (and so uncrossed) notes from his primary notebooks.[95] Joyce used these at times faulty transcriptions in the elaboration of his work along with the notebooks he continued to compile during those years.[96]

Each manuscript is a window on the text on its way toward becoming the work. By focusing critical analysis on the process of textual production as documented in the material artifacts of the creative endeavor, genetic critics uncover new dimensions of the text. As the following essays demonstrate, by exploring the texts that surround the public, published works, genetic criticism both grounds speculative interpretations in an historical, material context and opens up a broader horizon for critical and textual interpretation.

LC

A Brief Introduction to Genetic Criticism

Ever since Louis Hay coined the term *genetic criticism* skeptics such as Antoine Compagnon and Jean-Yves Tadié have wondered whether it is a new discipline at all or merely a research tool and whether it is really that different from textual criticism and scholarly editing. Some answers to these questions are contained in the important notion of "avant-texte" (pre-text), which denotes the result of the critical analysis, reconstitution, and organization of all the extant documents related to the writing process one intends to examine. In 1972 Jean Bellemin-Noël introduced this term in contrast to a more conventional notion of text. The prefix *avant-* therefore implies a retrospective view that raises—in that order—the three questions that are dealt with in this brief introduction: where does the *avant-texte* end, how does it progress, and where does it start?[97]

The end result of the writing process has traditionally been the main focus of textual studies. Even the Italian practice of *variantistica* and the early practitioners of *critiques de genèse* in France were limited to the most legible manuscripts and documents closest to the publication stages as a way to adjudicate between uncertain readings. A concrete example of such a problematic reading may elucidate how a genetic approach differs from scholarly editing. What appears as "Well down" (FW: 598.11) in the published text of *Finnegans Wake* is the result of a transmissional departure between two typescripts, from "well dawn" (BL 47488 f. 49v; JJA 63: 50) to "well down" (BL 47488 f. 50; JJA 63: 79). It is uncertain whether Joyce typed this document himself or not, whether he accepted the transformation while revising the typescript and decided to keep it that way, or whether he simply overlooked it. If the purpose of manuscript research is the production of a critical edition, the editor has no choice but to cut the Gordian knot. Often this will involve taking recourse to the notion of "passive authorization": since the author has revised the whole text and since he did not mark the change as an error, he approved it by default. Genetic critics do not employ this editorial strategy to settle such cases but prefer to draw attention to its unsettled nature. They attempt to understand the writing as a process rather than reduce its complexity, as is done in a traditional critical edition. What this approach can yield is an enhanced awareness of the tension between completeness and incompleteness and a revaluation of the work's progress.

The confrontation of a published text with all its previous versions gives the reader an idea of what they might have become. This attention to the text's potential energy is inextricably linked with genetic criticism's change of perspective. The main criticism against manuscript studies in the first half of the twentieth century is that their interest in the manuscripts works in the reverse direction. Pierre-Marc de Biasi notes, for instance, that archivists often arrange the manuscripts teleologically according to the final narrative structure. Therefore, he suggests a double-axis ordering in which the teleological *rangement* is followed by a chronological classification of the manuscripts (the so-called *classement*). In order to map all the hesitations and side paths of the writing process, it is necessary to try and study a work not only "counterclockwise" or in retrospect but also "in prospect." Daniel Ferrer has shown how every artifact inevitably involves a project, which means that it constantly "oscillates between an anticipatory perspective . . . and a retrospective vision."[98] This oscillation of perspectives is therefore a crucial strategy of genetic criticism. To a certain extent this double view becomes visual in Hans Walter Gabler's synoptic edition of *Ulysses,* with its edited text as a finished product on the right-hand side and a genetic representation of the textual evolution on the left-hand side. Gabler's edition partially draws on the German textual scholar Hans Zeller, who refers to the "synchronic structures" within the textual history as "versions" (*Fassungen*).[99] But no matter how crucial the notion of "version" is in German *Editionswissenschaft,* Gabler's is not considered a genetic edition according to French standards, since it does not present the different versions in extenso. Recent developments, however, show an enhanced attention to the writing process as such, not from an exclusively representational perspective. Hermann Zwerschina, for instance, presents different versions of Georg Trakl's poems in their entirety in order to gain a better insight into the creative process. Several American textual scholars have incorporated textual representations of more than one version of a work in scholarly editions. Donald H. Reiman suggests a multiversional representation or "versioning" as an alternative to "editing." Although this approach was not developed from a genetic point of view, draft stages are also taken into account. The main purpose of this textual approach is to offer readers and critics the opportunity to figure out for themselves how the work evolved during the writing process. Still, it is mainly concerned with representation and does not regard itself as a form of literary criticism, which is where genetic criticism differs from textual scholarship. Genetic critics try to reconstitute the writing process, not the "final" text of a literary work. The editorial results this research may produce are regarded as a by-product, not the aim of the investigation.[100] The recently coined term *genetic edition* comes closer to genetic criticism, but even in a documentary edition such as the Frankfurter Kafka edition, which was conceived as an archival rather than a critical edition, the main purpose is the presentation, not the critical study of the genetic material.[101] In comparison with Gabler's synoptic *Ulysses,* however, this kind of edition is less textually oriented because it offers facsimiles with diplomatic transcriptions, respecting the topography of the manuscript. Inevitably, this less textually oriented approach moves further away from the (final) text, which is reflected in Gabler's own shift of interest from the purely textual development to the topographical distribution of additions on the page.

Recent tendencies in French genetic criticism move even further away from a strictly textual approach and explore the *avant-texte*'s starting points in the author's personal library.[102] The edition of *The "Finnegans Wake" Notebooks at Buffalo* is an example of these efforts to establish what a writer reads, what he deems interesting enough to excerpt, and how these reading notes are processed and incorporated in the manuscripts. This expanding field of genetic studies comes closer to disciplines such as the history of reading. In a countermovement against a textual bias, paratactic reading notes receive ample attention. At the same time textual critics all over the world try to broaden their subject of research by focusing not only on the "linguistic code" but also on the "bibliographic code," including the material features of a publication and the meaning they carry.[103] The increased attention to these iconic aspects and the topography of manuscripts reflects a spatial interest. Nevertheless, the ultimate aim of these examinations is often the reconstruction of the writing chronology, for genetic criticism's main subject of research is the temporal dimension of writing, from "well dawn" to "well down" and vice versa.

DVH

Notes

1. For examples of the various debates concerning the nature of genetic criticism when applied to the *Wake* see Geert Lernout, "The *Finnegans Wake* Notebooks and Radical Philology," *Probes,* 19–48; R. J. Schork, "By Jingo: Genetic Criticism of *Finnegans Wake,*" *JSA* 5 (1994): 104–27; and Sam Slote, "Swerving Shores, Bendings Abeyed," *Papers on Joyce* 2 (1996): 117–24.

2. A. Walton Litz, *The Art of James Joyce* (New York: Oxford University Press, 1964), v.

3. See also Jane Lidderdale and Mary Nicholson, *Dear Miss Weaver* (London: Faber and Faber, 1970), 416.

4. This list of errata is now in the British Library (BL 57356; JJA 12: 176–81). See also Lidderdale and Nicholson 1970, 210.

5. The identification of VI.B.10 as the earliest notebook was made by Danis Rose and John O'Hanlon in "A Nice Beginning: On the *Ulysses/Finnegans Wake* Interface," *"Finnegans Wake": Fifty Years,* ed. Geert Lernout (Amsterdam: Rodopi, 1990), 165–73.

6. The "V" is presumably a caret mark indicating that a comma should be added.

7. As above, the "V" is a caret mark, in this case indicating the addition of the letter *s*.

8. The JJA inverted pages 1 and 2. A careful examination of the original shows the proper order of the pages. See *Buffalo VI.B.10,* 4–13.

9. See *Buffalo VI.B.10,* 18–20; Wim Van Mierlo, "Indexing the Buffalo Notebooks," *Writing Its Own Wrunes For Ever,* ed. Daniel Ferrer and Claude Jacquet (Tusson: Du Lérot, 1998), 168–90, 175–76; and Vincent Deane, "Greek Gifts: *Ulysses* into Fox in VI.B.10," *JSA* 5 (1994): 163–75.

10. Vincent Deane has traced most of these entries to the journal articles from which Joyce derived them. A good number come from the *Irish Times,* but many other papers were used. A cluster of notes on pages 61–74 deals with the murder trial of Frederick Bywaters as it was covered by the *Daily Sketch* and several other papers in December 1922. Some of these notes were eventually used in *Finnegans Wake,* chapter I.2–4 to partially characterize one aspect of HCE's crime. Deane discusses this in "Bywaters and the Original Crime," *"Finnegans Wake": "teems of times,"* ed. Andrew Treip (Amsterdam: Rodopi, 1994), 165–204. See also *Buffalo VI.B.10,* 9–10.

11. This source was first discovered by Andrew Norris, "The Plurality of Character in 'Finnegans Wake,'" Ph.D. dissertation, University of Leeds, 1989. See also Deane 1994, 166–75.

12. See Jed Deppman's incisive analysis in "The Return to Medievalism: James Joyce in 1923," *Medieval Joyce,* ed. Lucia Boldrini (Amsterdam: Rodopi, 2002), 45–77. Also see Deppman's chapter in this volume.

13. Thomas Sturge Moore, "The Story of Tristram and Isolt in English Poetry," *Criterion* 1.1 (October 1922): 34–49, 42.

14. See also WiT: 56–92. Danis Rose has disagreed with the importance Hayman ascribes to the Tristan and Isolde tale at this early date of the composition of the *Wake* ("The Beginning of all Thisorder of Work in Progress," *JJQ* 28.4 [Fall 1991]: 957–65).

15. It is also possible that Joyce's extreme interest in the Bywaters case (see note 10) derived from an analogy between the participants of that squalid love triangle and the story of Tristan, Isolde, and King Mark.

16. Georges Borach, "Conversations with James Joyce," trans. Joseph Prescott, *College English* 15 (March 1954): 325–27, 326. This quotation comes from a diary entry by Borach dated 21 October 1918.

17. Rose posits a lost notebook in between VI.B.10 and VI.B.3 (TDJJ: 46), but there are enough missing pages in these two notebooks to possibly account for any gap in Joyce's notes.

18. Vere Foster was the author of drawing textbooks, and his name was used as a brand of notebook. Joyce's 1904 "Portrait" essay was written in his sister Mabel's Vere Foster Ruled Exercise Book.

19. J. M. Flood, *Ireland: Its Saints and Scholars* (Dublin: Talbot Press, 1917), 105–6.

20. Deane notes that a popular cartoon figure called Pop appeared in John Millar Watt's strip "Reggie Breaks It Gently." This strip was run in several papers, including the *Daily Sketch,* a paper Joyce read regularly in the 1920s. It first appeared on 20 May 1921 (see *Buffalo VI.B.3,* 11–12; Deane 1994, 172 n. 13).

21. This entry derives from Flood's book on saints: "An Ollave poet had to possess a knowledge of seven kinds of verse, and to be able to compose extemporaneously in each" (1917, 86).

22. Frank Harris, *Oscar Wilde: His Life and Confessions* (New York: Horizon Press, 1974), 608. When Joyce used this passage in the "Here Comes Everybody" sketch, he obviated the elements that specifically referred to Horatio Lloyd (BL 47472 f. 97v; JJA 45: 3; FDV: 63). See Sam Slote, "Wilde Thing: Concerning the Eccentricities of a Figure of Decadence in *Finnegans Wake,*" *Probes,* 101–22, 105–6.

23. See Clive Hart, "The Earwickers of Sidlesham," *A Wake Digest,* ed. Clive Hart and Fritz Senn (Sidney: Sidney University Press, 1968), 21–22.

24. See "The *Finnegans Wake* Manuscripts" below. Also see Jorn Barger, "A Preliminary Stratigraphy of 'Scribbledehobble,'" Treip 1994, 127–37; see also his online article "A New Game," http://www.robotwisdom.com/jaj/newgame.html. Accessed March 2006.

25. In a note for *Exiles* about Bertha Joyce calls Isolde a "sister in love" (E: 157). See also WiT: 74–78.

26. See WiT: 93–114 and Hayman's book *Epiphanies* (Barcelona: Montesinas, 1996) and his essay "Epiphanoiding," *Geni,* 27–41.

27. Valery Larbaud reported that Joyce read him a draft of "Tristan and Isolde" in March (JJII: 554).

28. See WiT: 90–92 and Rose 1991, 961–63.

29. The new NLI manuscripts also include a fair copy of the material on BL 47480 f. 267v, but without "Nightpiece." Presumably, this draft was made in July before Joyce sent the sheet with the "Roderick" and "Tristan" drafts to Weaver (LI: 203).

30. Unlike the "Roderick O'Conor" and "Tristan and Isolde" sketches, the "Dympna" sketch uses a lot of material from the extant portion of VI.B.3 that had previously not been located in the manuscripts. Even with this new sketch, a great deal of unlocated material remains in VI.B.3, VI.B.10, and VI.A, which suggests that Joyce wrote still further drafts in early 1923 that may still come to light, perhaps even other new sketches.

31. For an examination of the evolution of *Wakean* language see Dirk Van Hulle's chapter in this volume and also Laurent Milesi, "L'Idiome babélien de *Finnegans Wake,*" *Genèse de Babel, Joyce et la création,* ed. Claude Jacquet (Paris: CNRS, 1986), 155–215, as well as his essay "Vico . . . Jousse. Joyce . . . Langue," *James*

Joyce: "Scribble" 1, genèse des textes, ed. Claude Jacquet (Paris: Lettres Modernes, 1988), 143–62.

32. See Bill Cadbury's essay in this volume and Bill Cadbury, "The Development of the 'Eye, Ear, Nose and Throat Witness' Testimony in I.4," *Probes,* 203–54.

33. On the Boston location for the letter's provenance see Adaline Glasheen's still-seminal essay "*Finnegans Wake* and the Girls from Boston Mass.," *Hudson Review* 7.1 (Spring 1954): 89–96.

34. This process of textual disjection is described in Dirk Van Hulle's chapter on Book IV in this volume. See also WiT: 166–77, JJA 46: xiii–xviii, and Laurent Milesi, "Metaphors of the Quest in *Finnegans Wake,*" Lernout 1990, 79–107.

35. See WiT: 30–55; David Hayman, "Nodality and the Infrastructure of *Finnegans Wake,*" *JJQ* 16.1–2 (Fall 1978–Winter 1979): 135–49; David Hayman, *Re-Forming the Narrative* (Ithaca: Cornell University Press, 1987), 73–104; and David Hayman, "The Manystorytold of the *Wake:* How Narrative Was Made to Inform the Non-Narrativity of the Night," *JSA* 8 (1997): 81–114.

36. See Jean-Michel Rabaté, "Lapsus ex machina," *Joyce Upon the Void* (New York: St. Martin's Press, 1991), 112–33.

37. Finn's Hotel was where Nora Barnacle was working when she first met James Joyce in 1904 (JJII: 156).

38. Danis Rose and John O'Hanlon, "The Name of the Book," *AFWC* 4.3 (Spring 1989): 41–50, 47–49. This article proposes the earliest formulation of the *Finn's Hotel* theory. See also TDJJ: 95–96.

39. See also Daniel Ferrer's review of *Textual Diaries,* "Opening up the *Avant-Textes,*" *James Joyce Broadsheet* 43 (February 1996): 1.

40. Joyce had also employed sigla in the earlier notebook, VI.B.11, but their use there seems tentative and unsystematized. See also TDJJ: 54–55. Some sigla also appear in earlier notebooks, but these were added into them after 1924.

41. In a later letter to Weaver Joyce remarks that Larbaud laughed at the sigla when he was shown them, but Joyce added, as a defense of his eccentric system, "it saves time" (LI: 216).

42. The first extended study of the sigla is Roland McHugh, *The Sigla of "Finnegans Wake"* (London: Edward Arnold, 1976). See also Jean-Michel Rabaté, "*Wakean* Cryptogenetics," Rabaté 1991, 69–111, 77–89. McHugh's study popularized the now widely used term "sigla," which he took from FW: 032.14, where it refers to the initials HCE. In his letters Joyce consistently referred to these odd characters as "signs," a term that Rose prefers (TDJJ: 44 n. 2). The *OED* defines "sigla" as initials or marks of abbreviation and thus allows both possibilities (see also *Buffalo VI.B.6,* 4–5).

43. This commentary is Thomas Josephus Lamy, *Commentarium in Librum Geneseos* (Mechelen: H. Dessain, 1883), vol. 1. See Ingeborg Landuyt, "Tale Told of Shem: Some Elements at the Inception of *FW* I.7," *Geni,* 115–34. See also her essay in this volume.

44. Gilbert incorrectly transcribed this as "Egan" in LI. I am grateful to Ingeborg Landuyt for pointing this out.

45. Léon Metchnikoff, *La Civilisation et les grands fleuves historiques* (Paris: Hachette, 1889). This source was discovered by Ingeborg Landuyt and Geert Lernout, "Joyce's Sources: *Les grands fleuves historiques,*" *JSA* 6 (1995): 99–138.

46. Landuyt and Lernout 1995, 112–15.

47. In VI.B.17 (April–May 1926) Joyce began using the siglum ⊣ in place of ⊥ for Issy/Isolde. If ⊥ was an inversion of T, then the new siglum allowed for mirroring with its complement ⊢. In this way both Isoldes could be designated. The K siglum here stands for Kevin; its use here shows that Joyce had already planned on using the Kevin sketch for the book's final chapter, or *ricorso,* which would follow Λd.

48. See Luca Crispi's essay in this volume for more on how III.4 sparked the idea for Book II. Also see TDJJ: 86.

49. See Sam Slote's essay on II.1 for more information about this plan.

50. Two days later he wrote that the *Dial* would publish the chapters but only after heavy editing. Joyce refused (LIII: 142).

51. See Geert Lernout's essay in this volume.

52. For an account of how the final sentence eventually dovetailed into the first see the essays by Geert Lernout, Dirk Van Hulle, and Finn Fordham in this volume.

53. Mary and Padraic Colum, *Our Friend James Joyce* (New York: Doubleday, 1958), 123.

54. See also James Stephens, "The James Joyce I Knew," *Listener* 36 (24 October 1946): 565–66.

55. Eugene Jolas, "Homage to James Joyce," *transition,* no. 21 (1932): 250–53, 252. Because of this hasty addendum to *transition* 6 "the page numberings of that volume . . . started to stutter around page 106, which was followed by 106a, 106b, 106c, 106d, 106e, 106f" (Jolas 1932, 252). See also Fred R. Higginson, "Notes on the Text of *Finnegans Wake,*" *Journal of English and Germanic Philology* 55.4 (July 1956): 451–56.

56. See Dirk Van Hulle, "The Art of Not Being Rude: The Encyclopedic Recycling of Wyndham Lewis' Early Joyce Criticism," http://www.antwerpjamesjoycecenter.com/lewis.htm. Accessed March 2006.

57. See R. J. Schork's essay in this volume.

58. See Sam Slote's essay in this volume.

59. See TDJJ: 169–81.

60. See Luca Crispi's essay in this volume.

61. See also Paul Léon to T. S. Eliot (JJ/PL: 179, 12 July 1936). In this letter Léon writes that Joyce thinks he will be done with all of *Work in Progress* within a year.

62. These are, under "Cyclops," "shot Buckley" (BL 49975 f. 7r; JJA 12: 7);

“[bl]Buckley & Russian general (bloody boy)” (BL 49975 f. 8r; JJA 12: 11); “Oxen of the Sun”: “How Buckley shot the Russian general” (BL 49975 f. 12r; JJA 12: 27); and “Eumeus”: “Buckley & Russian general” (BL 49975 f. 23r; JJA 12: 69).

63. See David Hayman’s essay in this volume for more detail and also WiT: 24–25, 39, 102 n. 13.

64. Rose claims that what is now the second half of II.3 was originally conceived to be II.4. But when Joyce “rediscovered” the sketches he grafted what had been intended as II.4 onto II.3 and then pieced together “Tristan and Isolde” with “Mamalujo” to form a new II.4. See TDJJ: 125–36 and the discussion above on Rose’s theory of “Finn’s Hotel.”

65. See Dirk Van Hulle’s essay in this volume.

66. For a detailed explanation of how Joyce grafted “Roderick O’Conor” into II.3 see Jed Deppman, “Hallow’d Chronickles and Exploytes of King Rodericke O’Conor from Joyce’s Earliest Draftes to the End of Causal Historie,” *Probes*, 179–202, 194–202.

67. These revised page proofs are part of the Paul and Lucie Léon/James Joyce Collection at the University of Tulsa; these were not reproduced in the JJA.

68. On the evening of 13 November 1938 Joyce telegraphed Weaver to tell her that he had finished *Work in Progress* that night (JJ/PL: 73). On 18 November he wrote Paul Ruggiero and exclaimed, “Hurray! I have finished this blasted book” (LI: 403).

69. See appendix 2 and also Finn Fordham, “The Corrections to *Finnegans Wake*,” *James Joyce: The Study of Languages*, ed. Dirk Van Hulle (Brussels: Peter Lang, 2002), 37–52.

70. Joyce also used a 1940 pocket diary to record lists of American and French expressions, mostly slang. This is now item VIII.C.2 in the Buffalo collection.

71. Stanislaus Joyce, *Ricordi di James Joyce* (Firenze: Fratelli Parenti Editori, 1941). This was translated into English by Ellsworth Mason and published as *Recollections of James Joyce* (New York: James Joyce Society, 1950).

72. Robert Spoo, “Unpublished Letters of Ezra Pound to James, Nora, and Stanislaus Joyce,” *JJQ* 32.3–4 (Spring–Summer 1995): 533–81, 575.

73. For a sequential listing of the *Finnegans Wake* manuscripts see Michael Groden’s *Index*, JJA 64: 41–69.

74. The notebooks were initially sorted and cataloged by Peter Spielberg; see *James Joyce’s Manuscripts and Letters at the University of Buffalo* (New York: University of Buffalo, 1962). I am preparing a new edition of the Buffalo Joyce collection catalog and in the interim revised and amplified bibliographical descriptions of the manuscripts will appear on The Poetry Collection’s website; see Luca Crispi, “ReCollecting Joyce at Buffalo: Revising and Completing the Catalog,” *Geni*, 13–26. The *Finnegans Wake* manuscripts in the Buffalo Joyce Collection arrived in four consignments: the initial acquisition of the Joyce family collection in 1950 (known as the Wickser Joyce Collection); the Sylvia Beach Joyce collection in 1960

(known as the Stafford Joyce Collection), which arrived in two parts; and a further acquisition of six *Work in Progress* galley proofs acquired from Maria Jolas in 1968. These proofs were uncataloged at the time the JJA was produced. The British Library's Joyce manuscript collection is cataloged online, but also see the various volumes of the JJA. Harriet Shaw Weaver initially planned on presenting the National Library of Ireland with her collection of manuscripts but Nora and Giorgio Joyce's reservations prompted her to alter her plans.

75. All the other known *Finnegans Wake* manuscripts are at the National Library of Ireland; the Beinecke Library, Yale University; the Firestone Library, Princeton University; the Harry Ransom Humanities Research Center, University of Texas at Austin; the Fromkin Memorial Library, University of Wisconsin–Milwaukee; the McFarlin Library, University of Tulsa; the Zurich James Joyce Foundation as well as in a few private collections. The NLI's holdings comprise four collections: manuscript material in the James Joyce/Paul Léon Collection; typescripts given to the Library by Jane Lidderdale (MSS 17,820); a variety of manuscript material acquired with the "Joyce 2002 Papers"; and six pre–*Work in Progress* manuscripts acquired in 2006. None of the NLI manuscripts appeared in the JJA. The Beinecke's holdings comprise the John J. Slocum collection of manuscripts as well as a wide array of other material. The Princeton holdings comprise various manuscripts acquired as part of Sylvia Beach's Shakespeare and Company collection. The HRC's holding comprise several sets of proofs acquired at various times. The Fromkin holdings comprise a single sheet of *transition* 13 proofs that ended up as part of *The Little Review* collection by accident. This sheet does not appear in the JJA. The McFarlin holdings comprise several settings of the final page proofs of *Finnegans Wake* acquired from Alexis and Marilena Léon as well as a variety of proofs for several deluxe editions of *Work in Progress* acquired at auctions. None of the McFarlin manuscripts appeared in the JJA. A partial description of these manuscripts can be found on their website. The various manuscripts in the Zurich collection were given as the Hans E. Jahnke bequest in 2006. None of this notebook and manuscript material appeared in the JJA.

76. In 1999 Geert Lernout was the first to document that it was actually in mid-November 1923, not October, as had been thought until then, that Joyce moved beyond the sketches to what would be *Finnegans Wake*, but because his eyesight prevented him from writing himself he dictated the seminal scene to Nora Joyce, and so it is her hand that we encounter on the first two pages of the copybook. He concludes: "The fact that this had not been noticed before does show how much basic philological work still needs to be done" (Geert Lernout, "Beginning Again," *JJQ* 36.4 [Summer 1999]: 984–86, 986).

77. These are reproduced in JJA 28–63.

78. A great deal more of the manuscript record of *Finnegans Wake* survives than for any other of Joyce's works but all the extant evidence suggests that he had developed his writing methods (both in terms of note-taking and use, as well as

the process of continuous accretion of the text on each version of the manuscripts) at least as early as 1904 and, although he refined it over the years, Joyce used the same techniques throughout his writing career, regardless of the increasingly experimental nature of his works. Some of the earliest evidence of Joyce's note-taking techniques for draft usage can be found in the recently discovered "Paris–Pola Commonplace Book" (NLI 36,639/2/A).

79. At this time Léon also sent her a sheaf of notes Joyce had used to write *Ulysses*.

80. Lidderdale and Nicholson 1970, 406.

81. See Hayman's "Draft Catalogue" (FDV: 286–330). Rose's draft codes as set out in the JJA have now become standard, and the manuscripts are usually referred to according to his arrangement in sections, subsections, and levels. Nonetheless, still further manuscript material has been uncovered since the publication of the JJA that will necessitate a further revision of the JJA's ordering and coding.

82. Since no new manuscript had appeared in about forty years, in 1999 most Joycean textual scholars presumed that few if any further Joyce manuscripts would come to light. Our perspective has been turned on its head in the twenty-first century. In 2000 the first new Joyce manuscript in decades appeared at auction at Christie's, New York. It was a later draft of the "Circe" (15) episode of *Ulysses* and was acquired by the National Library of Ireland (MS 20,030). A year later another new manuscript appeared at Sotheby's, London. It was an earlier draft of the "Eumaeus" episode of *Ulysses* and it is in a private collection (see Sam Slote, "Preliminary Comments on Two Newly Discovered *Ulysses* Manuscripts," *JJQ* 39.1 [Fall 2001]: 17–28). No one could have anticipated what happened next. In 2002 the NLI acquired a tremendous collection of notebooks and earlier and later drafts of *Ulysses* (comparable only to Buffalo's collection), as well as various typescripts and proofs of *Work in Progress* and *Finnegans Wake*: these "Joyce 2002 Papers" were catalogued by Peter Kenny (MSS 36,639). In 2006 the NLI acquired yet another collection of significant manuscripts, they are six pre–*Work in Progress* sheets. (I am preparing a revised descriptive bibliography of all the NLI's Joyce manuscripts.) Also in 2006 the Zurich James Joyce Foundation was given a substantial collection of books, letters, and manuscripts. Building on the expertise of Fritz Senn and the staff of the Foundation, these primary documents further establish Zurich an essential research center. There is no telling what new documents may appear in the future or how they may alter our currently held opinions about Joyce's creative endeavors but such are the joys and challenges of material textual studies.

83. Examples of printed text that Joyce revised for a subsequent publication is a copy of *transition* 8 that Joyce revised for the deluxe edition as *Anna Livia Plurabelle* and the published text of *Two Tales of Shem and Shaun* (Faber and Faber) that Joyce revised so that it could be set in galleys of what would be published as *Finnegans Wake*. During Joyce's writing career, galley proofs were the first setting

of the type and were single sided; page proofs, on the other hand, were often on better quality paper and were organized in signatures for publication.

84. Joyce's use of these bound copybooks allows for a more complete understanding of the genetic development of each section and chapter than was the case when he used loose sheets of paper. The initial development of *Finnegans Wake*'s structure was influenced in large measure by the material in which it was written.

85. These four copybooks are cataloged as BL 47471b (I.2–5, 7, and 8, November 1923–February 1924); BL 47482b (III.1–3, March–December 1924); BL 47482a (III.4, II.2, and I.1, September 1925–November 1926); and BL 47473 (I.6, summer 1927).

86. Listings of Joyce's serial and deluxe publications can be found in John J. Slocum and Herbert Cahoon, *A Bibliography of James Joyce* (1882–1941) (New Haven: Yale University Press, 1953), in the appropriate volumes of the JJA, and in TDJJ: 197–98, and in appendix 2 of this volume.

87. Joyce gradually initiated this practice of expanding his text on the at least two rounds of revisions of the *Ulysses* typescripts and then on the many sets of proofs provided to him by Beach and Darantiere. Of course, he was not the only author to take advantage of the opportunity afforded by a clean document to heavily revise his texts; other notable examples are Yeats, Balzac, and Proust.

88. See Eugene Jolas's account of the printer's distress when confronted with Joyce's revised proofs in "Remembering James Joyce," *Modernism/Modernity* 5.2 (April 1998): 1–29, 11.

89. These were acquired at auction from the Joyce family, following an exhibition at the La Hune Gallery. See Bernard Gheerbrant, *James Joyce: sa vie, son oeuvre, son rayonnement* (Paris: La Hune, 1949).

90. There are several notable exceptions to this over-simplified description of Joyce's general note-taking practices (VI.B.29 to name just one). In these notebooks Joyce was seeking very specific sources for particular uses in chapters for which he already had a well-defined plan in mind, such as for *Haveth Childers Everywhere* or *Anna Livia Plurabelle.* Since 2002 not all the *Work in Progress/ Finnegans Wake* notebooks are to be found in Buffalo. This new notebook material is in the National Library of Ireland and the Zurich Joyce Foundation (and presumably yet more could still appear).

91. Joyce used the same basic colored crayons throughout the sixteen years of harvesting from his notebooks: red, orange, green, blue, black, and brown. He had developed this technique as early as *Ulysses.* It would seem the color he chose at a particular stage had no intrinsic significance.

92. See Roland McHugh, "Chronology of the Buffalo Notebooks," *AWN* 9.2 (April 1972): 19–31; "Chronology of the Buffalo Notebooks (contd.)," *AWN* 9.3 (June 1972): 36–38; and "Chronology of the Buffalo Notebooks—Corrigenda," *AWN* 9.5 (October 1972): 100. The *Buffalo Notebooks* series continues to refine this chronology.

93. The JJA's arrangement of the pages side by side is thus deceptive of the nature of these notebooks. The *Buffalo Notebook* series includes color images of the "openings," thereby indicating the manner in which Joyce saw and used these sheet-length pages.

94. These forty-two remaining extant notebooks are all right bound, and Joyce used each page as a separate unit.

95. A notebook (VI.C. 7) contains transcriptions of a no longer extant *Ulysses* notebook that was transcribed and portions of which were used by Joyce in *Finnegans Wake.*

96. Spielberg designated a further group of notebooks VI.D.1–7. These so-called virtual notebooks are a record of the unused elements from notebooks that are no longer extant but were transcribed in the C-series of notebooks. Rose has postulated five further notebooks for which only collateral evidence exists (TDJJ: 25–34).

97. A new collection of translations of French genetic criticism provides a further introduction to *critique génétique*: Jed Deppman, Daniel Ferrer, and Michael Groden, eds., *Genetic Criticism: Texts and Avant-Textes* (Philadelphia: University of Pennsylvania Press, 2004).

98. Daniel Ferrer, "Clementis's Cap: Retroaction and Persistence in the Genetic Process," trans. Marlena G. Corcoran, *Drafts, Yale French Studies* 89, ed. Michel Contat, Denis Hollier, and Jacques Neefs (1996): 223–36, 225.

99. Hans Walter Gabler, "The Synchrony and Diachrony of Texts: Practice and Theory of the Critical Edition of James Joyce's *Ulysses,*" *TEXT* 1 (1981): 305–26, 309.

100. Daniel Ferrer, "Hypertextual Representation of Literary Working Papers," *Literary and Linguistic Computing* 10.2 (1995): 143–45, 143.

101. See Pierre-Marc de Biasi, "Édition horizontale, édition verticale: pour une typologie des éditions génétiques (le domaine français 1980–1995)," *Éditer des manuscrits: archives, complétude, lisibilité,* ed. Béatrice Didier and Jacques Neefs (Saint-Denis: Presses Universitaires de Vincennes, 1996), 159–93. See also Hans Zeller and Gunter Martens, eds., *Textgenetische Edition,* Beiheft zu *Editio* (Tübingen: Niemeyer, 1998); Roland Reuß et al., eds., *Kafka, Franz: Historisch-kritische Ausgabe sämtlicher Handschriften, Drucke und Typoskripte* (Frankfurt am Main: Stroemfeld/Roter Stern, 1996).

102. Such as Daniel Ferrer and Paolo D'Iorio, eds., *Bibliothèques d'écrivains* (Paris: CNRS, 2001).

103. Such as George Bornstein and Theresa Tinkle, eds., *The Iconic Page in Manuscript, Print and Digital Culture* (Ann Arbor: University of Michigan Press, 1998).

The Beginning

Chapter I.1

GEERT LERNOUT

As the case of *Finnegans Wake* shows, the first pages of a book do not always represent its genetic beginning. By the time Joyce was ready to write what would later become the first chapter, he had already written a substantial part of the book. Also, beginning and end were problematic concepts in the case of this book. When Joyce had only just started the drafting of the chapter, he wrote Harriet Shaw Weaver on 8 November 1926 about his decision to put "the piece in the place of honour, namely the first pages," and he added that "the book really has no beginning or end. (Trade secret, registered at Stationers Hall.) It ends in the middle of a sentence and begins in the middle of the same sentence" (LI: 246). The actual writing of the first part of this sentence, which closes the book, would have to wait for another twelve years. At that time Joyce even had trouble getting the second half of the sentence right, changing its basic rhythm on the last proofs.

First, I will describe briefly what, by the summer of 1926, Joyce had accomplished in his work on his new book and the circumstances in which Joyce began to write a chapter that is in many ways an overture and a prelude. Then I will look at how the notebooks Joyce had been using in the summer of 1926 supplied him with materials that would help in the writing of the chapter. Finally, I will turn to the different stages of the chapter's development.

In the summer of 1926 *Work in Progress* had not even a title yet: in a letter from Ostend to Sylvia Beach about the publication of the four watches of Shaun in the *Dial* Joyce asked Beach to tell Marianne Moore to use "some such title as Ford or Walsh or The Criterion used" (JJ/SB: 71). In any case, the existing parts of his new work had a logic and coherence that would be changed significantly by the addition of the new chapter. If we set aside the early sketches (which is what Joyce himself did at the time), *Work in Progress* at this moment had a real focus that had developed out of the HCE sketch: the story of HCE, of his wife and children. There were the adventures of Humphrey Chimpden Earwicker himself and the rumors about them in chapters 2–4, a description of his wife ALP's letter in chapter 5, a denunciation of his son Shem in chapter 7, and a dialogue about ALP in chapter 8. These texts, from the beginning of the "Here Comes Everybody" sketch to the end of "ALP," formed a unity: the first typescripts were still continuous and only later broken up when separate parts were published in journals. The story in Book III was less straightforward, but it was clear that HCE's other son, Shaun, was the central character. The earliest version of II.2 again has the two brothers as its central heroes, this time studying their mother's anatomy through a problem in Euclid. With the writing of I.1 Joyce would significantly alter his view of what the book was going to be.

In *The Textual Diaries of James Joyce* Danis Rose describes the peculiar circumstances of the late spring and early summer of 1926. On 7 June Joyce wrote to Miss Weaver that between the six HCE chapters and the Shaun sequence, there would be another "three or four episodes" (LI: 241). A few weeks earlier he had described a piece that was to follow the fourth watch of Shaun as "K's orisons" (LI: 241). Rose points out that not only the basic structure of the book was in place but the idea of a book of the night in itself is new: "This is the earliest adumbration of a chronological succession of episodes filling in the hours of a single night" (TDJJ: 91).

Joyce then began the piece that he had first called "night studies," then "the triangle," then, when it was published as one of the *Tales Told of Shem and Shaun,* "The Muddest Thick That Was Ever Heard Dump," which finally became section 8 of II.2. After a long process, breathtakingly described by Luca Crispi, Joyce took the drafts of the piece (and notebook VI.B.12, in which he had been making notes on mathematics and geometry) with him on his holiday to Belgium. From there he sent a copy of the four Shaun chapters to the American magazine the *Dial,* which had offered him $600. On his return from Belgium he sent the early version of II.2 to Wyndham Lewis, who had asked him to contribute to the first issue of a new journal, the *Enemy.*

Around 23 September, when Joyce was still in Brussels, the *Dial*'s refusal to print Λabcd, as Joyce called the early version of Book III, seemed to confirm Stanislaus Joyce's earlier objections to the new direction his brother's work was taking. A day later, in the letter in which he told Miss Weaver about the *Dial's* refusal, Joyce asked, since the "gentlemen of the brush and hammer seemed to have worked that way," if she could "order him a piece" (LI: 245). Miss Weaver did, in a letter dated 1 October and accompanied by a pamphlet by James Cropper about a giant's grave at Saint Andrew's in Penrith:

> To Messrs Jacques le Joyeux, Giacomo Jakob, Skeumas Sheehy and whole Company: Sirs: Kindly supply the undersigned with one full length grave account of his esteemed Highness Rhaggrick O'Hoggnor's Hogg Tomb as per photos enclosed and oblige
> Yours faithfully
> Henriette Véavère (JJII: 582)

The tone of this letter is interesting in the light of Joyce's earlier attempts to convince Miss Weaver of the value of his experimental method. Maybe as a sort of response in kind, Joyce's Maecenas jokingly adopts the book's punning. Although she added in the letter that she thought the pamphlet and the resulting order were "within the scope" of the present project, Miss Weaver concluded: "But what I would really like is to place an order well in advance when another book is under contemplation! But that time is far away." Joyce decided to ignore the implied criticism and to concentrate on the challenge.

The piece Joyce wrote for Miss Weaver became the opening of *Finnegans Wake.* As Richard Ellmann in his biography pointed out, the order supplied Joyce with a way to connect HCE with the giant interred in the Dublin landscape. With warrior Finn MacCool came the thematic clusters of building, conflict, war, sexual rivalry, the wake of Finnegan, whose wall brought in Humpty Dumpty and whose fall introduced Adam and Eve, and so on.

Rose suggests that most of this development, and thus most of chapter 1, was the result of Miss Weaver's happy order. In reality Joyce had been preparing a new sortie for almost two months. The last part of VI.B.12 is later than Rose assumes and dates in fact from the Belgian holiday. While he was still writing and rewriting the geometry lesson Joyce also began to explore Finn material. On pages 128–30 he made notes from an unidentified account of the story of Dermot and Grania, the Irish Tristan and Isolde (with Finn in the role of King Mark). Just a few pages further on we find Joyce reading *The Meaning of Meaning* by C. K. Ogden and I. A. Richards, covering the first half of the book and paying considerable attention to the authors' discussion of the power and magic of words. These notes are briefly interrupted on page 137 by a set of notes from J.-C. Mardrus's introduction to his translation of "the essential Suras" of the Koran. Joyce noted that HCE, like Mohammad, was illiterate, that the queen of Saba could be a "q[ueen] of Shebeen," that every word in the Koran could have seventy meanings, and that the Muslim holy book was written on "palmleaves, pebbles, shoulderbones, skins." These two sets of notes were destined for the first chapter of his own "all quorum." In conclusion he also noted "delta at end," which describes the typographical layout not only of the last page of Mardrus's Koran translation and the ending of a section in chapter 1 ("Daleth, who opened it, closes the door" [BL 47482a f. 78v; JJA 44: 87]) but also (starting in 1928, when the Crosby Gaige *Anna Livia Plurabelle* was published) of the beginning of I.8.[1]

References to things Belgian in notebook VI.B.12 start on page 100 ("suikerstuck" [piece of sugar]), but the earliest entries that can be attributed with some degree of certainty to the Belgian holiday (and not to the reading of guidebooks) are four references to Patrick Hoey, an old Dublin acquaintance whom we know Joyce met in a pharmacy the day he arrived in Ostend. On a postcard to Sylvia Beach and in a letter to Harriet Weaver, Joyce described Hoey as a Shaun figure: "He is in fact a very good Λ. . . . He very often uses the identical words I put into Λ's mouth at the Euclid lesson before coming down here" (LI: 244). The speech of the boys in the first drafts of section 8 of II.2 are indeed marked by a Dublin brogue.

Notebook VI.B.12 has four references to Hoey. The first is a puzzling "Hoey dillidantis" on page 164, and the last on page 178 is surely ironic: "Hoey—I haven't much of a brogue." Between them are two expressions that made it into *Finnegans Wake.* "Hoey—sure you'd write as good as that yrself. Pat" was first heavily Dublinized and then, with a number of French and Flemish words, almost immediately introduced into the fair copy of the geometry lesson as "(Sure, you could rite as foyne as that yerself, mick!)" (BL 47478 f. 11; JJA 53: 42). The second was destined for the "Museyroom" scene in chapter 1: "Hoey—Mind yr boot going out."

That Joyce was still using this notebook at the end of August is clear from a reference on page 186 to "Pas sur la bouche (Just a Kiss)," an apparently rather risqué operetta that was playing at the Théâtre de la Scala in Ostend at the beginning of September.[2] In addition, at the end of the notebook and starting on page 187 there are several references to Ghent, where Joyce and his family moved to on 13 September, although these could have been taken earlier, in preparation for the move, from a guidebook such as the *Gand guide illustré,* the title of which occurs in the following notebook. More important are two other references to Belgian history in VI.B.12, in this case to the Great War. The first appears on page 170: "/E wakes to find Great War Angel v Devil over." Ostend is just half an hour by car or bus from Flanders' Fields, and that Joyce had some interest in the Great War is clear. On the flyleaf verso at the end of notebook VI.B.12 he copied a number of notes from a publication by "the Army General Staff of Belgium" and published in French, Flemish, and English editions. In *General View on the Operations of the Belgian Army* the authors describe the Battle of the Yser between 16 and 31 October 1914. From this and from at least one other source Joyce copied examples not just of the military jargon ("gallants of the 42nd," "victorious onrush," "never there was") but also of the General Staff's awkward English ("up from the 27th," "Thus it were the remains"). The mixture of battlefield rhetoric and bad English would be helpful soon in writing the "Museyroom" sequence.

We do not have the notebook that Joyce began either shortly before or while already in Ghent. We only have the copies Mme Raphaël made in the thirties, in this case twice, in VI.C.9 and VI.C.16. With just a few exceptions there are few references to Belgium or to any of the themes that would be explored in chapter I.1, but their absence may well be explained by the fact that Joyce had already used and crossed out these items; Mme Raphaël only copied the uncrossed ones.

Notebook VI.B.15 was probably begun around the time the Joyces spent in Antwerp on their way to a longer stay in Brussels. What struck Joyce most about Antwerp were the swarms of mosquitoes: Joyce signed a letter to Sylvia Beach "With kindest regards / mosquitobittenly yours" (JJ/SB: 72), and in a letter to Miss Weaver five days later he wrote: "Antwerp I renamed Gnantwerp because I was devoured there by mosquitoes" (LI: 245), a pun he had noted down on page 9 of the notebook. In the same letter to Beach Joyce added that "the communal library of Dublin (Ga) ought to have an autographed copy of *Dubliners,*" which seems to suggest that Beach had written earlier about the Dublin counterpart in the southern United States. A few days later Joyce sent the signed copy back to Beach. In any case, the missing notebook may have contained notes on Dublin, Georgia, that Joyce used in writing I.1.

Significant for the development of I.1 was Joyce's interest in Antwerp's "freedom of the citz" (VI.B.15: 6). Twenty pages later there is a (Cockney?) version of part of Dublin's city motto: "the Hobedience of the Citizens is the Ealth."[3] When he incorporated it at the end of the "Prankquean" section, Joyce would substitute the Dutch word "burger" for "citizen." There are just a few references to Brussels around page 10 of the notebook and a few more to Waterloo, which Joyce visited on 22 September, between pages 47 and 54. Significantly, "Penrith" occurs on page 56, suggesting that Joyce had reached that page around the beginning of October, when the letter from Miss Weaver about the Penrith giant had arrived. Ten pages later we read "the giant's heart in / Rome" and "in sleep 'Self' leaves / Soma." Especially on page 67, Joyce seems to gather themes and motifs to be used in the new chapter: "adam was delvin and / madaman spinning / watersilks," "Δ wake & priest whole," "ᗰ sleeps," "ᗰ falls—pieces." At this point drafting and note taking go hand in hand.

The first pencil draft of this chapter was written in the large fiberboard-covered notebook in which Joyce had earlier written the first drafts of III.4 and II.2; in fact, the very first draft of the first section immediately follows the second draft of II.2. Joyce began by linking HCE's initials to the geography of Dublin: "Howth Castle & Environs! Sir Tristram had not encore arrived from North Armorica nor stones exaggerated theirselves in Laurens County, Ga, doubling all the time, nor a voice answered mishe mishe to tufftuff thouartpatrick. Not yet had a kidson buttended an isaac not yet had twin sesthers played siege to twone Jonathan. Not a peck of malt had Shem and Son brewed & bad luck to the regginbrew was to be seen on the waterface" (BL 47482a f. 83; JJA 44: 3).

Deftly, Joyce links the Tristan and Patrick sketches to the themes of doubling, of transatlantic Dublins, of the usurpation of power, of the family romance, Swift, Irish history, biblical precedents, Dublin detail. In any case, this is quite appropriate as a starting point of a new book, even as a prelude: nothing seems to have happened yet, everything is still possible.

HCE is central in this chapter; in fact, both the first and the last words of the first draft are marked by his initials, and both were taken from VI.B.15: "Howth Castle & Environs" from page 33 and "High Cost of Everything" from page 84 (in addition, the visit to the Museyroom ends with "Here Copenhagen ends"). But strangely enough these are exceptions: normally, Joyce wrote the earliest versions of the other sections of the book without much recourse to the notebooks.

The order in which Joyce composed the chapter is interesting. Quite quickly, on the recto pages 83 to 94 of the fiberboard notebook, Joyce wrote the first layer of the first section, from the beginning, which I quoted above, to the end of the "Museyroom" sequence: "Mind your boots going out" (BL 47482a f. 94; JJA 44: 21; FW: 010.23). He then revised what he had written, the last part so extensively that he had to recopy the "Museyroom" sequence on the following pages of the notebook, from pages 95 to 99.

Sometime after he began the first draft of section B (from the end of the "Museyroom" to the "Annals" [FW: 013.33–014.15]) and section D (from after the "Annals" to the beginning of "Mutt and Jute" [FW: 014.28–015.28]), continuing on page 99 and moving to the bottom of page 103. The "Annals" sequence was added on the facing page (continuing on the preceding 101v). Joyce heavily revised all of these passages and then began the still missing "Mutt and Jute" sequence, again writing backward in the notebook, using those verso pages (or parts) that had been left blank.

In a letter to Miss Weaver on 8 November Joyce explained that he had set to work at once on her "esteemed order" and that he had worked so hard that he almost "stupefied" himself and had to stop and read *Gentlemen Prefer Blondes* for three whole days. On the 8th he "started off afresh," probably by transcribing all he had written into a new notebook (LI: 246). He did find time to add at least one bit of information from his light reading, when he added a sentence about a "skierscape of an eyeful hoyth entirely" (BL 47482a f. 85v; JJA 44: 6). This is the way narrator Lorelei in *Gentlemen Prefer Blondes* spells the name of the famous tower's engineer.

The first continuous version of the first part of the chapter in the new notebook had reached this state quite quickly and certainly with considerably less effort and pain than the second half of Book III. But it is by no means a continuous narrative: after the title-setting (it is only on this second draft that Joyce added "brings us back to" before "Howth Castle & Environs") the sense of a beginning is stressed with the list of events that have "not yet" happened. Then follows the story of the fall, which presumably sets everything in motion because it also causes the fall of Finnegan, who with Humpty Dumpty and like Finn MacCool and the city of Dublin is interred in the landscape. All of history proceeds from this. Finnegan the builder is then described with words and rhythms taken from the song "Finnegan's Wake" and from other ballads: he is responsible for building the city of Dublin on the banks of the Liffey. He drinks too much, falls from a ladder, dies, and is laid out. His wake is a lively affair, with whiskey and ale, and the food at the wake (bread and fish) becomes the deceased himself to be sacramentally consumed. A new description of the dead or sleeping fish-giant in the landscape becomes more and more martial as

Dublin slowly turns into "charmful waterloose country," until the Mistress Kate leads us through the Museyroom, a "buddlefield" that extends far beyond Waterloo and includes all of history's wars and conflicts.

The most obvious link between the Dublin landscape and Waterloo is the Wellington monument in Phoenix Park, which blends with the Wellington Museum at Mont Saint Jean. But the visit in *Finnegans Wake* is more than a guided tour of a museum: the different exhibits also tell the story of the Battle of Waterloo and of all battles ever fought, although the battle between Napoleon and the rest of Europe keeps center stage. This is clear on the page facing the one in which the "Museyroom" sequence was first drafted. There we find a schematic representation of a battlefield, with the sigla representing the three sons of HCE facing their mirror forms across the battle line, an image that is repeated twice on the next verso page.

Out of the warm Museyroom again the "we" observe a "gnarlybird" collecting all kinds of artifacts from the midden of history. After a confused and confusing dialogue about the hills of Dublin the four historians, Mamalujo, make an appearance. They had been the central characters in one of the sketches (incidentally, the first to be published in April 1924 in the *transatlantic review*), but it would be 1938 before Joyce blended the material with another one of the early sketches. Earlier in chapter I.1 we had heard an echo of this section: the people at HCE's wake say grace, much like Mamalujo had done: "the way they used to be saying their grace before fish repeating itself for auld lang syne."[4] This phrase is repeated in various forms, and the version in the first draft of I.1 ("So pass the kish & pooll the begg. So sigh us!" [BL 47482a f. 89; JJA 44: 11]) could very well be its next incarnation. Joyce wrote a paragraph to link the wake with the four observers, borrowing again the rhythms and phrases of "Mamalujo" (fourfold narration, "adear, adear") and naming the speaker as "Mamaluijus," author of a "Grand Old Historiorum."

The next section may well be a quotation from this historical treatise. The landscape is described again but now with considerable emphasis on its peaceful nature. Here Joyce for the first time parodied the Quinet sentence that he had found in Léon Metchnikoff's *La Civilisiation et les grandes fleuves historiques.*[5] According to the French historian, flowers continue to grow in places where wars were fought, where civilizations have come and gone. In Joyce's version the long sentence has Ireland as its subject, with references to the mythical inhabitants of the country and to Dublin suburbs and villages. In addition, the sentence is followed by the suggestion that the flowers are multilingual temptresses and thus may well become the cause of future misunderstandings and wars.

Mamalujo also write the chiastic four entries of the "Annals"—the year 1132 plays a central role in the original sketch. The first half of the chapter ends with a meeting between two characters, Mutt and Jute, and their mutual misunderstandings. These two characters exemplify not only the problematic communication after Babel but at the same time the rivalry between two suitors of the same woman, two inhabitants of the same city or land, and all the enemy brothers of the book. Mutt and Jute are the prehistorical prototypes of antagonistic Shem and Shaun.

The different sections were for the first time integrated when Joyce copied in a neat hand a full version of the first half of the chapter in a new fiberboard notebook that opens with a big HCE siglum. On the basis of this draft (with some revisions but not all) Joyce had a typescript made of the first paragraph, which he dated 15 November (1926) and sent to Miss Weaver accompanied by "a key to same" as a sample form of the full order, which took another month to finish.

Most probably after but maybe while finishing the second draft in the fiberboard notebook Joyce returned to the earlier notebook. Starting on BL 47482a f. 94v (JJA 44: 90), at that time the first available blank verso page, and working backward, he wrote a fairy tale about one Sir Howther and a prankwench (the names were changed in the second draft). In a classic fairy tale structure the prankwench comes to the castle, where her uncle Sir Howther unkindly refuses to answer her riddle. She kidnaps one of his twins and refuses to come back. In strictly parallel descriptions this scene is repeated three times, and then some form of agreement is reached: the prankwench is given the dummy (both the twins' toy and their sister), the twins "keep their peace," and Sir Howther "was to get the wind up" (BL 47482a f. 87v; JJA 44: 93).

The overlay in this section became so dense that Joyce had to transfer the text to the fiberboard notebook, continuing on the next page after the end of the first half of the chapter. It is only here that the fairy tale ends with a moral, which turns out to be a Flemish version of Dublin's city motto: "Thus the hearsomeness of the burger felicitates the whole of the polis." Joyce now wrote a new section directly in the fiberboard notebook in which we once more return to HCE buried beneath the Dublin landscape. He is praised, now that he is dead, but there is a young lad, again in the form of a fish, ready to take his place. This is the first version of this passage, without additions or corrections:

> And be the hooky salmon there's a big lad now I am told, like a lord mayor (on show) the height of a brewer's chimpney, humphing his showlders like he's such a grandfallar with a pockedwife and three sly little clinkers, two twin bugs and one pucelle, and either he did what you know or he did not what you know and that'll do now but however that may be 'tis sure for one thing that he came to this place some time on another in a hull of a wherry and has been repeating himself like fish ever since are that he was of humile commune & ensectuous nature, as his you may guess from his byname, & that he is he & no other he who is primarily responsible for the high cost of everything. (BL 47471a fs. 37–38; JJA 44: 100–101)

Clearly, this section was needed to make the link with the beginning of chapter 2, which tells us about the origin of HCE's name.

But Joyce was not satisfied yet. On the basis of notes in several notebooks he returned to the description of the letter or the book that had occupied him in chapter I.5. Starting on BL 47482a f. 84v (JJA 44: 84) and again writing backward on blank verso pages, he began a detailed description of a book much like *The Book of Kells* but also reminiscent of the midden of history and of all holy books. For the first draft of this section (FW: 018.17–021.04) he relied on notes on writing, paper, and holy books in his recent notebooks, especially VI.B.12 and VI.B.15. From the first notebook he took the notes from Mardrus's introduction to the French translation of the Koran. The first draft has, among other references to the Koran, "A bone, a pebble, a ramskin" (BL 47482a f. 80v; JJA 44: 86) and "So you need hardly spell me that every word will carry 3 score & ten readings through the book of life till Daleth, who opened it, closes the door" (BL 47482a f. 78v; JJA 44: 87). A little design at the bottom of the page writes the letters ALP in the form of a triangle, which refers to the last note from Mardrus, and most of the other phrases also have a source in VI.B.12: at the bottom of the cover verso page we read "a closed book," and at the bottom of page 176 we read "daleth, page / delta, do." A lot of the revisions of this draft derive from VI.B.15, most of them from the cluster of notes taken from or inspired by Edward Clodd's *The Story of the Alphabet,* a book Joyce had asked Sylvia Beach to order when he was in Belgium. This is the source for the word "claybook" (VI.B.15: 156) and also "allaphbed," "abcedminded," "balfison," and "futhor" (VI.B.15: 159).

By the end of November 1926 and therefore after less than two months' work Joyce was ready for an ink fair copy that incorporated the latest versions of all the sections of the chapter in the final order but none of them in a finished form. At Buffalo Luca Crispi has discovered the first appearance of the word "river" in a newly discovered duplicate typescript of the first page.[6] When Joyce next copied the beginning from the typescript he also added the word "run" (BL 47472 f. 4; JJA 44: 105).

At this moment it is good to take stock of what had already been achieved. Although most of the narrative centers on the giant Finn-Finnegan, the builder of cities who is interred in the landscape, Joyce carefully worked references to the rest of his book into the text. Finn(egan) is HCE, his wife is the river Liffey, Mutt and Jute are Shem and Shaun but also the washerwomen at the end of I.8 who have trouble hearing each other. There are references to the protagonists of all of the sketches and the existing parts of Books I and III, to the four old men, the hen, the cad, the letter, Mamalujo. Apart from linking his protagonist with the mythic hero Finn and the ballad hero Finnegan (and thus moving, Danis Rose would argue, from the collection of short stories *Finn's Hotel* to *Finnegans Wake*), Joyce also echoes smaller textual elements from Books I and III and even *Ulysses*. The ballad of Hosty at the end of I.2 is echoed repeatedly (and appropriately, in a chapter so full of song parodies): "by the hump of the magazine wall, where our Maggies seen all" (BL 47482a f. 91; JJA 44: 15; FDV: 49) and "by the mausoleme wall. Finnfinn. Fannfann. With with a grand funferall. Fumfum fumfum!" (BL 47482a f. 100; JJA 44: 33; FDV: 53). "Stand up, mickies. Make leave for minnies" (BL 47471a f. 21; JJA 44: 66) mimics a line from I.4: "Move up, Dumpty, Make room for Humpty!" (BL 47471b f. 28; JJA 46: 47; FDV: 79). A book is described as "the bluest book in the race's annals" (BL 47471a f. 24; JJA 44: 69), which reminds us of the "Blue Book of Eccles" (FW: 179.27). And as we have seen, the section introducing the "Annals" consists of a combination of verbal echoes of the "Mamalujo" sketch.

But chapter I.1 is more than an overture in the same vein as the first pages of the "Sirens" episode of *Ulysses*. It has one ingredient that is absent from the chapters and sections that had already been written by the autumn of 1926. Although the conflict between Shem and Shaun entails some degree of violence and although the early misadventures of HCE were at least partly inspired by the Irish Civil War (the phrase "Move up, Dumpty, Make room for Humpty" was a parody of a note found on the grave of Michael Collins and threatening his successor, Richard Mulcahy: "Move up, Mick. Make room for Dick"), the first chapter centers from its earliest drafts on the issue of war.

The first page of the first draft has an addition in the top left corner: "to wielderfight his peninsular war" (BL 47482a f. 83; JJA 44: 3); more overtly, the verso of page 90 of the notebook has the names of four battles ("boyne / waterloo / magenta / golden spurs") crossed out when they had been used in the text (BL 47482a f. 90v; JJA 44: 14). Even in the introduction to the "Museyroom" sequence ("While beyind Ill Sixty, bagsides of the fort") there is an addition "over against this belle alliance" (BL 47482a f. 91; JJA 44: 15). The four entries in the "Annals" have as a refrain variants on "bloody wars in Dublin" (BL 47482a fs. 102v–101v; JJA 44: 37–38). Both the theme and a lot of the verbal echoes were the result of Joyce's visit to Waterloo and to other battlefields in Belgium, a country that boasts (at least according to the editors of *Trivial Pursuit*) more battlefields than any other nation.

The fair copy and the first typescript date from the early weeks of December. The chapter had become stable, and the changes and additions at this stage are cosmetic. Most of the elements introduced in these drafts come from VI.B.15, the "active" notebook at the time. As was his habit in working on later drafts, Joyce also went back to earlier notebooks, using items that seemed appropriate. From page 121 of VI.B.6 he added "eggs with sunny side up" (BL 47472 f. 15; JJA 44: 116), and a mention that the snake came in a cargo of fruit was added on BL 47472 f. 35 (JJA 44: 125). Joyce combined the word "worldwright," a neologism inspired by Otto Jespersen's *Growth and Structure of the English Language*, and a note about a copyist leaving a gap ("we can almost see from the illumination itself the very place where he was hurried from his work") from Sullivan's introduction to *The Book of Kells* into a longish addition (BL 47472 f. 33; JJA 44: 119) that also includes a number of words from VI.B.1, the following notebook.[7] This contained a number of references to prehistoric man (Cro-Magnon and Piltdown man), that Joyce was happy to introduce here. The most amazing alteration of an item from a notebook comes from VI.B.16, where Joyce on page 92 had noted author and title of Liam O'Flaherty's *Thy Neighbour's Wife*. Joyce crossed out the title and introduced it at the end of the same addition: "for taking that same fine sum covertly by meddlement with the drawers of his neighbour's safe" (FW: 014.25–27).

At the end of the fair copy Joyce's emendations became so extensive that he was forced to redraft several pages. Some of the additions were extensive: the voices with strong Irish accents that admonish Finnegan not to rise again were all added at this stage. Some of the elements were taken from extensive notes on pages 176 and 177 of VI.B.15, in their turn most probably taken from some Hiberno-English source.

The typescript has the same date as the last revised pages of the fair copy (16 December 1926), and this may explain why there are hardly any changes. Most of the emendations in the typescript are corrections of typist's errors. The only exceptions are the addition of words and phrases from pages 178, 182, and 183 of VI.B.15.

In 1927 this chapter became the first installment of *Work in Progress* in the first issue of *transition,* the literary magazine that would publish the work in the next ten years. Judging from the first set of page proofs, the writing process seems to have been finished. The changes are almost all printing or setting errors, except for the title, which was "Opening pages of Work in Progress," to which Joyce added a capital "A" before "Work." Most of the emendations restore readings of the typescript from which the text had been set, although occasionally minor adjustments are made.

When Joyce revised the *transition* version of this chapter for the book edition of *Finnegans Wake,* things were different. On the first copy of the first set, dated 16 July 1936, Joyce began quietly changing "waterface" into "aquaface" and "schute" into "pftjschute" (BL 47475 f. 3; JJA 44: 231), but from the second page onward more and longer passages were added. These do not introduce new thematic materials but extend existing clusters: Joyce adds another reference to Swift and Sterne and battlefields ("agincourting" and "crezy" [BL 47475 f. 5v; JJA 44: 236]) to the "Museyroom" sequence, and he extends "childers" into "happinest childer everwere" (BL 47475 f. 6v; JJA 44: 238). But he also brings materials from the other chapters back into his overture: the Twelve are echoed in the addition "To the continuation of that celebration until Hanandhunigan's extermination!" (BL 47475 f. 4v; JJA 44: 234), and he adds another version of the cad's question to the Mutt and Jute scene. With the exception of the "Prankquean," the last part of the chapter is most extensively added to: the Koran subtext is strengthened with a longer passage ("Can you rede [. . .] walked the earth" [FW: 018.18–24]) and a number of shorter additions to the section "True there was [. . .] closeth thereof the. Dor" (FW: 019.31–020.18). Joyce had found the material in VI.B.31, in a long index from *The Speeches and Table-Talk of the Prophet Mohammad.*[8] Interesting in the last set of additions is the strange punctuation at the end of the paragraph (BL 47475 f. 184; JJA 44: 274). Crispi has discovered that at this stage of the book's development Joyce had decided to use "the" as the last word of the book, so all through the book he added periods after the word "the."[9]

In the second set of *transition* pages Joyce does not seem to have become more adventurous, and not all the handwriting in this set is his own. Apart from retranscriptions of all the changes to the first set, the phrases "past

Eve and Adam's" and "by a commodious vicus of recirculation" are added to the first line. Joyce adds battle- or Napoleon-related words and sequences to the "Museyroom" scene: "solphereens," "stampforth," "after his hundred days in dulgence," "ousterlists."

In notebook VI.A, the Scribbledehobble notebook, we find an interesting list related to this chapter. On pages 744 and 746, in handwriting D, the following notes appear:

> Dublin (Geo) Isaac Butt, ^{r}Sosie Sizters, clap, Finnegan^{r}, bid-me-to-live, ego te absolve, there's hair, ^{r}elm, stone, Parr^{r}, To and to, ^{r}Eiffel, Lawrence O'Toole, Thomas a Beckett^{r}, wine vinegar, ~~crescent~~ crest, faigh-go-baile, automobile (VI.A: 744)

> ^{r}pftjschute^{r}
> First Paragraph
> ᗰ, T, ^{r}Peter Sawyer^{r}, P, /⊏, ⊥, /⊏, ꟻ Adam, Tristan, S Peter Sawyer, Isaac, S Patrick, Swift, Guiness (Noah), rainbow, ^{r}Allbrohome!, Ad sum, Kate tip^{r}, ⊏ sees jinnies through telescope, the ^{r}cagelanternhouse, 29, the boy Jones^{r}, while L (VI.A: 746)

These notes seem like a blueprint or schema for the famous opening of the book: in two bursts covering the same passage the notes follow the order of the first paragraph and then, more roughly, the rest of the chapter (continuing into I.2). Since some of this material originally comes from different notebooks, it is almost as if Joyce here reminds himself in which order he is going to write the first pages of his book. But something is wrong: first, not all of the items that do occur in the finished book are crossed out; second, the material entered the genesis of the chapter at different times.

In reality this is a late list, dating from the early thirties, when Joyce was preparing the *transition* versions of Book I for the printer of *Finnegans Wake;* thus the text of the chapter is the source of these notes, not their destination. They were most probably collected at the occasion of revising the text to be sent to the printers of *Finnegans Wake,* and they were destined to be distributed over the rest of the book, and most particularly the final chapters. Only one element is new and makes the trip in the other direction: "pftjschute" on page 764 of VI.A was entered on the first set of *transition* pages. All the other items that are crossed out reappear later in the book, mostly in Book IV, probably not just to strengthen the coherence but also to reinforce the circularity of the text. Examples of these include "Sosie" from VI.A.744, which becomes "O Sosay" as an addition to the typescript (BL 47488 f. 33v; JJA 63: 54; FW 601.12), and "Victoria Nyanza" from page 749 added to another typescript (BL 47488 f. 76v; JJA 63: 130; FW: 600.12). The "please stop" sequence of page 748 appears as part of a long addition to the typescript (BL 47488 f. 90; JJA 61: 153; FW: 609.07–9). The irony here is that a chapter that had functioned in 1926 as an overture, a repository of already existing thematic materials, was now used to give coherence to the (almost) finished book.[10]

Joyce's work was not finished when the printer had produced the galleys. On most of these galleys Joyce only corrected printer's errors, but he also added a few sentences (containing a number of words from a book on the language of Rabelais, which he had copied on VI.B.45), and more Koran lore as part of the answer to the question "What then agentlike brought about that tragoady thundersday this municipal sin business?" (FW: 005.13–14).[11] He added more Wellington battles to the "Museyroom," another section after the "peacefugle" passage (FW: 011.08–28), a description of the Buddhist chain of dependent origination (FW: 018.24–28), and two more passages with Rabelais words in the introduction to the "Prankquean."

The most intensive work was reserved for the end of the chapter: Joyce nearly doubled the last two pages. The additions again strengthen existing thematic materials (the phoenix, Vico's cycles, *The Book of the Dead*, American dialect words out of *Huckleberry Finn,* Hiberno-English expressions).[12]

But even these late additions were not the end. The final set of galleys, dating from the beginning of 1938, is the first to introduce chapter divisions. It was only on the page proofs, now at Tulsa, that the phrase "From swerve of shore to bend of bay" was added.

The genesis of the first chapter of *Finnegans Wake* is too straightforward to be typical: it went through drafting, fair copy, and typescript in a matter of months; it was printed only once and in the last stages of development; no new passages or narratives were introduced. The notebooks not only help us to see what Joyce was interested in just before (VI.B.12) and while actually writing the chapter (VI.B.15). A close reading of the drafts helps us to understand how one idea led Joyce to another and how he managed to incorporate materials from notebooks that were much earlier. After the publication in *transition* Joyce continued to read books and articles on themes he had touched on in his first chapter, and these notes in later notebooks made it possible to return to the text after almost ten years and enrich it considerably. In one notebook the text of the chapter itself became a source for note taking and thus for insertion in other parts of the book.

The first chapter of what was still called *Work in Progress* was conceived and written relatively late, at a time of crisis for the whole project. Joyce used Miss Weaver's order to create an overture that not only introduced all the major characters but linked his main hero, the origins of whose name would soon be explained in the next chapter, to the Irish mythic hero Finn MacCool and to the Irish American Tim Finnegan. It is in this sense that this chapter marks, perhaps, the beginning of the book called *Finnegans Wake.*

Notes

1. Here, as elsewhere, I confine myself to transcribing only the first level of inscription, not later emendations and corrections.

2. Joyce's stay in Ostend, Ghent, Antwerp, and Brussels was diligently researched by Tom Verheyden for a B.A. thesis, "'me Belchum': James Joyce in Belgium," University of Antwerp, 1997.

3. Sam Slote transcribed VI.B.15 and reported on his findings in "'Did god be come': The Definitive Exgenesis of HCE," *Writing Its Own Wrunes For Ever,* ed. Daniel Ferrer and Claude Jacquet (Tusson: Du Lérot, 1998), 103–18.

4. James Joyce, "Work in Progress," *transatlantic review* 1.4 (April 1924): 215–23, 215.

5. For a discussion of the Quinet sentence see Ingeborg Landuyt and Geert Lernout, "Joyce's Sources: *Les grands fleuves historiques,*" *JSA* 6 (1995): 99–138.

6. See Luca Crispi, "ReCollecting Joyce at Buffalo: Revising and Completing the Catalog," *Geni,* 13–26.

7. *The Book of Kells,* ed. Edward Sullivan (London: Studio, 1924), 8.

8. First identified in Roland McHugh, "Mohammad in Notebook VI.B.31," *AWN* 16.4 (1979): 51–58. Aida Yared has recently discussed the importance of the Muslim references in "'In the Name of Annah': Islam and *Salam* in Joyce's *Finnegans Wake,*" *JJQ* 35.2–3 (Winter–Spring 1998): 401–38.

9. Luca Crispi, "The word 'the' in *Finnegans Wake,*" forthcoming in *Genetic Joyce Studies.*

10. See also Finn Fordham's essay on I.1 at the end of this volume.

11. See Claude Jacquet, *Joyce et Rabelais: aspects de la création verbale dans "Finnegans Wake"* (Paris: Didier, 1972).

12. See the index in VI.B.32 of notes from a British Museum pamphlet about *The Book of the Dead;* see also Danis Rose, *Chapters of Coming Forth by Day*

(Colchester: A Wake Newslitter Press, 1982), 11–14. The dialect words from *Huckleberry Finn* appear in an index of pages 18–20 of VI.B.46 and another one of pages 82–83 of VI.B.42, both identified by Danis Rose, *James Joyce's The Index Manuscript: "Finnegans Wake" Holography Workbook VI.B.46* (Colchester: A Wake Newslitter, 1978), 18–31, and "More on Huck Finn," *AWN* 17.2 (1980): 19–20.

"The March of a Maker"

Chapters I.2–4

BILL CADBURY

Chapters 2–4, the first part of the *Wake* to be drafted, make up a self-contained narrative unit that presents the nature and history of the book's hero, HCE. It served as the beginning of the *Wake* until 1926, when Joyce drafted what would become chapter 1. Joyce's composition of the unit began in August 1923 with the drafting and revising of the "vignette" usually called "Here Comes Everybody," which was to take its place as the first section of chapter 2 (FW: 030–034.29). Then in the fall and winter of 1923–24 he drafted the rest of chapter 2 and chapters 3 and 4, though separation into the final chapter units only came later, to meet the requirements of serial publication. The vignette introduces HCE and gives his early history, and the rest describes a series of attacks on HCE both physical and verbal, in each of which he falls only to rise again. The final attack, in the first-draft version of chapter 4, is the courtroom trial involving Festy King, who ever more clearly throughout the revisions comes to seem ambiguously to be both HCE's attacker and HCE himself. The trial ends in comical disarray with Festy's acquittal, which is itself an instance of HCE's resurrection.

In the first drafts the trial is followed by the "Letter" from his wife, ALP, to and concerning HCE, and this is yet another attack—in effect, a fall like the other verbal attacks such as the poem that concludes chapter 2, "The Rann" (FW: 045–047)—in that it purports to defend HCE but in fact accuses him of various of the sins of which he seems always already guilty. Planned initially as the centerpiece of what will become chapter 5, the Letter will be moved in 1938 to Book IV, where its text thus follows rather than precedes its delivery. In the first-draft sequence the coauthors of the Letter, HCE's son Shem and ALP herself, are then described in chapters 7 and 8. After several stages of revision of these early drafts for Book I, Joyce turned, in another copybook, to the delivery of the Letter by HCE's other son, Shaun, which will become Book III.

2§1: Here Comes Everybody (FW: 030.01–034.29)

Chapter 2§1 is completed in the first draft, two holograph revision stages and a typescript before the first drafting of the rest. Because it is published early, in 1925, as "From Work in Progress" in the *Contact Collection of Contemporary Writers,* Joyce does not give it that extensive and extraordinary revision of the 1926 typescript that sets the style of the other parts as the chapters make their way toward *transition* publication in 1927. Joyce seems to have set it aside as having been elaborated already, and right through to the finished book its style remains comparatively simple.

In this first section of chapter 2 (2§1) we find how publican Earwicker got his name, his British connection, and his social position by involuntarily providing the occasion for a dumb play on words by the passing king, who enjoys noting how "we have for trusty bailiwick a turnpiker who is by turns a pikebailer no less than an earwicker" (BL 47477 f. 99v; JJA 45: 10; see FW: 031.26–28).[1] Thus even in the *Wake*'s plot, pure play with language has enormous consequences, since the story jumps to showing HCE's having achieved social position as a member of the Ascendancy. But somehow, between the encounter with the king and the appearance at the theater as "the father of his people" (BL 47472 f. 98v; JJA 45: 6; see FW: 032.21) surveying "the truly catholic assemblage" at the not very Catholic play *A Royal Divorce* (FW: 032.25, 33), malicious rumors have come to cling to his name, charges of "annoying soldiers in the park" (BL 47472 f. 98v; JJA 45: 7; see FW: 033.26–27) and of "having behaved in an ungentlemanly manner in the presence of certain a pair of maidservants in the rushy hollow" (BL 47472 f. 97v; JJA 45: 3; FDV: 63; see FW: 034.18–20).

HCE's sense of himself is thus from the start characterized by complacency in his accidentally achieved public place, along with undercutting guilt for acts and feelings both sexual and aggressive. Indeed, after *any* interpersonal encounter in the story, accusations that he is guilty of those two charges and/or accusations concerning whatever has happened in the particular encounter are at once made against him by others—this is the constantly repeated sequence of the plot. But since it is always ambiguous as to whether there *are* any "others" in the ordinary sense, these accusations always seem also to be projections, and the interplay between what on the surface seems to be HCE's sense of himself and others' sense of him is at root metaphoric of *intra*personal conflict. The "story" and its "characters" render Joyce's idea of the impulses and contradictions that make us up, his portrait of human nature. And we must note that although in Joyce's view human nature has a feminine component and women would have the same fundamental tendencies and contradictions as men, human nature in Book I is presented through HCE, from a male point of view. His name, like his story, tells us that "Here Comes Everybody," and though he comes sometimes with female aspect forward, this everybody *is* a "he."

HCE is our ancestor, "our Farvver" (FW: 093.20), then, in that his story is metaphor for the root and structure of human character, on the one hand (its paradigmatic aspect), and for the sequence of individual and social histories, on the other (its syntagmatic aspect). And so his story repeats itself again and again, for what it is to be ourselves is always, in every encounter with others and its consequences, to be HCE in his public and private contradictions.

2§§2–3 (FW: 034.30–47)

After this first vignette, with its centering image of origins in the encounter with the king, Joyce begins a new stage of the narrative in which he retells the tale from what seems a much later starting point and with a new root encounter that grounds the rest of the story. But despite its new look, the cad encounter in 2§2 (FW: 034.30–044.21) echoes the encounter with the king in 2§1, in their presentations of the relations between uncomprehending people of different social levels and in their hints of political and personal violence. The complacent king's place is filled by an equally complacent HCE. The encountered cad, while as much in the dark about the other's motives as HCE was about the king's, seems more accusatory than was the publican though perhaps equally dumbfounded at his interlocutor's incomprehensible carrying-on. After the encounter the story tracks the shredding of HCE's reputation through the cad's wife and various Irish types. Finally, the tale falls into the keeping of ne'er-do-wells who write and sing a ballad, a Rann, that becomes the final section, §3, of chapter 2 (FW: 044.22–47) and that emphasizes HCE's Scandinavian origins and his membership in the Protestant ascendancy as well as his sexual offenses. This sequence embodies Joyce's sense of the individual's way in the world, a way characterized by conflict: *always already we are where we do not deserve to be, and there we confront, in a moment of primal exchange and conflict, another who is also ourself, in the struggle with whom are mobilized all of our guilts and doubts as well as our (often humiliating) stratagems of defense and exchange.*

3§1 (FW: 048.01–061.27)

After his first revision of 2§2 Joyce drafted what eventually became the first section of chapter 3, though he did not draft the subunits of 3§1 in the order in which they were published. What becomes its final part is drafted first, the section usually called "the plebiscite" (FW: 057.16–061.27), in which we find public responses to the accusations made in the Rann that initially were planned immediately to precede them. These are responses to HCE's misconduct with "the two slaveys" and "the 3 drummers," and the section as first written in 1923 ends with a sketch of the fates of "the 2 maids" (BL 47471b f. 3v; JJA 45: 139).

But after writing it Joyce decided to precede the plebiscite on HCE with an account of the obscure fates of the first responders to him, the Rann-makers, and so he wrote what becomes FW: 048.01–050.32.[2] The plebiscite had begun by announcing the theme of decay and even transformation of information: "The data, did we possess them, are too few to warrant certitude" (BL 47471b f. 3; JJA 45: 138; FDV: 71; see FW: 057.16–17). And in the new unit Joyce emphasized that, even before the plebiscite gossip, information is decaying as it passes through characters with different motivations. Information about the characters themselves also slips: the narrator ends this part wondering if "the reverend, the sodality director" was in fact "the cad with a pipe encountered by HCE" (BL 47471b f. 3; JJA 45: 138; FDV: 69; see FW: 050.20, 31–32).

With the first drafts completed of the subunits that he intended to succeed each other directly, Joyce copied them, adding to the copy, however, a long addition (FW: 050.35–056.19) to come between the fates of the Rann-makers and the fate of HCE's reputation as detailed in the plebiscite.[3] The long addition takes its cue from the mistaking of the sodality director for the cad (though confronters of and commentators on HCE *are* always in some sense the cad), and the addition is the cad's retelling of the original encounter in so different a style that it too exemplifies the decay of information that at first seemed clear.

Joyce is developing the logic of his central theme throughout this sequence of additions. In the first section of chapter 2 the cheerfully pompous

English king had spoken patronizingly and self-revealingly to the gawking Irish publican HCE. In the second section of chapter 2 HCE had become an equally pompous (though now Irish) figure speaking patronizingly and self-revealingly to the lower Irish cad figure. And now in the long addition that Joyce places to follow the fates of the Rann-makers in the first section of chapter 3 the cad himself, "although it is no easy matter to identify" him, becomes a tawdrier but still pompous "individual in baggy pants" with Dublin accent but English "headquarters," speaking patronizingly and self-revealingly to "some broadfaced boardschool children on a wall," lower in age if not in station (BL 47471b f. 9v; JJA 45: 140; see FW: 051.06–7, 32, 11–12). He gets a "cad encounter" of his own, and the succession of social levels becomes thus a succession of generations, with "boardschool children" becoming types of the next generation, Shem and Shaun's. Throughout the rest of the book they always look back and up at their father and recapitulate his story while at the same time between themselves emulating the relation between him and them—exactly like HCE with the king, like the cad and then the Rann-makers with HCE, like the children with the clown in baggy pants.

The cad-turned-clown still has his characteristic pipe and revolver. Furthermore, the clown resembles HCE in having an aggressive side as well—HCE's watch in the original encounter had been produced "from his gun pocket" (BL 47471b f. iiv; JJA 45: 24; FDV: 64; see FW: 035.27).[4] And the pipe and gun have other embodiments as well: flowerpot on pole; fender; wooden bar; cigar; piece of wood; fart; turd; monolith; phallus; letter. A particularly evocative and mysterious term for it is "fender," as we will see, which suggests both offender and defender. The irreducible ur-object is emitted, offered, posted, delivered, valued, feared, swapped, used as weapon and as shield by HCE in the interchanges among the different parts of his (and our) self throughout his always-repeating story. This ur-thing is in effect the self as object, that which mediates between our internal lives and the world of others and of process that in some way we touch. One might be tempted to think that it *can* be reduced, via the phrase for defecation, "to post a letter," to a primal turd, core product of HCE the builder of cities.[5] But its phallic aspect, for one, is too strong. No, it is always all these things, and no doubt more: an "everintermutuomergent" (FW: 055.11) embodiment of our interface with the world.

But if he plays HCE to the schoolchildren from above, the clownlike narrator's perspective on the HCE about whom he speaks is as usual from below, and in the long addition (FW: 050.35–056.19) he tells of the grandiose figure who had "struck down Destrelle" (BL 47471b f. 9v; JJA 45: 140; FDV: 70; see FW: 052.29–30), as the Liberator O'Connell in fact struck down d'Esterre. The overblown account of the encounter emphasizes the striking gauntlet, then the offered cigar, and then again (as it will be yet again in the story of the Mookse in I.6 and elsewhere) the uplifted "hand protended towards the monumental leadpencil" when the story is told yet again by "one of that little band of factferreters" (BL 47471b f. 6v; JJA 45: 143; FDV: 71, 70; see FW: 056.11–12, 055.12–13), the children. Pride and shame, eroticism and aggression, homo- and heterosexuality sum up in the erection that is HCE's story. "Homo Capite Erectus" Joyce will call him in revision of the first typescript (BL 47472 f. 162; JJA 46: 63; FW: 101.12–13).

3§3 (FW: 067.28–74) and 3§2 (FW: 061.28–067.27)

As published, the plebiscite at the end of 3§1 comes after the report of the fates of the Rann-makers and the long addition in which the cad renarrates his encounter, just as in chapter 2 the Rann comes after HCE's introduction, the cad encounter, and the transmission of the cad's story leading up to the Rann. Chapter 3§1 thus seems an autonomous unit that re-presents HCE in confrontation with his Irish public and that culminates in that public's opinions of him, which are variously admiring and condemning and thus characteristic of father-son relations. And what Joyce drafted after fair-copying 3§1 is indeed a new rendering of the basic pattern. Again the higher, more English figure exculpates himself (though also revealing his guilt) in an encounter with a listening, lower, more Irish figure. But this time the mutually aggressive quality is more emphasized. The events from this point on seem less like distorted communications and more like direct attacks against HCE.[6] And as a narrative sequence this succession of encounters with their different connotations is itself a matter of decay and an extension of that theme of decay into the plot, the paradigmatic invading the syntagmatic. It is too hard to keep communication uncontaminated by the intrusion of our aggressive-defensive emotions, so efforts to do so tend to turn into battles.

But each of the remaining segments of chapter 3 that Joyce wrote next, 3§2 and 3§3, mobilizes the same material in a slightly different way, each way having strengths and weaknesses of continuity with what has come before. It seems most likely that Joyce drafted the sections as *alternatives,* only later deciding to use both rather than to choose between them and putting them in the reverse order from that in which he drafted them.

Joyce began with what will become 3§3 (FW: 067.28–74) and wrote that "First these outrages" that we have been hearing about may have been "instigated" by the "rushy hollow heroines" (BL 47471b f. 9; JJA 45: 160; FDV: 74; see FW: 067.29–30, 31) who had just been referred to at the end of the plebiscite, briefly reporting their later sad tales, their taking carbolic and necking in haymows. This reference to the crimes in the park and the heroines' later histories parallels the beginning of the previous unit, 3§1, which reported the later histories of the Rann-makers to follow the presentation of the Rann. And then Joyce's narrator explains why the two women "instigated" the outrages: offenses against women often lead to vengeful violence and thence to blackmail. Therefore, HCE's crimes in the park have led to aggression against him in the cad encounter and thence to slander (FW: 068.36–069.04). Thus the whole sequence 2§1–3§1 is recapitulated as the start of the new large narrative unit, good narrative practice.

But after this first paragraph Joyce continued to write as if the "these" of "these outrages" referred not to the outrages that preceded but to those that he is about to describe, beginning his next paragraph "First, there was a gateway" (BL 47471b f. 9; JJA 45: 160; FDV: 74; see FW: 069.15). He presents an outrage at that gateway, a violent attack on HCE culminating in "threats and abuse" (BL 47471b f. 9; JJA 45: 160; FDV: 74; see FW: 070.12) and the throwing of stones before the attacker leaves.[7] New imagery, supplementary to what was in 2§1–3§1, makes its appearance in the sketch of this attack, and it will come to dominate its later extension, 4§1A (FW: 075.01–091.33): the gate; a sheep later to be changed into a goat and pig; a mysterious "six pounds fifteen"[8] (BL 47471b f. 9; JJA 45: 160; FDV: 74; see FW: 070.01) stolen (until a typesetter for *transition* 3 misses a line at FW: 070.02)[9] from a "commercial stopping in the hotel" (BL 47472 f. 346; JJA 45: 267; see FW: 069.32–33); some "pegged" stones (BL 47472 f. 8v; JJA 45: 161; FDV: 74; see FW: 072.27).[10] This set of images comes into the story here just as previously a set of images was introduced in the cad encounter: pipe; revolver; watch; monument; raised gauntleted phallic hand, which is also a dropped turd. These sets are added to the imagery that is associated with HCE before the story even begins and that therefore seems always already to have been present, like original sin: the voyeuristic and homo-/heterosexual crimes in the Park involving three soldiers and two girls.

But after first-drafting what becomes 3§3, Joyce seems to have tried another version (3§2; FW: 061.28–067.27) of the "outrages" that carry so much thematic weight and characterize both what HCE does and what is done to him (BL 47471b fs. 10v, 5v, 4v; JJA 45: 151–53; FDV: 72).[11] The narrator begins this new version by asking, "Can it be that so diversified outrages" were actually "planned and carried out" against HCE? Amazing, and he such a "staunch covenanter" (BL 47471b f. 10v; JJA 45: 151; FDV: 72; see FW: 061.32). This opening reminds the reader of HCE's Protestantism, with which the section also ends as it presents the "scripture reader" Laddy Cummins, and that has not been much in evidence since the Rann (BL 47471b f. 4v; JJA 45: 153; FDV: 73; see FW: 067.11–12).[12] But it loses the elegant transition out of the plebiscite that 3§3 would have provided if it had immediately followed 3§1.

This second outrage, like the version drafted before it, centers on an attack at the "gateway" (BL 47471b f. 5v; JJA 45: 152; FDV: 73; see FW: 063.18–19), and this central section of chapter 3 also follows that attack with a defense concerning the girls in the parable (FW: 065.05–33) of "a fellow who calls on his skirt" (BL 47471b f. 5v; JJA 45: 152; FDV: 73; see FW: 065.05).[13] The parable is not unlike the discussion of "offended womanhood" and "levy of blackmail" (BL 47471b f. 9; JJA 45: 160; FDV: 74; see FW: 065.05–6), which had already been drafted as part of 3§3, though it will be placed to follow 3§2. But as well as following the attack in 3§2 with the parable, Joyce preceded it with an equally important narrative segment. The core of each section, 3§2 and 3§3, is a story of someone at a gate terrorizing HCE within, each derived—3§3 probably and 3§2 demonstrably—from newspaper accounts of criminal proceedings. The 3§2 account is a quite literal re-creation of a comical trial report in the *Freeman's Journal* of 21 November 1923, which Vincent Deane has recently discovered and shown to be the origin of six notes in VI.B.11: 146–47, from which Joyce crafted the anecdote.[14] The point of the story is a defendant's claim that he was banging on the gate of a store (which becomes the "Mullingcan Inn" by overlay to the second typescript [BL 47472 f. 240; JJA 45: 235; see FW: 064.09]) in order to open a bottle of stout, a feeble explanation of what was no doubt an attempt to break in and burglarize the store. But Joyce introduced and blended that story with what seems to be a different attack, set somewhere else entirely: "A tall man of his build carrying a suspicious parcel returning masked later to the old spot had a barking revolver put to his face by an unknown assailant not a Lucalizodite against whom he had been jealous?" (BL 47471b f. 10v, simplified; JJA 45: 151; FDV: 72; see FW: 062.28–33). This seems to take place outdoors; the "old spot" seems much more like the hill across which HCE billowed in 2§2 than it does the space at the gateway of his house; and the episode seems designed to recall the cad encounter.[15] Moreover, the cadlike "waylayer" has a revolver and "Humph" (BL 47471b f. 10v; JJA 45: 151; FDV: 72; see FW: 062.23) has a "suspicious parcel" that suggests both HCE's watch and his hump, especially when Joyce revised "carrying a suspicious parcel" to "humping a suspicious parcel" (BL 47471b f. 13; JJA 45: 155).

But after this introduction the telling of the simple joke about the hammering at the gate emphasizes that the social world can turn on you in your own house—like Bloom, you are never quite as much at home as you like to think you are. And the extension of the narrative from the end of chapter 3 into the beginning of chapter 4 will inherit the story pattern embodied in this opening of the central section of chapter 3 (3§2, FW: 061.28–067.27)—*something like a cad encounter leads to something like a Rann.* An outdoor back-and-forth struggle is followed by and reimaged in an attack at the juncture of the outdoors (at a gate, typically) and the indoors. Both types of attack throughout these chapters culminate in abuse of HCE, which is sometimes verbal and sometimes also physical (the slinging of words and/or stones) and which usually seems made against him by society itself, as when the first long section of chapter 4 (4§1A, FW: 075.01–091.33) climaxes with verbal abuse of HCE in the trial of Festy King. The narrative core is evident: we do our best one-on-one; the world puts us down; we rise to try again.

In terms of imagery, in 3§2 for the first time the watch/gun object, the "suspicious parcel" carried by "Humph," is called a "fender" when "the waylayer" with the "barking revolver" "pointedly asked him where he got the fender" (BL 47471b f. 10v; JJA 45: 151; FDV: 72; see FW: 063.05–7). Surprisingly, that fender is in the *Freeman's Journal* source (although the newspaper does not clarity what this object is), where it is said that a fender is carried by one of the attackers at the gate. Joyce combines it with another crucial term when he revises the reference (*currente calamo*) as he completes the 3§2 draft after the addition of the parable of the fellow and his skirt, so that "This ^1coffin1^" is "mistaken for a fender" (BL 47471b f. 4v; JJA 45: 153; FDV: 73; see FW: 066.27–28). Finally in this section, and filling the storehouse of essential imagery, "Next morning postman handed him a letter superscribed to Humphy Pot and Gallows King" (BL 47471b f. 4v; JJA 45: 153; FDV: 73; see FW: 066.10–18). The Letter here makes its first appearance in the text, and HCE's identification as "King," his assumption of that role from the initial sketch at the beginning of chapter 2, is restored, ready for its extension into Festy King in chapter 4.

In sum, both "outrages" sections of chapter 3 mobilize the same thematic materials, ordering and imaging them differently as they make use of notes from different sources. But despite a certain awkwardness in the transition out of the plebiscite, Joyce must have decided to use both, as it became clearer that the echoing and apparent repetition of episodes was to be a central aspect of his structure, carrying its theme. Therefore, as he follows his practice of copying his first draft (with copious changes) when it is completed to his satisfaction, he transcribes 3§2 to follow the revised copy of 3§1 where he has left room at its end in the copybook (BL 47471b fs. 13–16; JJA 45: 154–58). He begins the 3§2 copy on a fresh page, unindented, since he now conceives of it as a new chapter or episode to follow 3§1, which is at this point an episode in itself.

By using the later-drafted "outrages" passage (3§2) before the earlier-drafted one (3§3) Joyce loses the tight connection between references to the girls in the park that close 3§1 and open 3§3. But to use 3§2 first better establishes the sense of HCE's resurrection *from* his disappearance into the plebiscite and *to* the eternal sequence of being attacked and becoming an object of identification for others, as we can see from the sentence that follows the opening statement of the outrages and describes them:

> The city of refuge whither he had fled to forget & expiate manslaughter, the land in which by the commandment with promise his days apostolic were to be long with all good things with all things in it were, murmured, wd rise against him, do him hurt ghostly & bodily, poor jink, as were he made a curse for them, the corruptible lay quick, the saints of incorruption of an holy nation, the castaway in resurrection of damnation to convince him of their proper sins. (BL 47471b f. 10v, simplified; JJA 45: 151; FDV: 72; see FW: 061.36–062.21)[16]

HCE being discovered in or emerging from a refuge and being done hurt by society will be the essential sequence of the rest of the narrative of these chapters.

Having transcribed 3§2 into its waiting place after the first revision of 3§1, Joyce does not transcribe 3§3 to follow that, nor does he decide to drop it as a rejected alternative. He must have decided that its recapitulation would do well at introducing yet another major unit (4§1A) that he could extend on from it. And although 3§3 contains what has now become a redundant version of the attack at the gate, it also preserves explicit reference to the girls in the park. That is a subject that he is unwilling to let us lose sight of and one that he wants us to carry forward along with other versions of the cad encounter (since, after all, the three soldiers are a version of the cad) and subsequent gossip. Moreover, perhaps at this exact moment the decision to let 3§2 and 3§3 repeat each other leads to allowing 4§1A to repeat both yet again, with repetition by now decided upon as the principle of the composition as it is of the theme.

4§1A (FW: 075.01–091.33)

Rather than following his copy of 3§2 with a copy of 3§3, then, Joyce went in the copybook to the end of the first draft of 3§3 and wrote its seamless continuation, 4§1A.0 (BL 47471b fs. 8v, 8, 17, 7v, 18, 18v, 19; JJA 46: 3–9; FDV: 75–77; FW: 075.01–091.33).[17] The "bullocky" had "pegged" his stones (FW: 072.26–27) and left HCE at the end of 3§3 (BL 47471b f. 8v; JJA 45: 161; FDV: 74; see FW: 072.26–27), and at the start of what will become 4§1A HCE fantasizes patronizingly about this attacker's scapegoating others' crimes and becoming first of "a truly criminal class, thereby eliminating much general delinquency from all classes and masses" (BL 47471b f. 8v; JJA 46: 3; FDV: 75; see FW: 076.05–6).[18] But, knowing now that he is going to use *both* 3§2 and 3§3, Joyce goes back for an element of 3§2—the later drafted, therefore fresher in his memory—in order to carry what was unique about it forward into the extension. Recalling 3§2's stolen "coffin, mistaken for a fender" (BL 47471b f. 4v; JJA 45: 153; FDV: 73; see FW: 066.27–28), that the "aggravated assaulted" (BL 47471b f. 10v; JJA 45: 151; FDV: 72; see FW: 063.07–8) carried, he says in a new paragraph that "The coffin was to come in handy later" (BL 47471b f. 8v; JJA 46: 3; FDV: 75; see FW: 076.11–12). And indeed, Joyce concludes the cad encounter-like story of the "aggravated assaulter" (BL 47471b f. 10v, simplified; JJA 45: 151; FDV: 72; see FW: 062.34–35) by having HCE split himself off from others as he sinks into the "present of a grave which nobody had been able to dig much less to occupy, it being all rock" (BL 47471b f. 8v; JJA 46: 3; FDV: 75; see FW: 076.21).

From his grave HCE next emerges to begin a new round of encounters in which self and other meet and struggle and blend and divide again. Joyce began the next paragraph "The other spring offensive" (BL 47471b f. 8; JJA 46: 4; FDV: 75; see FW: 078.15), clearly signaling it as a new major segment, "other" than what has just concluded. And in the remainder of 4§1A (FW: 078.15–091.33) we have again an outdoor struggle and an indoor verbal abuse that ends with HCE's fall (to rise again) and the splitting off of his attacker, who, however, carries the same contradictions and thus also *is* the risen HCE. And this second repetition is again in two parts, with exactly the same narrative components and imagery.

The first part of this second repetition is reported to us now not with the cad encounter's "They tell the story" (FW: 035.01) but through the "statement" (connoting law and leading us toward the trial scene) of "Kate Strong, a widow" (BL 47471b f. 17; JJA 46: 5; FDV: 75; see FW: 079.36, 27). We have seen that Joyce began the 3§2 account, based on notes on the *Freeman's Journal* story of an attack at someone's gate, by changing the setting to "the old spot" (FW: 062.31), which is clearly outdoors and echoes the cad encounter. Similarly, here in 4§1A he carefully transformed another story derived from a newspaper report of a few days later (the *Connacht Tribune,* 24 November 1923). Whereas the setting of the crime reported in this newspaper article was indoors, Joyce has it occur outdoors, "on that resurfaced spot" (BL 47471b f. 17; JJA 46: 5; FDV: 75; see FW: 081.12–13).[19] The signs of the cad encounter, which as it recedes into the narrative past becomes ever more difficult to see clearly, are read from the "filth dump near the dogpond in the park" (BL 47471b f. 17; JJA 46: 5; FDV: 75; see FW: 080.06), where again "the attacker" (BL 47471b f. 17; JJA 46: 5; FDV: 75; see FW: 081.18) or "intruder" (BL 47471b f. 17; JJA 46: 5; FDV: 76; see FW: 082.18), who has a "long bar" (BL 47471b f. 17; JJA 46: 5; FDV: 76; see FW: 081.31), which he used to break in the door, and "a wooden affair in the shape of a revolver" (BL 47471b f. 17; JJA 46: 5; FDV: 76; see FW: 082.16), confronts "his chance companion who had the fender" (BL 47471b f. 17; JJA 46: 5; FDV: 76; see FW: 082.23–24).[20] The attacker, the "masked man" (BL 47471b f. 17; JJA 46: 5; FDV: 76; see FW: 082.04),[21] is losing the struggle, says "Let me go, Pat" (BL 47471b f. 17; JJA 46: 5; FDV: 76; see FW: 082.09), and after he drops his pretend revolver offers to pay the six pounds fifteen stolen last summer if Pat has change for a tenner—silly enough already, to offer to repay stolen money if the victim has change![22] But Pat, not having change, gives the attacker "four and 7 pence to buy whisky," at which even more ridiculous turn the "wouldbe burglar became calm" (BL 47471b f. 18; JJA 46: 7; FDV: 76; see FW: 083.02–3, 06)[23] and is naturally ecstatic—he was *losing,* after all! He leaves "gleefully" (BL 47471b f. 17v; JJA 46: 6; FDV: 76; see FW: 083.15), much as the cad in chapter 2 had left in wonderment at HCE's carrying on the way he did at a simple request for the time of day and as in chapter 3 the "bullocky" had left while the person attacked patronizingly salves his "wounded feelings" (BL 47471b f. 8v; JJA 45: 161; FDV: 74; see FW: 072.26)[24] by thinking about his attacker's reformation. And Pat, "the fenderite," HCE, then complains at the "watch house," where once again he is put on the spot by the raising of "the question of unlawfully obtaining" the "pierced fender & fireguard" (BL 47471b f. 18; JJA 46: 7; FDV: 76; see FW: 084.08, 18, 33, 34)—the second section of chapter 2 had established that the fender had been "removed from hardware premises" (BL 47471b f. 4v; JJA 45: 153; FDV: 73; see FW: 066.31). But the real question, the narrator says here in chapter 4, is the "political bias" of the man attacked while "walking along a public thoroughfare" (BL 47471b f. 18; JJA 46: 7; FDV: 76; see FW: 084.35, 085.09).[25] The question of political bias is a reminder of this episode's initial identification of the attacked as "the grand old whig in the flesh" and the attacking "wouldbe burglar [as] a tory of the tories" (BL 47471b f. 8; JJA 46: 4; FDV: 75; see FW: 079.02, 04), though the political connotations are weakened when the latter phrase is replaced on the first typescript by "ifsuchhewas bully on the hill" (BL 47471b f. 157; JJA 46: 33; see FW: 079.03–4), probably for a stronger identification with the cad.

In Joyce's first draft, as in the newspaper story, Pat berates the burglar and wrests the iron bar from him: "the attacker, though under medium, with truly native pluck tackled him whom he took to be ^[1]saying he wd have his life & lay him out & ^[2]made use of sacrilegious language &[2]^[1]^ catching hold of a long bar he had & with which he ^[1]usually[1]^ broke furniture" (BL 47471b f. 17; JJA 46: 5; FDV: 75–76; see FW: 081.18–32).[26] But in his fair copy of the first copy of the passage Joyce reassigns the cursing and the taking hold of the bar from Pat to the burglar, thus keeping the burglar from seeming too hapless and Pat from seeming more overtly aggressive than the HCE figure should be: "the attacker, though under medium, with truly native pluck tackled him whom he mistook to be somebody else to whom he bore some facial resemblance, making use of sacrilegious language to the effect that he would have his life and lay him out ^[1]as soon as he ~~said~~ ^[2]had[2]^ his prayers said[1]^ at the same time catching hold of a long bar he had and with which he usually broke furniture ^[1]he rose the stick at him[1]^" (BL 47472 f. 134; JJA 46: 24).[27] Yet, on the other hand, lest Pat be made to seem too much the victim, in the second typescript he becomes "the Adversary," with a Satanic suggestion (BL 47472 f. 262; JJA 46: 94; FW: 081.19–20). This even distribution of aggressive and defensive impulses, between attacker and attacked, allows the core event, the encounter on the hill, to be both an echo of HCE's challenge by the cad (in which, of course, it is never quite clear whether HCE carries a watch or a gun) and an instance of the fraternal struggle between Shem and Shaun. And this double perspective is the heart of Joyce's image of our primary encounter with the world, whether the outside world of interaction with others or the inside world of our own contradictions.

Finally, then, Joyce later added an extension to his first draft (BL 47471b fs. 18–19; JJA 46: 7–8; FDV: 76–77; FW: 085.20–091.33),[28] in which he puts together notes (VI.B.11: 48–49) he had taken from several stories in an earlier *Connacht Tribune* about actual court trials concerning ambush and attack, principally of the defendant, Festy King, against the plaintiff, Pat O'Donnell—conveniently, another "Pat." Again, the discovery of the source, the *Connacht Tribune* of 20 October 1923, is Vincent Deane's. With Joyce's use of this material in his draft we move into another, more public reconsideration of the encounter than the previous Pat's (Pat Byrne's, in real life) report at the watch house. In the *Connacht Tribune* stories, in addition to the plaintiff, Pat O'Donnell, there are two Festy Kings, father and son, as well as a number of other Kings, including a Simon King, whose name Joyce notes and uses. Also reported are two trials concerning altercations at different fairs between Pat O'Donnell and the Kings. In one trial Pat appeals his previous conviction for attacking the Kings. In the other, the one on which Joyce took his notes, the Kings and a certain Peter Naughton are accused of attacking Pat, who they say stole some sheep. Joyce's blending of it all in his draft renders the flavor the newspaper stories had of the accusations and counteraccusations of beatings and ambushings made by the various almost indistinguishable participants. This muddle allows him to mingle qualities of attacker and victim in both his characters.

As usual, the narrator's main point is that information is not clarified. He begins "but little headway was made when a countryman Festy King [. . .] was subsequently brought up on an ~~improper~~ ^[1]improperly framed[1]^ indictment" (BL 47471b f. 18; JJA 46: 7; FDV: 76; see FW: 085.21–28). Indeed, the same thing happens here as at the watch house, where Pat had complained of being attacked but was then accused of theft. During the trial the defendant, Festy, is clearly the attacker and the plaintiff, Pat, the one attacked. Likewise, in the previous episode the attacker had said to the attacked, HCE, "Let me go, Pat" (BL 47471b f. 17; JJA 46: 5; FDV: 76; see FW: 082.09). Moreover, the "wordwounder" of 3§3 had "pegged a few stones" (BL 47471b f. 8v; JJA 45: 161; FDV: 74; see FW: 072.27) at the gate, and in the first typescript Festy is renamed "Pegger Festy" (BL 47472 f. 160; JJA 46: 37; see FW: 091.01). In terms of parallelism of action, in the later 4§1B addition (FW: 092.06–24) Festy will abruptly leave the trial at its end, exactly like the "wordwounder" in 3§3 and the "wouldbe burglar," earlier in 4§1A, leaving their respective scenes.

Almost at once, however, "an eyewitness" countercharges that "he saw or heard a man named Pat O'Donnell unquestionably beat and murder another of the Kings, Simon" (BL 47471b f. 19; JJA 46: 9; FDV: 77; see FW: 087.11–18), and this testimony is augmented by Joyce's revisions of 1926–27 to the first typescript of 1923–24. These render the witness's testimony as a series of questions and answers (enormously expanded in later revisions) through which the witness describes Pat and his attack, though his testimony is impugned by the fact that "there was not as much light as wd ~~light~~ ^[1]dim[1]^ a child's altar" (BL 47471b f. 19; JJA 46: 9; FDV: 77; see FW: 088.03–4).[29] The testimony bulks so large that the original indictment of Festy King for having attacked Pat is lost sight of, the focus shifting to accusations against Pat/HCE himself. Joyce makes overt in revision of the galley proofs for *transition* 4 that Pat O'Donnell (who had been renamed "Hyacinth O'Donnell" in revision of the first typescript [BL 47472 f. 160; JJA 46: 37; FW: 087.12]) is HCE, calling him by an acrostic for "HERE COMES EVERYBODY," using names from the aristocratic Tollemache family: "Helmingham Erchenwyne Rutter Egbert Crumwall Odin Maximus Esme Saxon Esa Vercingetorix Ethelwulf Rupprecht Ydwalla Bentley Osmund Dysart Yggdrasselmann" (BL 47472 f. 376; JJA 46: 170; FW: 088.21–23).[30]

The eyewitness's testimony against Pat/Hyacinth/HCE is climactic, as it culminates in a description of the sexual offense in the park and a thunderword for whores (FW: 090.31–33). But, in full keeping with the confusions of the trials he found in the newspaper sources, Joyce then caps the comical confusion by having the original defendant, Festy, twice deny "to the perplexedly uncondemnatory bench" (BL 47471b 19; JJA 46: 9; FDV: 77; FW: 090.35) that he had thrown any stones (a detail Joyce drew from his notes on the newspaper source).

Festy and Pat derive, respectively, from the cad and HCE/Pat of the previous attack. But now Festy and Pat appear to commingle and become less distinct from each other, just as in the newspaper source, where victim and attacker seem to blend into each other. There are details that imbricate the role of the attacked HCE with that of the attacker cad, Festy. Mention of Festy's pig recalls that in 3§3 HCE's rent for his shack included "1 small pig, value 8^{d}" (BL 47471b f. 9; JJA 45: 160; FDV: 74; see FW: 069.18–19), and not only is the current pig connected with something like an attack at a gate ("This animal ate some of the doorpost ^[1], King selling it because it ate the woodwork off her sty[1]^" [BL 47471b f. 19; JJA 46: 9; FDV: 76–77; see FW: 086.24–28]),[31] but it is soon made clear, in Joyce's first copy of the draft, that the pig is sold "in order to pay off arrears of rent" (BL 47471b f. 26; JJA 46: 19; see FW: 086.29–30), which the fair copy of that first copy then specifies as "six pounds fifteen" arrears (BL 47472 f. 136; JJA 46: 27; see FW: 086.30), the sum stolen from HCE (see FW: 082.12–13) that he therefore needs to recover. Even Festy's trial, considered apart from the counteraccusation against Pat, seems in this sense one of the many trials of HCE, especially since that pig does return as a "goat" that is connected directly with a "coffin" (FW: 089.19–24), something that HCE stole in 3§2. Also, at stage 3 Joyce added that Festy had "a hyacinth" at the fair as well as a pig (BL 47472 f. 160; JJA 46: 37; FW: 086.14–15), and we have noted that Pat O'Donnell's name was changed on that typescript to "Hyacinth O'Donnall, B.A." (BL 47472 f. 160; JJA 46: 37; FW: 087.12–13).[32] After these changes the narrative seems ambivalent. The witness's testimony, as well as a countercharge that the plaintiff, Pat, had attacked Simon King, seems also to be a supplementary testimony against a codefendant, Hyacinth, who is Festy's crony. In this light it seems that Festy and Pat/Hyacinth were together at the fair, where they attacked various others who after various revisions do not even retain the name "King." Pat in the first draft (as in the newspaper story) had attacked "another of the Kings, Simon" (BL 47471b f. 19; JJA 46: 9; FDV: 77; see FW: 087.17–18), which phrase Joyce changes in his first copy to "another ^[1]two[1]^ of the Kings, Simon ^[1]& Peter[1]^" (BL 47471b f. 27; JJA 46: 21). He amplifies this a little in his subsequent fair copy to "another two of the Kings , Simon ^[1]D.[1]^ and ^[1]Roaring[1]^ Peter" (BL 47472 f. 137; JJA 46: 28) but alters that considerably in revising the first typescript to "Gush Mac Gale and Roaring O'Brien" (BL 47472 f. 160; JJA 46: 37). These names, especially after Joyce's fair copy of the first typescript changes "another two of the Kings" into "another two of the old kings" and "O'Brien" into "O'Crian" (BL 47472 f. 202; JJA 46: 76),[33] seem not only to have lost their connection with Festy King but hardly to be the names of real people at all. They seem most like those storms of the encounter in the park as recounted by the witness (FW: 090.06–12).

Both the scenes in the watch house and at the trial have turned Pat/HCE's victimization into the public appearance of guilt. Joyce does not after all report the trial's actual result, the plaintiff, Pat's victory and Festy's defeat. But Festy, Pat/Hyacinth, and the witness now differ so much from their originals, HCE and the cad, that as we follow Festy after the trial, who is now a version of Shem, it is as if HCE has disappeared again, dissolving into his inheritors. Just so, the departing "wordwounder," the attacker in

3§3 who also became the "haught crested elmer," HCE, fell into but "skall wake from earthsleep" (FW: 074.01–2), rising again after the usual fall.

The decision to make 3§1, 3§2, and 3§3/4§1A three separate units would not last long. Joyce preserved their autonomy by beginning each on a fresh page, the first line unindented, of the fair copy he made for the typist of the set of first drafts and first copies he had written of his whole book so far, 2§2–4§1A (BL 47472 fs. 108–16, 120–37; JJA 45: 46–54, 171–83, JJA 46: 22–28; FW: 034.30–091.33).[34] But the typescript made of this fair copy drops (surely at Joyce's instruction) the new start at 3§3 (FW: 067.28). This left as units 3§1 (BL 47472 fs. 147–51; JJA 45: 184–90; FW: 048.01–067.27) and 3§2/3§3/4§1A (BL 47472 fs. 152–60; JJA 45: 191–99, JJA 46: 30–37; FW: 067.28–091.33). Thus in the typescript the start of 3§3 becomes a middle rather than a beginning, and Joyce seeks to establish it as a structural division internal to the chapter by adding "Now to the obverse" (BL 47472 f. 154; JJA 45: 195; FW: 067.28). Despite that transition marker, the recapitulation, repetition, and transition seem odd in this final organization of the chapter, especially since the start of 4§1A, which had been intended to be a middle, becomes a beginning later, at stage 4. Only on the galley proofs of *transition* 3 were 3§1 and 3§2 joined.[35]

4§2

Joyce first wrote what became the close of chapter 4, 4§2, after making the fair copy of the whole unit 2§2–4§1 (BL 47471b fs. 27v–29; JJA 46: 46–49; FW: 096.26–103). It is clearly not intended to be the end of the previous major section, as it becomes in the book. Rather, it is the beginning of what Joyce conceives at this point as the *next* major section. It is an introductory passage that will be seamlessly connected with the Letter, which he then planned as the center of what became chapter 5. In fact, for the next three revision stages 4§2 begins chapter 5 rather than ending chapter 4, though it does so as usual by summarizing and reflecting on what has gone before.

As he usually begins units by emphasizing the theme of the decay of information, Joyce begins 4§2 with doubts about the information conveyed, about whether "the framing ^[1]up[1]^ of such fictions" could "bring any truth to light" (BL 47471b f. 27v; JJA 46: 46; FDV: 79; see FW: 096.26–27). But he assigns to what "[t]he ~~best~~ ^[1]soundest[1]^ opinion now holds" a summary description of the previous episode that "our highest common ancestor most effectually saved his brush" "by so playing possum" (BL 47471b

f. 28; JJA 46: 47; FDV: 79; see FW: 096.32–34),[36] that is, by taking refuge in the character of Festy King and denying everything. Again there is a recapitulation: HCE's struggles with the public are rendered as a fox hunt, which suggests identification with Parnell, like the earlier identification with O'Connell. His falls and rises throughout this passage are closely parallel to the pattern in 4§1A. The passage concludes by introducing ALP as "the scourge of Lucalizod" (BL 47471b f. 29; JJA 46: 49; FDV: 80; see FW: 101.11–12) and suggesting that her letter to and about HCE, purportedly intended to save his good name, contains "~~various~~ ^[1]vitriol of[1]^ venom" that a "quiet stamp could cover" (BL 47471b f. 29; JJA 46: 49; FDV: 80; see FW: 101.24–25).[37] As finally placed at the end of chapter 4, 4§2 thus begins to turn us toward ALP and the material *about* the Letter, which will be the content of chapter 5, though originally it was meant to introduce the Letter itself, which at that point lacked its introductions. Indeed, when in his first copy of the initial draft Joyce adds that, "[s]till believing that ^[1]the upper part of her[1]^ her face was the best part of her one nearer, dearer than all stood forth to crush the slander's head" (BL 47471b f. 36; JJA 46: 55; FW: 101.28–31, 102.07, 17), he clearly introduced the Letter, which is to be the mode of ALP's thus standing forth, and that copy continues from that point, with only a paragraph break, into the Letter itself.

In the first copy of his first drafts, then, Joyce planned 4§2/5§2 as a chapter that was to follow a chapter comprised of 3§2/3§3/4§1A. But in what has now become a familiar pattern, Joyce prefaces the Letter with introductory material in the first draft of 5§1 (BL 47471b fs. 33v, 34, 29v, 30, 29, 28v, 26, 27, 25v; JJA 46: 230–37; FDV: 84–87; FW: 104.01–113.22): the discussion of the "proteiform graph itself" (BL 47471b f. 33v; JJA 46: 230; FDV: 84; FW: 107.08). After giving this introductory material the usual transcription/revision treatment of a first copy (BL 47471b fs. 43–49; JJA 46: 240–46), Joyce places it after 4§2 in the fair copy made for the typist, which thus displays the unit 4§2/5§1/5§2: a recapitulation of HCE's career; a brief introduction to the Letter's author, ALP; and then the characteristics of the Letter and the Letter itself (BL 47473 fs. 3–10; JJA 46: 57–58, 247–52; FW: 096.26–112.02, 615.12–619.19). The turn at the end of the finished chapter 4 to ALP and Shem and thus toward the physical nature and authorship of the "mamafesta" (FW: 104.04) in chapters 5, 7, and 8 now reads smoothly. Only a hint that the Letter had been planned to come next survives, in the sentence exclaiming that "such a vetriol of venom" (FW: 101.23–24) could be covered by a stamp: the word "such" refers to what will be revealed 504 pages later.

4§1B

In 1924 and 1925 Joyce removed the Letter from I.5 and separated what became 4§2 from 5§1, thereby treating it as an entirely separate unit. Chapter 4§2 remained autonomous through several fair copies and typescripts until in 1927 it is included in the galley proofs of *transition* 4.[38] But earlier, in 1926 or early 1927 (the time period of the extensive revision of the first typescript), Joyce had drafted a new passage, 4§1B (BL 47471a fs. 6v, 3v, 2v, 1v, 7v, 8v; JJA 46: 38–43; FDV: 77–79; FW: 092.06–24),[39] which became the conclusion of chapter 4 until the integration into it of 4§2. This new sequence neatly divided the HCE portion of Book I from the ALP Letter with its introductions.

In 4§1B Joyce devises an exit from the trial that better fits the shape and themes of the text as it stood in 1927 than the far simpler ending it had in 1923. With the extensive revisions of the first typescript the focus is on the witness's description of Festy's attributes, as if the witness were testifying against not Pat but Festy. Therefore, the conflict is between two of HCE's main aspects: his socially adept, outward, Shaun-like part in the eyewitness against the awkward, inward, cad, or Shem-like part in Festy. And this contrast is emphasized even more in the new section.

The five segments of 4§1B were drafted as a set of one-page building blocks on versos of a copybook that contained the first revision of chapter 1 (BL 47471a fs. 1–3, 6–8; JJA 44: 44–46, 51–53). Unsurprisingly, then, 4§1B echoes many of the themes of the first chapter. But the draft order of these building block segments—1, 2, 3, 4, 5—was rearranged when Joyce copied the passage into his stage 4 fair copy, where it became 3, 2, 1, 4, 5 (BL 47472 fs. 204–7; JJA 46: 78–81). The segment that was drafted first narrates the trial's end very directly, as "The four judges Unchus Munchus, Punchus and Pylax could no more than pass the usual sentence of Nolans Brumans & King left his court trailing his tunic" (BL 47471a f. 2v, simplified; JJA 46: 40; FDV: 77–78; see FW: 092.33–094.21). It adds the Shaun and Shem connotations of the two inheritors who together make up HCE to the HCE/cad connotations of the witness and Festy. In that segment we initially follow Festy, who leaves the trial farting egregiously, to the disgust of "all the twofromthirty advocatesses within echo" (FW: 093.12). And then in the second-drafted segment (BL 47471a f. 3v; JJA 46: 39; FDV: 77; FW: 092.06–32) Joyce turns to the more socially acceptable type to establish the contrast in the women's response to *him:* how "the maidies [. . .] ~~clustered~~ fluttered & flattered around the willingly pressed" (see FW: 092.12–14) and kissed him "pizzicando at his ~~williwags~~ ^[1]woollywags[1]^" (see FW: 092.19–20). The initial letters of "willingly pressed" reestablish the "W.P." motif by which the "eyewitness" of the first draft of 4§1A (BL 47471b f. 19; JJA 46: 9; FDV: 77; see FW: 086.32–33) had become by the first typescript "an eye, ear, nose and throat witness W— P— described in the calendar as a word painter" (BL 47472 f. 160, simplified; JJA 46: 37; see FW: 086.32–33).[40] He will further be identified in a later elaboration of the passage (the galley proofs of *transition* 4) as "Show'm the Posed," as the departing Festy will be named "Shun the Punman" (Buffalo VI.G.1: 2, 3; FW: 092.13, 093.13).[41]

In the order of their composition, the two segments we have discussed narrate first a smooth exit from the trial just concluded at the end of 4§1A and then the transformation of the witness and Festy into Shaun and Shem. But Joyce must have decided that the transformation should come first. Therefore, in his next-drafted segment Joyce creates a new exit from the trial that begins with direct statement of the contrast between the WP witness and Festy: "The hilariohoot of Pegger's Windup contrasted so neatly with the tristitone of the wet pinter's as were they opposites" (BL 47471a f. 6v, simplified; JJA 46: 38; FDV: 77; see FW: 092.06–11). He will transcribe this segment in his fair copy as the first unit of 4§1B (BL 47472 f. 204; JJA 46: 78). In this new beginning the "P.W."/"W.P." opposition is supplemented by the "hilariohoot"/"tristitone" echo of I.1's "Hilary"/"Tristopher" pair that had been drafted and transcribed into this copybook shortly before (BL 47471a fs. 32–35; JJA 44: 94–97; FW: 021.05–023.15). Pegger Festy becomes a "P.W.," Pegger's Windup, though the "word painter," the"W.P." witness, receives a more Shem-like tinge as he becomes a "Wet Pinter."

This new introduction sets up the terms with which to follow the "W. P." and "P. W." characters separately, since "[d]istinctly different were their destinies" (see FW: 092.11). Nonetheless, as is always the case with versions of HCE and his antagonists, the blending of attributes is a reverse movement from the separation: because they were "opposites" they are also "polarized for reunion by the symphysis of their antipathies" (FW: 092.10–11). Thus as we follow the different destinies and concentrate on the "W.P.," the Shaun, part, Joyce focuses on how one of the maidies snuggles the witness, "the shay of his shifting into the shimmering of hers till the ^[1]wild[1]^ wishwish of her sheshay melted ^[1]moist[1]^ musically mid the ^[1]dark[1]^ deepdeep of his shayshaun" (BL 47471a f. 3v; JJA 46: 39; FDV: 77; FW: 092.31–33). Here Shem and Shaun are quite specifically combined, genders mingled as well.

Joyce seems by now to have decided to rearrange his segments into the order 3, 2, 1. In this order the scene that directly follows the trial states the opposition, reunion, and different destinies of "P.W." and "W.P." Then follows the narration of the destiny of the "W.P." as he is adored by the maidies (becoming more "P.W."-like as he "melt[s] moist musically"). With appropriate parallelism, then, after a brief statement of the judges' inability to judge (which now seems a little out of place), we follow the different destiny of the Shem figure as he leaves, in threadbare and disreputable exile, the social world into which the Shaun figure has been folded. With the two fates of Shaun and Shem laid out, Joyce can continue with the principal theme with which 4§1B was to conclude chapter 4 as it was then conceived: the climactic summarizing reflection of the judges on the nature and character of HCE in all the complexity with which he combines Shem and Shaun.

Therefore, the next segment of 4§1B, the fourth to be drafted (BL 47471a fs. 1v, 7v; JJA 46: 41–42; FDV: 78; FW: 094.23–095.26),[42] renders the reflection of the judges, Mamalujo, describing HCE as the "father behind the war of the two roses" (BL 47471a f. 1v; JJA 46: 41; FDV: 78; see FW: 094.33–36), who is as "I well remember him H_2CE_3" (BL 47471a f. 7v; JJA 46: 42; FDV: 78; see FW: 095.12). On the one hand, in this segment Joyce carries forward the Shem-like nastiness of the parting fart when Mamalujo complains of "the smell of him like the vitriol works" (BL 47471a f. 1v; JJA 46: 41; FDV: 78; see FW: 095.02–3). On the other hand, he also carries forward the Shaun-like (indeed, Tristan- or ShemShaun-like) blending with the woman. Mamalujo boasts that they remember "[w]hen I had her when I was in my grandfather" (BL 47471a f. 7v; JJA 46: 42; FDV: 78; see FW: 095.19–20). Finally, in the fifth and last building block of 4§1B (BL 47471a f. 8v: JJA 46: 43; FDV: 78–79; FW: 095.27–096.24) the "I" of Mamalujo fragments, and his different parts sag off to "contradrinking themselves" and to a valedictory "Be it soak!" (BL 47471a f. 8v; JJA 46: 43; FDV: 79; FW: 096.03–4, 096.24).

All these developments support the compositional rhetoric by which in 4§1B Joyce rounds out and closes the narrative of the falls and rises of HCE as the initial drafts of 1923 had left it. This 4§1B unit was intended to be the end of that narrative, since what became 4§2 was the beginning of the Letter (I.5). Stepping back from the trial, the narrative in 4§1B presents the broader perspective of Mamalujo and emphasizes that it is HCE whom we are always watching despite his falls and rises, splits and unions. Furthermore, this new narrative reorients the tenor of the larger narrative unit (2§2–4§1A), which was concerned with intermale struggles, toward the male-female relations that have always been at the heart of the crime in the park and the basic HCE/ALP union.

4§1B was fair-copied into stage 4 as the ending of 4§1A, and once again its summarizing is oddly followed by the resummarizing in 4§2. It is as if, just as there had been two "outrages" passages in chapter 3 and two versions of struggle in 4§1A, we were confronted with alternative but adjoined exits from the trial.

Final Shaping of the Chapters

In the spring of 1927 in the fair copy of the first typescript all the sections had been drafted and their sequence established. It only remained for Joyce to determine their final segmentation into episodes for publication in *transition* and to make the changes that would organize their proper symmetries and echoes.

During the revision of the first typescript in 1926 and early 1927 Joyce drafted the passages that effectively closed chapter 3 and opened chapter 4, though 3§3 and 4§1A were not yet separated. As it was in the fair copy of the early drafts, the "bullocky" (FW: 072.26) "proceeded in the direction of the deaf and dumb institution about ten or eleven minutes walk away" (BL 47472 f. 132; JJA 45: 183; see FW: 073.18–20), and in the next paragraph HCE continued to think about him: "It may be that with his deepseeing insight [. . .] H. C. E. prayed" (BL 47472 f. 132; JJA 45: 183; FW: 075.11–16). But on the typescript Joyce drafted additions that made a chapter break here plausible, though he did not find the proper division point within his additions until he revised the next typescript, made from the fair copy of the first typescript.

As he revised the first typescript, between the paragraphs Joyce added "It may be that the besieged ~~bethought~~ ^[1]bedreamt[1]^ him," which he then preceded with a simile for the dream of the besieged that will eventually open chapter 4: "As the lion in our teargarten remembers the nenuphars of his Nile" (BL 47472 f. 155v; JJA 46: 30; see FW: 075.03–5, 075.01–2). But then Joyce precedes the description and simile of the dream with a lovely narration of the falling asleep that leads to the dreaming: "Liverpoor? Not a bit of it. His brains ~~cold~~ ^[1]cooled[1]^ porridge, his pelt nassy, his heart adrone, his bloodstream acrawl, his puff but a piff, his extremities extremely more so. ^[1]Hypnos— —Humph is in his doge.[1]^ Words say no more to him than ~~the rain~~ ^[1]raindrops[1]^ to Rathfarnham. Which we like.

^[1]Rain.[1]^ When we sleep. Drop" (BL 47472 f. 155v; JJA 46: 30; see FW: 074.13–19). All these connected passage overlays describing the sleep and dream of HCE were copied, with changes, to the next stage (Joyce's fair copy of the first typescript) as the beginning of the 4§1A unit, which is there for the first time treated as separate from 3§3: its first word, "Liverpoor?" is brought to the margin, rather than indented, on a fresh page numbered "1" (BL 47472 f. 193; JJA 46: 67).

But before making the fair copy and after working out these passages on the first typescript (we can tell that it is afterward by its placement on the page), Joyce drafted on the same page of that typescript—indexed to precede "Liverpoor?"—a passage giving a fuller, richer ending for the departure of the besieger, the "bullocky": "But he made leave to many a door beside ^[1]of Finglas weald[1]^ for his cairns are ^[1]at browse[1]^ ~~on~~ up hill and ~~in down~~ coombe and on eolithostroton, at Howth or at Coolock or even at Enniskerry and Oliver's lambs we call them" (BL 47472 f. 155v; JJA 46: 30; see FW: 073.28–34). And this, again with changes, is copied into the fair copy as the end of the chapter 3 unit, where Joyce supplements it with an even richer addition: "and they shall be gathered unto him, their herd ^[1]and paladin,[1]^ in that day when he shall wake from earthsleep ^[1]in his valle of briers[1]^ and o'er dun and dale ^[1]the wulverulverlord protect us![1]^ his mighty horn shall roll, orland, roll" (BL 47472 f. 191; JJA 45: 218; see FW: 073.34–074.05). As the text stood on the fair copy of the first typescript, then, Joyce has two powerful passages about going to sleep. At the end of chapter 3 the departing "bullocky" enters into the "earthsleep" from which he will rise (BL 47472 f. 191; JJA 45: 218). At the beginning of chapter 4 the left-behind HCE goes to sleep before he dreams ("Liverpoor?" [BL 47472 f. 193; JJA 45: 219, JJA 46: 67]).[43] As they are separated on the fair copy there is only a little doubt about the different identities of the sleepers, but that little Joyce may well have sought out. What was intended at this point to *close* chapter 4, 4§1B, had already been drafted, and it presented similar effects of collapsings into each other and separations between attackers and attacked, brothers and father/sons. Moreover, the "Liverpoor?" paragraph does feel like an ending, not a beginning, and Joyce may have felt that both passages of going to sleep, a form of an end or fall, would do better as the conclusion of chapter 3 so that chapter 4 might begin with a sleeper dreaming, a form of a beginning or rise. And so Joyce emphasized the ambiguity between the identities of the sleepers by putting both passages of going to sleep at the end of chapter 3, with no hint that the sleeper in both passages is not the same character. The determining instruction, that the "Liverpoor?" paragraph should end chapter 3 and the "As the lion" paragraph begin chapter 4, appears on the typescript made from the fair copy during preparation of the two episodes for *transition* 3 and 4 (BL 47472 f. 253; JJA 45: 245, JJA 46: 89). With this decision the two we had been observing, "bullocky" and victim, become one again, the HCE we will continue to trace in his rise, splitting, and fall.

One final major adjustment brought the endings of the three chapters into a structural line, thereby making a pattern that holds the three together as a rhetorical unit. The climax of chapter 2 had always been intended to be the Rann, a satirical poem on the past of the Scandinavian immigrant HCE that emphasizes the crimes in the park. In the preparation of the typescripts for *transition,* for the ending of chapter 4 Joyce added the equally satirical poem "Sold him her lease" (FW: 102.31–103.07), in which HCE, as fish, swims in ALP's river with the result of "hues and cribies" for us all.[44] This moves us into the book's subsequent parts, the "feminine" half of Book I and indeed all the rest, which are no longer mostly about the patriarch himself but about his whole family, especially his wife and children. This poem is followed, as an end to chapter 4, only by the "Nomad may roam" paragraph (added in revision of *transition* 4 pages, in the 1930s), which even more specifically helps with Book I's turn toward ALP and chapter 8, since "we have taken our sheet upon her stones where we have hanged our hearts in her trees; and we list, as she bibs us, by the waters of babalong" (BL 47475 f. 42v; JJA 46: 190; FW: 103.08–11).

These poems are climactic in their chapters because they step outside the novelistic convention to summarize with the mocking dignity of satiric verse. We have just seen that during the same process of preparing the typescripts for *transition* Joyce amplified the rhetoric to end what became chapter 3, though without entirely forsaking novelistic decorum. But the catalog of epithets that the "wordwounder" pegs at HCE at the end of chapter 3 (FW: 071.10–072.16) is a structural analog to the satiric poems that end chapters 2 and 4. It effects the same pause in the narrative flow, the same stepping into a space of nonnovelistic writing. Its epithets define HCE's nature, his present, so to speak (appropriately for the middle chapter of the three), as the poems of chapters 2 and 4 define his past and future.[45] When on the third and last set of galley proofs Joyce instructed, concerning the epithets, "all in italics" (BL 47476b f. 333; JJA 50: 101), the visual effect offered to the reader of the finished book is the same in all three chapters. The narrative is interrupted at each chapter's end for an italicized block of satiric writing that encapsulates each chapter's point about the hero.

Notes

1. Cited quotations from the revision documents that are not identical to the corresponding passage in the finished book are indicated with "see FW: page.line."

2. It is possible that this subunit was composed before the plebiscite, and David Hayman notes that "it is difficult to ascertain which came first" (JJA 45: xi). If BL 47471b f. 2v was empty, why did Joyce not use it rather than cramming the margins of f. 3 so full? But if the plebiscite had not been written and f. 3 was open, why did he not continue this new unit onto it rather than squeezing its end into the margin of f. 2v? On balance, Joyce's habit of working backward, using the nearest available pages to the ones he had filled already, disposes me to think the plebiscite came first.

3. It is significant that the long addition is drafted, working backward in the copybook, on blank versos, namely, BL 47471b f. 9v and then, in a separate session, BL fs. 7v and 6v (JJA 45: 140, 142, 143; FDV: 69–71). F. 10v would have been open to begin it, but I think Joyce began on f. 9v instead because that is the verso facing the insertion point on f. 10—both the overlay and the insertion are marked with "V" carets. Placement on the pages proves that composition of this unit must precede 3§2.0, because that section starts on f. 10v and then jumps over 3§3.0 on f. 8v and the long addition continuations on fs. 7v and 6v to conclude on fs. 5v and 4v.

4. The suggestion of watch as revolver is heightened later at FW: 052.06–7: he "reprimed his repeater" in overlay on the first typescript (BL 47472 f. 148; JJA 45: 187; see FW: 052.06) "and resiteroomed his timespiece" in overlay on the second typescript (BL 47472 f. 229; JJA 45: 225; see FW: 052.07).

5. To "post a letter. To defecate: euphemistic: since ca. 1890" (Eric Partridge, *A Dictionary of Slang and Unconventional English,* 8th ed. [New York: Macmillan, 1961], 1230). In current use: "'I'll be back in a minute,' he says, 'I have to post a letter.' What he means doesn't dawn on me until I see him crouched in the rushes with his trousers down" (Hugh Carr, *Voices from a Far Country* [Belfast: Blackstaff Press, 1995], 27).

6. Perhaps Joyce intended a parable of Irish history. HCE versus the cad is the Anglo-Irishman versus the Celt, but the struggles that follow are those of the just-finished Irish Civil War. Perhaps it is too much to say that the HCE figure is de Valera and the cad figure Collins (though "Dev" has always been seen in Shaun), but something like that ratio seems to be connoted.

7. See VI.B.11: 144–45, 165 for the principal notes used for the breaking the gate/abusive names sequence. Other pages, both nearby and scattered throughout the notebook, provide notes as well.

8. The six pounds, fifteen shillings may be derived from a note on VI.B.11: 166: "[r]Later he said 'Was £6-15-d / taken from you,'" which is more fully quoted when the note is used again in chapter 4§1A (BL 47471b f. 17; JJA 46: 5; FDV:

76; see FW: 082.12–13), as we will see. In the *Connacht Tribune* story from which the note is taken the sum is "£6 10s." For the unusual occurrence of its being used twice, consider that three notes from close by in the notebook (though not from the same newspaper story) are also used in this 3§3 passage: "[r]found his coat disturbed," "[r]put a gate on the place / got up for the purpose" (VI.B.11: 167). I suspect that Joyce, when extracting those other notes, probably mined the previous page for "£6-15-d" before using it for the 4§1A draft as well, wanting the thefts linked, though obscurely.

9. On the second typescript, which was prepared in March–April 1927 for publication in *transition* 3, the text reads: "paying 11/- in the week, (Gosh, these wholly romads!) and he missed a soft felt and, take this in, six quid fifteen of conscience money in the first deal of July" (BL 47472 f. 248; JJA 45: 241; see FW: 070.01–3). When setting up the type for the galleys for *transition* the typesetter jumped from "romads!)" to "of conscience," omitting a full typed line (BL 47472 f. 346; JJA 45: 267). The text as set makes some sense but would make more if the conscience money were the important six pounds, fifteen shillings rather than the eleven shillings rent.

10. See VI.B.11: 144: "[r]pegged / stone at him."

11. Joyce's consistent practice in the copybook BL 47471b is to copy (with copious changes) a first draft on the rectos immediately following the conclusion of the first copy of the narrative unit he intends it to follow. But he did not copy 3§3 into the place waiting for it in the notebook after the first copy of 3§1, even though 3§3 would follow 3§1 with impeccable narrative and logical sense. Rather, he wrote what would become the middle section, 3§2 (FW: 061.28–067.27), on empty versos conveniently to hand, working (again in his usual practice) from the starting point backward in the notebook. The fact that he jumped from BL 47471b f. 10v to f. 5v, skipping over the pages that contain 3§3.0 and 3§1.1, proves that both of those must have been written first.

Three narrative units make up 3§2. The first two thirds of BL 47471b f. 10v, covering roughly FW: 061.28–062.26 on how the "covenanter" has fled and is "subjected to terror," relies heavily on notes from VI.B.11: 144–45. The second unit, covering FW: 062.26–064.16, drafted fast and with very little rewriting on BL 47471b fs. 10v–5v, describes an attack at a gate claimed as the noise of opening a bottle of stout built from notes in VI.B.11: 146–47, with a few phrases from nearby pages derived from a *Freeman's Journal* story, as we will see. The third segment (FW: 065.05–33; much later material intervenes), on the "fellow who calls on his skirt," continues on fs. 5v–4v in a different session, judging from ink color, also written with few changes or additions. It makes use of eleven notes scattered widely in VI.B.11.

12. See VI.B.11: 120–21.

13. "[A] fellow" is revised to "an old geeser" in the first typescript (BL 47472 f. 153; JJA 45: 193).

14. Vincent Deane announced this and several other discoveries mentioned below at the Antwerp James Joyce Center conference “Genetic Joyce Studies” (University of Antwerp, 29–30 March 2001), and I am grateful to him for allowing me to discuss them. In the trial three defendants were seen by a constable shoving at the gate of a store. One claims that “they were only trying to open a bottle of stout by hammering it against the gate” and another that “he had a lot of drink taken and was falling against the gate.” To much laughter the chief justice elicits from the caretaker, Maurice Behan, that he was in bed, heard the hammering, and did not think “the noise was like trying to open a bottle of porter,” which noise “would not rouse [him] from [his] sleep.” These and other phrases, and the story itself, are identical to those in the notebook and in Joyce's draft (BL 47471b f. 10v; JJA 45: 151; FDV: 72–73; see FW: 062.35–064.15).

15. The notebook entries underlying this sentence—“[r]the old spot” (VI.B.11: 148), “[r]revolver barking” (VI.B.11: 147), “[r]against whom he had / been jealous” (VI.B.11: 149)—suggest a newspaper source different from the *Freeman's Journal* article and thus a story not necessarily of an attack at a gate.

16. Ten notes on VI.B.11: 154–55 underlie this draft. The intention that “murmured” should be the main verb of a sentence of which “city” is the subject is finally thwarted in the process of revision of printed *transition* pages by a combination of Joyce's and a typist's misunderstandings (BL 47475 fs. 26v–27; JJA 45: 294).

17. The continuation, on BL 47471b 8v, begins below a few overlays at the end of the first draft of 3§3 that had intruded into its then bottom margin. Joyce is so sure that this 3§3–4§1A passage will be a new unit, entirely distinct from 3§2, that when he runs out of room on f. 8v and the space on f. 8 that had been left for the fair copy of the Rann (by now developed elsewhere) after his copy of the second section of chapter 2, he decides not to try to preserve his sequence of stage 1 copies in contiguous spaces, and he jumps from f. 8 to the next open recto (f. 17) after the completed copy of 3§2 and drafts away freely on fs. 18 and 19. There he finishes 4§1A with the disappearance again of HCE into his inheritor and antagonist Festy King.

18. Note that “much general delinquency” has become by *transition* 4 “from the oppidump much desultory delinquency” (BL 47475 f. 122; JJA 46: 193; FW: 076.06), but this is lost on the *Wake* galleys by printer's error, to the detriment of the grammar and meaning (BL 47476a f. 47; JJA 49: 99).

19. Again the discovery of the article in the *Connacht Tribune*—“Fierce Struggle / Man with Mask and Iron Bar. / Wooden Revolver”—is Vincent Deane's, announced at Antwerp. Joyce took extensive notes on the story on VI.B.11: 166, which he transcribed quite literally into his first draft though supplementing them with a few notes derived from different sources from elsewhere in the notebook and indeed also using two phrases from the newspaper account that are not in his notes, which suggests that he had both newspaper and notebook by him as he

drafted. In the newspaper account one Pat Byrne wakes to find that a masked burglar has used an iron bar to break in his door and is standing by his bed. They struggle. The burglar says, "Let me go, Pat," and asks if Pat has had six pounds, ten shillings stolen from him. As the burglar goes to the door trying to escape, Pat wrests the iron bar from him, and the burglar drops a wooden revolver and thereupon offers to pay back what was stolen last summer if Pat has change for a tenner—surely what attracted Joyce to the story was the comicality of a burglar offering to repay previously stolen money if his victim has change! But Pat has no money, the burglar leaves, and Pat goes to a neighbor's house (as Joyce's notes accurately summarize the news story) bloody but unbowed.

20. It will be remembered that the fender, assigned here as in 3§2 to the person attacked, was in the *Freeman's Journal* article of 21 November 1923 carried by one of the attackers at the gate. There is no fender mentioned in the *Connacht Tribune* housebreaking story.

21. Joyce introduces an inconsistency in a later revision when the "masked man" of the first draft and of the newspaper account becomes a "taller man" in revision of the first typescript (BL 47472 f. 158; JJA 46: 34), which is mistyped "toller man" in the second typescript (BL 47472 f. 263; JJA 46: 95), which last prevails. Since Joyce has specified that it is the "attacker" (changed to "attackler" on the first typescript [BL 47472 f. 158; JJA 46: 34]) who is "under medium" (FW: 081.18), the "taller man" would seem to be Pat, the attacked, just as at FW: 062.28 it is the attacked one who is a "tall man." No other detail suggests inaccuracy of the roles we have assigned, and this revision would seem rather to blur than to reassign them.

22. We saw that the VI.B.11: 166 note on the six pounds, fifteen shillings was used also in 3§3, though its main use is clearly here among the other notes on the newspaper story from which it comes, in which, however, the burglar asked if six pounds, ten shillings were taken from his victim. Joyce's change in the note from "10s" to "15 d" may be for thematic reasons—McHugh annotates: "6 Victoria 15: Act of 1843 against African slave trade," and Joyce's later change from "six pounds fifteen" to "six victorios fifteen pigeon" in the first typescript (BL 47472 f. 158; JJA 46: 34; see FW: 082.12–13) may support this connotation.

23. Joyce integrates here a note from several pages later in the notebook (VI.B.11: 168) that he must have taken from a different story source, though it certainly fits perfectly the burglar anecdote: "[r]I will give you £5 for / whiskey. At the mention / of whisky — became / calm."

24. See also BL 47471b f. 8v; JJA 45: 161; FDV: 74; see FW 073.01.

25. The change from the newspaper account's "neighbor's house" to "watch house" fits the transformation from a housebreaking story to one of an outdoor struggle and also repeats the pattern by which after these struggles HCE, though a victim, is in trouble with the community and its authorities. The victimhood is drawn from earlier in the notebook: "[r]exercising his right / walking along a crowded / well known thoroughfare / in broad daylight" (VI.B.11: 66).

26. The addition of the second overlay to the first draft makes the grammar ambiguous. Without it, the initial draft, "the attacker [. . .] tackled him whom he took to be catching hold," clearly assigns the catching of the bar to the victim Pat, and the first overlay preserves the assignment by making "saying" parallel to "catching." But "made use of" seems to be parallel to "tackled" and to say that the attacker was the one who cursed and caught hold, except that if that were the point, then "catching" should have been changed to "caught." But two factors militate against our assuming that Joyce's intention was blocked by this inadvertence. In the first draft there is a curious hook in the index line leading to the marginal overlays that could be mistaken for a comma after "him whom he took to be" (see FW: 081.21). Hayman in FDV supplies this comma, saying, in a note, "Joyce omitted this comma," apparently thinking that with it Joyce intended to assign the taking hold of the iron bar to the burglar. But the comma-resembling hook is the result of Joyce's taking two strokes to construct his index line, and they overlap in this deceptive way. And, more telling, the newspaper sentence has a faulty pronoun reference but is itself perfectly clear: "The burglar then went to the door and Byrne caught hold of a long bar he had and with which he broke in the door." Pat Byrne did not break in his own door, and it is certain that Pat takes hold of the burglar's bar. Joyce's note, the first he uses in his draft though the fourth of those that summarize the newspaper account, is "^{r}caught hold of a long bar / he had & with which he / broke in the door" (VI.B.11: 166). The marginal overlays in the draft are taken from earlier in the notebook, no doubt from other sources: "^{r}lay him out" (VI.B.11: 86); "^{r}made use of sacrilegious / language" (VI.B.11: 65).

27. Intervening changes to the first draft in Joyce's first copy (BL 47471b f. 24; JJA 46: 15), reflected in the text of the fair copy as quoted, begin to clarify the grammar, which is finally made unambiguous by the addition of a comma after "his prayers said" in Joyce's fair copy of the 1926 typescript (BL 47472 f. 198; JJA 46: 72).

28. We can tell that the drafting was discontinuous because there are overlays inscribed between the two parts on BL 47471b f. 18 (JJA 46: 7).

29. In making his fair copy of the revised first typescript Joyce placed the question/answer series *after* the statement about the dim light so that the refutation of the testimony seems to come before the description of its content. For details and for full description of the many revisions of the testimony see my "The Development of the 'Eye, Ear, Nose and Throat Witness' Testimony in I.4," *Probes,* 203–54, 220–22.

30. See VI.B.18: 83–84 for Joyce's two drafts of the list of names, the second of which revises the first so as to spell out "Here Comes Everybody." The second list differs only slightly from the draft.

31. See VI.B.11: 48: "^{r}pig ate woodwork / Alf said pig ate doorpost / of pigsty . . sold it^{r} / all for good of trade." These derive primarily from a *Connacht Tribune*

story of 20 October 1923 involving a merchant's complaint that a pig, being sold at the fair because it ate its sty at home, also ate the woodwork in front of her house on fair day. Though, except for "Alf said," Joyce's notes exactly summarize the newspaper story, perhaps David Hayman's speculation (private correspondence) that Joyce is referring to a story told by his father's friend Alf Landon could also be correct, at least as to a doorpost-eating pig. Hard otherwise to explain "Alf said."

32. The typescript errs with "O'Donnall," restored to "O'Donnell" by Joyce in his fair copy of the typescript (BL 47472 f. 202; JJA 46: 76).

33. The "Jr." was added in the second typescript (BL 47472 f. 267; JJA 46: 99). Also, Joyce changed "Gush" to "Gash" on this typescript, but the next typist did not notice the change, which is lost.

34. Joyce made the fair copy immediately after making and revising a first copy of the unit 3§3/4§1A (BL 47471b fs. 19v–27; JJA 45: 162–67, JJA 46: 10–21; FW: 067.28–091.33). Joyce had not made a first copy of 3§3 until he had first drafted all of 4§1A. He did not need to fair-copy 2§1, which, as we have seen, had already been revised, typed, and even published.

35. The last step of joining the parts of chapter 3 was that 3§1 appears at stage 6 joined by a missing instruction to 3§2 for *transition* publication, where the "diversified outrages" paragraph that begins 3§2 is indented for the first time on the *transition* galley (BL 47472 f. 339; JJA 45: 260; see FW: 061.28), all previous drafts of 3§2 beginning at the margin like all of Joyce's chapter beginnings.

36. Note that "highest common ancestor" becomes "hagious curious encestor" in the first typescript, the first revision stage at which Joyce begins to lard "HCEs" into the text (BL 47472 f. 161; JJA 46: 61; FW: 096.34).

37. In the fair copy of the first typescript Joyce changes "vitriol of venom" to the spoonerism "vetriol of vinom" (BL 47472 f. 211; JJA 46: 85). By one typesetter's error, *transition* 4 sets "vinom" as "vnomi," and a second typesetter's error on the galley proofs introduces the further error of "vetrio" for "vetriol" (BL 47476a f. 62; JJA 49: 137). On the first set of page proofs Joyce restored the l to "vetriol" but changed "vnomi" to "venom" so that the spoonerism is finally lost.

38. The Letter (5§2) was dropped from the typescript, 4§2/5§1/5§2, in January 1924. Chapter 5§4 was set to follow 5§1 at that time, though it was not certainly joined to it until February 1925, when Joyce's decision to print the unit, 5§1/5§4, in Eliot's *Criterion* also led him to separate 4§2 from 5§1 by cutting the typescript page (BL 47472 f. 63; JJA 46: 63) and renumbering 5§1/5§4 to reflect the new beginning—see BL 47473 f. 30 (JJA 46: 323), where what had been page 3 is renumbered as page 2 (the cut-off portion, which would have been page 1, is lost). Chapter 4§2 was fair-copied in March 1927, like the rest of the whole series 2§2–4§1B, but, like the other separate units planned at that point, it was given an unindented page beginning and numbered independently, until—the point when it joined chapter 4—Joyce renumbered the 4§2 pages that had been "1–5" so that they become "16–20" to succeed the last page, 15, of 4§1B (see,

e.g., BL 47472 f. 208 [JJA 46: 82], where "1" is renumbered "16"). Though the typescript, stage 5, made from this fair copy also ends 4§1B short on one page and begins 4§2, unindented, on the next (BL 47472 fs. 282, 285; JJA 46: 106–7), the typist numbered these consecutively "6" and "7," and the same behavior occurs on the next typescript, stage 6 (BL 47472 fs. 307–8; JJA 46: 151–52). It is barely possible, then, that it was only when Joyce included the 4§2 pages in what he sent to the printer for *transition* 4 that the decision to include it in chapter 4 was made. Either way, the join was made in early 1927.

39. Note that JJA 46: 1 designates 4§1B as revision stage 3, no doubt reading it as an extended passage revising the stage 3 first typescript rather than a first draft of an entirely new section. However, in the volume's preface it is referred to as "1B.*0" (JJA 46: ix), and it is included, entirely appropriately, in FDV.

40. Note that in his fair copy (BL 47472 f. 202; JJA 46: 76; FW: 087.13) of the typescript Joyce dropped "described in the calendar as a word painter" from the description of the witness and reassigned it to Pat O'Donnell, who had been renamed "Hyacinth" on the typescript.

41. The three folios of Buffalo VI.G.1 are the *transition* proofs not available for the JJA; they are indicated by the blank page JJA 46: 171. I am grateful to Luca Crispi for letting me see photocopies.

42. Note that the segment, drafted on the two widely separated folios, 1v and 7v, is the only building block of 4§1B extending beyond one page. That, after coming to the end of f. 1v in midsentence, Joyce leaps over the segments on fs. 2v, 3v, and 6v (as well as the chapter 1 overlay on fs. 4v and 5v) to conclude the passage shows that it was written after those segments. The final segment, on f. 8v, is less demonstrably written last, but I think it was. Hayman suggests this draft order: fs. 2v–1v–7v first, then fs. 6v–3v, and finally f. 8v (JJA 46: ix); however, I believe the first two steps cannot be right. Joyce would not have skipped over the blank fs. 3v and 6v when he ran out of room on f. 1v and then continued his sentence on f. 7v.

43. BL 47472 f. 192 is not reproduced in the JJA.

44. I agree with the JJA that the final poem was probably drafted on the now missing ribbon of which the carbons, which we have, are BL 47472 fs. 290, 291 (JJA 46: 126, 127). The missing ribbon with the draft poem was retyped (f. 314; JJA 46: 159), of which a carbon is f. 292 (JJA 46: 128). Though the JJA correctly designates f. 314 as draft stage 6, the fact is missed that f. 292 is a carbon of it, so that the latter is designated draft stage 5‡ rather than the draft stage 6' it should be. Note, though, that f. 314 was not prepared at the same time as the other stage 6 retypings of stage 5 pages, since the typewriter used for f. 314 is unique—no other machine used for any other page on stages 5 or 6 has a separate exclamation key, all their exclamations being combinations of period and single quotation mark. And, unique in these chapters, the carbon paper used for f. 292 is blue. Note too that, in an unpublished postcard of 28 May 1927 (BL 57349 f. 52v),

Joyce expresses concern to Harriet Shaw Weaver about the fact that the manuscript of the poem is missing, apparently lost in a Paris taxi when some pages fell off the seat.

45. That the total eventually comes to 111, the total of ALP's children (though not reaching that number until revisions on the page proofs and the corrections to the published book), would seem to undercut the claim that the catalog refers to HCE's present, but by the end of the revision process Joyce would have had no trouble thinking of HCE containing his children at every "present" time.

The Letter and the Groaning

Chapter I.5

MIKIO FUSE

In all of its dissimulating guises the Letter fulfills an integral function in *Finnegans Wake.* As a document of the family drama, it purports to defend (but yet betrays) "the crime or crimes" (FW: 107.26) allegedly committed by HCE. It was supposedly written by Shem and carried by Shaun on behalf of ALP, and, at times, it appears to be an incestuous message addressed by Issy to HCE. The Letter is thus an essential medium that relates the members of the "Doodles family" (FW: 299.F4) to one another. But the importance of the Letter does not end here, and a close examination of I.5, also known as the Letter chapter, is helpful in understanding the radical significance of the *Wake's* Letter, the more surprisingly so if we take its ur-textual development into account.

As David Hayman remarks, this chapter is significant not only because it had initially treated the conception and composition of the "Letter" sketch and the female plot but also because these two crucial components were eventually discarded from this chapter, only to be reintegrated elsewhere in the book in 1938 (WiT: 166 n. 22). In the published work I.5 consists of only two sections. The first section (FW: 104.01–113.22) postulates the hypothesized titles of the Letter and the question of its origin (who wrote it and who discovered it), while the latter (FW: 113.23–125.23) focuses on its content and the various elaborate attempts to interpret it. In addition to these two sections the chapter originally had two interceding ones that were abandoned within a few months of conception but were consequently relocated in two other books of the *Wake.*

One of the sections abandoned for I.5, "The Revered Letter" (the Letter itself, but only in a limited sense, as will be discussed below), ultimately contributed to the composition of the last two sections of Book IV (begun in 1938). The other abandoned section is the short and short-lived third section, "The Delivery of the Letter," which did not develop beyond the first draft and its revision (probably December 1923 or January 1924). Nevertheless, as a seminal sketch of the character and function of Shaun the Post it was soon to contribute both verbally and conceptually to Book III (started in March 1924).[1]

In my genetically informed reading of I.5 the chapter's development divides into three distinct stages, separated by two long breaks: Stage I (1923–25), Stage II (1927), and Stage III (mid-1930s–1940). These three periods are marked by two publications of the chapter as fragments of Joyce's *Work in Progress* (see table 1).

Stage I began with the writing of the first drafts of the four sections in December 1923–January 1924. Then, in spring 1924 Joyce abandoned the second and third sections, had the remaining two sections typed (now in the extant diptych format) in early 1924 (level 3), and ended with the publication of *Criterion* 3.12 in July 1925 (level 6). Stage II records Joyce's revision of the *Criterion* pages (level 7) and the subsequent galley proofs (level 8) for the chapter's republication in *transition* 5 in July 1927. Stage III started with Joyce's revision of the *transition* pages in the mid-1930s (level 9) and the subsequent galley proofs for *Finnegans Wake* (levels 10–13, July 1937–July 1938). The final level (14) is the errata for the first edition of *Finnegans Wake* that Joyce prepared with the assistance of Paul Léon in the summer of 1940.

Because of the crucial importance of the development of the chapter in Stage I, the main focus of my essay is a reading of the ur-textual corpus of

TABLE 1

	I.5§1 FW: 104.01–113.22	I.5§2 [FDV: 81–83]	I.5§3 [FDV: 90–91]	I.5§4 FW: 113.23–125.23
STAGE I (1923–25)	LEVELS 0–6	0–4	0	0–6
STAGE II (1927)	7–8		(III)	7–8
STAGE III (Mid-1930s–1940)	9–14	(IV§§4–5)		9–14

the initial stage, along with supplementary notes on the further development of the chapter in the two later stages.

To all appearances, the Letter motif plays a more crucial part in I.5 than the female plot.[2] The hen, introduced in the very first draft of the first section, is the only active feminine figure to survive in the published text of the chapter. However, her role is not entirely central, since she is only seen to be scratching at the Letter by Kev. Section 2 is indeed the most markedly feminine of the original four sections. It even contains the signature of the writer herself,[3] but even before its eventual displacement we have a piece of curious evidence in the first draft showing that Joyce attempted (but eventually deleted) an introductory passage suggesting that the "fair" hand could be that of "Shemus the penman" (§2.*0; BL 47482b f. 31; JJA 46: 255; FDV: 81). In section 3 the key figure is Shaun the Post, who delivers the Letter to HCE, who in his turn vituperates in an antifeminine manner. The first and fourth sections are dominated by the seemingly objective narrative voice (never markedly feminine) that scrupulously discusses the details of the Letter. Thus the original fourfold structure of I.5 enables us to see all the more clearly the Letter itself as the focus of I.5, with various *Wakean* figures (neither exclusively nor unequivocally female) involved in its authorship, writing, retrieval, delivery, and reading.

With the readers' perspectives shifting from the macroscopic to the microscopic, the chapter's sustained concern with the Letter leads us to suspect that it alludes to one and the same letter. Tindall observed that "the letter represents all literature . . . especially *Finnegans Wake.*"[4] Rose and O'Hanlon concur, arguing that the Letter is, "synecdochically, the *Wake*" (UFW: 75), but they go further, pointing out the analogy between the "ruled barriers" (§4.*1; BL 47482b f. 44v; JJA 46: 306; FW: 114.07) of the document and some of Joyce's notebooks, the pages of which are literally ruled (UFW: 81 n 2). Finn Fordham's study of the genesis of *Wakean* signs can be adopted to further pursue the *Wake*'s self-referential synecdoche, for he attributes their origin to Joyce's characteristic "revise mark" (§4.*2; BL 47473 f. 26; JJA 46: 318; FW: 121.02).[5]

Even if there is a synecdochic relation between the Letter and the *Wake,* this does not mean that the Letter's identity can be unequivocally reduced to it or, indeed, to any other single specific pretext. In this essay I propose to demonstrate *how* the seemingly different identities of the Letter are suggested to be identical in a certain radical perspective.

In the early versions of I.5 the various terms and functions (authorship, delivery, reading, etc.) ascribed to the Letter are markedly similar throughout all four sections. Indeed, even without recourse to the genetic information about sections 2 and 3, a number of correspondences between the two sections of the chapter survive in the published work.[6] On the other hand, the manuscript evidence of I.5 demonstrates how the whole chapter was composed so as to imply the identity and sameness of the Letter.

The correspondences between "The Boston Letter" of section 1 (FW: 111.08–24) and the second section, "The Revered Letter," are represented in table 2.[7] In the left-hand column the first draft text of "The Boston Letter" is given in full, along with selected passages from later drafts that further reinforce this correspondence.[8] In the right-hand column relevant passages from "The Revered Letter" are cited when appropriate.[9]

All the corresponding elements in sections 1 and 2 were written in the same, earliest period of the chapter's composition (probably December 1923). Therefore, the tightening of the focus on the transition from the first section to the second (or, alternatively, the "editing" of "The Revered Letter" into "The Boston Letter" of section 1) is a point Joyce deliberately established synchronically from the outset.[10]

"The Revered Letter" also has telling correspondences with some items in the list of the "names" suggested for "her memorial" (§1.*0; BL 47471b f. 33v; JJA 46: 230; FW: 104.04). Although they are said to be "many" (§1.*0; BL 47471b f. 33v; JJA 46: 230; FW: 104.05), Joyce began with *relatively* few in the first draft: "*Pro Honofrio,* The Groans of a Briton, An Apology for a Husband, Can you excuse him, The only true account all about Mr Earwicker & the Snake by an honest Woman of the world who can only tell the naked truth about a dear man and all his conspirators how they tried to fall him by putting it all around Lucalizod by a mean sneak about E— and a dirty pair of sluts, showing to all the unmentionableness falsely accused about the redcoats" (§1.*0; BL 47482b f. 33v; JJA 46: 230; FW: 104.14–107.07). The first item, which did not survive beyond the first stage, refers to "Humphrey" Chimpden Earwicker's "honour" and corresponds with "Honourable Mr Earwicker" of "The Revered Letter" (§2.*0; BL 47482b f. 31; JJA 46: 255; FDV: 81). The second item is not related to "The Revered Letter," but it does echo a passage in the third section, "The Delivery of the Letter" (as will be discussed later). The rest of the "names" obviously refer to the general tenor of "The Revered Letter," whose allusions to Earwicker's alleged disgrace, however, are oddly suppressed in the family-oriented Boston Letter. Furthermore, when Joyce revised the first typescript of the name list he added "The ^1Following1^ Fork" (§1.3; BL 47473 f. 30; JJA 46: 323; FW: 105.06), which suggests a passage in

TABLE 2

"The Boston Letter"	"The Revered Letter"
(§1.*0): Maggy well and everybody athome's general health well	(§2.*0): Majesty well (§2.*1): regards for self & dearest of husbands Papa Earwicker & self to dear [Mag] & all [athome] (§2.*2): with love to Mag and all at home [cf. FW: 617.16] (§2.*3): I am anxious about ye all
(§1.*0): and a lovely face of some born gentleman	(§2.*1): Always the born gentleman (§2.*3): he dreamt about me I had got a lovely face that day
(§1.*0): with a parcel of cookycakes for tea (§1.*1): cakes for dear (§1.*2): beautiful present; thank you	(§2.*0): I can show anyone the bag of cakes given to me by Mr Earwicker for our last wedding day. Thank you, beloved, for your beautiful parcel (§2.*1): I can show whoever likes the bag of one apiece cakes & Adam Findlater's best figrolls which was given to me on occasion of golden wedding day by dear Mr Earwicker
(§1.*0): well and must now close [transposed on §1.1; see below]	[see below]
(§1.*0): a grand funeral (§1.*2): don't forget unto life's end	(§2.*1): 3 p.m. Wednesday grand funeral of [McGrath] Brothers; Don't forget (§2.*2): who I'll be true to you unto life's end [cf. FW: 617.07]
(§1.*0): Maggy and hopes to hear from (§1.*2): Muggy well how are you (§1.*1): well & must now close	(§2.*1):Dear Majesty, I hope you are well, how are you? (§2.*3): how are we all? (§2.*0): and I shall now close [cf. FW: 616.33–34]
(§1.*0): with love (§1.*2): pee ess	(§2.*1): will now conclude the above epistle with best thanks (§2.*0): P.S. [changed to "N.B." on §2.*3]
(§1.*0): & four crosses from loving from a largelooking stain of tea.	(§2.*1): x x x x

"The Revered Letter" where the defender of her husband's honorable character declares, "he never chained me to a chair or followed me about with a fork" (§2.*2; BL 47471b f. 19v; JJA 46: 277; cf. FW: 618.24–26).

Although the identity/sameness of the Letter in sections 1 and 2 works in ways beyond the types of literal correspondences thus far noted, and although there are an impressive number of items in the name list and "The Boston Letter" of section 1 that can be linked with "The Revered Letter," we cannot simply conclude that the identity (or origin) of the Letter is "The Revered Letter." I would argue that one of the names given to the Letter allows for a most remarkable correspondence that points to a provocative reading of the identity/sameness of the Letter.

The third name in the first draft of the name list, "The Groans of a Briton" (§1.*0; BL 47482b f. 33v; JJA 46: 230; FDV: 84; FW 104.14), reveals a crucial thematic correspondence. As McHugh notes, the name refers to "the Groans of the Britons," the famous letter sent by the Britons (i.e., the Celts residing in South Britain) in 446 to Aetius, the Roman governor in Gaul. That letter was a plea to the Romans for aid against the invading Saxons: "To Aetius, now consul for the third time: the groans of the Britons. . . . The barbarians drive us to the sea; the sea throws us back on the barbarians: thus two modes of death await us, we are either slain or drowned."[11] In the second draft of the name list Joyce changed the gender of the sufferer to feminine, so that the name became "The Groans of a Britoness." Besides the initial characterization of the sufferer as a Celtic (or by extension Irish) husband groaning under the "barbarous" invasion of the Saxons (or Sassenach, while he himself might be the Irish betrayer, West Briton), the revised version now adds an overtone of maternal suffering of delivery.

"The Groans of a Briton" is exceptional among the names given in the first draft of section 1 because it links not to the second but to the third section of the chapter, "The Delivery of the Letter." Here is the corresponding passage in the first draft of section 3: "It was this last alone that at last gave H.C.E. the raspberry. Groaning of spirit, he lifted his hands & many who did not dare it, heard him say: I will give £10 tomorrow & gladly to the 1st fellow who will put that W in the royal canal" (§3.*0; BL 47482b f. 42, simplified; JJA 46: 295; FDV: 91). This literal correspondence between sections leads us to recognize a subtler thematic context that frames "The Groans of a Briton/Britoness," since the phrase "Groaning of spirit" also alludes to the following Pauline passage:

> For we know that the whole creation groaneth and travaileth in pain together until now. And not only they, but ourselves also, which have the firstfruits of the Spirit, even we ourselves groan within ourselves, waiting for the adoption, to wit, the redemption of our body. For we are saved by hope: but hope that is seen is not hope: for what a man seeth, why doth he yet hope for? But if we hope for that we see not, then do we with patience wait for it. Likewise the Spirit also helpeth our infirmities: for we know not what we should pray for as we ought: but the Spirit itself maketh intercession for us with groanings which cannot be uttered. (Rom. 8:22–26 [AV])[12]

"Groaning of spirit" in the first draft was subsequently changed to "With groanings which cd not be all uttered" (§3.*0+; BL 47482b f. 42, simplified; JJA 46: 295; FDV: 91 n. 44), making the biblical allusion even clearer.[13] Also on the first draft of section 3 Joyce made another significant revision in the same paragraph: "but when the facsimile of the letter written by the joint author finally reached the alderman's ears his surprise was practically complete so much so as to give him the raspberry" (§3.*0+; BL 47482b f. 42, simplified; JJA 46: 295; FDV: 91 n. 44). The deleted but still implicit word "spirit" is now countered by the "letter," which alludes to the famous Pauline antithesis: "the letter killeth, but the spirit giveth life" (2 Cor. 3:6 [AV]).[14]

There is sufficient evidence to prove that the literal correspondence with the Pauline groaning for the unutterable (but must be uttered) Word (the Truth, the Christ) is not just fortuitous but thematically important. As early as 1904 Joyce identified his artist figure as the giver of the Word in his essay "A Portrait of the Artist": "To those multitudes, not as yet in the wombs of humanity but surely engenderable there, he would give the word; . . . amid the general paralysis of an insane society, the confederate will issues in action" (PSW: 218). For all his prophetic self-definition, the Joycean artist (subsequently named Stephen Dedalus) never readily gave the Word—as is ironically suggested in *Ulysses* with the rumor that he too may be suffering from "g.p.i" (U: 1.128). Stephen's arduously self-imposed task of healing the paralytic through his Word may resonate in the discussion of "horseness," which Joyce added on the second draft (level 1) at the beginning of I.5 (FW: 111.26). McHugh notes that this discussion refers to Stephen's epistemological disquisition in "Scylla and Charybdis," where he continues to be concerned with the Word that is not just free from the paralysis of all human words but is in fact capable of healing it: "Unsheathe your dagger definitions. Horseness is the whatness of allhorse"

(U: 9.84). The question of "horseness" is introduced in I.5 as part of the argument that immediately follows "The Boston Letter" to explain the letter's apparently corrupt or distorted texture:

> Explain this.
> Well, [a]ny photoist worth his chemicals will tell anyone asking him at home that if a negative melts when drying well the resultant positive will soon be a grotesque distortion of horse values, and [horsey] masses. Well, this freely is what must have happened to this missive unfilthed by the sagacity of a slanteyed hen. (§1.*1; BL 47482b f. 49, simplified; JJA 46: 246; FW: 111.25–33)

Following Stephen's Hamletian, existential aporia, the question here is "to be or not to be—a horse."[15] At issue is the imperfect articulation that constrains us all in terms of the letter or language. As the wet ink dries to spell the word "horse," a "horse value" is clearly established—but only by excluding the other "horse values" of "allhorse," which in Joycean logic includes not only what a horse *is* or *may possibly be* but also what it *might improbably be*. Logically, "allhorse" might even encompass "nothorse," that is, what a horse *is not*. "Extremes meet," as Lynch's cap teasingly challenges Stephen to prove in "Circe" (U: 15.2098).

Joyce emphasized the inherent incompleteness of verbal articulation in the Stage I drafts by including allusions to "doubt," a term symptomatic of the artist's paralysis. It is not just the readers of this Letter who "may have irremovable doubts as to the whole sense of the text, the meaning of any phrase in it, the meaning of every word deciphered and interpreted" (§4.*0; BL 47471b f. 40v, simplified; JJA 46: 299; FW: 117.34–118.01), but the function of the letters (i.e., the graphemes) that constitute the Letter are equally tarnished with uncertainty. They "run, march, halt, walk, stumble at doubtful points, stumble up again in comparative safety" (§4.*2; BL 47473 f. 23, simplified; JJA 46: 315; FW: 114.08–9).

Furthermore, the fidelity of the letter carrier—or, for that matter, the letter (either epistolary or alphabetical)—to its role as mediator between the writer and the reader is also questioned. "The Delivery of the Letter" section describes the dubious function of Shaun the Post: "though his qualifications for that particular postal or office were known only to a limited circle of friends the spectacle of the Lucalizod lettercarrier, a most capable official of very superior appearance in his emptybottlegreen jerkin, at once gave doubtersful a vouch for his bilateralist zaal" (§3.*0; BL 47471b f. 35v, simplified; JJA 46: 292; FDV: 90). While this suggests that the "superior appearance" of the agent and his "most capable" skills in transmission might be able to overcome the inherent flaw in all letters, there is evidence to the contrary, for we are immediately reminded that "in the discharge of his important duty [. . .] he got a [number] of stumbles which appeared to startle him very much" (§3.*0; BL 47471b f. 35v, simplified; JJA 46: 292; FDV: 90). A fundamental aspect of the Letter is its incompleteness.[16]

From a skeptical point of view, all letters are fragments of the complete Letter that should give the Word (i.e., the "Word-Letter," as opposed to the incomplete "Letter" or all merely human letters). The sketch about "that hen" pecking up "certain fragments of orange peel" is a revelation of our partial access to the Word-Letter because our writerly/readerly manipulation/comprehension of the Letter is destined to imperfect (§1.*0; BL 47482b f. 28v; JJA 46: 235; FW: 110.22–31). Joyce's revision of "that hen" into "the original hen" resituates this incompleteness in the biblical context of "Original Sin" (§1.*1; BL 47482b f. 47; JJA 46: 244; cf. FW: 616.20 and 619.02). Another key epithet, "spontaneous," which was inserted before "fragments" in a later revision (§1.3; BL 47473 f. 33; JJA 46: 327; FW: 110.29), suggests that the "original" flaw can never be eradicated but always betrays itself of its own accord, however hard we may feign to be complete wherever the Letter is concerned.

The "groaning," in its biblical context, is a symptom of our alienation from the Word or the Truth. Even the Joycean artist, who aspires to be the healer of paralysis, is hardly exempt from the curse. Indeed, he is to suffer all the more because of his vigilance against the *general* paralysis of human language that inherently conditions his own mode of artistic expression. He may want to "talk straight turkey as man to man" (§4.*1; BL 47471b f. 44v; JJA 46: 306; FW: 113.26), speak "the *ipsissima verba*" (§4.*2; BL 47473 f. 26; JJA 46: 318; FW: 121.09), and "[settle] our ~~g~~ hashbill for us" (§4.*3+; BL 47471b f. 45v; JJA 46: 350; FW: 115.28), but he must acknowledge that all verbal expressions are alienated from the Word Itself because of the postlapsarian babelic confusion of human language. It is in this context that the readers of the Letter (be it *Finnegans Wake* or anything that is written) are reminded of "the confusion of its composition" in the very first draft of "The Delivery of the Letter" (§3.*0; BL 47471b f. 35v; JJA 46: 292; FDV: 90).[17]

For readers and writers (and even for the graphemes themselves) I.5 commends or commands "patience." The following passages refer to Pauline "patience" (Rom. 8:24): "Now, patience And remember patience is the great thing. And above all things we must neither be nor become impatient. Think of all the patience possessed by both Bruce Brothers & their Scotch spider" (§1.*0; BL 47471b f. 29v, simplified; JJA 46: 232; FW: 108.08–15) and "the penelopean patience of the paraphe tailed by a leaping lasso—" (§4.*0; BL 47471b f. 43; JJA 46: 303; FW: 123.04–6).

Section 4 of I.5 (which contains the second quotation given above) is a minute examination of the scribe's hand and of the letters that constitute the Letter presented in parodic imitation of Edward Sullivan's introduction to *The Book of Kells.*[18] Joyce's misappropriation of Sullivan's scholarly style is both salacious and gastronomic, thereby suggesting how readily we forget the essential "horse" discussion and digress to the mundane discussions of "whores" and "breakfast."[19] But the narrator's perspective here is also explicitly biblical. For example, Sullivan noted that "the unwearied reverence and patient labour . . . brought it into being,"[20] whereas the *Wakean* narrator exhorts "the headstrength revealed by a constant labour to make a ghimel pass through the eye of an iota" (§4.3; BL 47473 f. 36v, simplified; JJA 46: 332; FW: 120.26–27). The labor and patience of writing are amalgamated here with Jesus's parable that describes the difficulty for sinners to enter the Kingdom of Heaven (Matt. 19:24).

The impatience exhibited by various agents (both human and inhuman) of the Letter stands in stark contrast to the virtue of Pauline patience. The vituperating husband and the "anger" of the professor at the breakfast table perforating or punctuating the paper with his fork are examples of human agents' impatience (§4.*0; BL 47471b fs. 43v and 44; JJA 46: 304–5; FW: 124.09 and 124.14). There are a number of examples of inhuman (but humanized) agents' lack of patience, specifically in the microscopic scrutiny of the Letter in section 4: "the indignant whiplashloops" (§4.*0; BL 47471b f. 41v; JJA 46: 298; FW: 119.12), "the sudden petulance of a capitalized middle" (§4.*0; BL 47471b f. 43; JJA 46: 303; FW: 120.04–5), "the fretful eff" that "broods [. . .] paces with a frown [. . .] dragging its shoestring" (§4.*1; BL 47471b f. 47v; JJA 46: 310; FW: 120.33–121.08), as well as "the fatal ^[1]droopadwindle[1]^ slope of the damned ~~thing~~ ^[1]scrawl[1]^" (§4.*2; BL 47473 f. 27; JJA 46: 319; FW: 122.35).

Rather than become impatient, we must sustain "hope for that we see not," says Paul, who "against hope believed in hope" (Rom. 4:18). In the first draft, just before the description of the microscopic scrutiny of the alphabet, Joyce comments on the Letter as a type of necessary evil: "We ought to be deeply thankful that we have even a written on with now dried ink piece of paper after it all & cling to it as with drowning hands" (§4.*0;

BL 47471b f. 38v, simplified; JJA 46: 301; FW: 118.31–119.03). Joyce subsequently added a passage introducing an element of "hope" (although as yet unspecified) to counter this necessary evil: "hoping all the while that things will begin to clear up a bit one way or another and be hanged to them as ten to one they will too as they ought to" (§4.*1; BL 47471b f. 46v, simplified; JJA 46: 309; FW: 119.04–8). On the next level, Joyce further changed the "hoping" to "hoping against hope" (§4.*2; BL 47473 f. 25; JJA 46: 317; FW: 119.04), thereby making the reference to Paul's letter explicit.

Paul's words "hope that we see not" figuratively describe sinners as physically handicapped beings. The early stages of I.5 abound in quasi-biblical metaphors of physical impediment in relation to the Letter's various modalities of paralysis, including an allusion to another famous parable of Jesus: "Ah yes but one who deeply thinks will always bear in his mind that this downright there you are & there it is only all in his eye" (§4.*0; BL 47471b f. 38v; JJA 46: 301; FW: 118.14–17). In biblical terms, what is in the reader's eye is, of course, "the beam" (Matt. 7:3–5). Neither in the Bible nor in the *Wake* is blindness the only metaphor used for spiritual impediment (or paralysis).[21] There are also the deaf, the mute, and the lame, who, in the Bible, are all supplicants for Jesus's healing. In the first stage Joyce systematically added a remarkable number of allusions to the paralyses of the eye, ear, and mouth as well as the "lameness" of limbs to consolidate his appropriation of the biblical topos. For instance, where one would expect the maxim "advance from savagery to *civilisation*" (or "to *literacy*"), Joyce has "advance from savagery to barbarism" (§4.*1; BL 47471b f. 45; JJA 46: 307; FW: 114.13), because for him "literacy" *is* "barbarism" (the Greek term *barbaros* and the Latin term *balbus* are etymologically associated with "stammering").[22] That is, while the use of the letter is certainly one way for human beings to overcome their "savagery" or "illiteracy," nevertheless, it condemns us to verbal paralysis. Another example is the "zigzaggery" of the Letter's delivery that refers to its carrier's paralyzed or "sleepy" feet as well as to the devious ways in which its writers and readers must cope with it. Mr Deasy's motto "*Per vias rectas*" (U: 2.282), together with his innocuous concern with "foot and mouth disease," might be recalled here for further irony (§3.*0; BL 47471b f. 35v, simplified; JJA 46: 292; FDV: 90).[23]

In Pauline terms, what perpetually blocks our access to the Word is "the middle wall of partition" (Eph. 2:14 [AV]), which only Christ can break down. This stumbling block conditions our "continually more & less intermisunderstanding minds," or causes "the curt witty dash" to be "never quite at the truth letter" (§4.*0; BL 47471b f. 38v; JJA 46: 301; FW: 118.24; §4.*0; BL 47471b f. 43; JJA 46: 303; FW: 120.05). The biblical "wall of partition" is conflated with the Magazine Wall in Phoenix Park, thereby connecting it to HCE's alleged "crime." In Stage III Joyce explicitly links the wall and sin in the phrase "a makeussin wall (sinsin! sinsin!)" (§4.9; BL 47475 f. 47; JJA 46: 446; FW: 116.18), but even as early as Stage I there is an oblique allusion to the biblical "wall of partition" in the "partywall" against which the mysterious author is said to have written the Letter (§1.*0; BL 47471b f. 33v; JJA 46: 230; FW: 108.01).

Already in Stage I Joyce was concerned with all the various aspects of verbal articulation that constitute the "wall of partition." In many ways, spatial articulation is an essential prerequisite for literacy. The "ruled lines" (§4.*0; BL 47471b f. 40v; JJA 46: 299; FW: 114.07) on the Letter may not necessarily be explicitly drawn (e.g., as in some of Joyce's notebooks), but reading and writing presuppose those vertical and horizontal lines because they articulate the top versus the bottom and the right versus the left sides of the page, thereby orienting the writer/reader. This accounts for the allusion to "~~its recto~~ ^[1]the verso[1]^" and "^[1]its recto[1]^" (§4.*2; BL 47473 f. 28; JJA 46: 320; FW 123.34–36).

The change of "ruled lines" to "ruled barriers" (§4.*1; BL 47471b f. 44v; JJA 46: 306) is significant, since it reveals the double-edged nature of our spatial articulation. The "civilized" use of paper space presupposes ruled lines, but at the same time these constitute the "wall of partition" that constrains our pen and our eyes to follow a prescribed, although nonetheless "zigzag," course. By definition, the spatial articulation of the page is coordinate with paralysis.

Punctuation is another necessary component of spatial (as well as temporal) articulation. This topic is introduced in the first draft of section 4:

> The original document was what is known as unbreakable ~~script~~ ^[1]tracery[1]^, that is to say, it had no signs of punctuation of any kind. On holding it to the light it was seen to be pierced or punctuated (in the university sense of the word) by numerous ~~dots~~ ^[1]cuts[1]^ and gashes ~~inflicted~~ ^[1]made[1]^ by a pronged instrument. These paper wounds, four in type, were gradually [understood] to mean stop, please stop, do please stop, and O do please stop respectively and investigation showed that they were provoked by the fork of a professor at the breakfast table ^[1]professionary ~~trying~~ ^[2]piqued[2]^ to introduce tempo into ~~a surface~~ ^[2]a plane[2]^ by making holes in space[1]^. (§4.*0; BL 47471b fs. 42v–44; JJA 46: 302–5; FW: 123.31–124.12)

Joyce is again mimicking Sullivan, who writes that "[i]n the matter of punctuation, the written text of the Book of Kells is not a very good example of the Irish practice," since "[w]e find, as a fact, in the Book of Kells, many consecutive lines, embracing two or three fully completed sentences, where there is no trace of punctuation at all." According to Sullivan, there are three methods of "breaking" the text (corresponding to the professor's punctuating the document at his "breakfast table") adopted by the scribes of *The Book of Kells:* "(1) by three dots; (2) by one dot at half the height of the letter; (3) by omitting the punctuation mark altogether and beginning the next sentence with a striking illuminated initial." The last is the most common method, and so "one wonders why full stops should ever be introduced before so obvious an indication of a new sentence as is provided by these fine and constantly recurring initials." The fact that the "original document" has "no signs of punctuation of any kind" thus neatly corresponds to Sullivan's descriptions of *The Book of Kells* (§4.*0; BL 47471b f. 42v; JJA 46: 302; FW: 123.33–34).[24] Whether the text is punctuated or not, the reader must infer the presence of appropriate breaks in the text to make sense of it. The professor's puncturing is thus an allegory of how the reader or the writer, by punctuating, establishes a comprehensible text.

Although punctuation enables literacy, there is a coeval element of barbarism involved as well. The existence of impediment is revealed in the "anger" of the professor (§4.*0; BL 47471b f. 43v; JJA 46: 304; FW: 124.14), who was obliged to punctuate the unpunctuated "original document" (the Word-Letter) when his scholarly appetite for interpretation was provoked. His incitement is described in the double metaphor of sexual and gastronomic stimulations (his "hunger" and "anger"), but his appetite and his frustration are never assuaged, however hard his literary/sexual/culinary "pronged instrument" may work to perforate the object (§4.*0; BL 47471b f. 43v; JJA 46: 304; FW: 124.03). He is never to attain "it," which in a "[d]eeply religious" sense is the Word (§4.*0; BL 47471b f. 43v; JJA 46: 304; FW: 124.12), not because his ability to punctuate is inadequate but because his recourse to punctuation itself (or literacy in general) predestines an estrangement from the "body" of the material. The professor's frustration is soon to be literally presented *ad absurdum* (§4.3; BL 47473 f. 39; JJA 46: 337; FW: 124.07–12).[25]

Literacy requires a proficiency in grammar, which, at its most general, means understanding space and time. Ironically, this very skill is simultaneously paralyzing. Language articulates "local ^[1]colour[1]^ & personal ~~colour~~ ^[1]perfume[1]^" (§1.*0; BL 47471b f. 30; JJA 46: 233; FW: 109.26), but only by suppressing the "sequentiality of ~~impossible probables~~ ^[1]improbable possibles[1]^" where things that "may have taken place as any others which never took person at all are ever likely to be" (§4.*2; BL 47471b f. 29; JJA 46: 234; FW: 110.15–21). As the doubt-ridden "Mr Mayhappy Mayhapnot" nostalgically recollects, "Lucalizod was the only place in the world where the possible was always the improbable and the improbable the inevitable" (§4.*2; BL 47471b f. 29; JJA 46: 234, simplified; FW: 110.07–12).[26] Our barbarous literacy cannot help but localize "Lucalizod," for instance, as "Lucan/Chapelizod." Paraphrasing Hamlet, times are "~~separated~~ ^[1]disjointed[1]^" (§1.*1; BL 47471b f. 43; JJA 46: 240; FW: 104.05), while at the "origin" (or before our "barbarous" verbal articulation) "~~All~~ ^[1]Every single person place [or] thing[1]^ was moving, changing ^[1]every part of the time[1]^" (§4.*0; BL 47471b f. 38v; JJA 46: 301; FW: 118.21–23).

Another aspect of literacy's paradoxical blessing and curse is the split link between sound and sense. On the one hand, verbal articulation depends upon a connection between a particular "sound" and a particular "sense." That indeed makes for the "sound sense" of our language (§1.*1; BL 47471b f. 46; JJA 46: 243; FW: 109.15).[27] However, following from Saussure, the stability of language thus secured is questionable because the link on which we base it is fundamentally uncertain or arbitrary. Therefore, the assumed link between sound and sense actually depends upon their split. As Derek Attridge points out in *Peculiar Language,* punning depends upon and exploits this split.[28] The pun is an apparently aberrant but ultimately normal consequence of linguistic articulation, which depends upon the arbitrary link between "sound" and "sense." In a given system of language the same sound can have more than one referent, while the same referent can be linked with more than one sound.[29] Such confusion is amplified when many languages are brought together, as Joyce does in *Finnegans Wake* with his babelic puns.

The development of I.5 in Stage I demonstrates both how Joyce correlated language to barbarism as well as how he believed that writing might remedy paralysis, thereby striving to break down the "wall of partition" inherent in literacy. His literary experiments are inevitably "jocoserious" because, while artistically sophisticated, they must fail in the homeopathic healing of their own original sin.

The rotation of the HCE siglum is emblematic of the letters' jocoserious resistance to the conventional spatial articulation prescribed by the page's ruled barriers: "the curious Krismon sign m called Hec which moved watchwise [represents] his title HCE as the smaller Δ called alp or delta replaces or stands beside the names of his consort" (§4.*3⊢; BL 47471b f. 67v, simplified; JJA 46: 340; FW: 119.18–22). Rose notes that "Krismon" comes from Sullivan's commentary on the "Tunc" page of *The Book of Kells,*[30] but the "watchwise" rotation of the HCE siglum is Joyce's. On this manuscript page Joyce drew three of the four possible rotations of the HCE siglum and wrote out three of the six possible permutations of the initials "HCE" (BL 47471b f. 67v; JJA 46: 340).

When this idea was adopted in the typescript, the direction of the rotation was specified as "contrawatchwise" (§4.3; BL 47473 f. 36v; JJA 46: 332; FW: 119.18–19), thereby suggesting the sign's rebellion against temporal articulation as well. Petr Skrabanek points out that the HCE siglum appears four times in the *Wake* (although never "contrawatchwise") in the following order:

Ш (I.1§1A.*0; BL 47482a f. 89; JJA 44: 10; FW: 006.32)
Ǝ (I.2§2.5; BL 47472 f. 215; JJA 45: 74; FW: 036.17)
E (I.3§1.7; BL 47482b f. 351; JJA 45: 273; FW: 051.19)
ᗰ (I.5§4.*3⊢; BL 47471b f. 67v; JJA 46: 340; FW: 119.17)[31]

The dates of the first drafts document the order of the rotation of these turning signs. The rotation of the HCE siglum began in I.5 (1924 or early 1925) and was further deployed in I.1 (October–December 1926), then in I.2 (probably March–April 1927), and finally in I.3 (May 1927).[32] The published work also exhibits the mirroring of the upside-down "diagamma" (or inverted Fs, see also VI.B.18: 107: "F double gee"), whose "ambidexterous" (§4.7; BL 47473 f. 98v; JJA 46: 426; FW: 121.03–7) typological presentation was introduced later in Stage II.[33]

The text's further "ambidexterous" approaches to paper space oppose the inherent paralysis of spatial articulation. In another misappropriation of Sullivan Joyce has "the curious warning sign [. . .] indicating that the words which follow may be taken in any order desired" (§4.*2; BL 47471b f. 26; JJA 46: 318; FW: 121.08–13). Then in Stage II Joyce literally illustrates this practice by introducing a backward spelling in the description of the "hornful digamma": "*the Aranman ~~whispering~~ ^1 ingperwhis*1^ *through the hole of his hat*" (§4.7; BL 47471b f. 99; JJA 46: 426; FW: 121.11–12). Subsequently, in Stage III in the galley proofs, rather than just reordering the syllables within one word, he reordered the sequence of words in the phrase: "hole of Aran man the hat through the whispering his ^1ho1^" (§4.10; BL 47476a f. 72; JJA 49: 163; FW: 121.13–14).[34]

Joyce's jocoserious experiment of generating a word string that is a vertical mirror of "THE DREAM OF GERONTIUS" (the title of Newman's pious poem, which Elgar set to music) on VI.B.2: 110 is another, more complex challenge to conventional spatial articulation. Most of the deleted units on the notebook page were used to compose the first draft of the Mamalujo vignette, but Joyce did not use "The Dream of Gerontius" there—even though the theme of a dying old man's dream is appropriate to Mamalujo, until the galley proofs for I.5 (1937 or 1938), where it appears as "the drame of Drainophilias" (§1.11; BL 47476a f. 209; JJA 49: 441; FW: 110.11). Here the words are not inverted, but the subject-object of the dream is, for it is now the "tea/rain-lover's dream," that is, Issy's dream. Such a reversal was already planned in an extradraft note for I.5 in March 1925:

> 1) "Alice's["]
> 2) aphasia
> 3) speaking of Tiberias & other incestuish salacities ^[1]among gerontophils[1]^ (§4.*3+⊢; BL 47482b f. 118; JJA 46: 363)

These items are all concerned with the loss of patriarchal authority. Joyce used the word "aphasia" in "the aphasia of that heroic agony of recalling a once loved number leading slip by slipper to a general amnesia of misnomering one's own" (§4.*3+; BL 47473 f. 49v, simplified; JJA 46: 358; FW: 122.04–6). The first and third items, appropriate to the theme of an aberrant father-daughter relationship, were incorporated in the first draft of the passage at FW: 115.11–29. The third item appears as an insertion, while Joyce used the first in "we psychoes who have done our unsmiling bit on alices in the penumbra of the precoaxing room" (§4.*3+⊢; BL 47482b f. 118; JJA 46: 363; FW: 115.11–12; §4.*3+⊢; BL 47471b f. 118v, simplified; JJA 46: 364; FW: 115.21–23). Here the challenge to the conventions of spatial articulation is transposed to a challenge to the conventional family structure.

Joyce also experimented with other jocoserious challenges to the conventional orientation of reading to overcome our literary paralysis. Along with the rotations and permutations of the HCE siglum and cognomen Joyce played with various acrostic permutations on the name Shem (BL 47471b f. 122v; JJA 46: 341). Such acrostic patterns resist normal left to right reading and encourage a "zigzaggery" of sensibility (UFW: 86). There are riddles as well that challenge readers to free their eyes from the fixation on "normal" reading; for example, Joyce introduced a riddle on Shem's name in the first typescript of section 4 (§4.*3; BL 47473 f. 39; JJA 46: 337; FW: 124.24–28). Joyce added another riddle on Shem's name, although it is unrecognizable in the final text because of later additions, immediately after this on revision of the typescript (§4.*3+; BL 47471b f. 49; JJA 46: 357; FW: 124.36–125.02).

Only "that ideal reader suffering from an ideal insomnia" alone could be expected to read free from the "beam" in his eyes (§4.*3+; BL 47473 f. 42v; JJA 46: 344; FW: 120.13–14). This reader should never "blink," since he should maintain hope, abstaining from the temptation of false Words, "till his noddle sink or swim" (§4.*3+; BL 47473 f. 42v; JJA 46: 344; FW: 120.13). As nonideal readers who must take certain determinate points of view (spatial, temporal, personal, etc.), we cannot help clinging to one particular "soundsense" of the letter and must close our eyes to all the other possible "soundsenses" (and impossible "nonsense"): this constitutes the "wall of partition" and the betrayal of the Word.[35]

The identity of the Letter can now be established in a "deeply religious" understanding of the letter (whether epistolary or alphabetical). While it is a synecdoche of the *Wake* in that it exemplifies the ineluctable betrayal of the Word by both readers and writers, the Letter is equally *any* document that was, is, and will be articulated in any language, inasmuch as any iteration inevitably falls short of the Word Itself. While "that ideal reader" can read the Word without stumbling over "paralyzed" language, we (the real) readers must sin when reading. This is typified in our readings of the *Wake* because to make *any* particular sense out of it we inevitably betray the Word-Letter by focusing on only one or at most some of the many available senses it opens up. The *Wake* represents in a paradigmatic way that our access to the Word-Letter is inevitably impeded and paralyzed.

Insofar as it is iterated in language, the Letter can be any statement ever made by any person at any time: it has always been "the ~~work~~ ^[1]pen product[1]^ of a man or woman of that period & those parts," and "its compiler" is quite *capable* of "misappropriating the actual words of others" (§1.*0; BL 47471b f. 29v; JJA 46: 232; FW: 108.29–36). Joyce emphasized the all-inclusive identity of the Letter with some revisions on the first typescript. The date of "The Boston Letter" (§1.*3; BL 47473 f. 33; JJA 46: 327; FW: 111.10) was changed to "the ~~eleventh~~ ^[1]last[1]^ of the ~~fifth~~ ^[1]first[1]^" (§4.3; BL 47471b f. 38; JJA 46: 335; FW: 121.30–31) so as to include the alpha and omega of the history of the letter. Furthermore, its "lubricitous conjugation of the last with the first" is noted; and for its comprehension we are referred to "*Some Forestallings over that Studium of Sexophonologistic Schizophrenesis,* vol. xxiv, pp [2]–555" or to "*Later Frustrations amengst the Neomugglian Teachings abaft the Semiunconscience, passim*" (§4.3; BL 47471b f. 37v, simplified; JJA 46: 334; FW: 123.17–22).

As a counterpoint to the all-inclusive identity of the Letter as Every-letter, the digit 0 suggests the No-letter that the Letter fails to fully articulate. It appears the document was written in a temperature "below zero" (§1.*0; BL 47471b f. 33v; JJA 46: 230; FW: 108.02–3). Correspondingly, it was in "Midwinter" when the "poorly clad Shiverer," "little Kevin," witnessed the hen, appropriately "a cold fowl" that is "behaving strangely on the fatal dump" (§1.*0; BL 47471b f. 28v; JJA 46: 235; FW: 110.22–35). As she scratches (and one might say from scratch) the "mound" becomes a "[h]eated residence" (§1.*0; BL 47471b f. 25v; JJA 46: 238; FW: 111.33–34). This implies that it is "us" (FW: 111.36), the readers, who introduce the "heat" (of our gastronomic and sexual appetite) as we read the original writing by applying our "pronged instrument" so as to reduce the perfect Word-Letter to the imperfect Letter.[36] The writer of "The Revered Letter" also alludes to "the cold" and thinks that she "has to wear flannels to the skin" (§2.*3; BL 47473 f. 16; JJA 46: 284) to conceal "the naked truth" (§1.*0; BL 47471b f. 33v; JJA 46: 230; FW: 107.04).

Already informed of Leopold Bloom's ultimate identity revealed in "Ithaca," that is, "Everyman or Noman" (U: 17.2008), we may well wonder if our "Here Comes Everybody" (Everyman) might not at once be Noman to parallel the Letter's double identity of Every-letter/No-letter. As with the problem of "horseness" discussed above, HCE's designation as Everyman should necessarily include every possible subset of man, including Noman (i.e., what a man can *not* possibly be). In fact, it is said of HCE that "the great one is ^[1]3 syllables[1]^ less than a ~~name~~ ^[1]his own surname[1]^" (§1.*0; BL 47471b f. 29v; JJA 46: 232; FW: 108.20–21): "Ear-wick-er" minus 3 syllables makes a zero name, Noman. This is the case as early as the first draft of section 1: "Closer inspection of the bordereau would however reveal a multiplicity of personalities inflicted on the provoking document and a prevision of virtual crime or crimes unwarily be made before any suitable occasion for it or them had arisen. But under the very eyes of the inspector the traits which feature the sympathetic chiaroscuro coalesce, their contrarieties eliminated in a stable somebody" (§1.*0; BL 47471b f. 33v, simplified; JJA 46: 230; FW: 107.23–30). As Everyman, HCE is an all-inclusive mass of all verbal articulations or names that constitute "a man." The "crime or crimes" are all the sins universally committed as we take recourse to verbal articulation in giving HCE every possible name (whether incriminatory or extolling). According to this passage, the only way in which HCE can become a "stable somebody" free from incriminations (mankind's "groaning") is to eliminate the "contrarieties" that accrue to him through language. This freedom can only be attained were he to become Noman. Such is the state of Everyman in language.

In summary, the Letter plot was developed in Stage I to emphasize the essential identity of the Letter as Every-letter and as No-letter (synecdochically the *Wake*). As for the female plot in Stage I, "The Revered Letter," a notably feminine monologue, was ultimately displaced from this chapter. But even before it was removed from I.5 it contained a subversive introductory passage that suggested that its author was in fact Shem (§2.*0; BL 47471b f. 31; JJA 46: 255; FDV: 81). Although the entire passage was abandoned, its echo can still be heard in a first draft of a passage in section 4: "the ^[1]feminine[1]^ vaulting ~~ambition~~ ~~Δ[+]sex[+]Δ~~ ^[2]libido[2]^ of those interbranching ^[1]sex[1]^ ~~upsweeps~~ ^[1]up & insweeps[1]^ ~~continually~~ ^[1]sternly[1]^ controlled ^[1]and[1]^ ~~and led~~ ^[1]easily repersuaded[1]^ by the uniform ~~undeviating course~~ ^[1]matter of factness[1]^ of a ~~cold~~ ^[1]meandering[1]^ male fist" (§4.*0; BL 47471b f. 42v; JJA 46: 302; FW: 123.07–10). The hand guiding the "feminine libido" may be HCE's (as Shem), for it was originally conceived as a "cold" hand, suggesting the stable Noman. Although this may indicate the author of the Letter was male, the gender of its origin remains ambiguous because it presupposes a "feminine libido" prior to a male hand or "fist" guiding it. The male authorship is clear but in an officious way, somewhat reminiscent of Bloom's unsolicited eagerness to improve his wife's literacy. Before he began writing the Letter chapter, Joyce was concerned with the female authorship of the Letter: in a series of entries he noted from March to July 1923, "libido" was already a key link between the author of letters and the feminine.

> Volumes (Pop)
> [r]Mum—letterwriter[r]
> [br]Is—her libido
> the Beyond (VI.B.3: 123)[37]

The predraft articulation of "The Boston Letter" was addressed to "dearest Elly" and was originally conceived as having been written by "[r]her loving sister" (VI.A: 271). Even in early 1924, when Joyce had already begun I.5, he still ascribed a feminine origin to the Letter:

Shem jots down notes / for Δ (VI.B.6: 117; January–February 1924)

Letter written by [Shem], brother of Shaun, for ALP, mother of Shaun, all about Hek, father of Shaun. (III§1D.*0; BL 47482b f. 5, simplified; JJA 57: 11; FW: 420.17–19; March 1924)

The double authorship of the Letter is so dark an enigma that it was left unsolved in this chapter and remains ambiguous throughout the *Wake*. While maintaining the Letter's feminine origin, Joyce eventually chose to concentrate on its material aspect, that is, its letters. This now involves the (female) hen figure—as the reader and writer—exposing Shem's sham (male) authorship. When "The Revered Letter" was still in I.5, section 1 ended with "~~see~~ ^^{1}~~peep~~^{1}^ ^^{2}tour^{2}^ beyond the figure of the scriptor into the subconscious editor's mind" (§1.*0; BL 47471b f. 25v; JJA 46: 238; FW: 112.01–2). This was an invitation to read the apparently feminine words of ALP in defense of her husband. Initially, the "subconscious editor" was feminine: "Would we vision her (subconscious editor) with stereoptican relief" (§1.*0⊢; BL 47471b f. 35v; JJA 46: 239; see also WiT: 175). Subsequently, Joyce chose to redirect the reader's attention to the Letter itself rather than to its feminine "subconscious" or "libido." Correspondingly, another invitation at the beginning of section 4 asks us to "draw nearer to it" (§4.*0; BL 47471b f. 41v; JJA 46: 298; FW: 113.30–31) and "take our slant" at the letter (§4.*1; BL 47471b f. 44v, simplified; JJA 46: 306; FW: 113.31–32). Here, we find our guide is no longer the "slanteyed" hen (§1.*0; BL 47471b f. 25v; JJA 46: 238; FW: 111.33), and, to our further embarrassment, we see her beak magically transformed into the professor's amorous and culinary pronged instrument, whose pecking (reading and writing) never allows him (and us) to attain the Word-Letter Itself and Its Author, Noman. Needless to say, the suppressed "feminine libido" that is suggested to be Its origin is also unattainable.

Among the most important features elaborated in Stage II are the introduction of numerological and alluvial motifs and a premonition of the babelic range of human language (which was markedly expanded in the last stage). Stage I already contained abundant allusions to the digit 0, but it did not yet allude to other prominent *Wakean* numbers such as 2, 3, 4, 12, 29, 111, 1132. Although there were a few minor allusions to the digit 4 in Stage I, these did not refer to the Four Old Men but rather to the "barbarous" quadrupedal nature of human letters: "fourlegged ems" (§4.*0; BL 47471b f. 43; JJA 46: 303; FW: 123.01). References to the number 4 were increased in Stage II, with a significant quantity of allusions to Vico's theory of the fourfold cycle of history.[38] The digit 4 also suggests the all-inclusiveness of the "epistola" as well as its articulation into the four "cardinal" divisions of paper space.

As for the *Wake*'s other key numbers, for example, "2 (versus) 3," we see the addition of "~~three~~ ^^{1}two^{1}^ hoots [on] three jeers" (§4.*7; BL 47473 f. 102; JJA 46: 424; FW: 117.23) and "Abbrace of Umbellas or a Tripple of Caines" (§4.*8; BL 47471b f. 105; JJA 46: 431; FW: 106.32–33) in the second stage.[39] The digit 3 is typically symbolic of the tripartite identity of HCE: Shem, Shaun, and the mysterious tertium quid. The last must be "the third person [. . .] darkly spoken of" (§4.*2; BL 47471b f. 26, 27; JJA 46: 318–19; FW: 122.31), that is, HCE as Everyman and Noman. The number 111, which symbolizes ALP, figures in "Twenty of Chambers, Weighty Ten Beds and a Wan Ceteroom" (20 + 90 + 1 = 111).[40] There is also a trace of Issy here, since 28 + 1 (*ceterum* is Latin for "the rest") equal 29, the number of the leap-year girls.[41]

In Stage II there are other river references besides the "everflowing on the times," which is an allusion to Vico's *ricorso,* for example, "He's my O'Jerusalem and I'm his Po" (§1.8; BL 47471b f. 105v; JJA 46: 430; FW: 105.06–7). But of particular interest to our discussion of the Letter is "~~Said~~ ^^{1}Saith^{1}^ ~~the~~ ^^{1}A^{1}^ Sawyer ~~to~~ ^^{1}til^{1}^ the ~~Streams~~ ^^{1}Strame^{1}^, Ik dik dopedope et ^^{1}tu^{1}^ mihimihi" (§1.8; BL 47471b f. 105v; JJA 46: 430; FW: 104.10–11). This is the first instance in this chapter of the feminine "analphabet" or "preproniminal" subconscious (*strame* is Italian for "litter"), which acts as a countersign to the male's letter writing. He tills (*til* is Danish for "to") and sows or writes on her libido with his bulky "dik," or pen (*dik* is Dutch for "bulky"), giving it a name (*ik doop* is Dutch for "I baptize") and calling it "mine."

The memorable invocation that opens the chapter in the published work and that suggests its "feminine" orientation is a surprisingly late addition (probably mid-1930s): "In the name of Annah the all mazyful, the Everliving, the Bringer of Plurabilities, hallowed be her eve, her singtime [sung], her rill be run unhemmed as it is uneven" (§1.9; BL 47475 f. 43v; JJA 46: 443; FW: 104.01–3). The alluvial references added in Stage III go beyond the correspondence between this chapter's opening and the *Wake*'s first word. Joyce amplified the network of river symbolism at this level. HCE's multiform "Everyman" personality includes a quasi-feminine "Plurabelle" identity but is also tempered by his impersonal antithesis, a cold and stable "Noman." In contrast, the river symbolism in Stages II and III reveals

ALP's seamlessly streaming "libido" that always embraces but ever eludes "punctuation." Although she invites the "prong" of punctuation ("The river felt she wanted salt. That was just where Brien came in" [§1.11; BL 47476a f. 209; JJA 49: 441; FW: 110.01–2]), no punctuation can "stop" her ever-flowing libidinous being: "I have not Stopped Water Where It Should Flow" (§1.9+; BL 47475 f. 270; JJA 46: 452; FW: 105.24–25). This was foreshadowed earlier in Stage I with "stop, please stop, do please stop, and O do please stop" (§4.*0; BL 47471b f. 43v; JJA 46: 304; FW: 124.04–5). The symbolic river, the female, is not just a potent counterpart to Noman/Everyman but also a self-sufficient libidinous being that precedes the male's imperfect articulation: "From Victrolia Nuancee to Allbart Noahnsy" (§1.9; BL 47475 f. 43; JJA 46: 442; FW: 105.14). Both the male and female figures are symbolic entities rather than representations of "real" beings, but the female is "nuanced," whereas the male remains a riddle with "no answer": there is no negative term in the feminine "everflowing" being.

The famous name list of suggested titles for the Letter was only completed in Stage III. Tindall notes that in the final text two semicolons (FW: 104.24, 105.32) may divide this list into three parts: one for Issy (Anna the Young), one for Kate (Anna the Old), and the last for Anna herself.[42] But the first semicolon was only added on the second set of galley proofs (level 11), while the second had been added earlier on a copy of *transition* 5, which Joyce had revised for the printer to set the first galley proofs of *Finnegans Wake* (level 9++). We can thus see that even as late as 1938 Joyce was apparently unconcerned with establishing a tripartite structure for this list. Indeed, perhaps Joyce was never concerned with such a structure.

Although most readers, following Tindall, would expect the number of items on the list to add up to 111,[43] which would be symbolic of the ideal union of HCE and ALP, it remains impossible to determine the exact number of items in the list.[44] Neither the published work nor the many stages of its textual development clearly reveal a deliberate motivation to achieve this symbolic total. Furthermore, Joyce continually added more items to the list as it progressed through various draft stages. As late as the second set of galleys of *Finnegans Wake* (level 11) he had already exceeded 111 items.

The third stage also sees a number of remarkably systematic additions, many of which are based on particular notebook entries (from VI.B.45 and 46). These can be divided into two categories, cultural and linguistic. To the former belongs the introduction of allusions to Arabian, American Indian, Egyptian, and Chinese cultures; Bolshevism; Thomas Moore's *Irish*

Melodies; Rabelais; and Finn MacCool. Linguistic elements added at this level include words from Ainu, Persian, Albanian, Armenian, Ruthenian (Ukrainian), Polish, Norwegian, and so on.

Despite the comically extensive range of peoples and tongues registered in Stage III, the basic identity of the Letter as the groaning of all barbarous humanity persists. Because of the sustained recognition of the basic barbarity of all human language, the Letter achieves a Gargantuan assimilation of all letters—natural or artificial, international or regional. All human articulations necessarily promote, yet arrest, expression and communication through the "wall of partition." Thus the Letter—synecdochically the *Wake*—becomes the most typical exemplar of human language. Not only does it endorse Paul's words that "the letter killeth," but it also shows how the letter, being ever imperfect in perfection, is always already "killed," while the river of life, carrying all the "litters," runs on.

Notes

1. For discussions of the resuscitation of the two aborted sections see Dirk Van Hulle's and Wim Van Mierlo's essays in this volume.

2. See Roland McHugh, *The Sigla of "Finnegans Wake"* (London: Edward Arnold, 1976), 65.

3. "ʳDame Alice Barbara Esmond" (VI.B.10: 109) is probably "the earliest version of ALP's name" (WiT: 168–70). "Probably Alice Esmonde, the wife of Sir Thomas Henry Grattan Esmonde, M.P. and Papal Chamberlain, a great grandson of Grattan. According to *Thoms* 1925, 324, she died in 1922, so the entry may be from an obituary or commemorative notice" (*Buffalo VI.B.10,* 129).

4. William York Tindall, *A Reader's Guide to "Finnegans Wake"* (New York: Farrar, Straus and Giroux, 1969), 98.

5. See also Finn Fordham, "Sigla in Revision," *Geni,* 83–96.

6. See Bernard Benstock, "Concerning Lost Historeve," *A Conceptual Guide to "Finnegans Wake,"* ed. Michael H. Begnal and Fritz Senn (University Park: Pennsylvania University Press, 1974), 33–55, 37.

7. Laurent Milesi noted these correspondences and listed some of their thematic and lexical echoes in "Metaphors of the Quest in *Finnegans Wake,*" *"Finnegans Wake": Fifty Years,* ed. Geert Lernout (Amsterdam: Rodopi, 1990), 79–107, 95–96.

8. Level §1.*0 is on BL 47471b fs. 26v–27; JJA 46: 236–37. Level §1.*1 is on BL 47482b f. 48; JJA 46: 245. Level §1.*2 is on BL 47473 f. 10; JJA 46: 252.

9. Level §2.*0 is on BL 47471b fs. 30v–33; JJA 46: 254–59; FDV: 81–83. Level 2.*1 is on BL 47482b fs. 36–42; JJA 46: 262–72. Level §2.*2 is on BL 47482b fs. 14v–23v; JJA 46: 273–80. Level §2.*3 is on BL 47473 fs. 13–19; JJA 46: 281–86.

10. While the evidence of their literal correspondence suggests that "The Revered Letter" was written first, only to be "imperfectly" quoted in "The Boston Letter," the latter was actually the first to be conceptualized: "ʳon the N. E. slope of the dunghill the slanteyed hen of the Grogans scrutinised a clayed p.c. from Boston (Mass) of the 12th of the 4th to dearest Elly from her loving sister with 4 1/2 kisses" (VI.A: 271; see WiT: 21–22).

11. Gildas, *De Excidio Brittaniae et Conquestu,* trans. J. A. Giles (Willits, Calif.: British American Books, n.d.), 20. Also see Bede, *The Ecclesiastical History of the English Nation,* trans. Vida D. Scudder (London: J. M. Dent and Sons, 1910), 1:13.

12. According to Spiros Zodhiates, the Greek word *stenagmós* means "[a] groaning, sighing, as of the oppressed" (*The Complete Word Study Dictionary: New Testament,* rev. ed. [Chattanooga: AMG Publishers, 1993], 1310b). He notes another relevant Pauline passage: "I have seen, I have seen the affliction of my people which is in Egypt, and I have heard their groaning, and am come down to deliver them" (Acts 7:34), which includes an allusion to a passage in the Old Testament, "And God heard their groaning" (Exod. 2:24). Apparently, the fifth-century Britons allegorically figured themselves as the Israelites under Egyptian bondage.

13. The unutterable groaning of the Spirit contrasts with another Pauline passage, this one describing the Pentecostal miracle: "They were all filled with the Holy Ghost, and began to speak with other tongues, as the Spirit gave them utterance" (Acts 2:4).

14. Nathan Halper cites this passage to suggest the Boston Letter's connection with the Pauline letter ("Joyce and Eliot," *AWN* 2.3 [June 1965]: 3–10, 8).

15. Hamletian allusions are portentously scattered over sections 1 and 4 of I.5. For those added in Stage I see FW: 110.07, 104.05, 120.11, and 121.31–32. Joyce continued to add more Hamletian allusions in the second and third stages. Those allusion on FW: 123.32–33 and 114.19 were added in Stage II, while that on FW: 110.13–14 was added in Stage III.

16. The Letter's intrinsic incompleteness is to be articulated in the third stage as "all its featureful perfection of imperfection" (§1.11; BL 47476a f. 207; JJA 49: 437; FW: 109.09).

17. See also FW: 119.33 and 120.05–6.

18. Edward Sullivan, *The Book of Kells* (London: Studio Press, 1924). See §4.*1; BL 47471b f. 47v; JJA 46: 310; FW: 122.23; and VI.B.6: 35.

19. The topics of sex and food are introduced in "The Revered Letter" and persistently haunt the chapter throughout its three stages of development. It should be noted that "breakfast" etymologically carries a quasi-religious sense of turning away from "abstinence."

20. Sullivan 1924, 1.

21. See Mark 2:3 ff., Matthew 4:24, and so on, where the Greek word for "palsy" is *paralutikós.*

22. Epstein has pointed out that the passage is based on George Birdwood's *Sva*

(1910): "'the evolution of humanity from savagery to barbarism . . . Michael & his angels against the Dragon & his angels'" ("Yet Another Book at the *Wake*," *AWN* 7.2 [April 1970]: 29–30). As for Sullivan, he evidently endorsed the conservative dichotomy of barbarity versus civilization; he does not hesitate to use the term "barbarous" (or "barbaric") when pointing to artistically crude portions of the manuscripts (Sullivan 1924, 6, 21, and 43).

23. The other relevant passages in Stage I are FW: 111.33, 113.27–29 and 32–33, 114.08, 120.07–8 and 34, 121.07, 122.35–36, 123.11 and 20, as well as "amid a blizzard with low [visibility]" (§3.*0; BL 47471b f. 34v; JJA 46: 293; FDV: 90) and "this ^1~~bothered~~1^ ^2native2^ island [. . .]. Then them to go & say about him [Mr Earwicker] being ~~bothered~~ [. . .] he is ^1after his manner &1^ certified to be very agreeably deef in the matter of his hearing" (§2.*1; BL 47471b f. 40; JJA 46: 269; see FW: 619.07–10).

24. Sullivan 1924, 35.

25. Joyce exhibits a sustained interest in the different conventions of punctuation and other notational conventions for literary articulation in Stage I. For example, he alludes to "the symbol . . . known in Irish MSS. as 'head under the wing' or 'turn under the path' [which indicates] that the words immediately following it are to be read after the end of the next full line" (Sullivan 1924, 10) at FW: 121.08–13 (§4.*2; BL 47473 f. 26; JJA 46: 318; see Danis Rose, "Kells-Dublin-Rome-Trieste-Zürich-Paris," *AFWC* 2.1 [1986]: 1–13, 4).

26. McHugh notes that this echoes an aphorism of Oscar Wilde's mentor, Sir John Pentland Mahaffy: "In Ireland the inevitable never happens, the unexpected always."

27. The first draft reads "good sense" (§1.*0; BL 47471b f. 30; JJA 46: 233).

28. Derek Attridge, *Peculiar Language* (Ithaca: Cornell University Press, 1988).

29. Attridge's example is the word "port" (1988, 201–2).

30. Rose 1986, 8–9.

31. Petr Skrabanek, "The Turning of the Ш," *AWN* 15.6 (December 1978): 94.

32. In the last two instances Joyce left a blank space in the text of preceding drafts (I.2§2.*4, probably March 1927, and I.3§1.5, probably March–April 1927). When Joyce gave a set of the *Wakean* signs to Harriet Shaw Weaver in his letter of 24 March 1924 he explained the HCE sign as "Earwicker, H C E by moving letter round" (LI: 213).

33. Curiously enough, the signs Joyce added at this level were "∔ ^12^1^" and "1" that turn out to be the mirrored images of the respective signs as we have them in the printed text. See Ian MacArthur, "The F Sigla," *AWN* 15.4 (August 1978): 58; and Sam Slote, "Imposture Book through the Ages," *Geni,* 97–114.

34. See also Rose 1986, 4.

35. The relevant biblical context here is when, after his solitary prayer in the Garden of Gethsemane, Jesus returns to his disciples to find them all sleeping. He admonishes Peter by saying, "What, could ye not watch with me one hour? Watch

and pray, that ye enter not into temptation: the spirit indeed is willing, but the flesh is weak" (Matt. 26:40–41).

36. On a galley proof page not available in the JJA (early July 1927) "the reader" mentioned above was changed to "your pecker" (see §1.9; BL 47475 f. 45v; JJA 46: 445; FW: 111.36).

37. See also VI.B.3: 126: "^{br}my libido (Is)" and VI.A: 851: "^{br}libido."

38. "The lightning look, the birding cry, awe from the grave, everflowing on the times [. . .] a good clap, a fore marriage, a bad wake, tell hell's well" (§4.*7; BL 47473 f. 101, simplified; JJA 46: 423; FW: 117.03–6) and "this oldworld epistola of their weatherings and their marryings and their buryings and their natural selections" (§4.*7; BL 47471b f. 103; JJA 46: 424; FW: 117.27–28).

39. See also VI.B.18: 191: "^{bk}[A Brace] or a tripple of / [~~2~~] Umbellas [or 3] Caines."

40. §1.8; BL 47471b 105v, simplified; JJA 46: 430; FW: 105.03–4.

41. Further in Stage III Joyce added "ratiocination by syncopation in the elucidation of complications" (§1.9; BL 47475 f. 44v; JJA 46: 444; FW: 109.04–5). The repetition of *-tion* words is associated with the Twelve. Joyce also added "the ~~Forty~~ ^^{1}Twentynine^{1}^ Names of Attraente" (§1.9+; BL 47471b f. 270; JJA 46: 452; FW: 105.25). Issy is associated with the number 29 because of the leap-year girls. Both numbers are units associated with time (12 months and 28 + 1 days).

42. Tindall 1969, 99.

43. Ibid. Tindall's obvious typo "101" has been emended.

44. In fact, Joyce manages to do so in the list of HCE's "abusive names" in I.3 (FW: 071.10–072.16). See Bill Cadbury, "111 Epithets in 71–72," online posting, 28 September 1997, *Finnegans Wake* (by James Joyce) Discussion List, http://listserv.heanet.ie/lists/fwake-1.html, accessed 31 December 1999.

Genetic Primer

Chapter I.6

R. J. SCHORK

It is tempting to cite an epic parallel for chapter I.6 of *Finnegans Wake.* At first glance its form and function appear to be broadly modeled on the *Teichoscopia* (survey from the ramparts) early in the *Iliad* (3.161–244). In the Homeric episode King Priam calls Helen to the walls of Troy and asks her to identify—quite improbably, considering that the war is in its tenth year—various Greek heroes massing on the plain beneath the city's walls. Menelaus's wife, now the prize of Prince Paris, replies to the inquiries with capsule descriptions of Agamemnon, Odysseus, Ajax, and Idomeneus—swift-footed, man-slaying Achilles needs no introduction to the besieged. In the *Wake* Shem calls on Shaun to answer a dozen questions about the work's major characters and its strange "collideorscapic" point of view. The parallel from Homer, however, is only superficially valid. The characteristics of the *Iliad*'s warriors were established in tradition, and by the third book of the epic the actions of Agamemnon and Odysseus speak louder than Helen's synopses of their attributes. On the other hand, even after the first five chapters of the *Wake,* Joyce correctly judged that his readers needed as full and as meticulous as possible a description of the members of the Earwicker family, their locale, retainers, and presentation. That pass-in-review is the task of the chapter's twelve questions and answers.

Prior to a discussion of the ways and means that genetic criticism can contribute to a better grasp of this section of the *Wake,* it would be helpful to outline its compositional origins and narrative purposes.

Origins and Development

In his analysis of Joyce's "textual diaries" (the Buffalo notebooks) Danis Rose includes a brief chapter on "The questionnaire (I.6)" (TDJJ: 101–5). Joyce's

26 July 1927 letter to Harriet Shaw Weaver establishes the precise period of its initial composition: "I am working night and day at a piece I have to insert between [I.5 and I.7]" (LIII: 163). Evidence from securely dated drafts and notebooks (especially VI.B.4) indicates that the process of composition and revision continued, intermittently, until the spring of 1929. These dates are corroborated in additional correspondence with Miss Weaver. Seven years later, in 1936, Joyce expanded his description of HCE in Question 1 and came back to the VI.B.4 notebook and its transcription by Mme Raphaël (VI.C.15) to glean from them weird bits of diction and data. Finally, significant additions were made, primarily to the inquiry about HCE and to the Burrus-Caseous vignette, at the very last stage of composition on two sets of galley proofs corrected and embellished throughout 1937.

Purposes

While admitting that it is "marvellously entertaining," Rose also judges that "I.6, with its strings of attributes, does not add anything to the narrative" (TDJJ: 104). This opinion does not mean that the chapter serves no narrative purpose or that its only distinction is lexical and rhetorical finesse. Its expansive introduction, in schematic form, of the principal characters and primary precincts of the action constitutes a major contribution to the work in progress and its final form. For this there is a precedent: as early as the autumn of 1925 Joyce began to draft the first part of chapter III.4, a summary of the major participants in the *Wake* (FW: 555.01–558.31). (This first list, however, does not include either of the two impersonal items that appear in the later version, the book/pub/container [☐ in I.6] or the unique kaleidoscopic experience [⊕ in I.6].) It is reasonable to assume that Joyce eventually realized that a similar rundown of dramatis personae would not be out of place quite a bit earlier in the first part of his work, hence the night-and-day labor on the twelve-part questionnaire that he considered a necessary insertion into the composition. It introduces, by the numbers, (1) HCE, (2) ALP, (3) the Book/Pub, (4) the Four, (5) Sigurdsen, (6) Kate, (7) the Twelve, (8) the Twentynine Leap-Year Girls, (9) the Kaleidoscopic Dream, (10) Issy, (11) Shaun, (12) Shem. Moreover, as its text developed the chapter also became the repository for a fable about the Mookse and the Gripes, an alimentary allegory starring Burrus, Caseous, and Margareena, and flashes of comic diatribe aimed at several professorial incarnations of Joyce's hostile critic Wyndham Lewis. These accretions, of course, stimulate and/or vibrate to similar thematic and verbal elements throughout the entire text. Finally, the sheer exuberance of this chapter, especially the cascade of epithets for HCE, makes up for any detours it may impose on whatever passes for "narrative" in the *Wake.*

Genetic Opportunities

Chapter I.6 is particularly rich in material and method that offer opportunities to display the various types of genetic criticism. Rose has determined that the notebook that supplied phrases and terms for the first draft is now lost (VI.X.3; TDJJ: 29); but notebook VI.B.4, as will be shown below, has contributed many entries, in three significant clusters, to this section of the *Wake.* Paradigmatic documents (an article from the *Encyclopaedia Britannica* and two popular French books on the papacy) have been identified as the sources of Joyce's information for these long indexes. The opportunity to observe the strata of this material as it mounts, from documentary source to notebook to various drafts to printed edition, greatly helps in understanding Joyce's compositional strategy. In at least two cases (the Roman month-men and a Latin phrase from the New Testament) it would be almost impossible to detect and interpret the final text without the notebook entries and the permutations of early drafts. A predraft manuscript page also lists eleven of the twelve sigla that Joyce used as stenographic indicators of his characters; the unique twelfth siglum for the dream is found in a slightly later manuscript.

The facsimile publication of *The James Joyce Archive* opened a new era in research on the sources for and compositional history of the *Wake.* This type of scholarship, however, was not the first to concentrate on the text and structure of chapter I.6. From the pregenetic era Question 9 (answer: "A collideorscape!" [FW: 143.03–28]) was the topic of the initial Hart-Senn "Explications" in the first issue of the old *A Wake Newslitter.* Question 12 (answer: Issy, the "pepette" [FW: 143.29–148.32]) was the topic of the inaugural summer workshop at the Zürich James Joyce Foundation, justly proud of its growing collection of research material.[1] As mentioned above, a persistent thematic factor in chapter I.6 of the *Wake,* especially in Question 11, is ridicule of Wyndham Lewis's 1927 criticism that Joyce's writings are obsessed with time and unconcerned with space. The fable of "The Mookse and the Gripes," for example, begins with a take-off of the formulaic fairy-tale trigger, "Eins within a space" (FW: 152.18);[2] here the German word for "once" (*eins*) also suggests an abbreviated Einstein, and "space" is substituted for the expected "time."

The format and function of this *Genetic Guide* appropriately limit the space and time that can be devoted to the material for each section. Thus, what follows is a series of conspicuous examples designed to illustrate how various types of genetic criticism work (attention to sources, notebooks, and draft stages) and what specific insight they offer the reader of the *Wake*.

Sigla as Signposts

In a footnote near the end of "Night Lessons" (chapter II.2) readers meet a graphic version of "The Doodles Family, ᗰ, Δ, ⊣, X, □, Λ, ⊏" (FW: 299.F4). Understanding Joyce's use of these signs is important to many aspects of archival scholarship—and to grasping the genesis of chapter I.6. The most comprehensive examination of the function and scope of these sigla (Latin for "abbreviations," "little signs," "figurettes") is still the pioneering study by Roland McHugh.[3] As a 24 March 1924 letter to Harriet Shaw Weaver indicates, the signs were originally nothing more than Joyce's shorthand notation for the "chief characters" of the work in progress (LI: 213); Rose reasonably broadened their function by claiming that "Joyce frequently tagged a [notebook] quote with the signature of the character in whose development he intended to use that quote" (TDJJ: 42).

Slightly expanded versions of the list of sigla in the "Night Lessons" footnote also appear in the left margins of preliminary drafts of chapter I.6, each preceded by a number that specifies the question-answer to be posed in that portion of the chapter: "1 ᗰ, 2 Δ, 3 □, 4 X, 5 ⋜, 6 K, 7 O, 8 ⬭, 9 ⊕, 10 ⊣, 11 Λ, 12 ⊏" (BL 47473 f. 150v; JJA 47: 2; and BL 47473 f. 132v; JJA 47: 28).[4] In Joyce's partial fair copy of these early drafts of the chapter the corresponding sign is added, in the left margin of the texts, *before* the numbers for Questions 3–5, 9–10; in the second fair copy (July–August 1927) all twelve marginal signs precede the numbers. Although the hieroglyphic figures are not included in any of the printed versions of the final sections of this chapter, these signs on the various draft versions have helped commentators to pin down the objects of several of the more cryptic questions and their answers.

In Joyce's 1924 letter to Miss Weaver his terse announcement of the deployment of "signs for the chief characters" is followed by a list of ten sigla plus identifications. The final two items are "X Mamalujo" and "□ This stands for the title but I do not wish to say it yet until the book has written more of itself" (LI: 213). The sections of chapter I.6 keyed to those two sigla (X and □) raise problems in interpretation—and the obfuscation is part of its author's design. As he indicated in this letter, Joyce hoped to conceal the book's title. Thus, Question 3 (which is designated by the siglum □) begins with an ambiguous challenge: "Which title is the true-to-type motto-in-lieu for that Tick for Teac thatchment?" (FW: 139.29–30).[5] It is answered by a *Wakean* rendition of the motto of the city of Dublin. In the introduction to the chapter, however, Joyce warns his readers that Shaun Mac Irewick will "*misunderstruck and aim for am ollo* of number three of them" (FW: 126.07–8, emphasis added). The words that I emphasize in the quotation have been paraphrased as a "misinterpretation of a name for a motto," a proleptic apology for the topical confusion.

Joyce's introductory remarks also indicate that Shaun "left his free natural ripostes to four of them in their own fine artful disorder" (FW: 126.08–9). Throughout the *Wake* the "four of them" are a quartet of randy geezers, sometimes designated as the Four Annalists of Irish chronicles or the Four Evangelists, abbreviated as Mamalujo. Here, the number does double duty. In the answer to Question 4 (designated by the siglum X) the primary emphasis is geographical, falling on the capital cities of the four divisions of Ireland: "Delfas" (FW: 140.15) for Belfast in Ulster, "Dorhqk" (FW: 140.21) for Cork in Munster, "Nublid" (FW: 140.27) for Dublin in Leinster, and "Dalway" for Galway in Connacht. A whisper of the personal element is present, however, since each urban site unleashes, in the appropriate regional dialect and diction, a spate of romantic palaver that imitates the "free natural" speech of the Four Old Rakes, as opposed to the "fine artful" style that they employ in composing their histories or gospels. The long and the short of the matter is that a necessary topographical orientation to Questions 3 and 4 of chapter I.6 is provided by an examination of Joyce's draft-stage use of sigla that are applied, respectively, to shifting but significant objects/locations (3) and to the various manifestations of the male quartet (4).

The evolution of Question 7 (concerning O, the Twelve) can easily be traced by an inspection of the early draft stages of what became FW: 142.08–29. In the initial sketch (BL 47473 fs. 130, 135v, 131; JJA 47: 24–26) the "component partners" are distinguished as twelve sections of Dublin (from a draft "pré salés" to "Baldoyle"); these locales are sandwiched between a dozen of the hyper-Latinate "-ation" words that are the signature clues to the Twelve's presence.[6] On the first fair copy an initial group, the twelve "month-men," are added; one of the key abstractions is a switch from "association" to "miserecoration"; four temporal adverbs are inserted to regulate the parameters of the behavior of the dirty dozen: "*nightly* consternation, *fortnightly* fornication, *monthly* misereciation, and *annual* recreation"; the Hibernicized nicknames of the twelve apostles ("Matey" to "Jakes Mac Carty") join the other units at the end of the question; finally, an "Answer" is provided: "The Morphies!" (BL 47473 f. 188; JJA 47: 56). Thus, at a fairly early state of composition, Question 7 reached more or less its published form: four units of a dozen items each (month-men, areas of Dublin, "-ation" words, apostles).

Roman Month-Men

Another level of genetic inquiry, more complex than character identification and disposition, has something to contribute to a full understanding of the textual evolution and implications of this passage. On adjacent pages in a *Wake* notebook there are two crossed lists that contributed to the formation of Question 7.[7] The Irish nicknames of the apostles, crossed out with a large blue X (VI.B.18: 259), were transferred with only minor alterations—"Jorn" for "John," "Pedher" for "Peter"—to the end of the passage. Thereafter, the text was not changed in any way. The evolution of the second list, the month-men, is more involved and its interpretation more problematic.

In the final text of the *Wake* Question 7 begins by seeking the identity of "those component partners of our societate" (FW: 142.08). The last word is the ablative case of the Latin noun *societas;* the termination of that form also suggests a French state (*état*) or a Latin period of time (*aetate,* also in the ablative). Perhaps that latter possibility was the clue that urged McHugh to link a number of these terms with the months of the year. Such an identification also provides a time-oriented unit to balance the question's immediately adjacent space-oriented unit of a dozen Dublin districts. I suggest that each of the first six of Joyce's "partners" is associated with the ancient Roman calendar: "the doorboy, the cleaner, the sojer, the crook, the squeezer, the lounger" (FW: 142.08–10).

The first term, "doorboy," is certainly related to Janus, the guardian god of gates and beginnings. The "cleaner" is an allusion to Februa, the Roman festival of purifications. The third item, "sojer," is connected to Mars, since Roman soldiers, under his patronage, began their spring campaigns in March. The identity and purpose of the next three members of the list ("the crook, the squeezer, the lounger") require more extensive archival reference. In the original notebook index (which was crossed out with a large blue X) these three "month-men" appear as "priser, courter, lounger" (VI.B.18:

258; March–July 1927). When these items were added to Joyce's fair copy of this section, "priser" became "thief" and "courter" became "squeezer" (BL 47473 f. 18; JJA 47: 56; July 1927). In the next (and final) stage of revision "thief" was replaced by "crook" (BL 47473 f. 160; JJA 47: 72; late July–early August 1927). The entire process, from primary notebook entry to final text, was relatively short—five months at the most.

In Ovid's *Fasti,* a verse calendar of Roman religious festivals, the month of April is so named because it is then that spring "opens" (*aperit*) all things. In Joyce's versions the illegal opener (the "priser" with his jimmy) evolved into a more obvious "thief" and finally into a burglar-plus-tool ("the crook"). Ovid also indicates that the fifth and sixth months probably took their names from the elder (*maiores* = May) and the junior (*iuvenum* = June) citizens of Rome (*Fasti* 5.73–78). I suggest that, when he made his initial notebook entries, Joyce "translated" this age antithesis into a space-time antithesis; he then expressed the contrast in a pair of Franglish adjective-nouns: "court-er" (shorter) and "lo(u)ng-er" (longer). In the first draft "the courter" was replaced by "the squeezer," perhaps to emphasize that a younger courter tends to be more physically demonstrative than a mature (but patient) lounger. Some support for this mensural *coincidentia oppositorum* may come from a later exhortation to the people of Ireland to pray for the return of Shaun. His exile is a time of trial for all, "the old old oldest, the young young youngest"; their ways will wither until "their Janyouare Fibyouare [. . .] comes marching ahome on the summer crust of the flagway" (FW: 472.35–36, 473.02–5).

There are other archival considerations here. The "month-men" index appears one page before the notebook list of the six Latin terms for the dusk-to-dawn divisions of the night (VI.B.18: 258–59).[8] This collocation of Roman time terms argues strongly for some common source, perhaps in a yet-to-be-detected handbook or an encyclopedia article on ancient time reckoning.[9] Several other relevant entries appear on VI.B.18: 258: "[bl]asideration," a *Wakean* coinage that means "attention to the stars" (*ad sidera* in Latin); this word is found in the text right beside an allusion to Jupiter the Rain King, "shoepisser pluvious" (FW: 451.36). On the same notebook page there are two other uncrossed entries. The first, "mensural," refers to both a month (*mensis*) and to measurement (*mensura*); the second item is "calendar lunatic." Their archival combination looks like Joyce's personal comment not only on a calendar in which the months are calculated according to the phases of the moon (*luna*) but also on the ridiculously complicated computations involved in attempts to reconcile ancient solar and lunar calendars.

My demonstration that the first six months of the Roman year lie behind the January–June "partners of our societate" (FW: 142.08–11) shows how, in the maze of the *Wake,* from notebook to final text, it is possible for critics to follow a thread of Latin-French-English etymologies and wordplay. The last six months of the year are also present but in more contemporary forms: "the curman [dog days in July], the tourabout [vacations in August], the mussroomsniffer [peak fungus harvest in September], the bleakablue tramp [perhaps a demanding October pilgrimage], the funpowtherplother [the anniversary of the Gunpowder Plot, Guy Fawkes Day, 5 November], the christymansboxer [Boxing Day, a holiday immediately following Christmas, 26 December]" (FW: 142.10–11). This minor exercise in genetic scholarship also attempts to demonstrate that, more often than not, archival data favor the significance of one interpretation over another. Joyce put it nicely: plausibility is rarely a case of "six of one for half a dozen of the other" (FW: 446.19–20).[10]

Notebook Indexes and Their Sources

As just demonstrated, a primary aspect of genetic studies is a search for the sources and an examination of the compositional deployment of the entries from the *Wake* notebooks. The mass of material in notebook VI.B.4 contributed a large number of items to the text of two of the questions in chapter I.6. On the basis of internal evidence of the entries themselves and their first traces in the developing text, both Hayman and Rose give roughly the same date for this notebook, December 1928–spring 1929 (JJA 47: xii–xix; TDJJ: 29–30). This means that this notebook was not used in the first (mid-1927) draft of the chapter; the primary notebook has been lost, but its existence can be deduced from an examination of the growth of the earliest texts. Entries from notebook VI.B.4, however, were heavily deployed in the early 1929 additions to the text. Then, when Joyce greatly expanded the description of HCE in Question 1 during 1936 (BL 47475 fs. 228–41; JJA 47: 259–74), about twenty of the new phrases were based on entries (crossed out in blue or brown) from the second half of VI.B.4. These later additions to the text show that, seven years after his first forays into this notebook, Joyce returned to VI.B.4 and its transcription in VI.C.15 primarily for lexical inspiration, to spot "the catch word that is enough to set me off" (LII: 147).

In addition to their use in Question 1 during its final stages of composition, a large number of VI.B.4 entries were worked into the April–May

1929 revision of "The Mookse and the Gripes" episode in Question 11 (Yale 9.3 fs. 1–13; JJA 47: 210–23). With only a few exceptions, these items were crossed out in blue and come from two clusters of notebook pages, VI.B.4: 25–81 and VI.B.4: 308–34; many entries were used just shortly after they had been recorded in the notebook. This material involves two correlated topics that made major contributions to the final shape of the fable: the rivalry between the Catholic pope in Rome and the Orthodox patriarch in Constantinople.

As a prelude to an examination of genetic aspects of the "papal" dimension of "The Mookse and the Gripes" (FW: 152.15–159.18) it is necessary to summarize its action. Like a parallel episode, "The Ondt and the Gracehoper" (FW: 414.16–419.10), this incursion into Question 11 is roughly modeled on the animal fables of Aesop.[11] Joyce's protagonists can probably be traced back to the Mouse (who puffed himself up before a Lion) and the Grapes (which a frustrated Fox declared sour). In the *Wake* they represent, respectively, the rival twins, Shaun and Shem, as well as a number of other thematic opposites: Space-Time, Roman-Orthodox, Stone-Tree, English-Irish, Right Bank–Left Bank. Part of the fun is the implied mockery of Wyndham Lewis's literary-critical bulls that had anathematized Joyce. The most pronounced source of opposition in the fable is the encounter, perhaps on either side of a stream in the Vatican Gardens, between a fatuous pope and niggling patriarch. Both participants are described and converse in the jargon of their hierarchical and dogmatic offices. Granted Joyce's religious background (and several fortuitous sources described below), the Roman tradition, with its encyclical titles and *filioques,* gets more attention than the pseudo-Byzantine "synodals of his somepooliom" (FW: 156.16). On the other hand, Joyce's comic fable is far more than a mere allegory on the idiosyncratic blather of theological or jurisdictional controversy. From the genetic point of view, however, the following illustrations come from several notebook sections that are emphatically sectarian.

The first cluster of notes deals with the Vatican in general; the second index pivots around a contemporary instance of pontifical ceremony, Pope Pius XI's designation of 1925 as a Holy Year.[12] One of the objectives of this jubilee celebration was the reunification of the Eastern and Western Churches—under, of course, the primacy of the pope. Here, genetic techniques dispense an extraordinary bonus: Joyce's documentary source for each of these long clusters has been discovered.[13]

Papal embellishments were present right from the start of Joyce's version of the fable of "The Mookse and the Gripes." Such signature terms as "unfallable," "fresherman's blaque," a series of names from "Quartus V" to "Leo the Faultyfindth," and the declaration "I am superbly in my supreme poncif" were part of the first handwritten draft (BL 47473 f. 218v; JJA 47: 128) of the text that evolved into FW: 153.26–154.02. To work some personalized geography into his jabs at the pontifications of Wyndham Lewis, Joyce injected "Breakespeare," the family name of the only Englishman elevated to the papal throne (as [H]Adrian IV), into the August 1927 fair copy (BL 47473 f. 227; JJA 47: 136).[14] An Irish dimension—albeit bogus—was added in a series of Latin phrases, coming from a document known as the "prophecies of Saint Malachy."[15] This medieval work, falsely attributed to a genuine Hibernian monk-theologian, purports to predict future popes. Garbled versions of the allegedly prophetic mottoes were first inserted into the developing text of the *Wake* in April 1929.

Eastern Orthodox Elements

Another draft stage followed almost immediately, the typescript for *Tales Told of Shem and Shaun.* In its margins I detect the first ostentatiously Eastern Christian elements in the tale: the Mookse is "fore too *adiaptotously* farseeing," whereas as his rival the Gripes is "much too *schystimatically* auricular" (Yale 9.1 f. 10; JJA 47: 197; FW: 157.20–22). There is a notebook index—and a documentary source—for these exotic theological and linguistic data.[16] The italicized words in the previous citation are ostentatiously formed from the Greek roots for "infallible" (*ptotos* means "prone to fall") and "separated" (*schisma* means "rift," "split"). That dash of Orthodox vocabulary is considerably strengthened by the addition of an entire paragraph in the second set of proofs for *Tales Told of Shem and Shaun* (Yale 9.3 f. 7a; JJA 47: 217; April–May 1929). This passage (which became FW: 156.08–18) brings disputed dogma (procession of the Holy Ghost, Immaculate Conception, papal infallibility), as well as Greek, Russian ("haggyown pneumax," "breadchestviousness"), and pseudo-Latin ("philoquus") dogmatic terminology into play.[17] Also embedded in the paragraph are several references to various officials and governing bodies of the patriarchate of the Eastern Church at Constantinople: "the loggerthuds of his sakellaries [. . .] with the synodals of his somepooliom" (FW: 156.15–16). A *logothetes* is the most important Orthodox lay official; a *sakellarios* supervises the monasteries; the Holy Synod consists of the metropolitans, historically or ethnically preeminent bishops of the Eastern Church; the Symboulion is a mixed council of metropolitans and laymen.

In my judgment, the addition of the "Eastern Orthodox" material that I have just described has considerably influenced commentators' perceptions of the roles of the rivals in the fable. It is true that this paragraph is the latest (and longest) of a series of interpolations into this section of Question 11, and it is true that Joyce gave special emphasis to its exotic diction in an interpretative letter to Miss Weaver (LIII: 284–85). But, as stated before, the Mookse and the Gripes are, in fact, "characteristically" more than just *Wakean* stand-ins for the pope and the patriarch. (A clear and helpful commentary on the multiple tensions in this episode is Rose and O'Hanlon's *Understanding "Finnegans Wake"* [UFW: 96]; their succinct paragraph includes a three-column table of the contrasting roles and motifs associated with Shaun, Shem, and Issy in the fable.) Several additional aspects of the episode that illuminate its composition and components remain to be examined from a slightly different but still specifically genetic and decidedly Roman perspective.

Use of Source Material

First, a reprise of the long index of terms relating to the various ceremonies and documents of the reign of Pope Pius XI and to the 1925 Holy Year ("Annus Sanctus" [VI.B.4: 329]). This jubilee celebration was inaugurated on Christmas Eve of 1924 when the pope opened the Golden *Door* of the facade of Saint Peter's basilica by pounding on it with a *golden hammer;* at the conclusion of the Holy Year the *door* was *closed* and sealed with mortar applied from an *ivory-handled trowel.* Each of the italicized items appears as a separate entry on notebook page VI.B.4: 329. Here it must be pointed out that just as a scrutiny of the individual notes is usually the only way to determine the document from which they were copied, so too do the discovery and scrutiny of that document frequently enable a scholar to decipher unclear or purposely garbled entries in a notebook. Joyce's source also mentions several details that are directly linked to the vigorous missionary activity of Pope Pius XI:

"6 Chinois / 1 Japanois / bishop" (VI.B.4: 328) refers to seven native Asian bishops consecrated by the pope in 1926 and 1927.

"occident / S. Josaphat / Cyril & Methodius" (VI.B.4: 328; FW: 159.30–31) is an allusion to the pope's not very successful project to bring Eastern Orthodox Christians back into unity with Rome. Josaphat was the Uniat bishop of Polatsk in Belarus (the tricentennial of his martyrdom was commemorated in 1923); Cyril and Methodius were ninth-century brothers sent by the pope as missionaries to the Slavs.

"[bl]Singulare illud / Miserendissius Redemptor [*sic*; *miserentissimus* is the correct form]" (VI.B.4: 331; FW: 153.24, 154.06) are titles of documents issued by Pius XI in 1926 and 1928 and both have Joycean resonances: the first proclaims Saint Aloysius Gonzaga a patron of youth; the second dedicates the world to the Sacred Heart.[18]

Second, almost at the end of the notebook VI.B.4—just after the "Holy Year" cluster—Joyce interrupted his jotting of individual items to draft a complete sentence (VI.B.4: 331–34) that was transferred (with only a few adjustments and additions) into the evolving text of "The Mookse and the Gripes." An expanded version of this addition was then transferred to the top and the left margin of the second set of proofs for *Tales Told of Shem and Shaun* (Yale 9.3 f. 6; JJA 47: 215). That long insertion became FW: 155.23–29. In the final version an odd prepositional phrase at the end of the text is left unexplicated by commentators. Its genetic history and documentary source explain its unappreciated thematic relevance to the passage. The notebook version is "[bl]into one fold / one" (VI.B.4: 334); in the marginal insert into the draft the last three words are crossed out and replaced (above the line) by "umfullth onescuppered," which remains unaltered in the final text. Compositional retrospect points the way from the original "one fold" to the substituted "umfullth"; phonetic analogy suggests that "onescuppered" is a complementary distortion of an original (and elliptical) "one [shepherd]." The scriptural source is a parable from the fourth gospel in which Jesus advises his disciples to tend their diverse flocks with devout vigilance so that "there shall be one fold, and one shepherd" (John 10:16).[19] That exhortation is perfectly appropriate in its *Wakean* context as Joyce's pontifical pastor berates, chapter and verse, the Gripes and his errant schismatical sheep. The diverting substitution of "umfullth" for the original "one fold" may be intended as an echo of the German noun *Umfall*, which means "fall," "lapse," "sudden change of mind." In Roman Catholic terms the Orthodox patriarch and his flock have fallen away from the custodial grasp of the papal "crucycrooks" (FW: 155.17).

Third, a close examination of the entries shows that a significant number of uncrossed items from the last third of notebook VI.B.4 are in fact used in the text of "The Mookse and the Gripes." Several salient examples follow:

"pintacost acre" (VI.B.4: 298): "pintacostecas" (FW: 152.27–28): The entry itself is Greek-English for "fifty acre[s]" (and a mule?), perhaps Joyce's backhanded swipe to demonstrate to Wyndham Lewis his multicultural command of spatial local color; in Italian *pintacoteca* means "art gallery," the title that Pius XI gave to his new museum erected in the Vatican Gardens for the papal collection.

"lanca spezzata" (VI.B.4: 261): "*lancia spezzata*" (FW: 152.31): The phrase is Italian for "broken spear," a close approximation of the last name of Nicholas Breakspear, who became Pope (H)Adrian IV (1154–59). In the text it appears (as does the previous example) right at the start of "The Mookse and the Gripes."

"Cyril & Methodius" (VI.B.4: 328): "he's an nawful curilass and I must slav to methodiousness" (FW: 159.30–31): Joyce's archival evocation of the Apostles of the Slavs (and the inventors of the Cyrillic alphabet) is transferred into the text in a transition paragraph between "The Mookse and the Gripes" and the Burrus-Caseous episode.

The use of these and other uncrossed notebook entries, as well as the direct drafting of a three-page sentence, is not Joyce's usual mode of composition. The dates of the notebook and of the relevant draft stage (Yale 9.3 f. 6; JJA 47: 215) are roughly the same, April–May 1929. From both of these compositional procedures (which, again, are infrequent but not unique) I conclude that Joyce was working furiously to complete this episode against publication deadlines for *Tales Told of Shem and Shaun* (August 1929), a situation hinted at in his correspondence at that time.[20]

Fourth, as if to emphasize his interest in pontifical affairs, Joyce returns to Mme Raphaël's "recycled" notes during his late 1936 revisions: "^{g}papel blessing^{g} / 2 ^{g}finger^{g}" (VI.C.15: 173; FW: 138.22); "^{g}postulation of the / cause^{g} / beatified" and "^{g}Rite Expiatore" (VI.C.15: 174; FW: 392.22).

Electoral Procedures at the Vatican

Just as Shaun and Shem appear in "The Mookse and the Gripes" as the Roman pontiff and various rivals of his authority, so too does the presence of Issy display a punctilious awareness of papal protocol. After her introduction into the fable she finds it impossible to distract the twins, since they "were conclaved with Heliogobbleus and Commodus and Enobarbarus and whatever the coordinal dickens they did as their damprauch of papyrs and buchstubs said" (FW: 157.26–28). What is going on in this passage is a solemn assembly of cardinals to elect a new pope—and Issy cannot entice her "dogmad" (FW: 158.03) brothers to abandon the secret session to cavort with her. Strict regulations govern these conclaves: only cardinals participate in the deliberations; they may declare their choice by acclamation or by a series of votes (with the option of an immediate accession to a majority candidate); ballots that fail to achieve the necessary two-thirds majority are burned in damp straw, sending up a cloud of dark smoke, the signal that no decision has been made. When a new pope has been selected, he chooses his regnal name, is vested in the appropriate robes, and appears in public to bestow his first pontifical blessing.

These procedural details are synopsized in a compact series of notes in the same cluster that supplies so many exotic papal details for "The Mookse and the Gripes." After an uncrossed reference to "Pastor Eternus" (VI.B.4: 252) there appears the entry "[bl]Cardinal Dickens" (VI.B.4: 252). This item is not Joyce's co-option of the English novelist into the upper reaches of the Roman Catholic hierarchy but his archival distortion of the official title of the "cardinal deacons," who preside over various functions at an electoral conclave; in the *Wake* passage these prelates are further reduced in dignity to "coordinal dickens" (FW: 175.27). Following that entry are "[bl]by acclamation" and "[bl]accessit" (VI.B.4: 252). The first is the term used for a conclave's selection of a pope by the spontaneous hailing of an obvious candidate as the new leader of the Church; *accessit* is a Latin verb meaning "he comes toward," "he approaches"; it is the Vatican's technical term for switching one's vote on a second ballot to a candidate who is approaching the necessary majority. Both entries are reused slightly earlier in the text of the fable to describe the face-to-face meeting of the Mookse and the Gripes, "in an accessit" (FW: 153.21) and "by acclammitation" (FW: 153.25). Next comes an uncrossed "burned in / damp hay" (VI.B.4: 252); in the text this method of providing a smoke signal for an inconclusive vote is elaborated to include the ballot itself ("papyrs" [FW: 157.27]); the German word for smoke (*Rauch*) is appended to create "damprauch" (FW: 157.27), a compound that hints at the energizing presence of some Germanic steam (*Dampf*) with a touch of English "damp rot" ready to attack papyrus unless it is preserved in a humidity-controlled environment.[21]

Issy in the Papal Panorama

Although Issy is initially frustrated in her attempt to insinuate herself into the ecclesiastical action, she does finally cut a passing figure. Immediately after the entry on the "damp hay" but on top of the next page in the notebook is an uncrossed "nuvoletta" (VI.B.4: 253). This note is not the *direct* archival source for Issy's pseudonym in "The Mookse and the Gripes." The first draft (July–August 1927) calls the ingénue in the fable "a little cloud" (BL 47473 f. 220; JJA 47: 130). In the subsequent and considerably expanded fair copy her proper name is elaborated into "Nuvoletta" and "Nuvoluccia" (BL 47473 fs. 229 and 230; JJA 47: 138–39). These additions to the text date from August 1927, a year and a half before the compilation of VI.B.4. Nevertheless, there is a definite archival and thematic link between the adjacent "damp hay" and "nuvoletta" entries; the subsequent notebook entry is a fortuitous conjunction of a fact from its source and Joyce's prior selection of just the right term for her distinctly fluffy presence. The link is the moistened straw burned with conclave ballots to send into the sky above Saint Peter's a small cloud, *nuvoletta* in Italian.[22] As a matter of strict lexicological fact, however, the traditional Roman term for that indicator of an unsuccessful round of votes is *sfumata,* a puff of dark smoke. Joyce must have been aware of this bit of Vatican electoral idiom, since there is an archival note "[bl]sfumata" (VI.B.4: 309) to support the addition of "sfumatastelliacinous" (Yale 9.3 f. 10; JJA 47: 220; FW: 157.32) to the nearby text.

Pontifical Nomenclature

Genetic criticism can also bring into sharper focus the presence of another relevant item of papal terminology, first noticed by McHugh in the second edition of his *Annotations.* Two items after "nuvoletta" there appears another uncrossed entry, "1009 change fo [*sic*] / name" (VI.B.4: 253). In the year 1009 Peter, the bishop of Albano, became pope and adopted the regnal name Sergius IV, dropping his baptismal patron in deference to Saint Peter, the martyred apostle and first pope. The preelevation name of Pius XI, whose reign (1922–39) exactly corresponds with the period when the *Wake* and its notebooks were in progress, was Achille Ratti. Both components of the original name appear in the text of the fable: the Mookse bellows "Rats!" (*ratti* in Italian) after being confronted by the Gripes; when his Eastern nemesis persists in asking "what is the time, pace?" a pointed papal retort is flung at him: "Ask my index, mund my achilles" (FW: 154.07, 16–18).

The selection of examples of how various forms of archival research can enlighten a reading of chapter I.6 of the *Wake* has wound its way from a discarded Homeric model back to a pope with an Iliadic first name, through Roman months, fabulous Greek Orthodox functionaries, a contemporary Holy Year, and some evangelical sheep brought into one fold. Without the application of a modicum of genetic techniques most of these insights would lie obscured by the series of little clouds that Joyce arranged to dance over the surface of *Finnegans Wake.*

Notes

1. See Clive Hart, "Explications—for the Greeter Glossary of Code," *AWN* o.s. 1 (March 1962): 3–9; and Fritz Senn, "Explications—for the Greeter Glossary of Code," *AWN* o.s. 2 (April 1962): 1–5. A brief report on the Zürich Workshop by Vincent Deane appeared in *AFWC* 2.2 (Winter 1986): 1–2.

2. See Andrew Treip, ed., *"Finnegans Wake": "teems of times"* (Amsterdam: Rodopi, 1994) for a series of recent essays, many of which directly treat this theme.

3. Roland McHugh, *The Sigla of "Finnegans Wake"* (London: Edward Arnold, 1976). Jean-Michel Rabaté also deals with sigla in "*Wakean* Cryptogenetics," *Joyce upon the Void* (New York: St. Martin's Press, 1991), 69–111. A recent attempt to link Joyce's shorthand signs with the traditional proofreading marks is interesting but not convincing (Finn Fordham, "Sigla in Revision," *Geni,* 83–96). The term itself is used once in the *Wake* for the initials "H.C.E." (FW: 032.14), a second time for both ᗰ and Δ (FW: 119.17 and 19); Rose's objection (TDJJ: 44 n. 2) to this standard term of textual criticism flies in the face of convention.

4. In the first list no sign follows "9"; "⊕" appears for the first time in the second list. A vertical column of fourteen numbers (1–14), without the figures, appears upside down in the right margin of another sheet (BL 47473 f. 131; JJA 47: 44).

5. For the evidence that the siglum □ stands equally for the *title* of the work and for a *place* (HCE's pub) see Danis Rose and John O'Hanlon, "The Name of the Book," *AFWC* 4.3 (Spring 1989): 41–50. Their discussion helps to explain the appearance of a number of typical Dublin pub names in the reply to this question; also see Bernard Benstock, *Joyce-Again's Wake* (Seattle: University of Washington Press, 1965), 32–37. The minor catalog at FW: 063.23–25 is based on a very late notebook index (VI.B.44: 156–57).

6. In the reprise appearance of the collected Twelve (FW: 557.13–558.20) the number of -ation words used is two short of three dozen, but the total of the signature forms is exactly a dozen at FW: 551.17–21. This type of numerological and "morphological circumformation" (FW: 599.16–17) also appears frequently in clusters of four to signify the presence of the Four Old Men.

7. Strictly speaking, a third (uncrossed) series of entries on one of these pages also contributes to the detection of the "thematic" thrust of the two crossed lists: "Benjodan Julerube / Simashgad Zalisnap" (VI.B.18: 259) is a condensed version—

a mnemonic worthy of Leopold Bloom—of the names of the *twelve* sons of Jacob, the namesakes of the patriarchal tribes of Israel (Gen. 35:23–26 and Exod. 13:1–6).

8. This material is woven into the text at FW: 143.15–17, 244.13, 31–33, and 472.22–24. The terminology of time reckoning is cleverly distorted in at least two other passages: melancholy Anglo-Saxon days of the week (FW: 301.20–22) and Romance seasons of the year (FW: 548.28–29).

9. In an unusual archival move Joyce may have left a nearby clue to his source: "Chamber Encycl" (VI.B.18: 256) appears to be a reference to *Chamber's Encyclopedia,* a popular nineteenth-century compendium of useful information. I have not been able to locate a copy and to examine it for data on Roman months (and time periods of the night); but it is tempting to call the work Joyce's source here.

10. The "month-men" paragraphs are based on R. J. Schork, *Latin and Roman Culture in Joyce* (Gainesville: University Press of Florida, 1997), 242–51.

11. For a discussion of Joyce's use of the classical fable form see R. J. Schork, *Greek and Hellenic Culture in Joyce* (Gainesville: University Press of Florida, 1998), 226–32.

12. The specific date of this celebration is confirmed by another archival note, "[bl]holy year (1925)" (VI.B.26: 81), in a notebook that was certainly compiled in the summer of 1928; that entry reappears in the text just after the bell peals of Dublin churches announce "'Tis holyyear's day!" (FW: 569.13).

13. In a brilliant feat of archival detection Ingeborg Landuyt uncovered Joyce's two sources for the information in these extensive clusters. The first work covers the general locus of papal activity: Edourad Devoghel, *Le Vatican* (Paris[?]: Bloud & Gay, 1927); the second deals with the career of the current occupant of the apostolic throne: René Fontenelle, *Sa sainteté pie XI* (Paris[?]: Bloud & Gay, 1928). Both short works are part of the inexpensive series *Biblothèque catholique illustrée,* typical of Joyce's use of popular publications and reference works (as opposed to academic treatises) for exotic detail. Landuyt's identification of these works coincided with my writing this essay and thus illustrates another aspect of genetic scholarship: its potential for cooperative efforts in several different centers of research.

14. Landuyt has also identified Joyce's source of information for a shorter index (VI.B.4: 313–14 and VI.C.15: 166) on Breakspear: Edith M. Almedingen, *The English Pope (Adrian IV)* (London: Heath Cranton, 1925).

15. Joyce acknowledges this source: "Malachy the Augurer" (FW: 155.34). See James Atherton, "Sus in Cribro," *AWN* 9.6 (December 1972): 111–13; and Danis Rose, "Malachy," *AWN* 10.2 (April 1973): 99.

16. Dirk Van Hulle has shown that another archival cluster (VI.B.27: flyleaf–15) is derived from a favorite Joycean source, the *Encyclopaedia Britannica;* the article "Orthodox Eastern Church" supplied the data for the index in this mid-1929 notebook. For a longer discussion of this material see R. J. Schork, "James Joyce and the Orthodox Church," *Journal of Modern Greek Studies* 17 (1999): 107–24.

17. In the same draft stage Joyce supplied a hint of the linguistic virtuosity in the fable as the Mookse "gaddered togodder the odds docence of his vellumes, gresk, letton, and russicruxian" (Yale 9.3 f. 6; JJA 47: 215; FW: 155.26–28). In a 13 November 1906 letter from Rome to his brother Stanislaus Joyce claims to have been to a library to look up the details of the vote on papal infallibility at the First Vatican Council in 1870; this research prompted a revision of parts of "Grace" that deal with that doctrine (D: 168–70; LII: 192–93). Also note "Pastor Eternus" (VI.B.4: 252), the papal constitution by which Pius IX proclaimed infallibility for ex cathedra definitions; in 1854 he declared the dogma of the Immaculate Conception of the Virgin Mary.

18. Saint Aloysius Gonzaga appears several times in earlier works (P: 56 and 242; U: 12.1704 and 17.656); in *Dubliners* Mrs. Kernan has a special devotion to the Sacred Heart (D: 158). In a 23 July 1931 letter to Joyce Ezra Pound pokes fun at another recent encyclical by Pope Pius XI, *Casti Connubi* (Of a pure marriage) (see Robert Spoo, "Unpublished Letters of Ezra Pound to James, Nora, and Stanislaus Joyce," *JJQ* 33.3–4 [Spring/Summer 1995]: 565).

19. Several pages before the draft of the passage in the notebook Joyce jotted down a pertinent Latin entry: "Sit unum ovile / et unus pastor" (VI.B.4: 329); this is the Johannine verse as it appears in the Vulgate—except that the original has *fiet* (there will be), not *sit* (let there be).

20. Postcard (12 April 1929) to Miss Weaver: "I am very busy revising the fragment and don't feel at all well, tiredness and intermittent pains" (LIII: 186); letter (26 April 1929) to Miss Weaver: "You will scarcely recognise my fables now" (LIII: 189).

21. The final word of the citation, "buchstub," sounds like the German *Buchstaben* (letters of the alphabet); this is most probably an allusion to the fact that the procedures of a papal conclave are prescribed in minute detail—every move is laid out in ABC order. The citation's debauched Roman emperors, [H]Elagabalus, Commodus, and [A]Enobarbus [Domititian], allude, in acrostic form, to the patriarchal presence of HCE and remind readers that the Vatican was once the site of Nero's gardens (see Schork 1997, 70–73).

22. Dante used the same word in a simile describing the ascent of Elijah's chariot (*Inferno* 26.39).

Cain–Ham–(Shem)–Esau–Jim the Penman

Chapter I.7

INGEBORG LANDUYT

The accretive composition of I.7 entailed many successive revisions, like all of the chapters of *Finnegans Wake*. Much of the chapter's background and framework, as well as the several prototypes for its main protagonist, Shem the penman, were already integral parts of its first version. Nonetheless, these earlier elements were amplified and new motifs were introduced as the text developed, but since Joyce's writing technique was usually agglutinative, most of the earlier layers can still be recognized in the published chapter. This essay investigates the chapter's intertextual history and its main structural components as it developed through various stages. Obviously, such a study will remain incomplete because some of the manuscripts and notebooks have been lost and many of Joyce's sources may never be retrieved. Even though this chapter is relatively accessible for most readers, an analysis of its source contexts and the textual circumstances that generated it may help to elucidate which interpretative elements were relevant to its development and so may enrich our understanding of this chapter in general.

1924: Early Versions: Section 1 (FW: 169–187.23)

Writing to Miss Weaver on 16 January 1924, Joyce announced his intention to add a "description of Shem-Ham-Cain-Esau etc and his penmanship" to the "calligraphy expertise" (I.5) that he had just completed (LI: 208).[1] Hinting that the execution of these plans might be postponed for a while, he complained of being so tired that he was scarcely able to hold a pen. Apparently, this situation did not delay him long because about two weeks later he had what was most likely the first section of I.7 typed, and a few days later he sent the typescript to Miss Weaver.[2] Chapter I.7 was a logical consequence of the letter "plot" that Joyce had developed in 1923. In earlier chapters (I.2–4) Joyce had supplied an extensive introduction to his universal hero, Humphrey Chimpden Earwicker, and given particulars surrounding his hero's personal history and mysterious crime.[3] Then chapter I.5 introduced and elaborately described the ambiguous incriminating letter that his wife, ALP, had written with the help of "Jim" (in the first draft) or "Shem" (in the subsequent drafts) the penman.[4] A clear precursor of this chapter was that one of the diacritical signs in "the Letter" was compared to "the arbutus fruitflowerleaf of the *cain*apple" (FW: 121.10–11, emphasis added).

The improvised title Joyce wrote on his first draft indicates the chapter's varied ingredients: it would be about "Cain–Ham (Shem)–Esau–Jim the Penman" (BL 47471b f. 50; JJA 47: 331; FDV: 108). Apparently, he wanted to combine these several villains: Cain killed his brother Abel, Ham was guilty of irreverence toward his drunk father, Noah, when the latter exposed himself, and Esau planned to kill his brother Jacob. Although most of Shem's biblical models were not very prominent in the initial stages, Joyce added references to their fates throughout the revision process. For example, he added "Eden Quay" (FW: 172.15) early on, but a more obvious reference was an early version of Shem's complaint that "his pawdry's purgatory was more than a nigger bloke could bear" (FW: 177.04), which echoes Genesis 4:13: "And Cain said unto the Lord, My punishment is greater than I can bear."[5] When Joyce had Shem look "out of his westernmost keyhole" (FW: 178.29), he was alluding to the fact that Adam, Shem's biblical predecessor, and his descendants were to be found east of Eden, where they had fled. Of course, from Joyce's own geographical position, his compatriots could also be found in the west. The sole reference to Esau's mishap was the "hash of lentils" (FW: 171.05). Joyce first mentioned "Ham of Tenman's thirst" (FW: 187.22–23) in the last line of the second draft, attributing Noah's drunkenness to his son. Ham was also relevant in the overall context of the framework Joyce had set up so far because it serves as a background to HCE's exposure to the maidservants (I.2§1).

Most of Joyce's models in this chapter are eldest sons, but usually not the favored ones: Cain's sacrifice was not accepted, Ham's posterity was cursed, and Esau was cheated out of his birthright by the cunning Jacob, whose name Joyce included in this chapter as well.[6] The notorious forger, "Jim the Penman" (James Townsend Savard), was an alternative model for

Shem, as was Shemus, a character from Yeats's *Countess Kathleen* or, as Joyce has it, "countless catchaleens" (FW: 189.11), who sold his soul to the devil. It is noteworthy that Shemus is also Irish for James.

The first section of I.7 was primarily based on facts and rumors about Joyce's own life. In June 1921 Joyce wrote to Weaver that, depending on the source, he was supposed to be a cocaine victim, a spy, a weirdo, a dipsomaniac, almost blind, emaciated, consumptive and lazy, an owner of cinema theaters, going mad (see SL: 282; JJII: 510). Shem would similarly be characterized as a mad drug addict and an alcoholic with very peculiar eating habits who also suffers from "hereditary pulmonary T.B." (FW: 172.13). On 16 April 1924 Joyce even sent a picture of himself to Sylvia Beach with the note: "Here is the passport photo of Shem the Penman" (JJ/SB: 36). Furthermore, Shem was kicked "[a]s recently as 20 years ago [. . .] from 82 Dublin Square as far as the lefthand corner of [. . .] Europa Parade" (BL 47471b f. 52; JJA 47: 335; FDV: 110). Joyce wrote this in 1924—twenty years after he himself had embarked on his voluntary exile to the Continent from Ireland.[7]

Ulysses is also a prominent context for this chapter. Joyce characterized Shem's writings as forgeries and copies of "various styles of signature" (FW: 181.15).[8] Shem's subjects were either "nameless shamelessnesses about [. . .] everybody ever he met" or "endless portraits of himself [. . .] as a strikingly handsome young man with lyrics in his eyes and a lovely pair of inky Italian moustaches" (BL 47471b f. 50; JJA 47: 331; FDV: 109; see FW: 182.19–20); in other words, combinations of Joyce's earlier alter egos, Stephen Dedalus and Leopold Bloom.

The interior of Shem the penman's "house of [. . .] Shame" (FW: 182.30), which Joyce described in the second draft, is strewn with *Ulysses* references.[9] For instance, the "you owe mes" (FW: 183.15) are reminiscent of Stephen's debts (see U: 9.213: "A.E.I.O.U."), Shem's "borrowed brogues" (FW: 183.17) could be Mulligan's (see U: 2.255), his "worms of snot" (FW: 183.29) could be what Stephen left behind on the rocks (see U: 3.500), and the "ineluctable shadow" (BL 47471b f. 63; JJA 47: 357; FDV: 118; FW: 184.08–9; see U: 3.413) echoes Stephen's musings in *Ulysses*. There are also references that undoubtedly refer to Leopold Bloom; for example, "stickyback snap" (FW: 183.11), the "citizens' throwaway" (BL 47471b f. 63; JJA 47: 357; FDV: 117),[10] the "loveletter" (FW: 185.11), the "fireworks" (BL 47471b f. 63; JJA 47: 357; FDV: 118)[11] and concomitant "seedy ejaculations" (FW: 183.23), and the "whirling dervish" (FW: 184.06; see U: 15.2160). Furthermore, the garters (FW: 183.28), the "chambermade music" (FW: 184.04), the "ohs ouis" and all the other "yeses" (FW: 184.01–2), also in the same section, suggest his wife, Molly Bloom.

Shem's "inkbottlehouse" is probably based on the "Round House" or "The Ink Pot" in Martin's Row. Here, as in I.2, Humphrey Chimpden Earwicker's home is in "Lucalizod," a fictional setting combining Chapelizod and Lucan, both close to the "capital city" (FW: 181.07), Dublin. The fact that "the Thornton girl with her Kodak" (BL 47471b f. 52v; JJA 47: 336; FDV: 111; see FW: 171.31–32) saw Shem entering a "fruiterer & florist" suggests the shop where Boylan buys his present for Molly in *Ulysses* (see U: 10.299).[12]

Joyce further enhanced Shem's identification with Leopold Bloom with references to Dr. Joseph Collins's review of *Ulysses.*[13] According to Richard Ellmann, Joyce had met this psychologist in the spring or summer of 1921 and immediately added his name to the last *Ulysses* episode. Collins's admiration for *A Portrait* had induced him to ask some of his friends in Paris to arrange a meeting with the writer. Joyce lent Collins the *Little Review* installments of *Ulysses,* but of these Collins remarked to Myron Nutting: "'I have in my files writing by the insane just as good as this,' and gave a medical explanation of the deterioration of the artist's brain" (JJII: 516). Collins's discussion of *Ulysses* was written in a similar spirit and must have been an unpleasant surprise to Joyce:

> He [Joyce] is the only individual that the writer has encountered *outside of a madhouse* who has let flow from his pen random and purposeful thoughts just as they are produced. . . . When a master technician of words and phrases sets himself the task of revealing the product of the unconscious mind of a moral *monster,* a pervert and an invert, an *apostate* to his race and his religion, . . . he undoubtedly knew full well what he was undertaking, and how unacceptable the vile contents of that unconscious mind would be.[14]

Joyce accordingly also made Shem an "apostate" (FW: 171.33) in the first draft and a "monster" (BL 47471b f. 59; JJA 47: 349; FDV: 116; see FW: 177.15) in the second, accompanied by the remark: "But would anyone, short of a madhouse, believe it?" (FW: 177.13). Collins also described the writer's practice of using "every experience he has ever encountered, every person he has ever met."[15]

Joyce integrated more commentaries on *Ulysses* in his *Work in Progress.* Whereas his previous chapter (I.5) had absorbed some of the accusations that had been leveled at the book itself, this episode tackled the attacks of a more personal nature that Joyce found in "tress clippings from right, lift and cintrum" (FW: 183.29). Evidence of Joyce's interest in these reviews can be found in VI.B.6: 116–19,[16] in which he listed words and expressions from several reviews.[17] "The Scandal of *Uysses*" in the *Sporting Times* (or the "Pink 'Un") was the fiercest and thus most obvious source to complete the description of the "human outcome of dirt" (BL 47471b f. 65; JJA 47: 361; FDV: 119) that Joyce was compiling. The pseudonymous author, "Aramis," supported the verdict of the American judges who had convicted the publishers of the *Little Review* in 1921 for publishing "a very rancid chapter of the Joyce stuff."[18] Also via the notebook the "revolted demimondaines" (BL 47474 f. 8; JJA 47: 367) and "clean little cherubs" (see FW: 177.14), which are what Lenehan and Boylan are said to be compared to Joyce, were incorporated in this draft. An entire notebook page (VI.B.6: 116) was almost completely filled with fragments of the Aramis diatribe, among others, which Joyce used very soon afterward to fill in his description of Shem. Presumably, Joyce's readers were expected to recognize these references.

In his second draft Joyce had already added to the Latin description of Shem's ink manufacturing this motivation:

> Let ^^{1}the manner & the matter of^{1}^ it ^^{1}for these ^^{2}our^{2}^ sporting times^{1}^ be ~~veiled~~ ^^{1}cloaked up^{1}^ in the language of ~~blushing~~ ^^{1}blushfed^{1}^ cardinals ~~lest~~ ^^{1}that ^^{2}the^{2}^^{1}^ Anglican ~~cardinals~~ ^^{1}cardinal^{1}^, ^^{1}not^{1}^ reading his own ~~words~~ ^^{1}rude speech^{1}^, ^^{1}may always^{1}^ behold the scarlet ^^{1}brand^{1}^ on the brown of ~~the~~ ^^{1}her^{1}^ of Babylon yet feel not the pink one in his ^^{1}own damned^{1}^ cheek (BL 47471b f. 63v; JJA 47: 358; FDV 118; see FW: 185.08–13, my underlining)

In the following notebook pages Joyce continued to browse through his collection of press clippings, jotting down one word from this article, then again two lines from another, John Murray's review in *Nation and Athenæum.* He had exclaimed: "Every thought that a super-subtle modern can think seems to be hidden somewhere in its inspissated obscurities," "[those] who read it [*Ulysses*] will profit by the vicarious sacrifice," and "Mr. Joyce . . . seems to have dropped the illusion of truth for the truth, the effect of truth for the fact, which is, in art, to drop the bone for the shadow."[19] Joyce recorded "vicarious sacrifice," "inspissated," and "bone & shadow" (VI.B.6: 117–18) and wove them into his text (see FW: 179.25 and 184.08).

Ulysses was described as "a tome like a Blue-book" by Stephen Gwynn (see VI.B.6: 118; FW: 179.27),[20] and Shem was characterized as an "opprobious papist" (FW: 172.34). This also reflects Arnold Bennett's review in *Outlook:* "I must plainly add, at the risk of opprobrium, that in the finest passages it is in my opinion justified" (see VI.B.6: 117),[21] although the source for "papist," which is also in the notebook, has not been found.

Joyce incorporated the negative experiences he had had with his earlier writings in this chapter as well. For example, from *Dubliners* onward he had been "boycotted" (FW: 185.04) by several publishers who had refused to publish his works, one of whom was George Roberts or "George W Robber" (BL 47471b f. 64; JJA 47: 359; FDV: 118; see FW: 185.01), as Joyce has it in the second draft. As Robert Boyle has indicated, many elements from "Gas from a Burner" (1912), which Joyce wrote to vent his frustrations after his experiences with the Irish printers, resurface in this chapter: "The psalm, the urn, the writing material from the urn, the farts and the groans, and the writing upon the skin all appear."[22]

Like Shem, Joyce was also a tutor in his youth, accumulated debts, utterly disliked violence, and preferred a certain white wine: "Her Most Excellent Excellency's the Archduchess's most excellent piss (Pardon! Fendant de Valais [. . .])" (SL: 238). Joyce shared Shem's horror at the fighting that accompanied Bloody Sunday and the Irish Civil War. Michael Collins had called the treaty with England the "stepping stone to the Republic," but it was also the cause of a bloody war between Eamon De Valera's followers and the new Irish government.[23] Joyce noted that the "stepping stones" were "slippery with [the] blood of heroes" (VI.B.49c). Besides, Joyce's own wife had been in danger during the fights between Republicans and Free State soldiers, an incident he seems to have taken very personally. Shem's eating habits also betray his antinationalism: "He preferred the ~~mess~~ ^1hash1^ of ~~Europe's lentils~~ ^1lentils1^ in Europe to Ireland's tight little pea" (BL 47471b f. 54v; JJA 47: 340; FDV: 114; see FW: 171.05–6). The European "foodstuffs" Shem relishes are tinned salmon from the London soup maker, Lazenby,[24] Heinz's canned pineapples, and wine.

Joyce's depiction of Shem's criminal aspects was influenced by contemporary studies of the predestined delinquent such as the descriptions and investigations by the Italian sociologist Cesare Lombroso: "He [Lombroso] discovered . . . a criminal type, the 'instinctive' or 'born' criminal, a creature who had come into the world predestined to evil deeds, and who could be surely recognized by certain stigmata, certain facial, physical, even moral birthmarks, the possession of which, presumably ineradicable, foredoomed him to the commission of crime" (*Encyclopaedia Britannica* 11, s.v. "Lombroso"). Shem is typically marked by asymmetrical deformations, an obtuse sense of taste and smell, and a moral insensibility. Further references of this kind in this chapter are to his ambidexterity, the stink and filth in which he lives, and his tattoos and dark skin, which are other typical Lombrosian attributes.

Jean Crépieux-Jamin's *Les Éléments de l'écriture des canailles* (The elements of the writing of the rabble), from which Joyce took a long index of notes, was another significant source text for both I.5 and I.7.[25] The title itself gives an exact description of the contents of this popular book on graphology. Crépieux-Jamin focused his discussion on the *canaille* (blackguard), whom he defines as "un individu affligé de tares, c'est-à-dire d'insuffisances flagrantes ou de vices de caractère" [an individual afflicted by shortcomings, blatant insufficiencies, or character defects].[26] On the basis of numerous examples, he analyzes the properties of handwriting that indicate "débilité," "mensonge," "orgueil," "grossièreté" (weak-mindedness, mendacity, pride, crudeness), and similar defects. Apart from the technical graphological details, Joyce was interested in Crépieux-Jamin's psychological explanations, and he took notes on inhibition, respiration problems, and many other peculiar symptoms, complete with details on a number of cases. Joyce probably turned to this book for ideas for I.5, and most of the words that Joyce noted were in fact used to revise that chapter, but these notes influenced basic elements of this chapter as well. In one of the examples the handwriting of the *canaille* who "lives on loans & is 35" and was "never sentenced" (VI.B.6: 49; FW: 173.07) is described:

> l'auteur de la fig. 166, altère la vérité par faiblesse, par vanité, par paresse. Il a l'écriture tordue des débiles, le tracé petit et filiforme des déprimés, les *t* non barrés des négligents, les *d* enroulés des gens satifaits d'eux-mêmes, les *o* bien fermés et bouclés des impénétrables, et il met des majuscules à la place des minuscules comme des gens exaltés, dépourvus de jugement. C'est une *canaille. Il n' a jamis subi la plus petite condemnation,* mais ses tares profondes l'ont précipité avec sa famille dans une misère noire. *Il vit d'emprunt,* de mendicité, et *il a trente-cinq ans.*[27]

> [The writer of fig. 166 changes the truth because of weakness, vanity, and laziness. He has the twisted handwriting of the weak-minded, the small and threadlike tracing of the depressed, the unslashed *t*'s of the negligent, the

coiled *d*'s of people satisfied with themselves, the well-closed and curled *o*'s of the impenetrable, and he uses capital instead of small letters like fanatics, without common sense. He is a *canaille. He has never been sentenced,* but his profound shortcomings have plunged him with his family into black misery. *He lives on loans,* on mendacity, and *he is thirty-five.*]

Crépieux-Jamin rejects the methods advocated by Lombroso and other criminologists and especially condemns the latter's attempts at graphology. In Joyce's description of Shem we get a superficial mixture of the symptoms that each of the scientists gives to recognize criminals.

Notebook VI.B.6 provides us with some of Shem's other prototypes as well. Biblical Jacob and Jim the penman were not the only forgers Joyce had in mind. Joyce extracted the anecdote of how Saint Columba (Columcille) furtively copied Saint Finnan's psalter from John Sullivan's introduction to *The Book of Kells.*[28]

Another Irish saint, Patrick, was also introduced as a prototype for Shem. Based on notes taken from Otto Jespersen's *The Growth and Structure of the English Language,*[29] Joyce remarked on the saint's ability as the forger: "SP false coiner" and "SP coins words" (VI.B.6: 74 and 78). Although Saint Patrick is not discussed in the source, he is definitely relevant to the problematic issue of language, especially Latin. His vernacular was the debased provincial Latin of Roman Britain, and he even almost forgot that during his six years of captivity in Ireland. As a result, his writings display a rude style and a structure that is almost ungrammatical. Similarly, Shem's chapter also contains some amateurish Latin. The quoted psalm line "Lingua mea calamus scribae velociter scribentis" (BL 47471b f. 53v; JJA 47: 338; FDV: 112; see Psalm 45) reminds us of Patrick's *Confession,* where the saint repeatedly mentions his concern with his tongue.

The first draft (of the first section) of chapter 7 was probably composed shortly after 16 January and is very fragmentary. Joyce merely listed the ingredients for this chapter, most of which were taken from the notebooks he had filled by this time. The earliest *Finnegans Wake* notebook, VI.B.10, supplied Shem's situation when he "took a peep through his keyhole," he "found himself looking / into [the] barrel of [a] revolver" (VI.B.10: 57), a fragment that suggests a court case in a newspaper article. Shem's riddle, "when is a man not a man?" (FW: 170.05), was probably planned as early as March–July 1923, when notebook VI.B.3 was being compiled (VI.B.3: 30).[30]

Improperia: Section 2 (FW: 187.24–195)

As it does in the first section, the impromptu title of the first draft of the second section immediately establishes a coherent structure: "Improperia are the reproaches which in the liturgy of the Office of Good Friday the Saviour is made to utter against the Jews, who, in requital for all the Divine favours and particularly for the delivery from the bondage of Egypt and safe conduct into the Promised Land, inflicted on him the ignominies of the Passion and a cruel death."[31] The charges always start with what God did for the Jews in contrast to how he was treated in return:

> Popule meus, quid fecit tibi? Aut in quo contristavi te? Responde mihi!
> Quia eduxi te de terra Aegypti: parasti Crucem Salvatori tuo.
> [My people, what did I do to you? Or in what did I distress you? Answer me!
> Because I led you out of the land of Egypt, you prepared a Cross for your Savior.]

Thus episodes of Exodus are opposed to every detail of the Passion. Joyce copied this structure and rhythm in most of his charges. Even though not the original count (which is 3 + 9), the number 7 is the biblical (and Catholic) number par excellence, symbolizing completeness or perfection and reminding the believers of the seven days of creation, the seven years of plenty and famine in Egypt, the seven petitions of the Lord's Prayer, the seven words on the cross, the seven sacraments, and more septuplets. Besides, according to Malala, Cain would be punished sevenfold because he had committed seven crimes: envy, treachery, murder, killing his brother, first murder ever committed, grieving his parents, and lying to God.[32] Joyce made a similar, though not identical, list in the top right-hand corner of BL 47471b f. 65v (JJA 47: 376):

> <u>Charges</u>
> 1 Hell
> 2 Prop[agation]
> 3 ~~Doles~~
> 3 Prophecy
> 4 Shirking
> 5 Sins
> 6 Doles
> 7 Mother

Here Shem is one of the Jews who is called to account. There are several other biblical or Catholic references, usually slight transformations of the originals, such as "dust to dust," connected to "ashes" (Ash Wednesday service [Gen. 3:19]), "black sheep" (i.e., a scapegoat [Lev. 16]), and "repopulate the land" (see "replenish the earth" [Gen. 9:1]), to name just a few.

The Cain-Abel antagonism from Genesis 4 is one of the most important components of this section. Cain did not show the proper reverence for his God (Gen. 1), which was expressed by his neglect of a fitting sacrifice. The shirked office may be Joyce's transformation of this duty (number 4). But especially the fifth *improperium* is explicit: "There grew up beside you, on his keeping & in yours, that other [. . .] & him you laid low" (BL 47471b f. 67; JJA 47: 379; FDV: 121; see FW: 191.11–29, my underlining). In Genesis 4:9, after the murder, Cain replies to God's questions as to Abel's whereabouts: "Am I my brother's keeper?" And of course there is the "Cannibal Cain" (VI.B.6: 102) from the seventh charge.

Most of the accusations are even more relevant to Joyce himself: (1) though brought up in Ireland, he lost his faith; (2) he had not married, though he did "replenish the earth" with two children; (3) superstitious as he was, Joyce believed that his work had at least some prophetic quality; (4) the shirked office could refer to his refusal to become a priest, to find a job in Ireland (e.g., at Guinness's) or the fact that since Miss Weaver's donations began he had given up teaching and restricted himself to his literary activities, which were financially entirely insufficient; (5) he had conflicts with Stanislaus; (6) charity (Miss Weaver's gifts) mostly supported him (most of the money he received was spent quickly); and (7) possibly, he was influenced by the conflict preceding the death of his mother that was fictionalized in *Ulysses.*

These basic elements were all present in the first draft of I.7§2 and only needed rounding out. Joyce started a thorough research in order to be able to integrate the Genesis background properly. His notes on the subject, which were used in several drafts of this chapter, can be found in VI.B.6: 108–13 and were culled from a standard Latin commentary that was widely available in his days: Thomas Josephus Lamy's *Commentarium in librum geneseos.*[33] It presents a line-by-line exegesis of the whole book of Genesis, citing many alternative translations and interpretations. Not only does the source text locate more or less obvious references to the Cain-Abel conflict itself (such as possible reasons why Cain's offer was not accepted or the story from Jewish tradition that Cain was killed by Lamech, one of his descendants, while the latter was hunting), but it also lists all the different possibilities for the mark that Cain was given after he killed his brother: "torvum ac truculentum fuisse aspectum" [his face was both grim and ferocious], "maniam" (madness), or "tremorem quemdam capitis aut etiam omnium membrorum" [some sort of shaking of the head or even of all his limbs] (CLG: 256). Joyce noted these as "scowl," "maniac," and "epilepsy" (VI.B.6: 111). Furthermore, Lamy also gives alternative interpretations of the myth of Cain and Abel:

> VI.B.6: 111:
>
> (b) night kills day
>
> CLG: 253: Goldhiger vero in isto fratricidio discernit mythum quo esprimitur lucta diei cum nocte. [Goldhiger indeed in this fratricide discerns the myth in which the struggle of the day with the night is expressed.]
>
> (c) agricult — pastoral
>
> CLG: 253: J. de Liebig nihil aliud hic videt nisi symbolum, quo docetur agriculturam mortem inferre arti pastoritiae. [J. de Liebig sees nothing here but the symbol by which is taught that agriculture brings the death of the pastoral occupation.]
>
> (d) "jews — +"
>
> CLG: 253: Sic isti omnem pervertunt historiam. Abel a fratre occisis figura est Christi a Judaeis occisi. [Thus do they pervert the whole history. Abel killed by his brother is the prefiguration of Christ killed by the Jews.]

This meshes perfectly with Joyce's mingling of the *improperia* and the Cain and Abel story.

The "landmarks," "luxury" (FW: 192.05), and "gets others to work for him" (VI.B.6: 112) are the innovations Cain was supposed to have introduced in the history of humanity. Joyce systematically replaced the names Cain and Abel with the stylized letters ⊏ and Λ in his notes. Only later (at the end of notebook VI.B.6) did he start using ⊏ for Shem himself, and Abel evolved into Shaun in the following notebook, VI.B.1.

Further references to Cain were gradually introduced in later drafts. In the fair copy of section 1 Joyce added that the blood on the stepping-stone, like Abel's in Genesis 4:10 (VI.B.6: 111; CLG: 253–54), was crying to heaven (see FW: 178.11). Since the brother whom Cain buried was also the first human to die, Shem became a "premature gravedigger" (VI.B.6: 114; FW: 189.28) after "having buried a friend not long before" (BL 47471b f. 55v; JJA 47: 342; FDV: 114; FW: 171.35–36) in the first section. The "tree of the knowledge of beautiful andevil" (FW: 194.15) was also added.

Slightly transformed is the "firstborn and firstfruit of woe" (FW: 194.12). Lamy tells us that the Israelites were also believed to have sacrificed their first fruits and the firstlings of their flocks (CLG: 248; VI.B.6: 109).

The VI.B.6 index with *Ulysses* reviews was important for Joyce's revisions of this section as well: "Let us record the atoms as they fall upon the mind in the order in which they fall, let us trace the pattern, however disconnected and incoherent in appearance, which each sight or incident scores upon the consciousness."[34] This is how Virginia Woolf described the purpose of young novelists such as James Joyce. Her verdict was not wholeheartedly positive; though she acknowledges Joyce's merits, *Ulysses* fails "because of the comparative poverty of the writer's mind."[35] At VI.B.6: 116 Joyce recorded these "incoherent atoms" and "poverty of mind" (FW: 192.10). Several more insults were culled from the Aramis diatribe. "The main contents of the book are enough to make a Hottentot sick" was a comment often quoted by other reviewers.[36] More specifically, *Ulysses* "would also have the very simple effect of an ordinary emetic" (VI.B.6: 116; see FW: 192.14–15). How closely Joyce himself and Shem were to be identified can be deduced from the entry "Shemeries" (VI.B.6: 117; FW: 187.35–36), triggered by James Douglas's review in the *Sunday Express.* The critic complained of the "Joyceries," which would "out-rosse the rosseries of the Parisian stews."[37] That the book was "obscene" (VI.B.6: 117) could be found in many comments and had already been added to the first draft (FW: 194.18). Strikingly, in a note inspired by one of the other reviews, Joyce's name is not replaced by that of Shem but that of Tristan ("T his own poles, equator parallel of latitude" [VI.B.6: 118]).[38] Possibly Tristan was at this stage very much related to Shem. Not only did Joyce feel threatened by the many accusations and rumors in the reviews of his books, but the *Ulysses* trial probably also inspired him for Shem's summons. In his later revisions Joyce's defensive inclusions were especially triggered by negative comments relating to his *Work in Progress.* After *Ulysses* his new work would be another model for the letter: "*hic sunt lennones!*" (FW: 179.02) answered Judge Lennon's attack in *Catholic World* in 1931.

Joyce's letter of 4 February 1924 must have accompanied some manuscripts he left for Lily Bollach to type. Joyce wanted her to know that, after his last revision, he had taken the trouble of writing out again three of the pages for her. The typescript we have of the first section of the chapter indeed seems to have been produced in two separate parts. A first part is numbered from pages 1 to 6. A second is typed heavily and separately numbered from 1 to 5.[39] There is no evidence of a break in the fair copy, so the three pages rewritten by Joyce may have been lost. On 8 February his "nightman sketch," a piece of text intended to follow "after the words 'Shem the penman'" (LI: 211), was sent off to Miss Weaver. The second part of the Shem piece followed on the 17th of that month. An unpublished letter to Lily Bollach, dated 14 February, in which he specifies which passage to type, confirms the evidence.[40] Joyce wanted Bollach to type these pages heavily like the previous ones. To avoid blanks within the section she was to retype the page starting with "gallons" (BL 47474 f. 33; JJA 47: 419). Joyce probably lightly revised Bollach's typescript (in pen) and turned his attention to his next chapters.

1925: Preparations for Publication in *This Quarter*

In 1925 several magazines offered to publish Joyce's new work. "Shem" was promised to Ernest Walsh for the second issue of *This Quarter*. During the whole of June and the beginning of July Joyce tried to make his piece as finished as he could make it by revising the 1924 typescript (§1.3/2.3) and a second typescript (§1.4/2.4) of which several pages were retyped (§1.5/2.5). As his regular typist was away, Auguste Morel, the French translator of *Ulysses,* was engaged to take over. Joyce integrated explicit references to several new models for his alter ego: Tristan is repeatedly referred to ("a bladder Tristended" [FW: 169.20]; "a philtred love" [FW: 189.05]). Saint Patrick's "purgatory" (FW: 177.04), "wetbed" (deathbed) confession (FW: 188.01), and "adzehead" (VI.B.14: 163; FW: 169.11) made this draft more "patrician" (FW: 179.23). A suggested identification with Christ in earlier drafts was made more overt by the addition of the words "Fish" (BL 47474 f. 44; JJA 47: 456; FW: 177.12) and "stigmy" (FW: 193.17). The *canaille's* age was changed to "furtivefree" (FW: 173.07), Christ's age when he was "in honour bound to the cross," in this case of his own "cruelfiction" (FW: 192.19). Joyce also added a reference to Rabelais's Gargantua "de Trop Blogg" (FW: 169.05), possibly instigated by Muir's review, in which (as in many others) parallels had been drawn between Joyce and Rabelais.[41]

"Parnella" with his "kitty" (FW: 192.08), "O'Shea or O'Shame" (FW: 182.30), and Swift, accompanied by "stellas" (FW: 177.10) and "vanessance" (FW: 177.17), were new prototypes that induced a whole context of forgery and duplicity of their own. When the typescript was made Joyce left it with Sylvia Beach, and in letters to her he gave instructions about a few more changes and additions (JJ/SB: 54–55). On 21 July he wrote to Miss Weaver that he had sent off the piece (LIII: 122).

The (now lost) proofs (§1.6/2.6) arrived around 20 October and were slightly corrected in a hurry with the help of Joyce's two (at that time) most recent notebooks (VI.B.8 and VI.B.19) and sent off. Eventually, the issue (Autumn–Winter 1925–26) appeared.

1927: Preparation for Publication in *transition* (1.8/2.8)

In April 1927 Eugene Jolas started the serial publication of Joyce's *Work in Progress* in *transition.* Joyce started correcting chapter I.7 around the end of August and September 1927. He had just finished "The Mookse and the Gripes" fable for I.6 (*transition,* no. 6 [September 1927]) as a response to Wyndham Lewis's attack on him in *Time and Western Man.* But every publication of this "butcher" (FW: 172.05) was an occasion for Joyce to include some reaction in his own writings. Lewis had published *The Lion and the Fox: The Rôle of the Hero in the Plays of Shakespeare* in January 1927, and this book left several marks on Joyce's Shem chapter. Lewis's structuring device in this essay are Machiavelli's symbolic lion and fox, used by the latter "in the composition of his perfect human being."[42] He connects the lion with the Celtic, feudal, primitive mind, whereas the fox is represented by the Italian Renaissance artist and scientist. Lewis has two long introductory parts on the backgrounds of Tudor England and Renaissance Italy (part 1) and Machiavelli (part 2). This brings him to an analysis of Shakespeare's kings, heroes, and "colossi" but through them also to the workings of the playwright's mind itself as a conflict between these two opposing principles: "The figure used by Machiavelli to express this conflict is that of the *lion and the fox;* these two animals are chosen to represent the two forces in opposition, although his doctrine was directed to combining them. In Shakespeare, as in most of his contemporaries, with one foot in the old world of chivalrous romance and the other in the new one of commerce and science, they were imperfectly combined." The last chapters contain more loosely connected topics such as a comparison between Shakespeare and Cervantes in the light of the previously expanded opposition, a critique of Matthew Arnold's dichotomy of the "Creeping Saxon" and the "Celt,"[43] brief discussions of a few of Shakespeare's contemporaries, and so on.

Joyce definitely must have had this book or notes on it at his disposal.[44] Not only did he integrate the title repeatedly as "foxed fux to fux [. . .] with all the teashop lionses of Lumdrum" (FW: 177.36–178.01), "that foxy, that lupo and that monkax" (FW: 192.03), and the "Leon of the fold"

(FW: 193.04) but he integrated also a reference to "Nichiabelli" (FW: 182.20), and many Shakespeare quotations. References to "hammet" (FW: 193.11), for instance, include "*Hanno, o Nonanno, acce'l brubblemm*" (Italian for "They have or they have not" and thus a faint echo of "to be or not to be" [FW: 182.20–21]), "Reynaldo" (FW: 192.14), "and the cockcock crows for Danmark" (FW: 192.21). Though the most obvious of the Shakespeare references were not all taken from Lewis's book, they enhance this context. The title of the earlier short story "cattlemen's spring meat" (FW: 172.06–7) or *Cantelman's Spring Mate* (1917) may have been taken from the extracts from press notices at the end of the book. There are several other entries that could have been taken from *The Lion and the Fox*, but they are not specific enough for us to be certain.

In his corrected *This Quarter* pages (§1.7/2.7) Joyce also complemented his chapter with the titles of his short stories, such as "after the grace" (FW: 186.34–35), "eveling" (FW: 186.24), "countryports" (FW: 187.07), and all of the other *Dubliners*. In the proofs for *transition* Joyce integrated other personal references, such as a telegram with a request for money and the reply in which we can easily recognize him and his brother (FW: 172.22). That his "uncertain quantity of obscene matter" was "not protected by copriright in the United Stars of Ourania" (FW: 185.30–31) had been proven by Samuel "roth's" (FW: 176.23) pirated edition of *Ulysses* in *Two Worlds*.

A capital *A* (BL 47474 f. 89; JJA 47: 487; FW: 175.06–28) indicates where a long verse (of which the original is lost) had to be inserted with a recapitulation of several motives and themes from the earlier chapters: Adam and Eve, Napoleon and Wellington, Pierce Oreille, Noah and the rainbow.

Preparation for *Finnegans Wake*

VI.B.31 (late April–November 1931 [TDJJ: 31]) was one of the most important sources of new material for Joyce's revisions of his first set of *transition* sheets (§1.9/2.9). Joyce used the Canadian Protestant Charles Chiniquy's book *The Priest, the Woman and the Confessional* to add (in numerous stages) one more level to the confrontation between Justice "Justius" and his brother "Shem Macadamson."[45] With the help of notes on approximately the first thirty pages of VI.B.31, Shaun became a father confessor, a "handsome young spiritual physician" (FW: 191.16; PWC: 38) who is calling his black sheep to the fold: "I advise you to conceal yourself, my little friend, as I have said a moment ago and put your hands in my hands and have a nightslong homely little confiteor about things" (FW: 188.01–4, underlined words taken, with slight adaptations, from PWC via VI.B.31). On the one hand, Joyce could extract authentic references to the confessional and all that it involved from Chiniquy's text, such as the detailed questions the priest was expected to ask his penitent: "Quis, quid, ubi, quibus auxiliis, cur, quomodo, quando. Who, which, where, with whom, why, how, when" (PWC: 71; see FW: 188.08). The ex–Catholic priest also recounts several anecdotes about his and some of his confessors' difficulties with this Catholic institution, in one of which he rather unhappily informed a young woman: "The Church tells me also that you must give the details which may *add to the malice* or *change the nature of your sins*" (PWC: 15, emphasis added; VI.B.31: 7; FW: 189.02). Chiniquy's book, however, is not informative; it is a denunciation of the uses and abuses of the auricular confession, especially considering the role of priests and their relationship(s) with female penitents, who become Shaun's "dear sisters" (PWC: 14; VI.B.31: 6; FW: 188.22), "old Badsheetbaths" (PWC: 5; VI.B.31: 6; FW: 188.26), "accomplished women" (PWC: 13; VI.B.31: 6; FW: 189.14), and "debituary vases or vessels preposterous" (PWC: 159; VI.B.31: 30; FW: 189.21). The "horrible necessity" (PWC: 2; VI.B.31: 2; FW: 188.21) of sharing all sins and every secret thought with the priests resulted in many sinful relationships or, when not complied with, equally sinful sacrilegious confessions and thus caused the loss of innumerable souls, or so Chiniquy claims.

Joyce's use of this material is ambiguous. On the one hand, from his brother's point of view, Shem is obviously the sinner who needs to confess his many misdeeds to obtain absolution, and several negative elements in Chiniquy are coupled with this antihero and the accusations against him. When charged with the failure to "repopulate the land" of his birth (FW: 188.35), Shem is represented as a priest, an unattainable and thus doubly attractive prey for hordes of pursuing women:

> accomplished women, indeed fully educanded, far from being old and rich behind their dream of arrivisme, if they have only their honour left, and not deterred by bad weather when consumed by amorous passion, struggling to possess themselves of your boosh, one son of Sorge for all daughters of Anguish, *solus cum sola sive cuncties cum omnibobs* [. . .] mutely aying for that natural knot, debituary vases or vessels preposterous. (FW: 189.14–21, underlined words taken, with slight adaptations, from PWC via VI.B.31)

Part of this passage is derived from an anecdote that Chiniquy quotes from "Mysteries of the Neapolitan Convents" by Henrietta Caracciolo: "A young *educanda* was in the habit of going down every night to the convent burying-place, where, by a corridor which communicated with the vestry, she entered into a colloquy with a young priest attached to the Church. *Consumed by an amorous passion, she was not deterred by bad weather* or the fear of being discovered" (PWC: 30, emphasis mine). Another fragment was taken from the writings of Saint Jerome in which he warns his priests to take precautions against the temptations of the confessional: "*Solus cum sola,* secreto et absque arbitrio, vel teste, non sedeas" [Never sit in secret, alone in a retired place, with a female who is alone with you] (PWC: 122, emphasis mine). On the other hand, by hearing Shem's sins, plaintiff Shaun himself will be submerged into sin. Possibly the confession will not even be auricular but public, witnessed by the "dear sisters" of his congregation, Issy and her companions. That Shaun's relationship with them is dubious as well is also hinted by material from Chiniquy:

> And here, pay the piety, must I too nerve myself to pray for the loss of self-respect to equip me for the horrible necessity of scandalisang (my dear sisters, are you ready?) by sloughing off my hope and tremors while we all swin together in the pool of Sodom? I shall shiver for my purity while they will weepbig for your sins. Away with covered words, new Solemonities for old Badsheetbaths! (FW: 188.20–26, underlined words taken, with slight adaptations, from PWC)

The rest of Joyce's revisions touch diverse topics. A few expressions were culled from Basil Hargrave's list, *Origins and Meanings of Popular Phrases & Names Including Those Which Came Into Use During The Great War,* which was in Joyce's personal library.[46] Another minor source was *The Speeches and Tabletalk of Mohammad* by Stanley Lane-Poole.[47] The list of "flesh and blood" games that Shem refuses to play was considerably enlarged with material that Joyce extracted straight from the index of Norman Douglas's *London Street Games.*[48] Many late additions were also meant to extend important earlier motives within the chapter and references to the rest of the book, for example, of that "hereticalist Marcon and the two scissymaidies and how bulkily he shat the Ructions gunorrhal?" (FW: 192.01–3), the "flowerpot on the pole" (FW: 194.08), and so on.[49]

Galleys

The galleys for *Finnegans Wake* were made in March 1937, and they represented for Joyce a new occasion to incorporate additions. His text became more multilingual during his first series of revisions, with clusters of Hungarian and Russian words. The second set of galleys has numerous additions in Gipsy and Hungarian, Finnish from VI.B.45 and "Lieutuvisky" (VI.B.45: 520) or Lithuanian, Portuguese, and Irish (VI.B.46). The collection of heretics that Joyce had been accumulating in this chapter was also further added to with "Jansens Chrest" and "an Albiogenselman" (FW: 173.12). Part of Joyce's overlay was taken from the works of James Macpherson, another famous forger, and the names of several of his colleague writers were integrated (e.g., "larbourd" [FW: 178.28] and "Sharadan" [FW: 184.24]). Pulling together overall thematic webs, Joyce made more allusions to *The House by the Churchyard,* Irish songs, and English literature.

The result of Joyce's accumulations is a quite recognizable description and condemnation of his person and his methods as seen through the eyes of his critics that simultaneously should be read as his defense. One of the aspects of *Finnegans Wake* as a whole is indeed that it contained Joyce's answers to all attacks. Chapter I.7 is among the most obvious expressions of this concern, and most of the data that Joyce used were derived from his own life and writings and from the reactions they generated, complemented with elements from a wide range of negative prototypes for his antihero, the "still today insufficiently malestimated notesnatcher" (FW: 125.21–22) Shem the Penman.

Notes

1. Gilbert's transcription of "Egan" has been emended to "Esau."

2. See Joyce's letter to Harriet Weaver of 8 February 1924 (LI: 210) and an unpublished letter to Lily Bollach of 4 February 1924 (Stanford University M121).

3. See Bill Cadbury's essay in this volume.

4. See Mikio Fuse's essay in this volume.

5. Shem's characterization as a "nigger" may also be due to the fact that Ham fathered Cush, who, according to many biblical interpretations, is the father of certain Ethiopian tribes (*Encyclopaedia Britannica* 11, s.v. "Cush").

6. The Irish name "Seamus" ("Shemus" or "James") is an equivalent of the Hebrew "Yâkôb."

7. Joyce was born in 1882, which may account for the address in Dublin Square. In later revisions some of the more overt references were altered and camouflaged.

8. This had been one of the techniques in *Ulysses,* especially in "Oxen of the Sun," where Joyce imitated most major authors from the English literary canon.

9. Most of the litterings in Shem's lair (FW: 183–84) can be found in some form in *Ulysses.* See also, for instance, the eggshells (U: 16.275), the smut (U:

15.3053, 3249), a fallen Vesta or lucifer (U: 10.403), a hairshirt (U: 15.180), crocodiles' tears (U: 15.3218), wafers (U: 15.6, 18.621), carbon and oxygen (U: 17.132), globules (U: 9.87), and mercury (U: 15.213, 749).

10. This was cancelled on a subsequent draft and does not appear in *Finnegans Wake.*

11. This was cancelled on a subsequent draft and does not appear in *Finnegans Wake;* see U: 13.719.

12. The shop was James Thornton, fruitier and florist, 63 Grafton Street, Dublin.

13. Joseph Collins, "James Joyce's Amazing Chronicle," *New York Times Book Review and Magazine,* 28 May 1922: 6, 17.

14. Ibid., 6, emphasis mine. The first sentence was not in the reworked version of this article in Joseph Collins, *The Doctor Looks at Literature* (New York: George H. Doran Company, 1923).

15. Collins 1922, 6; see FW: 182.13 ff. Collins's *The Doctor Looks at Literature* is a collection of literary portraits with lengthy psychological interpretations, the first chapter of which is a slightly adapted version of the earlier *Ulysses* review. See also David Hayman, "Dr J. Collins Looks at J.J.: The Invention of a Shaun for I.7," *Writing Its Own Wrunes For Ever,* ed. Daniel Ferrer and Claude Jacquet (Tusson: Du Lérot, 1998), 119–50. See also Ingeborg Landuyt, "Tale Told of Shem: Some Elements at the Inception of *FW* I.7," *Geni,* 115–34.

16. Missing notebook VI.X.2, dated by Danis Rose to December 1923 (TDJJ: 26), may also have contained many interesting clues for chapter I.7.

17. See his letters to Miss Weaver of 23 December 1923 (unpublished) and of 26 February 1925: "I should be glad to hear Mr. Muir's article read to me before I send off the piece which is an indirect reply to criticisms" (LI: 114).

18. "Aramis," "The Scandal of *Ulysses,*" *Sporting Times* 34 (1 April 1922): 4, reprinted in *James Joyce: The Critical Heritage,* 2 vols., ed. Robert H. Deming (London: Routledge and Kegan Paul, 1970), 1:192–94, 192. This line was recorded on VI.B.6: 116 and appears at FW: 182.17.

19. John Middleton Murray, review of *Ulysses, Nation and Athenæum* 31 (22 April 1922): 124–25, 125, 124, 125.

20. Stephen Gwynn, "Modern Irish Literature," *Manchester Guardian,* 15 March 1923: 38–39, reprinted in Deming 1970, 1:299–301, 301.

21. Arnold Bennett, "James Joyce's *Ulysses,*" *Outlook,* 29 April 1922: 337–39, reprinted in Deming 1970, 1:219–22, 222.

22. Robert Boyle, "*Finnegans Wake,* Page 185: An Explication," *Critical Essays on James Joyce's "Finnegans Wake,"* ed. Patrick A. McCarthy (New York: G. K. Hall, 1992), 59–72, 65.

23. E. Rumph and A. Hepburn, *Nationalism and Socialism in Twentieth-Century Ireland* (Liverpool: Liverpool University Press, 1977), 71.

24. Don Gifford and Robert J. Seidman, *"Ulysses" Annotated,* 2nd ed. (Berkeley: University of California Press, 1988), 389.

25. Jean Crépieux-Jamin, *Les Éléments de l'écriture des canailles* (Paris: Flammarion, 1923). See VI.B.6: 40–55.

26. Crépieux-Jamin 1923, v.

27. Ibid., 288, emphasis mine.

28. See Danis Rose, "Kells-Dublin-Rome-Trieste-Zürich-Paris," *AFWC* 2.1 (1986): 1–13.

29. This source text was discovered by Vincent Deane.

30. The VI.B.3 note refers to the as yet unidentified "O'Gorman / Mahan" and "(LB)," or Leopold Bloom. Other notebooks used at this point were VI.B.25 and VI.B.11. Most of the items I could identify in this first draft, especially the additions, come from the first half of notebook VI.B.6.

31. *The Catholic Encyclopedia* (the 1913 edition, which Joyce owned), 7:703.

32. See S. Baring-Gould, *Legends of Old Testament Characters* (New York: Holt and Williams, 1872), 74.

33. Thomas Josephus Lamy, *Commentarium in Librum Geneseos,* vol. 1 (Mechelen: H. Dessain, 1883). Hereafter cited as CLG. The second volume of this book was in Joyce's personal library (now at Buffalo), although the notes I located come from the first.

34. Virginia Woolf, "Modern Novels," *Times Literary Supplement* 899 (10 April 1919): 189–90, reprinted in Deming 1970, 1:125–26, 125.

35. Deming 1970, 1:126.

36. Ibid., 1:193; see FW: 193.02.

37. James Douglas, "Beauty—and the Beast," *Sunday Express,* 28 May 1922: 5.

38. "Like Rousseau, Joyce derives everything from his own ego; he lives in a narrow world in which he himself is not only the poles, but the equator and the parallels of latitude and longitude" (Mary Colum, *Freeman's Journal* 123 [19 July 1922]: 452).

39. The first word of the second page 1 is "bluebook," but Joyce may have had Bollach retype and then add to a not completely filled last page of the preceding passage. The new paragraph on this page starts with "One cannot even begin to figure out how low" (BL 47474 f. 29).

40. Unpublished letter, held at Stanford University M121.

41. Joyce repeatedly mentioned the "sackful of notes" (LI: 227) he worked his way through for new additions to this passage. For the first typescript this was VI.B.14 but also VI.B.7, 2, 5, 19, 10, the first pages of VI.B.9, and probably several missing notebooks. VI.B.9 provided additional information for the second typescript. Page 154 of VI.B.9 refers to pages in the second (partially retyped) typescript.

42. Wyndham Lewis, *The Lion and the Fox: The Rôle of the Hero in the Plays of Shakespeare* (London: Grant Richards, 1927), 177.

43. Ibid., 11, 302.

44. According to Danis Rose's chronology, the missing notebook VI.D.6 was used while Joyce was revising his chapter (TDJJ: 29).

45. Charles Paschal Telesphore Chiniquy, *The Priest, the Woman and the Confessional* (London: Protestant Truth Society, n.d.). Hereafter abbreviated as PWC. For a more comprehensive discussion of this source see my article "A dive in the pool of Sodom: Joyce, the Priest, the Woman, and the Confessional," forthcoming.

46. Basil Hargrave, *Origins and Meanings of Popular Phrases & Names Including Those which Came into Use during the Great War* (London: T. Werner Laurie Ltd., 1932). This was used on VI.B.31: 86–87; see JJA 36: xv–xvi.

47. Stanley Lane-Poole, *The Speeches and Tabletalk of Mohammad* (London: Macmillan, 1882). See Roland McHugh, "Mohammad in Notebook VI.B.31," *AWN* 16.4 (August 1979): 51–58. See also VI.B.31: 44–69.

48. See Danis Rose and John O'Hanlon, "Norman Douglas' *London Street Games* Guess Where," *AFWC* 1.4 (1986): 85–92. Though an index from this book was recorded in VI.B.31, Joyce took his additions straight from the book itself.

49. The words "heretic Marcon" were taken from PWC: 125 via VI.B.31: 26.

Making Herself Tidal

Chapter I.8

PATRICK A. MCCARTHY

His voice eddying with the vowels of all rivers
came back to me . . .

—SEAMUS HEANEY, *Station Island*

We all know Anna Livia, the river-woman whose presence is implied in the "riverrun" with which *Finnegans Wake* opens and whose monologue closes the book. For over six hundred pages, however, Joyce presents Anna Livia to us almost exclusively through other characters, much as in *Ulysses* we hear what Molly Bloom has to say about herself only in the last chapter. The most extensive discussion of Anna Livia is in Book I, chapter 8, which Joyce variously designated "Anna Livia Plurabelle," "ALP," or "Δ" after its subject and her sign (or siglum). Almost certainly the most popular and well known of all of the *Wake*'s chapters, I.8 is an episode on which Joyce lavished even more than his usual generous measure of attention: he frequently calculated how much time he had spent on the chapter, noting, for example, that one important set of revisions had consumed twelve hundred hours (LIII: 164, 165, 167). Four times singled out for separate publication (more often than any other "complete" chapter),[1] recorded by the author, and translated into various languages,[2] this episode was clearly important to Joyce, who was confident of its artistic quality. In 1927 he told Harriet Shaw Weaver, "Either the end of Part I Δ is something or I am an imbecile in my judgment of language" (LI: 249), and later he declared himself "prepared to stake everything" on the revisions for the second published version (LIII: 163). I.8 has also been studied far more than most other chapters of the *Wake,* and it has the distinction of being the only chapter whose genetic history is laid out in a volume devoted to transcriptions of the various draft stages, Fred Higginson's *Anna Livia Plurabelle: The Making of a Chapter.*[3]

The popularity of this chapter may be attributed in part to its engaging and rhythmic style and its imitation of the gossipy language of two washerwomen. Like a river that expands as it flows along, eventually floods its banks, and finally disappears into the sea (or night), I.8 is an insistently fluid chapter, yet it has basic narrative, thematic, and stylistic elements that may be traced from the earliest to the latest drafts. More clearly than other chapters of the *Wake,* the genetic history of I.8 reveals the "continual embroidery upon a fixed pattern" that A. Walton Litz has argued is Joyce's typical method of composition in *Ulysses* and *Finnegans Wake.*[4]

Although it quickly developed a distinct character of its own, I.8 began as a continuation and extension of I.7, the Shem the Penman chapter. The earliest extant version of any part of the episode appears in the large copybook in which Joyce entered early drafts of chapters from Book I. Much as the first lines of I.7 were originally a continuation of I.5,[5] the opening lines of I.8 surfaced as an appendage to a preliminary draft of I.7:

> . . . your coalblack mummy is acoming, running with her tidings, skipping the weirs, ducking under bridges rapidshooting round the corners' R babbling, bubbling, chattering to herself, Anna Livia.
>
> O, tell me now about Anna Livia! I want to hear all about Anna Livia. Well you know Anna Livia. Yes of course I know Anna Livia. Tell me now. Tell me now. (BL 47471b f. 68; JJA 47: 381, JJA 48: 13; FDV: 123)

The end of *Finnegans Wake* I.7 and the beginning of I.8 (FW: 194.33–196.05) may be discerned in this draft, and one of their key characteristics is already evident: as in the final text, the "babbling, bubbling, chattering" river-woman quickly gives way to two gossips who "know Anna Livia" yet demand to hear more. The change of voices, indeed, was almost certainly why Joyce began a new chapter at this point, as it became clear that the shift in focus from sons to mother would be an extended one. Joyce helped to make the transition clearer in his second pencil draft of I.7, concluding with "gossipaceous Anna Livia" (BL 47471b f. 73; JJA 47: 391). I.8, then, is filled with gossip, as the rumormongers take up and elaborate on stories they have heard about ALP.

In a famous letter of March 1924 to Miss Weaver Joyce described the chapter in clear and simple terms: "It is a chattering dialogue across the river by two washerwomen who as night falls become a tree and a stone. The river is named Anna Liffey. [. . .] Her Pandora's box contains the ills flesh is heir to. The stream is quite brown, rich in salmon, very devious, shallow. The splitting up towards the end (seven dams) is the city abuilding. Izzy will be later Isolde (cf. Chapelizod)" (LI: 213). Joyce is referring to the earliest complete draft of the chapter,[6] composed early in 1924, fifteen years before the publication of *Finnegans Wake.* Although the first version lacks the rich verbal texture of later drafts, this description provides us with a fair entrée into some of the chapter's most important themes and narrative elements: the dialogue of the washerwomen, their transformation into tree and stone, Anna Livia's role as Pandora, and the concluding emphasis on the next generation.

The seventh chapter ends with Shem, the artist, lifting the "lifewand" to make "the dumb speak": picking up his pen to bring his characters to life or, alternately, using a magic wand to transform two inanimate objects, a tree and a stone, into the washerwomen, who serve as narrators.[7] The two washerwomen, later designated "Queer Mrs Quickenough and odd Miss Doddpebble" (FW: 620.19–20), have a lot to say—not all of it complimentary—as they wash the Earwicker laundry: "Look at the shirt of him! Look at the dirt of it!" (FW: 196.11–12). Washing Earwicker's dirty linen, they concern themselves with dirt of another kind, the scandal caused "when the old cheb went futt and did what you know. [. . .] Or whatever it was they threed to make out he thried to two in the Fiendish park" (FW: 196.06–11). The details of the infamous Phoenix Park incident are alluded to obliquely as well as other crimes both great and small: "Scorching my hand and starving my famine to make his private linen public" (FW: 196.15–16) connects him with the devastation of Ireland's land and people (and suggests exhibitionism as well), but the crime for which he was actually prosecuted, "illysus distilling" (FW: 196.21–22), combines the distillation of illegal whiskey with the "distillation" of a book like *Ulysses.*

The central subject of I.8, however, is not HCE's sins but ALP's response to them. It is appropriate that the waters of the Liffey, representing Anna Livia, are washing away the evidence of Earwicker's sins as the women speak, for (they tell us) she takes on her husband's guilt and redeems him; alternately, she is tainted with his crimes and regarded as an accomplice (at one point she is even charged with supplying him with prostitutes [FW: 200.29–30]). Later, however, she is said to have written a letter, declaring herself tired of her mate (FW: 201.05–20). The gossip digresses to her checkered past, retracing the course of the Liffey from the hills of Wicklow and alluding to her youthful affairs (FW: 203–204) before returning to a more recent sequence of events: the publication of Earwicker's guilt and his wife's revenge on his enemies. Borrowing a "mailsack" from her son Shaun the Post (the

Pandora's box Joyce referred to in his letter to Miss Weaver), Anna Livia "made herself tidal to join in the mascarete" (FW: 206.09–14). The puns here encapsulate the main events of the last part of I.8, as Anna Livia tidies up for an innocent evening party (a masquerade) that is also a deadly revenge spree (a massacre). She is of course "going out" in another sense as well: reaching the end of her course as a river, flowing out to sea, merging into the tide. This aspect of the story is suggested both by "tidal" and by the pun on French *mascaret,* "tidal wave in estuary" (McHugh).

After an extensive description of ALP (FW: 206–208) and a catalog of her presents (FW: 210–212), which also double as the items in her letter (and under her dress)—"All that and more under one crinoline envelope" (FW: 212.22–23)[8]—the washerwomen try to pick up the thread of the story, but their conversation is increasingly difficult because they are on opposite sides of the Liffey, which is wider near its mouth. It is also getting dark, and figures are hard to make out: do they see a statue of "the great Finnleader himself" (FW: 214.11) or merely "a blackburry growth or the dwyergray ass them four old codgers owns" (FW: 214.32–33)? Over the last few pages, moreover, the washerwomen are indeed transformed into tree and stone, as Joyce noted, a process that seems finally to be completed: "I feel as old as yonder elm. [. . .] I feel as heavy as yonder stone" (FW: 215.34–216.01). It is appropriate that at the end there are calls for tales of Shem and Shaun, who are also represented as the tree and stone and who underwent a similar process of transformation in I.6 at the end of "The Mookse and the Gripes" (FW: 158.25–159.05). But nothing is really static in this chapter, and the Elm (representing Shem and Mrs Quickenough) and Stone (Shaun, Miss Doddpebble) are also, as McHugh notes, names of rivers. This fact might help to account for the fluidity of their gossip; it also implies that they (and their stories) will be recirculated as surely as the waters that comprise ALP.

Although I have cited passages from the published text of *Finnegans Wake* in this summary, the same elements may be seen in every complete draft of the chapter, even though the earliest of these drafts, dating from February 1924, is well under half the length of the *Wake* version. As we shall see, Joyce's revisions of I.8 had little to do with introducing or rearranging narrative elements; rather, Joyce focused on the language of the chapter, which, like the river itself, began as a trickle and eventually reached flood stage.

The technique of elaboration through which Joyce expanded the chapter and enriched its texture may be illustrated through the evolution of the following passage, appended to the previous paragraph in Joyce's first separate but incomplete pencil draft of I.8: "But Why was she freckled? How long was her hair? O go on, go on, go on! I mean about what you know. I know well what you mean. I'm going on Where did I stop? Don't stop. Go on, go on" (BL 47471b f. 76; JJA 48: 7; Higginson: 25; FDV: 125). This passage, written in simple, common English words, contains the germ of the long *Wake* paragraph at FW: 204.21–205.15, commencing with "Drop me the sound of the findhorn's name" and concluding, "I amstel waiting. Garonne, garonne!" The preliminary draft has none of the verbal complexity of later versions, only questions about Anna Livia's freckles and hair length, repeated injunctions to continue, and the phrase "I mean about what you know," which hints at a crime that is well known but never expressed directly: you know what. Even in the earliest drafts this phrase appears in the first page of the chapter in "when the old chap did what you know" (BL 47471b f. 74; JJA 48: 3; Higginson: 23), which eventually became "when the old cheb went futt and did what you know" (FW: 196.06–7).

In the first complete pencil draft of the chapter the original passage is set off as a separate paragraph and has doubled in length: "Tell me the sound of the shorthorn's name and tell me why the something was she freckled as well and tell me too how long was her hair or was it only a wig she wore? Are you in this game or are you not? O go on, go on, go on! I mean about what you know. I know well what you mean. I'm going on. Where did I stop. Don't stop. Continuation! You're not there yet. Go on, go on!" (BL 47471b f. 84; JJA 48: 25; Higginson: 31).[9] Nothing from the previous pencil draft has been lost in this draft: freckles, hair, "what you know," "Don't stop," "Go on" are all still prominently featured here. Instead, the changes are almost entirely additions: the opening demand to "Tell me the sound of the shorthorn's name," which picks up on the preceding description of a time in Anna Livia's youth when she slipped past her sleeping nurse "and wriggled under a fallow cow"; the possibility that Anna Livia wore a wig; the impatient "Are you in this game or are you not?"; and the command, "Continuation! You're not there yet."

The fair copy that Joyce made from this revised draft contains a marginal note for an insertion directly after "I know well what you mean": "What am I rinsing now and I'll thank you? Is it a pinny or is it a surplice? Rinse it out and run along with you" (BL 47474 f. 120; JJA 48: 45). In the next stage, the first typescript of I.8, the addition has expanded greatly:

> What am I rinsing now and I'll thank you? Is it a pinny or is it a surplice? Arrah, where's your nose? And where's the starch? That's not the benediction

> smell. I can tell from here by the *eau de Cologne* and the scent of her moisture they're Mrs Magrath's. And you ought to have aired them. They've just come off her. Creases of silk they are, not crimps of lawn. The only pair with frills in all the land. So they are. Well, well! And there is her maiden letters too. Ell and a quay in scarlet thread. And an ex after to show they're not Laura Kelly's. O, may the devil twist your safety pin! Now who has been tearing the leg of her drawers on her? Which leg is it? The one with the bells on it. Rinse them out and run along with you! (BL 47474 f. 130; JJA 48: 77; Higginson: 40)

The remainder of the paragraph is essentially unchanged from the pencil draft and the fair copy. The insertion is typical of those in I.8 for two reasons: because it is mainly a digression and because the subjects of the digression, women's scents and women's clothing, are thematically significant. Note too that Mrs. Magrath, soon to be known as Lilith (or Lily) Kinsella (FW: 205.10–11), has been introduced, along with her embroidered initials, *LK*, followed by an *X* "to show they're not Laura Kelly's." There are few emendations of individual words at this stage, the emphasis being on the addition of new material.

In the next stage of composition—a series of typescripts and an abandoned set of galleys for the *Calendar of Modern Letters*—Joyce revised several words to reinforce the chapter's recurrent emphasis on the river's course. The repeated injunction to "tell" at the beginning of the paragraph becomes "Drop me the sound. [. . .] And drip me why. [. . .] And trickle me through" as Joyce opts for a variety of verbs with fluid associations (BL 47474 f. 192; JJA 48: 142; Higginson: 52).[10] The passage now begins with a drop, a drip, a trickle, once again suggesting the river's modest beginnings. "Are you in this game" becomes the more appropriate "Are you in the swim," and the ejaculation "Arrah" becomes "Arran," the name of a Dublin quay,[11] with the transformation of "not crimps of lawn" into "not crampton lawn" hinting at another quay. That Joyce was already thinking of quays is suggested by the phrase "Ell and a quay in scarlet thread" in the previous typescript, which here becomes "Ellis on quay in scarlet thread," a reference to Ellis Quay that would remain unchanged into the published *Wake* (FW: 205.07–8); another Dublin quay, Aston, appears near the end of the paragraph in "Rinse them out and aston along with you!" The frequency of quay references at this stage is somewhat surprising because most of the river names that dominate the final text were added later, but toward the end of the passage one obvious river name makes its appearance with the emendation of "Go on, go on!" to "Garonne, garonne!"

In 1927 Joyce marked further additions on the copy of the *Navire d'argent* text that he sent to the printer for the version published in *transition* (Yale 6.1 f. 66; JJA 48: 179). After "a wig she wore" Joyce inserted "And whitside did they droop their glows in their florry, aback to wist or affront to sea?"; after "not crampton lawn" he added "Through her catchment ring she freed them easy, with her hips' hurrahs for her knees' dontelleries"; after "scarlet thread," "Linked for the world on a flushcoloured field"; and after "your safety pin," "You child of Mammon, Kinsella's Lilith." Joyce also made changes on the galley and page proofs for *transition* (BL 47474 f. 216, 235; JJA 48: 196, 210; Higginson: 67), with the result that the passage is further enriched by river references: "drip me why in the something was she freckled" is changed to the more appropriate "drip me why in the flenders [Flinders river] was she frickled," for example, and "the scent of her moisture" becomes the only apparently redundant "scent of her oder." The shorthorn cow has now been submerged under the name of a river, Findhorn, while of the twenty-nine river names that Louis O. Mink spots in the final version of this passage, twenty—including Fleury, Back, Loth, Rance, Colo, Magra, Aird, Baptiste, Old, Welland, Nuble, Annan, Exe, and Wiske—are evident at this stage.[12]

Other additions to the *transition* text include "Baptiste me, father, for she has sinned!" (BL 47474 f. 235; JJA 48: 210): the washerwomen's adaptation of "Bless me, father, for I have sinned" converts an apparent confession into an accusation, much as Anna Livia's own defense of Earwicker often takes the form of an indictment. The allusion to baptism, an especially important sacrament in I.8, is appropriate, since it involves the use of water to wash away sins, which is what the women are supposedly doing as they gossip. Another addition, "You'd like the coifs and guimpes, snouty, and me to do the greasy jub on old Veronica's wiper" (Yale 7.7 f. 25; JJA 48: 222), reinforces the conflict between the two gossips while introducing other articles of clothing: *coif* is a term used for several forms of caps and headdresses, while French *guimpe* may signify a nun's wimple, a high-necked sleeveless blouse, or a tucker. One of the washers apparently resents having to wash a snotty, greasy old handkerchief ("Veronica's wiper"), while the other takes on the easier and perhaps less disgusting chore of cleaning coifs and guimpes. The additions to the passage abound in religious overtones, and the fact that baptism involves pouring water over the head while coifs and guimpes are forms of head covering suggests the process of association through which Joyce often developed his drafts.

When Joyce read galleys for the 1928 Crosby Gaige edition of *Anna Livia*

Plurabelle he added two brief exclamations—"Rother!" and "I declare!"—to punctuate the dialogue at this point (see FW: 204.28, 205.03). A more substantial addition to this passage, which itself increased in stages on different sets of galleys, was inserted directly after "Welland well!": "If tomorrow keeps fine who'll come tripping to sightsee? How'll? Ask me next what I haven't got! The Belvedarean exhibitioners. In their sculling caps and oarsclub colours. What hoo, they band! And what hoa, they buck!" (Yale 7.2 f. D20, 7.1 f. D20, 7.4 f. D20; JJA 48: 290, 304, 320; Higginson: 86). The dialogue has been expanded to include speculation on tomorrow's weather and possible sightseers, including schoolboys from Belvedere who have won examination prizes and are on the crew team; typically, their uniforms are introduced, since the speakers are constantly concerned with the clothing they might be asked to wash. The addition nicely echoes "who'll" and "How'll" against "What hoo, they band!" and "what hoa, they buck!" using a rather suggestive song title, "What Ho, She Bumps!" to set up the band/buck alternatives of pulling together and pulling apart.[13] These echoes may be heard again near the end of the chapter: "He had buckgoat paps on him, soft ones for orphans. Ho, Lord! Twins of his bosom. Lord save us! And ho! Hey? What all men. Hot? His tittering daughters of. Whawk?" (FW: 215.27–30).

By the time *Finnegans Wake* appeared in 1939 the passage in question was ten times its original length. Joyce had made virtually all of the changes in the passage by 1928: the 1930 Faber and Faber text of this excerpt is identical with that of the Crosby Gaige edition, and subsequent changes—either marked on a copy of the Faber text that was used to set type for *Finnegans Wake* or on the proofs for the *Wake*—consist of a few minor changes in spelling and punctuation, two rewordings ("cruisery caps" for "sculling caps" and "Laura Keown's" for "Laura Kehoe's," which had originally been "Laura Kelly's"), and two insertions. On the Faber text Joyce marked "I amstel waiting" for insertion before "Garonne, garonne!" (BL 47475 f. 83; JJA 48: 354), thereby juxtaposing a Dutch river, the Amstel, against a French one. At this stage Joyce's additions are written in the double language with which he had made himself familiar, so that the phrase "am still waiting" does not appear as such in any stage but is implicit in the reference to the Amstel, which may contrast the still waters of the Amstel with those of the more exuberant Garonne. In any event, the stop-and-go pattern of the excerpt (and the chapter generally) is enhanced by this contrast between waiting and continuing.

In the second and third sets of *Finnegans Wake* galleys Joyce expanded the opening sentence of this passage from "Drop me the sound of the findhorn's name" to "Drop me the sound of the findhorn's name, Mtu or Mti, sombogger was wisness" (BL 47476a fs. 266v, 267, 47476b fs. 416v, 417; JJA 49: 552, 553, JJA 50: 260–61). The last part of this insertion, with its implication that Earwicker's guilt was witnessed by some bugger, is easy enough to follow, but the possibility that either HCE or the witness was named Mtu or Mti is harder to account for unless we know that these are Kiswahili words for "man" and "tree." The final text of I.8 incorporates so many references to Africa that Sheldon Brivic argues that the chapter "seems to focus on Africa," with "an especially high concentration of Kiswahili words . . . between pages 198 and 209."[14] The same galley pages marked for insertion of "Mtu or Mti, sombogger was wisness" also direct the printer to insert a passage farther up the same page (now at FW: 204.03–4): "That was kissuahealing with bantur for balm!" Like these passages, the other Kiswahili words in I.8 are all late additions to the text: of the thirty-one Kiswahili puns noted by McHugh from 198.11 through 209.12, not one appeared in any form in the edition of *Anna Livia Plurabelle* published in 1930 by Faber and Faber.[15] Joyce introduced Kiswahili elements not by modifying words already in the text but by adding new phrases or even complete sentences to the Faber text, often clustering several Kiswahili words together. In this last stage of revision Joyce made few alterations in words already in the text, apart from an occasional minor change like the substitution of "drawars" for "drawers" at FW: 205.12, perhaps to reinforce the element of sexual conflict. He added new material to serve a specific purpose, as when the introduction of Kiswahili terms universalizes the chapter's themes and reinforces Anna Livia's associations with Africa.

The pattern of revision illustrated by the history of this paragraph is typical of I.8 generally. Joyce almost never relocated material in revising I.8, but he frequently inserted new material and either substituted one word or phrase for another or altered a spelling, as when "O go on, go on, go on!"—a simple repetition of the phrase—was changed to "O go in, go on, go an!" (FW: 204.27), and the final "Go on, go on!" became "Garonne, garonne!" (FW: 205.15). The repetition or echoing of phrases seen here is one of the most prominent features of I.8, suggesting a dialogue between two women who have trouble hearing each other and seek confirmation of what they have heard by repeating it; the strategy might also have been suggested by the example of musical repetition. In early versions of I.8 the repetition is often exact, but in later versions Joyce introduced more variety in the course of repeating a sound: an instance of the technique of "The seim anew" (FW: 215.23) or varied repetition that is basic to Joyce's technique throughout *Finnegans Wake*. Aside from examples of exact repetition that survive into the final text, such as "all about Anna Livia" (FW: 196.02–4), the opening page of I.8 includes striking examples of varied repetition: "Tell me all. Tell me now"; "butt [. . .] bend"; "threed to make out [. . .] thried to two"; "Look at the shirt of him! Look at the dirt of it!"; "steeping and stuping"; "Scorching my hand and starving my famine"; "wrists [. . .] wrusty"; "the dneepers of wet and the gangres of sin"; "a tail at all"; "Minxing marrage and making loof."

As the chapter proceeds the repetition often implies miscommunication. Ellmann traces "Fieluhr? Filou!" (FW: 213.14) to a story Joyce heard from Ottocaro Weiss in which a Frenchman on one side of the Rhine shouted "Filou!" (scoundrel, crook) at a German on the other side; the German, thinking he had heard "Wieviel Uhr?" (What time is it?), responded that it was 6:30—"Halber sechse" (JJII: 465 n.). Near the end Joyce openly alludes to the problem of translating from one language to another as the washerwomen refer sardonically to the pretensions of linguistic scholars: "Latin me that, my trinity scholard, out of eure sanscreed into oure eryan!" (FW: 215.25–26). The attempt to translate from "eure sanscreed into oure eryan" seems to place Sanskrit and Gaelic—the ancient languages of India and Ireland or Erin—in opposition, but the pun on Erin and Aryan destabilizes the opposition, since Sanskrit is one of the Aryan or Indo-Iranian languages; the pernicious and historically inaccurate use of "Aryan" to mean "Nordic" in Nazi propaganda may also be satirized in this passage, since the idea of a "pure" ("eure") race is as absurd as that of a language uncontaminated by foreign elements. Further meanings of "eure sanscreed" may be derived from the fact that the Eure is a French river and that "sanscreed," in addition to punning on "sunscreen," combines French *sans* (without) and English *screed,* a word whose many meanings include "a long roll or list; a lengthy discourse or harangue; a gossiping letter or piece of writing" (*OED*). Figuratively, at the end of I.8 we are "sanscreed" because the gossips' words are washed away, having been, like Keats's name, writ in water.

The chapter concludes with the washerwomen having increasing difficulty hearing one another or even finishing a sentence:

> Can't hear with the waters of. The chittering waters of. Flittering bats, fieldmice bawk talk. Ho! Are you not gone ahome? What Thom Malone? Can't hear with bawk of bats, all thim liffeying waters of. Ho, talk save us! My foos won't moos. I feel as old as yonder elm. A tale told of Shaun or Shem? All

> Livia's daughtersons. Dark hawks hear us. Night! Night! My ho head halls. I feel as heavy as yonder stone. Tell me of John or Shaun? Who were Shem and Shaun the living sons or daughters of? Night now! Tell me, tell me, tell me, elm! Night night! Telmetale of stem or stone. Beside the rivering waters of, hitherandthithering waters of. Night! (FW: 215.31–216.05)

This passage illustrates two striking stylistic features of the end of I.8. One is repetition that may derive from an attempt to restate what someone half hears and misunderstands, as when one woman asks if the other has not gone home, and the other thinks she has heard a question about Tom Malone, or when "A tale told of Shaun or Shem?" seems to be an attempt to understand "I feel as old as yonder elm." Another characteristic is fragmentation or inconclusiveness: several sentences end incompletely, with "waters of," and another—perhaps as a result of misunderstanding one of these—ends with "daughters of." Then again, which came first, the waters (mother) or the daughters? The previous paragraph concludes, "His tittering daughters of. Whawk?" and this emphasis on the daughters at the chapter's end may be traced to the earliest draft (BL 47471b fs. 89–90; JJA 48: 35–36; Higginson: 34–35; FDV: 128). Indeed, virtually all the important stylistic features of the conclusion are present in the first draft (February 1924), which concludes, "Nighty night! Tell me a tale of stone. Beside the rivering waters of, hither and thither waters of. Night!"

It is perhaps inevitable that as darkness falls and the women have trouble seeing (as well as hearing), one form would merge into another. One aspect of this blending of form is that the confusion of sexual identity that we find throughout the *Wake* is especially pronounced here. Earwicker, we are told, "had buckgoat paps on him, soft ones for orphans," but the orphans are at once exchanged for "Twins of his bosom"; these twins, the sons Shem and Shaun, are in turn converted into the "tittering daughters" who become indistinguishable from the "chittering waters" of the final paragraph. There, Shaun and Shem are "Livia's daughtersons" or, more elaborately, "the living sons or daughters of." This element of hermaphroditism is a prominent aspect of the conclusion from the earliest drafts on: apart from the first draft, in which Joyce originally wrote "sons and daughters" before changing "and" to "or," these daughter/son phrases appear in precisely the same terms in every draft of the passage.

The chapter's ending involves two forms of confusion: a blurring of distinctions and a tendency toward fragmentation or incompleteness. These two aspects of the conclusion may also be found throughout the chapter, for example, in the "narrative" itself. The chapter attempts to tell us "all about Anna Livia," yet the totalizing impulse implied by this phrase leads inevitably to a breakdown of narrative, to fragmentation, in part because one story constantly runs into another as tidiness gives way to tidalness.[16] David Hayman perceptively remarks that the first half of the chapter "is richly narrative," while the second half, in which Anna Livia delivers presents from her Pandora's box, has scant narrative content and is "little more than a simple list." Even the first part, he notes, is not a single story but "an agglomeration of possible narratives clustered beneath the dirty apron of the washerwomen's account, an accumulation of riverness, of flowing and overflowing liquid essence."[17] Margot Norris makes much the same point, observing that "the gossip of the washerwomen is never allowed to form a coherent story . . . because the red-haired woman they talk about keeps dissolving into the river."[18] Things fall apart; the center cannot hold—and all of this amounts to an excess of signification, an overflowing that Joyce associates with women and rivers.

As Eun Kyung Chun has noted, two dominant features of the gossip in I.8 are digression and a "repetitive return to the point of origin," a return that is frustrated because Joyce collapses "the distinction between digression and center."[19] Gossip feeds on itself, ultimately erasing all traces of its origins in a stream of talk that resists efforts to restrict it to a core of meaning. The movement outward from a single utterance—a request for the truth about Anna Livia—is symbolized by the chapter's opening, which suggests the delta (Δ) that represents Anna Livia:

> O
> tell me all about
> Anna Livia! I want to hear all
> about Anna Livia. Well, you know Anna Livia? Yes, of course, we all know
> Anna Livia. Tell me all. Tell me now. You'll die when you hear. (FW: 196.01–6)

Ironically, the river-chapter begins with a delta, which we would expect to find at its end, where the river "dies." Yet the chapter's opening includes a premonition of death: "You'll die when you hear"; moreover, the idea of the circular return is encapsulated in the "O" with which the chapter opens. The expansion of the text here, which Brivic likens to the gradual broadening of the river,[20] is one of the most striking typographic features of the *Wake* and one of the simplest but most significant changes Joyce made in the text. The triangular block of text is missing from Joyce's manuscripts and typescripts for I.8 and does not appear in the *Navire d'argent* or *transition* versions. A version of the delta first appears in the 1928 Crosby Gaige edition, which opens with a very large "O" centered on the first line, followed by "tell me all about" centered on the second line before reverting to standard margins; the Faber and *Finnegans Wake* versions both take this typographic experiment one line further. Perhaps Joyce needed to see the chapter in print in order to conceive of using so distinctive a typographic arrangement for the opening of his text.[21]

The text emerges through the "O," suggesting birth through the vagina as well as the emanation of words from the mouth.[22] Likewise, Joyce's method of revision involves an overflowing or continual expansion of text that may be seen in his scribbled-on manuscripts, typescripts, galley proofs, and even the copies of one printed edition that would provide a starting point for the production of the next stage. Joyce seems to have set out to demonstrate the impossibility of containing his story, or stories, within preset margins or banks, so that the addition of new matter typically demonstrates a principle already inherent in the text. The catalog of Anna Livia's presents (FW: 210.06–212.19), for example, increased at virtually every stage, with the final text coming to roughly four times the length of the original 1924 pencil draft (BL 47471b fs. 86v–88; JJA 48: 30–33; Higginson: 33–34; FDV: 127). Still, the beginning and end of this catalog were basically set from the first draft on, changes in those parts being largely a matter of stylistic embellishment. As with the chapter as a whole, the additions to this "pison plague" (FW: 212.24) of dubious gifts come in the middle: like *Finnegans Wake,* Joyce's catalogs are in theory infinitely expandable, all-inclusive, yet they tend to have a shape that is recognizable from one draft to the next.

Perhaps the most famous and controversial aspect of the chapter is its inclusion of references to several hundred rivers. Noting both Padraic Colum's defense of the river names as part of Joyce's attempt to capture the flowing, rhythmic character of the river and Edmund Wilson's complaint that they do not make the chapter "any more riverlike,"[23] Litz sides with Wilson, calling Joyce's inclusion of river names "almost an obsession" and contending that "no one can deny that many of the original and important aspects of *Anna Livia Plurabelle* are buried under river-names and allusions added in the last stages of revision." In his opinion Joyce overrevised his chapter, and it is only the vocal quality of the voices in the text, when read aloud, that makes the chapter "an artistic success."[24] Yet relatively few of the river names pose any significant hindrance to understanding. More often, they give readers the simultaneous impression of strangeness and familiarity: there is perhaps an intellectual pleasure to be derived from recognizing allusions to the rivers Cheb and Futa in "when the old cheb went futt and did what you know" (FW: 196.06–7), but this pleasure is secondary to our sense that some mysterious crime by the old chap has been summarized by the succinct expression "went futt [fizzled] and did what you know." Perhaps the recognition of references to the Yssel and Limmat is somewhat more important in our understanding of "Yssel that the limmat?" (FW: 198.13), but even without knowing the names of these rivers most readers who are attracted to the linguistic strangeness and luxuriance of *Finnegans Wake* would take pleasure in this odd way of asking "Isn't that the limit?" In any event, the defense of *Finnegans Wake* on the grounds that its style is imitative or expressive has its own limmats, and it is probably more useful to try to understand the text we are faced with than to wish for a simplified version that would call for less work on the part of readers.

Wilson's essay, published in the *New Republic* in 1939, was reprinted in *The Wound and the Bow* (1947). To the later version Wilson added a long note that amended his first impression of *Finnegans Wake* with the observation that, like *Ulysses,* the *Wake* "gets better the more you go back to it."[25] Wilson seems to have regarded the book's ability to grow on its readers not as an especially desirable quality but as a form of compensation for Joyce's lack of rapport with his audience. Yet the chapter's power proved irresistible to Wilson, who pronounced it one of the book's "wholly successful" episodes, much as Litz would judge it to be "an artistic success."[26] More than fifty years after Wilson's note about the way Joyce's books "gradually build themselves up for us as we return to them and think about them," many readers have experienced the way repeated readings of *Finnegans Wake* yield new insights and pleasures while frustrating the search for core meanings and for the realistic plot that Wilson hoped to uncover at the book's heart. Readers who return to the book find pleasure in gaining new knowledge of individual elements and their relation to one another; repeated readings also lead to a pleasurable sense of familiarity with the ryhthms of its language. Still, much of the attraction of *Finnegans Wake* lies in its irreducible strangeness and particularly in the rich, complex, comic language of this enduring book. The study of Joyce's notes and manuscripts may clarify the process through which a passage grew, often shedding light on meanings that likely would remain hidden if we had access only to the final published text. For me, however, an even more important consequence of genetic criticism is that it gives us insights into the book's design and enhances our appreciation of Joyce's artistry in this "letter to last a lifetime for Maggi beyond by the ashpit" (FW: 211.22).

Notes

For sage advice on this essay while it was a work in progress I am indebted to Luca Crispi, Catrin Siedenbiedel, Wim Van Mierlo, and especially Sam Slote.

1. James Joyce, "From Work in Progress," *Le Navire d'argent* 1 (October 1925): 59–74; James Joyce, "Continuation of Work in Progress," *transition*, no. 8 (November 1927): 17–35; *Anna Livia Plurabelle* (New York: Crosby Gaige, 1928); *Anna Livia Plurabelle* (London: Faber and Faber, 1930). Joyce planned to publish the earliest of these versions in the *Calendar of Modern Letters*, but when the *Calendar*'s printers attempted to censor passages they found offensive and refused to complete the galleys, Joyce sent the episode to *Le Navire d'argent* (JJII: 574). On the draft and publication history of I.8 see Fred H. Higginson, *Anna Livia Plurabelle: The Making of a Chapter* (Minneapolis: University of Minnesota Press, 1960), 16–19, hereafter cited as Higginson; A. Walton Litz, *The Art of James Joyce* (London: Oxford University Press, 1961), 100–114, 118–19 n. 65, 145–47; David Hayman, "Draft Catalogue," FDV: 302–4; JJA 48: vii–xv; JJII: 574, 602–3, 794–96; and Claude Jacquet, "Aspects de la genèse de *Finnegans Wake:* Anna Livia Plurabelle ou les métamorphoses du texte," *Genèse de Babel: Joyce et la création*, ed. Claude Jacquet (Paris: CNRS, 1985), 93–154.

2. Karen Lawrence's *Transcultural Joyce* (Cambridge: Cambridge University Press, 1998) includes essays on the French, German, Italian, Romanian, and Spanish translations: Daniel Ferrer and Jacques Aubert, "Anna Livia's French Bifurcations" (179–86); Fritz Senn, "ALP Deutsch: 'ob überhaupt möglich?'" (187–92); Rosa Maria Bollettieri Bosinelli, "Anna Livia's Italian Sister" (193–98); Laurent Milesi, "ALP in Roumanian (with some notes on Roumanian in *Finnegans Wake* and in the notebooks)" (199–207); Francisco García Tortosa, "The Spanish Translation of *Anna Livia Plurabelle*" (208–12).

3. Higginson divides the composition of I.8 into six basic stages, which he designates Texts A–F. The number of draft stages listed in David Hayman's FDV "Draft Catalogue" and in the JJA is far more extensive: Hayman lists twenty stages, including proofs for the *Wake;* the JJA lists seventeen main stages—not including *Wake* galleys—plus various revisions, insertions, late additions, extradraft material, and the like. One reason for the discrepancy is that Higginson omits some of the later draft stages altogether; another is that some of his draft stages are composites. For example, Higginson describes Text D as "a composite of a second typescript . . . a third typescript . . . and a partial set of galleys for the *Calendar*" (Higginson: 17). Higginson's text consists of reliable transcriptions that are far

easier to read than Joyce's manuscripts, and it may be available to readers who do not have access to JJA volumes; however, his conflation of draft stages makes it necessary to consult the JJA facsimiles for more detailed evidence. Whenever possible, I have referred both to the JJA and to Higginson. I have simplified all transcriptions.

4. Litz 1961, 89.

5. I.5, I.7, and I.8 were drafted one after another in relatively short order; Joyce conceived I.6 later. The emergence of I.7 from the ending of I.5 may be seen in the draft reading:

> [R]eluctantly the theory of the jabbering ape from Oxford was shortly dropped and the place usurped by that odious and even today insufficiently despised notetaker Shem the penman.
>
> Shem is as short for Shemus as Jim is jokey for Jacob. Originally of respectable connections his back life simply won't stand being written about. (BL 47471b f. 49v; JJA 47: 330; FW: 125.19–23, 169.01–8)

On the genesis of I.5 and I.7 see the essays by Mikio Fuse and Ingeborg Landuyt in this volume as well as Sam Slote, "Imposture Book through the Ages," *Geni,* 97–114, and Ingeborg Landuyt, "Tale Told of Shem: Some Elements at the Inception of *FW* I.7," *Geni,* 115–34.

6. Apart from the brief passage attached to the draft of I.7 there was one earlier partial draft of I.8, which Higginson designates Text A (BL 47471b fs. 74–78; JJA 48: 3–11; Higginson: 23–27). Since that draft does not include the list of items in Anna Livia's mailbag ("her Pandora's box"), the reference to Earwicker's "seven dams" (cf. FW: 215.15 ff.), or the metamorphosis into tree and stone, Joyce's description refers either to what Higginson calls Text B (BL 47471b fs. 78v–90; JJA 48: 14–36; Higginson: 28–35) or, as Litz (1961, 102) believes, to the fair copy made from this pencil draft (BL 47474 fs. 107–23; JJA 48: 40–51).

7. Joyce first added the phrase "He lifts the lifewand and the dumb speak" to the pages of the *This Quarter* "Extract from Work in Progress" (Autumn–Winter 1925–26) that were used to set type for the version of I.7 published in *transition,* no. 8 (October 1927); the "Quoiquoiquoiquoiquoiquoiquoiq!" with which I.7 concludes was added in 1936 to a set of *transition* pages used to set the text of I.7 for *Finnegans Wake* (BL 47474 f. 82; 47475 162v; JJA 47: 481, 550).

8. The phrase "crinoline envelope" first appeared as a handwritten addition to the second complete typescript of I.8 (BL 47474 f. 164; JJA 48: 95), dating to mid-1925, by which time Joyce had developed the extended analogy between envelopes and women's clothing in I.5.

9. Joyce originally wrote, "Tell me the name of the cow," later emending "name" to "sound" and changing "cow" to "shorthorn's name" (BL 47471b f. 84; JJA 48: 25; Higginson: 103 nn. 12, 13).

10. At this stage Joyce made two sets of emendations on different typescripts.

I am citing a duplicate typescript on which Sylvia Beach entered both sets of Joyce's corrections.

11. This emendation first appears in the crossed-out phrase "^{r}Arran (Arrah)" in notebook VI.B.8: 4 along with references to other Dublin quays: Sir John Rogerson's Quay ("^{r}Rogerson Crusoe" [cf. FW: 211.16]), Usher's Island ("^{r}ushered island" [cf. FW: 206.35]), "^{r}Wellington" Quay (cf. FW: 203.07), Aston's Quay (cf. FW: 205.13), Burgh Quay, and Wood Quay (cf. FW: 200.02). The last three items are not crossed out.

12. Louis O. Mink, *A "Finnegans Wake" Gazetteer* (Bloomington: Indiana University Press, 1978), 66–67. The exact mechanism through which Joyce added the names of rivers is still unclear: although the Buffalo notebooks contain many river names (e.g., "Thames," which is listed and crossed out on sequential pages, VI.B.9: 86–87), the surviving notebooks contain no large cluster of river names intended for inclusion in I.8. (Joyce used notebooks to compile information on cities for "Haveth Childers Everywhere"; see Jean-Michel Rabaté's essay in this volume.) Even so, river names and associated terms are scattered throughout notebook VI.B.1; for example, pages 31–35 contain numerous terms associated with the Nile, and notes on pages 88 and 89 include "Miss Sewery" and "Mrs Seepy," terms for the Missouri and Mississippi that did not find their way into the *Wake.* Joyce derived the notes on the Nile and various other rivers from Léon Metchnikoff, *La Civilisation et les grands fleuves historiques* (Paris: Hachette, 1889); see Ingeborg Landuyt and Geert Lernout, "Joyce's Sources: *Les grands fleuves historiques,*" *JSA* 6 (1995): 99–138, esp. 108–9 and 121–26.

13. In the "Circe" episode of *Ulysses* Virag refers to "What Ho, She Bumps!" in a sexually suggestive context (U: 15.2345). Zack Bowen's commentary and the excerpts he quotes make clear the relevance of this song to the *Wake* passage: in the song boys onshore watch two young ladies rowing a boat in rough waters, take delight at their bumping up and down, and repeatedly shout, "What ho, she bumps!" See Zack Bowen, *Musical Allusions in the Works of James Joyce: Early Poetry through "Ulysses"* (Albany: State University of New York Press, 1974), 278–79.

14. Sheldon Brivic, *Joyce's Waking Women: An Introduction to "Finnegans Wake"* (Madison: University of Wisconsin Press, 1995), 61; on the African theme generally see 54–67.

15. Higginson's textual appendix (99–101) lists all changes made between the Faber and Faber edition of *Anna Livia Plurabelle* and *Finnegans Wake.* A striking number of these passages include Kiswahili words and seem to have been inserted in the text to strengthen the chapter's African theme. These were first discovered by Philipp Wolff in 1962; see "Kiswahili Words in *Finnegans Wake,*" *AWN* o.s. 8 (December 1962): 2–4. Jack Dalton subsequently noted that all of the Kiswahili in I.8 was added to a single set of galleys ("Re 'Kiswahili Words in *Finnegans Wake,*'" *AWN* o.s. 12 [April 1963]: 6–12, 10; see also Jack P. Dalton, "Kiswahili Words in *Finnegans Wake,*" *A Wake Digest,* ed. Clive Hart and Fritz Senn [Sydney:

Sydney University Press, 1968], 43–47). This was the second set of galleys for Book I (BL 47476a fs. 261–75; JJA 49: 541–64), but the printer did not make changes in I.8 from this set, so Joyce reentered all of the corrections on the third set (BL 47476b fs. 411–25; JJA 50: 249–72). Joyce derived these passages from a list of Kiswahili words that he entered in the notebook that Danis Rose has edited (VI.B.46: 117–18; Danis Rose, *James Joyce's "The Index Manuscript": "Finnegans Wake" Holograph Workbook VI.B.46* [Colchester: A Wake Newslitter Press, 1978], 281–82). See also Jacquet 1985, 152 n. 67.

16. I have dealt with aspects of this issue in my essay "Totality and Fragmentation in Lowry and Joyce," *A Darkness that Murmured: Essays on Malcolm Lowry and the Twentieth Century,* ed. Frederick Asals and Paul Tiessen (Toronto: University of Toronto Press, 2000), 173–87, and in "Attempts at Narration in *Finnegans Wake,*" *Genetic Joyce Studies* 5 (Spring 2005).

17. David Hayman, "The Manystorytold of the *Wake:* How Narrative Was Made to Inform the Non-Narrativity of the Night," *JSA* 8 (1997): 81–114, 97.

18. Margot Norris, "*Finnegans Wake,*" *The Cambridge Companion to James Joyce,* ed. Derek Attridge (Cambridge: Cambridge University Press, 1990), 167.

19. Eun Kyung Chun, "The Intertexts of (Hi)story in James Joyce's *Finnegans Wake:* Paradoxical Textuality and Infinite Variations on 'The seim anew,'" Ph.D. dissertation, University of Wisconsin–Milwaukee, 1991.

20. Brivic 1995, 35.

21. Much the same thing happened during the composition of the "Aeolus" episode of *Ulysses:* one of its most memorable features is that the text is broken up by section headings that resemble newspaper headlines, yet these headings were not part of the chapter as it appeared in the *Little Review.*

22. In notebook VI.B.1: 65 Joyce wrote, "delta = pubic Δ." See also the obviously vaginal delta in the geometry lesson of II.2 (FW: 293).

23. Edmund Wilson, *The Wound and the Bow: Seven Studies in Literature* (New York: Oxford University Press, 1947), 263.

24. Litz 1961, 112–14.

25. Wilson 1947, 266.

26. Ibid., 268; Litz 1961, 113–14.

Blanks for When Words Gone

Chapter II.1

SAM SLOTE

It might be fair to say that in 1922, when Joyce began the jottings that would build, either directly or indirectly, into *Finnegans Wake,* he lacked a firm grasp on the beast he was unleashing. By 1926 his years of chaotic travails had at least produced a template of sorts: Books I and III had reached a relatively stable form, and he was beginning to consider the nature of the intermediary Book II. On 21 May 1926, with some confidence, he wrote to Harriet Weaver: "I have the book now fairly well planned out in my head. I am as yet uncertain whether I shall start on the twilight games of ⊏, Λ and ⊣ which will follow immediately after Δ or on K's orisons, to follow Λd" (LI: 241). Three weeks later he announced that the sequel to Δ would not just be a single chapter concerning the twilight games but rather an entire suite of chapters: "Between the close of Δ at nightfall and Λa there are three or four other episodes, the children's games, night studies, a scene in the 'public' and a 'lights out in the village'" (LI: 241). Here is sketched the broad outline of what eventually became Book II, a book that was written to complement and augment a pattern that had only recently begun to take shape (in Joyce's mind, if nowhere else). At this time Joyce drew up for himself a plan of the contours of Book II in a telegraphic style using the sigla (by then well developed) as markers:

> ? ~~A Blindman's Buff. ⊏ b~~
> Δ night!
> Driftwood on Δ. Trunkles. Contredanse. Hornies & Robbers. T devil ⊏. ⊥ angel Λ. ⊥ prisoner. The guess. (Pascal). Tug of love. ⊥ falls. /⊏ hide.

ᗰ beholds. ○ chuchotant. Δ picks up. Croon
Nascerà un melo. ᗰ∇ ab. ▭ & ○
round dance. Mulberry Bush. ~~Albion.~~ Coln
Maillard. ⊏ blindfold. ⊥Δ. X vident,
ᗰ all in!

———

Interior of hotel. O
Paschal lambtable ᗰ fights Δ (formerly)
Studies ⊏Λ⊣
⊥ tells story in bed to ⊏ (BL 47482a f. 2; JJA 51: 3, slightly simplified)

Beginning with the closing line of I.8, Joyce formulated a *précis* of Book II, with II.1 receiving the most emphasis. The still very much inchoate II.2–4 received only four lines in toto. Once ALP's night has fallen the twilight games begin. Already the importance of traditional children's games is established here with the whimsical mention of Cops and Robbers ("Horny" is English slang for policeman), Mulberry Bush, Tug of Love (i.e., Tug o' War), and Angels and Devils. Notable in this preliminary sketch is the presence of four rare sigla: ᗰ∇, ⊥Δ, ▭, and ⊏Λ⊣. Danis Rose plausibly suggests that ⊏Λ⊣ is an amalgamation of the sigla for Shem (⊏), Shaun (Λ), and Issy (⊣) (TDJJ: 111). The siglum ⊥Δ appears to be a combination of the sigla for Isolde (⊥) and ALP (Δ). The morphology of ᗰ∇ suggests that it is an inverted Δ superimposed over an ᗰ—perhaps as an indication of HCE and ALP engaging in copulation, as Wim Van Mierlo has suggested.[1] However these sigla may be construed, it is clear that Joyce had conceived of Book II as evolving out of the interactions of the extended "Doodles family" (FW: 299.F4). The sigla had become by this time relatively discrete entities—a convenient shorthand for notes and drafts—that could be combined and manipulated to generate new narrational possibilities.[2]

According to this early plan for II.1, Shem and Shaun play a game of Angels and Devils around Issy. This game devolves into a "Tug of Love," as well as other games, under the gaze of HCE. ALP gathers the children, who are ultimately told to reenter the home by HCE. Such a brief description fits in fairly well with the broad contours of the final version of the chapter, although specific correspondences between the chapter and its early plan are less viable.

This plan did not emerge Athena-like out of Joyce's head: one can see early versions of it in notebook entries prior to mid-1926. VI.B.11 (September–November 1923) contains some small clustered lists of children's games that were not used but indicate an early interest. The first clear note for II.1 can be found in VI.B.16 (April–May 1924), which has an entry that seems to intimate the chapter's guessing games: "name flower on undies / applaud" (VI.B.16: 111). VI.B.8, which was compiled almost a year before the Book II plan (late July–September 1925), also contains notes that point toward the games of II.1: "⊥ lay Eden / angels & devils / ᗯ Darby & Joan" (VI.B.8: 160). This entry uses the siglum ᗯ, an inversion of the plan's ᗰ siglum. "Darby and Joan" is a jocose term for an elderly couple who are "all in all to each other" (*OED*). The basic configurations for the 1926 plan of II.1 are already indicated in this brief note: the game of Angels and Devils around Isolde while HCE and ALP remain separate but nearby.

A later notebook, VI.B.17 (April–May 1926), contains a list of children's games directly preparatory to the early plan for Book II. These notes derive from the book *Les Jeux d'enfants* by Yrjö Hirn,[3] the title of which Joyce wrote on page 17 of the notebook. On pages 19–20 Joyce took down the names of various games from chapter 4 of Hirn's book. Two or three of these games also appear on the plan for Book II: "horneys & robbers" and "blindman's buff" (VI.B.17: 19). "Horneys and robbers" combines Cops and Robbers with Hornies, a Scottish game that Hirn describes as a variant of Blindman's Buff.[4] In his notes from Hirn Joyce did not record what he had to say about the game Colors or Angels and Devils.[5] Instead, he took an interest in games that involve romantic rivalry of some kind:

> [g]⊏'s game / ends with flailing[g]
> Λ's game — hipercalm
> T & ╧ ⊣ pray in ring (VI.B.17: 27)[6]

These entries follow some details of various rustic games that Hirn describes in chapter 5. A Swedish game Hirn analyzes in some detail involves a child playing the role of a farmer who attempts to gain admission to a ring, composed of the other players, by flailing his arms. Eventually, the "farmer" will be let into the ring and thus be allowed to choose a wife. Hirn states that this little drama creates "a complex and typical image of old-fashioned country life."[7] In his note Joyce has bifurcated the farmer into the unsuccessful Shem, left outside flailing his arms, and Shaun, calm because he has been admitted into the ring.

By July 1926, shortly after the completion of the plan, Joyce began work on the "Triangle" section of II.2 (see LI: 242). However, he became distracted from further work on Book II and did not return to it—with the exception of some revisions for the "Triangle"—until the early 1930s.[8] The 1926 plan thus languished for four years. Like a more fortunate, or perhaps less fortunate, version of Beckett's *innommable,* as soon as Joyce knew what he was doing he could no longer do it—at least for a while.

Let the Games Begin

By October 1930, when Joyce finally found himself writing II.1 in earnest, he most likely did not consult his 1926 plan for Book II (TDJJ: 111; JJA 51: vii); however, the chapter that Joyce produced does bear some affinities to the early plan. In November, after having completed a fair copy of II.1§2 (FW: 222.22–236.32), the earliest surviving draft for this chapter, Joyce sent it to Weaver along with a letter that described both his state of mind and the state of his text in considerable detail:[9]

> I enclose the final sheet of the first draft of about two thirds of the first section of Part II (2,200 words) which came out like drops of blood. Excuse me for not having written but I have had a dreadful amount of worry all this last month. . . . I think the piece I sent you is the gayest and lightest thing I have done in spite of the circumstances. . . .
>
> The scheme of the piece I sent you is the game we used to call Angels and Devils or colours. The Angels, girls, are grouped behind the Angel, Shawn, and the Devil has to come over three times and ask for a colour. If the colour he asks for has been chosen by any girl she has to run and he tries to catch her.[10] As far as I have written he has come twice and been twice baffled. The piece is full of rhythms taken from English singing games. When first baffled vindictively he thinks of publishing blackmail stuff about his father, mother etc etc etc. The second time he maunders off into sentimental poetry [bits] of what I actually wrote at the age of nine: 'My cot alas that dear old shady home where oft in youthful sport I played, upon thy verdant grassy fields all day or lingered for a moment in thy bosom shade etc etc etc etc.' This is interrupted by a violent pang of toothache after which he throws a fit. When he is baffled a second time the girl angels sing a hymn of liberation around Shawn. The page enclosed is still another version of a beautiful sentence from Edgar Quinet which I already refashioned in *Transition* part one beginning 'since the days of Hiber and Hairyan etc.' E.Q. says that the wild flowers on the ruins of Carthage, Numancia etc have survived the political rises and falls of Empires. In this case the wild flowers are the lilts of children. Note specially the treatment of the double rainbow in which the iritic colours are first normal and then reversed. (LI: 295)

The difficulty of writing that Joyce describes remained more or less continual throughout the writing of this chapter. In his letter the children's games, first cryptically outlined in 1926, benefit from a fuller, prosaic explanation. This initial installment essentially deals with the persecution of Shem by both Shaun and the Maggies. This could thus be seen as an extension of the fraternal rivalry first adumbrated in I.7, and indeed there are many echoes between the two chapters. However, in II.1 the tension between Shem and Shaun is not articulated from just Shaun's perspective. The emergence of their dialectic from a point uncontrolled by Shaun is perhaps the most important overall function of this chapter and demonstrates Book II's function as a balance to the HCE-dominated Book I and the Shaun-centric Book III.

In addition to Angels and Devils, the game that Joyce describes as the scheme for this section, the game Blindman's Buff might also be pertinent. Initially, Joyce had written "Blindman's Buff" on the plan only to cross it out and replace it with Angels and Devils (JJA 51: 3). Furthermore, in VI.B.17 Joyce has "blindman's buff / not to see / to hear / to feel he" (VI.B.17: 19). Hirn goes into some detail about this game and refers to Kant's claim that it "originates from the desire to prove the possibilities that pass in front of one's field of vision."[11] Hirn further mentions the obvious allure to children of a game that involves tactile and auditory sensation (this recalls Stephen closing his eyes while "walking into eternity along Sandymount strand" [U: 3.18–19] in *Ulysses*). The rules of this game, which dates back to at least the fourteenth century, are quite similar to Angels and Devils. A player is blindfolded, and then, in this position of disadvantage, he has to try to capture another player. "Thus great care is taken over the blindfolding, which is usually done with a scarf. It is tied tightly over the person's eyes, and he is repeatedly asked if he can see, and is tested with questions, 'What colour is my coat?' 'Who is the tallest here?'"[12] The first player to be apprehended then takes the blindfold and continues the action. An Italian variant of this game, *Gatta cecata* (blind cat), has the blindfolded player encircled by the other players in a dancing ring.[13] It seems that in II.1 Shem has to ascertain the Maggies' color from the handicapped position of being blindfolded. Hirn claims that the blindfolded player can be construed as representing an evil spirit or devil,[14] thereby allowing for a conceptual association between this game and Angels and Devils. The importance of Angels and Devils is that, in contrast to Blindman's Buff, it has an element of rivalry. This would be crucial for Joyce in setting up the antagonistic rapport between Shem and Shaun in this chapter.

Before the fair copy of II.1§2 was sent to Weaver a first typescript was prepared. As would become typical for other sections of this chapter, this typescript is marked by all sorts of errors. The archive for this chapter contains a large number of retyped pages that were an attempt to redress the typist's errors, but, sadly, these also introduced new blunders. Joyce then moved on to write the first draft of II.1§3 (FW: 236.33–240.04) immediately after the second typescript of II.1§2 was prepared. This section deals with Shaun's ascendancy with the Maggies in the aftermath of Shem's disgrace. This section went through a first draft, a fair copy, and a typescript. The two opening pages were then retyped under Joyce's supervision in order to properly accommodate the revisions made on the first typescript. The following section, II.1§4 (FW: 240.05–244.12), returns to describe Shem's shame and can be seen as a direct elaboration of the conclusion of the preceding section. On the typescript for this section Joyce added a few intimations of HCE's arrival into the scene of the children's games. This directly led to II.1§5 (FW: 244.13–246.36), which amplifies the intimations of HCE's reappearance. After being drafted separately these two sections were integrated onto one typescript. Joyce had the first draft of II.1§5 completed by mid-February 1931 and was encouraged by the quality of what he had written: "I am trying to conclude section I of Part II but such an amount of reading seems to be necessary before my old flying machine grumbles up into the air. Personally the only thing that encourages me is my belief that what I have written up to the present is a good deal better than any other first draft I made" (LI: 300).

The notebook or notebooks Joyce used in preparing these first drafts of II.1§§2–5 are now missing, and so the drafts themselves are the only textual record available.[15] However, Joyce did use VI.B.31 in revising the typescripts for these sections. On pages 185–98 of that notebook he recorded some items from Norman Douglas's book *London Street Games* that were added into the drafts in overlay on the typescript level.[16]

After February 1931 Joyce left II.1§§2–5 in typescript form. As Douglas's book was not published until May 1931, it would seem that at least some of the autograph revisions of the typescripts were not made until later in the year, but, in any case, his work on II.1 after February was minimal. This second hiatus in the composition of II.1 lasted until the middle of 1932, when, encouraged (or perhaps pestered) by Eugene Jolas, Joyce began revising II.1 for publication in *transition* (JJ/PL: 5). He began by drafting an introductory section, II.1§1 (FW: 219.01–222.21). This passage is a dramatis personae of the various characters in the chapter in the form of a theatrical advertisement or program. The initial drafts merely consist of a cast of characters and a short concluding paragraph concerning the staff involved with the technical aspects of the theatrical production. Since the characters had already been introduced in I.6, this particular cast has a different function, one that was amplified during the course of the composition of this segment. Chapter II.1 had begun life, in the 1926 plan, as a product of the interrelation of *Wakean* characters and sigla, and now, with the introduction, this dynamic is explicitly reinserted back into the text with the cast of characters. Daniel Ferrer calls this phenomenon "contextual memory": a text bears some trace of or reference to some element that had existed in a previous draft but that has since been excised.[17]

After composing the introductory vignette Joyce probably turned to II.1§6 (FW: 246.36–257.02), a sequel, of a sort, to the action thus far developed. This section reverts to Shem and his third and final attempt to guess the Maggies' color. This section was initially drafted in subsections and was not unified until the chapter as a whole was prepared for publication in *transition* 22.

The final section, II.1§7 (FW: 257.03–259.10), is very brief and only went through one, possibly two, drafts before the chapter was prepared for *transition*. This comparative paucity of draft levels suggests that this was the last section to be drafted before the chapter was integrated. This section deals with the end of the children's games and the resumption of adult order, expanded into an invocation of divine intervention.

The seven sections of this chapter, composed out of sequence, when taken together form a theatrical tableau in which the cast is assembled (§1), the games commence, and Shem is "divorced into disgrace" (FW: 220.01–2) by the Maggies (§2). Shaun then assumes the Maggies' favors (§3), while Shem ponders revenge (§4). Shem's fury leads to a gradual reemergence of HCE (§5). This point marked the original end for this chapter, but the concluding sections, added in 1932, expand upon the ominous implications suggested by HCE's return: in §6 Shem essays a third guess, the circumstances of which are less jovial and more sinister than the earlier games. Finally, the children are put to sleep, and the games come to an end (§7).

Once the various sections were drafted Joyce integrated them to prepare the chapter for publication in *transition* 22 in February 1933. Unfortunately, the manuscripts directly preparatory for *transition* have not survived.[18] However, a good deal of collateral information survives in a series of extradraft notes. These notes are quite heterogeneous: many contain brief phrases that wound up inserted in disparate locations throughout the chapter, and a good number of these are flagged by sigla. A large number of these notes derive from notebook VI.B.33. About a dozen small entries in the notesheets hail from VI.B.3 (used more extensively for II.2, which was also being drafted at this time). Certain sheets contain notes flagged by page numbers for insertion, and presumably these refer to the now-missing *transition* draft. Unlike the other extradraft notes of this time, the notes for the subsections of II.1§6 contain comparatively discrete drafts and protodrafts. Indeed, it was only at this level that II.1§6 began to take shape.

After publication in *transition* this chapter was prepared for separate publication as *The Mime of Mick, Nick and the Maggies* by the Servire Press in The Hague (see LI: 328). The marked-up pages for *transition* used to prepare this edition have not survived, but the number of changes made is relatively small. Beyond *The Mime* the draft history of II.1 is straightforward: two sets of corrected pages were prepared—one in autograph overlay and one with typed overlay—for the printer of *Finnegans Wake*. Then, in early 1938 Joyce was sent the galley proofs, and in late 1938 he was sent the page proofs.

Guessing Games

II.1§2, the first part of the chapter to be written, begins by establishing the polemic between Shaun (Chuff) and Shem (Glugg) within the roles prescribed by the game Angels and Devils:

> Chuffy was a nangel then and his soard fleshed light like likening. Fools top! Singty; sangty meeky loose, defendy nous in prayley boos. Make a shine on the curst. Emem.
>
> But the duvlim sulph was in Glugger, that lost-to-learning. Punct. He was sbuffing and sputing, tussing like anisine, whipping his eysoult and gmatsching his teats over the brividies from existers and the outher liubbocks of life. To part from thees, my corsets, is into overlusting fear. Acts of feet, hoof and jarrety. Djowl, uphere! (BL 47477 f. 6, simplified; JJA 51: 14; FDV: 130; FW: 222.22–31)

Shaun, the sainted sage angel, is here characterized as a guardian through a mild distortion of the prayer that concludes Mass. As such, he is associated with illumination and enlightenment. In contrast, Shem, the sulfurous devil, lacks Shaun's insight and certitude and is, instead, plagued with Sturm und Drang concerning matters ontological as well as the "outher liubbocks of life." Part of Shem's stress concerns his ability to see as he is "whipping his eysoult." This obviously alludes to Issy or Izod, the immediate cause of Shem's woes, as well as to Gertrud Eyesoldt, an early-twentieth-century German actress.[19] (This kind of theatrical allusion will be expanded in the subsequently drafted sections of this chapter.) Shem is placed in an interpretative role concerning Issy, "to catch her by the calour of her brideness" (BL 47477 f. 7; JJA 51: 15; FDV: 130; FW: 223.05–6). Already the children's guessing game is sexualized, since he tries to catch the *calor*—that is, the heat or passion—of her brideness.

Shem's predicament à propos Issy is analogous to HCE's with the Pranquean in I.1 in that they both have to solve a riddle. Issy's question—"With that hehry antlets on him and the baublelight bulching out of his sockets whiling away she sprankled his allover with her noces of interrogation: How do you do that lack a lock and pass the poker please?" (BL 47477 fs. 8–9; JJA 51: 16–17; FDV: 131; FW: 224.12–15)—explicitly echoes the Pranquean's riddle, "why do I am alook alike a poss of porterpease?" (FW: 021.18–19).[20] Shem has been asked a question, the answer to which—heliotrope—is already given: "what's that, O holytrooper^[1]s[1]^?" (BL 47477 f. 7; JJA 51: 15; FDV: 130; FW: 223.11).[21] Shem is surrounded by the name of the color that he is blind to in his guesses. Complicating matters, heliotrope is not just a color, it is a stone, a flower, and an orientation (*heliotropos:* turning toward the sun). Variants of the word "heliotrope" pervade this chapter from the first draft. It is as if the text itself holds the answer in abeyance in order to tempt the hapless Shem.

Analogies to the Pranquean were buttressed in subsequent drafts by the addition of a passage on the first typescript that characterizes Shem and Shaun's antagonism in terms reminiscent of HCE's scenario in the "Museyroom": "And they are met, face a facing: They are set, force to force. And no such Copenhague-Marengo was less so fated ^[1]scene[1]^ ~~for~~ a fall since in Glenasmole of Thrushes Patch Whyte passed O'Sheen" (BL 47477 f. 23v, simplified; JJA 51: 30; FW: 223.15–18). Copenhagen was the name of Wellington's horse (referred to variously in the "Museyroom" passage as Willingdone's "same white harse, the Cokenhape" [FW: 008.17]), and Marengo was Napoleon's horse.[22] HCE's "waterloose" (FW: 008.02) conflict is here being relived or reenacted by Shem and Shaun. The intergenerational conflict of I.1 has become intragenerational or internecine. Their "argument" (FW: 222.21) is thus not so much an actual disagreement that can be narrativized but rather an ontogenetic discord that fuels the scene of their games in this chapter.

There are three instances where Shem attempts to guess the Maggies' color, and each of these instances consists of three questions. As Joyce noted, the first two instances appear in II.1§2. In Shem's first attempt he appears to be trying to guess a stone. He fails to arrive at heliotrope, but the fact that in attempting to guess a color he postulates various stones shows that in being wrong he is tangentially correct.

This sequence is almost completely unchanged from the first draft:

> —Have you moonbreamstone?
> —No.
> —Or hellfeuersteyn?
> —No.
> —Or Van Diemen's coral pearl?
> No.
> He has lost.
> Off the clutch, Glugg! Forewhal! Shape your reres, Glugg! Forweal! Ring we round, Chuff! Fairwell! Chuffchuff's inner seven: all's rice with their whirl! (BL 47477 f. 10, simplified; JJA 51: 19; FDV: 131; FW: 225.22–28)

After guessing moonstone, flint (*Feuerstein* is German for flint), and coral pearl instead of heliotrope, Shem is left destitute. The tenor of Shem's guesses also betokens his status in the game as the devil: brimstone, hell-fire, demon. All these guesses are Germanic. Since Shem's guesses are wrong, the Maggies turn toward Shaun instead of gravitating to the devil. In so doing they *perform* heliotrope: they turn (*tropein*) toward Shaun or Chuff, the heavenly angel, their sun-god (*helios*). Patrick McCarthy has pointed out that the irony behind the setup of this game is that it inverts Eve's sin in the garden of Eden. Here it is the devil, Shem, who is tempted by Izod and the Maggies.[23] A further irony is that Shem is not so much a penman or a writer here as he is a *reader.* His task in this chapter is essentially an interpretative one: trying to divine the Maggies' color. In this he is bedeviled by his inability to have clear vision.

Part of Shem's problem is his difficulty in differentiating colors from out of the blur he is subjected to. In his letter to Weaver Joyce pointed out the double rainbow: "R is Rubretta and A is Arancia, Y is for Yilla and N for Greenerin. B is Boyblue with odialisque O while W waters the fleurettes of novembrance. Though they're all but merely a schoolgirl yet these way went they" (BL 47477 f. 12; JJA 51: 21; FDV: 132; FW: 226.30–34). On the retyped pages for this section Joyce added a line to the beginning of this procession that makes Shem's task in front of the Maggies' dance explicit: "Say them all but tell them apart, abelward from Haloeyes!" (BL 47477 f. 60; JJA 51: 55, simplified). Shem has to differentiate the dancing girls: to perceive them as a unity or sequence (RAYNBOW) and also as seven distinct apparitions (the iritic colors). The difficulty of this task is compounded by the redistribution of the colors: "And these ways wend they. And those ways wend they. Winnie, Olive and Beatrice, Nelly and Ida, Amy and Rue. Here they come back" (BL 47477 f. 13; JJA 51: 22; FDV: 132; FW: 227.13–15). The sequence is reversed (WOBNIAR), the names have changed, and the roles have shifted. In their dance they keep their secret.

The second series of guesses concerning the color is more complicated, both on a genetic and a thematic level. The first draft reads:

> For a haunting way will go and you need not make your mow. Find the frenge for frocks amd [*sic*] translace it into shocks of such as touch with show and show.
>
> He is guessing at hers for all he is worse. Hark to his wily geeses gossling by, ~~my~~ and playfair, lady.
>
> —Haps thee ore candy?
>
> —Now.
>
> —Haps thee mayjaunties?
>
> —Nowhow.
>
> —Haps thee per causes nunsibelli?
>
> —Nowhowhow.
>
> Get. (BL 47477 f. 18, simplified; JJA 51: 26; FDV: 133–34; FW: 233.08–27)

The goal is to "find the frenge for frocks," to glimpse her undergarments. The word "frenge" suggests French, which explains the Francophonic overtones to Shem's translaced and unsuccessful guesses here. The task is unclearly stated, expressed through a series of puns, and so its pursuit by Shem, and his "wily geeses," is likewise confused. Shem first asks if she has ore candy, that is, if she has something that is valuable (ore) to the eye. This is also possibly a pun on orcanet, a reddish plant (*Alkanna tinctoria*), or the name of the dye made from it. On the subsequent draft, the typescript, Joyce changed this question, possibly because he did not want a floral reference here or perhaps because he did not want to have a connotation of redness. The revised form of this question is "Haps thee ~~are candy~~ ^[1]jaoneofergs[1]^?"

(BL 47477 f. 31; JJA 51: 38).[24] This new question plays with the French word for yellow, *jaune,* and the Irish word for anger, *fearg,* as well as the English word "fear." This new nonce word also buttresses the allusion to yellow from the second question, mayjaunties (jaundice). Both the revised form of the first guess and the second guess have Francophonic overtones: Jeanne d'Arc and *mes gentils.* Instead of frocks Shem has settled on the French.

The third question also has a Francophonic ring, *non si belle* (not so lovely). It also seems to be a pun on the Latin phrase "per causas nuntiatas belli" [through the declared causes of war].[25] Patrick McCarthy sees this as an allusion to the Maggies' martial disposition, as evinced in the Museyroom and elsewhere.[26] The word "nunsibellies" also recalls an odd comment Joyce made to Italo Svevo in a letter dated 5 January 1921: "There is an oilcloth brief-case fastened with a rubber band having the colour of a nun's belly" (LI: 154). E. L. Epstein speculates that this color is yellow, certainly an appropriate hue for this jaundiced sequence, but one is tempted to ask how Epstein (or, for that matter, Joyce) came to know such privileged information.[27]

The yellowness of this passage is important. Shem's first guess involved stones, and so he was approaching, and missing, heliotrope from one direction. Here, he is approaching from another direction and still falling short. Sunflowers, which are heliotropic, are yellow. But the sunflower (*Helianthus*) is not the same as the flower known as the heliotrope (*Heliotropium*), which is purple. So the second guess revolves around another mode of heliotrope that is yet again misstated.

The first series of questions is Germanic and revolves around gems, whereas the second is Francophonic and concerns colors, specifically yellow. Neither proves successful. In the early phases of Shem's perplexity Shaun seems to be little more than an ambient nuisance. Shaun only comes to take on a more active role in II.1§3 once Shem becomes mired in failure. Perhaps the key line auguring such a transformation comes from within the description of Shem's shame: "He would split. Inform to the old sniggering publicking press" (BL 47477 f. 14; JJA 51: 23, simplified; FDV: 133; FW: 228.05 and 229.08). During the course of composition over a page of intervening matter was added between these two phrases, but their proximity here points to a colloquial sense of the verb "split." In addition to meaning to divide, to separate into pieces, to cause pain, to laugh excessively, and to quarrel—all appropriate senses here—the *OED* records that this verb can mean to turn evidence, to betray confidence. This sense is pertinent because of Shem's move to inform the sniggering press.

Another colloquial sense for "split"—to leave—is activated by an addition on the first typescript: "A wandering rogue" (BL 47477 f. 29; JJA 51: 35; FW: 229.14).[28] As this phrase also wandered away from the word "split," driven forth by the weight of freshly added text, Joyce added additional sentences to reinforce this sense of the word: "He take skiff with three shirts and a wind" (BL 47477 f. 57; JJA 51: 53; FW: 228.06–7).[29] For *transition* Joyce worked in a considerable amount of material that reinforces and builds upon the sense of departure, and he also added a great deal of information about voyages.[30] So while the sense of "informing" is retained, the sense of "leaving" is amplified.

Shem's failure to correctly guess the Maggies' riddle is echoed by the Quinet passage that closes II.1§2. This passage is, I believe, important to understanding why children's games are the locus of Shem and Shaun's rivalry in this chapter. Chronologically, this was the third Quinet passage to be installed into the text.[31]

> Since the days of Roamaloose and Rehmoose the pavanos have been stridend through their Struts of Chapelldiseut, the valusies have meed and youdled through the purly ooze of Ballybough, many a mismy cloudy has tripped tauntily along that hercourt strayed reelway and the rigadoons have held ragtimed revels on the plateauplainof Grangegorman; and though since then sterlings and guineas have been replaced by brooks and lions and some progress has been made on stilths and the races have come and gone and Thyme, that chef of seasoners, has made his usual astewte use of endadjustables and whatnot willbe isnor was those danceadeils and cancanzanies have come stimmering down for our begayment through the bedeafdom of po's greats, the obcecity of pa's teapucs, as lithe as limb free limber as when momie played at ma. (BL 47477 f. 21, simplified; JJA 51: 29; FDV: 134–35; FW: 236.19–32)

As with Joyce's other versions of the Quinet sentence, the temporal marker at the beginning is altered: instead of Quinet's Pliny and Columella, Joyce posits Romulus and Remus. Instead of ancient historians, Joyce has mythological founders. Furthermore, Quinet's flowers have become dances (a pavanes, valses, and rigadoons), an appropriate metamorphosis for this chapter, in which the Maggies dance around Shem as he attempts to guess their color. The point here seems to be that the dance endures through decay and entropy, much as children's games have lasted throughout history.[32] Children's games are, on the one hand, fleeting: by definition one (usually) grows out of them. On the other hand, they have persisted throughout the ages; individual players may grow up, but they will always be replaced by subsequent generations, thereby allowing for the continuation of the games. Indeed, Hirn begins his book by claiming that any study of human civilization and history would be incomplete without proper consideration of children's games.[33] James S. Atherton mentions other contemporaneous writers who have proposed that "children in play re-enact the history of their race."[34] If Joyce had been interested in children's games as early as late 1923 (as evinced in VI.B.11), then perhaps it was only through Hirn and Quinet (via Metchnikoff) that he was able to incorporate games into *Finnegans Wake.*

Children's games frequently represent adult activities as perceived through the prism of a child's imagination. Games enact something, usually some aspect of adult society that children have observed. Children's games reflect the world from which they are separate; they allow children to adopt the roles of adulthood within a space circumscribed by their own boundaries.[35] Children's games are a *mimicry* of adulthood.[36] The children's games in II.1 are thus a performative imitation or reenactment of the "drama" that had been suggested or implied in Book I but through the distorting lens of play. This performance in II.1 is, in some senses, the fulfillment of the drama of Book I: the adults have produced children who in turn replicate their ancestors' world into a new, youthful paradigm. History—specifically, the sexual history of HCE—repeats itself here in the farcical children's games. However, in the context of *Finnegans Wake,* if the children's games are an imitation, they are an imitation *without* an original. Just as HCE's crime appears to exist in Book I not in any actual deed but rather in the persistence of the accusations of such a deed, so too do the children's games allude to, perform, and repeat some nonspecified, ambiguous, and transgressive event.

The Quinet passage does not just signify a *thematic* repetition by the children of their parents' deeds, that is, the children reenacting or replaying their parents' lives. Beyond the thematic repetition, the repetition and endurance of a theme, the Quinet passage in II.1 also suggests a kind of narrative repetition unto the point of stagnation. In this chapter narrative progress is always belied and stalled by characterization: since Shem is a devil, his attempts to play the game—his attempts to engage in a narrative development or progression—are always jinxed by his very diabolic status. Because he is a devil he is stuck playing a devil in all sorts of diabolic modulations. The constant repetition of this status ultimately yields to a kind of stasis that can only be broken by the resumption of parental order at chapter's end.

Sunny Shaun and the Return of the Father

In the aftermath of Shem's having *split* (disseminated rumor), Shem and Shaun have fully *split* (separated) themselves into distinct characters. Shaun emerges from out of the Maggies' encomium in II.1§3:

> Enchainted, sweet dear Stainusless, dearer dearest, we herehear aboutobuds thee salutant Pattren of our unschoold, deliverer of softmissives, send us a wise and letters play of all you canceive of from your holy post. Sweetstaker, we toutes were drawpairs so want lotteries of ticklets. Will bee all buzzy one another again minmie for you are pollen yourself. We feel unspeechably thoughtless over it all so please kindly communicake with the original sinse we we [*sic*] are only yearning how to burgeon. It was milliems of centimants dead lost or mislaid on them bub we can change in the bite of a napple so long as we can see your quick. Behose, our handmades to the lured! To these nunce we are yours in ammatures but well come that day we shall ope to be ores. No more hoaxites! No more gifting in memnage! (BL 47477 fs. 34–35, simplified; JJA 51: 75–76; FDV: 135; FW: 237.11–239.13)

At the bottom of a retyped version of this passage sent to Weaver Joyce described it as the "begining of a prayer addressed to by the playing girls to Shaun who is their angel in the game of Colours or Angels and Devils" (BL 47477 f. 71; JJA 51: 90). The Maggies point to Shaun's postal authority, or "holy post," as the main reason for their devotion to him. Despite Shem's threat to split the news about HCE, the Maggies turn to Shaun to deliver to them news of the "original sinse." In a sense, by threatening to split Shem has created an alter ego to whom the Maggies (heliotropically) turn. But the Maggies also allude to a defect in the medium of communication: the dead lost or mislaid milliems of centiments. They conclude by promising themselves to Shaun, but nevertheless they hope for a time when they will no longer have to be subserviant to any male. They are Shan's "in amatures" but not in marriage: "No more hoaxites [German *Hochzeit*, "marriage"]. No more gifting in memnage." On the typescript Joyce mainly added terms that flatter Shaun and extol his prowess and abilities, such as: "Pattren of our unschoold, ^[1]pageant-master,[1]^ deliverer of softmissives, ^[1]round the world in forty posts,[1]^ send us jour adorables, a wise and letters play of all you can ceive of from your holy post" (BL 47477 f. 68; JJA 51: 83).

A passage added to the fair copy of this section accounts for Shaun's ascendancy in light of his brother's failure: "These bright elects they were waltzing up their willside with their princesome handsome angeline chiuff while in those wherebus there wont helds way oaths and screams and bawley groans with a belchybubhub and a hellabelow bedemmed and bediabbled the arimaining lucisphere. Lonedom's breach lay foulend up incouth not be brooched by punns and reedles" (BL 47477 f. 41, simplified; JJA 51: 81; FW: 239.28–36). The angel Shaun (the angeline chiuff) is favored over Shem, the devil, the bediabbled arimaining lucisphere. In the course of playing the game Shem's status as a devil remains unchanged. It is as if his diabolic role has been predetermined. He remains an outsider, excluded from the intimacy of the Maggies. His isolated status is registered here through a series of puns distorting lines from the children's song "London Bridge Is Falling Down," a song associated with a game since at least the late nineteenth century. Elements of this game are relevant to this passage. Two people form a bridge and sing the song, which, as its name suggests, recounts the collapse of London Bridge and proposes various means of rebuilding it, none of which will last:

> London Bridge is falling down,
> Falling down, falling down,
>
> . . . .
>
> Build it up with sticks and stones,
> Sticks and stones, sticks and stones,
>
> . . . .
>
> Sticks and stones will wear away,
> Wear away, wear away,
>
> . . . .
>
> Build it up with iron and steel . . .

As the song is being sung, other children pass under the "bridge." When the children playing the bridge reach the line "My fair lady," they trap the player passing through at that moment. This continues, with various modifications, until all the other players are caught. "The bridge is never mended, but it doesn't matter. You have a tug of war at the end."[37]

This game combines various elements pertinent to this chapter: exclusion (the entrapment of various players) and antagonism (the devolution of the singing game into a tug of war). Furthermore, the decay of London Bridge recalls the Quinet passage: monuments may collapse, but there will always be children there to sing and dance. However, here it is "Lonedom's breach"—as in Shem's exclusion as the "arimaining lucisphere"—that has been "foulend up." It is not just the "bridge" that is destroyed but its "breach" (or split): both junction and disjunction are fouled. This disrepair cannot be "broched by punns and reedles." "Broched" suggests both "broached" and the French verb *brocher,* to stitch (appropriate for the pun on pins and needles). The instruments that are insufficient to repair the foulend breach, "punns and reedles," are themselves the instruments of the decay of language in *Finnegans Wake* (puns and riddles). Indeed, the uncertainty of what exactly is foulend up (bridge or breach) is registered through a rather basic pun.

The fair copy of this section concludes with a final statement of Shem's dilapidation: "And you wonna make one of our micknick party. For poor Glugger was dazed and late in his crave, ~~i.e~~ ay he, laid in his grave" (BL 47477 f. 41, simplified; JJA 51: 81; FDV: 136; FW: 240.02–4). The description of Shem's destitution comes from the song "Old Rogers": "Old Rogers is dead and laid in his grave."[38] Through the taunts and mockeries perpetrated by Shaun and the Maggies during the games Shem is interred. His fate is thus all the more akin to HCE's: "Well, Him a being so on the flounder of his bulk like an overgrown babeling, let wee peep, see, at Hom, well, see peegee ought he ought, platterplate. Ш Hum!" (FW: 006.30–33). However, also like HCE, while Shem may be buried, he is not entirely gone. Nor is he entirely one, since he is part of the micknick party, that is, one half of one duo.

II.1§4 can be seen as a direct continuation of Shaun's shame as it works as an elaboration of the final line from the preceding section that concerns Shem's desistance. Shem rises again, but in so doing he also fulfills his characterization as a "low sham" (FW: 170.25): "But low, boys, low he rises, shivering. [. . .] Not true his portmanteau filled potatowards" (BL 47477 f. 42; JJA 51: 92; FDV: 136; FW: 240.05–241.01). He will keep on punning. This section is comparatively brief in its initial draft, but it received substantial additions in the subsequent typescript. The gist of the passage is Shem's invective, or split, against "this Heer assassor Neelsoen laslast great change of rehiring family buckle" (BL 47477 f. 42, simplified; JJA 51: 92; FDV: 136; FW: 242.01–3). He decries against his ancestor HCE in his guises as Nelson and the "last pre-electric king of Ireland" (FW: 380.12–13). Folded into Shem's invective are all sorts of tangential allusions to bizarre characters and incidents in a kind of semidigested blur of accusation. This collage of sin was already present in embryo on the first draft and was subsequently expanded considerably. Reincarnating the resurrected HCE, Shem also replays the persistence of accusation against his less-than-illustrious predecessor. The HCE whom Shem recounts is "more mob than man" (FW: 261.21–22), a conflation of so many details that no one individual can accommodate them all.[39]

Into this milieu of accusation HCE starts to intercede in the games. On the typescript for II.1§4 Joyce added two paragraphs, one at the bottom of the page that treats Shem's invective against ALP, HCE's helpmate: "Helpmeat too, his fiery goosemother" (BL 47477 f. 75, simplified; JJA 51: 95; FW: 242.25). On the facing page Joyce added a second paragraph with an insertion mark clearly indicating its position as coming before the ALP paragraph (BL 47477 fs. 74v–75; JJA 51: 94–95). However, on the following typescript (which also incorporates II.1§5) the ALP paragraph was incorrectly positioned before the HCE paragraph. As both paragraphs, especially the one concerning ALP, were considerably expanded during subsequent drafts, the typist's error appears to have been acknowledged by Joyce.[40] The HCE paragraph reads: "But who come yond with pire on poletop? He who relights the moon. And the hag they damename Coverfew hists from her lane. And haste, 'tis time for bairn to hame. Chickchilds' comeho to roo. Comehome to roo as chickchilds do" (BL 47477 f. 74v, simplified; JJA 51: 94; FW: 244.03–12). The time for playing has ended, and now the children must come home. The imposition of curfew—a reminder that the children still dwell within a world of adults—emerges from Shem's invective against HCE. Just as Shaun will "incarnate" HCE's voice in III.3, so too does Shem summon HCE here.

HCE's emergence in II.1§5 recalls Shem's "revitalization" in the previous section just as Shem's low rising there recalled HCE's own odd relationship with death and rebirth. HCE is recalled by Shem, who in turn recalls HCE. As noted above, II.1§5 was initially drafted separately from II.1§4, but the two were integrated on a typescript. This latter section is largely transitional; it elaborates the arrival of HCE augured in the previous section as a setup to the close of the chapter, where HCE will put the children to bed. It is important in that the focus shifts from children's antics to apparently broader concerns:

> It darkles, all this our fun nominal world. Man and beast are chill. In deeryard imbraced, alleged, injointed and unlatched, the birds even thumbtit, quail silent. Was vesper ere awhile. Now conticinium. No chare of beagles, frantling of peacocks, no muzzing of the camel, smtterring of apes. Lights, pageboy lights! When otter leaps in outer parts then Yul remembers May. [. . .] Bing. Bong. Bingbang: Thunderation! Welcome. Were you Marely quean of scuts or but Christien the Last here's dapplebellied mugs and troublebedded rooms

and sawdust strown in expectoration. Mr Knight, big tapster, buttles; his alewife's up to his hip. And Watsy Lyke looks after all rinsings and don't omiss Kate, put in with the bricks. (BL 47477 fs. 45–46, simplified; JJA 51: 96–97; FDV: 137; FW: 244.14–245.34)

The increasing castigation and abjection of Shem darkens the tenor of the games, and, likewise, night descends darkling the nominally phenomenal world of fun and games. On the typescript Joyce added the following qualifier after the first sentence: "We are circumveiloped by obscuritas" (BL 47477 f. 77; JJA 51: 101). The blindness of veiling and obscurity that had perplexed Shem during his interrogations has now become general. Any nightly redistribution of parts and players must cease at some point because of the inevitable nightly recurrence of night. The nightly desistance is characterized as falling over a zoo. The shift to a bestiary was made more explicit by an addition for *transition:* "Zoo koud" (*t:* 66; FW: 244.17); *koud* is Dutch for "cold." Within this zoo the sound of thunder calls forth Mr Knight (the knightly nocturnal hero) and his familiars, Watsy and Kate. Joyce considerably augmented the number and variety of the animals listed on the marked-up pages of *The Mime* (BL 47477 f. 173; JJA 51: 249). On the galleys he added another animal that helps to contextualize the emergence of HCE from this nightly zoo: "Panther noster. Send leadbarrow loads amorrow. While lovedom shleeps" (BL 47477 f. 286v; JJA 51: 424). Our father (*pater noster*) has been awakened from the zoo in which he sleeps. This suggests the Fluntern cemetery in Zürich (where Joyce is buried), which adjoins a zoo that Joyce had compared to the one in Phoenix Park.[41] Because of the fraternal quarrel HCE is raised in the cemetery by the zoo.

The Final Question

In a letter to Paul Léon dated 28 August 1932 Joyce wrote that he was preparing II.1§1 for publication in *transition* (JJ/PL: 5). This introduction was the first of three sections Joyce wrote in 1932 to augment the basic unit of §§2–5 drafted a year earlier. The first draft of II.1§1 is quite short: a brief elaboration of nine characters followed by a paragraph concerning the staff involved with the technical aspects of the theatrical production: "with battlepictures worked up by Messrs Blood and Thunder, costumes designed by Madame Delamode" (BL 47477 f. 3; JJA 51: 7; FDV: 129; FW: 221.18–25). This passage shows that this draft could not have been made earlier than late February 1931, since the phrase "[bl]blood & thunder" appears on VI.B.33: 5.

On the missing fair copy Joyce amplified this terminal paragraph to hyperbolically suggest a theatrical production of extreme historical magnitude. These changes are inferable from the typescript: "With battle pictures and the Pageant of History worked up by Messrs Thud and Blunder" (BL 47477 f. 24; JJA 51: 9; FW: 221.18–21). The typescript for II.1§1 could not predate early 1932, since at that level the phrase "Blood and Thunder" was changed to "Thud and Blunder" (BL 47477 f. 24; JJA 51: 9), a phrase found in VI.B.35 on page 27 and crossed out in blue. II.1§1 ends with the line "An argument follows" (BL 47477 f. 4; JJA 51: 8; FDV: 130; FW: 222.21), an appropriate segue into the children's games of this chapter.[42]

II.1§6 has the most complex draft history of any section in II.1. This section contains the final round of questions, but this was not present in the early drafts for this section and was only added to the chapter during the preparation for publication in *transition.* This section did not appear as a complete unit until publication in *transition* 22; until then it consisted of a series of six discrete subsections that were rewritten and drafted in a series of sometimes bizarre combinations. Three subsections—D, E, and F—do not have first drafts but instead make their earliest appearance on the extradraft notes. There also appear to be some missing drafts for these subsections (as well as for the overall drafts made to prepare the chapter as a whole for publication). Danis Rose's arrangement of the extradraft notes in *The James Joyce Archive* is nothing short of miraculous, as he has wrested a good degree of order out of the chaos of apparently unrelated pages. However, I disagree with some of his decisions in ordering the manuscript pages, and so I will not follow his numeration of the subsections. To simplify matters I have provided a table that outlines the subsections and their draft history.

As can be seen in table 3, portions of the subsections were rearranged for *transition* to accommodate some of the material produced on the extradraft notes. The first draft of subsection A announces a tone darker than what has come before. The more ominous implications of the children's merriment and gaming are explored and developed. This follows directly from the darkening announced in II.1§5 with HCE's return. The first subsection begins:

> Postreintroducing Jeremy. ^[1]The flowing tale that knows no brooking runs on to say,[1]^ His lasterhalft was set for getting the bester of his youngendtongend for control number thrice was operating the sibliminal of his invaded

personality. ^1He nobit smorfi endgo poltri & all the tondo gang bola del ruffo. Barto no know him mor, eat larti autruis with most perfect stranger.1^

He wept undeiterum. With such a tooth he seemed to love his wee tart when a buy. Highly momourning he see thee before him. Melanied from nape to kneecap though vied from thigh girders up. San Talto, sight most deletious! Lift the ~~black~~ ^1blank1^ ve veared as hell! Split the hvide, and aye seize heaven. ^1He knows for he's seen it in black and white.1^ ^1Tantamount to a clearobscure.1^ Prettymaide hues may have their cry apple, bacchanto, custard, dove, eskimo, fawn, ginger, hemalite, isinglass, jet, kipper, lucile, mimosa, nut, oysterette, prune, quasimodo, royal, sago, tango, umber, vanilla, wistaria, xray, yesplease, zaza, philomel, theerose. What are they all by? Shee. (BL 47477 fs. 114–16; JJA 51: 112–14; FDV: 138; FW: 246.36–248.02)

Shem has returned in the guise of Jeremy; his part has been redistributed. This passage describes Jeremy as an "invaded personality," suggesting that the distinction between Shem and Shaun is nothing if not porous. There is also an indication of the eventual third series of questions concerning the Maggies' color, even though these were not present at this draft level.

TABLE 3. Subsections of II.1§6

§6	FW page range	First draft	Fair copy	Typescript	Retyped pages
A	246.36–248.12 + 252.14–32	114, 115, 116, 117 (JJA 51: 112–15)	missing	118, 119 (JJA 51: 116–17) incomplete	120, 121, 122 (JJA 51: 118–21)
B	248.11–249.05	112v, 112 (JJA 51: 122–23)	127, 127v (JJA 51: 124–25)	137, 135, 136 (JJA 51: 126–28)	missing or none
C	252.33–253.36 + 255.12–256.10	128, 129, 130, 131, 132, 133 (JJA 51: 129–34)	missing	138, 139 (JJA 51: 135–36)	missing or none
D	249.06–252.13	88, 89, 93, 89v, 94, 95, 95v, 119v (JJA 51: 174–80, 184)	107, 108, 108v (JJA 51: 181–83) incomplete	missing or none	missing or none
E	254.01–255.11	96v, 97, 97v, 139v, 134 (JJA 51: 185–89)	missing or none	missing or none	missing or none
F	256.11–257.02	122v (JJA 51: 190), possibly other missing pages	missing or none	missing or none	missing or none

Note: All draft page references are to BL 47477. My division of the subsections does not correspond to Rose's in JJA 51. Prior to *transition,* subsections D, E, and F existed only on extradraft pages.

The first paragraph concludes with an overlay addition containing series of puns in Amaro, an Italian underworld slang.[43] The phrase "He nobit smorfi endgo poltri & all the tondo gang bola del ruffo" implies that Jeremy has supper and goes to bed (in Amaro *smorfire* means "to eat" and *poltriero* means "bed"), and then the whole world goes to hell (*tondo* means "world" and *bola dal ruffo,* literally "red city," denotes "hell"). This would suggest that Shem, the devil in the game of colors, has succeeded, since everyone else has gone to hell, his purview.

The second paragraph details Jeremy's sorrow at having failed in the guessing game. He has proven himself unable to gaze at the sight most deletious. He has succeeded only in ascertaining the blanks or the deletions and not the most delicious sight. An interesting adjustment occurs at this level. Originally Joyce wrote "Lift the black ve veared as hell." This would perhaps be a command to lift the darkness or veil that covers or obscures the hidden colors. This veil would be either the Maggies' outer garments or Shem's blindfold. If this could be done, then Shem would have won and thus be able to consign the Maggies to "hell." But at this level Joyce replaced "black" with "blank," which creates a more complex series of allusions that play off the pun "ve veared" (revered, be feared). Shem is left only with blankness, not even with blackness: an absence of even the absence of color. Joyce retained the sense of blackness in two distinct overlay additions: "^1He knows for he's seen it in black and white.1^ ^1Tantamount to a clearobscure.1^" This was complicated further on the missing proofs for *transition,* where this phrase now reads "Lift the blank ve veered as heil!" (*t:* 68). Hell now puns with both the Hitlerian salute and with veil. Instead of heaven Shem is consigned to hell, the provenance of the devil and, apparently, also of those who have failed the riddle. The paragraph concludes with a list of twenty-eight colors (the Maggies) of the veil for the prettymaide hues (the alphabet augmented by the two lagniappes philomel and theerose). Heliotrope is, unsurprisingly, absent from this list.

The typescript for this passage contains two slight modifications: hemalite becomes hematite and isinglass becomes isingglass (BL 47477 f. 121; JJA 51: 119). Both these changes are presumably due to a typist's error. The next extant level is *transition* 22, which contains two interesting changes. Fawn becomes feldgrau (German for "field gray") and ginger, the G entry, is absent altogether (*t:* 68). This means that the list is no longer 28 + 2 but rather 27 + 2. Since fawn was changed, Joyce must have made some alteration on a missing intervening manuscript, yet it is unclear if he also sanctioned the removal of ginger. Furthermore, it is possible that the new term, feldgrau, is supposed to combine the F and G entries. In any case, perhaps the absence of a G item could be analogous to the absence of heliotrope from the twenty-eight.

On the typescript for this subsection Joyce added a series of details that emphasize the antagonism between Shem and Shaun:

> Postreintroducing Jeremy, the flowing tale that ~~knows~~ ^[1]brooks[1]^ no brooking as it runs on to say ^[1], as it was ^[2]mutualiter[2]^ foretold of him, ^[2]by a timekiller to his spacemaker, velos ambos ^[3]and arubyat knights, with their tales within wheels & sucks between spokes,[3]^ on the hike from Elmstree to Stene and back,[2]^ how, running awage with the use of reason (sics) and ramming amok at the brake of his voice (secs),[1]^ his lasterhalft was set. (BL 47477 f. 118, simplified; JJA 51: 116)

Joyce here adds allusions to two modalities of the Shem/Shaun conflict: space and time and tree and stone (the latter one used in II.1§7 at 259.01–2, added on the galleys [BL 47479 f. 167; JJA 51: 445]). Joyce further expands the idea of the endurance of Shem's splitting (narrating prior incidents) by adding the phrase "tales within wheels" to the already-present idea of the flowing tale. This new addition recalls the early note from Scribbledehobble concerning modes of narration: "Arabian nights, serial stories, tales within tales, [g]to be continued, desperate story telling" (VI.A: 21; see also WiT: 23–26). Shem is desperately telling stories in which—both in the stories and in the act of narrating the stories—he is bifurcated.

II.1§6.A ends with:

> If you knew her in her prime make sure you find her complimentary. Or ^[1]by Angus Dagdasson & all his picciapiccions, on your very first occasion[1]^ she'll prick where you're proud with her speagle eye. Look sharp, she's signalling again from among the asters. ^[1]Turn again wishfulton loud mere ~~at~~ ^[2]of[2]^ Doubtluin. Arise, land under wave.[1]^ Clap your lingua to your pallet, drop your jowl with a jolt, tambourine until your breath slides, pet a pout and it's out. Have you got me, Allysloper?
>
> The bivetellines oxeye each other, superfetated, while the belles are in transfusion to know who is orthodox from whose heliotropic ~~that the great may be great and~~ ^[1]for exceedingly nice girls can have exceedingly hard times unless the rightly chosen's by to (what though of riches he have none & hope gainst hope's his heart's horizon)[1]^ their great moments be the greater. Till they go round if they go round again ^[1]before break par<t^ks^> and now dismiss.[1]^

> They keep. Step. Keep. Step stop. (BL 47477 fs. 116–17; JJA 51: 114–15; FDV: 138–39; FW: 248.03–10, 252.14–32)

The first paragraph points toward a further act of temptation performed by the Maggies, signaling again from among the asters. The second deals with a struggle between the twins (bivetellines) to gain the favors of the belles, who must decide which one of them is appropriate to them (orthodox to the heliotropic).[44] Clearly, something must have happened to raise such fraternal polemic. These two paragraphs remained contiguous for two further drafts, both typescripts. But in preparing the chapter for *transition* Joyce interpolated a new subsection (ultimately FW: 248.11–252.13) between them. This subsection deals with Shem's third attempt to guess the Maggies' color and his resultant "battle" with Shaun. It therefore expands upon the temptation built up from the first paragraph and leads up to the polemic announced in the second. The earliest draft of this subsection, which I call subsection D, exists on a series of extradraft notes.[45] Joyce made heavy use of notebook VI.B.33 (late February–early April 1931) for this subsection. The earliest draft of the third round of questions is as follows:

> All sing.
> ⊣ My name is Misha misha but call me Toffee tough. I mean Mettonchough.
> All laugh.
> They pretend to ~~help~~ ^[1]helf[1]^ him while they simply schutet at him
> —Willest thou rossy banders having?
> He pretends to be tight in ribbings round his rumpffkorp.
> —Are you Black hans that's hit on a shorn style?
> He pretends to be swiping the chimbley.
> —Can you ajew, ajew fro' Scheidan?
> He pretends to be cuttling up with a pair of sisserrs and to be buythings off their maiden ends pitting their heads into their face. (BL 47477 f. 93, simplified; JJA 51: 176; FW: 249.25–250.09)

The most important fact about this final exagmination (FW: 497.02) is that the roles are now reversed: the Maggies are asking the questions to Shem, as would be suggested by the use of the Issy siglum instead of a dash for the first question.[46] Joyce's subsequent additions tend to reinforce this impression. However, the word "schutet" (changed to "shauted" for *transition* [*t:* 70]) raises some problems. It obviously suggests the English "shouted," which implies that they are indeed asking the questions, but it also suggests (in both versions) the German *schautet,* "looked," which implies that they are silent and thus are not asking anything. Between Shem and the Maggies there is apparently a reversibility of voice and vision.

One element that suggests that this round of questions is somehow different from the earlier ones is a line also inserted into *transition* and found on a preparatory extradraft manuscript: "Twice is he gone to find her, thrice will they run to him" (BL 47477 f. 95; JJA 51: 179). This appears in *transition* and the final text as "Twice is he gone to quest of her, thrice is she now to him" (*t:* 71; FW: 250.27–28). This implies that the third time she presents herself to Shem he is not questing (looking for, asking questions of) her. This passage also follows from a notebook entry: "°⊏ returns 3 / times cf. Tristan / prankqueen" (VI.B.33: 50). The allusion to the Pranquean also suggests that it is the female who is asking the questions.

Apparently, if Shem answers appropriately he will be rewarded by the display of the Maggies' underwear (a most Bloomian delectation). She identifies herself with the name Misha Misha and the nickname Toffeetough, an obvious echo of "nor avoice from afire bellowsed mishe mishe to tauftauf thuartpeatrick" (FW: 003.09–10). (Mettonchough also echoes Metchnikoff.) The Maggies are enjoying this switch as they pretend to help him. However, Shem too pretends to answer their questions with a series of gestures. The direct verbal echo between the Maggies' pretense and Shem's was occulted for *transition,* where—instead of the thrice-repeated "He pretends"—Joyce has "He simules," "He makes semblant," and "He finges [Latin *fingere,* "to pretend"]" (*t:* 70–71). Notably, the terms describing Shem's gestures are Latinate, whereas the questions are Germanic. The final sequence of questions thus combines the individual linguistic traits of the first two series of questions.

The first question traces over some lyrics from the German children's song "Morgen ist die Hochzeit da!" (I'm getting married in the morning!).[47] The salient lines are "Willst du dieses Mädchen haben, mußt du rosa Bändchen tragen" [If you want the girl, you have to wear a pink ribbon]. This alludes to the old German custom of suitors announcing their intentions by wearing a pink ribbon. The issue here is somewhat confused, though, as the Maggies ask, "Willest thou rossy banders having." Joyce recorded the straight German version of this in notebook VI.B.33: "[bl]willst Du / Rosa Baenden / haben" [if you want to have a pink ribbon] (VI.B.33: 31). The sign of love is confused with its intended goal. The proposal of marriage to Shem, however confused it may be, reinforces the Maggies' earlier denial of marriage to Shaun: "To these nunce we are yours in ammatures but well come that day we shall ope to be ores. No more hoaxites! No more gifting in memnage!" (BL 47477 fs. 34–35, simplified; JJA 51: 75–76; FDV: 135; FW: 239.10–13).

Folded into this distortion of the German children's song is an inquiry concerning Shem's sexual orientation. *Bander* is French for "to have an erection,"[48] and *rossie* is both an archaic form of rosy and an Anglo Irish expression for "an impudent girl" (*OED*). Furthermore, in the context of an erection, rossy could be read as "raised." Apparently, the Maggies are asking Shem if he prefers boys or girls. His answer is to simulate some action involving his buttocks, his rumpffkorp,[49] perhaps miming anal sex. Joyce subsequently installed a prolepsis to this question in the galleys at the description of Shem's sorrow: "cursing sight, saint most deletious ^[1]to ross up the spyballs like exude of margary![1]^" (BL 47477 f. 289; JJA 51: 429; FW: 247.20–21). The verbal echo between these two passages suggests that the Maggies, in their interrogation of Shem, turn his aborted attempt to see their underwear against him.

The second question asks if Shem is a chimney sweeper all covered in soot, a black hans hit on a shorn style (German *Schornstein*, "chimney"). This question recalls a line from the song "The Lament of the Irish Emigrant": "I'm sitting on the stile, Mary."[50] The play between shorn style/stile and *Schornstein* entails an ambiguity as to Shem's location: is he at a height (i.e., on the roof, by the chimney), or is he not (i.e., on the stile, on the ground)? In other words, has he fallen yet? The question was modified slightly for *transition:* "Are you Swarthants that's hit on a shorn stile?" (*t:* 70). The name Swarthants (swarthy hans) is a Germanicization of black hans, and it also clearly echoes the name of a Germanic devil figure, Schwarzer Hans.

Shem's gestural response is to mime sweeping the chimneys. This response was indicated in notebook VI.B.33: "[bl]⊏ pretends to / sweep the chim- /ney" (VI.B.33: 33). The following notebook entry from the same page also provided the basis for the final question: "°adieu, adieu, frau / scheiden" [German *scheiden*, "to separate, to divorce"]: "Can you ajew, ajew fro' Scheedan." Here Shem is being asked, in effect, if he can *split.* The query "ajew" could follow from the previous question's "shorn stile" in that a style is a phallic implement, and thus a shorn style would denote circumcision. In sequence, all three questions impart some derogatory stereotype to Shem (homosexual, black, Jewish), and his responses, at least to the first two, seem to play along with these accusations. The final mime Shem performs has an obvious sexual component: he pretends to cut up their maidenheads.

For publication in *transition* Joyce added a key phrase to this passage immediately before the introduction of Misha Misha: "All point in the shem direction as if to shun" (*t:* 70; FW: 249.28). This suggests a fundamental ambivalence regarding the Maggies' interrogation: are they pointing to Shem to mock (shun) him, or are they pointing to Shem as if he were Shaun? This ambiguity implies that the "split" Shem announced earlier has reversed itself, and somehow he has become indistinct from his brother. In the various drafts before consolidation for *transition* this ambivalence between Shem and Shaun is muted, but, once they are consolidated, the struggle implied by the bivetellines passage becomes fully developed.

After Shem's third failure his role as devil is again emphasized: "Thrust from the light he spoors loves from her heat. He blinkth. But wraths but ire where those wreathe charity. For all of these have been thisworlders. Time liquescing into state, pitiless age grows angelhood. But, as he stands, most anysing may befallem, from a song of a witch to the totter of Blackarts, given a fammished devil, a young sourceress and (eternal conjunction) the permission of overalls" (BL 47477 fs. 107–8, simplified; JJA 51: 181–82; FW: 251.06–13). Much of this passage derives from accounts of witchcraft and rituals for summoning the devil.[51] Essentially, Shem's failure summons the devil in him to take over. This first appears in what seems to be a fair copy of II.1§6.D: "Thrust from the light he spoors loves from her heat" (BL 47477 f. 107; JJA 51: 181; FW: 251.06–7).[52] At this point Shaun intervenes. There is no surviving draft of this passage, and it appears for the first time in *transition,* immediately after Shem's satanic verses and immediately before the bivetellines paragraph that concluded subsection A:

> Which is why trumpers are mixed up in duels and here's Bowen meets Nolent for the prize of a thou.
>
> As he was queering his shoolthers. So was I. And as I was cleansing my fausties. So was he. And as way ware puffing our blowbags. Souwouyou.
>
> Come, thrust! Go, parry!
>
> —Now may Saint Mowy of the Pleasant Grin be your everglass and even prospect!
>
> —Feeling dank.
>
> Exchange reverse.

—And may Saint Jerome of the Harlots' Curse make family three of you which is much abedder!

—Grassy ass ago. (*t:* 72; FW: 251.33–252.13)

The format of this passage resembles those of the three failed encounters between Shem and the Maggies, but here it is a dialogue, of a sort, between Shem and Shaun: the "trumpers [threes, also the French *trompeur,* "deceiver"] are mixed up in duels [or duals]." Shem and Shaun appear as Browne and Nolan and are reduced to fighting. In the blur of battle they are indistinct in their exchange and reverse. The clearest apparition of Shaun in this chapter beyond being the Maggies' heliotropic ideal is this battle, in which he emerges as nothing more than the antagonistic mirror to Shem. This idea is buttressed by the two sentences Joyce added to the beginning of the bivetellines paragraph on the marked *Mime* pages to ensure a link between the battle of Shem and Shaun and the earlier-drafted passage: "And each was wrought with his other. And his countenance fell" (BL 47477 f. 180v; JJA 51: 264; FW: 252.14). This line echoes Genesis 4:5: "And Cain was very wroth and his countenance fell." Instead of just one belligerent brother desisting, *both* brothers have become aggressive. Shaun thus emerges fully only to become the antagonistic reflection of Shem through the scrim of other fraternal squabbles.

Subsection C begins the process of winding down the chapter by building into II.1§7, the concluding section:

> For the Producer (Mr John Baptiser Vickar) caused a deep abuliousness to descend upon the Father of Truants and, as a side issue, pluterpromptly brought on the scene, his cutletsized consort waighing ten stone ten, scaling 5 footsy five, and spanning 37 inchettes round the good companions, 29 ditties round the wishful waiter, 36 of the same round each of her quis separabits, 14 round the beginning of happiness and nicely nine round her shoed for slender. (BL 47477 fs. 132–33, simplified; JJA 51: 133–34; FDV: 140; FW: 255.27–36)

Here the deus ex machina, the producer, a certain Giambattista Vico, intervenes with "the Pageant of Past History" (FW: 221.18–19) that had been anticipated in II.1§1. The Mime ends with the creation of ALP, the cutletsized consort, like Eve taken out of the Father's ribs (Gen. 2:21). Shem may not have succeeded in his *splitting,* but apparently ALP has succeeded in her separabits. As per usual, ALP is left to pick up the pieces.

It is difficult to tell if II.1§7 was written before or after II.1§6, but since it received minimal alteration between its first draft and its appearance in *transition,* I suggest that this was the last segment of the chapter to be written prior to its integration. This section deals with the final, decisive return of the paterfamilias but concludes with the materfamilias. Joyce drafted a thunder word here to signify the crashing down of the curtain and the terminal applause (BL 47477 f. 145; JJA 51: 139; FDV: 141; FW: 257.27–28). But the play, like the Phœnix of its playhouse, will presumably be resurrected on succeeding nights. The thunder word here, then, is a perfect Vichian sigil of the end of a play: on the one hand, it is all sound and fury; on the other hand, it signifies nothing, except that even when the show has ended it must go on. After the thunder word Joyce writes:

> The play thou stagest, Game here endeth. The curtain drops by deep request.
>
> Byfall
> Uploud
> Byfall.
>
> For the Clearer of the Air from on high has spoken and the unhappitents of the earth have trembled, from firmament unto fundament and from twaddedumms down to twiddledeedee.
>
> Now have thy children entered into their habitations. Thou hast closed the portals of their houses. And thou hast placed thy messengers beside the portals of the habitations that thy children may read in the book of the opening of the mind to thy light err not in the darkness which is thy afterthought Pray your prayers, Timothy and Back to Bunk Tom.
>
> O Loud, hear the wee beseech of thees, of these thine unlitter ones! Give sleep in hour's time, O Loud!
>
> That they do not chill. That they may ming no merder. That they shall not gomeet mad howlattrees. Lord, heap miseries upon us yet entwine our arts with laughters low.
>
> Ha he hi ho hu
>
> Mummum. (BL 47477 fs. 146–47, simplified; JJA 51: 140–41; FDV: 141; FW: 257.29–258.10)

In II.1§7 the games have ended and it is bedtime, as the adult world has reimposed itself. Furthermore, this passage has a resonance of biblical ordination that underscores the weight of adult authority. Years later Joyce amplified the biblical tenor of this passage by including references to the book of Genesis and the construction and destruction of the Tower of Babel. Here, the separation between Shem and Shaun is phrased in such a way as to make them indistinct again. At the end, when they are differentiated, they blur again in their desistance. This desistance is phrased by the silencing word "Mummum." This terminal silencing recalls the original plan for Book II, which began with "Δ night!" ALP returns to silence everything in her maternal murmur.

Notes

1. Wim Van Mierlo, "Traffic in Transit: Some Spatio-Temporal Elements of *Finnegans Wake*," *"Finnegans Wake": "teems of times,"* ed. Andrew Treip (Amsterdam: Rodopi, 1994), 107–17, 109.

2. Jean-Michel Rabaté notes that Joyce continued to experiment with the sigla, producing all sorts of iconic variations, even after they had become relatively systemized (*Joyce upon the Void* [New York: St. Martin's Press, 1991], 85–88).

3. Yrjö Hirn, *Les Jeux d'enfants*, trans. (from Swedish) Lucien Maury (Paris: Stock, 1926).

4. Ibid., 64–65.

5. Hirn treats the game Colors, briefly, on page 103; Joyce's notes on VI.B.17: 29 bypass what Hirn has to say about it. Hirn mentions this game in his section on games that show an "eschatological tendency" (1926, 101). Clearly, this tendency allowed for Joyce to interlace the frivolity of the games with "loftier" matters. Indeed, once II.1 was under way Joyce continually emphasized the more diabolic as well as the more heavenly implications of Angels and Devils.

6. This is possibly the earliest notebook occurrence of the sideways Issy siglum, ⊣, which here replaces the crossed-out ⊥ siglum.

7. Hirn 1926, 81. All translations from Hirn are mine.

8. Joyce did not completely abandon II.1 during this time. He took extensive notes on children's books in VI.B.4 (which Rose dates January–late April 1929 [TDJJ: 29–30]), but none of these notes were used in the writing of II.1.

9. This fair copy was written on the back of the pages of the large typescript for III.4, as were the first draft and fair copy of II.1§3.

10. Iona and Peter Opie note that variants of this game (called either Angels and Devils or Colors) date back to at least the early seventeenth century and have been played in, among other countries, England, France, Italy, Germany, Austria, Spain, and the United States. In the Italian version one child is elected devil and another angel. They each take turns guessing the colors chosen by the other children. If a child's color has been guessed by the angel, he goes to Paradiso, if by the devil, he goes to Inferno. A German variant of the game, Blumen verkaufen, involves guessing flowers rather than colors (Iona Opie and Peter Opie, *Children's*

Games in Street and Playground [Oxford: Oxford University Press, 1969], 287–88). This German variant also appears in II.1.

11. Hirn 1926, 63.

12. Opie and Opie 1969, 117.

13. Ibid., 120.

14. Hirn 1926, 64.

15. In two letters to Paul Léon from August 1932, when Joyce was preparing II.1 for publication in *transition,* Joyce asked that Léon send him a brown notebook (JJ/PL: 4–5, letters from Joyce to Paul Léon, 17 and 28 August 1932). This notebook is now missing.

16. See Danis Rose and John O'Hanlon, "Norman Douglas' *London Street Games* Guess Where," *AFWC* 1.4 (Summer 1986): 85–92. Douglas's book was published in 1931 by Chatto and Windus, London. Items from this book were also used in other chapters, notably I.7.

17. Daniel Ferrer, "Clementis' Cap," trans. Marlena G. Corcoran, *Drafts, Yale French Studies* 89, ed. Michel Contat, Denis Hollier, and Jacques Neefs (1996): 223–36, 231–36.

18. These manuscripts were also missing to Joyce. In a letter to Weaver dated 11 November 1932 Joyce writes that there is "no trace of the MS." that Jolas wants him to complete for publication in *transition* (LI: 326). Presumably, this manuscript would be the unified typescript for II.1, which appeared in *transition* a few months later. In a follow-up letter to Weaver, dated 25 November, Joyce reports that although the manuscript never turned up, "I set to work on the notes you kindly sent over and patched it all up again" (LI: 327). This manuscript is now also missing.

19. Adaline Glasheen, *Third Census of "Finnegans Wake"* (Berkeley: University of California Press, 1977), 88.

20. The Pranquean element had earlier been suggested by "At last he listed back to beckline how she pranked alone so johntily" (BL 47477 f. 8; JJA 51: 16, simplified; FDV: 130; FW: 223.32–33).

21. In a letter to Frank Budgen written after the publication of *Finnegans Wake* Joyce divulged the color in reference to something in Book IV: "Page 626, line 17 (the word heliotrope appears here again after baffling Glugg in the mime, Isolde's colour too)" (LI: 406). "Who'll search for *Find Me Colours* now on the hillydroops of Vikloefells?" (FW: 626.17–18).

22. In the Museyroom Copenhagen is called a white horse, when actually Wellington's horse was not white. However, Marengo was white, so Willingdone's Cokenhape is already a conflation of Wellington and Napoleon's horses (Glasheen 1977, 62, 186).

23. Patrick A. McCarthy, *The Riddles of "Finnegans Wake"* (Rutherford, N.J.: Associated University Presses, 1980), 139–40.

24. The typist here mistyped "are candy" instead of "ore candy."

25. Brendan O Hehir and John Dillon, *A Classical Lexicon for "Finnegans Wake"* (Berkeley: University of California Press, 1977), 194.

26. McCarthy 1980, 147.

27. E. L. Epstein, "Interpreting *Finnegans Wake:* A Half-Way House," *JJQ* 1.3 (Summer 1966): 252–71, 256.

28. "Split" meaning "to leave" is primarily an Americanism. The earliest cited example of this use in the *OED* is from 1942. However, the *OED* also records an earlier cognate sense, "to break into factions," the earliest use for which is from 1730.

29. This addition is not in Joyce's handwriting.

30. James Joyce, "Continuation of a Work in Progress," *transition,* no. 22 (February 1933): 50–76, 56–57. Hereafter cited as *t.*

31. For more on the provenance of the Quinet citation see the introduction and Ingeborg Landuyt and Geert Lernout, "Joyce's Sources: *Les grands fleuves historiques,*" *JSA* 6 (1995): 99–138.

32. Iona and Peter Opie note that some contemporary children's games have their roots as far back as classical Greece: "If a present-day schoolchild was wafted back to any previous century he would probably find himself more at home with the games being played than with any other social custom. If he met his counterparts in the Middle Ages he might enjoy games of Prisoners' Base, Twos and Threes, street-football, Fox and Chickens, Hunt the Hare, Pitch and Toss, and marbles, as well as any of the games from classical times" (1969, 7).

33. Hirn 1926, 3.

34. James S. Atherton, "Sport and Games in *Finnegans Wake,*" *Twelve and a Tilly,* ed. Jack P. Dalton and Clive Hart (London: Faber and Faber, 1966), 52–64, 58.

35. "In the confines of a game there can still be all the excitement and uncertainty of an adventure, yet the young player can comprehend the whole, can recognize his place in the scheme, and, in contrast to the confusion of real life, can tell what is right action. He can, too, extend his environment, or feel that he is doing so, and gain knowledge of sensations beyond ordinary experience" (Opie and Opie 1969, 3).

36. Vico observed as much: "Children excell in imitation; we observe that they generally amuse themselves by imitating whatever they are able to apprehend" (Giambattista Vico, *The New Science,* rev. ed., trans. Thomas Goddard Bergin and Max Harold Fisch [Ithaca: Cornell University Press, 1984], 75).

37. Quoted in Iona Opie and Peter Opie, *The Singing Game* (Oxford: Oxford University Press, 1985), 62, see also 61–64.

38. Hirn 1926, 96. See also Mabel P. Worthington, "'Old Roger': Death and Rebirth," *AWN* 4.6 (December 1967): 121–22.

39. In a letter to Harriet Weaver dated 4 March 1931 Joyce indicated some of the topics he was considering, including in this passage "Marie Corelli, Swedenborg, St Thomas, the Sudanese war, Indian outcasts, Women under English Law, a description of St Helena, Flammarion's The End of the World, scores of children's

singing games from Germany, France, England and Italy and so on" (LI: 302). Many of these entries were noted in VI.B.33. See Danis Rose and John O'Hanlon, "Constructing *Finnegans Wake:* Three Indexes," *AWN* 17.1 (February 1980): 3–15.

40. Danis Rose postulates a missing draft between the first and second typescripts (JJA 51: 91); Hayman, on the other hand, suggests that the discrepancies between the two typescripts are all attributable to the typist's error (JJA 51: ix).

41. The proximity of zoo and cemetery in Zürich is alluded to at the beginning of I.4: "As the lion in our teargarten [*Tiergarten* is German for "zoo"] remembers the nenuphars of his Nile" (FW: 075.01–2).

42. I discuss the draft evolution of II.1§1 in more detail than I can here in my essay "Reading *Finnegans Wake* Genetically," *Text* 13 (2000): 203–20.

43. Joyce recorded many Amaro words in VI.B.35: 8–10. See Luigi Schenoni, "Amaro in *Finnegans Wake,*" *AWN* 11.4 (August 1974): 68–70. Rose dates this notebook at early and late 1932 (TDJJ: 31). If correct, this would place the drafting of II.1§6 as being comparatively late.

44. Like other passages in this subsection, this paragraph incorporates entries from VI.B.35.

45. The sequence of extradraft notes for subsection D do not form a contiguous and coherent subsection but rather a protodraft augmented by several pages of extradraft notes. It is very likely that at least one further draft stage existed prior to the integration of this section, and this chapter, for *transition.*

46. There is some ambiguity about this; see Margaret Solomon, *Eternal Geomater* (Carbondale: Southern Illinois University Press, 1969), 28–29, and McCarthy 1980, 148.

47. I am grateful to Karl Vitols for bringing this song to my attention.

48. This sense was used in the Museyroom in I.1 with the refrain "the Willingdone git the band up" (FW: 008.34, 009.09).

49. Changed to "rumpffkorpff" on a sheet of typed corrections for *transition* (JJA 51: 198; *t:* 70).

50. Matthew J. C. Hodgart and Mabel P. Worthington, *Song in the Works of James Joyce* (New York: Columbia University Press, 1959), 118.

51. The information Joyce used here derives from the *Grand Grimoire* and other books on the occult (such as Swedenborg's *Angelic Wisdom*). A good deal of this was recorded in VI.B.33. See Matthew Hodgart, "Music and the Mime of Mick, Nick, and the Maggies," *A Conceptual Guide to "Finnegans Wake,"* ed. Michael H. Begnal and Fritz Senn (University Park: Pennsylvania State University Press, 1974), 83–92, 85; and Roland McHugh, "*Grand Grimoire,*" *AWN* 14.3 (June 1977): 45.

52. No prior draft of this particular passage survives, but this page does include redrafted portions of an earlier extradraft note.

Storiella as She Was Wryt

Chapter II.2

LUCA CRISPI

The layout of the "night studies" chapter of *Finnegans Wake* immediately attracts the reader's attention, but this unique format is also what makes reading it such a disorienting experience. Even for those accustomed to reading the work's seemingly less "dense" parts, the narrative of the "central text" here is bewildering because something always seems to be deficient (and not in the same way as other chapters of *Finnegans Wake* are elusive).[1] Readers accustomed to find support in the apparatus of scholarly texts are encouraged by the appearance of the ostensibly familiar layout to seek the text's remainder in its margins. But as the reader is called from one side to the other and then, when prodded, to the outbursts down below, filling in the "narrative" of this tale remains an overwhelming task (especially since reading the text carefully only highlights the disjointed and abrupt flow of the narrative).

Joyce himself anticipated most readers' initial reaction to this chapter: "The part of *F.W.* accepted as easiest is section pp. 104 et seq and the most difficult of all [illegible] pp. 260 et seq—yet the technique here is a reproduction of a schoolboy's (and schoolgirl's) old classbook complete with marginalia by the twins, who change sides at half time, footnotes by the girl (who doesn't), a Euclid diagram, funny drawings, etc. It was like that in Ur of the Chaldees too, I daresay" (LI: 405–6, end of July 1939). Despite the chapter's obscure narrative, the visual clues of the text's format are sufficient to alert most readers to its performative purpose: it mimics and parodies the children's studies. Indeed, in the text as published a caricature of instruction and learning is the primary lesson performed. However, this pedagogical theme was not the chapter's rationale for the first eight years of its gestation: it had its own specific "plot" long before the chapter's form took precedence over its content.

This chapter is more difficult to read than most because of the piecemeal manner in which Joyce reformatted it, not because of the text per se. In fact, the tale told in this chapter would have been as obscure or as clear as most any other chapter in the *Wake* if the various transformations of the layout had not sacrificed narrative sense to a predominantly formal agenda. The tale told in "The Triangle" (§8; FW: 282.05–304.04) about the boys' initiation into the realms of geometry and feminine sexuality was coherent and complete for twelve years (from 1926 to 1938) through at least four drafts and two published incarnations. Then Joyce reformatted it to conform to what had (by 1935) become the chapter's distinctive format. The "Opening and Closing Pages" (§§1–3 and 9; FW: 260–275.02 and 304.05–308), in which the children bicycle ride home through the streets of Chapelizod, and the children's composition of the "night letter" at the end also developed over many drafts (from 1932 to 1934). They too underwent the gradual imposition of the new format. Finally, the remaining central narratives, "Scribbledehobbles," "The Letter," and "E. Q." (§§4→5,[2] 6 and 7; FW: 275.03–282.04), after having been set aside for about four more years, were all dismembered and recombined in both violent and subtle ways to conform with the chapter's new layout. As published, none of the constituent parts of the "night studies" were left unscathed by the reformatting process; their original narrative impetus and rationale were sacrificed to another performative program.

The Conception of the Children (September–December 1925)[3]

The beginnings of II.2 are found in what might at first seem an unlikely place: the final chapter of Book III, which Joyce began writing in September 1925.[4] From the very first fragment drafted through to its published version, III.4 begins with a scene of Shem as a child awakening from his *tumultuous sleep* because of a frightening (but undisclosed) dream.[5] Only partially awake, the young boy questions his mother and is comforted by her. When he recopied the fragments Joyce added another fragment of transitional material. Once it was revised and amplified that passage had a major conceptual impact on the structure and content of *Work in Progress.*

It set the scene by introducing the chapter's narrators, "the Four,"[6] as they peer over the (now three) children as they sleep: "nicechild Kevin Mary (who was going to rise to become a commander chief in the fireboys' brigade when he grew up [. . .])"; "nastybrat Jerry Godolphing (who was going to fall to remain a cardinal waiter of cruxnuts as soon as he was cured enough to leave the hospital)"; and "infantina sister Isobel (who was going to be when she grew up one Sunday a sister Isabelle the beautiful nun & next Sunday the beautiful nurse Isabelle but on Easter Sunday morning the beautiful widow Madame Isa la Belle, so sad & lucksome) for she was the only girl they loved" (BL 47482a f. 10; JJA 60: 17, simplified; FDV: 247–48; III.4.*0+; FW: 555.06–556.22). The description of the children outlined here established their characters (or, more precisely, their types), a subject Joyce further explored in Book II.

The conceptual and narrative development of the offspring *as children* in this chapter lead to the elaboration of the nucleus of Book II of *Finnegans Wake.* Chapters II.1–2 explore the dynamics of the sexual rivalry between the brothers for the attention and affection of their sister, specifically as young children who are destined to repeat their parents' history.[7] In III.4 Joyce described the elder male and female protagonists as young parents at a time when their conjugal life was still active. This cyclical repetition of the struggles of the parents in the role-play of the children provided Joyce with the structuring device he needed to bridge what he had already written of Books I and III.[8]

Joyce also composed at this time a detailed description of the interior of the publican's home in III.4 that became the setting of II.2. Amidst the hackneyed description of their commonplace home and then specifically in the description of the sleeping children in their rooms he explored the major themes he associated with them: their sexuality and their archetypal opposition. Along with their initial naming, these crucial descriptions of the family members would be the impetus for the elaboration of their roles in the new chapters of Book II.

In the first of the children's rooms the narrators encounter "Buttercup," the Porters' sexually provocative daughter. The twin brothers, "Kevin Mary" and "Jerry Godolphing," are sleeping in the next room. In their description their twofold nature, one evil, the other good, is emblematic of their character. The twins' double and reversible character is made explicit with the conjunction of their names as "kevinjerry" (see FW: 562.16–563.36). The fundamental ambiguity of their identity, signified by the slippage of their proper names, would become a crucial aspect of the narrative in "The Triangle."

Framing "Work in Progress" and the Idea of Book II (March–June 1926)

After having written III.4, Joyce was ready to begin Book II, but it would take him over a dozen years to complete it. From March through May 1926 he worked on two new notebooks (VI.B.20 and VI.B.17). Besides being the repository for additions and revisions for Book III, these notebooks also exhibit Joyce's other interest at the time: the work's expanding contours as well as his more specific concern with the themes and structure of what would become the children's chapters.

During this same period Joyce composed a new set piece for III.2 (FW: 461.33–468.19).[9] This transitional narrative piece presents Shaun's "proxy [. . .] Dave the Dancer," his "sneaking likeness [and] [. . .] alter's ego in miniature," whom Shaun leaves behind in his stead with his "dear sister" (FW: 463.06). This piece provided Joyce with a further impetus toward Book II because the presentation of Dave (as a mirror image of Shaun, a distinct but surrogate self), among other things, was crucial to the elaboration of the more general structural device of having Book II reflect and double Books I and III. The invention of "Dave" disclosed the narrative potential of presenting "Kevin" and "Jerry" as youthful surrogates of Shem and Shaun, as two brothers involved in the rituals of children growing up.

Even though it does so in just a few scattered entries, the extant portions of VI.B.17 document Joyce's investigation of the structural underpinnings of Book II as a whole. Indeed, more than any other notebook of the period it documents his exploration of the possibilities inherent in a conception of II.1–2 as a vicarious representation of the parents' lives in the varied performances of the children.

From the perspective of *Finnegans Wake,* the following conceptual note lays out the structure of II.2 in a nearly complete fashion. But from a genetic perspective, when it came to actually writing the chapters Joyce did not follow the schema, except in the most rudimentary manner. Actually, five more years would elapse before Joyce fleshed out the first line, and only in the most furtive way can it be said that "The Triangle" follows the schema's remaining trajectory:

home	∧ reading history (school)
tasks	⊥ " T & ⊥
	⊏ minus twos
	sock him snooping around (VI.B.17: 3)

For readers of the *Wake* the first line is recognizable as the chapter's principal scene: the children return home to their "home[work] tasks [of] reading history." Yet Joyce wrote those opening sections of II.2 (§§1–3; FW: 260.01–275.02) seven years after this note.

In mid-May Joyce sketched out a more comprehensive schema of Book II from heterogeneous material in VI.B.17 (BL 47482a f. 2; JJA 51: 3).[10] A horizontal line separates the detailed outline of the action of II.1 from what at this time was to be the other three (or four) chapters of Book II.[11] Only one line of the entire schema is devoted to II.2: "Studies ⊏∧⊢," which seemingly served Joyce as a shorthand title and description of the scene of the chapter: the three children (⊏, ∧, and ⊢: Shem, Shaun, and Issy) at their studies.

By the beginning of June Joyce had settled on both the content and the order of the chapters of Book II and confided his plan to Weaver: "Between the close of Δ [I.8] at nightfall there are three or four other episodes, the children's games, night studies, a scene in the 'public' and a 'light out in the village'" (LI: 241, 7 June 1926).[12] But, rather than start with the beginning, he jumped to II.2, writing the core of the "night studies," "The Triangle," first.[13]

"The Triangle" (July–September 1926): Revealing the Geometry Lesson

Thirst for knowledge seems to be inseparable from sexual curiosity.[14]

Although this section appears toward the end of the published text (II.2§8; FW: 282.05–304.04), "The Triangle" is the chapter's beginning: it was the first section written, and it remains the chapter's dramatic centerpiece. All the other sections of this chapter that Joyce wrote over the next nine years remain superfluous to the narrative climax depicted here.

Joyce compiled what was most likely his twenty-third *Finnegans Wake* notebook, VI.B.12, while he was in Paris from June until 5 August 1926, after which he left for a well-deserved holiday in Belgium (TDJJ: 28). During this same period Joyce also wrote the earliest (first through third) drafts of "The Triangle."[15] Joyce wrote out the following schema at the start of VI.B.12:

⊏ describes a circle (cuts)
∧ bisects a line

⊏ does theme for ∧
holds candle (VI.B.12: 21)[16]

Except for the candle, this is a skeleton of the action of the first draft of "The Triangle." Toward the middle of the same notebook, most likely just when Joyce was about to actually begin writing the chapter's principal scenes, he noted a possible scenario for the staging (the setting and action) of the first draft:

⊏ makes a castle of mud,
Δ runs to it (VI.B.12: 106)[17]

Once Joyce arrived at the seminal idea that Shem and Shaun will perform a geometry lesson by investigating their mother's element, the end of the river, the delta, the composition appears to have advanced relatively quickly and easily. It begins:

> Construct an equilittoral triangle. Can you do her? I con't, ken you? Simpl as kisshams. First, Take a mugful of mud. You take your madder river. Dump it at a point of coast to be called α but pronounced olfa. There's mud.
>
> After that you must draw the line somewhere. Given an inch make an ell. Now we see the line AL stops at lambda. Nodder island there too. Now with Olaf as centrum and Olaf's Lambtail as his spokesman, cumscribe a circlus. Hoop! O dear me! (BL 47482a f. 67, extensively simplified; JJA 53: 4; FDV: 160, 163; II.2§8AC.*0; see FW: 286.19–287.15 and 292.35–294.12)[18]

Unmistakably, the first line of the composition is also the "Problem ye ferst" (FW: 286.16) of Euclid's *Elements of Geometry*, something Joyce most likely remembered from his own schooldays: "Prop. I—Problem: . . . construct an equilateral triangle." It remained recognizable in all the versions of the text as published, and, though distorted, what followed were the boys' instructions for laying out that first Euclidean problem.[19]

Joyce now stopped composing the narrative and inscribed the geometrical figure that is both the object of the lesson and its subject, their *mother.*[20] The diagram itself was drawn after the paragraph that ends "O dear me!" and through its publication in "The Muddest Thick that was Ever Heard Dump" (1929) the diagram revolved around this phrase. But Joyce had a great deal more of the geometry lesson to write, and the next line begins with a reminder that more is to come. Having "cumscribe[d] a circlus," the boys are to "turn a sommersault" and "cumscribe" another (FW: 295.14–24). As the narrative will soon make explicit, it is the two young brothers (twin sons) who have drawn the diagram's centerline and then its outermost parameters. Readers of other chapters of *Finnegans Wake* may already recognize them as incarnations of Shem and Shaun. However, when redefining the brothers as children here, Joyce gave them a variety of different names (and seemingly, at times, he too confused their names). Even when named, their identities are so muddled as to make it difficult to assign a stable name to the one brother who is the instigator of the corruption and to the other who is the initiate.

These first paragraphs plot the mother as the sum and substance of the first and most fundamental geometry lesson. The mother is, of course, Anna Livia Plurabelle (ALP), whose sign is a triangle, a delta: Δ. Therefore, as the lesson's sum, the children delineate the mother's most intimate triangular contours, her pudenda. And as the lesson's substance, the mother is at the same time the "madder river" with whose mud the children are rendering Euclid's problem. After all, another of her many axiomatic names is "Anna Liffey." Here, in all of her guises, she is the figure of forbidden knowledge that initiates the boys into the most enigmatic realms: both the realm of abstract mathematics and that of basic feminine, maternal physiology. In this scene the sons do their homework by describing an equilateral triangle by means of her (written in mud), with her (in the shape of the triangle), and on her (as they gaze up her skirt).

Although the obvious sexual punning of laying out the "geomater" as the "first of all equilittoral triangles" was present from the onset, Joyce himself seems to have been ambivalent about actually naming the mother as the site of the lesson. At first he named her the "geomater" but then altered the watchword on the same draft to the more neutral "geometer" (someone who either measures the earth or specializes in mathematical abstractions).[21] The ambivalence continued: Joyce copied "geometer" to the second draft but replaced that indeterminate designation with "geomater" on the later draft. And this is how she resurfaces in the following draft and in all of the published texts.

Once the boys had surveyed her "centrum" lines from α to λ, they proceeded in different directions, the one to plot the "capital pee" down below and the other to contemplate her more "modest pie" (π) at the other end: and so here is our "A.L.P." They are then to connect all the points, one with solid, the other with dotted lines (or, as Joyce has it, "dotty links"), and thus they have mirror images of their mother: not one, but two triangles, the higher and lower.

> There's tewtricklesome poinds at which our two doubling run into eath the ocher. ^[1]~~Looksyhere~~[1]^ ^[2]Lucihere[2]^. I fee where you mein. I think as I'm squeezing the lemon I'd like to pore a capital pee there for Pride and you go & muck a ~~muddle~~ ^[1]modest[1]^ pie ~~at~~ ^[1]up[1]^ your end out of Humbles. Are you right there, Michael, are you right? Aye I'm right here, ^[1]~~ye Divel~~[1]^ ^[2]Nickel[2]^, ~~all right~~ ^[1]and I'll write[1]^ but it's the muddest thi<ng^ck^> that was ever heard dun. <u>Bene!</u> Now join alfa pea and pee loose ^[1]by ~~dotted lines~~ ^[2]~~slashes~~[2]^ ^[3]dotty links[3]^[1]^ and eelpie & ^[1]pale ale by trunk lines[1]^. Like that. I see. (BL 47482a fs. 67–67v, extensively simplified; JJA 53: 4; see FDV: 163–65; II.§8AC.*0; see FW: 295.14–24)

Having come this far, the brothers now call out to one another. Here Joyce gives only the most basic indication of the twin boys' identities in this game of initiation. They ask: "Are you right there, Michael, are you right? Aye I'm right here, ye Divel." On one level this is simply an echo of a popular song by Percy French, but it also suggests much more. Here Michael (the good brother) addresses the other as "ye Devil." Here too Joyce hesitated to name the evil one so manifestly, replacing this boy's name with one of Lucifer's less forbidding names in *Finnegans Wake:* "Nickel." With only this preliminary determination, all that is really known of the brothers is that they are polar opposites; so far they are simply archetypal incarnations of good and evil. As such, the text initially establishes which brother is expected to be the initiated or corrupting one and which is the uninitiated, the good (or simply naive) one: "Nickel" and "Michael." A reader may then expect the characters' actions to be predicated by their names, but such clear determinations are contrary to a fundamental formula in the *Wake:* opposites exchange roles and contraries commingle (see FW: 287.19–27). As he continued to revise the scene Joyce obscured who is who in this initiation; in fact, these explicit names for the boys do not recur in this section of the chapter. The boys' names are quietly diffused and transformed into a variety of evasive proper names, purposefully obscuring their particular identities.

The drama begins to unfold: the precaution to proceed "Kearfully!" is a forewarning of this sinister act of initiation, "this muddest thick that was ever done."[22] The exposure of this most covert of all primal scenes will reveal something diabolical, and the injunction against it developed as a theme as Joyce revised his text. For example, he added the already perilous call to "Looksyhere" and then altered it to the more ominous "Lucihere."[23] Next, one brother lifts up the hem of his mother's apron/skirt, all the way up to her belly, just so the other can gape at the mystery.[24] The corrupter instructs the other, innocent brother to "Waaaaaa. Tch!" In terms of the diagram, the triangle that was drawn below with dotted lines is being lifted up over the solid triangle above. The inversion of the triangle, the exposure of the mother, is the learning of the lesson: "And there's your muddy delta for you the first of all ^[1]~~equilittoral~~ equiltiteral[1]^ triangles" (BL 47482a f. 67v; JJA 53: 5; FDV: 165; see FW: 295.30–299.08).

Given the sinister appeal of the event, as the lesson proceeds something expectedly goes wrong. But the misapprehension is soon resolved when the initiated brother points out the proper stratagem for the vision: like a vision of the Almighty, this revelation cannot be seen directly but must be reflected, naturally enough, "in the water," in the mother's element.[25] Then the other brother sees it all, finally (see FW: 286.19–287.15 and 292.35–294.12).

Until now the narrative has left the identity of each of the twins undetermined: Who is playing which role in this initiation? They (if they are ever really two) were named before in III.4 as the twin(s) "kerryjevin." If such a disentangling is possible (since by any other name they are also "Shem" and "Shaun"), which of the two is corrupting the other? Here the twins reappear named "Jirrylimpaloop" and "Frankey" (presumably "Jerry" and "Kevin"):

> Whereapool would he nibble his mum to me in bewonderment of his chipper chuthor grafficking cyclopes after trigonies pursuiting themselves godolphing in fairlove to see allover waste of Nolan's Brown paper till that on him so poorin sweat the juggler's vein in his scrag forestood out bursthright taut tightropes. With best apologigs for again triposing on your bumficence. Signang away, happy nestcomplete. Intricatedly in years, Jirryalimpaloop. I romain to fallthereatyourfate hurryaswarmorose. [. . .] Hold the pen, man way I do. And this, look, is Lordbyrinazigazaggy. Ay. But efter all of his medley of muddlingisms thee faroots of cullchaw ate citraw, wouldn't able stab of the ruler do for him smarter, like it done for manny another of the hairy dary firstlings, anon would think Frankey who, to be plain, was misocain. Once one's won. And his countinance rose. (BL 47482a f. 68, extensively simplified; JJA 53: 6; see FDV: 165–66; see FW: 300.09–304.02)

Joyce named each of the twin brothers in this scene only after the deed was done and the secret revealed, that is, only once the loss of innocence had taken place. He only then individualized the one brother who knows, the "con," from the one who "con't do her."[26] On the other hand, even when finally named, the two boys are still conflated.[27]

The next phase in the enactment of this transgression is the translation and dissemination of the forbidden knowledge, and so the boys conspire to write a letter. This is the third element of the schema Joyce noted (on VI.B.12: 21). The brothers set about to write the "theme." But here their roles and identities remain undifferentiated. The ambiguity concerning the brother's names persists into the published work because it was not a rite of initiation but rather a conspiracy implicating them both.[28] Like the children's experience during their "geometry lesson," a genetic reading is a corrupting force because it assaults the univocal authority of the public, published work.

An Introduction and an Interlude

After having written these central paragraphs Joyce set about composing a new opening for "The Triangle." Its purpose was to provide the necessary transition to the geometry lesson by describing the uninitiated brother's insufficient knowledge. It recounts how, although "He" was good at "manual arith sure enough" and could count, "no boy better," on his "fingures," still, all the same, "He" got bad marks in geometry and algebra (or as Joyce has it, "nucleud and allgobrew"), and "O, it bate him up." This "hsaoc" (a metathetic jumble of "chaos") was "Binomeans to be comprehended" (BL 47482a f. 65v; JJA 53: 3; FW: 282.05–286.02).

Joyce now had written the opening as well as the central paragraphs: the narrative kernels at the core of the entire chapter. As he recopied and amplified his text Joyce was not simply adding material suggested by notebook entries, as he often does, he was also methodically adding set parenthetical phrases. These numerous and relatively clichéd phrases give both the texture and the bulk to the bare essentials of the first draft narrative. Joyce continued the redrafting process in this way and then began writing a new parenthetical interlude, but he only wrote about fifteen manuscript lines before stopping. This interlude (II.2§8B) is a first draft but is intermixed within the redrafting of the previously written text and introduces another, at first unnamed, figure who also first appeared simply as another "he." But "he" soon acquired the new name "Dolph, ^1Dean of Idles.1^" It tells the story of this boy's teaching days, of when he was "changing letters for them [his pupils] to *bonnes mottes* and blending tschemes" for the other boys (the Shauns of the world, the "mikes," as Joyce has it), before Dolph took on the task of instructing his own brother here in geometry. Here he is certainly a Shem-like figure who is also a Stephen Dedalus type (and thereby a young Joyce as well).

In this digressive interlude "Dolph" takes on the role of another St. Patrick (BL 47482a fs. 65, 62v, 63, 61v, 59, 60; JJA 53: 8–13; FDV: 160–63; II.2§8B.*0; see FW: 288.13–292.32). But Dolph also plays the role of another Tristan on his first landing in Ireland when he encountered Isolde. As part of this relatively long digressive interlude, while discussing the manner in which Dolph sets out to convert "the natives" by recalling long-lost languages and giving them new meaning, Joyce ironically reflected on the methods and implications of his Wakean language. The following burlesque, pedantic description captures the force behind Joyce's creative technique as well as accomplishes its own narrative tasks. His technique takes other writers' "stale words," making them his own (in notebooks). They are then sifted and sorted and only a fraction "woven" into new compositions, a process he describes here as "jazzfancy the fresh takinplace."

> for if an you could see peep inside cerebral saucepan of any adolescent you would see in that ouse of thought many a litter convolvuli suggestive of other times, lost or strayed, & lands, derelict or sunk, ay and other tongues too, and not alone that but, looking far into faturity, your own convolouli would reel to jazzfancy the fresh takinplace of what stale words were originally whlom found for woven on & fitted fairly featly too. (BL 47482a f. 62v, simplified; JJA 53: 9; FDV: 162; II.2§8.*0; FW: 292.12–21)

Joyce himself famously described *Finnegans Wake* as "the last word in stolentelling!" (FW: 424.36). Now, at the end of July, Joyce copied his second draft on loose sheets of paper and then slightly revised it further (BL 47478 fs. 4–12; JJA 53: 35–43). Having made various rounds of revisions to the fair copy manuscript, Joyce had finished with "The Triangle" for the present, and his interests were soon distracted by newer work, including the German translation of *Ulysses.*

"The Triangle" and *Enemy*

Joyce's attention soon returned to this piece, prompted, it seems, by a request from Wyndham Lewis.[29] Three months earlier (i.e., two months before he began composing the piece) Joyce described a meeting he had had with Lewis to Weaver:

> Wyndham Lewis rang me up twice last week. I arranged to meet him at the clinic and we went to the café. He told me he wanted to meet me because he is to bring out a critical review. [. . .] It is all to be critical and philosophic and contain no creative work. But he wanted to make an exception in my case and asked me would I give him something. I said I would with great pleasure. (LI: 240, 21 May 1926)

In the end Lewis did not publish Joyce's piece in *Enemy*, and that proved to be a decisive event in the shaping of *Work in Progress* and its reception. The reading of "The Triangle" as Joyce's most immediate response to Lewis's critique of him in "An Analysis of the Mind of James Joyce," which first appeared in *Enemy* 1 (January 1927) and then again in *Time and Western Man* in September, is contradicted by the chronology of the events. The narrative of Joyce's piece was already too well elaborated independently of Lewis's sustained attack on him: the piece acquired its fundamental thematic structure six months before Joyce read it. The few allusions Joyce subsequently inserted into the piece (on proofs for *transition* 11 in January 1928), which are precisely the hints that have provided what evidence there is for such an interpretation, were added over a year after the typescript had been prepared for Lewis. "The Triangle" simply happened to be his first piece published after Lewis's critique. Joyce often called Lewis's criticism the most insightful in print, but he never overtly bothered to answer it.[30] Rather, as was his practice, Joyce responded to Lewis by writing two new farcical fables. They both rehearse and counter Lewis's charges against the author and his works.[31] Unlike the superficial incorporation of a few hints of the controversy in the published versions of "The Triangle," the fables are an explicit rejoinder to Lewis's valuable, though misdirected, criticism of Joyce's aims and methods. It is precisely in analyses such as this that genetic criticism can sometimes disabuse literary history of certain of its accepted myths.[32]

The Fate of "Scribbledehobbles" (March 1931–Summer 1932)

What Joyce had written of the "night studies" by 1929 was textually complicated, but it was in no way comparable to the transformation the chapter underwent in the first half of the 1930s. The compositional development of "The Triangle" was characteristic of the process of most of the other chapters of *Work in Progress*. In contrast, the genesis of the subsequent sections, "Scribbledehobbles" (§4) and what came to replace it, "Storiella as She Is Syung" (§§1, 2, 3, and 9), would be extraordinary.[33] Almost six years elapsed between the time Joyce revised "The Triangle" for publication as "Muddest Thick" and the first publication of the other sections of II.2, the so-called "Opening and Closing Pages," in *transition* 23 in July 1935.

In 1930 Joyce put aside II.2 while he worked on the first chapter of Book II.[34] Even though he had not yet written any of it, as early as May–June 1926 he had planned the children's games chapter (II.1) as an opening to Book II that segues into the children's studies. For the next two years, until it was published in *transition* 22, the drafting and revising of II.1 and the newer sections of II.2 overlapped, and some of the same textual material (i.e., notebooks and extra draft sheets) and themes (e.g., the rivalry between the brothers for the affection of their sister) shaped the development of both chapters.

"The Triangle" had existed in a vacuum until 1930: although it was the most extended fragment of Book II yet written, it still only constituted a very circumscribed portion of its length in *Finnegans Wake.* When Joyce was finally able to turn his attention back to the "night studies" chapter (at the beginning of 1932) he had a practical objective. Needing a transition from the recently composed II.1 to the already well established but brief narrative of II.2, Joyce set out to write an introduction that would help counterbalance the length and complexity of the preceding chapter. The "Scribbledehobbles" section was to provide a solution to this exigency, but in the process of revising its sixth draft (the third typescript) Joyce followed a different (but related) path.

Both to aid in the revision of II.1 and probably also to gain a renewed perspective on II.2, which he had by now put aside for more than two years, Joyce made a concentrated effort to re-sort into new constellations notes from previous notebooks.[35] In their new constellation in notebook VI.A these notes were essential in the composition of the "Scribbledehobbles" piece.

As early as July 1923 Joyce had used this large, awkward notebook to help shape his thoughts on the work that was ahead of him. Now, in March 1931, Joyce filled its first unused pages with several hundred words.[36] During the next two months he once again turned to what were by then the notebook's first unused pages (VI.A: 744–62) and compiled yet more notes by recycling words and phrases from *Work in Progress* in *transition.*[37]

As David Hayman has shown, the "Scribbledehobbles" drafts are complex and fascinating because they present certain unparalleled curiosities in Joyce's compositional practices.[38] For example, although he was usually so parsimonious with his creative endeavors, Joyce chose not to publish it with the newly written opening and closing sections of the chapter in *transition* 23 (nor when he republished this material in 1937), even though he had expended a great deal of effort on its six (or more) drafts. Also unusual is that 58 of the 201 words in the most basic level of the first draft came from a mere seventeen entries in an ordered sequence from the first twelve pages of VI.A. This degree of seemingly automated creative technique is an unprecedented manner of composition for Joyce in a first draft.[39]

Joyce began "Scribbledehobbles" with the first word in the notebook, which, if not specifically destined for the studies chapter, obviously suggests one of the homework tasks set for the children: writing. He then systematically skimmed through the notebook's first pages and in a very craftsmanlike manner creatively constructed the first draft:

> Scribbledehobbles [1/1] are at their pensums. Trifid tongue [2/14] and dove without gall [2/15–16] to solve dulcarnon's [3/1] dilemma what stumped bold Alexander [3/3] and drove him to pulfer turnips. [3/5] But what a world of weariness is theirs! For how many guildens would one walk [4/12–13] now to the pillar? For one hundred? For one hundred's thousands? And to what will't all serve them in an after world. Will it make of one a good milker? [4/15] Will he go away and not be silly? [5/12] Or where will he find funds to smoke a whole box of matches [6/5–6] per day? Or if she makes an earth of heaven will she lilt Barney take me home again? [6/8–10] As long as Una reads serials in bummeltrain [7/12] the worst and last at least may happen, such as go to meet Mary, [8/5–6] miss Mamy & mary Meg. Why ask her sense from what she's read since every annual [9/4] has its own aroma? *Quid vobis videtur* [10/1–2]? And even the remembering a tree is too beautiful for her to listen. [10/4–6] Small blame to her then if she shook her shoe off [12/1] at geography class, doing rivers of India with a whisper of wilf[ulove] heard [12/1] round the world. (BL 47478 fs. 239–41; JJA 52: 148–50; FDV: 148; II.2§4.*0; FW: 275.20–276.08; the underlined words are followed by the page and line number of VI.A from which Joyce took them)

Joyce crafted the first and second drafts with elements from the recycled materials in VI.A. As is generally the case, but to an even greater degree here, the lexical material in this notebook had been thoroughly decontextualized from its various sources.[40] Although Joyce had carefully chosen his lexical material (at least twice in this case), based on the way in which these notes were molded together, it is not likely that he had any determined scheme of how this introductory piece would develop, beyond a vague notion that the children would be "at their pensums." Rather, Joyce allowed the elements to coalesce around a bare skeletal narrative setting. At this stage in Joyce's elaboration of his work he was able to compose in a manner that is analogous to artisans who, for example, construct a visual image from shards of material as they come to hand, possibly with only a faint idea of the "final work" but with an adept reliance on the quality of the found objects, on the one hand, and on their own ability to create constellations of artistic significance, on the other.[41]

This composition displays not only Joyce's clear vision of what he needed to accomplish but also a self-assuredness in his ability to achieve his goal with the material at his disposal; the degree and conspicuousness of the technique is all that sets this compositional process apart from any of his others.[42] Although the first draft does little more than set the scene and rehearse well-established motifs and relationships, even this early version provides an introductory setting for "The Triangle." That is, after coming in from playing outside, the children are now at their nightly homework tasks. Structurally, this was all Joyce needed to accomplish at this juncture.

This unusual writing procedure is accentuated by Joyce's continued, almost exclusive reliance on these notes to revise and expand the first level of the first draft. A remarkable proportion of the additions were taken directly from that same notebook, bringing the number of words in the draft to 266, of which almost half can be found virtually verbatim in VI.A.[43] This suggests that Joyce did not return to these notes out of frustration but, on the contrary, actually found this unusual mode of composing quite rewarding.[44] During the next three years he continued to refine, elaborate, and amplify this technique of transferring and juxtaposing lexical elements and textual fragments, eventually coming to rely upon it to compose and structure, among other compositions, the newer "Storiella" sections.

Joyce subsequently had a typescript made from his fair copy, indicating that he was satisfied with the development of the composition. He again adhered to the lexical material in this notebook to help him revise the typescript, but this time Joyce primarily used the notes he had compiled from the printed *transition* pages, a portion of which he had by then already recycled in other parts of Book I.[45] Furthermore, Joyce also used a note from a page (VI.A: 51) that was unconnected with the notes he had more recently transferred to this notebook.[46] This is an example, among so many, of Joyce's propensity to use words and phrases from his notebooks simply as they came to hand.[47]

The narrative of the "Scribbledehobbles" piece was fixed from early on. In fact, Joyce did not alter it vitally, except to add levels of details and refine his language. The subsequent revisions primarily elaborate the basic premise of the chapter as a whole: the children are at their studies preparing to repeat the lives, loves, and foibles of their parents. These themes were already there in the initial drafts: the three children, their task, the homework problems they are to solve, and a future in which they would reproduce the successes and failures of their parents.

In the spring of 1932, while still in Paris, Joyce had yet another typescript of "Scribbledehobbles" prepared.[48] Although its transformation into the sections published in "Storiella" would take place on these same typescript pages the following year, there was as yet no indication of a major reevaluation and reorientation; in fact, the manner of accretion here is similar to most other *Work in Progress* drafts. Joyce then left for Zürich in the first week of July, and whether he planned to work on II.2 as well as revise II.1 for *transition* is not clear; nonetheless, he managed to do both. He continued to revise and amplify "Scribbledehobbles," but a certain sense of closure and transition was indicated by the ultimate addition on its last page: "And. / But rather" (BL 47478 f. 286; JJA 52: 286). This formula signals both the completion of this piece and a segue to a retelling of the story of the children "at their pensums," at their geometry lesson. With this Joyce had accomplished his goal: he had written an introduction to "The Triangle," and so he may now have thought himself quite done with "Scribbledehobbles" and possibly with II.2. But this is only the beginning of the story of the "Opening and Closing Pages" of this chapter.

The Innovation of "Storiella as She Is Syung" (Summer 1932–August 1934)

This same last typescript page of "Scribbledehobbles" also documents the major creative breakthrough that became "Storiella" and the remainder of II.2 (BL 47478 f. 286; JJA 52: 286). On it Joyce added a further paragraph, the "Till Wranglers for Wringwrody" scenario, which set him out on another trajectory that would generate the present opening of the chapter (§§1–3) as well as three other sections (§§6, 7, and 9)—a full third of the chapter as published in *Finnegans Wake*. Nonetheless, Joyce did not abandon his work on "Scribbledehobbles" at this point out of frustration, as some critics have argued.[49] On the contrary, dissatisfied with its development for the specific purpose it had to serve (as a transition from II.1 and an introduction to "The Triangle"), Joyce appears to have followed his inspiration and in due course composed another, more expansive introduction.

The "Till Wranglers" sequel (that later became a prequel) repeats the story that is at the heart of both II.1 and II.2: the conflict of the boys at war with one another (FW: 266.07–275.02). This time they appear in Roman garb in a cowboy scene, with their self-righteous sister ambivalently looking on, egging them to combat. The physical disposition of the text on the page itself exhibits the manner in which the composition quickly outpaced the available space. Joyce then copied the first draft in a more legible hand with only a minimal amount of new material but with quite a bit of reordering and smoothing over of the text.

Inspired by the recopied piece, Joyce wrote still more fragments but probably without a clear notion of how he would orient the new material, and he was seemingly unconcerned at this stage about the situation as a structural problem for the chapter. He was simply generating more and more text, and experience had proven that he would find a way of integrating it later. In general, he composed these fragments as additional texts to be incorporated in various ways in or around "Scribbledehobbles." Joyce drafted several discrete fragments, which he titled with a variety of banners, including simply "X" or "Insertion," but two more provocative headings were "The Letter" and "*Te Deum.*"[50] Each of these fragmentary compositions became the core of several new sections that would ultimately constitute the remainder of the chapter seven years later.

A first-draft sketch, headed "Insertion / (address) ∧—sex at / virginity, Joanes Crescent / Floquet" (BL 47478 f. 116; JJA 52: 2), contained the pivotal notion of what became the opening of the chapter: "So let us follow them [the children]" through streets named after great artists and scientists from their play at the end of II.1 to the scene of the children "at their pensums" in II.2. At what became the other end of the chapter Joyce composed the finale, which he headed "*Te Deum* ^1antiphona after Δ ["The Triangle"]1^" (BL 47478 f. 124; JJA 53: 266), and, although the note specifying its placement most likely postdates its initial composition, the scene follows fluidly from the end of "The Triangle." It describes the two boys' jubilance after the geometry lesson but soon took on a more sinister tone. Joyce also began to group some of the more recently drafted texts under the title "The Letter", and they were all to be incorporated in what had already been written. On the other hand, the eventual differentiation of these newly drafted fragments was signaled by the emergence of "Till Wranglers" (§3) as a separate narrative entity, distinct from the "Scribbledehobbles" piece. In general, none of these newly drafted fragments necessarily precluded incorporating "Scribbledehobbles" in II.2, but the steady development of these fragmentary narratives marked the beginning of its abandonment.[51]

Joyce's departure from Paris in the spring of 1933 marked the beginning of a two-year surge of creative production.[52] Given his continuing personal difficulties, Joyce probably did not accomplish any writing or significant revision of II.2 before then. But after a six-month hiatus Joyce made a strenuous and prolonged effort to pull together the opening of the chapter around "Scribbledehobbles." Although this piece continued to be a relevant fragment in the development of the chapter as a whole for the rest of the year, after 1933 it was supplanted by the newer texts. Afterward, "Scribbledehobbles" lay dormant until 1937–38, when it was revamped and then reintegrated in II.2 for publication in *Finnegans Wake.*

Before leaving for Zürich Joyce gathered together some of his newly written fragments and imposed a semblance of order on them by having the first and/or second drafts of the various sections typed.[53] The scope and purpose of these opening sections (§§1 and 2) was quite straightforward: after their play, the children ride home through the streets of Dublin (FW: 260–263); and what follows is a pastoral scene in Chapelizod, describing the Liffey and the area around the tavern where the children live (FW: 264–266.19).

Once the first paragraph of "Till Wranglers" (§3) was recopied it remained virtually unchanged, although slightly amplified, until Joyce altered the chapter's format. This text is a sexually charged bucolic scene with an emphasis on Issy: she is "[a] one of charmers, yet Una Unica" who went walking "under the branches of elms, in shoes as yet unshent by stoniness," with her sisters arm in arm "all thinking all of it, the It with an itch in it [. . .] the business each was bred to" (BL 47478 f. 130; JJA 52: 18; FDV: 146; §3.2; FW: 267.24–268.06). Then it became a moral tale for young girls, recounting how soon the brothers would be at war, over math and mating, while the sister sits on the sofa knitting, ignoring her studies. But she is reminded of some traditional advice from her "gramma," which is appropriately couched in grammatical terms, since that is the focus of the children's studies at the moment. She says that while it might be fitting to flirt with the boys while Issy is a young girl, she must think of the time when she too will grow old and should therefore look for a man to marry (see FW: 268.09–270.28).

From its first drafts this text closely corresponded in compass, content, and theme to the "Scribbledehobbles" narrative. Although the newer texts may well have been composed to be incorporated within the "Scribbledehobbles" piece, it is likely that when "Till Wranglers" grew into an independent narrative it was too commensurate with "Scribbledehobbles" for both of the pieces to appear in print, side by side, without a major alteration of one or the other (or both). Nonetheless, at this stage these textual considerations were not yet an issue for the author.

Joyce and his family again set off for Zürich on 4 July 1933, and, with a renewed sense of focus and urgency, he asked Paul Léon to find the by now well represented quotation from Edgar Quinet in a notebook he had left in Paris (VI.B.1: 84–85).[54] The Quinet quotation at this stage was supposed to be part of the opening, but ultimately it was not included in the published versions of the chapter's "Opening and Closing Pages." In 1933 sections 3 and 7, the material that would become FW: 266.20–279.09 and 280.01–282.04, were still all part of a single but unintegrated narrative that introduced "The Triangle."

That summer Joyce revised the already well developed "Scribbledehobbles" piece (4.5') and his newer typescripts, and he wrote still newer textual fragments. All of this work was actually part of a unified project to amplify "Scribbledehobbles" as the introduction to "The Triangle." During this round of revisions he also began to consolidate "The Letter." Six years later this text would become the long footnote on page 279. The composition of "The Letter" (§6) presents certain genetic features that resemble the "Scribbledehobbles" early drafts and also foreshadowed the techniques Joyce would employ several years later to incorporate previously unused material in the final preparation of *Finnegans Wake.* Here he composed ten discrete sentences, mostly from his notebooks, with little forethought to their eventual interrelations and without ascribing to them a predetermined order (BL 47478 fs. 302, 302v, 303v, 304, and 305; JJA 52: 227–31). Only afterward did he forge this material into a coherent draft, without altering it significantly or adding much material, simply by numbering the fragments, probably in (at least) two different stages.[55]

Like the new material added to the "Till Wranglers" piece, this composition is centered around Issy, specifically, what little she knows about life, sex, and her studies. It describes her youthful, manic, self-centered, flirtatious exuberance; her thoughts of suicide; her relationships with boys and her father; and her thwarted attempts to write and pass herself off as intelligent. Only from the summer of 1932 onward (i.e., six years after Joyce first composed "The Triangle") did the theme of Issy's sexuality and its relationship to the process and intent of writing come to dominate the new sections of the "night studies." This particular fixation, so pronounced in the published texts, only now came to occupy a central place in II.2.

During the autumn of 1933 Joyce may not have had the time or the creative energy to do any further work on the scattered fragmentary texts of II.2, but he most likely returned to them in the first half of 1934. He then made complex revisions to "Till Wranglers" that were extensive enough to prompt the retyping of its second page (BL 47478 f. 131; JJA 52: 19). The revision process of the "Till Wranglers" piece is unusual because a notebook (VI.B.34) was not Joyce's only source of lexical material. He still had a good deal of previously written first-draft fragments that had not yet been integrated. Therefore, presumably not liking to waste material, he used them to augment his latest typescripts. Joyce was now extending the technique of composing by collage: just as he had used disjointed notes and fragmentary sentences before, now he was using fragmentary paragraphs and blocks of text dispersed on various sheets of paper to create his narrative.[56]

After the typist had incorporated all of the additional material it was further revised as Joyce patched together parts of sentences from diverse first drafts and improvised other sentences in dictation.[57] The new material (FW: 270.29–275.02) moves the children's studies from one topic to another, that is, from grammar/rhetoric/logic to history, a lesson that is not part of either the trivium or the quadrivium. Here the lesson is both familial and universal. It begins by rehearsing what the children should have learned from their history books; but Issy (here called "Mutua"), as she stares at herself in the mirror, is not paying attention; nor are the boys, who are hiding their heads in a tub. Predictably, here the *history* is rendered in paradigmatic *Wakean* fashion as a repetition of the supposed crime in the park. But this time the cast of characters (HCE, the two girls, and the three soldiers) is played by Julius Caesar, two druidesses, and the Roman triumvirate: Octavius, Lepidus, and Mark Antony. The scene is also resituated in a more heavenly sphere, the time of the Fall in the garden of Eden, complete with Eve, the apple, and the snake.

Joyce must still have been unsure how he would incorporate all of these various fragments into a unified draft. Nonetheless, the "Till Wranglers" piece was the core of the new material in terms of both its development and its themes; but it and what became FW: 280–282.04 (§7) were still constituent parts of a single narrative unit at this stage. They continued as such until the two parts of §7 were typed and expanded to the point where they took on an identity of their own (much in the same way as "The Letter" became an independent text) and were segregated from §3.

Probably in the winter or spring of 1934 Joyce turned to all of the new typescripts and revised them again as a group. He also wrote a considerably longer addition to the "Scribbledehobbles" piece: a repetition of the Prankquean drama (that is, Joyce's version of the Grace O'Malley tale) that is echoed throughout the *Wake.*[58] After this "Scribbledehobbles" was set aside (along with §7) in favor of the new opening, and he only returned to it several years later to dismember and then recast it.

Joyce's further work on the opening was probably undertaken when he realized that the texts he had written since "Scribbledehobbles," with their more elaborate description of the children's ride home and the description of the field around it, functioned better as a dramatic transition from the children's games outside to their home and their studies. Arguably, the newer opening was neither as interesting nor as lyrical as the "Scribbledehobbles" piece, but Joyce may simply have favored the more recently written texts because they gave a more prominent voice to Issy, whose place in II.2 up till then had been minimal.[59]

At some point between the autumn of 1933 and the winter/spring of 1934 Joyce had the opening, the "Till Wranglers," "The Letter," and the closing pieces retyped (§§1–3, 6, and 9). This decision implies a resolve not to have the "Scribbledehobbles" and the Quinet pieces (§§4 and 7) included among the still active texts.[60] The eventual ordering of the material most likely occurred over an extended period of time, slowly and hesitantly and with little premeditation. Up through its revision in late 1934 "The Letter" section remained a constituent element of this, the first integrated typescript. But after it was initially revised along with the other typescripts it joined the "Scribbledehobbles" and Quinet pieces in limbo until the preparations for the publication of *Finnegans Wake.*

Reformatting "Storiella" (September 1934–July 1935)

In the twenty or so pages Ellmann devoted to the period from July 1933 to July 1935 Joyce's biographer focused almost exclusively on Lucia's condition and her treatments rather than on Joyce's continuing literary work (JJII: 667–86). He did not even mention that the July 1935 issue of *transition* 23, the first new issue of *transition* since February 1933, published Joyce's only new *Work in Progress* fragment in over two and a half years. Understandably, Joyce's daughter's well-being as well as concerns for his own health were most certainly Joyce's overwhelming personal preoccupations at the time. Nonetheless, it was precisely during this same difficult period that he accomplished the transformation of the layout of this chapter, giving it the appearance that characterizes II.2 in *Finnegans Wake.* Fortunately, the manuscripts present a fairly complete account of this gradual and piecemeal development.

The overhaul of the layout of II.2 (i.e., making the text performative by having the participants *voice* their comments on their studies) established this chapter as a milestone in the development of *Work in Progress/Finnegans Wake.* On the other hand, the momentousness of a textual and aesthetic strategy in which form(at) takes precedence over content is tempered by the realization that this procedure was not revolutionary for Joyce but rather a continuation of the creative techniques he had employed before.[61] The mimetic strategy of structuring the chapter as an example and parody of the children's own studies, with commentaries and asides, seems obvious once accomplished, but the genetic, textual evidence indicates that Joyce achieved it slowly and fortuitously.

The initial stage of the revision process was similar to all of the preceding ones: Joyce simply added more text. These revisions were made only to the "central" text, as there was as yet no marginal text to be revised. This chapter's format still resembled its previous states and all the other chapters of *Work in Progress.* Then, when Joyce began to add the marginalia, he did so *only* on the left side. Only later, on the subsequent level (the fair copy), did he also add marginalia on the right side. Finally, the extant fair copy was itself further revised to include the footnotes, the text of which were written as afterthoughts on the versos of the manuscript pages.

Some extradraft material documents Joyce's strategy of adding left- and right-side marginalia. He seems to have begun by simply compiling a list of short fragmentary and unrelated sentences on one of the sheets (BL 47478 f. 154; JJA 52: 49), apparently without recourse to his notebooks. Then he made the notation "Left side" in the top right corner of the page: this is the first indication of a plan to incorporate *any* marginalia. Joyce subsequently assigned these sentences the letters *a* through *y* in red crayon. Finally, when he began to incorporate this material as left-side marginalia he simply crossed through the sentence in blue crayon and noted where each belonged with corresponding letters (also in blue crayon) in the margins of the typescript (BL 47478 fs. 138–51; JJA 52: 31–48).

In general, these short sentences are not particularly integral to the text, but most already have the juvenile tone that is so evident in the published work. These marginal comments are all somewhat sardonic, irreverent, and irrelevant, that is, somewhat *Shemish.* The list itself does not seem to have been compiled with the idea of having one side of the marginalia speak with a specifically "frolicking tone" in contrast to the "academic tone" of the other. In fact, the manuscripts indicate that the plan of distinguishing the voices in dialogue, which characterizes the dueling marginalia in the published version, had not yet been conceived. There were as yet only similar left-side marginalia, and Joyce had not yet planned to have the voices switch sides by the close of the chapter.[62] These structural innovations happened later and slowly.

The other sheet documents the decisive moment of the format's second structural innovation: the addition of the right-side marginalia (BL 47478 f. 155; JJA 52: 80).[63] Joyce divided this page into three parts with horizontal lines and began using the text in the middle of it for more left-side marginalia, continuing his list with the letters *z* through *Ω*. Then, later, he specifically designated two other entries in the bottom portion of the page with the directions "R." and "L.," thereby indicating their placement as marginal comments on *either* side of the central text. This is the first explicit evidence of the creative breakthrough of the balancing, right-side marginalia.

The stock Latin phrase "Unde et Ubi" that Joyce used as the first right-side comment may also be the first indication of yet another permutation of the format, the assigning of *personalities* or *voices* to the opposing marginalia.[64] These sentences have a ponderous professorial, academic tone that characterizes the right-side marginalia in the published work: they generally tend to resemble fragmentary thesis topics. They are de facto evidence of the establishment of the more scholastic, Latinate voice that characterizes the right-side marginalia, which only slowly came to contrast the mocking, sarcastic voice on the left side.

In general, nothing about either the compilation of these lists or their initial use suggests that Joyce had such an explicit strategy. The uniformity of the contrasting structure that characterizes the *voices* of marginalia in the published text emerged fortuitously, at least initially. But, on the other hand, the relevance of the marginal comments to the central text became more pronounced as the personalities of the speakers in the margins became more distinct.

The revision, the accretion, and the reformatting accomplished at the next stage (the fair copy) are so substantial that it became a completely altered version of the narrative. The fair copy resembled its published incarnation more than any draft that preceded it most obviously because both the right-side marginalia and the footnotes all appeared in it for the first time.

A commonplace in the exegesis of this chapter has it that the footnotes are the place where Issy finally gets her say about the children's homework tasks. Based as it is on the published versions of the text, such an interpretation is convincing. But, as was the case with the development of the distinct voices of the marginalia, here too the textual evidence suggests that this was an afterthought, a voice or personality imposed on the footnotes after many of the footnotes, which are not Issy-specific, were already in place.[65]

Back in Paris Joyce had recourse to other material besides his own notebooks to further revise his text, including the second notebook Mme Raphaël had compiled. Like all the other second-order notebooks, it was an aggregate of the unused notes from several primary notebooks. Joyce's practice of relying on these notebooks is the most explicit example so far of his penchant for using texts that had been thoroughly divorced from their source contexts. His concern was evidently not any integral contextual unity that the notes may have had in the source or that may have accrued to them in his first-order notebooks. Almost mechanically, Joyce was looking for lexical data to provide the material inspiration for his creative process.[66]

Tailoring II.2 for *Finnegans Wake* (July 1936–September 1938)

II.2 became the integral narrative of the children at their studies that readers of *Finnegans Wake* would recognize only between November 1937 and September 1938. In that ten-month period (i.e., over ten years after the first draft of a part of II.2 was composed) its nine disparate, constituent sections were revised (§§1–3 and 9), reformatted (§8), reconfigured (§4→§5), and reintegrated (§§6 and 7).

In July 1936 a year after the publication of *transition* 23, Joyce's attention returned to the "night studies" when he received a request from the fledgling Corvinus Press asking whether he had something they might publish. And so began a two-and-a-half-year process of getting this elaborately designed fragment published. *Storiella as She Is Syung* was the last, most beautiful, and most expensive deluxe edition of an integral fragment of *Work in Progress* that was published before *Finnegans Wake*.[67]

By the winter of 1937 the text of "Storiella" was the only reformatted portion of II.2 ready for publication. Joyce's next task was the reformatting of "The Triangle." The text of this section, the centerpiece of II.2, had not been revised since the summer of 1929. Its revision at this stage illustrates Joyce's usual method of overlaying several networks of themes onto an already fully elaborated narrative. In fact, Joyce only added some of the networks of leitmotifs that readers of *Finnegans Wake* recognize as integral to this chapter's design at this late stage.

Joyce used five colors of ink (black, purple, red, green, and blue) and at least four notebooks (VI.C.7, VI.C.17, VI.B.42, and VI.B.46) at various times to revise this section.[68] The first notebook he probably used is unusual among the second-order notebooks because of the seven primary notebooks transcribed here; four were actually late *Ulysses* notebooks.[69] Intriguingly, Joyce used twice as much material from the missing *Ulysses* notebooks as from any other of the other notebooks transcribed in VI.C.7. The next notebook Joyce used, on the other hand, is more typical of the rest of the author's second-order notebooks because it was made up of at least three *Work in Progress* notebooks. Nonetheless, it too is peculiar because one of its constituent primary notebooks was transcribed in an inverse sequence.[70] Only the uncrossed notes were transcribed from the original notebook, which, coupled with the peculiar mode of transcription employed here, further disrupted any integral cohesion the notes may have had as initially compiled. Its use as transcribed also illustrates Joyce's general disregard of the original context of the lexical material, whether in the sources or in his notebooks.

In November or December 1937 Joyce probably had this preliminary version of the revised manuscript typed.[71] The next notebook Joyce used to compose further additions to the new typescript is important because it contains at least three indices (i.e., lists of words, phrases, and fragments from single sources) that contributed significant leitmotifs to II.2 as published. Although the first half of VI.B.42 presumably spanned a relatively wide assortment of sources, from page 136 onward there are three primary indices from which Joyce harvested material for this revision: W. B. Yeats's *A Vision* (the 1938, revised edition), Mark Twain's *The Adventures of Huckleberry Finn,* and Sheridan Le Fanu's *House by the Churchyard.*

The connection between the several diagrams in *A Vision* and the one in this chapter must have been an immediate attraction to Joyce, and his additions from it were primarily concentrated in the text around his diagram. Otherwise it is difficult to account for Joyce's eclectic choice of specific lexical material, and thus his practice here resembles his attitude toward the majority of his sources. The notes Joyce had compiled are primarily an appropriation of Yeats's vocabulary and puns on it. The superficial character of this index undercuts the critical importance of Yeats's work as a significant intertextual source for Joyce's text. The relation between the source text and Joyce's fragmentary compositions is tangential: the two texts are not mutually explanatory and are dependent upon one another only in the most superficial manner.[72] The relationship between them is based more on Yeats's lexicon than on the conceptual meaning or semantics of his descriptive ontology. They are friends of circumstance, much like the authors. Unlike the example of Joyce's confrontation with Lewis's critique, Joyce here simply appropriates the terminology of Yeats's text, usurping it without any overt critical engagement. Even though Joyce uses only enough of the words and syntax from the source text to draw the reader's attention to Yeats, the generative structure of *Finnegans Wake* allows the reader to reflect on a myriad of possible associations between the two texts and the two artists as well as their divergent aesthetic creeds and practices.[73] Although Joyce's appropriation of Yeats's text and its concepts is quite mechanical here, the artistry of Joyce's citation brings the two texts into a much more dynamic relationship than would a more traditional critical disputation.

This type of textual (mis)appropriation is also evident in Joyce's use of *The Adventures of Huckleberry Finn.* He had no more than a superficial knowledge of this work and was possibly only interested because of the name *Finn* in its title. Even though readers have recognized the characteristic voices of *Huckleberry Finn* in the published work, the genetic evidence indicates that it too was not a structurally or thematically significant source.[74] Predictably, Joyce's composition sets itself off from the specificity of its source texts; nonetheless, by simply (mis)quoting the conversational language of the source the two texts enter into an indeterminate relationship, an ever-changing constellation of reference, that readers of *Finnegans Wake* can explore but never stabilize.

Sections 4→5, 6, and 7 (FW: 275.02–282.04) share the same textual materials and similar draft histories. These texts were all compositions that Joyce had written, revised, and either fair-copied or had typed in 1933–34 as unified, although fragmentary, narrative units. But so far he had not incorporated them into II.2. Joyce most likely found the various sheets that comprised these sections at the same time and began reintegrating all of them as a unified narrative: they were to be the transition from the opening sections (§§1–3) to "The Triangle" (§8).

Like the "Scribbledehobbles" piece, §6 ("The Letter") and §7 ("E. Q.," a text centered around a flawed version of the Quinet quotation and a form letter that the children are to learn and mimic in turn) were also fully developed, although fragmentary, compositions that Joyce had suppressed twice when he published the opening and closing sections of II.2. Now, in November and early December 1937, under continuing pressure from Faber and Faber, Joyce turned his attention back to these fragmentary sections, divvied up the same textual material, and revised and recomposed them (or had them retyped) as a single textual unit.

Joyce now set about dismembering the text of the "Scribbledehobbles" piece, amputating its constituent elements and mutilating its integral narrative structure. He then reconstructed it as an altogether different piece. By cannibalizing his fully developed piece (§4) he created a more concise but, at the same time, more discontinuous and aberrant narrative (§5). By the time it appeared in *Finnegans Wake* (FW: 275.03–279.09) the "Scribbledehobbles" piece had been more radically altered and distorted from its previous textual incarnations than any other section of II.2; it was a mere skeleton of the previous tale.[75] The narrative sense and artistic integrity of the piece as developed over the preceding seven drafts were irrevocably squandered as Joyce literally broke up this draft into pieces to compose a radically deformed and much more delimited narrative piece. In fact, the piece that appears in *Finnegans Wake* pales in comparison with its previous textual incarnations. It is therefore one of the tasks of the genetic critic to salvage and reconstitute it as an alternative textual moment in the developmental history of this work in process.

To incorporate the "Scribbledehobbles" piece in the reformatted chapter Joyce had to reconfigure it to accord with the new layout of II.2. He began by perusing all of the top copy of the typescript,[76] crossing through in crayon the majority of the text on each of the pages to retailor the piece. Here Joyce was using his fully developed narrative as he usually used his notebooks, using the constituent elements of the narrative as disassociated lexical material that could be ripped out of their contexts and dispersed in radically different ways in another composition. This is the first example of Joyce using a fully developed composition as fodder for a new one, and it is most violent, utterly unlike the accretive, expansive techniques Joyce employed in turning a word or phrase from his notebooks into yet more phrases, sentences, and paragraphs in his compositions.[77] Here painstakingly developed, expansive phrases and sentences were sacrificed to create much shorter textual units (sentences and fragments of marginalia). In the end, most of the text of the previous "Scribbledehobbles" piece *does not* appear in *Finnegans Wake,* the new text is *missing* all of the text Joyce crossed through in crayon, and thereby the narrative is rendered much less descriptive. Although grammatically coherent, the retailored opening lost some of its more evocative phrases, specifically, several lines of vivid commentary concerning HCE, ALP, where they live, their love, and their children. This type of squandering of descriptive detail was a common fate for much of the poetic color in this new piece and here amounted to a loss of precisely those phrases that are considered exemplary of Joycean language and narrative description.

Joyce incorporated the varied texts that constituted §§6 and 7 into II.2. He reincluded "The Letter,"[78] which up till then had been an integral but unused narrative piece in a straightforward manner: he simply crossed through the typed title, "THE LETTER," and wrote over it in ink the directions for its placement: "Footnote." Unlike Joyce's technique in transforming §4 into §5, here he incorporated the entirety of the text, with all of its additions, as a single long footnote (FW: 279). This text underwent virtually no alteration from how it was typed and revised in 1933–34 to its only published version in 1939. It was in fact already suited to Issy's point of view as put forward in most of the footnotes.

The transformation of the Quinet section (§7) as drafted, revised, and typed in 1933–34 was a more complicated process. In contrast to the transformation of the "Scribbledehobbles" piece, the incorporation of what became FW: 280–282.04 further illustrates the fluidity with which Joyce could convert (when he wanted to) previously unused textual fragments into a new text for *Finnegans Wake* without sacrificing any of its constituent textual elements, smoothly integrating the previous text into the expanding narrative of II.2. Here Joyce constructed the section's opening (FW: 279.09–281.13) piecemeal,[79] but verbatim, out of two separate texts using the letters *a* through *g* alternately on the two pages to patch together this new composition. Now the text was complete and sent to Faber and Faber.

Predictably, because they were unaware of the different format of this chapter, the typesetters encountered problems situating the marginal comments beside the relevant text on the galley proofs. Nor were these the typesetters' only problems. Naturally, because of the odd format of the text in this chapter, each new addition (on both the two sets of galleys and the two sets of page proofs) had consequences for the placement of the footnotes. The final problem Joyce (and the typesetters of *Finnegans Wake*) had to face was that on the page proofs the left and right marginalia had inadvertently switched sides on the even-numbered pages: what were to be the capitalized right-side marginalia were on the left, and what were to be the italicized left-side marginalia were set on the right. Therefore, another (but final) set of page proofs was printed, and the text of II.2, as it is known to readers of *Finnegans Wake,* was established.

Notes

1. "If Chapter IX [II.1] is denser than what preceded, Chapter X should be densest; but chapter XI is even denser. A more elaborate comparison of adjectives is called for. Lacking it, we must content ourselves with calling Chapters IX, X, and XI the densest part of the *Wake*" (William York Tindall, *A Reader's Guide to "Finnegans Wake"* [New York: Farrar, Straus and Giroux, 1969], 171). Rose writes of this chapter: "There is only periodically a sense of narrative continuity and in some sections a bewildering lack of it even from one sentence to the next. This effect may or may not have been intentional" (UFW: 144).

2. The editors of the JJA have designated this section as §4 through its more than six earlier drafts and then as §5 after Joyce reconfigured the piece in 1938.

3. In March 2006, the National Library of Ireland acquired six previously unknown Joyce manuscript sheets, all of which date from 1923. They are some of Joyce's earliest writings after completing *Ulysses* and document a period of his creative activity, which although much studied remains quite problematic. In fact, these manuscripts require that previous conceptions of what Joyce was working on before he set off on the path toward *Work in Progress* will have to be reconsidered. Joyce wrote the second of these sheets from 12 to 27 March and it is a short sketch, a self-contained narrative. It is a delightful tale of a young girl's prudence, her "learning in geog," her charm; her health; her piety; her "learning in zoog," her domestic economy, her pity, and her charity. Although remarkably similar in theme and scope to the "Night Lessons" chapter of *Finnegans Wake,* Joyce did not return to this manuscript in 1926 when he actually began writing II.2. Therefore, although intrinsically interesting from a genetic perspective, this early sketch only has a tangential textual relationship with the actual composition of the chapter under discussion here. See the Introduction, as well as my article "*Enter Tristan, Briefly*" (forthcoming in *Genetic Joyce Studies*) for a more comprehensive discussion of these crucial newly-discovered manuscripts.

4. Since it precedes III.4 in the published work, some readers may assume that this was also the sequence of their creative production. In fact, a genetic analysis reveals how Joyce's creative experience with III.4, with its emphasis on the children's perspective, became the catalyst for the elaboration of (at least) two other, wholly separate chapters (II.1 and 2). See Daniel Ferrer's essay in this volume.

5. "What was thaas? Fog was whaas? Too mult sleepth. Let sleepth" (FW: 555.01–2).

6. They are the "Four Masters" (Mamalujo of II.4) who may have "witnessed" the comforting interaction between mother and son.

7. This antagonistic dynamic may have been implicit in the chapters of *Work*

in Progress already composed, but it was presented here for the first time as an intragenerational contest between the brothers for their sister, as opposed to the intergenerational contest that characterized the rivalry between father and sons for the attention of the daughter, which was explicit in the already written chapters of *Work in Progress* (see also TDJJ: 86).

8. For a discussion of what Joyce had written of Books I and III by 1925 see the compositional history in the introduction of this volume.

9. See Wim Van Mierlo's essay in this volume for a discussion of the "Dave the Dancekerl" interlude as well as David J. Califf's "Clones and Mutations: A Genetic Look at 'Dave the Dancekerl,'" *Probes,* 123–47.

10. See Sam Slote's essay in this volume.

11. The remaining chapter(s) only get a sparse four lines in all.

12. For evidence that Joyce was also concerned at this time with the transitions between the two Books he had already written (I and III) and the two Books he had yet to write (II and IV) see Joyce's letter to Weaver of 21 May 1926 (LI: 240).

13. No direct textual (or external) evidence has been uncovered that explains why Joyce decided to start working on II.2 before II.1. This is especially odd, since the notes Joyce took on games and for the studies in VI.B.17 show an almost equal interest in both topics.

14. Sigmund Freud, *Collected Papers,* vol. 3, trans. Alix and James Strachey (London: Hogarth Press, 1925), 153. This quote from the "Little Hans" case study, which Joyce did not note, appears on a page from which Joyce took some of the notes on Freud in VI.B.19. See Daniel Ferrer's essay in this volume.

15. Joyce must have made the decision not to pursue the theme of the children's games by the time he started VI.B.12 because it seems there are no notes on that subject in this notebook.

16. Rose and O'Hanlon have transcribed the third line of the schema as "⊏ does theorem for Λ" (UFW: 156; see also TDJJ: 92). Although the narrative context of the soon to be written drafts would support this interpretation, I read it as "theme."

17. These are elements in a longer list of ideas for Book II. Also see Joyce to Weaver, 15 July 1926 (LI: 242).

18. Due to the way in which the JJA (and to an extent the FDV) is organized, it was not relevant for those editors to indicate that fs. 67–68 were most likely written before the opening on f. 65v and that it was only in the second draft that the two pieces of the section acquired the order they would retain through to the published work.

19. The first line of the schema "⊏ describes a circle" (VI.B.12: 21), which can be detected in "cumscribe a circlus" in the first draft, is part of the instructions for the first problem of Euclid. For discussions of Joyce's probable use of John Casey's *The First Six Books of the Elements of Euclid and Propositions I-XXI of Book XI, etc.,* 17th ed. (Dublin: Hodges, Figgis & Co., 1902) and the clear connection between

Euclid and Joyce's draft see William York Tindall, *A Reader's Guide to James Joyce* (New York: Farrar, Straus and Giroux, 1959), 283; Thomas E. Connolly, "Joyce's 'The Sisters,'" *College English* 27.3 (December 1965): 189–95, 172 n. 21; and Fritz Senn, "The Aliments of Jumeantry," *AWN* 3.3 (June 1966): 51–54.

20. Glasheen has pointed out that the diagram is also the vesica piscis, "Re 293, 'The Geometrical Figure,'" *AWN* 1.2 (April 1964): 13. See also Roland McHugh, *The Sigla of "Finnegans Wake"* (London: Edward Arnold, 1976), 67–71.

21. Joyce showed the same ambivalence about actually naming the mother in the extradraft version of the line.

22. This first draft already included an early version of the title Joyce gave the piece when he further revised and published it three years later as one of the *Tales Told of Shem and Shaun.*

23. Joyce made the revision right above the appellation "ye Devil," which most likely suggested the addition.

24. Joyce noted this dramatic action on VI.B.12: 50: "⊏ holds Δ's skirt / as child."

25. It seems that Joyce had second thoughts about revealing this secret too: he obscured the rules of the stratagem by deleting "in the water" and replacing it with the more vague instructions "You must look upon the reflection below." Thereby Joyce reinforced the infernal aspect of the boys' act by replacing it with the proverbial residence of the devil down below and also situating the mother in a heavenly sphere above.

26. Again Joyce masked the more explicit naming of one of the boys as the Devil, simply calling him a wretch (BL 47482a f. 67; JJA 53: 4; FDV: 160; FW: 286.19–21).

27. "The Triangle" is the first narrative instance in *Work in Progress* in which the brothers confront one another directly; until now they have usually been speaking about one another in the other's absence.

28. This is often case in the *Wake,* as, for example, with HCE and the Cad in I.2–4; see Bill Cadbury's essay in this volume.

29. Although the initial letter from Lewis requesting a piece from Joyce does not survive, subsequent correspondence gives some indications of its request. Almost three months after reading Lewis's brief first attack on him in "Mr. Joyce and Mr. Jingle" in *The Art of Being Ruled* (London: Chatto and Windus, 1926), Joyce seemed to have overcome his initial displeasure with Lewis. For a discussion of the way in which Joyce answered Lewis's first "volley" in "Dave the Dancekerl" see Joyce's published and unpublished correspondence with Weaver that spring, as well as Califf, 1995, and David Hayman, "Enter Wyndham Lewis Leading Dancing Dave," *JJQ* 35.4–36.1 (Summer–Fall 1998): 621–31.

30. See, for example, Joyce to Harriet Shaw Weaver, 22 July 1932 (LIII: 250).

31. "The Mookse and the Gripes" (FW: 152.18–159.18) appeared in *transition,* no. 6 (September 1927). Of it Joyce wrote to Miss Beach: "In question 11 I

have allowed Shaun to speak with the voice of the Enemy" (JJ/SB: 129, 14 August 1927), and the controversy is rehearsed again in "The Ondt and the Gracehoper" (FW: 414.16–419.08).

32. Once Joyce had sent the typescript to Lewis he put aside "The Triangle" until January 1928, when he received the galley proofs of *transition* 11. In general, the emendations and additions he made for its appearance in *transition* did not alter the narrative: the alterations are mostly verbal, multilingual puns or further distortions of what would otherwise be ordinary English words. Besides sporadic allusions to Lewis, references to Swift's life and works were also only added at this stage of the chapter's development.

33. Throughout this essay "Scribbledehobbles" (in quotation marks) refers to the draft section II.2§4 (and subsequently §5), whereas Scribbledehobble (without quotation marks and a final *s*) refers to the notebook VI.A.

34. See Sam Slote's essay in this volume.

35. The notebook in which Joyce transferred the notes, VI.A, has come to be known as the Scribbledehobble notebook after the first word in the notebook.

36. VI.A: 1–20, 22–47. Although Joyce primarily interspersed these notes among the other chapters of Book I as leitmotifs, the following year some of the remaining notes were also used to compose and revise the early drafts of "Scribbledehobbles." Unlike Joyce's other entries throughout this notebook, which, although small, are quite legible, these newer notes were in a far less careful or legible hand; in fact, this material is in a hand that resembles his usual notebook or first-draft handwriting.

37. This recycling of words, phrases, and themes from previously written (and here published) texts for use in newer compositions is similar to the technique he had employed in the late revisions of *Ulysses* ten years earlier, in 1921. See Michael Groden, *"Ulysses" in Progress* (Princeton: Princeton University Press, 1977), 196–200, and Phillip F. Herring, *Joyce's Notes and Early Drafts for "Ulysses": Selections from the Buffalo Collection* (Charlottesville: University Press of Virginia, 1977), 37–52.

38. Forty years ago, in his pioneering analysis of II.2§4 in "'Scribbledehobbles' and How They Grew: A Turning Point in the Development of a Chapter" (*Twelve and a Tilly: Essays on the Occasion of the 25th Anniversary of "Finnegans Wake,"* ed. Jack P. Dalton and Clive Hart [Evanston: Northwestern University Press, 1966], 107–18), David Hayman was the first to document Joyce's reliance on VI.A. and analyze the unique nature of Joyce's compositional practices here. All the subsequent studies of "Scribbledehobbles" are indebted to his groundbreaking work.

39. Joyce's creative output in the 1930s is striking: in contrast to what one would expect, an inverse correlation exists between his personal and artistic difficulties and the amount and quality of work he accomplished. Even during his most difficult periods Joyce managed bursts of creative productivity.

40. Although the sources for these notes have yet to be uncovered, Joyce's note-taking process has been well documented, and, as with most of Joyce's notes, presumably the majority of these notes have a textual source in the newspapers and books Joyce was reading at the time.

41. Just this kind of technique was also employed by other modernist artists such as Picasso, Braque, and Matisse, to name only the most obvious.

42. Although this draft was generated with an almost unprecedented dependence on his notes, it would be just as unprecedented a situation for Joyce to compose (or, more often, revise) a draft without relying on the lexical storehouse that his notebooks represented in his by now well tuned creative machinery. Joyce consistently needed an already distilled system of lexical material to spur on his creativity, and the notebooks provided just this sort of intellectual and verbal filtering system. For Joyce the notebooks were invariably a way of keeping the information and the world in check. This composition is an example of the writer's scissors and paste technique taken to its logical extreme.

43. Of the sixty-six new words added to the first draft a remarkable fifty words were culled verbatim from the notebook. As Joyce found notes in the later pages that fit into earlier parts of the draft he inserted them as additions.

44. Joyce had fair-copied the first draft with a continued reliance on VI.A for inspiration and elements. Its first three lines are new to the draft and are composed of elements that follow in sequence, but not as formulaically as with the first draft, on the pages from which the additions to the first draft were made.

45. Joyce had inserted some elements in other parts of Book I to reinforce thematic links between the various texts he had already written, but here he was extending this method to the drafting of new material in Book II and so establishing further intertextual links.

46. These notes, under the heading "Eveline," had been transferred to VI.A in 1923 and (if nothing else) were visually unmistakably different from the newer notes.

47. A long paragraph Joyce added to the first typescript (BL 47478 fs. 248–51; JJA 52: 160–63; §4.2) is genetically interesting because it also marks the interpolation of the first material from another notebook (VI.B.14), which also inspired the majority of the other additions to this typescript. This marks the juncture at which Joyce returned to his more tried and proven techniques of reliance on several notebooks to revise a draft.

48. The typescript survives in two copies: a top copy (4.5') and at least one carbon (4.5).

49. Hayman established an interpretation of this section as a failure of Joyce's writerly self-confidence and creative powers.

50. See *Buffalo VI.B.3,* 71.

51. In fact, Joyce's further revisions of its typescript indicate that "Scribbledehobbles" was still a developing concern and continued to be for at least another year.

52. Joyce and his family had returned to Paris on 20 October 1932. He then became involved with the publication of *Two Tales Told of Shem and Shaun,* choosing not to include "The Geometry Lesson" among them. During what some have considered a period of writer's block and seeming creative uninterest, the composition of new texts as well as Joyce's continued revisions are intriguing.

53. Although these fragments did not attain their final order for another year, it is convenient to describe them in terms of their final placement in their published versions.

54. As Ingeborg Landuyt and Geert Lernout have demonstrated, Joyce did not transcribe the quotation directly from Quinet but rather mistranscribed it from Léon Metchnikoff's *La Civilisation et les grands fleuves historiques* ("Joyce's Sources: *Les grandes fleuves historiques,"* *JSA* 6 [1995]: 99–138). Léon found the quotation and sent a transcription two days later (see JJ/PL: 10). Coming across a fragmentary draft that he had composed the previous summer on which he had inscribed the initials "E. Q." most likely sparked Joyce's renewed interest in Quinet (BL 47478 f. 122; JJA 52: 21).

55. The scarcity of added material on the next extant draft (6.2) indicates his confident reliance on assemblage as a compositional technique.

56. Joyce's use of BL 47478 f. 122 (JJA 52: 21) is an interesting case in point.

57. Not wanting to stop work when he lacked the right phrase, Joyce seems to have instructed the typist to leave room for even more material, which he added when he had settled on the right words.

58. See, for example, the first and most complete version of the tale in I.1 (FW: 021.05–029.36). Why Joyce made such an extensive addition to a now out-of-date document is not clear.

59. Issy subsequently made herself heard much more vocally, even if it is principally from down below in the footnotes.

60. The inclusion of "The Letter" (§6), which was also later set aside, in this new typescript indicates a deliberate exclusion of the other two pieces; and their exclusion cannot be attributed either to simple forgetfulness or to a lack of decisiveness, as has been suggested by Rose (TDJJ: 119–20).

61. The most obvious and exemplary instance of Joyce's prior use of a technique of this kind is the transformation of the "Aeolus" episode of *Ulysses* in galley proofs (JJA 18: 3–10); see Groden 1977, 64–114.

62. Initially, Joyce added the "Shemish" marginal comments all on the left side, even to the closing section (§9), and all from the same list (on BL 47478 f. 154; JJA 52: 49). But by the time he had prepared the next level (the extant fair copy) of the close of this chapter he had decided that the voices would have changed sides here; that is, here the more ponderous voice was on the left and the more frolicking one on the right. He could only have made this determination at a later stage (than this typescript) after he had settled on having marginalia on both sides and after having assigned specific voices to each side.

63. It is not possible to precisely determine the sequence of creative events here because Joyce did not incorporate this material on the typescript and fair copies do not document most of the inevitable false starts or the breakthroughs that are so important to genetic analysis. Nor did he tag (e.g., with letters) most the text that he used as right-side marginalia on this sheet.

64. One of the repercussions of the piecemeal implementation of the format is that inconsistent remnants of text that had been added before the assignment of voices to the marginalia (including the footnotes) persist in the published version; for example, see "*Non quod sed quiat*" (FW: 263.L3–4).

65. The second footnote on BL 47478 f. 171v (JJA 52: 69) is the first explicit indication that the footnotes are to be Issy oriented (as the note in VI.B.36: 138 that inspired it was Issy tagged). Interestingly, at this stage Joyce seems to have been especially attentive to the structural balance of the marginalia, specifically trying to distribute an equal amount of text in the footnotes and margins.

66. More often than not the use of the note has nothing to do with the material source. For example, see the last footnote on BL 47478 f. 192 (JJA 52: 95; FW: 268.F1), which has a curious history in its original notebook (VI.B.6: 75) and illustrates once again the general pattern by which Joyce creatively appropriated his textual material.

67. This summary statement excludes the small fragment of II.1 (FW: 244.13–246.02) that was printed in the lavish Parisian journal *Verve* (1.2) the following month (March 1938) as well as the last fragment of *Work in Progress* (II.3§4–5) that was published in *transition* 27 in May 1938.

68. Joyce used two colors of ink (purple and black) to revise §8.12 *before,* one color of ink (red) *during* the typing process, then two more colors of ink (blue and green) *after* the typing had been completed. He undertook this elaborate method to indicate precisely to the amanuenses and typist(s) the newer levels of additions so that only they would be incorporated at each stage of the text's development. He had employed a similar technique to revise *Ulysses* and most recently while revising the galleys of Books I and III. For Joyce's own description of this technique see Joyce to Curran, 14 July 1937 (LI: 392).

69. In his 1962 catalogue description of Buffalo manuscript VI.C.7, Peter Spielberg postulated this portion of the transcribed notebook as constituting the uncrossed units from a single presumably lost notebook, VI.D.4 (*James Joyce's Manuscripts and Letters at the University of Buffalo,* New York: University of Buffalo, 1962, 134). These four *Ulysses* notebooks only resurfaced in 2002 when they were acquired by the National Library of Ireland as part of their "Joyce 2002 Papers." Mme Raphaël transcribed most of the uncrossed units from NLI MSS 36,639/5/A–B (these are two distinct notebooks) on VI.C.7: 136–234, 36,639/4 on pages 235–54, and 36,639/3 on pages 255–69. Joyce originally compiled the three other *Work in Progress/Finnegans Wake* notebooks transcribed in VI.C.7 in 1925 and 1926.

70. VI.B.37 was transcribed from the end of the primary notebook to its beginning, backward, page by page (verso to recto), from the top to bottom of each page, filling the new notebook, VI.C.17, in this disjointed sequence. The *only* notes Joyce used from VI.C.17 were those transcribed from VI.B.37 and all for this revision process.

71. This manuscript is §8.13; BL 47478 fs. 84–115; JJA 53: 230–64.

72. See BL 47488, BL 47478 fs. 253 and 257; JJA 53: 228–29.

73. For example, Joyce turns one of the most important and recognizable conceptual terms in *A Vision,* "gyres," into a mere childish pun: "Gyre O, gyre O, gyrotundo!" (FW: 295.23–24), which a reader may recognize as a rendition of the Italian version of the nursery rhyme "Ring-a-ring o' Roses." This gloss already happened to have a suitable place in Joyce's text, before the Italian "Hop lala!" (which is said, e.g., after a stumble) and the description of Humpty Dumpty, who falls to the ground "As umpty herum as you seat!" both of which were already part of the text of "Muddest Thick" (FW: 295.24–25).

74. See Joyce to David Fleishman, 8 August 1937 (LIII: 402).

75. Joyce turned to the less revised top copy of the third typescript 4.5'. Therefore, additions from the typescript pages that were not copied from the carbon copy (4.5) to the top copy (4.5') by the amanuensis fell out of the textual line of descent. In all, the eleven-page typescript of 4.5' became a four-page holograph draft that is only four pages of printed text in *Finnegans Wake.*

76. The manuscript is BL 47478 fs. 288–98; JJA 52: 197–208.

77. In contrast, consider the variously fluid ways in which the sketches were incorporated into II.3, II.4, and IV as described in David Hayman's, Jed Deppman's, and Dirk Van Hulle's essays in this volume. Also see TDJJ: 121–31, 132–36.

78. This manuscript is §6.2, BL 47478 fs. 309–11; JJA 52: 235–37.

79. BL 47478 f. 316, 317; JJA 52: 248–49.

Male Maturity or the *Pub*lic Rise & Private Decline of HC Earwicker

Chapter II.3

DAVID HAYMAN

At the risk of being thought outrageous, I'll begin by saying that chapter II.3 has a stranger and longer history than any other chapter in the book. We can, after all, with a bit of effort trace parts of it back not only to the notes for *Ulysses* but also to some of that book's most challenging and rewarding chapters: to "Scylla and Charybdis," where the argument is presented within a theatrical form; to "Cyclops," where fantastic asides magnify the aura of a trivial pub tale about the activities in an ambiguously presented pub and where an outsider's reputation is humorously demolished; to "Oxen of the Sun" or, rather, to its raucous concluding polylogue, of which the penultimate segment of II.3 is an elaboration of sorts; and to "Circe," in which subconscious conflicts are given a dramatic rendering. We can go further. Of course, the parallels, to which we will return, are richer, firmer, subtler, and more ambiguous than I am suggesting.

Primordial Traces

Somewhat more basic is the mysterious foreshadowing underscored by Joyce himself when he called the chapter he planned to write "A Painful Case" (LI: 242, 15 July 1926).[1] At this point I can do no more than suggest that he could already have been thinking of the Chapelizod setting for the chapter, but perhaps he was also thinking back to one of his earliest conceptions. At any rate, in January–February 1923, when he was preparing to begin work on his final project, he took notes under the heading "A PAINFUL CASE" in VI.A, or Scribbledehobble.[2] The topic of those notes was not the story of sour Mr Duffy, who has retreated to the village of Chapelizod, and the notes are not transparently predictive of II.3. Their focus is a closely observed, quirky (and witty) Establishment villager called simply "Pop." An article could be written on the entries under this heading: their inner coherence, their use in the *Wake,* their relationship to the Chapelizod context of both the short story and II.3, and how they function to record the traits of an eminently caricaturable type of Irish burgher. Digging deeper, in the Trieste notebook first transcribed by Robert Scholes for *The Workshop of Daedalus* we find a premonition of this figure in the notes Joyce took in 1909 on his "Pappie" (Cornell 25: 37; JJA 7: 145–47).[3]

Let's pause briefly to record part of the "painful" sequence. Think of the following as related to an ur-HCE:

> Pop sits back to sea: Naturfreund: saving daylight: the noise of the explosion was so disagreeable that the night polishman retired to his box and slept: his Anglican ethics: he sang Sweet Sacrament: R[euben] J. Dodd since old times think he was a hundred: solicthur's: writing pen: went with whore as aperitif: [. . .] this year made up of anniversaries: broken check: la mia signora: in W[ater] C[loset] blotting paper: spitoon: doorplate [with the message??]—polish [?] feet etc: sleeps in park, paper over face: joy to sit under grating: breaks on bed: publishes description of Is: specs at back, protected by beechtree umbrella: (VI.A: 121)[4]

Pop's daughter is already called "Is" after Isolde, who gave her name to the village. A careful reading suggests that, while focusing on Pop, Joyce was imagining him as his daughter might see him. This reverses the field of both the short story, which sees the world and Mr Duffy ostensibly through his eyes, and the chapter, where (under the most "realistic" scenario) the conscience and consciousness of HCE dominate how we experience the taproom. Still, it is possibly in the voyeuristic quality of many of these notes that the roots of II.3 lie buried.

Depending upon our reading, the entries under the heading "THE SISTERS" may contain some of the most significant foreshadowings of the oral narrative underpinnings of II.3. Narrative and especially oral narrative was Joyce's topic under that heading; it is also a major aspect in our chapter. Most interesting for our purposes is a remarkable list of tale titles, among which we find "The Tale of the Storyn of the Hundred Bottles," later associated with "Roderick O'Conor" but also applicable to the chapter as a whole. In the earliest available draft of the opening we find a reference to HCE as "the host of a bottlefilled" (BL 47479 f. 4; JJA 58: 5;

FDV: 168; FW: 310.26), an allusion that captures both the bellicose and the hospitable aspects of the notebook entry.

Also in the list is "The Story of how Buckley shot the Russian General," a comic narrative that, perhaps because of its Hamlet-like hesitation, voyeurism, plebeian conquest, and Oedipal violence, seems to have haunted Joyce.[5] This is reflected in the very early references to Buckley's exploit in *Ulysses* and the *Wake* notebooks. Indeed, the foundations for HCE's paranoid reaction to the pub gossip/tales were laid as early as the Scribbledehobble notebook and VI.B.3, in both of which the incest theme is implied. Beyond that, the crime, the encounter in the park, the trial setting, the exculpatory Letter of ALP, together with the accusatory broadside, or "Rann," were all very much in place as early as 1923. Oddly, the tale of the Norwegian Captain is not in "THE SISTERS," though it too appears in the notebooks, specifically in VI.B.17, compiled in 1926, when Joyce was contemplating Book II. There we find a curiously tentative reference to Joyce's godfather McCann's version of the joke (VI.B.17: 21). These are only some of the foundational materials so necessary for the construction of a capstone chapter, but it is easy to get lost in such matters even before we begin our study of the chapter as a complex formal and pseudonarratological unit.[6]

Beyond this ur-prehistory, the *Finnegans Wake* notebooks reveal a remarkable amount of preparation over the years for the composition of what was arguably the first chapter to be conceived and the last to be written.[7] As we know, the first passage written for the *Wake,* and the first of the foundational sketches, was the Cycloptic pastiche/parody "Roderick O'Conor," which was drafted on 10 March 1923. Surprisingly, given the time Joyce had for his preparations, that passage, revised to bring it into line with the by that time richly elaborated book, is the only one specifically to predate the body of the chapter it now concludes (FW: 380–382).

A Nod toward the Novel

II.3 is among the most complex formally but, as "narrative," it is one of the most accessible of the chapters. Its accessibility derives from its fairly conventional (for our days) novelistic structure. Readers of *Ulysses,* to say nothing of those of us immersed in post-*Ulysses* fiction and film, would not be put off by an overarching narrative that treats obliquely and simultaneously through narrative vignettes the rise and fall of a protagonist in relation to the history of a city and a culture. It is no longer unusual for such a tale to be told episodically in a sequence of radically disparate narratives, genres, and even modes. (This is, of course, testimony to the conditioning and sophistication of the modern reader, though, surprisingly, we can find quite early precedents.) Still, given the range of approaches taken in the earlier chapters, it would appear that Joyce has taken a giant step backward in framing the underlying discourse of this II.3. There is even a psychological dimension, that of the wary, conscience-stricken publican.

Narrative in Joyce, even the young Joyce, was never limited by established procedures. This does not mean that in 1922–23 he had twenty-twenty foresight into the shape and significance of what he was preparing to write. Still, the list of titles, the conceptual notes, and the short, even atrophied, foundational narratives (or sketches) were crucial both to the development of the book and to its very existence. The fact that none of the sketches ever reached the critical mass of "story" and that we have trouble seeing them as elements in a narrative unit rhymes with the book's revolutionary nature. Joyce's problem began with and remained how to accommodate their disparity within the *Wake*'s immensity. More specifically, he had to find the proper emplacement for what became the book's narrative sheet anchors.

Perhaps Danis Rose is right,[8] and Joyce lost sight of his primal insight at times during the book's development. Perhaps he needed to be serendipitously reminded in the late 1930s of his early efforts. Still, the early sketches were so quickly and thoroughly accommodated by the evolving text that we can reject that idea. In my view, the oral tale that is so basic to all cultures (and religions) was seen by Joyce as integral to the vision of a universal (cultural) history whose vehicle rapidly became the universal family. By placing the pub at the center of his epic structure Joyce seems to have recognized in that epicenter of Irish and Dublin male life the narratological center of male awareness and "spirit." Female tales are part of the book's fabric elsewhere, but here, as in the real pub of his day, the male universe and voice are dominant and (for HCE at least) predominantly destructive. This is the hub of what I have called the "male plot" (see WiT: 109–10 and passim).

There are precedents for II.3 in *Ulysses*. In "Circe" the embattled male psyche is the center of activity. But here that center is both muted and virtually unfocused; the reader must supply it, as is the case in "Cyclops." Indeed, the latter chapter with its graphic use of words and behavior progressively elicited by "liquid courage" (FW: 313.29) provides the most immediate source of its procedures. There, deprived of Bloom's thought, repelled, informed, and engaged by the predatory dun, we are pleasantly distracted by the mainly antinarrative asides. In opposite equivalence II.3

punctuates the pub tales through which HCE's evolution is developed with side-glances at the pub keeper as a constant presence. That is, the tales foreground a self-assured maleness while building, like "Cyclops" and in another sense like "Oxen of the Sun," toward a drunken climax, a gargantuan chaos. If Bloom rises, somewhat shakily and absurdly, to his climactic Cycloptic outburst, HCE achieves his maudlin collapse into senility after a sequence of Circean self-exposures, and the clients explode into an Oxen-like polylogue.

Heroic Evolution

There are many ways to read the "action" of II.3, but beneath all of them is the focus on HCE as a dispenser of liquids and recipient of cash ("the pilsener at the baar, still passing the change-a-pennies" [BL 47479 f. 7; JJA 54: 11; FDV: 170; FW: 313.14–16]).[9] That position and that role make of him both an emblem of power and a mainly mute and vulnerable, almost sacrificial, presence. Though he is effectively off-center, without him the center would simply not exist. Seen globally, however, the chapter is concerned less with the behavior of the clients than with HCE's self-involvement. His "agenbite of inwit" leads him to see himself as the focus of the barroom talk in the first half of the chapter and then to defend himself and face the dethronement due to the carnival king, whose position he occupies throughout the *Wake.*

The reader will inevitably sympathize with HCE and to some degree share his perspective. Consequently, our relationship to HCE in II.3 is close to our relationship with the scapegoated Bloom of "Cyclops." But let us not minimize the differences. After all, though both are outsiders, HCE is legitimately at home behind his own bar. Joyce assures us that, on the one hand, the pub context is somehow analogous to the mind of the "pilsener had the baar" (FW: 313.14). On the other hand, it is the domain, the virtual living room, of the clients, who function as a gossipy jury presided over by four Gilbert and Sullivan judges similar to those trying HCE's attacker in I.4. Even though we hear the twelve's characteristic "-tion" phrasing only late in the chapter (on FW: 369), it is presumably their words, real or imagined, and their presence that eddy around and through him.

Telling Tales: The Chapter's Structure

All of this brings us to the obligatory consideration of the tales-told aspect of II.3 and to its essentially elusive but superficially clear narrative structure, whose development was closely followed by the genetic procedures. What might be called "The Painful Case of the House of the Hundred Bottles" begins with a brief introductory description of the pub radio, followed by the tale of a larcenous Norwegian Captain who is finally brought to land and married to a Dublin girl. We know that the origin of this tale is a joke told by Joyce's godfather, Phil McCann: the story-teller Kersse says, "[H]e was ^[1]one[1]^ my godfather when he told me saw" (BL 47479 f. 7; JJA 54: 11; FDV: 170; FW: 313.09–10).[10] It was also a favorite of Joyce's father. The original tale concerned a hunchbacked sailor who couldn't be fitted by the Dublin tailor, J. H. Kerse.[11]

In II.3 the Norwegian Captain's tale is presented as an oral narrative recounted by several (perhaps four) narrators and eliciting responses from its audience. The *Wake* treats it as at once a typical Dublin pub tale, a bit of drinkers' gossip, and even as a radio broadcast complete with weather reports. Though its details are spare and nebulous, its action redundant, and its language opaque even in the earliest version, we may read through it to an account of the gradual accommodation of the lawless Viking invader to a civilized urban existence and his eventual absorption into the native population.[12] The marauder/outlaw/trickster of the first incursion becomes by turns the vandal, the disillusioned client, the slick merchant-trader, the captive bridegroom, and the Dubliner doing business from the harbor formed by the mouth of the river Liffey. On the other hand, the tale can be read as an allegorical rendering of the pub keeper's own development from a young wiseacre into a settled and respected businessperson. Such a reading may approximate the one given to it both by the pub clients and by HCE.

These are, of course, no more than superficial and perhaps arbitrary readings of a tale that has acquired epic allegorical dimensions through the scrim of *Wake* language. Others are both possible and necessary to complete our sense of what is "going on" in the opening tale/skit. I would add that the events, though they are presented here in the past tense, occur in a sort of narrative present, recalling, for example, how Christ can be seen as crucified and risen in the permanent present of the theological vision. The present-time action, seen from a mythical, prehistoric, and even an historical perspective, takes place in the mists of time or across undetermined nautical distances. No wonder the narrative seems exceptionally nebulous to the reader.

Returning now to our overview. The Captain's tale was followed by the first major interlude, marked by the entrance of Kate the slop summoning

HCE to attend to his paternal duties, a passage that segues into the second panel, a rendering in dialogue of another pub tale, "How Buckley Shot the Russian General." Formally, this is the central panel of a vox populi triptych, but it is presented in a manner reminiscent of "Circe," complete with surreal stage directions and interludes. If the first tale comes to us as though over the radio, the second comes as though on a futuristic television screen. If HCE as Captain and businessman (or perhaps Shem and Shaun as invader and native) represents the movement of authority from tentative/uncontrollable to stable and in control, "Buckley" shows us a corrupt and/or vulnerable power through the eyes of an emerging popular consciousness. Here the sons seem bent on taking over from HCE as father.

The interlude that follows is crucial for HCE's development. In it he sets himself up for his fall by revealing his decadent tastes in art and literature during a monologue in a register very different from the "Amtsadam" passage climax to III.3. This leads to a full, and fittingly equivocal, "Amtsadamic confession": "—Guilty but fellows culpows!" (FW: 363.20), which in turn leads into deliberation and conviction/sentencing by the twelve clients. The latter is less a narrative than a record of the degeneration of the pub scene into a drunken confusion at closing time, a recasting of the conclusion of "Oxen of the Sun," itself a reenactment of the polylogical picnic in Rabelais's *Gargantua.* Neither a radio broadcast nor a television show, this passage, which seems to take place in something close to real time and in a *Wakean* approximation of real voices, rises to a rendition of Hosty's scandalous "Rann" before slipping into the register of the judges or Mamalujo as the "for eolders" (FW: 372.34). In the course of the Rann the pub has turned subtly into a boat, and the judges are left (in more than one sense) at sea. We seem to have come full circle, from the invader's boat to the "steamadories" (FW: 395.09) of "Mamalujo" and "Tristan and Isolde."

The verdict having been delivered, the twelve clients having left by the "gangstairs" (gangplank and gangsters), the undifferentiated voices of departing drunks are heard. This final polylogue (FW: 373.13–380.05) consists of a single paragraph rehearsing a multitude of *Wake* motifs. The voices come to us in an extranarratorial continuous present tense, underscoring the arranged aspect of this complex chapter. Still, close attention to the content reveals a subtle transition through the strands of HCE's guilt toward the "Roderick O'Conor" passage, the account of his drunken collapse in both "present" and "historical" time. When revising that primal sketch, Joyce recast it in the voices of the four,[13] thus providing another sort of transition to II.4 with its fourfold shipboard voyeurism designed to counter and perhaps complete the threefold spying of the soldiers in the park.

Digging up the Viking Midden

One of the most striking aspects of the manuscript development of II.3 is the relative absence of genetic anomalies. With the exception of the "Roderick" passage, there are no major passages with clear roots in the genetic past. On the other hand, since the chapter consists of three major panels plus a coda (or *ricorso*), and since the panels differed widely in subject matter and treatment, Joyce's major problem was how to soften the differences, how to make it a coherent unit without making it seem mechanical or forced. In practice, that meant he had to establish organic transitions that function more like secondary developments or skits than caulking. How he accomplished this is a subject for a coda to this essay. For now, suffice it to say that the discovery of the transitions is the single large surprise in II.3's genetic history. Second to that is the evolution of the third panel, the trial and conviction of HCE. For reasons to be assessed later, in that seemingly amorphous unit we see a radical shift in Joyce's method. Apart from that, what is startling about this long and complex chapter is the fact that it was drafted sequentially, that there was so little backing and filling. In short, the most anomalous aspect of II.3 is the paucity of "incidents," or details that would indicate a major compositional crisis, evidence that Joyce needed to rethink his procedures.

It is easy to ascribe this to the obvious fact that the chapter's composition capped an incredibly long period of preparation. Not only did the author know what he was about, he had for years been writing directly in *Wakese.* However, since nothing in the creative process of this book happened without ample preparation, the genetic critic must look beyond the manuscript to find evidence of creative cognition: to the *Ulysses* notes; to the *Wake* notebooks, some of them dating from the very beginning of the project; to the chapters and tactics of *Ulysses;* and to other passages in the *Wake* itself. It would be very hard to follow all of these exhaustively, but some effort must be made here to rationalize the germination process. I propose to do so piecemeal, dealing with each major episode as a unit and in sequence and doing the same for the transitional interludes.

We will begin, therefore, not with the tales but with the opening paragraphs on the pub context. The earliest available draft, a fair copy, leads us directly into and indeed incorporates major themes of the "Norwegian

Captain" tale while evoking the presence of the "host of the bottlefilled" (BL 47479 f. 4; JJA 54: 5; FDV: 168; FW: 310.06). However, in the early drafts it lacked two important elements. The opening "Guinesses" statement with its teasing "but" was added to the third typescript (BL 47479 f. 114; JJA 54: 148). Along with it came the paragraph describing HCE as an Egyptionized host cleaning his ear with a pencil so as better to hear the gossip: "So he sought with the lobster claw of his propencil the clue in the wickser of his ear. O, Lord of the barrels, comer forth from Anow" (BL 47479 f. 114, 83; JJA 54: 148–49; FW 309.01 and 311.10–12).

Joyce's method had long been associative and accumulative. Thus, the reference to the "balk of the deaf" introduced in the first draft was bound to elicit echoes and development.[14] The allusion is already simultaneously to the postmortal "book" and to the very lively auricular function, themes further developed in our paragraph, in which the pub, the server, and the (divine) authority are all present. Earwicker's hearing is the faculty that enables him to become the silent collector of oral histories and hence something of a threat to his overly vocal clients. His insect name suggests that along with his stutter, an impediment to speech, he suffers from (possibly a self-imposed or professional) deafness. It seems that he "hears" with an inner ear. Already in the opening his behavior makes him suspect, since he is sharpening his hearing as ruler of the nocturnal universe of brew and barrel, but the passage also suggests the depth of his suspicions, along with his vulnerability to the attacks on his already fragile reputation. Typically, these themes are far more complex than my summary indicates. After all, the clients-cum-worshipers would want their orders/prayers to be heard by the powerful server/receiver, and so on.

The Radio

A great deal of thought had gone into the revision and typing of the opening segment before Joyce found an effective way to elaborate on the speaking/hearing, expanding it to introduce the idea of an external source for language, sound, and action. The third typescript, which Joyce prepared for *transition* 26, had been revised by the time he conceived, researched, and finally wrote the elaborately technical description of the radio, an account that segued into an equally technical treatment of the anatomy of the ear (of HCE) (BL 47479 fs. 75–78; JJA 54: 180–83; FW 309.11–310.23). In the description of the client's donation we have a possible source of the sound and of the hearing. The radio broadcasts at least some of the sounds the landlord hears with his inadequate ears.

In preparation for this passage Joyce had taken extensive notes in VI.B.37 (on pages 106–10 and 122–26) on radios in highly technical terms, drawing on encyclopedias but perhaps also newspaper advertisements. The sequence of notes on ears definitely comes from an encyclopedia. When he took it he was preparing to write the "Russian General" segment, his second narrative, but he was also collecting from an as-yet-unidentified source notes on Viking mythology and Scandinavian nautical terms, some of which he incorporated in his revisions for the "Norwegian Captain" episode.

Exceptionally, the radio and ear passage was compiled rather than accumulated. That is, Joyce seems to have done little more than connect the dots between notes he had collected on ten tightly packed notebook pages. The result is surprisingly close to the final version of this paragraph, which was drafted as an addition to the typescript made from the first draft. The coincidence of a tightly organized note sequence taken exclusively on one topic and probably from a very limited number of scholarly (or commercial) sources is relatively rare. Still, it illustrates in brief Joyce's rapid creative modification of source materials at this late stage in the book's development.

The radio and ear passage does much more than simply accommodate these notes, even though they are themselves altered only slightly. Joyce was able to turn technical terms rapidly into puns based on homonyms while integrating the radio into its pub context. To this end he returned to the notebook source and drew from it further references as he revised and retyped. Beyond that, a number of these focused notes were used in other passages to reinforce the radio theme in II.3.[15] Typically, and in accord with what I would call Joyce's "aesthetic of ignorance,"[16] a reader unfamiliar with these terms would register the radio associations but be at a loss to explain specific functions.

The following come from the second cluster (VI.B.37: 122–28) but contributed most heavily to the major paragraph:

VI.B.37: 122: °29 tube / high fidelity / equipped with magn / link / supershield antenna / coupling system / man made static / distance jetty / vitaltone speaker° [BL 47479 fs. 75–76; JJA 54: 180–81; FW: 309.14–19] / electric eyes

VI.B.37: 123: °skybuddy / Chief Ski . anders [FW: 309.20] / lackslip [BL 47479 f. 77; JJA 54: 182; FW: 310.05] / Plight, calvitousness [BL

47479 f. 115; JJA 54: 161; FW: 318.34] / harbour craft [FW: 309.20] / dial [FW: 309.14] / in the ohmes [BL 47479 f. 75; JJA 54: 180; FW: 310.01]

VI.B.37: 124: bypass condenser / input voltage / °for all the earth° [several possible applications] / the 2nd being [play on Second Coming] / °twintriode [BL 47479 f. 75; JJA 54: 180; FW: 310.04] / univalve [BL 47479 f. 75; JJA 54: 180; FW: 310.04] / as modern / as tomorrow [BL 47479 f. 75; JJA 54: 180; FW: 309.14–15]

VI.B.37: 125: oscillascope[17]/ °rugged construction / up to the minute / appearance [BL 47479 f. 75; JJA 54: 180; FW: 309.15] / gives [?] continual / megacycles / range° [BL 47479 f. 77; JJA 54: 182; FW: 310.07] / calibrated

VI.B.37: 126: °harm[?] shock [FW: 308.11] / kecy [sic for "key"] click / vacuum cleaner° [BL 47479 f. 75; JJA 54: 180; FW: 309.20–21] / heating pads / °magazine battery [BL 47479 fs. 75–76; JJA 54: 180–81; FW: 309.20–23] / harmonic condenser [FW: 310.01]

VI.B.37: 127: Ear [heading] / °pimna [*sic* for pinna] / auricula / meatus / conch / tympanus / Eustatia° [BL 47479 fs. 77–78; JJA 54: 182–83; FW: 310.12–16] / fenestra rotiva / . . . ovalis / °hamerbone [BL 47479 f. 78; JJA 54: 183; FW: 310.19][18]

VI.B.37: 128: °anvil inces [?] / stirrup° [BL 47479 f. 78; JJA 54: 183; FW: 310.19] / tensor / ~~b~~ °labyrinth° / petrous pall / spiral & coils [?] / °rods of Corti [BL 47479 f. 78; JJA 54: 183; FW: 310.19]

Note that, though most of these items were included in the first draft, some were added later. Though the terms were often used with no alteration, some were significantly altered to fit and enrich the context. Not all of the entries seeing service were crossed through when used, nor were the notes always used sequentially and in the order of appearance. I should add in passing that, though the extent and concentration of technical terms here is unusual, there are plenty of other sequences in this notebook that are tightly focused by a particular theme (e.g., the tailor's craft, navigation, or Scandinavian and Viking lore). Here is the first draft with the notebook contributions underlined (underlined also are elements taken from an earlier sequence):

whyfor had they donated him,[19] as mysterbolder, forced in their waste, that their tolvetjubular high fidelity, ~~equipped with~~ as modern as tomorrow afternoon in appearance up to the minute, (hearing that anybody schemed

> to ~~have~~ halve the wrong type of date) equipped with supershield antennas for distance getting and connected by ^[1]the magnetic[1]^ links ~~with~~ of a Bellini-Tosti[20] coupling system with a vitaltone speaker capable of, capturing sky-buddies harbour craft emittances,[21] key clickings, vaticum cleaner, due to woman formed mobile or man made static and bawling the whowle hamshack ^[1]and wobble[1]^ down in an eliminium soundspound so as to serve him up a melogoturny manygoraumd[?], eclectrically filtered for allirish-earths and ohmes. This harmonic condenser enginium ~~(known as~~ (The Mole)[22] they caused to be worked by a magazine battery (called his Mimim Bimbim~~)~~ patent number 1132, Thorpetersen and Synds, Bergen) which was tuned up by twintriadic singulvalvulous pipelines [(]lackslipping along as if liffing deepunded on it) with a howdrocephalous enlargement, a gain control of circumcentric megacycles ranging from the antidulibnum onto the serostaatarean (BL 47479 fs. 75–78; JJA 54: 180–83; FW: 309.11–310.08)[23]

With the next sentence Joyce moved by way of the "pinnattrat[ion] inthro an auricular forfickle" to his consideration of HCE's ear as a combination loudspeaker and receptacle or "meatous conch culpable of cunduncing Naul and Santry." In the process he introduced or reinforced both the public and the private ear, suggesting for the first time that the tales we are hearing have their origin in a broadcast received, on the one hand, privately by HCE's inner ear and, on the other, publicly by the clients and HCE or perhaps that the radio is simultaneously contributing to the tale and providing a kind of static.

Notice how many words have been quickly reshaped to fit the situation and how the situation has been expanded. For example, "eclectrically filtered for allirish earths and ohmes" was generated by the implied homonym of the original note: "in the ohmes." The association through olms with homes leads naturally to the idea that Irish homes will have their broadcasts eclectically censored (see the technical terms for which Joyce needed no notebook preparation: "electrically" and "filtered"). Similarly, the earlier sequence, which prefigures this domestic reference ("key click"), probably suggested the house key and led to "vacuum cleaner," "heating pads," and "magazine battery." Three of these lend themselves to homely connotations in conjunction with a further static-kinetic and hence male-female association and the noise factor of "bawling" in the howl-filled home or "hamshack." The radio serves up an eclectic and melodious mulligatawny soup not only to the pub clients but to the less than harmonious "allirish" hearth and home. This is of course only the beginning of an analysis, a way of pointing up how, even before he drafted his passage, Joyce had sowed the seeds of a reading in his notes, but also how he managed to play associative games with those seeds. Significantly, he saw fit to preserve these details in the *Wake.*

Since the typescript to which the radio paragraph was appended was used for the first setting of *transition* 26, we know that the passage was written against a fully elaborated treatment not only of the "Norwegian Captain" but of later passages as well. That is, both the pub context and the narrative frame were well established, and the Captain had long since completed his forays and been grounded, bonding with the town of Dublin.

What sets this chapter off from other, perhaps equally reflexive chapters is precisely its lateness and the smoothness of its growth out of largely preexistent substance. It is as though Joyce had been building toward this moment over the years, preparing to write lengthy passages like the "Norwegian Captain," "Butt and Taff," and the trial and conviction of HCE by his pub clients but also the shorter transitional passages. In form and content the "Norwegian Captain" has its nodal antecedent in the pithy narrative of the lady pirate Grace O'Malley, whose comings and goings are recounted in I.1, a tale upon whose three plus one structure it reflects at much greater length. Here the tricksters' sex roles are more than switched. The female adventurer gets Jarl van Howther's children, while the Viking gradually becomes a settled husband to ALP, marrying the Liffey.

Perhaps because it reaches into the mists of Dublin's past, which, like the Celtic and Norse myths, epics, and sagas, was so badly mauled in transcription, I find this tale and its telling unusually obscure even after fifty years of study. Still, the outline of the action is relatively clear. Along with the history and content of "my godfather,"[24] McCann's joke about the hunchbacked sailor whose shape defied the skills of the tailor Kersse, the details of narration and reception, the various levels of implication, and even the nature of the voyages and the setting of the three major panels of the narrative are all elusive. Even the humor tends to be murky. Are we really supposed to be laughing along with the pub audience at the discomfiting of the tailor and the ship's husband, who may also be a sailmaker? Aren't our laughter and our interest focused elsewhere? One thinks of "Cyclops."

One of the problems II.3 gives the geneticist is the complexity of even the earliest drafts. True, complexity has characterized the language of such drafts since 1926, but it reaches its apogee here. This is partly due to another anomaly: some of the earliest available draft materials for the opening episode appear to be fair copies rather than the usual first drafts. That would make what would already be complex more so.

All the more strange, then, the level of polish evident in the first of the original opening paragraphs, which, with its *Book of the Dead,* mountain, and river images, lacked only the primal desert and the "Grander Suburbia," the rural and the cosmopolitan. The second (and what is now the third paragraph) provided colorful introductions to the belligerent "host of the bottlefield." HCE's routine behavior behind the bar, where he uncorks bottles and manipulates levers, is leavened even in the first draft by all manner of historical and folkloric references comically inflating his presence: he has "canterberry bellseyes" that gaze "wickeding indtil the teller"; he is about to pull a cork or "on a bout to be unbulging and o'connells," and so on. We even get graphic representations of the behavior of the liquids. The transition is made by the phrase "These two got there's," a reference both to the pub clients and to the antagonists in the Captain's tale, which opens with the traditional "Once upon a time" combined with the equally traditional "It was long ago." The words "It was long after once there was" introduce a set of ambiguous temporal markers: after, more recently, and not before. Obviously, the reference here is to the opening of I.1 with its sequence of "not yet" clauses. Our paragraph concludes with Kersse's "jerkin" and the Captain's being "buttonhaled."

The radio paragraph eventually provided further and much-needed transition as well as the by-then-necessary focus on tavern/radio talk and the host's (un)hearing ear: the paranoid center of the ensuing (non)action. We should remember that nothing out of the ordinary happens in the projected pub setting of the longest and most complex of the *Wake's* chapters. Further, we may suppose that, though both seem to prefigure the host, the antagonists of this tale are remarkably close in their nature and behavior to the archetypal brothers putting on a show for their father.

Granted that the first segment of the telling was already in polished form and, consistent with what we will see elsewhere, there is ample evidence in the draft of heavy first-draft writing later on, for example, in the paragraph originally beginning "That if all our proud invisors" (BL 47479 f. 10; JJA 54: 17; FDV: 172;[25] FW: 316.02–10). There, the bulk of the paragraph was built around the nonsentences "While they either took a heft. Or the other swore his eric," which combine to frame once again the antagonism. Passages like this one were quickly filled with broadening qualifiers that characterize the northern courage, will, and violence of the Captain: "[H]is ulstravoliance led him infroraids striking down and landing alow" while introducing a Swiftian "Dane and Tysk and Handry." The "landlord," on the other hand, becomes himself somewhat waterborn when we see him "noting, nodding a coast to moor [customer] was cause to mear."[26] (This prepares us for the boat references in the last two segments of II.3.) Toasting and drinking ensue: "Heirs to you, Brewinbaroon." Joyce is doing more than simply enlarging the context. As usual, he is larding the passage with historic and literary themes and local color. Before publication he added a further and clearer reference to the radio and perhaps to current (Nazi) events with "against our aerian insulation resistance"[27] and a bit of nautical drinking jargon: "Heaved to, spluiced the menbrace."

One striking characteristic of this complicated segment (and indeed of this chapter) was Joyce's practice of lettering his draft additions, enabling us to keep accurate tabs on the numerous levels of revision (BL 47479 fs. 3–43v; JJA 54: 3–55; FDV 168–81; FW: 312–335).[28] Passages were revised as many as nine times and as few as two, and though a given pass often resulted in only one addition, some yielded as many as six.

The structure of the "Norwegian Captain" segment echoes that of the chapter as a whole in that the narrative sequences include longer paragraphs and contain references to the pub audience's response, while the three plus one episodes are punctuated by interludes. Both developments become increasingly longer and more complex as the tale evolves. By splicing the fairy-folktale "Prankquean" format onto the otherwise simple pub tale, a form subject to any number of asides and embellishments, Joyce has reintroduced the pantomime procedures highlighted in II.1. This will be accentuated in the "Butt and Taff" dialogue. Conventions from the pantomime in fact underlie the whole chapter if not the whole book.[29]

Introducing Kate

Typically also, the end of the sequence, which follows the grounding of the Captain and dramatizes his splendid wedding, constitutes a theatrical and disruptive entr'acte: "Enterruption. Check or slowback. Dvershen" (FW: 332.36).[30] A virtual curtain has dropped, and we experience the intrusion into the male universe of the eerily servile figure of Kate the slop, a pantomime dame. How fitting it is that the only female presence actually to penetrate this male chapter/sanctuary is cast in a stage Irish role usually acted by a man in drag.

The postsexual Kate was introduced in I.1 as the museum guide at the "Museyroom," but in the next sequence she was identifiable as the "gnarlybird" scavenging on the battlefield, a sort of banshee. Here, she is a stage Irish slavey portending war as she penetrates the male ranks to summon HCE to respond to his wife's ambiguous request that he come upstairs and say goodnight to the kids. The ALP she serves is the bride of the Captain's tale turned into a demanding wife. One can also read her as a Judy match for the hunchbacked sailor's Punch or a mate for his Scandinavian follower, Sigerson. Consistent with the dual function of this interlude, Kate is not only an emissary of the hearth but also a camp follower like Brecht's Mother Courage. Beyond that and consistent with the dual function of the interlude, she recalls the crone who guided us through the battle won by the Irish Duke of Wellington on a field urine-spotted by the temptresses or Jinnies. It follows that, sheelike, her presence portends the carnage at Butt's "Sea vaast a pool" (BL 47480 f. 2; JJA 55: 3; FDV: 182; FW: 338.14) after which another gnarlybird could collect the spoils.

The draft history of the interlude reflects its function. When Joyce added it the Captain's tale had already been drafted and revised and then typed and revised as a unit. (These sets of pages were separately numbered by Joyce.) It is significant that the revisions for the ink draft were made mainly on verso pages and lettered for insertion. The same goes for the typescript, which I believe was made under Joyce's close supervision so that important alterations occurred even as that mechanical fair copy was produced.

Support for the view that what Danis Rose and I had labeled fair copies are in fact first drafts comes from the clean state of what is obviously the first draft of Kate's entry. Like the opening segment and though it was quite brief, the transition was quickly typed for further (light) revision and then extended. It is on the second typescript, which was originally an extension of the third typescript of the "Captain," that Joyce lavished the most care, and it was there that he actually developed his detailed comic portrait of the slavey.

The primitive draft, obviously designed as a male transition from tale to tale, did not mention Kate. In fact, she made her ignominious entry only through a lettered addition, a paragraph written and revised on what amounts to a verso page. Note that this passage already contains allusions to her guided tour of the Willingdone Monument in I.1: "Dip. This is me vulcanite smoking, profused ~~Mr~~ 'Bonaparte Nolan' under the notecup. Dip" (BL 47479 f. 185; JJA 54: 303). The original transition began as a quick reference to the Captain/HCE's capture by ALP, "with her harpoons sticking all out of him." At that time it was followed immediately by a mock-Russian exchange: "Sdrats ye, Gus Paudeen! Kenny's thaw to ye, Dinny

Oozle." Joyce was obviously preparing for the Crimean setting announced at the paragraph's close by a Kiplingesque, though hardly Crimean, "booths, booths, booths." The original paragraph preemptively moved him from the battle of the sexes toward the treatment of a male war.

His next move was not to Kate but to the conjunction of the Crimean fiasco with Napoleon's defeat in the exchange cited earlier. Joyce must have realized that this leap needed mediation, the key to which was already provided by Kipling's "boots" and Kate's Waterloo voice. So he created and quickly revised the image of the "aged, crafty, nummifeed, confusionary, over insured, everlapsing, accentuated Kate" who "clopped, clopped, clopped" between armed camps. The revisions, some of which were in another hand, were so complicated and numerous that, immediately thereafter, he had a reasonably faithful and independent typescript made. As frequently happened in this chapter, he then tacked a few lines onto its end. (At this point the Kate passage is not yet explicitly an interruption.) A second typescript quickly followed, but this time the passage was treated mainly as an extension of the "Norwegian Captain." That is, it was typed beneath an early version (from a missing typescript) of the plebiscite paragraph that marked the conclusion of the wedding celebration (FW: 331).

Leaving aside the question of the whereabouts of the remainder of this typescript, what is important is that, like the "radio" passage and at approximately the same time, this transition was begun as a free-floating offshoot of the second typescript. It too filled an important thematic role as well as a transitional one. The difference is that the Kate interlude contains significant dramatic action: Kate arrives for the stated purpose of delivering the summons. To drive that point home Joyce added heavily to the Kate passage, but its burden is contained in two brief segments of the first draft. The first shows us how Kate slips into the room (as a manifestation of being and becoming!): "An interruption what, ^1sezame open,1^ is the doer doing? The door is being. How, ^1the thingajarry1^ miens but this being becoming in the doer? Sooftly ~~she~~ ^1annislavey1^ ^1, sezishe1^ is Sloowjanka" (BL 47479 f. 191; JJA 54: 311; FW: 332.36–333.05). The second segment tells us why she has come, relating her appearance to events outside the pub context: "And the message she braught below from the missus she bragged above that had her ^1agony1^ stays outside her chemise, fed to the chaps with the working medicals, and the forty pins in her hood, was to mountainy mots in annas plain language how she was a wanton for De Marara to take her genial glow to bed" (BL 47479 f. 190v; JJA 54: 310). In this way

Joyce set Kate's intrusion and ALP's request within the larger pub context, giving us a revised impression of the life led by the Captain when married. It should be noted that II.3 gives its hero only the illusion of grandeur. This is an epic of the ordinary even when it calls up images of stature. (Think of it as an inversion of the procedures of *Ulysses.*) The Norse sagas and myths that underlie the Captain's tale and figure prominently in the preparatory notes are treated in the text as subjects for pantomime. All elevation is to be seen primarily as mock elevation. In *Finnegans Wake* the king is always the carnival king, and here the "narrative" procedures resemble most closely those of the "Circe" episode of *Ulysses,* with the difference that in the latter the protagonists are returned to normality.

In the dream world of the *Wake* there is, properly speaking, no realistic norm beyond the one wishfully imagined by the reader. Here the action, both in the pub and in the sketches, is "realized" only if we find it, in ourselves, to establish a viable relationship with what we filter through a linguistic field that is in perpetual motion. As I suggested earlier, the deepest and perhaps the most accessible situation is that of a paranoid perceiver, a pub keeper who imagines that his person and life are the subject of all that transpires in a sound-saturated environment over which he presides as a deposable authority figure.

The entry of Kate, next to Sigerson the most limited of the *Wake* personae, a readily accessible caricature of enormous potential power, is unsettlingly funny. In the published version she insinuates herself softly like a magical ("open sesame") being out of *The Arabian Nights' Entertainments* into the male ambiance but clops clops "weepovy willowy dreevy drawly" even while she carries about her a horsey whiff of battle from the "mewseyfume" (FW: 333.16). Her message is bound to embarrass the dominant male, the one with the hunchback's "krk n yr nck," forcing him to pay his "reverence to her midgetsy the lady of the comeallyous," ALP. Given his guilt feelings, how can he keep from hearing in the background the sexual gossip of his clients, who speak of "the punchy and the jude." In the smoky, beery haze of this passage we too hear references to Waterloo, Humpty Dumpty, "Millikan's pass" (or Manikin Piss), and the Prankquean, all of which will soon cede their place to the strains of Tennyson's guns that "woollied and flundered" in the Crimea. So the passage that began with Kipling's "boots" has ended with the chromolithograph that hangs on the tavern "mizzatint wall," which may be the immediate "realistic" inspiration for the next pub tale. These are the bounds of the transitional passage's first panel, these and the entrance and exit of Kate.

A study of the lettered additions shows how they made their separate ways into the text. At this stage in the novel's development Joyce had ready to hand the vocabulary of thematic touches needed to bring to mind a variety of nodal systems. Indeed, he was so well prepared that in three astonishingly rich and probably quick passes he could write and assemble what is now FW: 334.19–335.04. At first glance it seems that he had in his head the overall appearance of this particular portion of his four-dimensional jigsaw puzzle and could summon at will the pieces required, slipping them unerringly into place; but an inspection of the nine shorter notes on these pages modifies that impression. Yes, the thematic vocabulary has been established after thirteen years of effort, but significant fresh effort went into the accumulation, shaping, placement, and so on. In fact, it took him eight separate revisions to complete this particular sequence.

The same process was followed when he appended the second phase of this transition to the same typescript (that passage was also subjected to eight revisions). There, many of the motifs were repeated, with significant additions. But if the first half focused on the transition from the Captain's tale to the intrusion of Kate with her message, the second half treats the allegations of the clients and HCE's response to matrimony, to the crime, and to the message (or letter).

Further, though our passage functions as a transition to the tale of "How Buckley Shot the Russian General" and though it begins with a reference to the chromolithograph of the Light Brigade, the references to the tale are extremely muted until we reach the final paragraph, which opens with the demand, "We want Bud . . . [t]he man that shunned the rucks on Gereland" (BL 47479 f. 220v; JJA 54: 362). Joyce added that paragraph in almost its final form in 1937 to §4.3, the typescript made after he had drafted not only the dialogue but also the stage directions. The page in question, resembling in its form and integrity the one containing the Kate additions, is an instance of pure transition. Its contents suggest the existence of an audience while embodying the voice of a faceless mob. Immediately before Butt's opening dialogue we read,

> How Burghley shuck the rackushant Germanon. For Ehren, boys, gobrawl! A public plouse. Citizen soldiers. (FW: 338.01–4)

For Eire and Honor indeed! A public place or house, applause. Butt and Taff must ultimately be citizen soldiers, but the idea of the citizen implies civilian, about which more later.

How Buckley Became: Prehistory

Buckley's tale, like that of the Captain, began as a simple pub joke, another of John Stanislaus Joyce's favorites. It was on Joyce's mind when he was preparing to write the "Cyclops" episode. "Buckley & Russian general (bloody boy)" (JJA 12: 11) is among the notes that Joyce was probably collecting in Zürich.[31] It was there that he told his father's story to his friend Ottocaro Weiss during a discussion of Freud. Ellmann gives this account:

> Buckley . . . was an Irish soldier in the Crimean War who drew a bead on a Russian General, but when he observed his splendid epaulettes and decorations, he could not bring himself to shoot. After a moment, alive to his duty, he raised his rifle again, but just then the general let down his pants to defecate. The sight of his enemy in so helpless and human a plight was too much for Buckley, who again lowered his gun. But when the general prepared to finish the operation with a piece of grassy turf, Buckley lost all respect for him and fired. Weiss replied, "Well that isn't funny." Joyce told the story to other friends, convinced that it was in some way archetypal. (JJII: 398)[32]

Several details of this story should detain us. First, there is the Freudian association, which prefigures not only the Oedipal nature of the occurrence but also the excretory imagery in the crime sequence and in II.3. Second, Joyce told the story repeatedly.[33] Third, it is divided in three distinct parts. (The tripartite development was dictated by the dialogue's joke/tale conventions, but the Vichian conventions of the *Wake* dictated the tardy creation of a coda/*ricorso.*)

Aside from the Scribbledehobble reference under "THE SISTERS," we can point in VI.B.3: 80–83 (begun in March 1923) to a suggestive sequence of Buckley notes that falls in the midst of preparations for the "Tristan" and "St Kevin" sketches:

> VI.B.3: 80: °Blanco Buckley is the / wild goose
> VI.B.3: 81: Crimea [*sic*] War (Buckley) / arabesque of Buckley / 'limewhite mansions'
> VI.B.3: 82:[34] So Buckley shot the / Russian general[35] but / who shot B— / T[36] said negrily / I was that mad (he / was furibund) I was that / mad (he was foaming / with rage) it was / in the Crimean War / on the Black Sea / (it was raging with foam)

VI.B.3: 83: The turd swiftsure / Flew down the sewer / & the sleuce-hounds / Flushfleshed after (*Buffalo VI.B.3,* 67–69)

As a sequence and individually this is remarkable. First, there is the incipient dialogue format, which includes a speaker and a commentator, though nothing like the comic music hall pair of enactor/reactor Joyce finally established. We are already well beyond the simple pub rendition with its third-person protagonist. Second, Joyce already sees Buckley as the archetypal "wild goose," though he was still far from seeing the General as an equally Irish father figure. Third, he advances the idea of an "Arabesque," a term referring here to the Turkish alliance and the actual setting of the war, buttressed by a vision of limed eastern houses. This could perhaps be enlarged to bring in not only the East but also the elaborate form it implies, the form the dialogue eventually achieved. Fourth, Joyce seems to be advancing the idea of Buckley as a potential victim, an idea that he did in fact develop. Fifth, in drafting the scatological verses he has inserted a homely domestic absurdity into an exotic context, one that would become increasingly important when the dialogue was written and located in HCE's pub/house. At this stage in the book's development it would have been entirely possible to give the tale a cloacal context. Indeed, such a context is implied by HCE's response to the enactment of the tale, by the situation of Butt and Taff in the stage directions, and even by the outhouse featured in the Captain's tale.

More significant is the long dialogue sequence, which appears to have been written in the heat of inspiration, to judge by the spontaneous-looking scrawl (a visible written gesture if ever there was one). Though the actual words were not used, the exclamatory register and even the content of these lines, which read like a preamble, eventually informed the dialogue. Here are the opening dialogues in their earliest form:

Taff—All was flashning and krashning bloodymoriaty bluchedred?
Butt—Sea vaast a pool! (BL 47480 f. 2; JJA 55: 3; FDV: 182; FW: 338.05–14)

Along with the Crimea (Sevastopol) and the raging (Black) sea, Butt/Buckley's rage is also available in this, the earliest draft.

Given the associations already present in the notebook, we may wonder why Joyce failed to develop this theme in 1923 and why he seems not to have considered writing a Buckley sketch in addition to his six original pantomime burlesques. The answer is ready to hand in the fact that the sketches are not so much narratives as frozen vignettes, very brief, nearly stop-action moments rather than developments. Like the Norwegian Captain's tale and unlike "Roderick O'Conor," the "Buckley" narrative involves us in a complex series of actions and relationships that have important psychological and archetypal dimensions. In a sense "Tristan and Isolde" has a comparable charge, but when exploiting that well-known tale Joyce chose to take a different tack. He found a way not only to freeze an essential moment from it, the shipboard seduction, but also to incorporate moments from the romance in a nodal system. There, a variety of contributing moments generated a complex subplot and eventually II.4.[37] "Buckley" does not lend itself to so expansive a treatment.

We can point to other foreshadowings and preparations for "Buckley" in (later) notebooks, but most striking because quite early are two direct reflections of these notes, both of which are seeds sown for a modest nodal system. The first is in the first draft of I.3's opening paragraph, where we learn the fates of HCE's plebeian attackers: "O'Donnell is said to have enlisted at the time of the Crimean war under the name of Buckley" (BL 47471b f. 2v; JJA 45: 137; FDV: 69; FW: 049.04–15). Significantly, the very next version is even closer to the crossed-through note with its "wild goose": "O'Donnell, somewhat depressed by things, is said to have accepted the (Saxon) King's shilling on the outbreak of the Crimean war, enlisting under the name of Blanco Buckley" (BL 47471b f. 10; JJA 45: 141). The final version expands on this and explicitly mentions the goose.

In the most primitive version of I.4's conclusion, in a paragraph that served to introduce ALP as gossip, we find an elaboration of the hastily written first note on VI.B.3: 82: "Who then was the scourge of Lucalizod, it was wont to be asked as once what became of Peabody's money or who shot Buckley though every schoolgirl knows that it was Buckley who shot and the Russian general & not Buckley who was shot" (BL 47471b f. 29; JJA 46: 49; FDV: 80; FW: 101.15–22). Clearly, although in the fall of 1923 he probably did not yet know how to present the tale, Joyce had Buckley on his mind.

When push came to shove, narrative was only a tiny portion of the development in the "Captain" and "Butt and Taff."[38] Just as the former depended on the procedures of the Prankquean in I.1 to achieve the necessary heft, Buckley's tale needed the precedent and conventions of music hall stage so beautifully reconfigured by Flaubert in *Bouvard et Pécuchet,* readapted by Joyce himself in "Circe" and later revived in Beckett's *Godot.* The necessary discovery was made precisely where so many of the other models are found, in I.1, which seems to have functioned as an idea bank for II.3. Joyce had to wait until 1925–26 for the discovery of Jute and Mutt (Mutt and Jeff of cartoon fame), the prehistoric native and invader duplex that marks the threshold between prehistory and history, the point at which races and languages merge to "swop hats and excheck a few strong verbs weak oach eather" (FW: 016.08).

It was the form and tactics of their exchange that enabled Joyce to invent the naked first-draft version of the tale-telling as enactment and to discover an archetype for the plebeian interaction/conflict. In the event, the II.3 procedure was, already at its inception, far more sophisticated and adaptable than the primitives' elementary dialogues, first in I.1 and later in IV, both of which are sketchlike moments rather than fully evolved events.

Initiating the Dialogue

The basic draft "Butt and Taff" seems to have grown directly out of the typescript-cum-draft (§2.2) of the transition. It is an incredibly compact piece of writing, stripped down to the basic nuances of the dramatic situation. Two "citizen soldiers," clowns, jack priests bearing witness to the archetypal event, are performing a comic and/or tragic Mass to celebrate and participate vicariously in the Oedipal act of Buckley. The triumphant and guilt-ridden common soldier has shot the authority figure, the (presumably Irish) Russian General, who has been rendered vulnerable by the act of "creative" defecation.

Almost fifty years ago I published an essay called "Dramatic Motion in *Finnegans Wake*" that consists of a very close reading of the most basic draft, elaborating on and attempting to rationalize the developing action.[39] My results, by which I mean what the manuscripts revealed to me, were perhaps preordained by my approach, but I still find them suggestive: at any moment this text includes all of the elements of its action, though the emphasis shifts as the action progresses. The predetermined part, my readings of the structure of comedy and tragedy, has not aged well, but the idea of the passage as something like a rolling transparent barrel on which the whole is imprinted sequentially has retained its force, at least for me. In my current, far less detailed reading I shall try to nuance and deepen my genetic reading. Unfortunately, it is impossible to push this reading to the limit and still outline the remarkable manuscript record. (Only the history of the late-developing "Storiella as She Is Syung" for II.2 rivals that of "Butt and Taff" in its compexity.)[40]

The sequence, which features a stage Irishman and a stage Welshman ("Taffy was a Welshman") rehearsing Buckley's adventure, began as a spare and naked dialogue headed "Repliques" (BL 47480 fs. 2–3, with heavy revisions on 47479 f. 194v and 47480 f. 2v; JJA 55: 2–5). Even from the unrevised primitive version it is clear that the dialogue is from the start much more complex than Jute and Mutt, and that there is a subtle psychological conflict here between two not-quite-equal-opposite figures, whatever roles we assign them. The story they react to and reenact is, of course, yet another version of the crime, focusing on HCE's defecation and the spying soldiers rather than on his female-oriented voyeurism.

There is another new wrinkle, however, one that points up the nature of the plebes. If, as one reading would have it, Butt and Taff are enlisted men telling of the exploit of an earlier soldier, then the absent soldier is in effect the tie that binds them, the third element "sundering" the twins in relation to their father. Absented by time and place, the figure of Buckley is present in Butt's reenactment and in Taff's gradual implication in the action. The text dramatizes the seduction of the auditor (see the role of the literary text), his progressive engagement in a tale he has requested. "Conscribe him tillisk, unt!" he demands in the third dialogue, seemingly identifying a scribal Butt with the Ondt while echoing the unnamed washerwoman's demand in the opening of I.8. Indeed, for an analogue of the relationship developed between the clowns we should turn to that early precedent in the fluvial register.

Here, on the other hand, we begin with recognizably antagonistic types whose names bestow on them some semblance of function and even personality: Butt may well be confessing to Taff, who, like the instigating washerwoman, repeatedly prompts him to be more forthcoming and direct. If she says, "Tuck up your sleeves and loosen your talktapes. And don't butt me—hike!—when you bend" (FW: 196.08–9), Taff shouts at Butt, "Say your piece! Bucker to!" (BL 47480 f. 2; JJA 55: 3; FDV: 183). He goes further in an early addition to the third dialogue where he asks for clear and simple words: "The good old gunshop monowords for manosimples" (monosyllables for a simple man), to which he appends the suggestive psychoanalytic appeal, "And may it be untrepidation of our dreams when we 1st forgot at wiking in the bleakfrost chilled our revery soughts" (BL 47479 f. 194v; JJA 55: 2; FDV: 182). It follows that the dialogue can also be read as a psychoanalytic session with Taff as an inexpert practitioner whose empathy runs amok.

If at the start Taff is somewhat hostile, by the end he is full of praise for

Butt, who increasingly identifies with Buckley as the defender of, among other things, his honor as a heterosexual against the old bear. In our citation Taff is proposing a Freudian dream interpretation while accurately describing what happens to our dreams when we awaken. The draft was enormously expanded in the course of seven revisions, by the end of which our dialogue went far beyond the tale proper to evoke repressed memories: "I've a boodle field of maimeries in me buzzim." Among them are the crime, the encounter in the park, the Ondt and the Gracehoper, military life, and other battle scenes.

Growing the Sequence

Returning now to the complex history of the "Buckley" skit, we find that Joyce began with the naked dialogues, headed "Repliques," under which heading he drafted them, adding revisions that quadrupled their length and immensely complicated their content. In the fair copy he systematically embellished each dialogue element with the "stage directions" that enrich the identities and activities of the protagonists: Taff is described as "a smart boy, thirty seven," raising an umbrella before/after ("privious to") looking through the "roof" of what seems to be a privy. Butt has a "clerical appearance," but he is seen as a Wilde-like poseur "supposing to be the sorry jester" (BL 47480 f. 9v; JJA 55: 18). After Butt's description of the General's multinational uniform, Taff is described not only as astonished but as reflecting somehow in his eyes the magnificent absurdity: "his starseers razzledazzlingly full of eyes, full of balls, full of holes, full of buttons, full of stains, full of medals, full of blickblackblobs" (BL 47480 f. 9v; JJA 55: 18).

From the start these stage directions function more as asides than instructions. Like those in "Circe" but more so, they record what the protagonists might be imagining rather than what we might actually see on a television screen. Significantly, the accompanying dialogue registers astonishment before affirming doubt: the description is magnificent ("mangraphique"),[41] but it is not as good as a daguerreotype, and the comic opera uniform is not appropriate to the war context. The fact that the notes for these additions were compiled on separate pages rather than in the notebooks illustrates how quickly and systematically Joyce was working at that time.

The first typescript, following consecutively the opening sections and including a new beginning for HCE's reactive monologue, received several revisions. Joyce was clearly getting winded when he appended to that draft a handwritten instruction to his typist: "Please change where they occur (too tired to hunt for them)" (BL 47480 f. 37; JJA 55: 71). Echoing the tripartite structure of the pub tale, the dialogue had three movements, concluding with the shooting, but two things were still lacking: the necessary intermezzi or scenic breaks and a fourth or ricorso movement. Both of them were added to the second typescript, a draft that for the first time numbered Butt and Taff's pages as a separate unit, distinct both from what preceded it and from what was to become the next interlude.

Intermezzi

The intermezzi, doubling as (radio) news flashes, are four in number plus a final added item: an echo of the brother battle in II.2 and of Shaun's manual arithmetic, or the "pump and pipe pingers" (thumb and five fingers). These pastiches were written consecutively for insertion in the typescript, but from their lettering it is clear that Joyce did not at first know where he would place them. What became the first one, the hilarious sexual horse-race version of the crime, bears the letter C. The second, with its comic Christmas and New Year's greetings and containing an overt, if strongly Germanic, reference to television ("The other foregottheneds are during swishinsight teilwiesioned" [BL 47480 f. 62; JJA 55: 94; FW: 345.35–36]), is labeled A. The third, arguably most interesting, is an astonishingly accurate account of television, which was, after all, a *very* new mode of communication in 1937, when the passage was written. It is labeled D. Joyce seems to have felt the need to incorporate in his text the technology of the future.[42]

It is worth studying, however briefly, the way he turned the General's ghost into a televised emanation and how the technology is presented:

> Following a fade of transformed Tuff and pending a reglow of beaming Butt the *bairdboard*[43] *bombardment field* of tastefully taut geranium satin, tends to *teleframee* and step up to the *charge* of a *light barricade.* Down the *photoslope in syncopanc pulses,* with the bitts bugtwug their teffs, the missledhropes *glitteraglatteragutt,* born by their *carrier wave.* Spraygun *rakes them from a double focus:* shellite, grenadite, alextronite, nichilite: and the *scanning* spot traverses the rutilanced illustred sunksundered lines. Shlosshh! A gaspel truce leaks out over the *caeseine coatings.* Amid a *fluorescence of spectracular mephiticism* there *caoculates* ^1 *through an iconoscope*1^ *a still,* the figure of a fellowchap in the hwoly ghast, Popey O'Donoshough. (BL 47480 f. 63; JJA 55: 107; I have italicized the technical terms)

Joyce must have taken notes on this topic, but I have yet to locate many of them in the relevant notebooks.[44] Television had been in existence in crude form for over a decade when he wrote these lines, but the most important development had been a recent one: the inauguration of BBC television in 1936.[45] I suggest that, when he began work on the dialogue, Joyce did not yet see the action as televised. Sometime between the production of the original draft and the composition of the interludes he became aware of the potential of this new medium and imagined its use in a pub. On the other hand, there is evidence that he was following the development of this device as early as 1927. At that time he drafted for the *transition* 6 galleys of I.6 the passage on Lucien Lévy-Bruhl containing the following: "Looking [. . .] through the faroscope of television ^1(this ^2nightlife2^ instrument needs still some subtractional betterment in the adjustment of the mover refrangiblity angle to the squeals of the hypothesis on the outer tinsides)1^" (BL 47473 f. 145; JJA 47: 113, simplified; FDV: 100; FW: 150.32–35).[46] Another important aspect of the ghastly scene is the discovery or at least the projection of the viceversion of Butt and Taff, which enabled him to write the *ricorso* to the episode.

The last and shortest of the interludes, originally labeled B, is the famous "abnihilisation of the etym." It was to be inserted immediately before the final pair of typed dialogues, where it has remained. Despite the arrangement in *The James Joyce Archive* it appears that the composition, revision, and fair copying of both the "Butt and Taff" ricorso and the "pump and pipe pingers" interlude/finale (BL 47480 fs. 68, 66, 67; JJA 55: 129–31) occurred very shortly after the composition of the other interludes. (Significantly, some of the revisions for that passage are to be found on the page containing the revisions for the television/teleframe interlude.)

There are so many discursive levels and levels of activity in Buckley that any account is bound to shortchange it. In fact, the only account that has value will be the one constructed by the active reader willing to let the hyperactive text work its magic. Still, in watching Butt take on the character, motivations, and actions of Buckley while Taff moves from the role of interrogator to that of partner, we become, like the pub clients and HCE, engaged in its timeless action. The joke/tale takes us into a universal dimension and a complex temporality in which heroism, impulsiveness, scatology, piety, treachery, and buffoonery mingle. The all too familiar crime takes on fresh shadings that are both accessible and beyond categorization. Above all, this is a masterpiece of clownish mockery in which the clowns typically engage us in an inversion of values.

HCE in/on the Spot: The Second Interlude

Focusing as I have on the dialogue, I have only touched on an important fact, one that distinguishes this segment from the others: from the outset, "Butt and Taff" (now FW: 338–55) was integrated with the crucial transitional passage recording HCE's reaction to the Buckley tale (now FW: 355–60). Once written and perhaps fair-copied, the transition was dropped long enough for "Butt and Taff" to be developed, polished, and typed twice as a distinct unit. It is hard to say precisely when Joyce returned to the transition, but when he did he gradually extended it until he had in place what amounts to the third major narrative, which would in turn open into another interlude transiting into "Roderick O'Conor."

Joyce was at great pains to anchor this chapter in narrative reality. The behavior of the clients in the pub and HCE behind the bar, the description of the radio and the insertion of broadcast passages (weather reports, racing news, music, etc.), the implication that Butt and Taff are visible (perhaps only in the imagination of the pub keeper) on a television screen that was somehow generated by the "Findlater's" calendar image, and the formal expulsion of the clients at pub-closing time: these are only some of the seemingly naturalistic grounds for what is in other respects a phantasmagoria.[47]

Through the end of Butt and Taff the focus is intermittently on HCE's professional behavior, but following that sequence we perceive him differently. In an anguished present and with the historical scrims lifted, he stands naked before his hallucinated judges and jury, ready to be destroyed. In terms of the *Wake*'s carnival thematic the carnival king has become vulnerable to the attack of those who contributed, however ambiguously, to his rise.[48]

When we finish Butt and Taff it is a shock to find ourselves once again in the pub context listening to what appears to be HCE's voice, rather innocently identifying with the sacrificial victim and then pleading extenuation. Strategically, this is a very significant development. Until this point Joyce had given HCE voice only in III.3. There he speaks as the city father. Here, in a hilarious and disturbing pastiche of urbane decadence, a pub keeper divagates on culture before a group of semiliterate drinkers.

With a Bloomlike gesture HCE asked his clients for "advice, free of graces, scamps encloded." Then, with naive enthusiasm he proceeds to praise a "surpressed book" with "illustrative plates" whose "leaves" he has "been turning over" while "on the lamatory," only to find himself "big altogether" or aroused (BL 47480 fs. 2v–3; JJA 55: 4–5; FDV: 187; FW: 356.05–358.16). We should be aware that we are listening to a particularly personal confidence given in a voice we are told is the pub keeper's. The informal tone and decadent content of this utterance are very different from the tone and content of the city-fatherly presence that closes the inquest of III.3 in a stellar passage with which II.3 nevertheless emphatically rhymes. The figure announcing himself as "Amtsadam" (FW: 532.06), having been dredged up from the body of Yawn, is not so much confessing frailty as asserting with hollow pride the gifts he has bestowed on Dublin and Anna Liffey. The utterance of the pub keeper is in the register of the confidence-giver, one who speaks *entre amis.*[49]

Though "Butt and Taff" outstripped the transition in complexity,[50] lending itself to an isolated development, it appears that very early on Joyce had a clearer vision of their integration than he did of the relationship between the Captain's story and the Kate interlude, which appears to have been written more or less simultaneously with it. Furthermore, there is an impressively organic quality to the development of the third pub event out of the interlude, even though in its details that development was piecemeal.

One factor facilitating the semiunitary treatment of this expansive development was the nature of the post-Butt material. An enormous amount of notebook preparation was needed to build the historical tapestry of Dublin into the Norwegian Captain's tale, with its roots in piracy, colonization, assimilation, and the growth of mercantile trade. There, the language and history of the Vikings in particular and the Scandinavians in general had to be explored, digested, and displayed. Similarly, since "Butt and Taff" is grounded in the posited origins of the Celts in the Crimea as well as in the Viking incursions into Russia, Joyce built not only on the historical war but also on prehistory. Along with this, we have the collision of cultures that the war occasioned and the subculture of the Irish wild geese. Notes on all of these topics, and especially on the war and the Russian language, abound.

On the other hand, as he approached the Irish present with its readily available divisions, though he needed documentation, Joyce's materials were more readily available, and the composition process needed and had somewhat less of a prehistory. It may seem strange, therefore, that this segment had a complicated draft history. Content and strategy combine to suggest why that is so.

An Unlikely Source

Still, there some peculiarities in the draft history, and here is perhaps the most striking one. In 1977, when preparing my introduction to VI.B.14

for *The James Joyce Archive,* I noticed a sequence of notes used by Joyce when he drafted HCE's description of the "(suppressed) book" (FW: 356.20). At the time I was puzzled by the fact that in August 1924 Joyce would be able to compile so coherent a preview of some of HCE's most striking and damning words and that his source was so obviously a devout Christian one. Until Roland McHugh discovered the heavy use of Dean Kinane's squishily pious *St Patrick: His Life, His Heroic Virtues, His Labours, and the Fruits of His Labours* (Dublin: Gill, 1889), I had no idea what text he was using. Until Chris Bjork handed me his photocopy of that Book I had no way of knowing that Joyce was systematically harvesting the bits of pious cant that season the letters by princes of the Church modestly included by the good Dean Kinane as the bulk of his prefatory material.[51] As McHugh has shown, Joyce turned back to the prefatory materials *after* he had systematically worked his way through the book, filling sixteen notebook pages (34–49).[52] Only a few of those notes, which contain a great deal of specific data about Patrick and his followers, were used in *Work in Progress* before the notebook was transcribed between 1934 and 1936. The same goes for the five pages drawn sequentially from the clerical blurbs, but the latter had a more focused and potent impact.

In 1938, using Mme Raphaël's transcription, Joyce mined these notes for HCE's decadent utterance in a way that parallels his use of the radio and ear notes. The difference is that these entries were incorporated in a single level of the first-draft revisions rather than built into (and constituting the bulk of) the basic draft. Here, as transcribed and mistranscribed, are some of the raw materials for HCE's book review, potsherds extracted from the midden of clerical "Approbations" (Kinane's term):

VI.C.12: 37: could give anything / like an adequate / idea of his singularly / varied & edifying / [bl]the letterpress is / eminently legible, / the paper fixed [*sic* for "excel"] / could scarcely be / better

VI.C.12: 38: if he were [*sic* for "ere"] long / I cannot hope for / absolution from you / for any [*sic* for "my"] long silence / a glance thro it / how wholly my time / is taken from me / [bl]works [*sic* for "worthy"] of previous publicity[bl] / interspersed / [bl]It is, I can see[bl] / O way [*sic* for "Owing"] to continuous / absence from home

VI.C.12: 39: [bl]eagerly seized on[bl] / it is time I shld [*sic* for "shd"] thank / you / busily engaged / I cd. only open / volume here / & there till lately / since— march [*sic* for "much"] / from home / [bl]I augur[bl] / engaged in my / visitations & taking / it up from time / to time

This takes us only halfway through Raphaël's transcription, but it should convey Joyce's method of selection first from the letters used by Dean Kinane and second from his own notes. Clearly, no attempt was made to check the transcriptions; but then, accuracy was not a desideratum. Joyce was more interested in style than substance. Selecting some of the juiciest bits of the clerical letters, he was able to convey the ripe decadence that became useful in conveying HCE's appreciation of an expensively produced book, the centerpiece of his hilarious and damaging (to say nothing of distinctly odd) monologue. It is singularly appropriate and wonderfully ironic that, when trying to divert attention from a potentially embarrassing topic, HCE describes his "suppressed" book in language borrowed from the clerics.

The following (simplified) rendering of the second draft will show how clerical preciosity was made to complement and nuance the publican's decadent appreciation of his cloacal reading experience (the incorporated notes are underlined):

> —I have just, let us suppraise, been reading in a (suppressed) book ^[1](it is by measures long and limited) the letterpress is eminently legible and the paper fixed upon could scarcely be buttered in works of previous publicity, enough, however, have I read of it to augur in the hurry of the times that it will commend the widest circulation and a reputation coextensive with its merits when ~~intrusted~~ ^[2]inthrusted[2]^ into safe & pious hands upon so edifying a mission as it, as I can see)[1]^ with expurgative plates accompaigning the action passim with my warmest venerection before the wordcraft of this early woodcutter, Mr Aubey Birdsly. (BL 47480 fs. 152v–153, simplified; JJA 55: 270–71; FDV: 190–91; FW: 356.19–357.03)

To compile this elaborate aside Joyce selectively and artfully jiggered his source notes, using minimal distortions to make the language his own. While the introduction of the clerical notes was tardy, the move was heralded earlier by the word "suppraise," which was destabilized by both "(suppressed)" and "venerection." In the course of revision the elements of this passage evolved into the substance of two sentences, gaining considerable polish and complexity while maintaining their integrity and strengthening the bibliophile, the cloacal and clerical messages:

> I have just (let us suppraise) been reading in a (suppressed) book—it is notwithstempting by meassures long and limited—the latterpress is eminently

> legligible and the paper, so he eagerly seized upon, has scarsely been buttered in works of previous publicity wholebeit in keener notcase would I turf aside for pastureuration. Packen paper paineth whomto is sacred scriptured sign. Who straps it scraps it that might, if ashed, have healped. Enough, however, have I read of it, like my good bedst friend, to augur in the hurry of the times that it will cocommend the widest circulation and a reputation coextensive with its merits when inthrusted into safe and pious hands upon so edifying a mission as it, I can see, as is his. It his ambullished. (FW: 356.19–30)

It is worth noting that Joyce made only minimal alterations in the notebook materials themselves, concentrating on placement and punctuation. On the other hand, he amplified the context by inserting two interpolated sentences and the phrases "wholebeit in keener notcase would I turf aside for pastureuration" and "like my good bedst friend." Still, such changes taken together significantly alter the tone and broaden the implications of the borrowed language. Viewed in the context of the whole passage, that language contributed to the pretentious and mock humble qualities of HCE's discourse. On the other hand, the pieties and their situation are overshadowed by the larger context with its rich trove of comic detail and allusion, to say nothing of its attitudinal reach.

The landlord or host of II.3 seems to have just returned from the toilet/outhouse, where he has been indulging his erotic imagination. He has been doing what the Russian General did but in a more private place and with a different purpose: we can't accuse the General of masturbation-cum-defecation. If HCE has indeed "just" come back, perhaps he has not seen (or heard) the story and, again like Bloom, would not know that he was suspected of having broken a behavioral code when he reenters the pub.

From the start, however, he is openly and in all innocence admitting from behind the bar to a series of embarrassing actions. As the passage evolved and expanded those actions were tied increasingly to "decadence," and particularly to literary and sexual decadence. Already, in the first draft HCE identifies the artist responsible for the illustrations in the book he has apparently (ab)used as well as perused. It is Aubrey Beardsley, or "Aubey Birdsly," whose unfinished parody of *Lohengrin,* the polymorphously perverse *Under the Hill,* is a beautifully illustrated and funny banned text.

Later on Joyce introduced other "precious" works, notably Mallarmé's *Un coup de dès,* the reference to which is predicted by a covert allusion to gambling and a lucky seven in "his roundhouse of seven orofaces" (BL 47480 f. 152v; JJA 55: 270; FW: 356.05–6). Mallarmé and his beloved

Poe became inescapable in "the hasard you asks is justly ever behind his meddle throw!" (FW: 357.04–5) and in "*Culpo de Dido!* Ars we say in the classies. *Kunstful,* we others said. What ravening shadow! What dovely line!" (FW: 357.15–17).[53] Indeed, in the course of revision Joyce stuffed the monologue with literary references that underscore poor HCE's decadent tastes and style and open him up to the accusations that follow in the next segment.

Jenny and Florence in the Park

The remainder of what became the transition to and motivation for the trial passage grew directly out of HCE's statement. To the first fair copy Joyce added a damning radio broadcast or diffusion: "We are diffusing (toyou, toyou,) among our wordless lovers of our sequence the dewfold song of the naughtingels (Alys, Alys allo!) from their sheltered position on the heather side of Waldalure, Mount St John's" (BL 47480 f. 3, simplified; JJA 55: 5; FDV: 188; FW: 559.30–33). Here, in a relatively simple state of a soon to be delightfully complex sentence, we find our clue to the source not only of this passage but also of Kate's role in the previous interlude. Significantly, both of these passages are predominantly and intrusively feminine.

The generative words "dewfold" and "naughtingels" can be traced to a development in VI.B.37, one of the source notebooks for II.3. The earliest reference to "Fl Nightingale" follows immediately after "c'est magnifique mais pas Daguerre,"[54] located, appropriately enough, within a sequence of Crimea notes (VI.B.37: 163–64). The next entry falls in a conceptual sequence that includes the first reference to Jenny Lind.[55] I will cite the relevant (crossed-through) items in their context to illustrate how Joyce's mind was working:

> VI.B.37: 179: °interruption / for Irish Florence / nightingal [?] / slavey° / premen[?] world / bogland[56]
>
> VI.B.37: 180: °alliance / ([wedding] ring) / jenny lind° / Russians had / no rifles

A third entry follows a punning reference to Beethoven and is followed by two patently American fashion references:

> VI.B.37: 185: °more beethoken° / made to masure[?] / streaked across the / blue / sensitized to / black light

VI.B.37: 186: ghost star / °Jenny Lind / Flo Nightingale° / shiftwaist / Gibsen [*sic*] girls

Here the association was clinched, but the relevant onomatopoeic passage was not added until the second draft: "(floflo floreflorence) sweetishsad lightandgale, twintwin twosingwoolow" (BL 47480 f. 153v; JJA 55: 272; FW: 360.02–3). Since that draft already contained the "beethoken" reference, it seems likely that there was a considerable time lapse between our entries, the time it took to revise heavily and recopy the bird/music paragraph.

Clearly, we are in the park, the scene of the crime, possibly in the position of the soldier spies. (Whereas "Butt and Taff" and HCE's self-exposure deal with defecation and homosexuality from the points of view of two plus one soldiers, the interlude emphasizes the role of the girls.) Bird and radio references gradually bring into play Lewis Carroll, *The Arabian Nights' Entertainments,* the Egyptian *Book of the Dead,* Lord Byron, Shakespeare, Macpherson's Ossian, and a variety of classical writers and musicians.

Of Trial and Judgment

Though situated in the depths of the night, our third panel gives us what is arguably the most detailed rendering of setting and action in the book, with the exception of the more openly (and perhaps misleadingly) realistic Porter household in III.4. I should add that HCE's inculpating monologue and the treatment of the pub as a courtroom were never completely separated during the drafting process. My own decision to deal with the latter as a distinct but highly ambiguous narrative reflects a formal reading along Vichian lines and a belief that the chapter is best viewed as a pseudotheatrical development similar to that of "Scylla and Charybdis." Here as there we find acts and interludes, though the pattern is closer to that of the Christmas pantomime than to Shakespeare and the action is more expansive than that of "Scylla."

Lacking the clearly delineated three plus one form, the frequent dialogue dashes of the Captain segment, and the (mock-)theatrical accoutrements of "Butt and Taff," the trial and judgment segment is, nevertheless, the most immediate and paradoxically the most theatrical. This extended passage serves to equate the internal flux of HCE's mind with a projected external flux of pub life. While the clients as jury and judges become drunker, HCE is returning willy-nilly to his Scandinavian roots, aging backward, so to speak, finally being identified with his curate, Sigerson. It is this ancient avatar who expels the clients, forcing them to empty their glasses quickly and angrily. The mimesis of all of this, while adding to the incoherence, increases the dramatic impact.

Flaubert may be said to have introduced and perfected the use of synchronous or hyperrealistic action in the novel with the famous agricultural fair chapter of *Madame Bovary;* Joyce carried it much further in *Ulysses* with "Wandering Rocks," "Sirens," "Oxen of the Sun," and, arguably, "Circe." In II.3 and especially in this third panel he turns it to radically fresh ends. There is, of course, a good deal of synchronous action throughout this chapter, where the pub talk, plus the behavior of HCE behind the bar, plus what HCE hears of the talk, plus the rich historical and cultural analogies are developed in tandem with the narrative line of the "Norwegian Captain," "Buckley," and the trial sequence.

In preparing for and conceptualizing his third "tale" Joyce faced special problems. First, having committed himself to a Vichian arrangement, he needed to impose a way to convey both democracy and expulsion for the dependents-clients and disempowerment and isolation on the diminished leader.[57] The process had to be gradual but not necessarily calibrated. The focus had to be more than ever on the host as a threatened leader. HCE had to survive the rage generated by unrequited thirsts and the mounting opprobrium. The result would be both a climax and a transition to the previously written anticlimax or *ricorso,* the "Roderick O'Conor" sketch. Building from an unwary confidence to a confession of "Guilty but fellows culpows," the sequence had to lead up to a judgment, but the development through democracy would logically lead to a muted chaos rather than a neat conclusion.

Procedural Matters: First Inserting, Then Adding

The draft history of this segment exhibits several peculiarities. The transition was blocked in as an organic extension to "Butt and Taff." It consisted of the material surrounding and including HCE's remarks (now FW: 355.08–359.20) followed by the shorter radio broadcast of the temptresses and the music in the park (now FW: 359.21–361.31). Though, after the second draft, these pages were revised separately, they were never divorced from "Butt and Taff." Indeed, the first typescript, made when the chapter had grown to include FW: 161–70, was numbered consecutively with the first typescript of the primitive "Butt and Taff," a development too subtle to rationalize here.

It is the second draft that reveals the most startling developments. To begin with, when revising the transition segment Joyce drafted on verso pages and on separate pages (BL 47480 fs. 153v, 154v, 156v, 158; JJA 55: 272, 275, 278, 281) long and elaborate passages, as opposed to the usual brief snippets, for insertion in the body of the text. This draft grew so complex that he seems to have made a quasi-simultaneous fair copy in four (perhaps five) stages. That is, as he revised each segment he made (or in one case had someone else make) a fair copy. The procedure was necessitated by extremely heavy and complex revision, especially of the later pages. The segments include (1) HCE's first statement preceded by two lead-up paragraphs (FW: 355.21–358.16); (2) the girls in the park broadcast (FW: 358.27–360.16); (3) "Bulbulone" and the "moon priestess" continuing the girls topic while introducing the treatment of "the sixdigitarian legion" as accusers (FW: 360.17–363.20); and (4) HCE's guilty plea and defense (FW: 363.21–367.06). It is in relation to the last two segments, or rather with the second half of (3), that the final anomaly occurred.

After a cursory revision of the fair copy Joyce stopped to have a typescript made of the whole chapter. At that time he suspended work on the post-Butt material, thus initiating its separate development. When he did turn back to the typescript he added heavily to the "Bulbul" paragraph, building the girls' presence, buttressing their pantomime seeing or "peeptomime" with hearing ("Mr. Eustace"), and even writing (see the Irish tree alphabet in the "quicken in tongue irish: Quicken, aspen, ash, and yew").[58] He further expanded the "Guilty" address. But, most significantly, he continued the process of extension begun with the previous draft.

A second typescript was made, revised, and extended. Then he inaugurated a complex and puzzling new procedure. Perhaps, since galleys for this chapter were already in progress and the pressure was on, he began what can only be called piecemeal production of text. That is, not only did he revise and extend the typescript, he also set about drafting fresh passages in near-final form on separate pages. Many of these were marked by a double slash in the upper right-hand corner to indicate their status as discrete paragraphs. Only one of them, the sixfold "So many needles to ponk out to" (BL 47480 f. 213; JJA 55: 367; FDV: 197–98; FW: 369.23–370.14), bears witness to a difficult birth and heavy revision. On the other hand, and *very* exceptionally, two paragraphs never made it into the *Wake*. The first, dedicated to Mamalujo, may have captured the writer's mood at the time:

> ^[1]Item.[1]^ He was hardset then and he wanted to go (somewhere) while he was weeting. ^[1]Utem.[1]^ He wished to grieve on the good persons, that is the

> four gentlemen. ^1Otem.1^ And it was not a long time till he was feeling true forim he was godda purssia and it was a short time then till he was fooling mehaunt and mehynte he was an injime robber. ~~He~~ ^1So much so that he was1^ at his ~~thinker's aunts~~ ^1tinker's dance1^ to give (the four gentlemen) ~~a corse~~ ^1the presence (of a corse).1^ ^1Etem.1^ He ~~fund~~ [?] ^1found1^ the ~~found~~ ^1~~pond~~1^ ^1pound1^; and they fond the hurtled stones; and they fell in with the gravy duck; and he got the roast of the meat. ^1Atem.1^ (BL 47480 f. 210, simplified; JJA 55: 363; FDV: 197)

The paragraph was retyped and lightly revised (BL 47480 f. 237; JJA 55: 411) at least once, but it was omitted from the galleys and hence from the *Wake*. The second lost passage concerns Issy as "Vela, Lady Pressygrows": "It is so long till I thanked you but I do so much now. Thank you[.] You introduced me to forks. Have I assisters? Who is this she was? So they ~~told you~~ ^1squealed1^! The cads! It makes the wildfire break out all over me. What he did. The brute. I'll behead his old porterant, the wrex" (BL 47480 f. 36v; JJA 55: 371). Whether or not the omissions were deliberate, it is clear from the typescript that the procedure was complex. Joyce must have been very nervous. As he revised and as he drafted fresh material he had frequent recourse to his typist, who apparently transcribed the new materials under his direct supervision. This was done in several batches, probably as the revision was completed. The segments are usually less than two pages long, with the second page breaking off after a dozen or so lines. It seems outlandish, but one thinks of Balzac and Dickens.

Introducing the Two, the Twelve, the Four, and the Six

Central to an understanding of the generation of this section of II.3, along with the introduction of HCE's voice(s), is the methodical introduction and development of numerical sets, what could be called actor clusters. Though hardly new in the *Wake*, exceptionally here, the manipulation of such groupings helps give structure to the process of devolution.

By the first typescript Joyce had introduced and developed the presence of the One, or HCE, and the Two temptresses/birds in the park. The Twelve were inserted in the second draft along with the thematic of respectability between the park passage and HCE's guilty plea. These clients react directly to the broadcast of the girls' accusation with "condomnation ^1of his totomtation1^ for the duration ^1till his repepulation1^" (BL 47480 fs. 156v, 159; JJA 55: 278–79; FDV: 193; FW: 362.03–4). Joyce had also already introduced the number six in the context of the twelve. I won't pretend to understand this subgroup, but it is implied by the word "sixdigitarian" appearing in a brief but direct allusion to twelveness. Their presence is confirmed by the allusion in the paragraph that originally followed the "Item" paragraph to Six men and Six Jack- or Joyce-built actions contributing to the "hoose that Joax pilled."

Presumably, inebriation is well advanced when HCE makes his incriminating statement, and the jury/demos is already less than lucid; but the progress of drunkenness along with the progressive degeneration of HCE's position had to be conveyed. Then, since no force or development in the *Wake* is unaccompanied by a countervailing one, mounting chaos must find a response in some sort of order and continuity. This role is eventually and partly filled by the assertive Sigerson, who in expelling the clients at pub-closing time provokes by means of control.

An earlier source of control would be the "wisdom" and "judgment" of those compass points, the four elders. During the drafting process Joyce reintroduced the admittedly decrepit (and perhaps tipsy) chroniclers as observers before establishing them as the recorders of Roderick O'Conor's fall. They had long since been seen as judges in I.4 and as the voyeurs spying on the mutual seduction of Tristan and Isolde. In II.3 Joyce gradually developed the presence of these watchers and their identity as the type of codgers one finds in any pub. In this way he distinguishes them from the surrounding mass of vociferous celebration.

The four and six seem to function as subsets to the twelve, but clearly the four remain in the pub or at least in the pub narrative after the others leave. They had begun to make their presence felt after the introduction and elaboration of the girlish voices of the temptresses and where they had made explicit the identity of the twelve clients. (By that time the nautical references that were to become so important were already present. Boat references were, of course, central to the "Norwegian Captain" segment and long since part of the "Tristan" and "Mamalujo" sketches.)

Mamalujo's presence became explicit late in the revision of the first typescript, where they figured as an extension:

> —Look about you Tutty Comyn!
> —Remember and recall, Killykeg!
> —When visiting Dan Leary try the corner house for thee
> —I'll gie ye credit for sixmence more if ye'll be lymphing our four avunclulusts.

> And ^[1], since three^[2]se[2]^ slory sorratelling was much too many,[1]^ they maddened and they morgued and they lunged and they jowled. Tell the Juke done it. (BL 47480 fs. 191v–192; JJA 55: 330–31; FW: 367.10–19)

Several things are noteworthy about this forceful introduction of the "avunculusts." First, like so many of the additions to this segment, this appended passage is astonishingly close to the published version. Second, the words in the four voices come to us as a radio advertisement for a pub rather than as voices of the clients. Third, the reference to Mamalujo by their names is cast not as dialogue but as third-party observation of their frustration. Finally, the references to Kevin ("Comyn"), Patrick's King Leary, storytelling/Tristan ("threesestory") combined with the Mamalujo suggest that, as he wrote, Joyce was already preparing for the inclusion of the sketches in II.4 and IV.

It is a characteristic of this section that once a motif was introduced Joyce proceeded to ground it. To the second typescript he added the "Like Jukoleon" paragraph with its nautical references and "old thalassocrats." To this soon came the next paragraph with its four "Guns," "greatgrandgosterfosters," and "fourlings." The piecemeal development proceeded through the "There is to see" paragraph, with its graphic evocations of the oldsters and their dress: "Squarish large face with the atlas jacket" (FW: 368.30–369.05). Joyce added the latter to the bottom of BL 47480 f. 210 (JJA 55: 363), a page that already contained the "Item" paragraph discussed above. Even without that abortive paragraph he had powerfully established the presence of the fabulous four by the time the piecemeal third typescript was made, thus laying the groundwork for their doddering description of Roderick's fall, the preamble to their star turn in II.4. The two-page Mamalujo concentration was punctuated by an important prohibition or rules or negative vows,[59] a rather long pendant to the threatening "Guns" sequence establishing the authority of the four, whom one must never "underrupt." Joyce followed this with a direct address to the twelve: "You were in the same boat," a paragraph that kicked off the last transition leading into what we might call the endgame.

Only Connect

This is a good time to pause for a consideration of a neglected aspect of *Finnegans Wake:* transitions. Readers who have followed Joyce's fictions should be aware of two things: Joyce's Flaubertian dedication to the principle that form fits matter and his increasing reliance on parataxis as a tool. The development can be traced back to *Dubliners,* where each tale finds its appropriate formal presence and, as is normal in the short story, there are significant gaps between tales. It is more obvious but less disruptive in *A Portrait,* with styles that adjust to the maturity of the protagonist and chapter breaks whose abruptness requires considerable reader adjustments. It reaches its zenith, of course, in *Ulysses.* Up to this point one could say that Flaubert's example had applied, and Joyce was his "schoolboy." Suddenly, he has pushed Flaubert beyond Flaubertian, making parataxis the rule, a parataxis that turns the reader into an intellectual acrobat. Joyce's major innovation was to virtually eliminate transitions, obliging readers to bridge demanding gaps. To enable this process and make the book readable if challenging he resorted to any number of ingenious devices into which we need not go here. In the process he pushed parataxis very close to the limits of its viability in narrative, obliging readers to readjust to shifts in style, an approach designed to universalize the particulars of situation.[60]

All of this points up an important and neglected convention, that of providing all aspects of the *Wake* with discrete but powerful transitions. Here, universalization is unnecessary, since *everything* is inscribed everywhere. Instead, Joyce needed to find ways to impose order on his development, establishing connections and smoothing over on all levels the radical disparities between his chapters and their subdivisions. This was always a balancing act, since he had to be careful not to create fresh imbalances by introducing meanings that would call for further amplification and unwanted implications. Usually, imbalances could be adjusted for in multiple revisions,[61] but by this time in the book's development there was little time for such adjustments.

Let's pause now for an accounting of the curious concatenation of events that accompanied the revision of "Butt and Taff." As mentioned earlier, Joyce appended a transition (§6B.*0), beginning with HCE's appearance and speech, to the primitive draft of that section. Included were the sound effects paragraphs beginning "We are diffusing" and "Bulbul bulbul!" The former, with its "dewfold song of the naughtingels," clearly emanated from a radio. Joyce made a second draft of this transition along with the second draft of "Butt," but he set it aside until the second typescript of "Butt," revising it at about the time he was writing the scenic breaks. I have dwelt on these rather technical details because they help explain the evolution of some of the chapter's most memorable passages.

It was probably in December 1936, though in the absence of dated letters the dates are fluid, that Joyce finally recognized the importance of radio and television as means to ground and rationalize in terms of our age the dissemination of the pub tales. (Note that in that way he also foreshadowed the alienation process we see today in which entertainment comes to us prepackaged like the rest of our groceries.) That was when he followed up on the "slavey" note, doubtless wishing to increase the female participation in the pub action. After all, Kate's entry is a direct reflection on ALP's harpooning and hauling in the Captain. That memorable passage was drafted on the same yellow paper that Joyce used when he organized his radio and ear notes in the radio paragraph. We know that the ground already existed for this development, but by writing it Joyce turned the hints into a statement. At this point, still using yellow paper for his first drafts attached to the second typescript, he seems to have written the interludes for "Butt and Taff." It was there that, following up on the early hint, he firmly grounded the television broadcast. Note that he has not and did not introduce an actual television set into his by now futuristic pub.

All of these crucial transition amplifications are linked thematically to women and communications. All reflect an awareness of the need to fill in the links between disparate parts of the chapter without eliminating the shock of difference. Joyce must have felt that need when he ceased to think of the parts as separate and began to concentrate on the chapter as a functioning and accessible megaunit. By that point he had effectively polished the complex pub sequence and was ready to phase in the clamor of the departing guests.

Enter Sigerson, Exit the Twelve

Joyce attached his introduction of the Scandinavian pub curate to the direct-address paragraph, writing it in a quick, small hand (BL 47480 f. 208; JJA 55: 369; FDV: 198–99; FW: 370.23–29). Those paragraphs were separated only in the typescript. A crucial organic move, it initiated the final transition. His second portrait of a comic servant begins on a fairy-tale note by establishing a giant astonishment ("Stunner of oddsbones on bluebeeding boarhorse!")[62] before descending to the menial level of the fellow who "dusts both sides of the seats of the bigslaps" and "was rancing there smutsy floskons." Suddenly, we find ourselves watching the passive-aggressive Sigerson persona, who, despite his thick Scandinavian brogue, emerges as an elderly double for HCE, returning us to the root cause of dublinity, the Viking incursion. Compare his appearance to that of Kate in the first interlude. The balance was doubtless intentional. It is certainly consistent with Joyce's practice here and elsewhere.

This ousting presence now dominates a full *Wake* page. Joyce drafted the better part of it (FW: 370.30–371) as a succession of paragraphs leading up to the announcement "Tide, genmen, plays, She [*sic*] been goin shoother off almaynoother onawares" (BL 47480 f. 254; JJA 55: 447; FDV: 200; FW: 370.25–27). He followed this passage with two short paragraphs, the second of which is a refrain from the Rann, "Ostia, lift it!" Very soon after this he drafted on a verso page the intermediary paragraphs designed to anticipate the pub closure, describing the clients "cupturing the last dropes" and motivating the introduction of a kind of rann (see "O'Ryne O'Rann" [FW: 372.32]) with the call, "Ostia [Hosty], lift it! Lift at it, Ostia! From the say!" declaring that condemnation of HCE to be an emphatic "Him-him!" or hymn.[63] Tucked within the "Sockerson" sequence, these paragraphs set the pace for the exuberant remainder, rendering immediate the sound and presence of the twelve merrily singing their scurrilous verses. In the process Joyce incorporated references to the primal themes of chapter I.1 while casting forward to II.4 and the "for eolders aspoloutly at their wet-send in the mailing waters."

Drafted with minimal revision, this synchronous sequence paved the way for one of the most extraordinary paragraphs in the book, the last marked dialogue in this polyvocal chapter, a seven-page polylogue. For some time the pub had been turning into a boat, but it was much later that Joyce completed that development. To do so he devised the paradoxical Rann verses that expel the roisterers: "The gangstairs , ^^{1}^^{2}strain^{2}^ noise^{1}^[64] [under the client's weight] and ~~angers~~ ^^{1}anger's^{1}^ up As Hoisty rares the can and cup To speed the bogre's barque away O'er wather parted from the say" (BL 47480 f. 156v; JJA 55: 278; FW: 373.09–11). At this point the narrative seems to bifurcate, or rather we seem to leave our firm pub base for an unspecified outer space. In textual terms, we seem to have been plunged into a place of unfettered utterance.

Polylogism

The dialogue dash preceding this long paragraph seems anomalous. This is, after all, neither a choral utterance nor an individual one; nor is it more oral than the dashless scurrilous verses that have preceded it. But then the whole question of who speaks in II.3 is a teaser. At first glance, the closest things to this superparagraph may be the *Wake*'s catalogs of titles in I.5, of traits in question 1 of I.6, and of water-born gifts in I.8. Much closer than any of these in both form and function is the drunken rout that closes "Oxen of the Sun." Both "Oxen" and "He should be ashaped of hempselves" owe much to Rabelais's picnic. All three assault us with a rush of undifferentiated and unattributed drunken utterance. What distinguishes this drunken polylogue from the close of "Oxen" and relates it to Rabelais is the fact that since the pub clients have no individual identities, Joyce, like the good French monk, had to find strategies to make the prolonged (perhaps operatic) outburst pertinent.[65] After all, an underlying pertinence has characterized every aspect of this chapter if not the *Wake* as a whole.

One could argue that since our Shemish Joyce has systematically "squirtscreened" (FW: 186.06) his content, narrative logic does not pertain. Indeed, I have argued similarly myself,[66] and I admit to an apparent contradiction. Still, while thwarting conventional coherence and narrative conventions at every turn, Joyce deliberately included in this daunting block of hyperactive prose a variety of buffers to incoherence. They are (1) logic of situation—drunken rage at HCE induces a chaotic response; (2) thematic logic—well-developed motifs are incorporated; and (3) logic of structure—there is an underlying coherence of development. None of this is evident on a first reading that carries us through the lush comic complexity of the wordplay, confusing us in a way that parallels the jagged utterance in "Oxen's" rout, tantalizing us with flashes of the familiar.

All in all, it seems a curious transition into the "Roderick" finale. Its success is obvious when we note how the emergence into the narrative light (in two senses) of the sketch comes as a relief, a shock, and a delight but also as the next necessary step. How it works is another matter, as is why Joyce lavished so much energy on it to the point that it is literally the last thing written for the *Wake.*

As often happens in the drafting of longer sequences, the most primitive version established the tone and included the paragraph's beginning and ending. These three pages (BL 47480 fs. 262, 263, 264; JJA 55: 457, 459, 461; FDV: 201–3; FW: 373.13–374.08 and 379.06–380.05) were written fairly rapidly in a clear hand and revised with numbered additions on their versos. They were part of a sequence of unnumbered pages that began with the "Hray!" and the "The for eolders" paragraphs. But, unlike those paragraphs, both of which were drafted in near-final form and subjected to only minimal revision, the polylogue was from the start what could be called an open-form unit.[67] That is, it was by its nature expandable, capacious. In this it resembled superficially the various catalog passages, most particularly the catalog of ALP's flood-born gifts in I.8.

Unlike other cumulative passages, however, it gathered its forces very rapidly, growing severalfold in the course of three extremely irregular drafts plus the first set of galley proofs for the *Wake*. Those galleys, dated 23 November 1938, include everything that follows "Butt and Taff." (A duplicate set properly locating the changes made on this one is missing. So is a fresh set incorporating those changes and containing further revisions.) Significantly, though minor additions, revisions, and corrections were made on every galley, the great bulk of the additions were to our maxiparagraph.

The urgency behind the development of this key passage was evident from the start, as was its bridging function. The basic first draft began as now "He shook be ashamed of hempshelves," with its play on mercery and death by hanging.[68] The brief text from the opening pages (373.08–373.17) ends with a reference to the "Anonymays left hinted palinode" of ALP, which runs seamlessly into the claim that "Errorsure [HCE's] the mannork of Arrahland." This allusion to Roderick is followed by HCE's personal thunder word, the display of his name in "fusefiressence on the fashmurket," and the dream or "traum" thunder word (BL 47480 f. 262; JJA 55: 457; FDV: 202; FW: 378.06–10). Though these three pages were written in a relatively clear hand, variations in spacing and size indicate that Joyce paused periodically to regroup.

He seems to have composed by sentence and/or topic: the thunder and lightning sequence is followed by an attack sequence ("There's a light there still, Bung! Bring out your deed! Bung!"), which leads to an extended Letter sequence ("So it will be will be quite a material what May farther be unveloped for you"). Playing upon the scholarly commentary in I.5, this treatment of the Letter concludes with the most striking visual feature of this basic draft: the words "BINK . . . BUNK . . . BENK BANK . BUNK" are double-underlined. Indeed, these words, suggestive of stones being thrown at the pub by the clients, were written with strong emphasis and varying dimensions, suggesting rhythmic variations. Understandably, though the typescript bears evidence of Joyce's attempts to reproduce these effects, later versions omit them.

The early introduction of the Letter and its climactic presence leads me to suggest that, from one angle, the polylogue can be seen as a combined meditation on and performance of that missive. But that is only one of many teasing considerations. Another is the fact that, after making and heavily amending the first typescript, Joyce introduced a paragraph break in the second. His self-inflating monolith was at that point divided precisely at the "Errorsure" alluded to above (BL 47480 f. 296; JJA 55: 503; FW: 378.06). By that time the Letter theme had been partly submerged in other thematic clusters, including a long passage recasting Mamalujo as Roman soldiers or "the 4 crucifixioners throwing lots inside." These are the "Four ghouls to nail" in the shadow of the cross: "Isn't it great he is swaying above us for his good and ours" (BL 47480 f. 296; JJA 55: 503; FW: 377.23–378.01). The treatment of the four at this point suggests that their behavior could provide another frame for the polylogue, in which case the break is a logical one and doubtless intentional. At any rate and to good effect the paragraph break was undone in the next typescript.

This is not the place to solve all the puzzles raised by the evolving paragraph, but it may already be clear how what appears to be a polylogue, a potpourri of angry voices, can also function as a smooth and coherent transition to the chapter's climax: the *Wake*'s initial sketch. The last high king, after having sat on the sidelines since March 1923, is by this time ready to assume his place, his tale reformulated as the word of the four. The form of the chapter has been completed: three major episodes are capped by a fourth lesser one. Echoing this, there are three significant and memorable intermissions introduced by the radio paragraph as a prelude, and on a smaller scale we have the "Butt and Taff" interludes in the center of the chapter, giving it the formal elegance so dear to its author's heart.

Joyce's "boring parties" have broken through the last major barrier to the location/incorporation of not only this sketch but also the five other unpublished primal sketches. The latter will soon become the two component parts of II.4 and the three-part armature of IV.

Having reached this point in my own argument at the end of a painful three-year struggle, I think I have some inkling of what Joyce must have felt after nearly two decades of single-minded toil. One wonders whether, when he drafted "Roderick," Joyce had any inkling of the joys and torments that would fill the remainder of his creative life.

Roderick!

In our description of II.3's evolution, "Roderick O'Conor" comes almost as a footnote, a footnote that signals the fresh opening to the end. Everyone is doubtless familiar with the originary event: "Yesterday, I wrote two pages—the first I have written since the final *Yes* of *Ulysses*. Having found a pen, with some difficulty I copied them out in a large handwriting on a double sheet of foolscap so that I could read them" (LI: 202). In the event, Joyce revised that fair copy so heavily that a second fair copy was immediately essential. Written in a small, neat hand on two double pages, that version was eventually typed up by Miss Weaver. In September 1938 Joyce returned to that typescript, updating it for its new context.

One might expect, after the astonishing growth of the polylogue, to say nothing of the "Butt and Taff" dialogue and staging, that Joyce would want to beef up his sketch, introducing elements from various nodal systems. In fact, he did add references to clothing, to the radio, and to the solar breakfast egg: "till that hen of the heavens shows her beaconegg" (BL 47480 f. 272v; JJA 55: 464). More important, he introduced Mamalujo-like plural narrators: "under the grass quilt on us" and "we to lather and shave" (BL 47480 f. 264v; JJA 55: 462).[69] So little of substance was added that Joyce needed only one further typescript typed and numbered consecutively and then revised. Given the unstable state of the galley text, it seems probable that the printer received a carbon that included those last revisions. Finally, the otherwise unenhanced galleys had to be improved by a battery of commas, suggesting that Joyce failed to parse his text before he handed over what may have been a carbon copy to the printer.[70]

It is striking that in those same galleys the polylogue was so greatly amplified, making even more striking the contrast between the baroquery of the client's discourse and the Eumean miracle of "Roderick." In short, despite the lapse of so many years and like the other sketches, "Roderick" appears today much as he did in 1923. Like the other sketches, it is among the most accessible passages in the *Wake*.

Though at the time he could have had only the vaguest sense how he would get there, it is possible that when he drafted his foundational skit Joyce really did know where he wanted his "universal history" to go. From the start "Roderick" was a tour de force, a breathless paragraph punctuated as a single sentence carrying the reader along by sheer verbal energy toward an inglorious anticlimax. Though we may think of him as the historic loser, Roderick was ready to become the majesty of ALP's Letter long before that missive was imagined. More surprisingly and long before the advent of HCE, he is a publican in his "house of the 100 bottles" (VI.A: 21). Like a pub keeper, he is so abstemious, so reluctant to drink his profit, that he can get drunk on the meager leavings of his guests. He is also a "polemarch," an ancient Greek military leader. As the host at a "last supper," a lowly "beanfeast," he is a Christ celebrating "the anniversary of his

1st coming." Already, that is, we have the carnival king as sacrificial victim and the pantomime event in the form of a truncated shaggy dog tale, an action that is also a narrative, a told behavior.

By building on and reversing the procedures of *Ulysses,* by placing the explicit event in an historical past rather than an absolute and realistic present, Joyce had already established the unfixed temporality of what would become the *Wake.* Whether or not he had already imagined something like the situation of II.3, he had already written in 1923 the necessary conclusion to HCE's agony in the barroom. Or rather he had already set the bar for that chapter to leap. What could be more appropriate for that "host of a bottlefilled" (FW: 310.26) haunted by real and/or imagined scandal than for him to find unaccustomed solace in stale spirits after his resentful guests had left?

Notes

1. The sentence is enormously suggestive: "I have done a piece of the studies, ⊏ coaching Λ how to do Euclid Bk I,1. I will do a few more pieces, perhaps ⊣ picture history from the family album and parts of O discussing . . . *A Painful Case* and the m-Δ household etc" (LI: 242). Clearly, in 1926, though the book had yet to be fully plotted, the story Joyce thought the least successful in *Dubliners* would provide fodder for II.3, a chapter that takes place in a Chapelizod pub with twelve clients or O.

2. Thomas Connelly, *Scribbledehobble* (Evanston: Northwestern University Press, 1961), 63–64. Though not quite accurate, Connelly's transcriptions can help us read the notes, as can Mme Raphaël's considerably less accurate versions. Serious readers should always consult the JJA or even the original notebook in Buffalo.

3. This notebook dating from 1909, when Joyce returned to Dublin, is one of the earliest direct sources for some of the preparations for *Finnegans Wake* as well as *A Portrait* and *Ulysses.* It deserves close scrutiny. Right now I am trying to rationalize the possible overlap, for example, of John Stanislaus Joyce or "Pappie" and "Pop," but there are many other topics begging for study. See also Robert Scholes and Richard M. Kain, *The Workshop of Daedalus* (Evanston: Northwestern University Press, 1965), 103–4.

4. I am reproducing with virtually no apparatus the first quarter of the notes. In the service of simplicity I have not indicated which notes were crossed out and when and where and how they were used, and I have not included the interpretation needed to support my suggestions. Inclusion of such materials here would unduly complicate this presentation. They will be included in my follow-up essay on this note sequence. For now, it must suffice to say that only one sequence of *Dubliners*-related ink notes (among the earliest to be found in this notebook) is

longer than this one, while one is about as long. Under "THE SISTERS" Joyce included/transcribed a whole page of closely written notes on storytelling, discussed below. The notes under "EVELINE" are devoted mainly to Is/Isolde/Lucia in a sequence that can be seen as complementary to that of the Pop notes that dominate "A PAINFUL CASE."

5. Other titles are possibly of genetic interest, but of them only "[bl]the Story of Tristan and Isolde" (VI.A: 21) was crossed through on the notebook page. That crossing was doubtless done when Joyce drafted the second of his foundational sketches in 1923. The fact that neither the Hundred Bottles, which contributed to the first of his parodic narratives, nor the Buckley tale was crossed through suggests that Joyce was saving these topics for the actual composition of II.3, which occurred more than thirteen years later.

6. For my own best shot at the function of narrative in the *Wake* see "The Manystorytold of the *Wake:* How Narrative Was Made to Inform the Non-Narrativity of the Night," *JSA* 8 (1997): 81–114.

7. Nothing is unequivocal in either the *Wake* or its history, but a case can be made in terms of the amount of earlier draft materials found in both II.4 and IV and the paucity of the same in II.3. This small fact helps me build my pile of genetic peculiarities.

8. See the argument woven into the fabric of TDJJ.

9. This is from the basic draft of FW: 313 in a paragraph that from the start emphasizes both the serving/receiving functions of HCE and his equivocal and paranoid position as the clients "pushed their whisper in his hairing."

10. In the first half of 1926, when he was planning Book II, Joyce wrote the suggestive series of notes alluded to above: "[Ned] Thornton [Joyce's model for Tom Kierney in *Dubliners* and *Ulysses*] / fair time / McCann, Kersse & Norwegian Captain / behind the fire / K's bread 124 Russell St & at S[aint] P[atrick's] Bakery / Studies from I[rish] History / Stopford Ewer" (VI.B.17: 20–21). The bibulous Protestant Kierney, the pub tale, perhaps even Kennedy's bread, and certainly Dublin/Irish history all seem to suggest the shape of things to come. I say "seem" because I am still not sure how this isolated configuration should or could be interpreted.

11. See Ellmann's account in JJII: 23 and 705, where he quotes from a letter to Alf Bergan (LIII: 399) in which Joyce spells the name "Kersse" as it is spelled in the *Wake.*

12. We can perhaps assume that a parallel development takes place in the native community.

13. For a fine reading of the genesis of this seminal passage see Jed Deppman's "Hallowed Chronicles and Exploytes of King Rodericke O'Conor from Joyce's Earliest Draftes to the End of Causal Historie," *Probes,* 179–202.

14. It seems to me that what Danis Rose and I called a fair copy in the JJA is in fact the first draft of this segment.

15. Though the defining cluster of radio and ear references is located on FW: 310 in a powerfully focused paragraph, terms from the notebook clusters were used in transitional passages to help locate the wandering mariner before his various returns to Dublin. Thus, we find lesser clusters on FW: 313–16 and 325–26. Since this is a minor node, we are not apt to find references outside the "Norwegian Captain" section. As I have shown in WiT, Joyce's nodal systems vary considerably in importance and extent.

16. By this I mean that Joyce's major works and those of other modernists were designed to be so rich in implications, complications, ironies, and even privileged information as to defy exhaustive readings. The reader is obliged to accept ignorance as a sign of inexhaustible possibilities and challenged to accept and even delight in the proliferating challenges. I suggest that, given Joyce's command of his medium, such readerly "ignorance" can be and should be aesthetically satisfying and that it is more common than many are willing to accept. Perhaps it is also closer to our experience of reality than we care to admit. Furthermore, it is a corollary to the view that the work is ultimately about itself and beyond explanation. One result of this attitude and practice is of course what Umberto Eco has called the "open work."

17. The presence of "oscilloscope" in a context so methodically focused by radio suggests that the radio concept was already somehow linked to the idea of a television presentation of the second pub tale, "How Buckley Shot the Russian General." But Joyce did not incorporate it in the appropriate interlude.

18. This is corrected in the manuscript to "hummer."

19. This is of course a significant echo of another gift. Basic to chapter I.4 is the gift of a grave to HCE. The primitive draft of the relevant passage reads: "The coffin was to come in handy later & in this way. A number of public bodies ~~presented him~~ ^[1]made him a present of[1]^ a grave which nobody had been able to dig much less to occupy, it being all rock. This he blasted and ~~then~~ ^[1]carefully[1]^ lined the result with bricks and mortor, encouraging the public bodies to present him over & above that with a stone slab" (BL 47471b fs. 8v–8r; JJA 46: 3–4; FDV: 75; FW: 075.11–077.37). There are other verbal and conceptual parallels between these two passages. It seems clear that the opening pages of II.3 usher us into a postmortal setting like Valhalla.

20. VI.B.37: 106: "audion / Bellini-Tossi / systems."

21. VI.B.37: 106: "°bright emitter."

22. VI.B.37: 120: "°Mole / 1132."

23. Like a few other words on these pages, this one has a complex history.

24. In the very first draft Joyce seems to be commemorating the original telling: "as sober as a ship's husband he was my godfather when he told me saw[so]" (BL 47479 f. 7; JJA 54: 11; FDV: 170; FW: 313.09–10).

25. Alas, readers will note that the page reference in the FDV is off by one line here.

26. Insufficient notice has been taken of the extent to which the pub is throughout water-born. An argument can be made for II.3 and perhaps all of Book II taking place in a variant of the Noah's ark setting, but I won't try to make it here. On the other hand, not only is the first segment focused by nautical imagery and the presence of a sea-going protagonist, but the nautical imagery proliferates in the Trial sequence and colors the later versions of "Roderick O'Conor." The chapter ends on shipboard, floating us into the fluid ambience of II.4.

27. See VI.B.37: 108: "°insulation / resistance."

28. Where he did not use letters he generally used numbers. This practice permits us to ascertain the logic of his revision process. There are as many as eight separate levels of revision on these pages.

29. James Atherton gave us a brilliant introduction to Joyce's use of pantomime in II.2 ("*Finnegans Wake:* The Gist of the Pantomime," *Accent* 5 [1955]: 14–26). I have carried this argument further in "Farcical Themes and Forms in *Finnegans Wake,*" *JJQ* 2.4 (Summer 1974): 323–43.

30. This paragraph was added in stages to a later draft.

31. Phillip F. Herring, *Joyce's Notesheets in the British Museum* (Charlottesville: University of Virginia Press, 1972), 114, 1.38 (JJA 12: 11).

32. Ellmann claims that Joyce used the tale in *Ulysses,* but the only reference to a general in that book is to a Finn named Bobrikoff. Perhaps that name figures in the joke, but the Crimean context is missing, as is Buckley, the Irish soldier.

33. It would be nice to know under what circumstances and to whom he retold the tale, but Ellmann failed to annotate this remark. He mentions only Samuel Beckett, whom he credits with the idea of the insult to Ireland, Joyce's punch line.

34. VI.B.3: 82–83 seem to have been filled rather quickly and when Joyce was suffering from eye trouble (perhaps in June 1923). These pages may even originally and inadvertently have been left blank. The hand is very loose, and there is some overwriting. But then there is overwriting and curious spacing on pages 84–86, which are otherwise more regular. The biggest anomaly is the large amount of space left beneath the "poem" on page 83.

35. It is significant that the word "general" is not capitalized as it will frequently be in the *Wake.*

36. Note the presence of Tristan here in an uncrossed sequence that corresponds very closely to the earliest version of the passage in II.3.

37. I have developed this more fully in WiT.

38. On the problem of narrative in the *Wake* see WiT.

39. David Hayman, "Dramatic Motion in *Finnegans Wake,*" *Texas Studies in English* 37 (1958): 155–76.

40. See David Hayman, "'Scribbledehobbles' and How They Grew," *Twelve and a Tilly,* ed. Jack Dalton and Clive Hart (London: Faber and Faber, 1966), 107–18. See also TDJJ: 117–20 and passim. Rose, whose reading relies heavily but without acknowledgment on my discoveries, gives a breezy and quirky spin to the

chapter's development and to the role played by the Scribbledehobble notes, which exceptionally, like the radio notes for II.3, served as a source for the great majority of the abortive version of that text.

41. On VI.B.37: 164, amidst Butt and Taff preparations, we read "^{bl}C'est magnifique mais pas Daguerre."

42. Too bad he couldn't know about either the computer or the Internet, which Donald Theal claims he must have known. Does that ignorance tarnish his self-generated reputation as a prophet?

43. Joyce was obviously aware of the work of John L. Baird, who transmitted images across the Atlantic in 1930.

44. Aside from a reference to "oscilloscope" in VI.B.38, the only note I have found is one isolated reference taken in VI.B.35 while he was working on revisions for II.1, probably in 1933. In VI.B.35, probably in reaction to a newspaper article, he wrote "^{bl}2 way television" (VI.B.35: 70). Obviously, inventors of the day could imagine uses that are only now becoming current.

45. It is typical of Joyce to include references to the latest communications technology in his notes and eventually in the *Wake*. As part of the joke Joyce included in the midst of the general's confession this devowellized exclamation: "Hll, smthngs gnwrng withth sprsncswtch!" [Hell, something's gone wrong with the speaker[?] switch!]. The final version is only slightly different. In the next sentence we find him confessing "to all his tellavicious nieces."

46. The *OED* gives us some hints about where Joyce was getting his information from so early in the history of the device. There seems to have been a flurry of interest in 1927–28, mainly in the *Glasgow Herald*, which Joyce was unlikely to have read. Doubtless such reports traveled elsewhere. From the *British Weekly* the *OED* quotes, "Televisionists will expect their heroes to stay put." By 1936 great strides had been made in that "nightlife instrument."

47. There is no room here for a potentially illuminating study contrasting the ways in which the radio contributes throughout the other parts of II.3 with the function of television in "Butt and Taff." The radio seems to be a more or less constant element, intruding on and mingling with the pub activities during the first and third sequences. Television displaces it as a/the major source of "Butt and Taff." Significantly, mention of both media, though crucial to a reading of the chapter, came rather late in the development. Perhaps they both figured in Joyce's basic plan, but their tardy appearance suggests that the idea came to him only after he began to feel the need to ground his narrative, to establish its "real-time" sources. As it is, they certainly help orient the reader's perceptions without subverting hallucinatory thrust and the dream context. The contrast between this procedure and the tactics used in "Circe" is suggestive.

48. I have argued that, from the start, one could say from the foundational sketches that Joyce has used the carnival situation (and the Christmas Pantomime) as the nocturnal foil for diurnal reality. HCE has consistently come to us

as the carnival king raised from obscurity only to be ignominiously dismissed. The pattern is evident in the tripartite account given in "Here Comes Everybody." Of course, never content with a static rendering, Joyce rings changes on that theme. In II.3 the development is powerfully immediate, subtle, and expansive. Here the carnival king is a Punch whose rise and fall take on profound psychological implications with an aura of sad joy.

49. For a fuller reading of this sequence see my "'The Pilsener Had the Baar': HCE's Sorry Case," *Papers on Joyce* 1 (1995): 39–52.

50. Transitions are always more accessible than the major panels.

51. In his unpublished transcription of VI.B.14 Chris Bjork has done an admirable job of filling in the gaps left by McHugh in his pioneering "Dean Kinane in VI.B.14," *AFWC* 1.2 (Winter 1985): 21–33.

52. Bjork has added two pages to McHugh, who begins on page 36.

53. See my *Joyce et Mallarmé,* 2 vols. (Paris: Lettres Modernes, 1956).

54. This is of course a clichéd reference to the origins of photography (VI.B.37: 164) and by inference to the post-Daguerreotype photography used so effectively in the Crimean War. In the fifth dialogue of Butt and Taff it was united with an earlier reference to General Todleben (VI.B.37: 163), "Toadlebens! That is mangraphique, yet is it not daguerre" (BL 47480 f. 2; JJA 55: 3, simplified; FDV: 183; FW: 339.21–23). It is worth noting that the first draft of the dialogue sequence is especially rich in materials taken directly and even sequentially from VI.B.37.

55. I regret that the decorum (and bulk) of this essay prohibits my paying adequate attention to the contribution of the note taking both to the conception and to the elaboration of many aspects of our chapter. In addition to important conceptual notes there are plenty of indexes, heavy concentrations of notes taken and often used to flesh out major and minor themes. VI.B.36, 37, and 38 all merit critical inspection. Because of their richness and the diverse problems they raise, I find the prospect of treating them even in a separate essay or two daunting. Nevertheless, I am already tunneling through VI.B.38 with the goal of showing what a global and "readerly" approach can yield. My experience so far has shown me that these notebooks, which are not in themselves works of art, are almost as demanding, frustrating, inviting, and rewarding for the critic bent on analysis as is the *Wake* itself.

56. The Kate implications of "interruption" and "slavey" establish the link in the creative process between the women whose presence in II.3 is most marked in the two main interludes. They also suggest that Kate's presence grew out of the Nightingale-Crimea association.

57. Though history seldom intervenes in the *Wake,* it is worth noting that when he was writing this chapter Fascism with its massification of the demos and deification of the leader was on the rise. Democracy was seriously threatened along with values that Joyce certainly held. The trial with its generalized and chaotic explosion may have been written partly, if obliquely, in response.

58. Suggestively, much of this material was first rough-drafted under the heading "Extras for Nightingels" (BL 47480 f. 193; JJA 55: 334). When arranging, transcribing, and embellishing this page Joyce crossed through many lines, but, exceptionally, he left some lines uncrossed and unused.

59. See *The Book of the Dead*'s negative commandments.

60. See my essay "Toward a Postflaubertian Joyce," *James Joyce: "Scribble" 2, Joyce et Flaubert,* ed. Claude Jacquet and André Topia (Paris: Lettres Modernes, 1990), 13–32.

61. I have illustrated this process in "From *Finnegans Wake:* A Sentence in Progress," *PMLA* 73 (March 1958): 136–54, revised for *Bibliography and Textual Criticism: English and American Literature, 1700 to the Present,* ed. O. M. Brack, Jr., and Warner Barnes (Chicago: University of Chicago Press, 1969), 256–94.

62. Compare this to our first sighting of Bloom through his monstrous appetites: "ate with relish the inner organs" (U: 4.01).

63. McHugh identifies this as the refrain of a Dublin street ballad.

64. This word was indeed added first, though it makes little sense now. "Strain" seems to have been added late, perhaps by the typist.

65. The term *polylogue* is not in my dictionary, but it served as a title for Julia Kristeva's 1977 book (Paris: Éditions du Seuil). There it serves brilliantly to describe the method of her husband, Philippe Sollers's remarkable *H.* Sollers has written a novel entirely composed of dialogue by unidentified voices. It is worth noting that Joyce got there first, using the word both in the *Wake* ("pollylogue" [FW: 470.09]) and in notebook VI.B.10: 37. In the *Wake* it describes the prattling of the "February Filldyke" girls over Jaun. In the notebook it qualifies the technology of the radio broadcast after a brief exploration of narrative voicing: "Stories 1 monologue / pers to 1 / 1 — 2 / 2 — 1 / 2 — 2 polylogue (broadcasters)" (*Buffalo VI.B.10,* 54).

66. See Hayman 1997.

67. It would be hard to overstate the complexity of the process at this point. This should be clear from the discrepancies in the accounts given in the draft catalog for the FDV, Danis Rose's arrangement, and in my rather lame attempt to rationalize it in the introduction to JJA 55. In fact, in an unusual lapse, Rose's arrangement fails to make an account of this important segment (see JJA 55: 445 ff.). I hope that I have finally gotten it (almost) right in what follows. Joyce was obviously hard-pressed to complete the chapter before the scheduled publication date and his birthday. Pressure or no pressure, he was clearly intent on completing and polishing his polylogue. There is no gainsaying the evidence for his felt need to enable a passage designed to carry its weight both as a climax in its own right and as a bridge to Roderick's climactic slide. Others may disagree, but in my opinion Joyce succeeded magnificently, producing a tour de force worthy of his keystone chapter under extreme pressure.

68. Joyce added "heaving that shepe in his goat," identifying the hunchback captain with the ship's husband and the tailor.

69. See Deppman 1995. This is the most exhaustive and insightful treatment of the sketch to date. I have done little more than add only a few further observations.

70. Again, perhaps because of the publication pressure, errors were made in the punctuation, and typos were overlooked. Another galley and perhaps a set of page proofs followed. In them the errors and omissions were rectified.

A Chapter in Composition

Chapter II.4

JED DEPPMAN

In 1938, fourteen years after writing, rewriting, and setting aside the short sketches "Tristan and Isolde" and "Mamalujo," Joyce combined them to form chapter II.4 of *Finnegans Wake.*[1] Because this process involved too many resources and drafts to discuss in a single essay, I will limit myself to some of the most fundamental genetic questions: What can be said about Joyce's intentions for and composition of chapter II.4? Why and how did he write his "Tristan and Isolde" and "Mamalujo"? What were the significant features of these sketches when they were put aside in 1924? Finally, how were they put together in 1938?

"Tristan and Iseult: passim."

In a famous letter to Harriet Shaw Weaver, written in 1926 at a time when he had few allies, Joyce rather enigmatically suggested that the "Tristan" material was going to have an important role in his new book.[2] He sent her a short, dense sample of the new text, ultimately the *Wake*'s opening paragraph, and then justified its significance by detailing its references, that is, providing a "key."[3] He closed with unusual deference:

> brings us back to Howth Castle & Environs.
> Sir Tristram, violer d'amores, had passencore rearrived on the scraggy isthmus from North Armorica to wielderfight his penisolate war; nor had stream rocks by the Oconee exaggerated themselse to Laurens County Ga, doublin all the time; nor avoice from afire bellowsed mishe to tauftauf thuartpeatrick; not yet, though venisoon after, had a Kidscad buttended a bland old

isaac; not yet, though all's fair in vanessy, were sosie sesthers wroth with twone jonathan. Rot a peck of pa's malt had Shem or Shen brewed by arclight and rory end to the regginbrow was to be seen ringsome on the waterface.

James Joyce

Paris. 15/xi/926

Dear Madam: Above please find prosepiece ordered in sample form. Also key to same. Hoping said sample meets with your approval

yrs trly

Jeems Joker

Howth (pron Hoaeth) = Dan Hoved (head)
Sir Amory Tristram 1st earl of Howth changed his name to St. Lawrence, b in Brittany (North Armorica)
Tristan et Iseult, passim
viola in all moods and senses (LI: 247)

Probably because it tries to do so much, the letter is a rather tense negotiation between playful and serious moods. Joyce was straining to keep things light ("Jeems Joker"), trying hard to please ("Hoping said sample meets with your approval"), and also trying to market his odd new writing style to a skeptical but important investor. Since he could neither mislead nor frighten Weaver then when he most needed her support, his glosses on the book must be taken literally, as aids to interpretation, and rhetorically, as attempts at persuasion. On both counts the "key" was and is unsatisfying, for while it is informative and user-friendly, it is also conspicuously and worryingly incomplete. Not a full collection of meanings, an unveiling of allegory, a stylistic cheat sheet, or a paraphrase of the disorienting effects of the text, it does nothing, in fact, even to address the obvious question of why a literary text would require a key.[4] John Bishop's general comment on the predicament faced by all *Wake* readers well captures what Weaver must have felt when she read the letter: "Even if we consult the available reference works and have the allusions and foreign words explicated for us, they only render what is already unintelligible a little more clearly unintelligible."[5] Despite the fact that Weaver, in her response, referred to the "comprehensive key and glossary" Joyce had sent, she was clearly uneasy with the way the text seemed incomprehensible without it (and perhaps with it). And, as Ellmann reports, she ultimately went so far as to suggest that Joyce consider publishing two editions of his new work, one "ordinary" and one "annotated" (JJII: 583–84).

Weaver's idea for a bitextual compromise suggests that in the early 1920s Joyce either purposely downplayed or legitimately underestimated how difficult it would be for others to detangle the playful erudition of his new book. Perhaps he did both; while his comments on the book's density and difficulty have become famous, in fact he tended more often, and perhaps more seriously, to stress its assembled, allusive, syncretic nature and to imply that a knowledge of its source materials would really help readers solve its riddles ("Miss Beach will send you a book of spirit talks with Oscar Wilde which will explain one page of it" [LI: 224, 1 January 1925]).[6] Yet no matter how many of its so-called sources have been revealed, the *Wake* has always been hard to read and explain. The genetic mystery is how Joyce could have understood his own writing in a way shared by so few readers, including highly literate readers who had cut their teeth on *Ulysses.*

One good example of the gap between the author's expectations and those of his audience is the glossy phrase "Tristan et Iseult, passim" in the key sent to Weaver. What does it mean? On the one hand, taken as an offhand comment, the Latin locution suggests that whether or not he had already done so in 1926, three years after stopping work on the "Tristan" sketch, he generally intended for Tristan and Iseult to be here, there, and everywhere in the *Wake.*[7] On the other hand, offhand or not, the phrase implies a paradoxical textual logic in which the two lovers would be both omnipresent and—since they wouldn't really be *visible* everywhere, even in the short sample included in the letter to Weaver—also somehow skulking around behind readers' backs and under their eyes and noses. Who, what, when, and where *were* "Tristan et Iseult," and *how* could they get away with so much uninhibited textuality? It is another difficult genetic question: according to what understanding of the nature of his own developing text could Joyce have written "Tristan et Iseult, passim" to explain it?

The answer tacitly depends upon the answers to many other questions. Joyce's explanatory "passim" and air of control are problematic, since, famously, the presence of everything and everyone "in" the *Wake* is virtual or uncertain. On the level of characters such as Tristan and Isolde, Adaline Glasheen asks: "Who is who when everybody is somebody else?" And whether we are (post)structuralist, (post)semiotic, or lay readers, we also wonder in what sense letters, words, images, sounds, ideas, and other phenomena of all kinds and sizes "are" really "there," that is, whether the mechanisms of presencing proper to this singular text are comprehensible according to recognizable categories of fictional or poetic being.

If they are, then they are complex, for early in the *Wake* process Joyce's ever-expanding ideas of writing began to demand that he himself consider, imagine, and try to control the sense-giving possibilities of every letter, sound, and graphic pattern. If he complained repeatedly about his failing and overtaxed "memory," "vision," and "power of attention" in the 1920s, it was partly because he was attempting to guide, align, and contrast so many referential orders and textures: "In this atmosphere I found my memory, vision, power of attention all gradually getting worse yet I knew that if the books or even the Mss and notebooks were left here I would go on. [. . .] To write a book like this I should have a study of my own where I could quickly get at my books and papers. Otherwise it is impossible" (LI: 214, 24 May 1924). Such comments, scattered about in his letters and in the memories of his friends, are proof that to write his new book Joyce needed not only his powers of creativity and originality but also more information, sources, and details than his mind could carry. Yet, as the letter also suggests, while preliminary research and a room of his own were necessary for him to write "a book like this," he was also dependent on the actual physical presence of his source material, that is, the manuscripts, notebooks, and other "books and papers." For the *Wake* to follow the laws of its own fusion, its author required a high-speed connection to his books and *avant-textes*; "otherwise," he glumly concluded, it was "impossible."

There are signs that this comment was not hyperbole. His unromantic admission—"I knew that if the books or even the Mss and notebooks were left here I would go on"—confirms that in 1924 not only did Joyce not think he could continue writing if he were entirely cut off from his sources and drafts but he also had in mind a rough hierarchy—"*or even* the Mss and notebooks"—in which his books were more important resources than the sketches and notes that he himself had written. This bibliophilia strongly suggests that he intended to use his eclectic reading list for more than just ideas, information, styles, structures, or echoes of great themes; he also meant to incorporate and represent some aspects of those sources that defied his own memory, such things as precise quotations, references, and the graphic and visual layout of the pages. That Joyce carried out this plan to produce a multisourced and multilayered text involving many means of attracting and repelling a reader's consciousness is borne out by the history of II.4.

Overview of the Composition of II.4

In 2006, the National Library of Ireland acquired Joyce manuscripts written in April 1923 that shed new light on the composition of II.4. Together with other *Archive* materials from the period, they reveal a Joyce experimenting with the characters of Tristan and Isolde and using narrative voices—hagiographical, historical, nostalgic, bombastic, adolescent—in a chaotic Menippean satire with moving parodic targets. Apparently less interested in the story itself than in its main characters and possible ways of telling it, Joyce uses four old Irishmen and a group of seabirds to provide interpretive commentary on Tristan and Isolde's famous transgressive kiss. Perhaps testing the potential of each group as narrators for the book he is planning, he assigns them similar voices: the birds sing a biting song that mocks King Mark and the four men recite a draft—much more bitter than the version later published in *Pomes Penyeach*—of Joyce's own short lyric about the betrayal of love and memory, "Tutto è Sciolto."

This use of a poem he had written much earlier in Trieste hints at an element of autobiographical self-criticism in these drafts, one strengthened by his subsequent attempt to put the poem "Nightpiece" into Tristan's mouth (FDV: 210–11). Taken this way, Joyce can be interpreted as teasing both his former Tristan-self and his later Mark-self; and since some of the new manuscripts also play on words like glaucoma and cataracts, and were written when Joyce's own eyes were failing and he was forced to dictate to Nora, it seems likely that he was connecting the idea of physical blindness to the metaphorical, epistemological, and narratological failures of historians and other storytellers, including himself. Ultimately, those connections were plentiful and promising enough to endow the study of the four old men with a consistency independent of the Tristan plot, and he separated the two sketches by the summer of 1923. By April 1924 Joyce had stopped working on "Tristan and Isolde" entirely and his "Mamalujo," which had given him "great trouble," was still not definitive but was the most advanced work he had completed to date—"the only sidepiece" he was prepared to publish. (After months of drafts it appeared in the *transatlantic review* under the title "From Work in Progress.") The finished chapter of II.4 exemplifies par excellence Joyce's famous and still mysterious writing method of "fusion,"[8] a process to which Walton Litz, a pioneer of genetic scholarship on the *Wake,* was among the first to draw attention:

> In 1923 the ultimate structure of *Work in Progress* was still unclear, and Joyce had no narrative framework such as the *Odyssey* to follow. Therefore he adopted the technique of getting the book's major figures and motifs on paper as quickly as possible, feeling that these were "not fragments but active elements" which would "begin to fuse of themselves" in time. His favourite

analogy for this mode of composition was that of an engineer boring into a mountain from different sides.[9]

Saying that the "elements" of his text would "fuse of themselves," Joyce almost managed to sound quixotic and humble at the same time. Ultimately, however, he was neither: in 1938, when the time came to finish chapter II.4 for the *Wake,* he found, unsurprisingly, that the elements had not fused with the passage of time.[10] When he took matters into his own hands he was not content with the "humble" practices of clarifying, tightening, prettifying, juxtaposing, cannibalizing, embellishing, or kneading the materials he had so carefully developed years before—indeed, none of the usual soft metaphors for the editorial process adequately captures his method. Resembling a modern subatomic physicist more than a copyeditor, he actively pulverized and recombined his textual elements, notably shattering "Tristan" and scattering *its* pieces into "Mamalujo," not the other way around. As we will see, he was also not content to isolate passages or sentences by theme, to create dislocated constellations of miniature or fragmented narratives, or to filter in material by paragraphs or other large blocks. Even practices as confusing as these would not have allowed II.4 to match the radical textural thickness and nonnarrativity of the rest of the *Wake* as it neared completion. Instead, the "Tristan" atoms, varying in size from words (often recast as puns) to phrases (often divorced from their narrative or vocal contexts) to full paragraphs (often separated from their narrative flow) were transplanted, often nonsequentially, into the text.

Without yet delving into the details of this, I offer the following simple formal diagrams in order to give a sense of the essential mechanisms of Joyce's creative process. In 1938 two long-dormant sketches awoke before his eyes:

"Tristan and Isolde" (Sketch from 1923. 5 typescript pages, about 1200 words.)

TTT TTTTTT TT TT TT T TT TTTT TT T TTT T TTT T T T TTT T TTTTTTTTTTTT TTTTTTT TTTTTTTTT TTTTTTTT. TTTTTTT TTTTT TT T T T T TTTTTT TTTTT T T TTTTT TTT TTTTTTTTTTT TTTTTTTTTT TTTTTTTT TTTTTTTTTTTT T T T T T TTT TTTT TTT TT TTTTTTT TT T T T T T T. TTTTTTTT TTTTTTTT. TTT. TTTTTTT. TTTTT TTT TT TTTT TTTTTTTTT. TTTTTTT T T T T TTTTTTTTTTTTT T T TTTTT TT TT TTTTTTT TT T

"Mamalujo" (Sketch from April 1924. 20 typescript pages, about 4300 words.)

MMMM MM MMMMMM MMMM M MM MM M M MM MMMM-MMMM MMMM MMM MM MMMMMMMM M M M MMMM-MMM MM MMMM MMMM MMMM M MMMMM M MMMM M M M M MMMMMMMMM M M M MMMMMMM M MMMMM-MMMMM MMMM MMMMMMM MMMMM M M M MMMM MMMMMM MMMM MMMMMMM MMMMMM MMMMMMM-MMM M MMMMMMM MM MMMMMMMM MMMM M MMM-MMMMM MMMMM. M MMMMMMMMM MMMMMMM MMMM MMMM. . . .

The first additions to each page of "Mamalujo" were usually, but not always, from Joyce's own mind or from sources other than the "Tristan" sketch (below, additions 1–2, simulated by "XXXX"). The next additions (possibly made during an entirely new read-through) were fragments of "Tristan." Joyce placed both kinds of additions onto sheets opposite the "Mamalujo" typescript, writing numbers to indicate where the insertions would go. Typical 1938 corrections of "Mamalujo" looked like this:

[Corrections for "Mamalujo"] [General corrections]	[Corresponding page of "Mamalujo" typescript]
1. XXXX XXX	MM[4] MMMMM[1] MMMM
2. XXXX XXXXXX	MM MMMMMMM M MMMMMM
["Tristan" fragments]	MM MMMM M MMM MM
3. TTTT TTTTTTT	MMMM MMMMMMM
4. T T T T TTTT	MMMMM MM[3] MMMM M
5. TTTT T TTTTT	M[6] MMM MMMMM[2] MMM[5]
6. TTTTTTTT	MMMM MMMMMM MMMM

and thus a genetic reader of the published text of *Finnegans Wake* II.4 sees this:

XXXX MMMM TTT TTTTTT MM MMMMM MMMM M MM MM M M MM MMMMMMMM MMMM MMM MM MMMMMMMM M M TT TT M MMMMMMM MM MMMM XXXX MMMM MMMM T M MMMMM M. XXXX MMMM M M M M MMMMM-MMMM M M M MMMMMMM M TTTTTTT TTTTT TT T T T T TTTTTT TTTTT T T TTTTT TTT TTTTTTTTTT

TTTTTTTTTT MMMMMMMMMMM MMMM MMMMMMM MMMMM M M M MMMM XXXXXXXXXX MMMMMM MMMM MMMMMMM MMMMMM MMMMMMMMMM M MMMM-MMM MM TTTTTTT T MMMMMMMM MMMM M MMM XXXXX MMMMM MMMMM. M MMMMMMMMMM MMMM-MMM MMMM TT T. MMMM.

This is an abstract genetic diagram of the chapter. Clearly, however, we have gotten ahead of ourselves, for we have not yet inquired into the separate origins of each of the sketches.

Tristan and Isolde

Why would Joyce have wanted to write an episode from the Tristan and Isolde story? The long answer required by this simple question stands as a figure for the difficulty facing all *Wake* geneticists: Joyce had read, written, thought, and lived so much by the time he began his last book that every inquiry into his intentions is complicated and deeply rooted.

Certainly, Joyce's literary stereotypes were always capable of becoming archetypes (just think of the Citizen or Tim Finnegan), and from the start his Tristan and Isolde were caught up in that abstractive process. This series of notes from VI.B.10 reveals something more:

T. Moore wishes for 5 ears
ʳBulbul
Ahaga Kelly / Lassam
won its dancing / spurs / buggareaus / (seeds)
Val. Vousden[11]
Several Greeks wrote / Medea / Ital. Hamlet //
Tristan—Binyon / Tennyson / Wagner / Michael Field / Swinburne / Arnold / Debussy / Gordon Bottomly (VI.B.10: 14–15; *Buffalo VI.B.10,* 30–31)[12]

We see that after *Ulysses* Joyce was still interested in the fascination certain mythic heroes had for certain cultures: the Greeks repeatedly conjured up Medea, the Italians Hamlet, and, French and German composers aside, the list of literary Tristans is English. Perhaps after musing over this Anglo-European fascination with Tristan Joyce decided to redirect, or correct, the national legacy of the legend by Celticizing it: according to a note in VI.A, he saw something essentially Irish in the story's famous love potion: "Tristan Tantris Tantrum: philtre love to hate, essence of Erin."[13] Indeed, Joyce's post-Wagnerian pan-Celtic aim is already discernible in these VI.B.10 notes, namely, the "dancing spurs" and the Irish musicianship of Val Vousden and Thomas Moore.[14]

Geert Lernout has also found distant connections between Joyce's use of Wagner/Tristan material and George Moore's books *The Lake* and *Hail and Farewell*.[15] Joyce probably noticed Moore's *Memories of My Dead Life* as well, a book that, as its title suggests, has thematic parallels with the *Wake* and also includes a provocative, speculative, and orthographically *Wakean* meditation on art, adultery, and famous love triangles:

> All love stories are alike in this; they all contain what the reviewers call "sordid details." But if Tristan had not taken advantage of King Mark's absence on a hunting expedition, the world would have been the poorer of a great love-story; and what, after all, does King Mark's happiness matter to us—a poor passing thing, whose life was only useful in this, that it give us an immortal love-story? And if Wagner had not loved Madame Wasindonck, [*sic*] and if Madame Wasendonck [*sic*] had not been unfaithful to her husband, we should not have had *Tristan*. Who then would, for the sake of Wasendonck's [*sic*] honour, destroy the score of *Tristan?* Nor is the story of Tristan the only one, nor the most famous. There is also the story of Helen. If Menelaus' wife had not been unfaithful to him, the world would have been the poorer of the greatest of all poems, the *Iliad* and the *Odyssey*. Dear me, when one thinks of it, one must admit that art owes a good deal to adultery.[16]

To the *Iliad* and the *Odyssey*, of course, one must add *Ulysses*. Moreover, as Lernout has also shown, Joyce had recently read and taken many notes from the English version of Édouard Schuré's *Woman: The Inspirer*, a book that enthusiastically recounts the affair between Mathilde Wesendonck and Richard Wagner.[17] Therefore, Joyce had fresh in his mind an intriguingly romantic description of why another large-scale artist had undertaken a *Tristan*. According to Schuré, Wagner

> had just read for the second time the poem of Gottfried von Strasburg on *Tristan und Isolde*, an imitation of the French poems of the Middle Ages on the same subject. The story of the trusty knight Tristan accompanying the Queen of Ireland to the abode of King Mark, his uncle, and, during the crossing, both of them drinking the love philtre which unites them with bonds that cannot be broken, offers a certain analogy with Wagner's own situation

> between his protector and his friend. Impressed by what he read, and yielding to his own feelings, he saw the outlines of a poignant and tragic drama appear in the picturesque setting of the old Celtic legend. One day, finding himself alone with Frau Wesendonck, he told her that he was writing the text of a musical drama on *Tristan und Isolde*. This drama was to be mysteriously dedicated to her, and would express all that had ever passed between them, all that was to remain unknown to the world.[18]

Besides finding a lush pasture for pastiche in the way Wagner's art and personal life imitated and perhaps demonstrated key aspects of the Tristan romance, Joyce had several other good reasons for taking up the Tristan theme.[19] The specifically Celtic and/or medieval nature of the tale complemented the other early *Wake* sketches, since "Roderick O'Conor," "St Patrick," and "St Kevin" all dealt with medieval Irish history and hagiography. There were also the timely inspirations of two articles written by George Moore's brother, Thomas Sturge Moore, summarizing modern versions of Tristan, Joseph Bédier's recent scholarship and reconstructed version of the tale, and countless other modern dramatic, prose, and poetic renderings of Tristan.[20] Beyond this, one need merely consult Glasheen's *Census* to see how many parallels to the Tristan story Joyce knew and ultimately used in the *Wake*.[21] Lastly, Joyce naturally found in the Tristan cast a set of morph-figures for his earlier literary characters, his family, and himself.[22]

At any rate, a few months of work in 1923 resulted in a five-page typescript centering on Tristan and Isolde's kiss. It is at once a coherent narrative, a ridiculous pastiche, a brief character study of the two lovers, and a snapshot of their interaction on the ship crossing from Ireland to Cornwall.[23] (See figure 1, the first page of the "Tristan and Isolde" typescript.) In a deliberately overwritten but quite understandable English—precise stylistic precursors are to be found in "Nausicaa" and "Cyclops"—Joyce deflates both the tale and the lovers, mocking the high opinion they have of themselves. Tristan takes on the somewhat contradictory roles of effete, "wannabe" artist-romancer, and athletic rugby star, while Isolde, star-crossed and starstruck, becomes part ditzy flapper, part innocent Irish lass, and part Hollywood actress.[24]

Together in the dark the "brineburnt sixfooter" Tristan and the dolled-up Isolde—"quite charming" in her dress of "oceanblue brocade"—dance the "bunnyhug" and then sneak away to a loveseat, where Tristan fondles his "dinkum belle" (BL 47481 f. 101; JJA 56: 20). To extend the precious moment and cool her gypsy's lust, Isolde gives a "firm order" for the "six

"Tristan and Isolde" ~~F.W. II.IV~~ excerpt only used ne copied for Mr. Joyce 19.8.38 (duplicate) 101

As slow their ship, the sea being slight, upon the face of waters moved by courtesy of God that handsome brineburnt sixfooter Gaelic, rugger and soccer champion and the dinkum belle of Lucalizod quite charming in her oceanblue brocade and an overdress of net darned with gold well in advance of the newest fashion exhibits bunnyhugged scrumptiously when it was dark whilst they dissimulated themself on the eighteen inch loveseat behind the chieftaness stewardess's cabin whilst also with sinister dexterity he alternately rightandlefthandled fore and aft on and offside her palpable rugby and association bulbs. She, after a cough, murmurously then gave her firm order for tootsweet if he wouldn't please mind though not too much of the six best national poetry quotations reflecting on the situation so long as it was a stroke or two above it's a fine night and yon moon shining bright and all to that, the plain fact of the matter being that being a natural born lover of nature in all her moods and senses, by the light of the moon, of the silvery moon she longed to spoon before her honeyoldmoon at the same time drinking in long draughts of purest air serene and revelling in the great outdoors. That mouth of mandibles vowed to pure beauty promptly elocutionised to her a favourite lyrical bloom *bellclear in iambic decasyllabic* hexameter:

— Rollon thoudeep anddark blueo ceanroll!

Lady, it was just too gorgeous for words, the whole sensation. The sea, of a lovely tint and embellished by the

Figure 1: BL 47481 f. 101 (JJA 56: 20)

best national poetry quotations reflecting on the situation," and when her magnetic hunk delivers—"Rollon thoudeep anddark blueo ceanroll!"—her sublime feeling overrides his mechanical pronunciation.[25] The narrator then softly satirizes Isolde's bliss—the weather is wonderful, the sea is beautiful, and she has exactly the right man—to boot, the quote, right on cue, has made everything "ever so much more delightful." At the height of this heavy-handed literary happiness Tristan emits a few of the self-important pataphysico-theosophical Schopenhauerisms with which Wagner had seduced Wesendonck, and then, finally, "with grand passion," that is, with absurd melodrama, he breathes out "Isolde" three times.[26] Joyce may once have intended to complete this derisory parallel by recounting the fervorous vicissitudes and deaths of his poet and pixie, but, perhaps tiring of his own effusive pen, he cut it short.

It is hard to know what was planned in 1923 for this pixilated piece because the idiosyncratic nature of Joyce's notebooks and writing methods makes it possible to maintain very different hypotheses about it. David Hayman cogently argues that Tristan and Isolde were originally meant to be the core characters or narrative entities of the inchoate book, though he also suggests that Joyce had abandoned this idea by the summer of 1923. As we've seen, Joyce had the lovers, or their tale, constantly in mind, so that "Tristan" may vaguely be said to have conditioned or colored, passim-style, the material that followed it. On the other hand, Joyce may have written the "Tristan" sketch, set it aside, and left it alone until returning to it or even rediscovering it in 1938 with the task of incorporating it into the book. The truth lies closer to the first of these two extreme positions: at first "Tristan" promised, and delivered, a basic, comic pattern of love and betrayal, and later it provided a key template for the universal family.

How shall we grasp the changing roles of "Tristan" material in the development of a text that, unlike others and to the utter dismay of its first readers, did not and does not seem able to speak for itself? Let us try again to read the phrase "Tristan et Iseult, passim." Hindsight allows us to see four important and interrelated levels, or referential strata, of T & I that Joyce may have intended, however cryptically, to hint to Weaver:

1. Universal theme. Joyce meant that the theme of Tristan, as one of a "dozen original themes" of world literature, carried with it basic, recurrent, existential situations of illicit love, love triangles, aging, conflict, duty, betrayal, and so on that were central to human experience. The

algebraic logics of these settings, rather than any single dramatization of them, would dominate his work.

2. Character. Joyce meant that the characters (or archetypes, personality traits, models, etc.) of the Tristan cast—Mark, Tristan, the two Isoldes, Brangein, Kurvenal, Wagner's Melot, and/or Bédier's four felons—were in and out and all over the book, exchanging identities and splashing in and out of other characters in water-in-water fashion.
3. Myth. Joyce meant that the historically and mythically situated legend of *Tristan and Isolde* was to inform the whole of the new book in the *Ulyssean* sense (modified for the *Wake* by Joyce's application of Vico's philosophy) that the medieval tale would establish a set of formal and ritual parallels to be reawakened in and contrasted with modern forms, rites, and modes of living. Joyce's use of the French (*Tristan et Iseult*) suggests that it was to Bédier's rather than Wagner's reconstructed version, and more distantly to the French tradition of Thomas and Béroul, that he owed his archetypal plot. Conceivably, Joyce was also suggesting to Weaver that the *wholeness* of the tale—its implied values, worldhood, ideology, or other deep cultural, historical, or mythical structure—would echo allusively throughout or provide frameworks for his developing text.[27] Since Joyce had a complex understanding of the medieval period as well as of the Tristan legend (a legend with precise, late-twelfth-century historical roots of which he was certainly, and recently, aware), this thesis could be developed at great length.[28]
4. Ireland. Joyce meant that within this specifically Celtic tale was embedded a study of Ireland that he meant to feature in his book. In the early sketch Tristan is a "Gaelic rugger" and Isolde is "Ireland's bonniest," a "Miss Erin" who asks for six of the best "national" poetry quotations. Joyce also meticulously and prominently placed a great number of allusions and references to the Irish music of Thomas Moore and Thomas Osborne Davis in the sketch.[29] It opens, for example, with the phrases "As slow their ship, the sea being slight, upon the face of waters moved by courtesy of God," and in this short overture we can already hear several musical allusions: (1) "As slow our ship" (Moore); (2) "The West's Awake" (this song begins "When all beside a vigil keep / The West's asleep, the West's asleep" [Davis]);[30] (3) "As a Beam o'er the Face of the Waters May Glow."[31] The songs of Moore and Davis provide a focus for an Irish experience that is simultaneously preserved, idealized, and satirized in the sketch. These archetypal Irish songs are quoted neither as indirect speech nor as

> interior monologue; rather, the third-person narration of the dreamer/storyteller insistently establishes a maudlin aura of traditional, well-known rhythms and, more generally, a lyrical mood of Ireland.[32]

After discovering references in *Finnegans Wake* to 124 of the 126 *Irish Melodies* by Thomas Moore, the critics Matthew Hodgart and Mabel Worthington asked themselves why Joyce might have gone to such "fantastic lengths" to include them. Ultimately, they argue, his method was naturalistic, since nearly every Irish household had a copy of the *Melodies,* and also encyclopedic, since the songs summarize basic historical, mythological, political, and romantic aspects of Irish life.[33] It is also true that Joyce was attracted to "tummy moor's maladies" (FW: 492.31) and to Moore himself because of the way both music and musician were historically transitional and multifaceted. The *Irish Melodies,* as Joyce well knew, were quintessentially composite: while the airs were remnants from the medieval Irish bardic tradition, Moore wrote the words. As "The Bard of Ireland" Moore substantiated and voiced the Irishness of the chapter, and as the erstwhile religious pioneer, political rebel, and companion/biographer of Lord Byron he embodied several important romantic and historic literary moments and attitudes of the "essence of Erin."[34] Perhaps most important, with his life and work he gave modern expression to traditional rhythms of Ireland, making the *Irish Melodies* a classic Celtic corpus, like the *Annals of the Four Masters, The Book of Kells,* and *Finnegans Wake.*

Together these four bedposts of interpretation suggest that, by the mid-1920s, Joyce wanted his "Tristan" sketch to be a channel between Celtic cultural history and universal human experience.

Mamalujo

Joyce seems to have had as many goals, or exigencies, for "Mamalujo" as he had had for "Tristan." While the conceit of men turning into the waves of Ireland or Homeric "old men of the sea" is a multivalent and protean one and may well have its origins in the "Proteus" episode of *Ulysses,* Joyce's more immediate aim seems to have been to express the process and result of aging, senility, and failing memory while also lightly satirizing the bold colors and melodrama of Irish history and its historians.[35] Many of the core elements are present in the very first "draft" (1923) of "Mamalujo":

> ⌈Arrah na Pogue
> Woman squash

> Dion Boucicault
> mouth water / make —
> Matt Gregory / Marcus Lyons
> Auld Lang syne[r]
> [bl]Gone are the days[bl]
> [r]Luke Tarpy / Johnny MacDougall[r]
> ah well
> [r]sure you won't go / & leave out // a cup of kindness yet (VI.B.2: 98–99)

Here Joyce reincarnates Matthew, Mark, Luke, and John as modern old Irishmen. He assigns them a characteristically repetitious and colloquial phrase, "ah well, sure you won't go & leave out," and provides them with a symbolic central focus for their memories: Dion Boucicault and his play *Arrah na Pogue.* The nostalgic formula "Gone are the days" is echoed by the two references to the nostalgic song par excellence, "Auld Lang Syne," and with the notes on the physical degeneration that accompanies old age—mouth watering, "woman squash," and confusion—the stage is set for a harsh picture of senility.

Mainly because Joyce later sharpened the pettiness, myopia, and self-absorption of the four barons from Bédier's *Tristan* and transferred them to the portrait of the four, Glasheen and other critics have agreed that the sketch is satirical.[36] To the large extent that the four do represent a sexually voyeuristic and kaleidoscopically geriatric Michael Cusack from "Cyclops," Joyce is clearly poking fun at the tendency of some Irish to fantasize forgetfully and fretfully about Irish life as it once was or was not. Unsurprisingly, then, much of the creative and intellectual groundwork for "Mamalujo" is to be found not in the *Finnegans Wake* archive per se but in the texts and *avant-textes* of *Ulysses,* for just as the fabrication of Gerty in "Nausicaa" provides the best context for understanding the construction of Isolde, the use of Irish history and mixture of styles in *Ulysses,* especially the "Cyclops" episode, is a propaedeutic for "Mamalujo."[37] Some of the basic ideas for the sketch are first mapped out there, such as the ironically romantic and homesick evocation of myth: "[A]ll these moving scenes are still there for us today rendered more beautiful still by the waters of sorrow which have passed over them and by the rich incrustations of time" (U: 12.1461–64), or the humorous juxtaposition of the four evangelists and the four masters: "No need to dwell on the legendary beauty of the cornerpieces, the acme of art, wherein one can distinctly discern each of the four evangelists in turn presenting to each of the four masters his evangelical symbol" (U: 12.1441–44).

However, "Mamalujo's" divergence from "Cyclops" emerges clearly in notebook VI.A, where we find a series of conceptual notes, important for both "Mamalujo" and the rest of the *Wake,* that reveal Joyce's interest in patterns of preconscious or subconscious thought: "[D]ream thoughts are wake thoughts of centuries ago / unconscious memory / great recurrence / race memory / repressions / fixations / signs by" (VI.A: 104). Curious about the ways "unconscious" memories in old men's minds carry and express the Irish "race memory" and "thoughts of centuries ago," Joyce may well have intended for the sketch to caricature, interrogate, or extend the nostalgic tendencies of four famous members of the Gaelic Revival: significantly, on the same page of VI.A he writes the ages of four Irish writers (A.E., Yeats, Shaw, George Moore) a generation older than he is: "Aet 56, WBY 58 GBS 67 GM 71."[38] Whether or not these writers are ultimately targeted in the final text of II.4, and there is little explicit evidence that they are, Joyce does make a concerted stylistic attempt to create an aura of repetition, "great recurrence," uncertainty, and forgetting, doing everything he can to represent and interlace the cyclical processes of an aging mind and culture. One strand of additions to the early sketch demonstrates how serious Joyce was about this process:[39]

BL 47481:
f. 29: "forget and" "repeating itself"
f. 31: "not forgetting" "was it?" "there like forgetmenots" "or 1169"
f. 32: "to forget the past and all" "not to forget" "or 1169 or 1798" "dinna forget"
f. 33: "forgot himself making" "now, forget and forgive, and"
f. 34: "it and forgetting about" "and repeating themselves"
f. 35: "forgetting to say" "so forgetful" "repeating yourself"
f. 36: "and by the world forgot" "repeating ourselves and all now" "we never never shall forget" (JJA 56: 71, 73–78)

Careful reading of the final text also reveals that the chapter is fixated on both the historical past and the grammatical past tense. In fact, despite the overwhelming resistance of the *Wake* to traditional linguistic analysis, a survey of some basic time words in the sixteen published pages of II.4 gives interesting results: "when" occurs twenty-seven times and "then" twelve times, both of these words almost always referring to a past moment; "At the time" occurs once; "at that time" five times; "were" twenty-seven times; and "used to" nine times. By contrast, "are" is used as a verb only three times, and the word "will" is used only once, as a noun. There is simply no clear reference to the future.[40] This last fact makes it possible to appreciate the studied nature of Joyce's use of time words and to disconfirm the popular critical opinion that "Mamalujo" conflates or telescopes "all times" into one date, 1132. It also suggests that for Joyce the sketch was both an analysis and an illustration of Thomas Moore's most sentimental lyrics:

And thus, as in memory's bark we shall glide,
To visit the scenes of our boyhood anew,
Though oft we may see, looking down on the tide,
The wreck of full many a hope shining through;
Yet still, as in fancy we point to the flowers,
That once made a garden of all the gay shore,
Deceiv'd for a moment, we'll think them still ours,
And breathe the fresh air of life's morning once more.[41]

As Joyce writes of Mamalujo, "thoh the dayses gone still they loves young dreams" (FW: 398.21–22). Yet while the sendup of Irish nostalgia is easy to see, it is still only a small portion of Joyce's aim. Similarly, there is little direct parody of historical or biblical authority: dates, phrases, voices, and topoi from these and other resources are mixed into a nonnarrative and synesthetic blend that does not lend itself to satire. Even Joyce's brother Stanislaus, who disliked "Mamalujo" intensely, recognized that the sketch was not trivial, small-minded, or unidimensional—"I have no doubt that you have your plan, probably a big one again as in 'Ulysses'" (LIII: 103)—and in fact Joyce's plan was too big, too multifaceted, or at least too open-ended to be considered a mere joke by any of its early readers. Another indication of Joyce's hubristic multitasking is revealed in a letter to Weaver in which he lists the modern Irish names for the four old men and establishes parallels and correspondences between them and the four masters, the evangelists, pronouns, liturgical colors, days, provinces, accents, even "ores."[42] However, these correspondences and their implicit interactions remain little elucidated in the final text—they too are only a fragment of the "Mamalujo" story.

The first few drafts show that "Mamalujo" was in part intended to limn and telescope three different levels of old age and senility. The metempsychotic, Vichian, and Hegelian Joyce was beginning to write a new universal history and had in trifocal view the cyclical human experience of individuals as (1) unique subjects with particular memories and experiences,

(2) members of (a nineteenth-century generation of) Celtic culture with shared experiences, and (3) members of the human race with the shared basic experiences of all people: food, speech, marriage, burial, and other rites.[43] While, eventually, the *Wake* would bring this collapsive strategy to its limits by correlating and contrasting the individual mind of the dreamer with the movements of universal history, it was not until 1938 that Joyce was willing to transgress in II.4 the limits that his own brand of naturalism had imposed upon the project. Significantly, the first few sketches of "Mamalujo" do not include references that four modern old Irishmen would not have known: their aggregate database is dominated by Irish geography, history, and local culture. Yet it is important to note that Joyce did eventually take the important step of widening the text beyond the conscious and subconscious minds of the four Irishmen by including in II.4 many of the ubiquitous and universal *Wakean* epithets, sources, and motifs—such things as *The Book of the Dead,* the P/Q split, "up guards, and at them," Armenian and Greek vocabulary, and so on. This helped him sluice the chapter into the book and the book into the chapter.

Thus in 1924 we find personal experiences, nineteenth-century literary, theatrical, and musical memories, and historical, mythical, and religious memories all converging and diverging wildly, all half-remembered and half-forgotten by the four.[44] Yet while all three of these levels were ultimately important in their own right, Joyce was especially careful to allow the activity of Mamalujo's collective unconscious to enact the dispersive and binding processes of communication between levels.[45] The radical uncertainty of their memory in fact became a form of radical freedom, a means of enabling unpredictable metonymic and metaphorical transfers between all levels of (imagined) experience. Singular and collective, Mamalujo's active and error-prone memory was Joyce's first model for expanding the activities of dreams and puns to the metaphysical and material levels of history.

Joyce's progressive development of Mamalujo's catalytic ability to set particulars and universals in communication lies behind the fact reported by Richard Ellmann that the four were intended from the very start to be the "chorus for the action" of the rest of the book.[46] The generic "choral" possibilities of which Joyce availed himself were indeed numerous: as Matthew, Mark, Luke, and John, Mamalujo used biblical, epic, and eschatological forms; as the four masters they acted as (naively) historical, objective, and truthful chroniclers. As four modern old Irishmen they indulged in chatty, forgetful meandering and popular, intimate colloquialism—restless and oral blends of all the other genres. By the time the book was published the old men's minds were actively and passively negotiating with the *Wake* dreamer's voices and visions throughout the chapter, and the narration of II.4 had become an *om-nescient* form of polyvocality, a way of writing that both includes and erases everything.

Starting with the first drafts of "Mamalujo," various memories of "Dion Boucicault, the elder" (FW: 385.03) federated symbolically to form the high-water mark of the four's floating nostalgia. Cascading across the pages in murky ways, "all wishening for anything at all of the bygone times" (FW: 386.06–7), the four used the "good old bygone days of Dion Boucicault" to represent and regurgitate especially well the Irish fetishization of ancient history over and against the infirm present. Indeed, if Thomas Moore was crucial to the referential aura underlying the "Tristan" sketch, then Dion Boucicault's life and works played the same role in "Mamalujo," and this parallelism is one of the keys to understanding Joyce's willingness to marry the two sketches. Not only did Boucicault write *The Shaughraun,* a play that provided Joyce with the setting of a wake in which an Irishman comes back to life, but the dramatist's own quintessential Irish character, humor, and melodrama—as visible in his colorful rags-to-riches-to-rags life as in his plays—helped give shape and language to the memories of the four. Boucicault's famous peripatetic wanderings between America, France, England, and Ireland, the well-documented inconstancies of his fortunes, his controversial status as a near-plagiarist and "channeler" of existing plots, and his self-conscious attempt to speak, through drama, the contemporary historical truths of Ireland are things that make him, like Moore, a consummately pied and transitional figure. No doubt Boucicault, a specialist in Irish stereotypes whose so-called Irish plays (*The Colleen Bawn, Arrah-na-Pogue,* and *The Shaughraun*) were a fixed presence in "Mamalujo" starting from the earliest versions, was also meant to combine thematically and stylistically with the four masters and other narrators of the Irish past.[47]

Joyce must have especially appreciated the showy way Boucicault had of constantly reinventing and restaging his own "true" Irishness, an especially eye-catching feature of the bill he wrote to accompany his first production of *The Colleen Bawn:*

LAURA KEENE'S THEATRE.
A New Play By
DION BOUCICAULT

Ireland, so rich in scenery, so full of romance and the warm touch of nature, has never until now been opened by the dramatist. Irish dramas have hitherto been exaggerated farces, representing low life or scenes of abject servitude and suffering. Such is not a true picture of Irish society.

THE COLLEEN BAWN
Founded on a true history
First told by an Irishman
And now
Dramatized by an Irishman.
THE COLLEEN BAWN
Or
The
BRIDES OF GARRYOWEN[48]

Boucicault ultimately became the lead deity in a pantheon of "Mamalujo" playwrights, a group that in 1938 would provide a generically theatrical counterbalance to the operatic and filmic qualities of "Tristan."[49] In fact, the selection of Boucicault and his plays as an important axis for the collective memories of Mamalujo was a decision with deep roots in Joyce's own lifelong engagement with questions of Irish nationality, myth, and history. Boucicault's plots and performances reinvigorated those questions, while his melodrama and optimistic political nationalism opened them up to various forms of ironic renovation.[50] In short, the plays not only gathered up many of Joyce's favorite strands in the fabric of the Irish past, they also asked to have their plots, characters, and cultural contexts recombined in many of the same ways as the legend of Tristan and Isolde. Indeed, like Bédier's *Tristan,* Boucicault's plays and players were broad and permeable enough to invite endless analogues—more than osmotic enough, therefore, to allow "Mamalujo" to take in the "Tristan" material.

"Tristan" and "Mamalujo"

"Tristan" and "Mamalujo" were wed in 1938. To recapture the event it will help to look at a few snapshots (figures 1, 2, and 3) and recall some details of the ceremony:

1. Joyce incorporated "Tristan" fragments of various sizes, from single words to full paragraphs, into "Mamalujo."
2. "Tristan" fragments were sometimes placed into "Mamalujo" sequentially, sometimes not.

3. Roughly 60 percent of *Finnegans Wake* II.4 was originally written for "Mamalujo." Some 20 percent was written for "Tristan," and the rest of the material, drawn from various sources, was added during the final drafting process.
4. Sometimes Joyce transformed "Tristan" material before placing it into "Mamalujo," sometimes not.
5. Out of some 126 additions Joyce made to "Mamalujo" to form *Wake* chapter II.4, about half were fragments drawn from the "Tristan" typescript.
6. Much but not all of the "Tristan" material was used in "Mamalujo." Some unused material was discarded, and some was used in the elaboration of III.1–2.[51]
7. As Joyce proceeded he grew hastier and/or more comfortable with the inclusion of "Tristan" material. He started to transplant larger and larger segments, sometimes whole paragraphs. He crammed over a page of "Tristan" in large chunks into the last two or three pages of "Mamalujo."
8. Joyce tended to mine "Tristan" page by page, treating each separate page as a complex visual puzzle or artwork from which to draw material.
9. Similarly, he treated each page of "Mamalujo" as a unit, scattering reference numbers all over it and starting again with 1 on the next page.

Everything suggests that Joyce carefully read and reread each page of both typescripts, pondered where to put new material, and continued to hold the pages in his mind even as they were transforming. The sequence of numbered insertions on the sample "Mamalujo" page (figure 2) is typically nonsequential: 2, 4, 1, 6, 14, 8, 7, 10, 11, 16. Joyce wrote some corrections directly onto the typescript (e.g., between 2 and 4 and after 16) and recorrected some numbered corrections before they were even placed in the text (17 added to 9, 15 to 2, etc.). It is crucial to see that Joyce's new text required him to have a strong visual, aural, orthographic, syntactic, and grammatical memory of each page. Without these various forms of grasping, accessing, and linking his own material Joyce could not have controlled in the way he did the pullulating sights and sounds of his additions. Litz made this point a long time ago:

> Joyce's work of the 1930s may be distinguished from his earlier efforts by the complete control of his material that it exhibits. No longer was composition a process of exploration, a search for structural solutions or the perfection

1 F.W. 114

(in so hattapoucy

And there they were too listening in as hard as they
(by the tourneyold of the wattarfalls with their vuofens and they kemin)
could in Dubbeldorp the donker (only a quarterbuck askull for
the last acts) to the solans and sycamores and the wild geese
and gannets and the migratories and mistlethrushes and the aus-
pices and all the birds of the sea, all four of them, all sighing and sobbing, and listening.

They were the big four, the four maaster waves of Erin,
all listening, four. There was old Matt Gregory and then besides old Matt there was old Marcus Lyons, the four waves, and
oftentimes they used to be saying grace together right enough
~~xxxxxxxxxxxxxxxx~~ Bausnabeatha, in Miracle Squeer ; here now
we are the four of us : old Matt Gregory and old Marcus and old
Luke Tarpey : the four of us and sure thank God there are nomore
of us : and sure now you wouldn't go and forget and leave out
the other fellow and old Johnny Mac Dougall : the four of us
and no more of us and so now pass the fish for Christ sake,
Amen : the way they used to be saying their grace before fish
repeating itself for auld lang syne. And so there they were
with their palms in their hands like the pulchrum's proculs,
spraining their ears luistering and listening to the oceans of
kissening with their eyes glistening all the four when he was
kiddling and cuddling his colleen bawn, an oscar sister, the
hero, that was ~~very~~ wrong and ~~most~~ improper, and cuddling her
and kissing her, Isolamisola and whisping and lisping her about
Trisolanisans, how one was whips for one was two and two was lips
for one was three, and dissimulating themself,
with his poghue like Arrah-na-poghue, the dear dear annual, they
all four remembored who made the world and how they used to be
at that time in the vulgar ear cuddling and kiddling her after

Figure 2: BL 47481 f. 114 (JJA 56: 171)

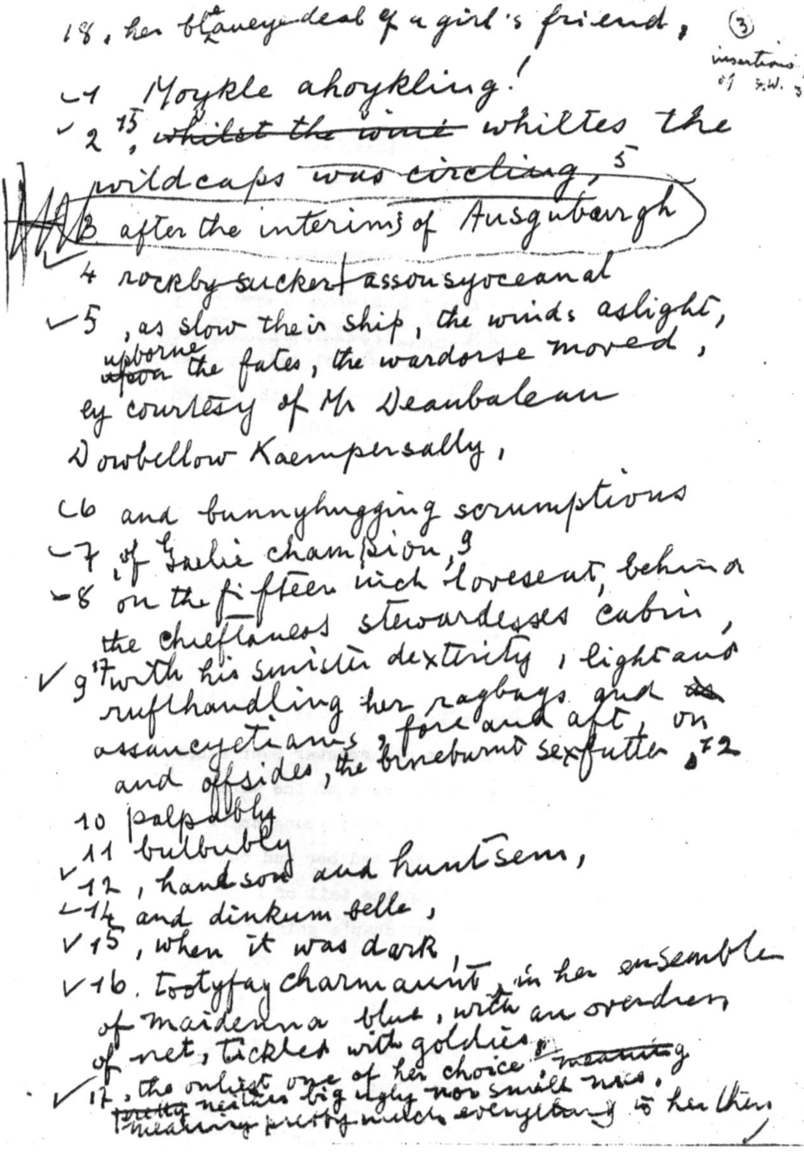

18, her blaneydeal of a girl's friend, (3)

insertions for of S.W. 3 & 3

✓1 Moykle ahoykling!

✓2 15, ~~whilst the wind~~ whiltes the wildcaps ~~was circling,~~ 5

3 after the interims of Ausgubargh

✓4 rockbysuckerassousyoceanal

✓5 , as slow their ship, the winds aslight, ~~upon~~ upborne the fates, the wardorse moved, by courtesy of Mr Deaubaleau Dowbellow Kaempersally,

6 and bunnyhugging scrumptious

✓7 of Gaelic champion, 9

8 on the fifteen inch loveseat, behind the chieftaness stewardesses cabin,

✓9 17 with his sinister dexterity, light and rufthandling her ragbags and assaucyetiams, fore and aft, on and offsides, the bineburnt sexfutter, 12

10 palpably

11 bulbubly

✓12 , handsom and huntsem,

✓14 and dinkum belle,

✓15 , when it was dark

✓16 . tootyfay charmaunt, in her ensemble of maidenna blue, with an overdress of net, tickled with goldies, 8

✓17 , the onliest one of her choice ~~meaning~~ ~~pretty~~ neither big ugly nor small nice, meaning pretty much everything to her then

Figure 3: BL 47481 f. 113v (JJA 56: 170)

> of linguistic devices. Instead the ultimate form of the book was fixed in his mind, and—as in the last stages of writing *Ulysses*—he elaborated like a mosaic worker upon a predetermined pattern. His friends of the time who were familiar with his methods, especially Louis Gillet and Eugene Jolas, have recorded their impressions of Joyce at work, and they attest that he held the incredibly complex form of the *Wake* in his mind as a single image, and could move from one section to another with complete freedom.[52]

Intense scrutiny and visual awareness of his own text helped Joyce create subtleties, riff on words, and plan micro- and macroconnections between rhythmic, visual, linguistic, oral, and many other orders of presencing throughout the book. In this increasing complexity we see how much Joyce pressured himself to refine and reproportion not only the novelistic tendencies of his book (e.g., the sequences of images, narrative developments, voices, and characters) but also its more material, poetic, and nonnarrative aspects (effects of alliteration, rhythm, allusion, etc.). One reason he could not work additions easily and sequentially into the *Wake*'s stretched but usually visible virtual structures of grammar and syntax is that there were several logical, narrative, rhythmic, and other referential mechanisms in place and acting simultaneously, passim, in his text.

Since genetic criticism has the task of revealing something of this multiplicative presencing, let us look at and listen closely to the first five changes Joyce made to the first page of the "Mamalujo" typescript (figures 2 and 3):

1. Moykle ahoykling!
2. ~~whilst the wind~~ whiltes the wildcaps was circling
3. after the interims of Ausgubargh
4. rockbysucker / assousyoceanal
5. , as slow their ship, the winds aslight, ~~upon~~ upborne the fates, the wardorse moved, by courtesy of Mr Deaubaleau Dowbellow Kaempersally. (BL 47481 f. 113v; JJA 56: 170)

These first five of eighteen additions softly began to pipe "Tristan's" Irish music into "Mamalujo." Addition 1, "Moykle ahoykling," carried both the Moore tune "Silent Be, O Moyle" and its traditional air, "Michael Hoy";[53] in 2, "the wildcaps was circling" we hear Moore's "The Wine-cup Is Circling"; in 5, "as slow their ship," we hear Moore's "As Slow Our Ship"; also in 5, "the winds aslight," we hear the line "the West's asleep" from Davis's "The West's Awake," and in "upborne the fates" we hear Moore's "Upon the Face of the Waters."[54] On those who are familiar with the songs the effect is powerful—the textual equivalent of sampling or of turning on several CD players in rapid succession. While the resulting noise is confused, fragments of it are comprehensible, and the more one fiddles with the knobs the more one receives of the clipped, competing Irish sounds.

We also see that Joyce favored effects of assonance and alliteration: oykle / oykle / . . . whil / wil . . . after / inter / Aus . . . Deaubaleau / Dowbellow. This poetic/musical effect of echoing or doubling sounds (very hard to explain, incidentally, if the *Wake* is just a dream narrative, a universal history, or a vision) also has several important conceptual counterparts, both on this first page of additions and throughout the end time of the *Wake*'s composition.[55] Indeed, the whole process of infusing the text with aural and conceptual doubling is so meticulous and complex that it merits further explication.

First, there is an echoing étude on the phrase "Rugby and Associational balls," which Joyce found in Otto Jesperson's 1922 book *Language: Its Nature, Development and Origin.* While the phrase may have originally attracted him because it showed how the words "rugger" and "soccer" derived from "Rugby" and "Associational," Joyce's *Wake* usages, doubling all the time, both incorporated and transcended this light philology. In additions 4, "rockbysucker / assousyoceanal," and 5, "ragbags and assaucyetiams," there is grist for pages of commentary, from the "rock, suck, ass, anal" sequence in 4 to the sassy, saucy, ragtag Latin in 5—"etiam" can mean such timely, doubling things as "still," "as yet," "already," "indeed," "certainly," and "again." Following a genetically obstreperous and peculiarly Joycean editorial logic in which the rejected forms of words, phrases, and other textual phenomena are not suppressed or repressed once and for all but are preserved in the new forms, which they haunt noisily, everything in 4 is also in 5, and thus each version of the "r & a" phrase tends to carry its previous incarnations with it in a process that quickly exceeds our grasp.

Joyce also included ordinary, colloquial, and proverbial pairs of binary opposites, a process he began in the early "Mamalujo" sketch and later linked to Bruno's philosophy. Consider the way Tristan plays with Isolde's breasts in addition 9 (figure 3): "[W]ith sinister dexterity he alternately rightandlefthandled fore and aft on and offside her palpable rugby and association bulbs." *Sinister* and *dexter* are Latin for "left" and "right," and "rightandlefthandled" is "right and left" and "light and rough" all at once, and there is also "fore and aft" and "on and off." For better or worse and from start to finish Joyce included many such back-and-forth duets in II.4, using their status as clichés to install a dialectical humor and an oral feel.

Still another counterpart to the foregoing processes is the twingling of male and female, another studied feature of II.4.[56] In the final text the four, who "were four dear old heladies and really they looked awfully pretty" (FW: 386.14–15), are characterized less as sexless than as epicene. The "manowoman" (FW: 396.05), the feminized "roi" in "*A Royenne Devours*" (FW: 388.07), and countless other examples in the chapter suggest that Joyce saw old age as a time when male and female experiences and, perhaps more metaphysically, "principles" draw closer together and mingle.

These binomial expansions are not only Shem/Shaun and Patrick/Kevin-style antinomies but also examples of "Mamalujo's" function of bridging or channeling between disparate realms. With this in mind, one could theorize the gap between the 1924 and the 1938 Joyce by seeing the latter's inclusion of layering effects as an expansive but recognizable development of the former's use of the inherently intertextual techniques of pastiche.

Let us test this idea by looking at some examples. In 1924 Tristan is Isolde's "beau ideal of a true girl's friend." This kitschy cliché is drawn from the pages of "Nausicaa," where Joyce, exploiting the tropes of a commercialized, saccharine romanticism, had young Gerty dream of Tommy in similar language.[57] In addition 18 (figure 3) he changed the phrase to "blaueyedeal of a girl's friend" and then, correcting the correction, added an *e* to make this: "bleaueyedeal of a girl's friend." The reworked phrase maintains the original "beau ideal" but hydrates it (*eau*); *Work in Progress* had changed so dramatically that the "eau" that was orthographically present in 1924 took on semantic value in 1938. Also added were a "blow" (bleau), the color blue (blau, bleu), and such higher-level comment-puns as "eyedeal" (ideal; "deal" of the eye; "I"-deal; "I(solde)-deal"; "why-deal"; "Y(seut)-deal"; "below-eye-deal"; "below-ideal"; "blue-eyed deal"; etc.). Some readers will even see a "blue-eyed eel" and others anything "ideally" blue—but why should we deal with those possibilities? Can we really subordinate such puns to a theme (the puns touch aspects of the "Tristan" tale), a descriptive system (they are part of a referential node/web/network), or a literary technique (they are Joyce's way of writing an encyclopedic, comic, and universal text)?

Before addressing this let us look at another simple example of literary description: in 1924 Isolde was "quite charming in her oceanblue brocade and an overdress of net darned with gold," that is, she was a superficial and delightful girl similar to Lorelei Lee from Anita Loos's *Gentlemen Prefer Blondes* (1925). By 1938 Isolde was "tootyfait charmaunt in her ensemble of maidenna blue, with an overdress of net, tickled with goldies." Joyce added French (*tout à fait charmant[e]*); Italian (*tutti*); a horn (toot); some birds (goldies = goldfinches); and a toothy comment on Isolde, who, as Mark's wife, was logically Tristan's "charm aunt." In "maidenna blue" there is Madonna blue, or Medina blue, and an extra ironic emphasis, perhaps, on Isolde's (lost) maidenhood.

Reading in this way we may just be tempted to believe that the characters and narrative of the tale of "Tristan," together with the comic and dispersive processing power of "Mamalujo," are enough to provide conceptual control over the changes and additions Joyce made to the text. Indeed, this is the most tempting of all genetic assumptions, that Joyce's composition was governed by a matrix of ideas that, however complexly entangled, is ultimately localizable or recoverable. In its strong form this is a pipe dream (appropriately nostalgic in the context of "Mamalujo") because, first, puns inherently open up meanings and contexts well beyond the resources of II.4, its *avant-textes,* and the *Wake* itself, and, second, the many senses of every pun open windows onto different genetic histories, the vast majority of which cannot be made explicit. In its soft form, of course, it is the hope that sustains geneticism: perhaps it *is* possible to recover something of Joyce's proliferating and layering textual logics and their links to his life and times.

Now often bracketed by critics as a problem too well known or thorny to address directly, puns and other kinds of paronomasia nonetheless represent one of the core aesthetic commitments of the *Wake* and greatest divergences from Joyce's previous works. Taken seriously, they are also infinitely productive of commentary, so I will only be able to discuss a few examples. An explosive one is the benign-looking "bulbubly" (cf. figure 3, addition 11): "the brueburnt sexfutter, handson and huntsem, that was palpably wrong and bulbubly improper" (FW: 384.28–29). At first it seems to condense, extend, and conceptually collapse the preexisting "palpably" (figure 3, addition 10) and "bulbs" (figure 1), this last already a pun (humorizing Isolde's breasts) on the Rugby or Associational "balls." The onomatopoetic "bulbubly" also recalls the champagne phoneme "bubbly," with its overtones of effervescent times and personalities, and Tristan and Isolde's philter of love and death. Perhaps we also hear echoes of the words "bauble," "babble," "bobble," and "probably/doubly improper," all of which seem relevant in the context of Tristan's bullish groping of Isolde.

Yet Joyce intended still more presence than this in the phoneme: Roland McHugh reasonably proposes "balbus," which is Latin for stammer,[58] and, perhaps even more obviously, Joyce was referring to the popular cage bird, the bulbul. Certainly present as well is William Percy French's 1877 swashbuckling song "Abdullah Bulbul Ameer" (or "Abdul the Bulbul Ameer"), which recurs repeatedly in II.3 and elsewhere.[59]

With so many animals,[60] birds, and birdcalls on the brain as he writes II.4, Joyce may also be recalling to himself and his readers the way Simon Dedalus appeared to Stephen as a buzzard in "Circe."[61] His aerial exhortations featured the word and sounds of the "bulbul":

> That's all right. (*he swoops uncertainly through the air, wheeling, uttering cries of heartening, on strong ponderous buzzard wings*) Ho, boy! Are you going to win? Hoop! Pschatt! Stable with those halfcastes. Wouldn't let them within the bawl of an ass. Head up! Keep our flag flying! An eagle gules volant in a field argent displayed. Ulster king at arms! Haihoop! (*he makes the beagle's call, giving tongue*) Bulbul! Burblblburblbl! Hai, boy! (U: 15.3944–50)

Buzzards, asses, eagles, beagles, and bulbuls—this erratic fray of nature's noise is dimly audible in the *Wake*'s word "bulbubly." In the context of the *Wake* the extreme linguistic mutability of this group of letters is also noteworthy: the sounds of both the bulbul bird and the beagle baying occur in the "Circe" word "Bur*blbl*bur*blbl!*" and Joyce, later in the same chapter, also turns the sound into a verb: "*beaglebaying, burblbrbling*" (U: 15.3955).

Beyond this it must be allowed that there are striking visual and dramatic parallels between the situation of impropriety and insobriety evoked in "Circe" (especially among Simon, Stephen, and the whores) and the bulbubly improper "seatuition" (FW: 385.30) of Tristan, Isolde, and Tristan's surrogate buzzard-father, Mark, in II.4. Of course, these and other thematic parallels of sex, infidelity, and parental and filial duty, if pursued, would only lead to more tangents.

Thus we face, in "bulbubly," a series of typically unanswerable genetic questions: how much of the foregoing discussion, and what else, was properly implied when Joyce added the word/letters/sound/musical intonation/birdcall imitation "bulbubly" to his list of corrections? What pressures, thoughts, texts, memories, or other references are copresent here? Clearly, no theoretical tool could hope to quantify and hierarchize the simultaneous presences of the Percy French song, the meanings of "stammering" and "a cage bird," the scene from "Circe," and so on. To quiet the clamor we would need, at the very least, to select appropriate contexts; yet this is very difficult, not only for the reason John Bishop has given, that the dream texture of the *Wake* makes it likely that relevant contexts for a given word or situation are distant from it in the space-time of the text,[62] but also because, even if we take the chapter, plot, node, or nearby words as the primary contextualizing units, the meanings of those elements are, like "bulbubly," themselves hard to freeze, characterize, or enumerate.

This is precisely the difficulty that David Hayman has attempted to resolve with his theory of nodality.[63] His flexible, nuanced theory of *Wakean* contextualization combines a careful genetic study of the *Wake's* early development with a phenomenological attentiveness to the wandering power of the reader's consciousness: "Nodal systems in the *Wake* may be built around or evolved from narrative sequences, descriptive tropes, clusters of words in an exotic language, song tags—indeed from anything remarkable enough to be isolated by the reader" (WiT: 37). The recurring problem for geneticists is that by 1938 many "words" in the *Wake* had many genetically defiant undercurrents "remarkable enough to be isolated by the reader," that is, the same liquid tendency to join with many nodes and to ripple outward indefinitely, for example, the 1924 "sixfooter" that in 1938 became "sexfutter." In 1924 "sixfooter" *described* Tristan, and it meant, first, that he was rather tall and fit Isolde's childish, preconceived ideas of attractiveness and, second, that Joyce was punning on poetic "hexameter": Tristan the six-foot-tall specialist of "six-footer" poetry came up a little short with his decasyllabic, Byronic verse to Isolde.[64] In 1924 the pun was relatively easy to decode, drew little attention to itself, and was perhaps even exhausted by those two specific meanings of the English word "sixfooter." In 1938, however, Tristan became a "sexfutter." This linguistic bit, vocable, phoneme, or nonword "sexfutter" brings to mind "sixfooter," no doubt, but also "sexfooter," "sexe-foutre," "sexe-fouteur," "six fuck her," "sex fuck her," "sexfucker," "sex-father," "sex-fooder," and "sex-fodder," among other things.[65] As we know from other places fluttering in the *Wake*—"may be matter of fact now but was futter of magd then" (FW: 129.03–4)—Joyce's opportunistic spooneristic tactics must also be taken into account: perhaps Tristan is a fuck-sitter, facts-checker, or fox-suitor.

While all of these multifarious messages, languages, and registers of discourse can always be massaged, with muscular contextualization and good humor, into relevance for the "Tristan and Isolde" tale or some other controlling set of ideas, readers will always sense that the sights and sounds emitted by signifiers like "bulbubly" and "sexfutter" and their surrounding text invite many other substitutions as well. If we open the spigot wide, we see that the first syllable, "sex," invites such readings as socks, six, sacks, sax, shacks, shocks, soaks, sucks, Saxe, such, sicks, sics, checks, shucks, chicks, Czechs, seeks, chokes, sheiks, shakes . . . in English alone. The point is that by 1938 Joyce had not only destabilized words by changing or removing a few letters, he had radicalized enough of the text on enough of its readable levels to splash suspicion upon every textual order. In other words, he had created a hermeneutically excessive circumstance in which even the most innocent word in II.4—a word like "word" (FW: 385.05), which is spelled the same as the word "word"—could be suspected of polygraphy.[66] While the patterning power of consciousness will tend, as theorists as different as Kant, Saussure, Iser, and Hayman have shown, to sift these possibilities into certain forms, and individual readers will always wipe their glosses with what they know, the *genetic* critical consciousness has the task of bringing into view and maintaining, in a pluralizing (if paralyzing) copresence, as many possible genetic stories and layers of meaning as possible, no matter how ephemeral or unlikely. Yet what started out as a geneticist-friendly environment in which Joyce's text offered itself as a progression through *avant-textes*—books, papers, manuscripts—has turned into a frenzied semantic situation that defies evolutionary accounts.

Some passages were transformed on the wing as Joyce copied them for use in "Mamalujo":

> 1924: Praises be to fair sea (BL 47481 f. 97; JJA 56: 13)
> 1938: (praisers be to deeseesee!) (BL 47481 f. 116v; JJA 56: 176; FW: 386.35)

In "Praises be to fair sea" there was nothing very problematic. In 1924 the phrase was essentially a trite rhetorical formula uttered with some degree of sarcasm. However, in the 1938 word "praisers" (FW: 386.35), different by one letter, we hear many new things: "pressers be," "prayers be," "pleasures be," "phrases be," "phrasers be," "poseurs be," "Battersby," "precious be," "praise us be," "preserves be," "pleasers be," "players be," "pacers be," "placers be," and many more combinations. It would be a spectacular genetic mistake to think that Joyce added the simple letter *r* to one simple word and transformed it into another simple word or set of words. In fact, the semantic and epistemological breadth, "denoted content," and homophonic copresences have been wildly multiplied and mutated. Perhaps this even occurred *mechanically*, as a result of the entropic dynamics of the text, more than it did *creatively*, as a result of Joyce's linguistic inventiveness.[67] Indeed, the genetic point to make would be that the *r* need never have been added, for the surrounding text would have suggested its presence even if Joyce had not written it, as in the case of the absent/present/passim apostrophe in the book's title. The ugly truth is that this *r* so Derrideanly *différant* may even have been implied in the earlier drafts, in the 1924 "praises," for example, in such a way that it was virtually present as an absence before it was present as a presence.[68]

In every example such paradoxical examples abound. Note the fairescapading leap that Joyce made from "fair sea" (1924) to "deeseesee" (1938). In the latter set of nine letters we can see and hear the deep, deep sea (perhaps an echo of "Deepsleep Sea" [FW: 37.18]), "disease-y," "the deceased," "this Issy," and "the sissy." Moreover, the phonemes "deeseesee," when pronounced, become letters (DCC) that, when written, become numbers, that is, the Roman numerals for 700—perhaps a medieval date recalling the Vikings, the reign of Dagobert (FW: 394.18), or *The Book of Kells.* Listening again, perhaps we hear "decease-y," "d'Assisi," "dis, si si," or simply "this is he."[69] Decisive readers or linguistic pharisees may find this easy or dizzying, and French readers in particular may feel momentarily *dessaisis,* that is, dispossessed, but only by patiently examining, rather than disparaging, such lists and examples will we acquire an idea of the genetic development, or intention, of the *Wake.*

In 1924 Joyce described Isolde as "a natural born lover of nature in all her moods and senses" (BL 47481 f. 96; JJA 56: 12). In 1938 the phrase became "natural born lovers of nature, in all her moves and senses" (BL 47481 f. 114v; JJA 56: 172; FW: 385.19–20). In 1924 the phrase was a cliché appropriate for Isolde and a fairly well hidden pun, perhaps, on the title of the book by the American classicist W. W. Goodwin, *Syntax of the Moods and Tenses of the Greek Verb.*[70] This example reveals an interesting substructure: Joyce was generally more dedicated to keeping such phrases as "natural born lover of nature" and "in all her moods and senses" in the text than in maintaining their narrative contexts. He unhooked the descriptive phrase "natural born lover of nature" from Isolde's portrait, gave it an extra *s,* and reattached it to Mamalujo: "It brought the dear prehistoric scenes all back again, as fresh as of yore, Matt and Marcus, natural born lovers of nature, in all her moves and senses, and after that" (FW: 385.18–21).

The larger point is that deictics, narratives, voices, grammar, syntax, and the other integuments that usually hold pieces of novelistic text together as they are edited lost much of their cohesive power as Joyce continued to build "Tristan" into "Mamalujo." Above those things Joyce prized discrete atomic families of linguistic and literary fodder and their deep roots in historic, mythical, etymological, cultural, and other sources. In fact, he may even have been counting on some turns of phrase such as "rollon thoudeep anddark blueo ceanroll" and "natural born lovers" to reproduce or represent circumstances, texts, and contexts that he himself had forgotten or failed to fully imagine or notice in the first place. He may have been hoping or expecting, even in the early years of the writing of the *Wake,* that his language was pregnant with meanings to which he himself was or would become blind—a circumstance that would have been just as hard to explain to Weaver in the 1920s as it is hard for geneticists to swallow now. Accepting the idea that Joyce himself was a self-conscious Mamalujan "channeler" would, among other things, make it very, very difficult to use the *avant-textes* to clarify the final text, or vice versa.[71]

Ultimately, so many patterns form and unform in the meeting of the early and late waters of the *Wake* that it is a veritable genetic revelation to compare the published text of II.4 by the 1938 Joyce with *Work in Progress* by the 1923 Joyce. Indeed, it is like comparing the Quixotes of Cervantes and Pierre Menard. The earlier Joyce, to take one last example, wrote: "They were the big four, the four maaster waves of Erin, all listening, four. There was old Matt Gregory and then besides old Matt there was old Marcus Lyons, the four waves, and oftentimes they used to be saying grace together" (BL 47481f. 114; JJA 56: 171; see figure 2). Written in the early twenties, written by the archmodernist Joyce, this allegorization was a mere echo of *Ulyssean* procedures, an allusive and layering form of textual parallelism and a rhetorical eulogy of ancient and modern mythic connectedness. The 1938 Joyce, on the other hand, wrote: "They were the big four, the four maaster waves of Erin, all listening, four. There was old Matt Gregory and then besides old Matt there was old Marcus Lyons, the four waves, and oftentimes they used to be saying grace together" (FW: 384.06–9). Matthew, Mark, Luke, and John were alive and living in Ireland—the idea was astounding. Joyce, a contemporary of Heidegger, did not see the gospellers as the origins of an eschatological framework. Rather, he sensed their destining presence shining forth anew in modernity in the everyday lives of ordinary old Irishmen.

Equally vivid is the contrast in styles. The 1924 Joyce placed the extra *a* into "maaster" in order to add length and breath to the titles of the four "master waves," that is, the four annalists and gospellers. This clean rhetorical flourish enabled the ironic modernist both to approach and to distance himself from the massive traditions of Western history and Christianity. The 1938 Joyce, on the other hand, concentrated the abundant presence of the gospels, the tradition of biblical commentary, and the whole of

Christian culture into the infinite space-time of a single letter. Stepping through the thick, dark syntactical surface, Joyce wrote "maaster" with an extra *a* in order to bring forth the name of the Reverend Anthony John Maas, author of *The Gospel According to Saint Matthew: With an Explanatory and Critical Commentary, The Life of Jesus Christ According to the Gospel History,* and other important Christian works.[72] Of course, in 1938 Joyce meant to include much more than a broad evocation of Christianity, so the *a* in "maaster" was also called upon to reproduce the magisterial, classical, and literary presence of the great Ernst Maass (1856–1929), author of the capacious *Goethe und die Antike,* a volume whose name and 655 pages contained and represented central aspects of Western culture other than Christianity (e.g., rationalism, romanticism, neoclassicism) as well as debts to non-Christian ancient civilization.[73] Beyond this, Joyce was also careful to inscribe, as plainly as he could, with this same extra *a* in the word "maaster" the names of musicians Louis Philipp Otto Maas (1852–89) and Gerald Christopher Maas, whose famous book on violoncello technique was first published in 1923, the very year Joyce began work on *Finnegans Wake.*[74]

Thus, in the final version of chapter II.4, Joyce gathered Anthony, Ernst, Otto, and Gerald Maas together, all saying grace within the confines of a single pun. Different readers will want to see and hear a different Maas: some will wish to know objectively and prove which Maas, if any, was important to Joyce and why. Most will sense the Pynchonian futility of such projects, not only because these four, and surely at least four more, will always be clamoring for attention but because their genetic traces are not recoverable. No Maas is the best Maas, and the genetic lesson, so laboriously necessary to construct, is that the *Wake* has an aleatory and encyclopedic system of reference that is simultaneously most visible and most fleeting on the level of the individual word. This system—we cannot accuse Joyce of being unsystematic—forcefully and inexorably Mamalujizes any genetic critical consciousness. Indeed, because geneticists always try to relate the mass of bulbuble undecidabilities in the *Wake*'s language to its structures, rhythms, and voices, it is ironically none other than the creatively forgetful "Mamalujo" who best demonstrates how to allow these different orders to communicate and contaminate.

From a more general perspective, the relative weights in II.4 of "Mamalujo" (some 60 percent) and "Tristan" (some 20 percent) in the published text of II.4 may therefore emblematize the proportional importance of modalities of enunciation and interpretation versus plot, character, and theme in the *Wake* as a whole. While "Tristan," however complexly, provided a set of plot mechanisms for II.4, "Mamalujo" furnished a still more expansive set of inscriptive, vocal, and (anti)narrative modalities. When the sketches were finally joined, the setting of the ship on the way to Cornwall became layered with cultural, historical, medieval, sexual, Celtic, existential, universal, comedic, tragic, symbolic, and other associative pools. Mamalujo's narration then joined with the reader's and the universal dreamer's consciousnesses and cocreated a series of voyeuristic and nostalgic acts of seeing and forgetting.

Notes

I am grateful to Oberlin College for grants that enabled me to examine the Joyce manuscripts at the National Library of Ireland and to this book's editors for their helpful comments on this essay.

1. "Tristan and Isolde" is at BL 47481 fs. 94, 94v, 267v; JJA 56: 2–7; FDV: 208–12. "Mamalujo" is at BL 47481 fs. 2–4; JJA 56: 26–35; FDV: 213–19. Like the rest of the book, the "Tristan" and "Mamalujo" materials were elaborated from notes in notebooks. The best and most nuanced work on these notes and their evolution has been done by David Hayman. See "Tristan and Isolde in *Finnegans Wake:* A Study of the Sources and the Evolution of a Theme," *Comparative Literature Studies* 1.2 (1964): 93–112. Hayman expanded and nuanced this essay in chapters 4 and 5 of WiT. Those who are interested in the difficult question of the precise dates of composition of the early II.4 sketches should consult Danis Rose's review of Hayman's Wit: "The Beginning of all Thisorder of Work in Progress," *JJQ* 28.4 (Summer 1991): 957–65, and Hayman's reply: "Transiting the *Wake:* A Response to Danis Rose," *JJQ* 29.2 (Winter 1992): 411–19. The following is a short list of critics who have also dealt with important aspects of the development of II.4: A. Walton Litz, *The Art of James Joyce* (New York: Oxford University Press, 1961); Beryl Schlossman, "Tristan and Isolde or the Triangles of Desire: Jealousy, Eroticism and Poetics," *Probes,* 149–78; Grace Eckley, "Tristan and Isolde," *Children's Lore in "Finnegans Wake"* (Syracuse: Syracuse University Press, 1985), 50–57; UFW; TDJJ; Fred Radford, "Anticipating *Finnegans Wake:* The United Irishman and La Belle Iseult," *JJQ* 33.2 (Winter 1996): 237–43; David Hayman, "Substantial Time: The Temporalities of Mamalujo," *"Finnegans Wake": "teems of times,"* ed. Andrew Treip (Amsterdam: Rodopi, 1994), 95–105; Andrew Treip, "Lost Histereve: Vichian Soundings and Reverberations in the Genesis of *Finnegans Wake* II.4," *JJQ* 32.3–4 (Spring–Summer 1995): 641–56; Wim Van Mierlo, "*Finnegans Wake* and the Question of Histry!?" *Geni,* 43–64; Timothy Martin, "Joyce and Literary Wagnerism," *Picking up Airs,* ed. Ruth Bauerle (Urbana: University of Illinois Press, 1993), 105–27; and Jed Deppman, "The Return of Medievalism: James Joyce in 1923," *Medieval Joyce,* ed. Lucia Boldrini (Amsterdam: Rodopi, 2002), 45–77.

2. In August 1924, for example, Joyce's brother Stanislaus had harsh words for the "Mamalujo" he had read in the *transatlantic review.* He called it a "nightmare production . . . the witless wandering of literature before its final extinction" (LIII: 102–3).

3. Joyce had asked Weaver to "special order" a piece of writing, and this is it. Cited below are the first five of thirty-two entries in the key explicating the paragraph. See also Hayman's discussion in WiT: 13 n. 28 and the essay by Geert Lernout in this volume.

4. Joyce makes no comment, for example, on the nonnarrative quality of the text or its use of foreign languages. Of course, the problem of "when to stop" providing glosses is a basic problem for every reader of the *Wake.* Roland McHugh, latter-day high king of annotators, admits that it "is not always entirely obvious what items are, and what items are not, in need of glossing" (McHugh, vi).

5. John Bishop, *Joyce's Book of the Dark* (Madison: University of Wisconsin Press, 1986), 27.

6. Consider also "I have sent away four-fifths of my books, keeping only dictionaries and books of reference . . . I am also trying to conclude section I of Part II but *such an amount of reading seems to be necessary* before my old flying machine grumbles up into the air" (LI: 299, 16 February 1931, my emphasis). Geneticists ask, If the author cannot write his text without "such an amount" of "necessary" reading, then can the reader read it?

7. David Hayman once remarked that Tristan and Isolde are "everywhere one cares to look" in *Finnegans Wake* (Hayman 1964, 94).

8. As the last chapter in this volume suggests, Book IV is a similar product of compositional fusion, formed in part by the joining of the Berkeley and Patrick sketches. It differs significantly from II.4 in that a good deal more material, for example, ALP's Letter, is included besides those sketches.

9. Litz 1961, 80.

10. It should be noted that by the time of its publication in the *transatlatic review* Joyce had already begun the process of fusing "Mamalujo" and the other early sketches. Included in "Mamalujo" were direct references to Berkeley and Patrick, the reign of Roderick O'Conor, and Tristan and Isolde.

11. Val Vousden was a popular nineteenth-century Irish singer and performer: he played popular tunes such as "The Irish Jaunting Car" (see FW: 050.15).

12. The source for this note is Thomas Sturge Moore's essay "The Story of Tristram and Isolt in Modern Poetry," *Criterion* 1.1 (October 1922). I have argued elsewhere that Joyce's pastiche of the Tristan legend also directly targeted Moore's two "Tristan and Isolde" *Criterion* essays (Deppman 2002).

13. Joyce's use of Latin declensionese to mutate Tristan's name into the word "Tantrum" is just one indication of the way his text, even more than Bédier's reconstructed romance, transformed the legend's famous "childlike medieval innocence" into pure childishness.

14. Thus Richard Ellmann is only partially right to suggest that "Joyce deals in his books with the theme of Tristram and Iseult that his fellow-Dubliners were freshening up, paradoxically, with the more ancient Irish names of Naisi and Deirdre, but the love story interests him hardly at all, his interest is in the common-place husband" (JJII: 5). While Bloom is in fact a modern "common-place" Mark figure and the *Wake's* Tristan is a youthful, single HCE, Joyce was also interested in the love story. In the wake of the grandly thematic *Exiles* and *Ulysses,* the "Tristan" sketch sails along as a humorous renewal of cuckoldry, passion, and betrayal.

15. Geert Lernout shows that Moore was aware of and perhaps influenced by the controversy occasioned by the publication of Wagner's letters. See "The *Finnegans Wake* Notebooks and Radical Philology," *Probes,* 19–48, 40–41.

16. George Moore, *Memories of My Dead Life* (1906; London: Heineman, 1915), 134–35.

17. See VI.B.3: 66–71 and 75–77.

18. Édouard Schuré, *Woman as Inspirer,* trans. Fred Rothwell (London: Power Book Co., 1918), 16.

19. Joyce's engagement with Wagner dates to his youth. On 25 January 1903, in a letter to his mother, he wrote: "Tell Stannie to send me *at once* (so that I may have it by Thursday night) my copy of Wagner's operas and if he can to enclose with it a copy of Grant Allen's 'Paris'" (LII: 25). Fred Radford has demonstrated that Joyce read carefully the contemporary coverage of the first Dublin performance of Wagner's *Tristan und Isolde* (December 1901) in several papers, including the *Irish Times* and Arthur Griffith's nationalist paper the *United Irishman.* Tim Martin has charted Joyce's evolution from youthful "Wagnerism" to serious interest in Wagner's work, convincingly demonstrating that many of Joyce's favorite books and authors were heavily imbued with all manner of Wagneria: D'Annunzio, Symons, Dujardin (this author of *Les lauriers sont coupés* was also the devoted editor of *La Revue Wagnérienne*), George Moore, Yeats, Shaw, and others (Martin 1993, passim).

20. Thomas Sturge Moore's articles were published in the October 1922 and January 1923 issues of the *Criterion.* Joyce carefully read the *Criterion* and took notes from different issues. On 13 December 1923 he asked Ford Madox Ford for a copy of the October issue (LIII: 84). Joyce took many notes and ideas from Joseph Bédier's book (*Le Roman de Tristan et Iseult* [Paris: l'Édition d'Art, 1926]) and, as Hayman has shown, eventually used many of its settings and plot twists in the *Wake.* On 7 June 1926 Joyce wrote to Harriet Shaw Weaver: "Have you finished *S. Patrice?* If so, I should like you to read St John Irvine's *Life of Parnell* to begin with. It is not good but you ought to know some of the facts. For instance the word 'hesitency.' Irishmen usually remember the Piggott trial by this catchword. I shall send you Bédier's *Tristan et Iseult* as this too you ought to read" (LI: 241).

21. Glasheen writes: "In FW, the Mark-Tristan-Isolde triangle moves in and out of identity with the Finn-Dermot-Grania, Arthur-Lancelot-Guinevere, Captain O'Shea–Parnell–Mrs O'Shea, etc., pattern. This primitive love triangle is bright,

brittle, unsoftened by moral consciousness or sentimental education. Ten thousand emotional miles from Wagner's, Bédier's *Tristan and Iseult* is an ur and unslick bedroom farce peopled all with tricksters. Mark and his four barons . . . would trick the lovers, and the lovers out-trick them, but the lovers are fatally out-tricked by the wife Tristan has wronged with cold" (Adaline Glasheen, *Third Census of "Finnegans Wake"* [Berkeley: University of California Press, 1977], 289–90).

22. Using his observations of Lucia as his *materia prima,* Joyce developed a child character named "Is" in the *Wake* notebooks. See VI.B.3: 56–60 and passim. In a complex manner that is much too long to trace here, this "Is" character contributed both to the Isolde of the *Wake* sketch and to Issy, the young ALP, as in "Is is" (FW: 620.32).

23. See BL 47481 fs. 94, 94v, 267v; JJA 56: 2–7; FDV: 208–12.

24. Along with VI.B.3, VI.A is an important source of many ideas and notes for both "Tristan" and "Mamalujo": "Trist 12 cent.," "Trist a film star," "In 6 months I shall be a theosophist" (VI.A: 88).

25. This line was originally written by Byron in canto 4 of *Childe Harolde* and was cited by Henry James in a book by Ezra Pound: "As Henry James has said 'It was a period when writers besought the deep blue sea to roll'" (Ezra Pound, *Instigations* [New York: Boni and Liveright, 1920], 16). Joyce may also be linking Tristan to likeable swain Little Billee from George De Maurier's bestseller *Trilby*: "For Little Billee was much given to monologues out loud, and profuse quotations from his favorite bards. Everybody quoted that particular poem ["Break, break, break"] either mentally or aloud when they sat on that particular bench—except a few old-fashioned people, who still said, 'Roll on, thou deep and dark blue ocean, roll!' or people of the very highest culture, who only quoted the nascent (and crescent) Robert Browning; or people of no culture at all, who simply held their tongues—and only felt the more!" (George Du Maurier, *Trilby: A Novel* [New York: Harper & Brothers, 1894], 269–70).

26. Note that in the romance Tristan says Isolde's name three times and then dies as he tries to say it again. See Bédier 1926, 220.

27. Joyce had important contemporary critical precedent and encouragement to read the Tristan legend in this structural, symbolic, and allegorical way. Bédier and Sturge Moore, in particular, saw the tale as a pure materialization of the structures of medieval codes, especially codes of justice.

28. Bédier had gone to his normal scholarly lengths to show that Thomas's *Tristan* dates to 1155–70. Joyce was more interested in Irish history than the Frenchman and therefore made more of this date's coincidence with the English invasion, the fall of Roderick O'Conor (see FW: 380–382), and the beginning of English rule in Ireland. I have explored this topic at greater length in Deppman 2002.

29. Moore was a constant element in all of Joyce's life and fiction. Zack Bowen has shown that "The Dead" uses many Moore songs and probably owes its title to "O Ye Dead" (*Musical Allusions in the Works of James Joyce* [Albany: SUNY Press,

1974]). Matthew Hodgart and Mabel Worthington have shown how Joyce used Moore's "Silent, O Moyle," a song featured in the first drafts of "Tristan," in a complex manner in *Dubliners:* "A street harpist is described in 'Two Gallants': 'One hand played in the bass the melody of "Silent, O Moyle," while the other hand careered in the treble after each group of notes. The notes of the air sounded deep and full.' This air later becomes the vehicle for the cadger Lenehan's desolation: 'The air which the harpist had played began to control his movements. His softly padded feet played the melody while his fingers swept a scale of variations idly along the railings after each group of notes'" (*Song in the Works of James Joyce* [New York: Columbia University Press, 1959], 2). Moore's presence in II.4 is especially worth examining because it represents Joyce's early and determined commitment to include all of the *Irish Melodies* in his new work.

30. See Thomas Osborne Davis, *National Ballads, Songs, and Poems* (Dublin: James Duffy, 1869), 38. See also James S. Atherton, *The Books at the Wake* (Carbondale: Southern Illinois University Press, 1959), 105. Here is a typical and difficult genetic question: Shall we choose to "hear" the song at this stage or not? While there is little in "the sea being slight" to suggest the lyrics at first, the fact that Joyce later changed the phrase to "the winds aslight" (FW: 383.20), thereby clearly invoking "the West's asleep," raises the question of when the first reference or referential intention really occurred.

31. Genesis 1:2 is also blended in: "The spirit of God moved upon the face of the waters." While the reference to God is only very distantly present in the final text, Joyce does add references to Moore's "The Wine-cup Is Circling" and its air, "Michael Hoy." He also adds the phrase "when it was dark"—a reference to a book by that name written by Ranger Gull (a.k.a. "Guy Thorne"), whose name may have attracted Joyce, since he was attempting to write the sounds of gulls (see *When It Was Dark: A Story* [London: Greening, 1903]). See also FW: 383.19–21.

32. Joyce had used Davis in the same way in "Cyclops": "a remarkably noteworthy rendering of the immortal Thomas Osborne Davis' evergreen verses (happily too familiar to need recalling here)" (U: 12.915–17).

33. Hodgart and Worthington 1959, 11. Hodgart and Worthington's insightful analysis of the reasons Joyce used and produced so much music in the *Wake* should be kept constantly in mind: "The dreamworld of *Finnegans Wake* is firmly based on demotic culture, mainly that of early twentieth-century Dublin but also the common Anglo-Saxon culture of Joyce's lifetime. He was interested in slang catch-phrases, American comic strips, movies, jazz, advertisements, and even *Punch* jokes. . . . But song is used more frequently than any of these other elements, because it was a more essential part of the Dublin *ambiance,* because it is more suitable for refilling with meaning, and because its rhythms are stronger" (1959, 9).

34. In 1793 Moore was one of the first Roman Catholics to enter Trinity College. For Gabriel Conroy in "The Dead," Moore's songs were precisely the poetry that uneducated Irish could understand and appreciate. "He was undecided about

the lines from Robert Browning for he feared they would be above the heads of his hearers. Some quotation that they could recognise from Shakespeare or from the Melodies would be better" (D: 187).

35. Stephen meditates on "wavespeech" in "Proteus." As he urinates he even imagines a kind of narrative: "Listen: a fourworded wavespeech: seesoo, hrss, rsseeiss, ooos. Vehement breath of waters amid seasnakes, rearing horses, rocks. In cups of rocks it slops: flop, slop, slap: bounded in barrels. And, spent, its speech ceases. It flows purling, widely flowing, floating foampool, flower unfurling" (U: 3.456–60).

36. Rose and O'Hanlon's characterization of "Mamalujo" is typical: "From inception it was a semi-comic portrait of the Four Masters as senile, garrulous gentlemen historians, old men metamorphosed into sea waves that splash endlessly against the planks of passing ships. They are represented as aquaceous, amorphous, undifferentiated; their personalities are interfused and their collective consciousness is turbid, feeble and limited. They are or have been annalists, dry-as-dust academics, greyhead geographers, professors of history, gospellors, chroniclers, evangelists: four morose, diseased, jealous, petty, vain, reiterative recorders of time past who live, if life it is, vicariously" (UFW: 201).

37. The "Tristan" sketch also continues certain mocking ideas introduced in "Cyclops," for example, its aura of romantic pastiche ("Lovely maidens sit in close proximity to the roots of the lovely trees singing the most lovely songs while they play [. . .] And heroes voyage from afar to woo them" [U: 12.78–83]) and its maudlin celebration of Irish music (U: 12.16–17).

38. The Struldbrugs of Joyce's beloved *Gulliver's Travels* are also obvious precursors.

39. These notes also illustrate a stylistic difference between the Tristan sketch and "Mamalujo." "Mamalujo's" setting was Joyce's own invention, and in its development he relied much less heavily on quotations and borrowed speech than he did in the case of "Tristan" and the other early sketches.

40. The exception is the seagulls' song, which opens the chapter and taunts Mark about what will happen between Tristan and Isolde.

41. Thomas Moore, "And Doth Not a Meeting Like This," *The Poetical Works of Thomas Moore,* ed. Francis Waller (New York: P. F. Collier, 1879), 22.

42. Joyce's various ways of referring to this sketch reflect the many demands he was placing upon it. In different letters written on the same day in March 1924 Joyce referred to it as a "proof of the four masters or evangelists" (LIII: 91) and "the piece about the four old men" (LIII: 92). Elsewhere he called it "the four masters bit" (LI: 209), "the foursome episode" (LI: 205), the "Mamalujo episode" (LI: 210), "the four old men, Mamalujo" (LI: 213), and "the four eminent annalists" (LI: 204).

43. In late 1923 Joyce wryly, slyly, and pseudosimplifyingly suggested again that there was a "theory of history . . . set forth" by the four. Somehow in "Mamalujo" the lead ideas, as Joyce understood them, of metempsychosis, Hegel,

and Vico would coalesce: "I am sorry that Patrick and [?] Berkeley are unsuccessful in explaining themselves. The answer, I suppose, is that given by Paddy Dignam's apparition: metempsychosis. Or perhaps the theory of history so well set forth (after Hegel and Giambattista Vico) by the four eminent annalists who are even now treading the typepress in sorrow will explain part of my meaning" (LI: 204, 9 October 1923).

44. "[T]hey all four remembored who made the world and how they used to be at that time in the vulgar ear" (FW: 384.35–36); "It brought the dear prehistoric scenes all back again, as fresh as of yore" (FW: 385.18–19).

45. Joyce carefully orchestrates the recurrences of two songs in II.4 to accentuate the binding power of alcohol and nostalgia. "Auld Lang Syne" recalls New Year's celebrations; the drinking song "One More Drink for the Four of Us" unites the Irishmen just as it did Joe and the Citizen in Barney Kiernan's pub (U: 12.238 ff.).

46. Ellmann continues: "Joyce evolved four old men, representing the four evangelists, whose names he coded as Mamalujo (Matthew, Mark, Luke, and John), the four masters who wrote a history of Ireland, and sometimes manifesting themselves as six rann singers or as twelve customers in Earwicker's pub. He drafted the Mamalujo episode as 'a study of old age,' he told Miss Weaver, and finished its first version in October 1923" (JJII: 555).

47. See figure 2, for example, "with his poghue like Arrah-na-poghue" (BL 47481 f. 114; JJA 56: 171). It is typical of the *Wake*'s texture that it produces disagreements about how much Boucicaultian "presence" there is in the *Wake.* The question of how much Joyce's Shaun owes to Boucicault's Shaun the Post is especially instructive, for it has produced two very sure but very contradictory views by two of the best readers of the book. "Beyond his name," Brendan O Hehir contends, "the character Shaun the Post contributes very little distinctive to the chuffy young champion of *Finnegans Wake.* But in the initial run of *Arrah-na-Pogue* in Dublin and London, the part of Shaun was played by Dion Boucicault himself, and the career of Boucicault is one that remarkably resembles that of Shaun in *Finnegans Wake*" (Brendan O Hehir, *A Gaelic Lexicon for "Finnegans Wake"* [Berkeley: University of California Press, 1967], 360–61). For Atherton, however, it is "the character of Sean [*sic*] the Post which is Joyce's main borrowing from Boucicault. I would almost describe it as being his main borrowing from any single source. . . . It is surprising how much of the character of Sean the Post goes over into the Shaun of *Finnegans Wake*" (1959, 159–60). My own view is that Joyce's Shaun incorporates both Shaun the Post and Boucicault.

48. See Townsend Walsh, *The Career of Dion Boucicault* (New York: Dunlap Society, 1915), 74. Although it is quite possible that Joyce consulted this book, he would not have needed it to write his "Mamalujo" sketch.

49. There is a great deal of theater in "Mamalujo" apart from Boucicault: Ibsen's *Lady from the Sea* (FW: 390) and *A Doll's House* (FW: 395 and elsewhere); W. G. Wills's *A Royal Divorce;* Gerald Griffin's *The Collegians* (FW: 388) (this story was

the source for *The Colleen Bawn*—Boucicault refers to it when he writes that his play was "Founded on a true history, First told by an Irishman"); Ord and Mackay, *Paddy the Next Best Thing;* Shaw's *Candida* (FW: 396); and many more.

50. Stephen Watt distinguishes between the *theatrical emphasis* of the theater managers and Boucicault's *dramatic emphasis* in the comedies. He shows that while audiences and critics in the 1880s enjoyed the *theatrical* confrontation between stage Irishmen and villains, Boucicault's plays displayed a deep *dramatic* sensitivity to the political strains between England and Ireland. He concludes that *Arrah-na-Pogue* and *The Shaughraun,* two plays particularly important in chapter II.4, are generically more complicated than most comedies, since they "contain ideological material and historical perspective that most comic melodrama lacks" (Stephen Watt, *Joyce, O'Casey, and the Irish Popular Theater* [Syracuse: Syracuse University Press, 1991], 72). In 1876 the always outspoken Boucicault wrote an open letter to Benjamin Disraeli "demanding the release of Irish political prisoners from British prisons" (ibid., 72).

51. See Wim Van Mierlo's essay in this volume.

52. Litz 1961, 92–93.

53. Joyce had previously used this song in "Two Gallants" to carry great patriotic and nostalgic significance. When Lenehan and Corley turn into Kildare Street they suddenly encounter a harpist playing "Silent, O Moyle," and Joyce's description strongly suggests that an allegory of all Irish history is operative: "His harp too, heedless that her coverings had fallen about her knees, seemed weary alike of the eyes of strangers and of her master's hands [. . .] The notes of the air throbbed deep and full" (D: 50).

54. Joyce crosses out "whilst the wine" and writes "whiltes the wildcaps," typically mutating a phrase to preserve its basic meaning and to evoke new ones: "whiltes" visually suggests "white" and "whilst," while "wildcaps" suggests the "winecup" but adds the "whitecaps" of a roiling ocean.

55. Joyce doubles many letters, sounds, and words as he brings the sketches together. "Deaubaleau Dowbellow" includes "w/w" (5); "palpably" (10) plays off "bulbubly" (11); Tristan is a handsome huntsman, not a hands-off husband: "handson and huntsem" (12).

56. In fact, this gender blending was one of Joyce's earliest intentions for the chapter. On 23 October 1923 he wrote to Harriet Shaw Weaver: "Many thanks for your letter and kind appreciation of the foursome episode. It is strange that on the day I sent off to you a picture of an epicene professor of history in an Irish university college seated in the hospice for the dying etc after 'eating a bad crab in the red sea' I received a paper from Dublin containing news of the death at the age of 41 of an old schoolfellow of mine in the hospice for the dying, Harold's Cross, Dublin, professor of law in the university of Galway who, it seems, had lately returned from the West Indies where his health collapsed. More strangely still his name (which he used to say, was an Irish (Celtic) variant of my own) is in

English an epicene name being made up of the feminine and masculine personal pronouns—Sheehy. It is as usual rather uncanny" (LI: 205).

57. "No prince charming is her beau ideal to lay a rare and wondrous love at her feet but rather a manly man" (U: 13.209–10).

58. See VI.B.2: 92: "Old men stammer, / their broken voices."

59. Hodgart and Worthington have located echoes of this lighthearted tune on pages 355, 360, 365, 476, and 597 of *Finnegans Wake* (1959, 173). Some of these usages introduce still more meanings (e.g., the "Bablyon" in "Bulbul, bulbulone!" [FW: 360.21]) that one may also wish to hear in the "bulbubly" under consideration here.

60. A prominent motif in II.4, "Noah's ark" is announced on the first page of the chapter (FW: 383.09). Joyce manages to include a flock of bird names in the chapter as well as a menagerie of animals, for example, a horse, orangutan, beaver, ewe, ram, leopard, and hen in rapid succession on FW: 396. Horses and racehorses are especially privileged: in Boucicault's *Arrah-na-Poghue* Shaun asks: "Have I been singin' to the auld mare till I've got a quadruped voice?" a phrase that is probably repeated in II.4's "quad rupeds" (FW: 397.15–16). Isolde has a "paddock weight," and her height is measured in "hands" (FW: 396.08–9). The "ark" doubles as Tristan and Isolde's ship, the barroom from II.3 ("the stout ship *Nansy Hans*" [FW: 382.28]), the ships that carry Irish immigrants abroad ("The new world presses" [FW: 387.36]), a church, and other self-contained microcosms.

61. At first Joyce placed the famous bird song "*Three quarks for Muster Mark!*" (FW: 383.01) at the *end* of the whole sketch, making it a commentary, analysis, coda, chorus, or note of summary. He eventually decided to move it to the front of the chapter, making it "auspicious" in the various senses employed by Homer, Virgil, Greek tragedy, and Vico. Since it is written in the future tense and foretells Mark's downfall, it also has a strong feeling of cruel prophecy: "*Tristy's the spry young spark / That'll tread her*" (FW: 383.11–12). Ellmann reports that Joyce intended for the song to mimic the sounds of seagulls (JJII: 555). Mark is figured as a buzzard and a rooster in the chapter.

62. "Rather than moving linearly through a text 'imitative of the dream-state,' drawing on the compromised instruments of orthodox rationalism, it might better make sense to proceed much as we might in interpreting a dream" (Bishop 1986, 39).

63. See the chapter "Nodality" (WiT: 36–55).

64. See VI.B.2: 81: "Trist. Alexandrine."

65. Joyce showed his predilection for "futter" on VI.B.10: 40: "John Sebastian Bach / Super Marie Antoinette / arsefuttered her." See also the "Canon Futter" of the Museyroom episode (FW: 009.19–20) and other uses in the *Wake*.

66. Useful also sometimes is reading backward: "Exeunc throw a darras Kram of Llawnroc, ye gink guy, kirked into yord. Enterest attawonder Wehpen, luftcat revol, fairescapading in his natsirt" (FW: 388.01–3).

67. With world enough and time one could attempt to follow the imbricated logics in many of Joyce's other corrections. The word "waters" from "As a Beam o'er the Face of the Waters may glow" is transformed into "wardorse" in the phrase "wardorse moved." One could speculate extensively on how and why the waters moved, or the warhorse, or the warders, orders, borders, boarders, oarers, hoarders, whorers, warriors, and so on.

68. Ironically, readers of the final text tend to skip over such letters as the added *r* in "praisers" precisely in order to render the text as readable as the first drafts. (Of course, those same first drafts were judged unreadable by many of *their* readers.) The final text of the *Wake* devours the placenta of its previous drafts, notebooks, and source materials and ultimately transforms them, including anything signed "Joyce," into *Wakean* textuality.

69. The genetic rhyzomes of this phrase may extend to some notes in VI.B.3. Located near other "Tristan" material we find "the A (Ah) C is at the / door. Thought. Ass He / J.C.??? Assisi?? Very / Handy for Georgie / Bus!" (VI.B.3: 72).

70. William Watson Goodwin, *Syntax of the Moods and Tenses of the Greek Verb* (Cambridge: Sever and Francis, 1860). Geneticists are made uncomfortable by moments like this: we will probably never know if Joyce meant the phrase "in all moods and senses" innocently, as a use of speech, or self-consciously, as mentioned speech, that is, as a reference to the title of a well-known book. See Brendan O Hehir and John Dillon, *A Classical Lexicon for "Finnegans Wake"* (Berkeley: University of California Press, 1977), 347. The phrase also stays in Joyce's mind long enough to appear in the key he sends to Weaver: "viola in all moods and senses" (LI: 247). One wonders whether Joyce's list of "all the moods and senses" of "viola" would look like the lists I have generated in this essay.

71. In the example under consideration the phrase "natural born lovers of nature" *seems* to be appositively juxtaposed to "Matt and Marcus" (FW: 385.18–21), that is, it seems to function as a lightly ironic description of them. Yet the comma separating the two clauses may not mean apposition—the lovers of nature may be Tristan and Isolde.

72. These books were published in St. Louis by Herder Press in 1898 and 1904.

73. Ernst Maass, *Goethe und die Antike* (Berlin: W. Kohlhammer, 1912).

74. Gerald Christopher Maas, *Finger-exercises and Scale-studies for Violoncello* (New York: G. Schirmer, 1923).

Shaun the Post

Chapters III.1–2

WIM VAN MIERLO

Around midnight the *Wake's* narrators stumble across a dozing but vituperative Shaun, who "was after having a great time [. . .] in a porterhouse" (FW: 405.21–23). They question the postman about the significance of the missive he is carrying, but Shaun, apprehensive about being slighted, is on his guard, and the placating narrators never get a straight answer from him. There is a sudden flurry of movement as Shaun's barrel starts to float away, and the questioning is over. Shaun is "passing hence" (FW: 427.18). Now, taking leave of his sisters, the "twenty nine hedge daughters" (FW: 430.01), he delivers a lengthy sermon, larded with self-aggrandizement and full of jealous admonitions about her sexuality. To guard them, he introduces his double, Dave the Dancekerl, to take care of her, and from the sound of it, he will do so in more than one sense of the word. The happy-go-lucky Rainbow Girls hate to see him leave. As they flirtingly promise him to remain pure, he obligingly announces his resurrection and return.

The plot of chapters III.1–2 (the first two of Shaun's watches were originally composed as a unit) does not pose many serious problems. Yet readers commonly feel uneasy about the beginning of Book III, because the narratives and themes of these chapters give the impression of turning away from the *Wake*'s "familiar" archetypes: the patriarchal Earwicker, the matriarchal Anna Livia, the warring brothers, and the artist Shem. Evaluating the first "Watches of Shaun" Joseph Campbell and Henry Morton Robinson write: "It is difficult to make the transition from Earwicker's dream of the bliss of Tristan and Iseult to the material of Book III."[1] Michael Begnal recognizes a chronological sequence between Books II and III but sees "no other ties between them."[2] The exigency that these critics identify is indeed real, and it is structural in nature. Chapters III.1–2 in fact follow I.8. The chapter's opening reveals some "garments of laundry" on the riverbank that were left behind by the washerwomen in the ALP chapter (FW: 404.02). The composition history bears this out: chapters III.1–2 were composed to continue the narrative of I.8; Book II was later constructed as a long interruption. In other words, the problem these readers have does not exist in the organization of Joyce's book but in the limitations of a synchronic approach. A linear reading does not reveal the structural complexity of the book as Joyce conceived it.

Regretting that Book III does not fit chronologically with the rest of the "story," Campbell and Robinson also point to the marginal position of Book III, and especially of chapters 1 and 2. Begnal, in turn, accedes that Shaun "is heard most insistently and most often throughout the pages of *Finnegans Wake*. . . . He is certainly the most forward of the Earwicker family," but his loudness and forward nature are a negative quality. His exhortations are reprehensible in all their "pettiness, repression, and self-importance."[3] He is not the genius artist who can be identified with Joyce himself but (following Ellmann's biographical schema of artist-genius versus jealous brother) with the berating Stanislaus. The critical response to Shaun and Book III seems to be one of impatience. The *Wake*'s "central" characters, HCE, Shem, and ALP, appear to be displaced by Shaun, a dishonest and weak character who fails in his duty to deliver the Letter.[4]

In spite of the negative reception of the Shaun chapters, their place in the *Wake* is quite significant, as I will try to show in the following pages. Thematically, chapters III.1–2 find their *raison d'être* in the Letter and its discontinuous placement in the book as a whole: although Shem is the artist, his art comes to nothing without the mediator Shaun. From a narrative perspective they tell the story of the son usurping the position of the father, of one plagiarist stealing the writing of another plagiarist, while Book III as a whole narrates the regression in space and time. Structurally, therefore, the chapters offer a second leg in the telling. They do not quite fit in the grand Vichian schema as the age of the people (although Shaun appears quite common, he is nonetheless associated with Hermes, the god of mediation); instead, these chapters comprise a counterpart to what came before. The development of Shaun's preoccupation with space forms an alternative device—or, perhaps appropriately for the Λ siglum, a second leg—for the idea of time/history developed in Book I.[5] From an evident but limited connection with space, Shaun's role as postman branches out gradually, from a traveler in a barrel/on a *via crucis* to a spokesman of spatial philosophy in "The Ondt and the Gracehoper." Ultimately, Joyce set up the exploration of Shaun's postal/spatial mission in III.1–2 to make him, rather than the artist Shem, the primary mediator of *Finnegans Wake.* This idea becomes apparent when we track the genetic evolution of the first two Shaun chapters in correlation with their protodevelopment in the Buffalo notebooks. In other words, the early structural design of *Work in Progress* was set up to reflect a now well known thematic concern with space and time in which Book III has a much more prominent role than is generally accepted.

The structural role of chapters III.1–2 and their relative position to the other segments of the book have changed in the composition process owing to Joyce's continuous expansion of *Work in Progress.* The composition of new chapters in Book III and elsewhere led directly to a displacement of the chapters in terms of location as well as conception in what is one of the most elaborate turning points in the history of *Work in Progress.* This displacement takes place in the course of one and a half to two years since the inception of Shaun's postal mission. In this evolution three stages can be discerned: the drafting of a protoversion, the composition of III.1–2 (and the rest of Book III), putting in place a contrapuntal movement, and the final positioning of Book III.[6]

~

The first stage in this evolution is quite brief. Around New Year 1924 Joyce drafted a short piece, describing Shaun's delivery of the Letter, that contains the seminal idea for chapters III.1–2. The episode was intended to accompany the "Revered Letter" and the other episodes on the Letter that now comprise chapter I.5. The "Delivery," however, only contains a provisional draft, consisting of two subepisodes: a description of the postman and his superior character (which now corresponds to chapter III.1) and HCE's unpropitious reaction to ALP's Letter (which perhaps foreshadows the pub setting in II.3).[7] As such the episode forms a triptych of sorts with the "Letter."[8] On the one hand, the episode introduces a number of situations that are reminiscent of the later version in III.1, though different in detail. The "Lucalizod letter carrier" is "a most capable official of very superior appearance" (BL 47471b f. 35v; JJA 57: 2) who manages to deliver only those packages that contain "bullion or eatables" (BL 47471b f. 34v; JJA 57: 3).[9] Because he is quite intoxicated he veers to the "North & South sides of the roadway" (BL 47471b f. 35v; JJA 57: 2). On the other hand, we get elements that have not been developed elsewhere: Earwicker's indignant surprise and fierce reaction to Anna Livia's "confession" (BL 47471b f. 35v; JJA 57: 2) and the notion that the Letter was brought "by two sons of wild earth" who have since become "sainted scholars" named Shamus or Iacupos Pennifera and Johannes Epistolophorus (BL 47471b f. 34v; JJA 57: 3). The double authorship of the Letter—"written of Shem" and "uttered for Alp" (FW: 420.17–18)—is therefore temporarily expanded to a joint venture of the brothers-scholars who scrutinize the manuscript in the manner of the Four Old Men. Finally, a larger theme of doubling unfolds itself when Earwicker receives a facsimile of the Letter, not the original.[10]

Joyce, however, did not pursue the idea of the delivery any further. The episode, like some of the other very early materials relating to "Tristan and Isolde" and "Mamalujo" now at the National Library of Ireland, remained quite fragmentary, not even reaching that quasi-finished state of a sketch, suggesting that Joyce abandoned the idea of having the Letter delivered before it was fully developed. This turning point in the writing can be explained in two ways. Joyce may have considered the contents of the passage as already outdated, because by this time the Letter's contents had already receded to the background in favor of a physical description of the document. In a parallel move he then transformed the delivery into a description of the personality of the letter carrier and his postal mission. Or the "Delivery" can be seen as a direct addition to the physical aspects of the document. In particular, the opening phrase—"and congruously enough the confession of its composition was fitly capped by the zigzaggery of the delivery" (BL 47471b f. 35v; JJA 57: 2)—echoes the description of the spiral convolutions of the handwriting in the Letter.[11] In this case the transformation to Shaun has to be seen as part of Joyce's general strategy of centrifugal expansion.

Yet Joyce would retain one crucial idea, penned in at the bottom of the sketch: "postman & style of narration symbolical of our time" (BL 47471 f. 42; JJA 57: 5). This surreptitious note became the basis for the contrapuntal complementation of Books I and III, the first treating Earwicker's past, the history of his name, his family, and his sin, the second dealing with Shaun's presence, his role in mediating the story of that past, his usurpation of Earwicker's position. After he had finished the "Delivery" Joyce read in a book by Léon Metchnikoff, *La Civilisation et les grands fleuves historiques:*

> Il n'y a qu'une seule loi, celle du progrès. . . . Au-dessus de toutes les lois auxquelles les anciens et les modernes ont tenté d'assujettir les mouvements

de l'humanité, au-dessus de tous les cycles, de toutes les alternatives, de tous les flux et reflux, de toutes les lignes droites ou brisées, en spirale ou en zigzag, de tous les rythmes, *itus reditusque,* comme dit Pascal, *corsi e ricorsi,* comme dit Vico, il n'y a que cette seule loi de progrès qui pour ainsi dire surnage.[12]

[There is *only one law, progress.* . . . Over all the laws to which the ancients and the moderns have attempted to subjugate humanity's movements, over all the cycles and all the alternatives, all the ebbing and flowing, all the lines whether straight or broken, in spirals or in zigzags, all the rhythms—*itus reditusque,* as Pascal said, *corsi e recorsi,* as Vico said—this single law of progress alone remains afloat, so to speak.]

To Joyce this passage must have suddenly appeared like a déjà vu. It came, so to speak, as a vindication of his own creative enterprise, and it prompted him to record in his notebooks: "Λ zigzag v spiral / ʳcorsi ricorsi Vico" (VI.B.1: 29). One of the earliest allusions to Vico in the *Wake*'s textual dossier, this note has still to do with any three- or fourfold patterns of cyclicality, but the idea of flux and reflux, a movement to and fro, comprises for the first time an element of the book's larger unifying design. We might identify this note as a turning point, a first indication of a contrapuntal structure that Joyce was beginning to develop.

The second stage in our story begins in March 1924 with the drafting of chapter III.1–2 proper. Even though this stage is comprised of four consecutive drafts, Joyce was only concerned with establishing a plotline. The clock strikes twelve. A nightly interview takes place regarding Shaun's "annunciation" and the sanctity and royal significance of his postal mission. But the focus of the interview soon turns to derision, when Shaun accuses Shem of conspiring to write the Letter with his mother, until a sudden, careless movement brings Shaun's barrel out of balance, and it starts rolling backward. Shaun now floats up the river and begins to take leave from his sister Issy by delivering a protracted sermon, which we can read as a parody of Laertes' warning to Ophelia as he sets sail for France, not to lose her heart and honor to a venturing Hamlet. She responds amorously and gives him a lover's gift. Soon after Shaun disappears out of sight, and the chapter ends with "noises of morning" (BL 47482b f. 8; JJA 57: 17).

Pushing the actual delivery of the Letter to the background, Joyce shifted his point of view and focused more on the characterization of Shaun.[13] At the same time Joyce exchanged the third-person narrator of the "Delivery" sketch (and of the entire Book I as it then existed) for a first-person narrator. The opening of the chapter introduces Johnny McDougall's "poor ass" (FW: 405.06), who notices the light shining from Shaun's lamp.[14] In the final version the Ass is no more than a temporary interloper for the narrator, for when Joyce was preparing the chapter for publication in *transition* 12 in 1928, he added the "fogbow" passage (FW: 403.06–17) as a prelude to the appearance of the Ass and Shaun, recovering the third-person voice of the narrator. In the early drafts, however, the Ass is the narrator before whom Shaun appears; presumably, he is also Shaun's interrogator.[15] Fittingly, the questioner's voice resembles that of the Four Old Men, and many of the notes upon which Joyce based the interrogation derive from renditions of courtroom proceedings (probably intended to parallel Earwicker's trial in chapter I.4).[16] Nonetheless, the narrative does not identify the Ass explicitly as the questioner: "Shaun in proper person [. . .] was before me and he spake. And lo meheard the voice of him sighed to the scented night as softly as the tall telegraph masts at Clifden sigh secrets to Nova Scotia listening ladies" (BL 47482b f. 4; JJA 57: 9). There is no indication either that Shaun directly addresses the Ass. Moreover, in the first fair copy Joyce changed the interrogator's first-person singular to a plural "we," introducing a grammatical differentiation between narrator and questioners. With this change the Ass cedes his voice to an unnamed personage.

Undoing the identification creates a greater ambiguity, whereby, within the logic of the *Wakean* night, the rainbow girls could possibly be the questioners. (Joyce emended "listening ladies" in the above passage to "listing sister poles" [BL 47482b f. 4; JJA 57: 9], retaining "to listen" in the poetic *to list*, but also playing on to make a list as well as to desire or wish for, or even heel to one side.) In the narrative of the first draft the girls appear only metaphorically as receivers: Shaun sighs as softly as the telegraph masts sigh secrets to the girls across the Atlantic. But the allusion to the first transatlantic telegraph connection between Clifden, Connemara, and Nova Scotia, Canada, should caution us: after all, radio and wireless often play tricks in *Finnegans Wake*. The change from "I" to "we," the endearing use of "dear Shaun," and the fact that Shaun is "staring upon the girl he so loved" (BL 47482b f. 4; JJA 57: 9) all would suit the sisters as questioners.[17] But Joyce later in the composition partly undid the ambiguity of the questioners' identity in the scene of Shaun's "passing" when he has the *narrator* admonish in a characteristically Mamalujean voice: "Musha, be thinking of us ^[1]poor twelve o'clock scholars[1]^ sometime or other" (BL 47483 f. 52; JJA 57: 176; FW: 427.33–34).

Apart from the changes in point of view between the "Delivery" sketch and the early-draft version of the chapter, Joyce also changed Shaun's personality from a local notoriety as the Lucalizod letter carrier in the sketch to a fuller and more saintly character who receives his legitimacy from "on high" (FW: 410.01) in the name of God, Mary, and Saints Patrick, Brigid, and Columkille. These patron saints of Ireland put Shaun's mission in a nationalist perspective, while Shaun is turned into a stage Irishman, a rural Haun (FW: 471.35) who wears a frieze and whip coat (FW: 404.15, 17) and who is associated with Shaun, the main protagonist of Boucicault's play *Arrah-na-Pogue.*[18] If his "emptybottlegreen jerkin" (BL 47471b f. 35v; JJA 57: 2) already marked him as a stock character, in the third draft (fair copy) Shaun's uniform expanded to contain the familiar seven items of clothing that identify him as an avatar of Earwicker. What is less known is that in expanding Shaun's character and the events in chapters III.1–2 Joyce created an episode that abounds with reverberations from his own rendering of "Tristan and Isolde."[19] The correspondence might already apply to the "Delivery" sketch, for some important elements are featured among the Tristan notes in Scribbledehobble that, although uncrossed, have been translated to fit Shaun: "Trist's way for entering house (zigzag)" (VI.A: 301) became "the zigzaggery of the deliverery" (BL 47471b f. 35v; JJA 57: 2); another one identifies Tristan as letter carrier: "King! (I speaks) le beau T carries Letter" (VI.A: 301). Another note prefigures Shaun's captive audience, the girls of Saint Brigid's: "What is it? / Chorus of / Females — Love!" (VI.B.3: 14). Neither of these early notebooks, filled a year prior to the composition of III.1–2, contains any conceptual development directly relevant to the themes in Shaun's first watches, but a few ideas seem to have lingered, and they were used heavily during composition of III.1–2. Returning to his indexes with material on "Tristan and Isolde" and the earliest development of Issy's character, Joyce seemed particularly interested in the lovers' discourse.[20] He constructed Shaun's leave-taking as a continuation of "Tristan and Isolde" and drew on materials from the earliest, abandoned versions of his own sketch as a basis for this expansion. The lovers' gazing "to stardom" (BL 47480 f. 267v; JJA 56: 6–7) echoes Shaun's (FW: 426.19–20); Issy's gift of her handkerchief to Shaun echoes Tristan, who courteously picks up the handkerchief Isolde had dropped. But particularly the following passage reads as a protoversion of Shaun's departure: "He took leave of her and circulated as bidden. Hearing his name called before many instants had passed he most sagaciously ceased to walk about & turned, his look now charged with purpose" (BL 47480 f. 267v; JJA 56: 6–7). Before this passage in this sexually frank first draft, Tristan asks Isolde "whether she had ever indulged in clandestine fornicationm," a proleptic echo of Shaun's admonitions to Issy to adhere to the "ten commandments" (FW: 432.27–28) during his absence.[21] In ensuing versions of the Shaun chapters, Joyce continued to add subtle allusions to the archetypal couple.

Before Joyce copied out his second fair copy of chapter III.1–2 he explained on 24 May 1924 the meaning behind Shaun's postal mission in a well-known letter to Harriet Shaw Weaver: "[It is] a description of a postman travelling backwards in the night through the events already narrated. It is written in the form of a *via crucis* of 14 stations but in reality it is only a barrel rolling down the river Liffey" (LI: 214). Joyce's explanation, uncharacteristically clear and free of riddles as it is, has nevertheless puzzled critics and readers to the point that some have even dismissed such conceptual matrices as "vestigial" and utterly "unimportant."[22] Where are the Stations of the Cross? What are the events, if any, that are being retold?[23] And, of course, what is reality in the *Wake?* Like with "Oxen of the Sun," where Joyce wanted the gestation of language to be "linked back [. . .] subtly with some foregoing episode" (LI: 140), we could assume that Joyce simply abandoned the idea of rehearsing prior events.

Such solution, however, is too facile to accept readily, especially in light of the idea's prominence in Joyce's notebooks. VI.B.1, which lies at the basis for copious insertions in the first drafts of III.1–2, contains the following conceptualizations: "∧ stations of † / [. . .] / [r]∧ walks backwards" (VI.B.1: 76; FW: 426.34); "for ∧ it is past / for reader— present / we can't see actual present" (VI.B.1: 160); "∧ swings back / [. . .] / ∧ inverse" (VI.B.1: 161); "See history retrograde if / leave E faster than lux" (VI.B.1: 165);[24] "[r]St[ations] of † / ⊏ blacker & blacker / ∧ whiter & whiter" (VI.B.1: 166; FW: 472.04); and "∧ ray of light / travelling backward / antipodes" (VI.B.1: 167). In a consecutive notebook the same concepts are repeated: "[r]pilgrimage to the past" (VI.B.16: 9); "thinking retrograde / [. . .] / travelling back" (VI.B.16: 25);[25] and "[r]∧ turn back / ∧ dearest Jesu" (VI.B.16: 90). Possibly, the idea of a regressive journey originated in an entry from a few months earlier on the currents in the river Liffey: "winds blow from S— [South] / liquid flotsam / °barrels begin to come / back" (VI.B.6: 34). The note itself may have been inspired by the floods that hit Paris in January 1924, as it was reported for instance in the *Irish Independent*: "Paris Face with Disaster / Seine Still Rising / To-day's way of passing the time was fishing for wine barrels. Hundreds of persons of both sexes and of all ages brought ropes with hooks to capture cases and barrels of choice vintages being swept away from the huge wine storage yards of Bercy (known throughout the world) and drifting down the river" (quoted in *Buffalo VI.B.6*, 27). But it is highly significant that Joyce hits upon the idea of a regressive journey at the time when he is reading historical geography: he makes a connection between rivers and history in VI.B.1 when he reads Metchnikoff's *Les Grands fleuves* and, presumably from other sources, draws numerous other connections between rivers and culture or history. The obsessive rehearsal of the idea of regressive repetition of events in various notebooks, even when the chapter was already well on its way, underscores its central importance to the reeling and dealing of Shaun the Post.

Shaun's travels have a triple destination on three different levels of reality. On the most abstract level of the text he travels to death (which Clive Hart associates with the setting sun) in search (but also in imitation) of his father.[26] The entire chapter, especially the passage of Shaun's leave-taking from his sister, is interspersed with allusions to "passing" and the afterlife, and he admonishes her to "create no scenes in my poor [. . .] wake" (FW: 453.02–3). He does not want his sister to participate in any kind of rambunctious drinking and fighting, in any mayhem for which Irish wakes are known, but neither does he want to see any "ugly lemoncholic gobs" in the "sewing circle" (FW: 453.07). (Joyce's subtext here is "The Sisters" and the old ladies' drapery shop.) Shaun's rather strange prohibition to mourn his person seems to make sense only when we read it as an amplification of its original Good Friday context. But the Passion is reverted to a fatalistic expression of barroom frivolity: "Now cheer up all. We'll all soon be dead and happy," to which Joyce later added: "Drink it off, ladies, please" (BL 47482b f. 6v; JJA 57: 14 and BL 47482b f. 15v; JJA 57: 32; FW: 453.31–32 and 35). Imitating or parodying Christ's Passion, Shaun announces his death and resurrection as an Easter egg: "I'll make ye all an Easter egg of myself the moment that you name the day" (BL 47483 f. 25; JJA 57: 151; FW: 453.22–23). This is probably more serious than it sounds: the custom of eating Easter eggs is presumably of pagan origin, but a later Church tradition interpreted the Easter egg as a symbol of Christ's recreation of mankind (*The Catholic Encyclopedia,* 1913, s.v. "Easter").

On the next level, closer to events in the narrative but also playing on the interconnection between time and narration, Shaun undertakes a "pilgrimage to the past" (BL 47482b f. 8; JJA 57: 17), a journey that engenders a conflation of present with presence and of past with absence, reminiscent of the Four Historians' "Vichian" relationship to time/tense and the past: Shaun supposedly "ʳmakes absent present" (VI.B.16: 75).[27] During Shaun's absence "life . . . will be a dream" for Issy, a "lapsus temporis" or "slip of the time" (BL 47482b f. 8; JJA 57: 17); his departure creates a temporary vacuum, one that Joyce underscores by substituting "dream" with "blank" in the second fair copy (BL 47482b f. 61; JJA 57: 123). The significance of this pilgrimage to the past pertains to the contrapuntal design of Book III. When Joyce reworked the passage for the second draft, he introduced some of the conceptual components from his notebooks to enhance the symbolical meaning of the chapter: "while you are away ^1as the beam of light we follow receding1^ on your pilgrimage to ^1the antipodes of1^ the past" (BL 47482b f. 18; JJA 57: 37). The antipodes, in this case, are not only an allusion to the "torrid austral Hell" of "Australia's antipodal position"[28] but also a symbolical point of oblivion very much like the final dot that closes Ithaca and Bloom's day.[29] If at the beginning of chapter III.1 Shaun wakes up, he falls asleep again at the end of III.2, having "followed through [his] upfielded neviewscope the rugaby moon cumuliously godrolling himself westasleep" (FW: 449.34–35), curiously echoing the ingredients—rugby, moon, and cloud—from "Tristan and Isolde" (BL 47481 f. 94; JJA 56: 2–3, and BL 47480 f. 267v; JJA 56: 6–7).

Finally, on a literal level Shaun's regression in time coincides with his journey to the west, again in search of his father, or his father's toes, who sent "an unquiring one well to the west in quest of his tumptytumtoes" (FW: 003.20–21).[30] Like an (un)characteristic Saint Patrick, he blesses all to the west (FW: 469.24–26). In Patrick's life story Ireland's patron saint did not travel to convert the remote western lands but blessed the people of Kerry from his vantage point in Limerick before heading south. Shaun, in his own scathing manner, casts his eye far beyond the West Country.[31] He does not intend to leave Ireland in exile via Holyhead to the Continent, like his artist brother; instead, like Saint Brendan, John McCormack, and many other of his countrymen, he takes a more "customary" way out: emigration to America. At the end of chapter III.1 he is a remittance man (VI.B.16: 93; FW: 428.25), supporting the family back home with his new earnings in the land of opportunity. A note dating from spring 1926 reiterates Shaun's intentions: "Λ writes to ⊓⊓ he / is going to U.S.A" (VI.B.17: 96). Apart from these modern connections, Shaun's narrative ties in with a tradition of Irish voyage tales, such as St. Brendan's, but also a monastic tradition that regarded "pilgrimage overseas . . . as a sign of greater dedication and devotion than pilgrimage within Ireland."[32] Shaun, of course, turns this tradition upside down as Joyce's after-the-fact recording of a popular tale regarding Saint Columkille insinuates: at Port-na-Curraich in Iona the saint erected a pile of stones popularly called Carn-cul-ri-Erin, "Cairn of the Back Turned to Ireland."[33] Joyce transformed this monument into "The Cairn of thy / Cul Turned to I—" (VI.B.34: 153).[34]

Even though place, like time, is always in a state of flux in the *Wake,* the early drafts give us some indications about Shaun's itinerary. Like Bloom's "crumpled throwaway" in "Wandering Rocks" (U: 10.294 and 753), Shaun is carried by the tide. (Joyce, however, did not allude explicitly to this fact until he changed Shaun's "timeshackled wrists" to "tide shackled wrists" when the episode was published in *transition* 12 in March 1928 [BL 47483 f. 109; JJA 57: 328; BL 47486a f. 80; JJA 61: 22; FW: 426.20].) Toward the end of his interview Shaun, sleepy and tired from talking, gazes up at the stars, and "he overbalanced by weight of the barrel and rolled ^1backwards1^ [. . .] in the ~~Inchicore~~ direction ^1of Delgany1^ before being ^1<~~set~~^put^>1^ righted" (BL 47482b f. 6; JJA 57: 13). In other words, Shaun floats upstream: Inchicore is a district in West Dublin between the Liffey and the Grand Canal; Delgany is a village in county Wicklow south of Bray near Glen of the Downs.[35] The introduction of Delgany into the text means that Shaun first drifts for a moment toward the sea until the incoming tide catches hold of his barrel and pushes him westward. His next stop is "at the weir by Lazar's Walk" (BL 47482b f. 6; JJA 57: 13; FW: 429.06), where he will deliver his Lenten sermon. Lazar's Hill is now Townsend Street (between Tara and Luke Streets behind the Tara Street Station), where the south bank of the Liffey used to be in the seventeenth century.[36] At the end of chapter III.2 Shaun has traveled "nine furlong mile" (FW: 473.12), 9 miles being the distance from Dublin Bay to Island Bridge, the point up to which the Liffey is tidal (9 furlongs, though, is only 1.125 miles).[37] Thus, Island Bridge, near the southeastern corner of Phoenix Park, is the farthest point Shaun can travel in a floating barrel. At this point, however, the realistic underpinnings of the chapter come to an end. Implicitly, Shaun's barrel should drift back east (Joyce, after all, wrote that Shaun's barrel was "rolling *down* the river" [LI: 214, emphasis added]), although the narrative does not bear this out.[38] Joyce did not carry through any impression of literal movement in later chapters of Book III, but if Shaun continues on his westward journey, it is purely on a symbolical level, "like a shot off a shovel" (U: 12.1918). Another passage, earlier in the *Wake* but added later, has Shaun leave "The Barrel," an area in Meath Street where the Friends' Meetinghouse stood, setting off to wander across Dublin via "thrie routes and restings" on the Underground (FW: 041.17–18; cf. McHugh). Such wanderings befit his role as postman, but they also underscore the circular aspect of his travels, for at the end of chapter III.2, effectuating his final farewell, Shaun waves his hand across the sea and sets off again "to the left," "making a fresh sta[r]t" (BL 47482b f. 8; JJA 57: 17; BL 47482b f. 18; JJA 57: 37; FW: 471.11).

So far, however, Shaun's backward movement has only played itself out on a thematic level in the early drafts of chapters III.1–2. Joyce's conceptual notes in VI.B.1 referred to above intimate some broader, more structural implications as well. Beside the actual direction of Shaun's itinerary, these notes also suggest that the chapters were to be an inversion, not a repetition, of what came before, in which past and present are turned inside out or substituted for each other. In this respect, Joyce built on an idea from his original "Delivery" sketch in which the events surrounding the Letter's delivery do not happen "for the 1st time in history" (BL 47471b f. 35v; JJA 57: 2).[39] Coincidentally, a notebook that predates the "Delivery" has "the son's life / repeats the / father's. He does / not see it [—] Make / the reader see it / he—" (VI.B.3: 13), and some scattered situational notes from the same early period, such as "addressed girl's school!" (VI.A: 24), clearly suggest that the son's life was intended as an extension of the father's.

Nevertheless, in chapters III.1–2 Joyce did not realize a full doubling of events from Book I but rather a mirroring of the work's architecture.[40] The contrapuntal function of the chapters is the result of a subtle but long and strenuous process of rethinking the entire conceptual framework of the book that took place during ten months prior to and after Joyce's Letter on Shaun's rolling barrel of 24 May. On 15 March he had written: "On Monday I shall try to start Shaun the Post. This would make the second part of the book fairly complete with the Letter. The first part is not written yet" (LIII: 90). At this moment, Shaun the Post was still an afterthought, a separate piece following the washerwomen episode. In the opening paragraph of the first draft Joyce clearly tied the new episode to the washerwomen's business when the narrator spots "sundry articles of laundry reposing upon the greensward" (BL 47482b f. 3; JJA 57: 8); it is likely that Shaun's "return" was intended to close off the book.[41] But gradually the piece detached itself from "Anna Livia Plurabelle" and became itself the second part, maybe because it was "long, long as the night he travels through" (BL 57347 f. 148v), while the other episodes, so carefully listed in VI.B.1: 163, took the place of the unwritten first part.[42]

How this transformation happened is not possible to make out with any precision, but traces of it are discernible in Joyce's letters. On 24 March, predicting characteristic difficulties with the composition, he wrote: "Shaun is going to give me a very great deal of trouble" (LI: 213). On 6 April: "I hope to resume with Shaun tomorrow. I had done about a third. But he (already a dawdler) will be longer on the road" (LIII: 92). On 25 April: "I have finished the second draft (not the final) of the first part of Shaun the Post. [. . .] The second part (far more difficult) I dare not even attempt yet" (JJ/SB: 37). Presumably, this second, more difficult part of Shaun is his cross-examination by the Four Old Men in chapter III.3, which he would not start until late 1924. On 7 May: "He is now halfway" (BL 57347 f. 148v). On 13 May, working on extensive revisions: "I shall try to finish the first half of Shaun before the next big event—whatever it may be" (BL 57347 f. 154). On 2 June, after the letter introducing Shaun's mission as a reversed *via crucis*: "I cannot remember accurately the first page of Shaun and he is not here to aid me" (LIII: 97). Joyce had packed up his books and manuscripts and left them with Sylvia Beach because he urgently needed to rest before his fourth eye operation on 11 June. On 4 June, illuminatingly: "Perhaps I was wrong to begin such a difficult book after having ended *Ulysses.* I began to see fairly clearly this morning the fusion of the second and third parts. How often in the day have I to resist the temptation to go down to Miss Beach's shop and get out, at least, the typescript or even the unfinished MS of Shaun!" (BL 57347 f. 165v). On 16 August he still had not resolved the problem: "But it is true that I have been thinking and thinking how and how and how can I and can it—all about the fusion of two parts of the book—which my one bedazzled eye searches the sea like Cain-Shem-Tristan-Patrick from his lighthouse in Boulogne. I hope the solution will presently appear" (LI: 220). On 14 October: "I have been working hard revising Shaun and in the middle of unloading of boxes, bundles, trunks, etc." (BL 57347 f. 213v). On 9 November: "I think that at last I have solved one—the first—of the problems presented by my book. In other words one of the partitions between two of the tunneling parties seems to have given way" (LIII: 110). Finally, on 27 January 1925: "Tomorrow I shall send you MS and typescript of the first two watches of Mr Shaun (what I read, slightly revised) and the day after MS and typescript of the rest. There is an interruption near the middle (indicated in the MS)" (LI: 225). After the typist returned the chapter Joyce would not work anymore on III.1–2 for over a year.

When Joyce embarked on the composition of Shaun the Post in March

1924, he realized that the drafting would be considerably slower than the previous passages (partly because the writing was interrupted by another eye operation). It soon struck him too that the chapter—quite appropriately for Shaun's spatial preoccupation—was taking up a lot of space—"30 pages of my large notebook, foolscap size" (LI: 214; actually sixteen rectos)—perhaps too much space to function as a suitable coda for the book. At the same time, the writing spawned the idea for further Shaun sections, a "second part"; even though this part would remain unwritten for quite a while, Joyce entered Shaun's variant name in one of his notebooks: "°Λ Yawn" (VI.B.16: 26). Yawn's presence in a notebook of this period indicates that Joyce was already conceptualizing what would become chapter III.3. Following orders from Dr. Borsch, Joyce took a much-needed break away from his manuscript, but even though he was not laboring on it any longer, Shaun the Post did not leave him alone. At first Joyce complained that his mind was dulled, unable to remember even his own writing, but soon he was preoccupied again with the architecture of the book: in his mind, if not in actual composition, Shaun the Post had become part three of the book, with part two wrapped up in a composite typescript at Shakespeare and Company and part one still not written—and it never would be. But with this separation of Shaun from the rest of the book he was faced with what was already a persistent problem in the composition of *Work in Progress*—how to fuse together the distinct parts. Joyce's solution had everything to do with the "partition" that gave way "between two of the tunneling parties." What Joyce meant by this "partition" is not clear, but, ironically, the problem of fusing the different parts only presented itself because the Shaun chapter was firmly fixed as an independent leg in the narration: the sections on the history of Earwicker and his family (part two of the book or Book I in the *Wake*'s final version) are one side of the mountain, the "Watches of Shaun" the other.[43] As soon as a zealous and invigorated Joyce resumed revisions of Shaun—after recovery and an extended but intellectually fertile vacation in Brittany (his notebooks swelled with Breton themes), a trip to London, and a move to a new and bigger apartment in the avénue Charles Floquet—he would never again mention any unwritten first part.

With all this—Shaun's backward itinerary and the chapter's contrapuntal structure—the problem of the *via crucis* is intertwined. In an early tradition of the *via crucis,* pilgrims started from Calvary and proceeded backward to Christ's sentencing at Pilate's house (*The Catholic Encyclopedia,* 1913, s.v. "Way of the Cross"), although there is absolutely no evidence to support that Joyce had this tradition in mind when he had Shaun travel backward. What Joyce did mean, however, is not immediately clear. Many critics have attempted to identify the Stations of the Cross as if Joyce had hidden the solution in a crossword puzzle.[44] Not surprisingly, the proffered solutions show a large degree of variation, and, with just a few exceptions, none of them is entirely convincing. Jesus's successive falls (Stations 3, 7, and 9) could correspond to Shaun's "footslips" (FW: 442.15); Veronica wiping the face of Jesus (Station 6) to Tizzy's gift of her handkerchief (FW: 457.34). Most other identifications, however, do not ring true because they were not yet part of the text when Joyce revealed his schema to Miss Weaver.

Perhaps a less literal interpretation of Joyce's clue needs to be considered, whereby Shaun's "heaviest crux" (FW: 409.17–18) symbolizes the Way of the Cross and the entire Good Friday ordeal. Following a suggestion James Atherton made in *A Conceptual Guide to "Finnegans Wake,"* Ingeborg Landuyt argues that the fourteen questions parthenogenetically match the fourteen Stations of the Cross, an assertion that has some credibility, for it replicates the means by which Joyce often strove for coherence in or between particular passages.[45] Joyce seemed indeed to emphasize that he was after a rhetorical device, "written in the *form* of a *via crucis*" (LI: 214, my emphasis), each question representing a "devout meditation" of sorts. But this solution is not entirely satisfactory either. The difficulty is that the *via crucis* appears only in the first half of a chapter that is as yet undivided. Moreover, as Landuyt correctly observes, III.1 is comprised of only thirteen questions until the addition in 1928 of a transitional question that introduces "The Ondt and the Gracehoper."[46]

The idea of the Stations as a rhetorical device might play itself out differently. For one, the Good Friday motif in the *Wake* is not limited to chapters III.1–2 only.[47] The whole idea might have sprung from an insignificant notebook entry, recorded about six months prior to the writing of Shaun the Post: "stations of Earwicker / Earwicker (Adam) wake & / finds Eve" (VI.B.2: 31), an entry that concentrates on the Resurrection, or *Pascha resurrectionis,* rather than on Shaun's *Pascha crucifixionis* (*The Catholic Encyclopedia,* 1913, s.v. "Easter"). In that sense Shaun bears at the same time the burden of his father and of the Letter. Historically, moreover, the *via crucis* originated as a devotional practice in imitation of a pilgrimage to sacred places in Jerusalem (*The Catholic Encyclopedia,* 1913, s.v. "Way of the Cross"). The narrative in the chapter indeed emphasizes a journey rather than individual stations, while an early cluster of fragmented notes, recorded about four months prior to the drafting of Shaun the Post, loosely associates the Stations of the Cross with Shaun's travels: "⌈last long journey / [. . .] / stations of cross along route / [. . .] / It is prayer all the time / in the suburbs of the / heavenly gardens" (VI.B.11: 70; used at FW: 431.27 and 454.28–30). In Shaun's mouth these notebook entries become a blasphemous derision of Catholic devotions along with his own anticipated death and resurrection. In this sense, Shaun at the same time does and does not represent Christ. His postal mission—simultaneously an honor and a burden—becomes itself, parodically and symbolically, the *via crucis.*[48] Each station (to adopt freely an idea from Derrida) is a poste restante along the river, and Shaun is performing his devout exercises at each station of his journey either as a reenactment of the Passion or as a part of Good Friday celebrations.[49] He is trying to outsmart his father's own "Christlikeness" (FW: 033.29). But as with the individual stations, we cannot identify the individual exercises either. At most, Shaun is saying his "prayers regularly" (BL 47482b f. 5; JJA 57: 11; in the final text, "grocery beans" of the rosary [FW: 411.16–17]), and he receives an indulgence for forty days from his sister (BL 47482b f. 31; JJA 57: 63; FW: 458.03–5).[50] In the notebooks Joyce associates these prayers with the *via crucis:* "Rosary—Teulhan / Stations of †" (VI.B.11: 116) and "Irish litany" (VI.B.11: 117). Strangely, Joyce includes with these notes part of the litany in French.

Even if the individual exercises cannot be recognized (it is quite significant to note that the Church does not prescribe a regulated set of devotions for the stations either), there is still a broader connection that is related to Shaun's postal mission as it was enunciated in Saint Columkille's prophecies (FW: 409.28). The most recognizable allusion here is to the numerous "spurious 'prophecies'" attributed to Columba.[51] However, Victor Branford's sociological theory of sainthood in his *St. Columba: A Study of Social Inheritance and Spiritual Development* (1913) provides a context that is of much interest. Joyce listed Branford's monograph in one of his notebooks. Whether he read it or not is uncertain, but Branford's book tentatively helps us understand the archetypal nature of Shaun's travels. According to Branford, there are three "primal pastoral institutions—the Quest, the Mission, and the Pilgrimage"—that define the sociological origin of heroism and sainthood, institutions that can be said to parallel loosely the underlying motivations behind Shaun's postal mission.[52] The motivation behind sainthood centers around "the transmutation of dream into deed," but this deed can only be realized when "a dead point of inertia" is surmounted with "heroic effort": "The ecstasy of feeling which the vision of the ideal produces, fades into the lethargy of inaction, unless there are tense muscles awaiting the command of the will, to carry the aspiration into act and make real the dream."[53] Branford thus connects the ethos of the healthy body of his and Joyce's time—the Sandowian ethos of the gymnasium positing that a healthy body will lead to a healthy, morally just mind and a strong will—to the ethos of sainthood and monasticism. The saint overcomes mind *and* body; Shaun, however, will not quite overcome his inertia.

Zeroing in on the pilgrimage, Branford discusses among others "The Old Irish Life of Columba," a text that expounds a theory of the "Perfect Pilgrimage" in a curious mix of Gaelic and Latin:

> Translated into the half-technical, half-popular terms of current sociology, it means that the perfect pilgrim is one who has been able to rid himself of the prejudices of his own people and incorporate the best ideals of other peoples. And the state of perfect pilgrimage is to be objectively reached, if possible, by travel and sojourn amongst foreign peoples, until one can possess and practise their particular virtues; or if we may not do it by actual voyaging, then we may approach indefinitely near by cultivating goodwill towards foreign ideals and all the human personalities which they have formed and animate.[54]

Branford's description of the holy wayfarer's modern pendant again aptly fits Shaun's antipilgrimage: the Perfect Pilgrimage originates in the Old Testament with Abraham's journey to the Land of Promise; to Shaun this becomes "the land of breach of promise" (FW: 442.13–14). More particularly, the pilgrimage itself, which Irish monasticism associated with the third call from God (that of a religious vocation), consisted of the following characteristics. It began with a filiopietal "visit to the ancestral tomb" to remember and revere the deceased parents; this visit engendered a sudden spiritual awakening in which the mind was lifted upward from the tomb or temple "to the contemplation of the starry heavens"; the force of this cosmic vision usually transformed the pilgrim, inducing a process of rejuvenation of himself and his people that resulted in a desire to guide his people to a Promised Land.[55]

These events seem to reverberate in chapters III.1–2, where Shaun visits the porterhouse and undergoes a friendly interrogation about his family and his duties; he experiences a change and decides to abandon his postal mission (even though it is a holy one) and "strike off hiking" (FW: 448.27); finally, to complete the reversal of the Perfect Pilgrimage toward spiritual rejuvenation, he looks up at the heavens and takes leave. But there is more. He promises that after he returns he will engage himself in various kinds of social work, such as taking care of the poor and cleaning up the muck-ridden streets of Dublin. As such, the narrative operates within a mode of double time that is characteristic of much of the early stages of *Work in Progress* and reminiscent of Branford's ideas about the sociohistorical archetype of the saint. Shaun's roles of holy man (as saint or Christ) and social activist are not simultaneous occupations but archetypal duplicates.

In this context of social archetypes Shaun's pilgrimage, like the *via crucis,* is both a subjective and objective pilgrimage.[56] According to Church tradition, the Way of the Cross is a pilgrimage of the mind that does not require actual displacement to a holy site, but at the same time the pilgrimage is rendered concrete by means of a simulacrum, a set of reproductions that duplicates Christ's Passion as well as the actual locations of the *via dolorosa* in Jerusalem. In another sociological study of sainthood that Joyce was interested in, Stefan Czarnowski's *Le Culte des héros et ses conditions sociales: Saint Patrick, héros national de l'Irlande* (1919), Joyce found another interpretation of Good Friday that was similar in nature to Branford's archetypal interpretation of sainthood and his own treatment of Shaun: "Le héros est mort une fois pour toutes. Le dieu sacrificié subit la mort chaque fois que le sacrifice s'accomplit. La passion de Jésus est quotidienne. La mort sacrifielle d'Osiris se réitère à toutes les fêtes et tous les jours." (The hero died once and for all. The God who is sacrificed undergoes his death each time the sacrifice takes place. The passion of Christ is repeated every day. The sacrificial death of Osiris is repeated during every feast every day.)[57] Because Christ's death is commemorated and reenacted in religious celebrations, it is not a one-time event. Joyce recorded: "°Λ oriented † / [. . .] / every day in a passion" (VI.B.14: 213). Possibly in this sense, too, Shaun "travels through the events already narrated."

~

For the third stage in the architectural evolution of chapters III.1–2, the moment the Shaun chapters are pushed back from part two to Book III, we need to retrace our steps to when Joyce began drafting chapters III.1–2 in order to look at two additional but related events in the composition and organization of the chapters: the development of the "Watches of Shaun" and the division of III.1–2 into two separate chapters. I am not postulating any direct causal relationship between these developments and the creation of a new center for "Work in Progress" that consigned Book III to its final position. It needs to be understood that Book III will retain its contrapuntal position, even in the *Wake*'s final version. Gradually, Book III received a somewhat greater degree of autonomy in relation to the rest of *Finnegans Wake,* particularly as Shaun's regression expands in chapters III.3 and 4. His consciousness, as it were, grows dimmer and dimmer—he first becomes Yawn and then the sleeping child Kevin with "the Four speaking through the child's brain"—until he practically disappears from the narrative.[58] All the while "elvery stream winds seling on for to keep this barrel of bounty rolling" (FW: 565.28–29)—Shaun floats continuously through the whole of Book III. However, these developments will only partly overshadow its contrapuntal role, not remove it entirely.

From the text of chapters III.1–2 we can surmise that Shaun is himself the watch who holds his nightly vigil; his "belted lamp" (FW: 404.13) serves a double purpose of postman's and nightwatcher's lantern (both officials are definitely "[r]nightwalker[s]" [VI.B.16: 31]). Sigurdson, who is commonly known as the "warden of the peace" (FW: 429.19), makes only a brief entry in chapter III.2. However, since Sigurdson is a new character in the history of *Work in Progress*—a transformation from the "quidam" who is hired by the "watch warriors of the vigilance committee" (FW: 033.35, 034.04), or "Vigilence Cie / Watch & Ward" (VI.B.3: 119) who appears as "petty constable Sigurdson" in "Shem the Penman" (FW: 186.19)—he is presumably at this stage of the composition a Shaunian emanation rather than a full protagonist. An unused note identifies the sleeping watchman as Shaun: "Λ asleep at's post" (VI.B.16: 27). But apart from this connection there is little evidence of the watches' conceptualization in the *Wake*'s genetic dossier, except for another early note that harks back to *Ulysses.* Under the heading "Eumeus" in Scribbledehobble Joyce wrote "asleep on watch" in a context containing snippets of police and/or court stories (VI.A: 803).

The idea of the "Watches of Shaun" has again been the subject of much speculation, ranging from the unlikely to the overdetermined, among *Wake* scholars who mostly focused on the fourfold structure of Book III.[59] But the idea originated separately from the fourfold structure, for in the margin of the first draft next to the opening paragraph Joyce added "watches of the night" (BL 47482b f. 3; JJA 57: 8). The use of the plural in this marginal notation, along with another one in the notebooks ("[r]set the watches" [VI.B.11: 6]), indicates that there was more than one, but this evidence does not yet indicate that there were going to be four watches, divided among different chapters. The end of the first draft simply marks a closing with "(noises of morning)" (BL 47482b f. 8; JJA 57: 17). The finality of the impending dawn, however, disappears when Joyce introduces "[r]Yawn"

(VI.B.16: 21). This entry, however, was used as "Shaun yawned" (FW: 427.28) in the original watch, but it already contained the inspirational seed for a new chapter, a new watch, and a new embodiment of Λ as the waking Yawn. Almost immediately following this entry Joyce envisaged Shaun's postal mission as a postal relay: "^{r}Λ hand letter to Yawn" (VI.B.16: 30). Soon after, continuing to expand what had become an elaborate theme of telecommunications,[60] he would note down the following cluster, introducing yet another Shaun personage:

Yawn	telegraph
	telephone
Dawn	wireless
	thought transference (VI.B.5: 68)

Yet a more extensive conceptualization of the watches would only take place when Joyce had almost completely drafted all four chapters of Book III in the summer of 1925. At this point, however, Joyce attempted to bring the chapters closer together thematically by paving the watches with roads—the idea that "Λd ought to be about roads" (LI: 232) is an elaborate spin-off from the "traffic in transit" segment in chapter III.1 (FW: 448.08–9)—and structurally by building a sequence of "gradations" into the text—the word "degree," each inserted around the same time, occurs exactly once in each of Shaun's watches: "a poor hastehater of the first degree" (BL 47483 f. 35; JJA 57: 169; FW: 408.10–11), "be flummoxed to the second degree" (BL 47483 f. 114; JJA 57: 181; FW: 438.29), "You're a nice third degree witness" (BL 47484a f. 49; JJA 58: 189; FW: 522.27), and "to the last degree" (BL 47482a f. 43v; JJA 60: 190; FW: 572.26). In one sense, this preoccupation with the coherence of the various chapters was necessary to retain the underlying impression that Shaun is continuously floating up the river through the consecutive chapters.

The earliest indication that Joyce was expanding the "watches of Shaun" into separate chapters hangs together with the earliest, tentative indication that chapters III.1–2 had become separate entities. The first unequivocal indication of a splitting occurs on 27 January 1925, when Joyce wrote to Harriet Shaw Weaver: "Tomorrow I shall send you MS and typescript of the first two watches of Mr Shaun (what I read, slightly revised) and the day after MS and typescript of the rest. There is an interruption near the middle (indicated in the MS)" (SL: 305).[61] The third fair copy indeed contains such a mark alongside the present chapter division (BL 47483 f. 14;

JJA 57: 140). Later Joyce made the separation part of the narrative when he added to the opening of the second watch: "the first leg of his [Shaun's] being pulled through" (BL 47483 f. 163; JJA 57: 263; FW: 429.02–3).

Nonetheless, even though the chapters were conceptually disassociated, they would remain a physical unit until their publication in *transition* 12 and 13, respectively. Joyce still intended the first two watches to be published together, since the first proofs for *transition* were still a composite set.[62] All the while Joyce continued to see chapters III.1 and 2 as a unit. On 17 April 1926, when he was preparing Book III to be retyped, he wrote: "Today I copied out the sheets of Λa which were unreadable [. . .] Tomorrow and Monday I shall do, I hope, the same for Λb. Then Λc will take three or four days." These copies resulted in what is now in an ink fair copy mixed with less heavily revised pages of an older typescript, but chapters III.1–2 are still continuous.[63] Indeed, in the same letter Joyce informed Miss Weaver, "I am to read it Λab, interval, and Λc to a small group" (LIII: 140). Although the chapters had grown apart, in Joyce's mind they still belonged together.

What prompted the conceptual division of chapters III.1 and 2? The exact reasons are not apparent, although it is clear from the beginning that Shaun the Post consisted of two identifiable segments—the interrogation and the sermon—poised around an unexpected turning point: Shaun's "overbalancing." Perhaps as a result of Joyce's frantic method of revising and expanding, adding layer upon layer of verbal material, the halves of Shaun the Post simply drifted apart. Yet it is also possible that the separation is finalized as the result of a real if not psychological response to the drafting of three new episodes: "Dave the Dancekerl," "Twilight Games," and "The Ondt and the Gracehoper." The first and the third only induce the separation of chapters III.1 and 2, since they consist of elaborate expansions of the text; the second, an entirely new episode, clinches Book III in its final position in *Finnegans Wake.*

Drafted between the fall of 1925 and the spring of 1926, "Dave the Dancekerl" is a raucous sketch that jars with the prohibitive moral lesson of Shaun's sermon. Having admonished his sister to heed "college swankies" and any other "lapwhelp or sleevemongrel" (FW: 438.32 and 441.31–32), Shaun would "give three shillings [. . .] for the conjugation to shadow [see] you kissing her from me leberally all over as if she was a crucifix" (FW: 465.24–26). Adaline Glasheen and most other *Wake* critics identify Dave with the artist Shem, an identification that is unambiguously supported in the notebooks: in the text Shaun calls Dave his "innerman," a name derived from "[g]⊏ inner man of Λ" (VI.B.9: 12; see FW: 462.16). But the Shem-figure that appears here in the text as well as in the notebooks is unmistakably a Shaunian emanation that resulted from "a sidesplitting nature" (FW: 454.08), creating a deliberate ambiguity between the essential selves of the protagonists.[64] This confusion perhaps originated from the introduction of a protagonist who was relatively new to *Work in Progress:* Λ⊏ or the brothers as two-in-one. A good number of notes used for the composition of "Dave the Dancekerl" come from notebooks in which this siglum features prominently, most specifically: "[g]Jean Jacques Λ⊏ / jeanjakes Λ⊏" (VI.B.8: 19). For this reason, Dave's characteristics in the early drafts could almost be mistaken for Shaun's, whereas the more explicit allusions to Shem in the final version were actually added at a later date, partly obfuscating the ambiguous characterization of Dave. Hence, in the early drafts Dave's attributes resemble Shaun's; for example, "he fell out of space" (FW: 462.31), and he is "draped in mufti" (FW: 462.32), that is, he wears plain clothes although he has the right to wear a uniform (McHugh).[65] His skull is shaved like "Nuntius' piedish!" (FW: 464.09); that is, he has been tonsured, and he is thus, like Shaun, a holy man, but Latin *nuntius* also means "messenger," which makes Dave a Hermes figure too, like Shaun.

Given these interconnections we can see that the intruding episode expanded the text, but it also constituted a departure, if not in form at least in content, from the surrounding narrative. The new direction that the episode brought to the text is concomitant with the kind of expansions that took place while Joyce was revising his typescript in early 1926. In the typescript, prepared in the fall of 1924, the plot is fully in place; the revisions Joyce now applied resulted for the first time in the kind of full-blown *Wakese* that is characteristic of the final text. He introduced puns and linguistic deviations that make any "original" meaning unrecognizable; for example, the tower clock strikes "agoodmantrue" instead of "atwelve," while "scotsmost" replaced "Irish" (BL 47483 f. 33; JJA 57: 167). Also, an increase in thematic doublings took place; for example, the text's "partisanship" is confused when "British ^[1]and Irish[1]^ objects [become] nonviewable" (BL 47483 f. 33; JJA 57: 167; FW: 403.23); before, the text only mentioned invisible British objects. On the whole, the text received a multilingual rather than Irish outlook; for example, Shaun's Irish words "Also, alack, allauna, aroon!" (*alanna* means "my child, my darling"; *aroon* means "my beloved") changed to "Allo, alass, aladdin, amobus!" (BL 47483 f. 35; JJA 57: 169).[66]

Yet these expansions do not imply that Joyce lost sight of the narrative coherence of his writing: a seemingly insignificant emendation responds meaningfully to the inclusion of "Dave the Dancekerl." Originally, in the second fair copy of chapters III.1–2, Joyce had introduced the following passage: "Something of an amusing nature must have occurred to westminstrel Jaunahaun. A grand big hearty laugh hopped out of Jauny at the bare thought" (BL 47482b fs. 54v–55; JJA 57: 110–11). The moment of parting is an occasion for merriment and laughter as Shaun foresees the happy times of his return and reunion with his sister. In the mixed fair copy that follows the typescript, to which the sketch was added, Joyce changed the passage to "Something of an sidesplitting [*sic*] nature must have occurred" (BL 47483 f. 148; JJA 57: 238).[67] With this change Joyce tried to make Dave's appearance in the narrative more functional but without sacrificing the overall intrusive effect, an effect that probably profiles for the first time in *Work in Progress* the unusual love-hate antagonism between the brothers. The sketch itself is literally a side splitting—but also a kind of random amusement, a sideshow—because it was inserted in the middle of Shaun's leave-taking speech. As such it performs a double function: it brings about Shaun's exit without his being fully gone, but as a tale about Dave told by Shaun it postpones his exit, for Dave never appears in the flesh; Shaun only invokes his coming.

Unlike "Dave the Dancekerl," the fable of "The Ondt and the Gracehoper" (probably begun in February 1928) interferes more radically with the narrative of Shaun's postal mission.[68] Obviating the growing incompatibility of the chapter halves, Joyce now paired Jaun's sexual innuendo in the sermon with the Gracehoper's "ungraceful overtures" (FW: 414.24) to the insect girls ("commence insects" [FW: 414.26–27] puns, naturally, on *incest*), but by the time Jaun delivers his warnings to his sister, Shem, in the guise of the lustful Gracehoper, will already have consummated his liaison with the girls. The most striking level of intrusion, however, is the change in the range of Shaun's attack: whereas the questions and answers in chapter III.1 turn around Shaun's dislike for Shem's writing, the fable extends the ad hominem attack on Shem's morality, resembling very much the diatribe of accusations in chapter I.7.

An equally radical expansion of the narrative comes with the fable's various philosophical tenets. From the fable's early drafts Joyce started weaving the names of philosophers and thinkers into the text obviously in mockery of the text's—and the Gracehoper's—obscene "joyicity" (FW: 414.23). The method is reminiscent of the Anna Livia chapter, where Joyce added more river names to make the narrative more fluid. It is a method that Joyce applied repeatedly (but one that is not always easy to recognize in the final version) throughout *Work in Progress.* Joyce used these genetic clusters, which form a structuring device somewhere in between Clive Hart's motifs and David Hayman's nodes, more or less like a trellis.[69] At least from a genetic point of view, the philosophers in "The Ondt and the Gracehoper" are thus a parody of Joyce's prospected use of Vico and Hegel in the "Mamalujo" sketch, where they functioned as the underlying principle that would tie the early historical sketches together (LI: 205). The names are here to give a more philosophical outlook to the fable.

As a companion piece to "The Mookse and the Gripes," the fable of "The Ondt and the Gracehoper" had its own specific philosophical intent in a literary rejoinder to Wyndham Lewis's rejection of time-oriented writers like Stein and Joyce in *Time and Western Man.* However, within the narrative of chapter I.6, "The Mookse and the Gripes," written in the summer of 1927, is a popularizing retelling of the "Talis" debate and Professor Loewy-Brueller's exposé (FW: 149.34–152.03).[70] The space-time controversy in "The Ondt and the Gracehoper" does not respond to an earlier question but seems to appear out of the blue in Shaun's question-answer session; the sister-girls themselves suddenly interrupt their interview for no apparent reason, adapting Shaun's own stopgap "So be it" to ask for a song, but Shaun would rather spin a philosophical tale.[71]

In spite of the interruption, however, Joyce intended the fable of "The Ondt and the Gracehoper" in Shaun's first watch to provide more unity to *Work in Progress* as a whole. The "Λ *doctus*" section with Professor Loewy-Brueller—itself an intrusion in the sequence of questions that comprises chapter I.6—was originally intended "as a ballast and the whole piece is to balance Λabcd" (SL: 327). When Joyce returned to revising the Shaun chapters, he probably felt that the pendant in Book I in turn needed a pendant (in all likelihood the "Mookse" was already composed as a way to compensate for the narrative's jarring voices, because Joyce felt that "Λ *doctus* is a bit husky beside the more melodious Shaun of the third part" [SL: 327]). But the upshot of the debate in either fable is different: the argument between the Mookse and the Gripes remains unresolved because of ALP's interruption, when she summons the children home; but even though the Ondt takes advantage of the Gracehoper's mistakes and wins the insect girls for him, the Gracehoper has the last word and checkmates the Ondt in the space-time debate: "*Your genus its worldwide, your spacest sublime! / But, Holy Saltmartin, why can't you beat time?*" (FW 419.07–8). The outcome of both fables has structural implications: whereas in "The Mookse and the Gripes" any resolution can lie only in the fusion of the brothers as /⊏, the Ondt's defeat in a chapter devoted to Shaun's postal/spatial mission underscores that time is indispensable.[72] Thus Joyce ensures through an intricate system of balancing and counterbalancing that Book III forms a counterpart to Book I at a time when this is no longer obvious in the narration and architecture of *Work in Progress.*

What has happened in the composition process, namely, is the introduction of another interlude, the Children's Games, a process that anchored Books I and III in their final position in *Finnegans Wake.* On 21 May 1926 Joyce wrote to Miss Weaver: "I have the book now fairly well planned out in my head. I am as yet uncertain whether I shall start on the twilight games of ⊏, Λ, and ⊣ which will follow immediately after Δ or on K's orisons, to follow Λd. But my mind is rather exhausted for the moment" (LI: 241). Conceptually, these episodes originated in the themes of Shaun d (children and dawn [TDJJ: 90]), but what Joyce had in mind here for the architecture of the entire work is reminiscent of a structural expansion of *Ulysses* that was never realized. In October 1920 Joyce had dreamed up an entr'acte to follow "Scylla & Charybdis," a dead middle point in Bloomsday that would have "absolutely no relation to what precedes or follows" and that would be balanced with a short opening "*matutine*" and closing "*nocturne*" (LI: 149). In *Finnegans Wake* the new episodes have a closer bearing on the rest of the narrative, but it is important to note that even though the episodes follow Shaun's fourth watch thematically, they precede the Shaun chapters to form the book's middle and end. (Five months later Joyce would also embark upon a prologue, chapter I.1; with the exception of Book IV, this nearly completed the broad and final outline of *Finnegans Wake.*) Notwithstanding the rapid growth of the middle part (in just a few weeks' time Joyce envisioned no less than "three or four episodes" between ALP and the Watches of Shaun [LI: 241]), its writing effectively separated Books I and III. With the completion of this architectural plan the Watches of Shaun now occupied their final position within *Finnegans Wake,* but, ironically, their primary structural function—a thematic counterpart for part I—seemed to have been obscured. Moreover, after the publication of the chapters in *transition,* Joyce would not return to chapters III.1–2, except for the incorporation of "The Ondt and the Gracehoper" in *Tales Told of Shem and Shaun* (1929), until he started preparations for the final printing of *Finnegans Wake* in the mid-1930s.

In 1928 the genesis of Shaun's journey—the gradual expansion of Shaun's role as postman from a simple traveler floating in a barrel on the Liffey tide to a mediator of spatial philosophy in "The Ondt and the Gracehoper"—seems to have arrived at its final halt. The concluding stages of this expansion began in March 1926, when Joyce started revising the first typescript (draft level 5) and added "Dave the Dancekerl" and some other, mainly motival additions; it was completed when chapters III.1 and III.2 (after their split had been realized) were published in *transition* 12 and 13 (March and June 1928) and "The Ondt and the Gracehoper" was added to the text. The passage from chapter III.1 that I quoted at the beginning of this essay, depicting Shaun's starward gaze and overbalancing in the first-draft version, now reads:

> And big hottempered husky pugiliser such as he was he all but broke down on the moorherhead, getting quite jerry over her, overpowered by himself with the love of the tearsilver that he twined through her hair for sure he was the soft slob of the world and as innocent and undesignful as the freshfallen calef. Still he laughed it off with a wipe at his pudgies and a gulp apologetic. Mind you, that he was in the dumpest of earnest orthough him jawr war hoo hleepy hor talk urthing hurther. Like that only he stopped short in looking up up up from his tide shackled wrists through the ghost of an ocean the wieds of pansiful heathvens of joepeter as they are telling not but were and will be, all told, scruting foreback into the fargoneahead, to feel out what age in years tropical, ecclesiastic, civil or sidereal he might find by the sirious pointstand of Charley's Wain (what betune the spheres sledding along the lacteal and the mansions of his blest turning on old times) his thumbs fell into his fists and, losing the harmonical balance of his ballbearing extremities, by the holy kettle like a flask of lightning over he careened (O the sons of the fathers!) by the mightyfine weight of his barrel (all that prevented the happering of who if not the asterisks betwink themselves shall ever?) and, as the wisest postlude he could playact collaspsed in ensemble and rolled buoyantly backwards in less than a twinkling via Rattigan's corner out of farther earshot wit his highly curious mode of slipashod motion, surefoot, sorefoot, slickfoot, slackfoot, and by Killesther's lapes and falls, with corks staves and treeleaves and more bubbles to his keelrow a fairish and easy way enough as the town cow cries behind times in the direction of Mac Auliffe's, the crecethouse, before he was really uprighted ere in a dip of the downs he miraculously disappaled and vanesshed from circulatio. Ah, mean![73]

The passage is almost that of the final version in *Finnegans Wake*. From now on the genetic history of chapters III.1–2 is merely one of further accretion. Joyce kept expanding his text, but ultimately the additions barely altered the structural and conceptual outlook of the chapters. As if Joyce had finished the "exploratory work," A. Walton Litz suggests, he now labored at perfecting his "final style."[74] These additions and expansions are nonetheless significant for the final meaning of *Finnegans Wake,* particularly because Joyce's concerns were broader still than just style.[75] Publication of the chapters in *transition* may have concluded the third stage in the structural development of the first two watches of Shaun, but it marked the actual beginning of their "universalization" in *Work in Progress.*

Shaun's characterization has come a long way from a drunken postman who zigzags along the road to a "general omnibus character with a dash of railwaybrain" (FW: 444.02). Metaphorically, Shaun has come to represent travel, movement through space. He resembles a bus that does not appear to have a fixed route but also, underscoring his alleged contributions to the writing of ALP's Letter, a book "containing [. . .] several reprinted works by a single author or works of the same kind" (*OED,* s.v. "omnibus"). His "general omnibus character," then, takes away from the linearity of his backward journey to death/the past/the west. Significantly, Joyce added the phrase to his text at the same time he added one of the first explicit allusions to Vichian cyclicality: "The Vico road goes round and round to meet where ends begin" (VI.G.7: 6; FW: 452.21).[76] Quoting this same passage, Beckett even made the suggestion, pregnant with meaning, that Vico's (or Joyce's?) "insistence on the inevitable character of every progression" could actually work retrogressively.[77] Taking it all together, we can see an intricate network of connections emerging that blend together Shaun's expanded spatial function with HCE's spatial capacity as prime mover, for Earwicker too is identified as omnibus (FW: 088.01, 099.10; Latin *omnibus,* "for all," "for everybody"); particularly in one section, which resonates the opening passage "In the Heart of the Hibernian Metropolis" of "Aeolus," Earwicker's "mausoleum" emanates into or "faulter[s] along the tramestrack by Brahm and Anton Hermes!" (FW: 081.06–7), combining father and son.[78] This blending of spatial attributes emphasizes in a different way the centrality of Shaun as mediator in the *Wake,* especially because of the Vichian elements that clinch the connection.

As I have tried to show, it is necessary to see the thematic development of chapters III.1–2 in conjunction with the chapters' structural development. Particularly, the changes in the chapters' structural significance have caused certain themes—such as the idea that Shaun's travels consist of a *via crucis*—to be left unfulfilled in whole or in part. Yet Shaun's development as a postman can be readily traced from the notebooks to the drafts. During the establishment of the plot, Joyce was especially concerned with the thematic unity of *Work in Progress* on a specific level. In this respect, chapters III.1–2 clearly rely on a continuation of the Tristan and Isolde theme. After the plot was in place chapters III.1–2 were subject to Joyce's typical method of accretion, adding layer upon layer of material of various themes and motifs. On the one hand, this method seems intended to explode any kind of unity in the chapters, especially when the "Dave the Dancekerl" section deliberately confuses notions of characterization or when "The Ondt and the Gracehoper" interrupts the narrative flow. On the other hand, the "Dave" episode and particularly the later fable about the notions of space and time are intended to provide a larger, more philosophical unity to the chapters.

On a synchronic plane of reading Shaun may have become a universal figure, a "general omnibus character" (FW: 444.02), but his active contribution to the events in *Finnegans Wake* seems to have dwindled. As postman delivering Anna Livia's letter he was an active force in driving the events of the plot; in the guise of Hermes he mediated a good deal of the *Wake*'s narrative voice. However, such acceptance of loss is erroneous. Whereas the contrapuntal role of Books I and III might not be evident anymore and other aspects—in fact, commonplaces of *Wake* criticism, such as Vico's ever-present mythology of recirculation, a language of the night that all too readily effaces linguistic, social, and historic identities, and Finnegan's usurpation as the book's universal archetype along with another unironic portrait of the artist in Shem the Penman—have ostensibly overshadowed the centrality of Shaun's role to the *Wake*, this metamorphosis does not mean that Shaun's structural and narrative significance has suddenly disappeared from the text. As I have described it, the centrality of Shaun's presence in the *Wake* has been displaced. His primary importance to the narrative simply lies buried underneath layer upon layer of meaningful material, apparently invisible but nonetheless recognizable, as long as readers do not forget that *Finnegans Wake* is the result of a long and laborious composition process. Any reading that does not take into account at least the broader tenets of the *Wake*'s diachronic structure does not do justice to Joyce's work, for *Finnegans Wake* is not a linear book, nor was it written that way.

Notes

I wish to thank Ingeborg Landuyt and Bill Cadbury for responding diligently to my interminable barrage of questions and queries during the writing of this essay. I am also immensely indebted to Luca Crispi for sharing so generously with me a small set of recently uncovered proofs for *transition* 12 and 13.

1. Joseph Campbell and Henry Morton Robinson, *A Skeleton Key to "Finnegans Wake"* (New York: Viking, 1961), 256.

2. Michael H. Begnal and Grace Eckley, *Narrator and Character in "Finnegans Wake"* (Lewisburg: Bucknell University Press, 1975), 76.

3. Ibid., 47.

4. Ibid., 114.

5. Andrew Treip neatly summarizes what several critics have noticed before him: "The passage from one book to the other is a moment of transition from E to Λ or from father to son; it is also a moment of transition from the penning and discovery to the subsequent posting and reading of the *Wakean* Letter; and it is probably a transition from the Irish past to the Irish present" ("Lost Histereve: Vichian Soundings and Reverberations in the Genesis of *Finnegans Wake* II.4," *JJQ* 32.3–4 [Spring–Summer 1995]: 641–57, 646). Clive Hart recognizes an "inverse relationship" between Books I and III (*Structure and Motif in "Finnegans Wake"* [London: Faber and Faber, 1962], 67, 251). A. Walton Litz, writing from a genetic point of view that is not much different from mine, suggests that Joyce soon abandoned his two-part design because work on the watches of Shaun had advanced so far as to interfere with the book's structure as a whole ("The Making of *Finnegans Wake*," *A James Joyce Miscellany*, 2nd series, ed. Marvin Magalaner [Carbondale: Southern Illinois University Press, 1959], 209–23, 211).

6. I do not use these novelistic terms like *narrative* and *structure* lightly, and I do not think of the *Wake*'s pretexts in terms of a simplified, purified origin either. My point is that a reading into the history of the composition process can *circumvent* (but not necessarily *solve*) some of the critical despair associated with the *Wake*'s notorious unreadability in offering some sort of foothold that readers often seem to crave. The early stages of Joyce's work show a descriptive sequence of events—no more complex than the later chapters in *Ulysses*—that years of accretion have obscured. Yet none of these elements has disappeared from the text (the information has simply been buried too deep), and they continue to be part of the semiotics of the text. The *Wake*'s drafts, metaphorically speaking, are the unconscious of the text; along with Joyce's notebooks they reveal insights into themes, structures, and character development that a synchronic reading cannot yield.

7. Extradraft notes for this segment contain Norwegian phrases, or "Sayings of HCE" (BL 47471b f. 42; JJA 57: 5).

8. The JJA editors speculate that the episode—which they named "The Delivery of the Letter"—was intended to precede the "Revered Letter," but the evidence

possibly indicates that Shaun's delivery precedes the "Letter," while Earwicker's response follows it. First, Earwicker's response follows in the notebook the end of a protoversion of ALP's Letter: "^[1]Her mark and seal[1]^ Dame Lara Prudence Earwicker (valued wife of——)" (BL 47471b f. 30; JJA 57: 4). Second, in a letter to Miss Weaver Joyce mentions "three further passages" that are to precede the "Letter" ("a description of Shem-Ham-Cain-Esau etc and his penmanship, Anna Livia's visits and collaboration and delivery of the memorial by Shawn the post"), but he makes no reference to HCE (LI: 208).

9. All draft quotations in this essay have been edited to produce a simplified reading version, unless the argument makes a genetic representation necessary.

10. In the "Revered Letter" the double authorship is introduced by an abandoned phrase that establishes Shem as author of the Letter: "Alone one cannot have [misread] it for the hand was fair. We can suppose it that of Shem the penman, a village soak, who when snugly liquid limed" (BL 47471b f. 31; JJA 46: 255).

11. This description of the handwriting, partly derived from Edward Sullivan's introduction to *The Book of Kells,* was added to the text around the same time as the composition of the "Delivery," probably January 1924 (BL 47473 f. 26; JJA 46: 318).

12. Léon Metchnikoff, *La Civilisation et les grands fleuves historiques* (Paris: Hachette, 1889), 8. See Ingeborg Landuyt and Geert Lernout, "Joyce's Sources: *Les grands fleuves historiques,*" *JSA* 6 (1995): 99–138; see also *Buffalo VI.B.1,* 54.

13. Nonetheless, the delivery theme still lingers in the first draft, where Shaun is remembered as "you, who so often delivered us tidings of great joy [. . .] into our never too late to post box" (BL 47482b f. 8; JJA 57: 17). The earliest allusion to an actual delivery of the Letter in the chapter was only added between 1933 and 1936 on *transition* pages in preparation for the final text for the printer: "And the topnoted delivery you'd expected be me invoice!" (BL 47486a f. 85v; JJA 61: 32); Shaun delivers here simultaneously a letter and a song.

14. In the *Wake* a close association exists between Shaun and the fourth of the Old Men. Johnny MacDougal is a "hiker" (FW: 475.30), while Shaun is "Johnny the quickest," later "Johnny Walker" (BL 47482b f. 33; JJA 57: 67; BL 47482b f. 61; JJA 57: 123; FW: 473.03–4; see Adaline Glasheen, *Third Census of "Finnegans Wake"* [Berkeley: University of California Press, 1977], 178).

15. Glasheen 1977, lviii, 18.

16. For example, "Had you a man named / O'Neill with you // that night / I haven't seen him for / 6 month[s] / Did you change a PO / for him that day / What has that to do / with it? / Was he in yr home then / You know they follow / O'Neill / Well. I saw him / coming into house / Do you do his washing" (VI.B.1: 112–13); "[r]Q Did you? / A I wd not like to swear[r]" (VI.B.1: 121; FW: 421.28); "what time of night / begin the shouting / [r]Well, no[r] [FW: 411.26–27] / What distance cd that be / [r]I asked you did you —[r] [FW: 409.08] / he thought to — / Was he able to speak / he — — to shout / [r]Now you suggest[r] / to the man / [r]None whatsoever[r] [FW: 413.32]" (VI.B.1: 146).

17. When he copied this sentence in the second draft Joyce changed it to "Alas, Shaun said, staring upon the *native soil* he loved, how all too unworthy am I for such eminence" (BL 47482b f. 10; JJA 57: 21, emphasis mine). While the emendation attempts to bring out Shaun's connection with his native land, it also identifies Ireland as a young woman.

18. James S. Atherton, *The Books at the Wake* (Carbondale: Southern Illinois University Press, 1959), 99, 159; James S. Atherton, "Shaun A," *A Conceptual Guide to "Finnegans Wake,"* ed. Michael H. Begnal and Fritz Senn (University Park: Pennsylvania State University Press, 1974), 149–72, 152. Atherton also mentions the character of Shaun Buie McGaveran in William Carleton's *Tales and Stories of the Irish Peasantry* as a possible model for Shaun (1959, 59), but neither Boucicault nor Carleton has been conclusively identified as used by Joyce.

19. Conceivably, this underlying theme might be another reason to identify Issy as Shaun's questioner.

20. "What is it? / Chorus of / Females — Love!" is not an evident allusion to the legendary couple, but it may become so when it is considered in light of one of Joyce's intertexts for *Tristan and Isolde*, Édouard Schuré's *Woman: The Inspirer* on the relationship between Mathilde Wesendonck and Richard Wagner and the lovers' discourse that he borrows from this source. The following entry, for instance, might again be applicable to the situation in Shaun the Post: "love born beneath / the shade of / friendship" (VI.B.3: 67); Joyce took his note from this passage: "Now began the delightful innocent period of gift-making, when love, born beneath the shade of friendship—like the modest rose tree under the bushy linden,—discloses so many secret intentions and delightful allusions. She sends flowers, a lamp, a silver" (Édouard Schuré, *Woman as Inspirer*, trans. Fred Rothwell [London: Power Book Co., 1918], 11; see also Geert Lernout, "Woman the Inspirer: Wagner in VI.B.3," *AFWC* 6 [1990–91]: 1–11; *Buffalo VI.B.3*, 7–8, 59–60).

21. The extradraft material, which Joyce wrote on the verso of the first draft of the "Roderick O'Conor" (BL 47480 f. 267v; JJA 56: 6–7), is now the second half of the first-draft version of "Tristan and Isolde" at the NLI.

22. Hugh Staples, "Growing up Absurd in Dublin," Begnal and Senn 1974, 173–200, 174.

23. Clive Hart believes that one of the frames of reference for chapter I.7 "is a full set of allusions to the fourteen stations of the cross" that "until now does not seem to have been noticed" (1962, 172). If this is true, we have a clear repetition of events, but Hart does not provide any further evidence. Roland McHugh in his *Annotations* has not picked up on his suggestion either.

24. This entry is reminiscent of Bloom's observation in "Calypso": "Travel round in front of the sun, steal a day's march on him. Keep it up for ever never grow a day older technically" (U: 4.84–86).

25. These later entries, from which the Shaun siglum is absent, appear in the notebook among entries concerning ALP and the Liffey flow: "°Δ run in the wash°

[FW: 208.14] / thinking retrograde / reactionary / travelling back / °catch it a 2nd time" (VI.B.16: 25). The connection between river and history is one that Joyce first explored when he read Metchnikoff's *La Civilisation et les grands fleuves historiques* (see Landuyt and Lernout 1995, 108).

26. Hart 1962, 115.

27. See Van Mierlo, "Question of Histry!?" *Geni,* 43–64, 60, and Treip 1995, 648–50 on the business of present/absent and its Hegelian undertones.

28. Hart 1962, 118.

29. Notebook VI.B.16 contains the telling association "down under (Austr) / un Irish" (VI.B.16: 8); another cluster of notes also mentions Australia but does not identify it uniquely as Shaun's destination: "where is he / Λ walks back / [. . .] out of touch / [. . .] from Toronto in / Australia" (VI.B.16: 61–62).

30. On an unconsciousness level of the text, as it were, the West is linked with death, because Joyce changed his note and source text from "When he died, he looked for me in the sky" (Sigmund Freud, "From the History of an Infantile Neurosis" ["The Wolf Man"], *Collected Papers,* vol. 3, trans. Alix and James Strachey [London: Hogarth Press, 1925], 471–605, 566; VI.B.9: 39; VI.B.19: 90) to "Look for me always at my west" (FW: 457.20). For a more extensive discussion of Freud's case histories in these chapters see Wim Van Mierlo, "The Freudful Couchmare Revisited: Contextualizing Joyce and the New Psychology," *JSA* 8 (1997): 115–53. See also Daniel Ferrer's essay in this volume.

31. No source has been identified for Joyce's note, "ʳI bless you all to the west / SP to Kerryboys" (VI.B.2: 7), but see Dean Kinane, *St. Patrick: His Life, His Heroic Virtues, His Labours, and the Fruits of His Labours* (London: R. & T. Washbourne, Ltd., 1888), 146; and *The Catholic Encyclopedia,* 1913, s.v. "St. Patrick."

32. Richard Sharpe, introduction, Adomnán of Iona, *Life of St. Columba,* trans. Richard Sharpe (Harmondsworth: Penguin, 1995), 12.

33. Raymond O'Flynn, "St. Columcille (521–597)," *The Irish Way,* ed. F. J. Sheed (London: Sheed and Ward, 1932), 52; see also Sharpe 1995, 15.

34. On Shaun, Saints Brendan and Columkille, exile, and particularly a discussion of Joyce's source see Wim Van Mierlo and Ingeborg Landuyt, "Catholicism, Nationalism, and Exile: *The Irish Way* in VI.B.34," *Genetic Joyce Studies* 2 (online).

35. Louis O. Mink, *A "Finnegans Wake" Gazetteer* (Bloomington: Indiana University Press, 1978), 350, 283.

36. Ibid., 377.

37. The first draft read "10 furlong mile" (BL 47482b f. 8; JJA 57: 17), but it was changed to "nine furlong mile" in the following draft.

38. To explain this contradiction between Joyce's description of the barrel "rolling down the river" and Shaun's westerly movement in the narrative of *Finnegans Wake* Clive Hart infers a double movement induced by "an optical illusion"—Shaun only "*appears* to be floating eastward down-river . . . but in fact travels westward" because, he generalizes, "progress in one direction generates a reaction

in the other" (1962, 115, emphasis mine). Supporting his claim, Hart quotes—out of context—an earlier passage from the *Wake:* "most easterly (but all goes west!)." The passage, however, reads in full: "Butt's, most easterly (but all goes west!) of blackpool bridges" (FW: 085.15). Butt bridge is the last bridge, nearest to the mouth of the Liffey (Mink 1978, 246); in other words, "easterly" does not indicate movement but a location, whereas Shaun—and the whole of the *Wake*'s historical narrative, for that matter—"wurm[s] along gradually [. . .] backtowards motherwaters so many miles from bank and Dublin stone" (FW: 084.31–32).

39. Even in this early context the events are not merely repeated, for the "Delivery" sketch suggests that one incident always triggers other incidents of a similar nature: "just as it has been more than once pointed out, the demise of one parish priest or curator is sure to be followed sooner or later by other parochial demises of an allied nature" (BL 47471b f. 35v; JJA 57: 2). This is a variant of the *ewige Wiederkehr*, the "seim anew" (FW: 215.22); but here the emphasis is not on repetition, but, almost fatalistically, on what triggered history. The concern of early *Work in Progress* with origins is in this case portrayed as moving inevitably towards some *vague* goal.

40. Apparently in preparation of Shaun the Post, Joyce compiled in reverse a list of episodes he had executed so far: "[r]Anna Livia / Cain / Shem (when hvorledes) / Collaboration on MS[r] / Hen finds Boston Letter / Δ writes petition / ? is ! / the Kings / the Attack / the coffin / Batter at Gate / plebiscite / train dialogue / Sunday evg Bognor (Cad) / Hosty's ballad / lodging house / lodginhouse [*sic*] / races / sodality / cad in park / Sin / ! riches / origin of name" (VI.B.1: 163; note that the list comes *after* the conceptual notes discussed above). For two opposed but illuminating interpretations of the list see TDJJ: 58–71, and David Hayman, "To Make a List: Two Preparatory Puzzles on the Threshold of Book III," *Probes,* 255–79, 270–78.

41. We can be relatively certain that in his Letter of 15 March, despite his mentioning the "Letter" sketch, Joyce referred to the first draft of chapters III.1–2 (composed in March 1924), not the "Delivery of the Letter" (probably December 1923–January 1924). The "Delivery" was unmistakably drafted in conjunction with the "Letter," whereas Shaun the Post follows the drafting of ALP, which was finished on 7 March (see unpublished letter to Harriet Shaw Weaver, BL 57347 f. 136, and LIII: 90).

42. There is no indication whatsoever as to what this unwritten first part was to entail; perhaps we can speculate that it somehow involved the abandoned sketches written in early 1923, "Roderick O'Conor," "Tristan and Isolde," "St Kevin," and "St Patrick."

43. Rose suggests that the drafting of chapter III.3, begun in November 1924 around the time of Joyce's Letter, comprises the manifest solution to Joyce's problem of fusing the book (TDJJ: 77), but since this is a new chapter, it cannot be one of the "tunnelling parties." Chapter III.3 is rather a result of the partition that

gave way, meaning that the solution somehow involves the conceptual material on Saint Patrick, Tristan and Isolde, and the entire Breton connection that Joyce gathered during his vacation in the summer of 1924. One significant note reads: "licorsi [*sic*] in T and ⊥ itself" (VI.C.5: 21). Oddly, Joyce's solution did not affect chapters III.1–2 in any directly recognizable way; the third fair copy, dating from late 1924, has only been moderately revised.

44. William York Tindall, *A Reader's Guide to "Finnegans Wake"* (New York: Farrar, Straus and Giroux, 1969), 237–39; Atherton 1974, 155; see also Ingeborg Landuyt, "Words in Distress: A Genetic Investigation into James Joyce's Early 'Work in Progress,'" Ph.D. dissertation, Universitaire Instelling Antwerpen, 1999.

45. In Joyce's mind tiny, unobtrusive textual elements often carry symbolic and structural importance. To Anna Livia Plurabelle Joyce added river names to make the chapter more fluid; in "Mamalujo," he inserted fourfold patterns to suggest through structured repetition a concurrence of historical events (see Van Mierlo 1999 and also my discussion below on the "four degrees" in Book III).

46. Landuyt 1999, 168–69.

47. The passage in which Biddy "rounded up lost histereve" (FW: 214.01) originally read "rounded up last Fridayweek" (BL 47474 f. 182; JJA 48: 132). The "Anno Domini" poem that closes chapter II.4 has "*It was of a wet good Friday too she was ironing and, as I'm given now to understand, she was always mad gone on me*" (FW: 399.24–27).

48. According to *The Catholic Encyclopedia,* the *via crucis* did not become widespread until the end of the seventeenth century; in 1742 Pope Benedict XIV encouraged all priests to adorn their church with the stations (s.v. "Way of the Cross"). Is this perhaps Shaun's "Benedictine errand" (FW: 452.17)?

49. "ʳposte restanteʳ / — haste" (VI.B.16: 19) is used to describe Shaun, "propped up, restant, against a slumbering warden of the peace, one comestabulish Sigurdson, who had fallen on sleep at the curing station" (BL 47482b f. 26; JJA 57: 53).

50. Perhaps Izzy's gift contains another remote connection with the *via crucis,* for indulgences were attached to every station (to the accompanying crucifix, not to the pictorial scene), although priests were prohibited from disclosing the exact number of indulgences that could be gained (*The Catholic Encyclopedia,* 1913, s.v. "Way of the Cross").

51. Atherton 1974, 156; McHugh.

52. Victor Branford, *St. Columba: A Study of Social Inheritance and Spiritual Development* (Chelsea: Patrick Geddes, 1913), 54. To my mind, the pastoral is an important aspect of the various historical layers of *Finnegans Wake.* On several occasions Joyce's book evinces a yearning for a lost state of purity that is most clearly expressed in Anna Livia's final monologue (and her emotional plea to "mememormee!" [FW: 628.14]) or in the setting of the entire narration: Chapelizod, next to the Edenic Phoenix Park, functions as a pastoral environment, especially in chapter I.2 and the original sketch of "Here Comes Everybody" but also,

for instance, in Joyce's use of Sheridan Le Fanu's nostalgic romance *The House by the Churchyard* throughout the *Wake.*

53. Branford 1913, 63.

54. Ibid., 34.

55. Ibid., 35.

56. Ibid., 56.

57. Stefan Czarnowski, *Le Culte des héros et ses conditions sociales: Saint Patrick, héros national de l'Irlande* (Paris: Librairie Félix Alcan, 1919), xlv.

58. Samuel Beckett, "Dante . . . Bruno. Vico . . . Joyce," *Our Exagmination Round His Factification for Incamination of Work in Progress,* Samuel Beckett et al. (New York: New Directions, 1962), 1–22, 21.

59. The origin of the watches has not been satisfactorily explained. David Hayman suggests that the watches correspond to the four watches of Buddha (FDV: 220 n.), which is highly unlikely; Atherton suggests Macrobius's *Saturnalia* as a possible source (1974, 250; see also R. J. Schork, *Latin and Roman Culture in Joyce* [Gainesville: University Press of Florida, 1997], 238), but no evidence exists to corroborate either of these assertions.

60. See Ingeborg Landuyt, "Shaun and His Post: *La Poste et les moyens de communication* in VI.B.16," *Papers on Joyce* 3 (1997): 21–48. Landuyt identified Eugène Gallois, *La Poste et les moyens de communication des peuples à travers les siècles: messageries, chemins de fer, télégraphes, téléphones* (1894) as the source for some of these notebook entries. See also Wim Van Mierlo, "Traffic in Transit: Some Spatio-Temporal Elements of *Finnegans Wake,*" *"Finnegans Wake": "teems of times,"* ed. Andrew Treip (Amsterdam: Rodopi, 1994), 107–17, 107–12; and Schork 1997, 251–52.

61. An earlier trace appears between August and late November 1924: "[g]poppy Λb" (VI.B.14: 206); because this is an isolated case, however, it does not count as evidence to support the idea that Joyce was already conceptualizing the four watches. The entry, rather, is associated with Oscar Wilde, and it was used in chapter III.3 in a context replete with allusions to Wilde (FW: 476.20).

62. In the duplicate set of first proofs for *transition* 12 and 13 Joyce indicated with an asterisk in the margin and a pencil line through "Jaunty Jaun as I was shortly before that made aware" where the text should be divided (BL 47483 f. 68; JJA 57: 289). Perhaps reasons of space eventually effected the physical separation of chapters III.1 and 2, for the chapters combined would have comprised forty-seven pages, about double the size of most other chapters from "Work in Progress" that were published in *transition.*

63. See draft codes III§1A.6/1D.6//2A.6/2B.4/2C.6 and III§3A.5/3B.5.

64. Similarly, Michael Begnal asserts that Dave the Dancekerl is "a surrogate of Shem that Shaun *creates*" (Begnal and Eckley 1975, 50, emphasis mine), but other critics, in fact, do not recognize Shem's presence at all. John Gordon sees Dave as an "exercise in self-induced schizophrenia," resulting in a hypersexualized

double (*"Finnegans Wake": A Plot Summary* [Syracuse: Syracuse University Press, 1986], 233).

65. A mufti is also an official interpreter of Muslim law; in the notebooks this personality is in the first place associated with HCE: "mufti = lord chancellor" (VI.A: 742), "[b]mufti !" (VI.B.12: 12). One entry associates mufti with Shem: "⊏ mufti / (public scribe)" (VI.B.8: 18).

66. Apart from an allusion to the *Thousand and One Nights,* the only language present is Latin in the declination of *amo, amas,* and so on (McHugh) and in the word *amoeba,* but the phrase also "sounds" like any of the artificial international languages with which Joyce would be preoccupied in the late 1930s. Coincidentally, in the notebooks this bit of artificial language is also connected with the doubling of Shaun as /⊏: "[g]Allo, alass, amarum, amobus, /⊏" (VI.B.8: 150). The phrase is also reminiscent of a nonsense lyric by John O'Keeffe that appeared in his play *The Agreeable Surprise* (1781): "Amo, amas, / I love a lass, / As cedar tall and slender; / Sweet cowslip's face / Is her nominative case, / And she's of the feminine gender. / Horum quoruom, / Sunt divorum, / Harum, scarum, Divo, / Tag rag, merry derry, periwig and bobtail / His, hoc, harum, genitivo."

67. No textual witness is present for this change to support authorial intervention, but note the ungrammatical "an sidesplitting," suggesting that Joyce made the change on the spot during copying.

68. The initial drafting of the "Ondt" coincided with revisions on the proofs for *transition* 12 and 13. Moreover, the fable is only one of several larger additions to the first watch; there are also the "white fogbow spans" episode, a new opening passage for III.1 (FW: 403.06–17) that puts down a pastoral setting referring to Vergil's *Eclogues* (Atherton 1974, 288), Shaun's own version of the Letter about the "defunct Mrs Sanders" (FW: 413.03–26), and the famous list of incorrect addresses (FW: 420.09–421.14).

69. Hart's motifs are "a mass of cross-correspondences" (1962, 157) that exist only in the synchronic text. Hayman's nodes, like Hart's motifs, derive from "narrative sequences," but they exist simultaneously in the synchronic and diachronic text, and they have the capacity to act as structuring devices (WiT: 37). The genetic clusters I have in mind here, however, only exist in one uniquely circumscribed segment or chapter of Joyce's text.

70. Laurent Milesi, "Killing Lewis with Einstein: 'Secting Time' in *Finnegans Wake,*" Treip 1994, 9–20, 13.

71. Gordon suggests that, like "The Mookse and the Gripes," Joyce used "The Ondt and the Gracehoper" to clarify a preceding point in the narrative that was left deliberately obscure (1986, 224). That is not the case, however. The question and answer that give Gordon so much trouble (FW: 413.27–414.01) are extremely circumlocutory as a result of textual accretion, but they are not quite incomprehensible: in the first draft the sisters want to know the history ("biography") of Shaun's uniform; Shaun replies that he has given away his uniform among the

poor evicted tenants and therefore he is now clothed in one of Guinness's registered barrels (BL 47482b f. 5; JJA 57: 11). The confusion starts in subsequent additions to the drafts as Shaun feels pressed to explain this unusual state of affairs more clearly and, like Earwicker, talks himself into trouble: "What I say is and I am no fool, permit me to tell you:" (BL 47482b f. 23; JJA 57: 47); the colon, which disappears from the text in later drafts, would suggest inadvertently that there is more to the story of Shaun's uniform or his charitable act (the allusion, of course, is to Saint Martin, who donated half his cloak to a beggar). One possibility is that the rabble cheated him out of his possessions (in the fourth draft "fool" is replaced by "greenhorn" [BL 47482b f. 41; JJA 57: 83], a simpleton who is easily fooled or cheated out of money) or that he pawned it for a drink (in the sixth draft Shaun explains that he had not "spent it. It went" [BL 47483 f. 38; JJA 57: 172]). Thus inadvertent self-incriminations pile up, but the ensuing fable in no way elucidates or supplements the unfortunate story about Shaun's uniform.

72. Milesi 1994, 18–19.

73. James Joyce, "Continuation of a Work in Progress," *transition*, no. 12 (March 1928): 7–27, 25–26.

74. Litz 1959, 217.

75. Litz gives a more extensive overview of the genesis of these early and late stages in the drafting of Book III (*The Art of James Joyce* [London: Oxford University Press, 1961], 76–100). Yet he rather narrowly appoints the turning point between exploration and elaboration to 1926–27 (76, 88; see also Litz 1959, 217).

76. In the final text "ends" becomes "terms." The reference to Vico was added on the duplicates of the third set of proofs for *transition* 13 (JJA draft code 2A.10'/2B.8'/2C.10', dated May–June 1928) together with some Egyptian allusions. This new cluster is in itself an echo of an earlier allusion to Vico in "The Ondt and the Gracehoper," where his name appears among material from *The Book of the Dead* (FW: 417.06).

77. Beckett 1962, 8.

78. Van Mierlo 1994, 116–17.

The Fourfold Root of Yawn's Unreason

Chapter III.3

JEAN-MICHEL RABATÉ

And the etymology of gas? Could it be the same word as chaos? Hardly. Chaos was yawn.

—SAMUEL BECKETT, *Murphy*

The idea of "genetic" approaches to chapters of *Finnegans Wake* is bound to promise more than it can hold: what is often tantalizingly proffered is the disclosure of new meanings, of deeper and more thorough annotations, even as a revolutionary interpretative horizon bridging the gap between original hermeneutic strategies and an array of verifiable empirical and textual data, whereas what is really given is a little more "sordid," or perhaps I should say "sordomutic" (FW: 117.14). Sordid, because in the end we only get another story, for the new "understanding" sends us back to that useful but predictable reminder: "There are sordidly tales within tales, you clearly understand that?" (FW: 522.05–6). However, since the story provided also aims at being an account of the process of Joyce's writing, it will try to reach the roots of this writing, roots to be extracted in Schopenhauerian fashion through a fourfold method of systematic investigation. Its unfolding may not so radically revise what we know or think we know about the chapter but will I hope throw a different light on it, follow its rhizomatic ramifications or nodalities (to use David Hayman's term) in all their intertwined interbranchings. Hence the possibility of a glimpse into not just "woman't seeleib" (FW: 505.08)—that is, the body and soul of woman—but also the "odd" process by which family, language, and culture are spliced together: "and her leaves [. . .] sinsinsinning since the night of time and each and all of their branches meeting and shaking twisty hands all over again in their new world through the germination of its gemination from Ond's outset till Odd's end" (FW: 505.09–13).

Another reason why it is important to provide such a genetic narrative in this context is that III.3 remains one of the most baffling chapters of the book, and, if not technically the longest, it is indeed one of the longer sections and obviously one of the most complex if not outright demented. In III.3 Joyce wishes to portray the densest climax of the dream just before dawn approaches in a recapitulation of all the themes in the book, a strategy that could easily be compared with that deployed in the "Circe" episode of *Ulysses*. Through their joint investigation of sleeping Shaun's psyche, the Four Masters unfold the deepest recesses and layers of fears, wishes, and perversion lurking in the closets of the Earwicker family. The narrative technique is relatively simple if not straightforward, since it consists in direct dialogue with questions and echolalic answers bandied back and forth between prying investigators and a mediumistic sleeper who incarnates all the other characters in turn. Yawn's answers are at times limited to stichomythic one-liners with the kind of rhyming effect that marks the washerwomen's dialogue in ALP. At times they give birth to wholly independent speeches through which other characters come alive and explain themselves fully, often merely apologizing by lying shamelessly or hiding further in the coils of their opaque dream images. Thus is Shaun's "dream monologue" replaced by his "drama parapolylogic" (FW: 474.05): this Bakhtinian polylogue will imply the use of a different reason, a methodical madness mimicking the irrationality of dreams while calling up the little cosmos of the pub and the Earwicker family with which we have by now become thoroughly acquainted.

Joyce's progression in the writing of this chapter can be divided into three strikingly delimited periods. A first moment of intense creation in the early twenties launches what David Hayman has called the "revise-and-complete method" (FDV: 12), a method best suited to a dramatic passage relying on a polyphony of voices. The first moment finds its culmination in the earlier version of the III.3 that *transition* published in 1929. (The proofs for this issue, number 15, are dated January 1929 by the printer.) The second moment begins soon after with a more individualizing approach beginning at the hinge of 1929–30, when Joyce makes the decision to split the chapter into two subsections, III.3A and III.3B. Then III.3B, otherwise known as "Haveth Childers Everywhere," was soon published as a separate book in June 1930. Each subsection followed a different logic before a later process of reunion began in 1936 with the preparation of a continuous text for the final version of the *Wake*. For this Joyce revisited once more all his notebooks and inserted the remaining items he culled under the heading of ∧c. I will provide some examples so as to describe in more detail each of these three "campaigns" of writing.

Nowhere can Joyce's creativity be better measured than in the first moments of the composition of III.3. A careful examination of the manuscripts gives the sense that Joyce's outburst of energy in November and December 1924 was unprecedented, at least since the writing of *Ulysses.* This explains why Hayman needed to reproduce the first drafts of the first pages in a different way from his usual synthetic manner in his *First-Draft Version.* Here is how he describes the technique: "Pausing at the end (or near the end) of each substructure or chapter to revise and recopy, the author would then append to the redrafted material a fresh passage which would in its turn be revised, recopied, and lengthened" (FDV: 12). This process led to a different style of transcription in order to reproduce the subtle overlays. Hayman decided to follow the chapter "through two or three drafts, repeating each time the material which the author repeats" (FDV: 228 n. 1). To understand how this works, let us examine the opening of the earliest version of the first paragraph:

> Lowly, longly, a wail went forth. Pure Yawn lay low. <I^O^>n the mead of the hillock he lay, the brief wallet by his side, one hand still loosely on his staff of citron ~~wood~~ ^^{1}briar^{1}^. Distressfully (but how successfully!) he waited, his golden locks downflowing, his lashful lids at closing time, and out of his sidewaysopen mouth the breath of him, as sweet as any golden syrup could buy. Yawn in a semiswoon was wailing. And, O, his sweetness! O the dulcitude! As though you were to go and push a pin into hinterplush of a chubby ~~angelic~~ ^^{1}angelboy^{1}^. (BL 47482b f. 62, first layer; JJA 58: 3; FDV: 228)

The text, whose style hesitates between sentimental comedy and the parody of Victorian clichés similar to the style deployed with Gerty MacDowell in "Nausicaa," takes up the upper half of one page where it is immediately peppered with interlinear and marginal additions that double its size. Subsequently, Joyce rewrites the paragraph in the bottom half of the page, beginning with a number 1 that was probably added at a later stage before spilling over to the left-hand side but because of the numerous previous jottings once more in the bottom part only. Only then the Four arrive and are identified in very helpful parentheses that allow one to distinguish the voices of Marcus Lyons, Matthew Gregory, Luke Tarpey, and Johnny MacDougall. I'll just quote the first version: "He is giving, the wee lad (Mw). Y has lived" (BL 47482b f. 63; JJA 58: 5; FDV: 229). Or again:

> Why so? (Luke)
> Is he sick or what? (Mk)
> Yes. Listen. (Mw)
> Why so? Speak up, some of ye. (Lu)
> The wind's from the wrong cut, so it is. (Jy) (BL 47482b f. 63; JJA 58: 5; FDV: 232)

The Four Masters (who are obviously also the four evangelists) come upon the scene followed by their ass, and they seem pleased with what they discover: "The present is a good time" (BL 47482b f. 64; JJA 58: 7; FDV: 232). In view of the general confusion that reigns among enunciators—for, despite McHugh's efforts in his revised *Annotations* to identify the Four, it turns out that most of the time we cannot help feeling lost, as Hayman shrewdly noted in a recent study—the global effect is that of a polyphony with the usual themes and functions determined by the set of the "sigla" but devoid of subjective characterization.[1]

A subsection beginning with "And as the buzzer of the light brigade" is numbered 2, and then a third section is identically numbered 3: "3) The four claymen clomb together to hold their sworn inquiry on him" (BL 47482b f. 65; JJA 58: 9; FDV: 232). A fourth section begins with "The proto was traipsing." It is interesting to note that even if the draft contains apparently more paragraphs, these numbered sections correspond to the first four paragraphs of the final version. They constitute a sort of general introduction leading to the dialogue itself. The numbers stop with 4, since the text is now engaged in direct dialogue.

A third draft of 3A follows hard upon this layer, again from November 1924. This time Joyce goes once more back to the beginning, progressing in the questions and answers until he reaches the climactic moment of the "Zinzin" motif. Then one discovers a curious and funny telephonic exchange in French that seems to have been omitted from the final version by mistake:

> —Now, we're getting it. Hello!
> —Zinzin.
> —Hello!
> —Abride!
> —Hello there ^1Ballymacaret!1^ Am I ~~throu~~ ^1thru,1^ ^1~~θ~~1^ ^2~~mess~~2^ ^3miss3^?
> —True!
> —Hello hello!

—Zin. *Comment, six heures?* Up zin. *Ecoute, Charles!* ^[1] *Godasses de qui?*[1]^ *Up zin. O la la! Ca c'est fort.* Up zin. Up zin. *Oui mon petit. Mais oui mon petit.* Petitzin. Petitzin. Petitzin. Petitzin.

—Now just permit me for a moment. Now hello there. Dingle beach. Now very good. Now about this massacre & so on. Do you remember ~~the~~ ^[1]that[1]^ night ~~after~~ ^[1]following[1]^ ^[1]the fair day[1]^. (BL 47482b f. 85; JJA 58: 45; FDV: 240)

It is a pity that this expansion of the Parisian argot at the telephone should have been lost in the myriad revisions; we had here a continuation of the exchange begun much earlier with "Epi alo, ecou, Batiste, tuvavnr dans Lptit boing going" (FW: 054.15–16) in which we heard an unidentified telephonist telling a certain Baptiste that he should go to a restaurant called curiously Le petit bon coin (instead of Au bon petit coin, which is more common).

A rapid overview of the following handwritten revision shows that Joyce stopped in his rewriting at "Hellohello! Ballymacaret! Am I thru, miss? / True!" (BL 47484a f. 15; JJA 58: 116), which left a small blank space; he then continued the dialogue on another page. This remains in the first typed version—the page numbered 13 ends with "—Hello! / Abride! / —Hellohello! Ballymacarett! Am I thru, miss? / True!" (BL 47484a f. 70; JJA 58: 152), followed by a space of approximately eight lines before the dialogue starts again with "Now. Just permit me a moment? Are you there? Hello? Sybil Head here" (BL 47484a f. 71; JJA 58: 153). In a subsequently revised version of the typescript Joyce sees the blank space and cannot resist an insertion; the first two lines are typed, the last one handwritten: "—Hellohello! Ballymacarett! Am I thru, miss? / True! / What is the ti . . . ?" (BL 47484a f. 102; JJA 58: 183). The following snatch of dialogue is also handwritten and inserted at the top of a typed sheet: "—Now just permit me a moment. Clear the line, priority call! Sybil!" (BL 47484a f. 103; JJA 58: 184).

When Joyce returned to the chapter more than a year later, in April–May 1926, he did not change that passage, and when it was set for *transition* 15 in April 1928 the gap followed by a capitalized "SILENCE" (Princeton f. 29; JJA 58: 289) survived all the successive versions with slightly different emphasis. The elision of the Beckettian scene in which a man is woken up at six o'clock by a certain Charles who insists upon talking about old shoes and finds this fantastic is due, like so many others, to the complexity of the manuscript and to its numerous voices that make skipping lines a statistical probability.

Let us note in this context how obsessed Joyce shows himself with technology, as if he had anticipated that Derrida would use his work to coin the phrase *être au téléphone* in an effort to update the Heideggerian "being for death," or *Sein zum Tode.*[2] Not only is this development anticipated but so also is the idea that in our new "wireless age" (FW: 489.36) the tangled telephone exchanges that loom so large in III.3 provide an image of a technological apparatus as living source and origin of presence: truth can no longer be identified with the little voice we hear in our heads when we talk to ourselves, or think, in other words: "with his I've Ivy under his tangue and the hohallo to his dullaphone, before there was a sound in the world? [. . .] If you hored him outerly as we harum lubberintly, from morning rice till nightmale, with his drums and bones and hums in drones your innereer'd heerdly heer he" (FW: 485.21–28). While Proust still rhapsodizes on the "ever-irritable handmaids of the Mystery, the umbrageous priestesses of the Invisible, the Young Ladies of the Telephone," Joyce invents both collective conference calls and the *trou téléphonique* with its anonymous numbers rallying lost souls that so delighted Marguerite Duras in *Le Navire Night.*[3]

This chapter is also one of the most replete with psychoanalytical allusions, and it looks as if this had been one of Joyce's earliest motivations. As early as the third draft of the beginning, that is, around November–December 1924, one finds the long section devoted to Coppinger and Cockshott as part of an investigation of "early bisexualism" (BL 47482b f. 102; JJA 58: 72). Yawn resents the forceful Freudian prying into his psyche and replies angrily: "To hell wi' ye and yer coprulation! Pelagiarist. Y'are obsexed, so y'ere" (BL 47482b f. 102; JJA 58: 72). A later version displaces this bisexualism to the young girls, but the passage is introduced by another question about Yawn's impartiality: "~~— Are you a~~ tonedeaf in our noses? You're a ^[1]third dregree[1]^ nice witness. Can you distinguish ~~right~~ ^[1]the sense[1]^ from ~~wrong~~ ^[1]the sound[1]^, we <p^b^>ray" (BL 47484a f. 49; JJA 58: 189). Around April 1926 this is then recopied in longhand and becomes "—You're a nice third degree witness. Do you think we are tonedeafs in our noses to boot? Can you not distinguish the sense, prain, from the sound, bray? Get yourself psychoanalysed. / —I can psoako-onaloose myself any time I want without your interferences" (BL 47484a f. 110; JJA 58: 230).

On the whole, the more technical jargon is inserted after the *transition* 15 proofs; in the same passage, then typed, one finds handwritten insertions dating from late 1928: "You have homosexual cathexis of empathy between narcissism of the expert and steatopygic invertedness" (BL 47484a

f. 222; JJA 58: 379), a good example of pure mumbo jumbo barely mimicking psychiatric diagnosis. In the same writing campaign a very dense sheet shows many additions to the Issy motive, like "Languishing hysteria? Le clou historique" (BL 47484a f. 283; JJA 58: 389). Joyce keeps adding and complicating the psychoanalytical theme, which could be described as having evolved from condescending rejection to parodic inflation and reaching finally a global semantic saturation that permeates all levels of meaning. This is why Joyce continues heaping allusions quite late, as when we see him adding an entry in longhand to a list of additions ("—Paterpatruum cum filiabus familiarum. Or" [BL 47486a f. 164; JJA 61: 237]), preceded by an *h* to be inserted at the beginning of a line in a *transition* page (BL 47486b f. 339; JJA 61: 452).

Incest, homosexuality, bisexuality, hysteria, narcissism—these are only some of the diseases ascribed to the Earwicker family via Yawn. But this is slippery ground, and we should not get carried away into new theoretical or rhetorical issues, at least not before pursuing the genetic rationale for the chapter I had so boldly promised.

This genetic pattern can be followed if we try to understand why Joyce decided to divide a compact text with a clear dramatic structure into two different entities. There again, chance may have had a role to play: without Henry Babou and Jack Kahane's offer to do a separate book publication (JJII: 628) Joyce might not have taken the second half of an already published *transition* chapter as the point of departure for *Haveth Childers Everywhere.* But a deeper divisive logic seems to be at work and is quite visible in the sequence of drafts.

From the start, the speech beginning "Sir to you! I am known throughout the world as a cleanliving man"—a speech obviously attributed to Earwicker, so far chased with great zeal by the Four throughout the meanders of the family's psyche—is part and parcel of the general interrogation. It comes as a reply to "—I want to hear the old lad himself. Hey, there, Bohermore! Are you old Pradamite? Kithogue?" (BL 47482b f. 90; JJA 58: 55). However, after a few revisions we reach the page numbered 114, on which "Sir to you" begins the whole sheet (BL 47482b f. 114; JJA 58: 95). This may be due simply to chance, since the previous page, numbered 113, ended at the bottom with "Truly" (BL 47482b f. 113; JJA 58: 85). A curious coincidence seems to force "true" or "truly" to conclude each section or development. This seems to be confirmed when we realize that in the next installment, a longhand fair copy of the whole chapter, a break has been inserted there. We see first "—That's enough. I mean to op the top of this. And will too. The governor general himself no less. Here, come, evildoer" (BL 47484a f. 25; JJA 58: 126), which has a generous blank space at the bottom of the page, while the next page begins with "—Sir, to you. I am bubub brought up under a camel act of a dynasty long since out of print" (BL 47484a f. 26; JJA 58: 127).

The reader who could have concluded that this was the seed of the bifurcation in the chapter would be disappointed by the next stage: the typescript for *transition* 15 shows no such break or gap; one goes very smoothly from "Here, come, evildoer" to "—Sir to you" (BL 47484a f. 80; JJA 58: 162) or from the subtly different "Ho, call evildoer! Doff!" to an identical "Sir, to you" (BL 47484a f. 52; JJA 58: 195) without noticing anything particular. The numerous later versions, whether typed or longhand, all adhere to this global unity, which of course dominates in the *transition* 15 version as printed. Something happens, however, between the printed version, that Joyce could not read and revise as usual because of his failing eyesight, and the several retyped versions of the same chapter, which were typed either in capitalized letters or double spaced. This has to do with a new focus on cities in general and not just Dublin, as was the case before.

We see this new cluster taking shape in the handwritten additions to pages typed in the "legal size" that enabled Joyce to decipher them and dated around January 1929. On BL 47484a f. 251v (JJA 58: 320), for instance, we discover an interesting unfinished list of cities:

> whom certain orbits assertant re ~~poot~~ humeplace of Civitads Ei,
> 1)
> 2) Rhode Island
> 3) Capetown,
> 4)
> 5)
> 6) Argyll
> 7) and

After a few revisions this almost empty structure will generate the list of the different birthplaces of Homer, provided fully in the final version: "—Ouer Tad, Hellig Babbau, whom certayn orbits assertant re humeplace of Chivitats Ei, Smithwick, Rhonnda, Kaledon, Salem (Mass), Childers, Argos and Duthless" (FW: 481.20–22). The list was inserted into a typed section of the first part in which cities in general would be called upon to situate and define the Father grammatically and geographically by his "locative":

"I have your tristich now. It recurs in three times the same differently. And speaking of this same famous sire of yours, Mr. Tupling Towns, would he reoccur now in city or country if you know the difference" (BL 47484a f. 251–251v; JJA 58: 319–20). Anyway, it would be premature to speak of a dominant theme: in 1929 Joyce was still multiplying approaches and strategies, expanding the psychoanalytic theme, rather than using cities in view of a polyphonic saturation of semantemes.

One finds on BL 47484a f. 285v (JJA 58: 392) another allusion to Dublin as a "City of God" in another handwritten addition: "—Wallpurgies! And it's this's your deified city! And it's we's to pay for his conversions?" around the end of the first half (otherwise known as IIIA) of the chapter. Then on the next page (BL 47484a f. 233; JJA 58: 394) one witnesses the crucial insertion of "Amtsadam" just before "—Sir, to you!" that had so far marked the beginning of that subsection. But despite the fact that "Mannequins Passe" is added on the following page to send us toward Brussels, we can safely conclude that city entries are still inserted without consideration of a structural divide between 3A and 3B. The motif of "*Urbs in Rure*" (FW: 551.23) that dominates, as we will see in "Haveth Childers Everywhere," had been announced almost too early and in the first part, while the Dublin names predominate in all the insertions throughout this 1929 campaign of writing (a few Dublin lists are added).[4]

The real new departure came after a moment of crisis that almost blocked the writing of the *Wake*, and it has been well documented by Richard Ellmann and Stuart Gilbert. Gilbert notes on 31 January 1930 that Joyce has resumed his work on the *Wake* by making extensive use of the *Encyclopaedia Britannica:*

> At last J.J. has recommenced work on Work in Progress. The de luxe edition by? soon to come out—about the old lady ALP I think. Another about the city (HCE building Dublin). Five volumes of the Encyclopaedia Britannica on his sofa. He has made a list of 30 towns, New York, Vienna, Budapest, and Mrs. [Helen] Fleischmann has read out the articles on some of these. I "finish" Vienna and read Christiania and Bucharest. Whenever I come to a name (of a street, suburb, park, etc.) I pause. Joyce thinks. If he can Anglicize the word, i.e. make a pun on it, Mrs. F. records the name or its deformation in the notebook. Thus "Slotspark" (I think) at Christiania becomes Sluts' park. He collects all queer names in this way and will soon have a notebook full of them.[5]

One can recognize the city notes that went into notebooks VI.B.24 and VI.B.29. The word "^{r}Slotspark" is indeed to be found in notebook VI.B.24: 227, and it generates "Slutsgartern" in the final version ("in Kissilov's Slutsgartern or Gigglotte's Hill, when I would touch to her dot" [FW: 532.22–23], adding to "slut" the complement of some sly "garters"). And "in Slutsgartern" was inserted on BL 47484b f. 356 (JJA 59: 86), a typescript of a version prepared for *transition* 15 on a page dated July–August 1929 by the editors of *The James Joyce Archive.* It is in this typed version that many city names are added (e.g., on BL 47484b f. 365 [JJA 59: 93] we find "Brixton" and "Schottenhof" inserted intralinearly, the latter word coming from the Vienna list in VI.B.24: 225; from the same list "Elserground," barred and in another hand in VI.B.24: 225, is inserted in Joyce's hand on BL 47484b f. 375 [JJA 59: 99] as "from elserground"). Joyce had another draft typed in view of this collective effort that allowed other amanuenses such as Paul Léon, Padraic Colum, Stuart Gilbert, and Helen Joyce (some of whose hands are also visible in the lists found in the notebooks, as is the case of the Vienna entries just alluded to) the opportunity to add various interlinear words. Among them one distinguishes "in Kissilov's Slutsgarten" written in Joyce's own hand, immediately changed into "Slutsgartern" by the addition of an extra *r* (BL 47484b f. 356; JJA 59: 86). There is a single entry on the blank left-hand page close of BL 47484b f. 386v (JJA 59: 118) in Joyce's hand: "Bulafests onvied me, Corkcuttas graachted" (an entry typical of Joyce's wish to pair off foreign cities as couples of complementary opposites), while the many other intralinear insertions are in someone else's hand (as "tunes like water parted fluted up from the west-inders while from gorges in the east come the strife of ourangoontangues" added to BL 47484b f. 393 [JJA 59: 119]).[6] Joyce is not really modifying the original concept of a subsection devoted to the self-aggrandizing and all too righteous projection of Earwicker's accomplishments as a city builder; he merely expands and universalizes.

III.3B was retyped in March 1930, when Joyce was busy preparing the typescript for *Haveth Childers Everywhere* that was to be published in June 1930. In this version one finds the new rhetorical opening marked by a double salute: "Amtsadam, Sir, to you! Eternest cittas, heil!" Simple periods had to be replaced by handwritten exclamation marks. A little earlier, in the summer of 1929, Joyce had decided to insert "Eternest Cittas, heil!" (BL 47484b f. 351; JJA 59: 63) to duplicate pages of *transition* 15. Was he guessing that the German salute would soon become a new "wake-up call" for Europe? Whether it is identified with Rome or New Amsterdam, the "eternal city" embodies all the cities in the world only if it carries its onus of guilt, betrayal, and totalitarianism. One may notice that at the same time as he added "Eternest cittas, heil!" to the *transition* 15 proofs Joyce added on the very last page the telling phrase "Roamer Reich's rickyshow with Hispain's king's crombeteer" (BL 47484b f. 354v; JJA 59: 70). Whatever he had in mind, this allusion to a Germanized *Römer Reich* trumpeted throughout Spain resounds curiously in the historical context of the thirties.

In the second version (BL 47484b f. 426; JJA 59: 165) the reference to "Kissilov's Slutsgartern or Giglotte's Hill" is now typed in. We have here a fleshed-out version of HCE's defensive speech by which he awkwardly tries to exculpate himself of various sins (here, just "malfeasance trespass against parson with the person of a youthful gigirl") while accusing himself all the more damningly in his stammering confession. Other cities than Dublin seem merely to provide a backdrop of universal gossip, facing which Earwicker's reputation seems to have suffered. The adjective "bad" is thus transformed twice: "~~baad~~ ^[1]bahad[1]^, nieceless to say, to my reputation on Babbyl <~~m~~^M^>alket for daughter-in-trade being lightly clad" (BL 47484b f. 426; JJA 59: 165).

What is, then, the significance of the addition of echoes taken from at least forty (if not even more—I have counted, in fact, forty-two cities) cities of the world chosen from entries in the *Encyclopedia Britannica?* Let us return to Joyce's composition as described by Stuart Gilbert. In this case his associative and collective method implies enlisting the help of many other people and induces a mechanical linguistic process. Three persons at least are needed in order to constitute this atlas of puns, this Baedeker of spoonerisms. Gilbert remains highly critical of a method he finds both too simple and too complicated:

> The system seems bad for (1) there is little hope of the reader knowing all these names—most seem new even to Joyce himself, and certainly are to me. And supposing the reader, knowing the fragment dealt with towns, took the trouble to look up the Encyclopedia, would he hit on the 30 Joyce has selected. (2) The insertion of these puns is bound to lead the reader away from the basic text, to create divagations and the work is hard enough anyhow! The good method would be to write out a page of plain English and then rejuvenate dull words by injection of new (and appropriate) meanings. What he is doing is too easy to do and too hard to understand. (PJ: 21)

We may agree that the method is frustratingly simple and opaque at the same time. The notebooks bear evidence to the presence of numerous word lists, along with cryptic allusions, half-elaborated portmanteau words, random jottings that look like the weird game invented by a demented lexicographer who would have, on top of that, thrown overboard all philological probity. However, there is something perverse in imagining that Joyce requires that his readers should be looking around for encyclopedias and travel guides and grapple in vain after thousands of local names only to find the key to a few dubious puns. Such methodological flippancy triggers Gilbert's scorn, as when he describes Joyce "curled on his sofa, while I struggle with Danish or Rumanian names, pondering puns. With foreign words it's too easy. The provincial Dubliner. Foreign equals funny" (PJ: 21). The severity evinced by such a close "anticollaborator" betrays a stubborn belief in classical textuality. Indeed, why not write in "plain English" first, and then only add polyglot and intertextual allusions? "The good method would be to write out a page of plain English and then rejuvenate dull words by injection of new (and appropriate) meanings. . . . I think I shall try my hand at the simple method myself" (PJ: 21). This explains why Gilbert never became a novelist, in spite of real literary gifts (evinced, e.g., in his excellent translation of Dujardin's novel *Les Lauriers sont coupés*). Gilbert's position corresponds to that of the reductive reader who imagines that a first-draft version of *Finnegans Wake* would be written in "normal" English and would provide a "basic text" from which the reader might produce a continuous narrative or a "skeleton key." This view, such is my contention, would go against the grain of Joyce's method, a method that is not either perverse or both too easy and too difficult because it supposes an ideal reader who is identified to an interpretative community.[7]

We could meditate at some length on the meaning of Joyce's curiously "collective" compositional practice in order to build the city words that loom larger and larger in the second half of III.3. The questions we could pose stem directly from Gilbert's reservations. Is Joyce's method "sound" or is it "crazy"? Is there a link, can we establish a structural homology between this allegedly mechanistic and collective way of writing and the "content" or theme, sketched more or less by the idea of building cities, or should we simply condemn Joyce's absorption in these linguistically complicated but fundamentally simple language games? Is it true, moreover, that Joyce simply Anglicizes the words he culls from the *Encyclopaedia* in a way that betrays his provincial chauvinism?

If we take as a counterexample those words that are already in English, as when Joyce (or, rather, an amanuensis in this case) takes notes on New York, we can see that the technique is identical with the other more exotic cities. His aim is always to create puns that are less gratuitous than the "Slutspark" example might indicate. Some are obvious, as when he transforms "^{o}Bronx" (VI.B.24: 205) into "bronxitic" at FW: 536.13 or when "^{r}Gramercy Park" (VI.B.24: 206) is reintroduced as "by gramercy of justness" (FW: 534.13). Others imply the constitution of a dense network that keeps on adding layers to itself; for instance, the notes "^{r}Fifth Avenue / Avenulceen!" (VI.B.24: 206) generate "avenyue" (FW: 549.20) with a rich reinscription of the New York theme, while "^{r}Tombs (city prison)" in VI.B.24: 206 is spliced with Dublin in a hardly legible insertion to BL 47484b f. 357 (JJA 59: 87), where Joyce inserts by hand "under my duskguise of whippers ~~by~~ ^^{1}through^{1}^ tombs and deempseys," which becomes in the final version "through toombs and deempeys" (FW: 532.28). The phrase splices the acronym for Dublin Metropolitan Police with the famous New York prison while maybe losing an allusion to Jack Dempsey's fists. Joyce's tendency is thus to shake the drifting signifiers until they are caught in a sort of verbal clinamen, a verbal vortex creating new couplings and compounds while offering glimpses and vistas to the reader who can still make out elements on the map.

For instance, two discrete items that have also been crossed in red, "^{r}Mulberry Bend Park" and "^{r}Coney Island" (both found on VI.B.24: 206), are chiasmically inverted so as to cross their properties: "and I did spread before my Livvy, where Lord street lolls and ladies linger and Cammomile Pass cuts Primrose Rise and Coney Bend bounds Mulbreys Island" (FW: 553.04–6). Not only do London (with Camomile Street and Primrose Street) and New York overlap, but these very signifiers allegorize "coupling." On the one hand, geography is not inanimate but caught up in a spiral of love and carnal desire: we never forget that HCE uses the recitation of cities as a way to praise his wife and sing their love. On the other hand, the puns carefully collected from the enormous repertoire provided by the dense entries in the eleventh edition of the *Encyclopaedia Britannica* function as so many "passages," to take up Walter Benjamin's concept. When Benjamin attempted to allegorize Paris as the "capital of the nineteenth century" in his voluminous and unfinished *Passagenwerk,* Joyce's universal city based upon Dublin becomes a dream landscape upon which all the cities in the world can be superimposed. Moreover, both Joyce and Benjamin know that they cannot simply provide an encyclopedia of the universal city, and thus both face the issue of presenting this vision in a mimetic and performative language.

If we look at the notes collected under "Warsaw" in VI.B.24: 223–24, the picture becomes clearer. Interestingly, we notice that the name of the city first occurs on VI.B.24: 190 in a Dublin context, already transformed into "^{r}Warshow." Most notes have been left uncrossed, and it is clear that Joyce was not extremely stimulated by the reading of this entry. The notes are in his hand, and it looks as if he was more inclined to capture the sounds than to be accurate. Hence potential puns are produced, stressing negative elements, as with "Muckatucksy Parade" (VI.B.24: 224), which distorts "Mokotowski parade ground," or "Przedndmessy," from the "Przedmiescie Street" said by the *Encyclopaedia* to be the finest in Warsaw. The notes begin with a few signposts, like "Sliwicki," "Luzyenky" for "Lazienki gardens," and "Sasky Ogrot" (VI.B.24: 223) for "Saski Ogrod" (Saxon garden), but Joyce gets tired after a short while and stops when he is halfway through the description of the Old Town and then moves on to Madrid on the same page (VI.B.24: 224). The uncrossed entries "Wolla" (for the suburb of Wola) and "stare miast" for "Stare Miasto" (old town) later blend with Prague's own "Staremesto" (old town) in the rather poetic coining of "under starrymisty" (FW: 539.21).

The Madrid notes are probably in Helen Fleischman's hand, and they quickly spill over to Vienna: after two barred entries ("^{r}Puerta del Sol" and "^{r}Buen Retiro" [VI.B.24: 224]) one reads "Plaza," followed by "^{r}AMIENS" and "RASTRO" in uppercase letters, and then "^{r}Kaiserlane" and "^{r}Kaisersstadt." The top of the following page (VI.B.24: 225) also mixes up hints to Madrid (with "PRADO") and a list of terms taken from Vienna, all in uppercase letters and crossed out: "^{r}RINGSTRESS" opens the list, a distortion of "Ringstrasse" that finds its way into the final version as "ringstrasse" (FW: 547.32), followed by an illegible entry and then by "^{r}SCHOTTENHOF / FREIUNG / RATHOUSE / GRABEN / STOCK IM EISEN." They are all kept more or less intact in the final version, with "Schottenhof" (FW: 538.32), "freiung" (FW: 538.27), "ratshause" (FW: 535.17), "graben" (FW: 545.34), and "my dart to throw" (FW: 547.21) developed by "a tritan stock" (FW: 547.24) to call up the Viennese grove marked by a stump of a tree with a piece of iron in it. It looks as if the relative literality was due to the amanuensis, who did his or her best to copy the exact spelling of the *Encyclopaedia* entry, while Joyce himself was taking more liberties. On the whole, most of the entries are not substantially modified once they have generated a pun (or even without a pun) in the notebook. All of this tends to confirm that the description given by Gilbert is faithful: Joyce did work with a team of friends, he did not really know the meanings or references of the names he worked from, he was interested in adding overlays of meaning applied to the text in an almost mechanistic manner. And yet it is in this very method that he gained access to a different and original generation of meaning.

If we know that the notebooks belong to the creative process I have sketched, then Gilbert is mistaken when he believes that the earlier versions contained either in the notebooks or in the drafts keep intact the plot and essence of the text's meaning. When he suggested, as we saw, that a better method would write the text in "plain English" and then "inject" new meanings (PJ: 21), he forgot that Joyce had in fact another text from which he was working, Yawn's dreamy "polylogue" in which Yawn's disembodied voices call up HCE praising his wife and defending himself from calumny in front of the Four. The automatic word machine systematized by Joyce in the winter of 1930 after a period when he seemed to have lost interest in his own work in progress was designed to radically alter a previous text. The number of layers piled up on the first-draft version is staggering, and we see this happening in the very typescript for *Haveth Childers Everywhere.*

The building materials used to transform the interaction between HCE and ALP into a hymn to all the cities of the world are complex but distinguishable. We find, first of all, a rich layer focusing on Dublin, documenting its history and present situation, with notes taken from books such as Ada Peter's *Dublin Fragments: Social and Historic,* Dillon Cosgrave's *North Dublin—City and Environs,* David Alfred Chart's *Story of Dublin,* and a few others.[8] Then we reach the forty or so cities taken from the eleventh edition of the *Encyclopaedia Britannica* (Amsterdam, Athens, Belfast, Belgrade, Berlin, Bern, Brussels, Bucharest, Budapest, Buenos Aires, Cairo, Christiania, Constantinople, Copenhagen, Delhi, Edinburgh, Kabul, Lisbon, London, Madrid, Mecca, Melbourne, Mexico City, New York, Oslo, Ottawa, Paris, Peking, Philadelphia, Prague, Rangoon, Rio de Janeiro, Saint Petersburg, Sofia, Stockholm, Teheran, Tokyo, Vienna, Warsaw, Washington, D.C., and Wellington), all of which provide some key elements taken from their signifiers. I have added Philadelphia, which is represented by at least one entry, "°liberty bell" (VI.B.29: 41).

Another layer is provided by direct quotations carefully copied in the notebooks. Besides the numerous city words already mentioned, we can "catch" a few supernumerary layers; a typed version of the infamous charter by which Dublin was granted to the inhabitants of Bristol by King Henry II in BL 47484b f. 374 (JJA 59: 141); a tourist guide view of Dublin that takes up Holinshed's often quoted description of the beauties of Dublin in his *Chronicles* in BL 47484b f. 437 (JJA 59: 178); long passages taken more or less literally from B. Seebohm Rowntree's book on the phenomenon of urban poverty he observed not in Dublin but in York, a primordial source extensively studied by James Atherton in *The Books at the Wake;* all of Ibsen's plays and characters, quoted with a curious equanimity; the list of all the Lord Mayors of Dublin, all bringing something to HCE; the eight main statues of Dublin that one encounters going down from Parnell Square to College Green; the list of the fourteen main architects of Dublin (Cassels, Redmond, Gandon, Deane, Shepperd, Smyth, Neville, Heaton, Stoney, Foley, Farrell, Van Nost, Thorneycrofdt, and Hogan), all neatly copied in an amanuensis's longhand and added to BL 47484b f. 455 (JJA 59: 198), except for poor John Van Nost, whose name was first distorted as "Zmot" and then became just Vnost—as he still survives in the final text on FW: 552.12.[9]

One is tempted to shout in despair "Enouch!" as the text suggests on FW: 535.22 in a wry allusion to the city built by Cain after his murder and flight "East of Eden." The issue remains that one will not necessarily recognize all these references; one would thus need much more than the volumes of the *Encyclopaedia Britannica* to feel at home in this curious feat of linguistic excess. The very excess might lead to the contention put forward by Danis Rose in his 1978 *Index Manuscript* and taken up again in UFW that all the words in the *Wake* derive from some written source mediated by the notebooks (see UFW: xiii–xiv). When all the sources are provided, then and only then can the text's meaning be revealed. This might take a few centuries, but in the end the riddle will be solved. It seems that a category mistake is performed when we labor under the illusion that either genesis or source hunting is interpretation. I think that "Haveth Childers Everywhere" is a good passage to work from in order to try to put the genetic fallacy to rest.

When, as in this case, we have retrieved almost all the sources from which the text is constructed, can we say that the meaning of the text is finally provided? Does Joyce want to depict Dublin as a universal and eternal city? Probably. But why does he insert the "heil!" salute at FW: 532.06? Moreover, is he poking fun at HCE's sexual hubris ("since I perpetually kept my ouija ouija wicket up" [FW: 532.17–18]) and its link with the imperialism of the English language ("in pontofacts massimust, I am known throughout the world wherever my good Allenglisches Angleslachsen is spoken" [FW: 532.09–11]), or is he condoning it in the name of some mythical reunification of all and sundry? Is he depicting Earwicker as quasi-Nazi chief saluting his city's renaissance, or is he attacking a possible collusion between British imperialism and Fascism? In other words, is this picture of a Dublin containing all the other cities in the world political, or are we to allow Joyce to perform the "eternizing" metaphor of essentialist or Jungian myth making?

One of the keys to this crucial question seems to lie in the composition indeed, but at the level of the interaction between the "first draft" and its overlays. Or, to narrow down the focus, the issue is what took place between January 1929, when Joyce was revising the proofs for *transition* 15 (February 1929), and May 1930, when Joyce had finished revising the sixty-four pages of the Babou and Kahane edition of *Haveth Childers Everywhere.* The final version of "Haveth Childers Everywhere" in III.3 (FW: 532.06–554.10) does not significantly differ from the slim book published in 1930. The flurry of activity recorded by Gilbert in the early months of 1930 should also be explained by the relatively short time Joyce disposed of to alter the meaning of his piece.

A survey of the first proofs for the last pages of III.3 in *transition* 15 discloses familiar features; Earwicker betrays himself, as we have seen, through slips, double entendres, and stutterings while he reminisces on his marriage, the foundation of his family, the expansion of his commercial endeavors. His love for a fluvial ALP is embodied in the typical geography of Dublin:

> But I was firm with her: and I did take the hand of my delights, my jealousy, and did raft her riverworthily and did lead her overland the pace whimpering by Kevin's port and Hurdlesford and Gardener's mall to Ringsend ferry and there on wavebrink did I uplift my magicianer's puntpole and I bade those polyfizzyboisterous seas to retire with himselves from us (rookwards, thou seasea stammerer!) and I abridged with domfire Norsemanship her maiden race, my baresark bride, and knew her fleshly when with all my bawdy did I her worhsip, min bryllupswipe. (Princeton f. 43; JJA 58: 303)

The 1928 *transition* pages already insist on the prototype of a male dominator who remains in control of his wife ("and I did encompass her about, my vermincelly vinegarette, with all loving kindness as far as in man's might it lay and enfranchised her to liberties of fringes" [Princeton f. 43; JJA 58: 303]), but there is no other voice that could offer a discordant commentary or take a critical distance.

When we reach the same passage in the 1930 *Haveth Childers Everywhere* version (I use the printed version here simply to make the transcription simpler), it is less the insertion of allusions to other cities ("whimpering by Kevin's creek and Hurdlesford and Gardener's Mall, long Riverside Drive"; "and to ringstresse I thumbed her with iern of Erin" [BL 47484b fs. 486v–487; JJA 59: 256–57]) that creates a different atmosphere than the sheer excess of references. Earwicker's jealousy leads him to chain ALP to a chastity belt ("I chained her chastemate to grippe fiuming snugglers, her chambrett I bestank so to spunish furiosos" [BL 47484b f. 487v; JJA 59: 258]), and the very presents he offers sound so dismissive that they turn truly ridiculous: "[A]nd I gave until my lilienyounger turkeythighs soft goods and hardware (catalogue, passim) and ladderproof hosiery lines [. . .] trancepearances such as women cattle bare" (BL 47484b f. 488; JJA 59: 259). HCE's unbearable paternalism and vainglorious praise of his prowesses appear clearly as the equivalent not only of British imperialism but also of the expansion of commerce identified with Irish capitalism.

Another passage from "Haveth Childers Everywhere" indicates a more critical mode of writing:

> Like as my palmer's past policy I have had my best master's lessons as the public he knows, and do you know, homesters, I honestly think if I have failed lamentably by accident benefits through shintoed, spitefired, perplagued and cramkrieged, I am doing my dids bits and have made of my prudentials good. I have been told I own stolenmines or something of that sorth in the sooth of Spainien. Hohohoho! Have I said ogso how I abhor myself vastly (truth to tell) and do repent to my netherheart of sun<~~d~~^t^>ry clothing? The amusin part is I will say, hotelmen, that since I, over the deep drowner athacleeath to seek again Irrlanding, shamed in mind, with three plunges of my ruddertail, yet not a bottlenim, ~~poisted~~ ^[1]vaneed[1]^ imperial standard by weaponright and platzed mine residenze, taking bourd and burgage under starrimisty and ran and operated my brixtol selection here. (BL 47484b f. 474–474v; JJA 59: 231–32)

Here, we are closer to an open confession of guilt, denouncing all the "absurd bargains" (FW: 538.19) that have made Dublin what it is, not excluding Henry II's charter giving away Dublin to Bristol. This is why it is not a coincidence to see Joyce insert the text of the charter itself: the typed text ("Wherfor I will and firmly command that they do inhabit it and hold it for me and my heirs firmly and quietly, amply and honestly, and with all the liberties and free customs which the men of Tolbris have at Tolbis, and through whole my land.") ends here on a period in the original addition.

Then one can see Joyce's hand adding the more pointed words "fee for farm, enwreak us wrecks" (BL 47484b f. 374; JJA 59: 141). These words echo the nursery rhyme Stephen sings to himself in "Proteus": "Feefawfum. I zmellz de bloodz odz an Iridzman" (U: 3.293) and suggest that the "freedom" implied by the charter spells out slavery for the natives of the island. Put together in the final version of "Haveth Childers Everywhere" (BL 47484b f. 483v; JJA 59: 250) and then in the *Wake* (FW: 454.14–23), the effect is devastating.

It comes as the climax of a long paragraph stretching over six pages and beginning with a recapitulation of the changes wrought on the city by history. The paragraph is announced by the voice of a guide inviting visitors to discover "Drumcollogher-la-Belle" and then takes stock of legal, financial, and political changes: "Things are not as they are. Let me briefly survey. [. . .] The end of aldest mosest ist the beginning of all thisorder so that the mast of their ~~benbailiffs~~ ^[1]hansbailis[1]^ shall the first in our sheriffsby" (BL 47484b f. 476; JJA 59: 235). Another variation on the Dublin motto ("Obeyance from the townsmen spills felixity by the toun" [BL 47484b f. 476v; JJA 59: 236; FW: 540.25–26]) is followed by a series of platitudes that debunk their own optimism: "Our bourse and politico-ecomedy are in safe with good Jock Shepherd, our lives are on sure in sorting with Jonathans wild and great. Been so free! Thanks you besters! Hattentats have mindered" (BL 47484b f. 476v; JJA 59: 236; FW: 540.26–28). The mention of two famous English criminals both hanged for their crimes could leave one skeptical about the future of the Dublin "Bourse" (both stock exchange and purse). This does not seem to embarrass the speaker, because these are precisely the methods he extols: "By fineounce and imposts I got and grew and by grossscruple gat I grown ontreachesly: murage and lestage were my mains for Ouerlord's tithing and my drains for render and prender the doles and the tribute" (BL 47484b f. 477–477v; JJA 59: 237–38; FW: 541.07–10). This paean to financial exploitation is not of course limited to Dublin ("Bulafest onvied me, Corkcuttas graatched" reappears here on BL 47484b f. 477v [JJA 59: 238; FW: 541.16–17]) but applies to all imperialist political formations, which includes the United States: "In the humanity of my heart I sent out heyweywomen to refresh the ballwearied and then, doubling megalopolitan poleetness, my great great greatest of these charities, devaleurised the base fellows for the curtailment of their lower man: with a slog to square leg I sent my boundary to Botany Bay and I ran up a score and four of mes while the Yanks were huckling the Empire" (BL 47484b f. 480; JJA 59: 243; FW: 542.35–543.06). Once more, the

Dublin Metropolitan Police is taken to task and metamorphosed into a megalopolitan expansion that keeps "doubling" all the time while severely punishing the inferiors. The law and economy go hand in hand in this exploitative process, since one hears the name of de Valera in "devaleurised" meaning that base money has been devalued, which calls up Swift's campaign against the devaluation of the pence in Ireland. The cricket terms calling up some foul play and the allusions to Huck Finn suggest that the business of empire building is indeed dirty, while the assertion that there are twenty-four cities named Dublin in the United States merely sets off the fact that the speaker seems satisfied with a world limited to the quadrangle in Trinity College (Botany Bay).

Then a mention of the Dublin people who should all be grateful in front of the display of such good deeds ("in hommage all and felony" [FW: 543.21]) ushers in the long insertion of the jumbled notes taken from Rowntree's book *Poverty: A Study of Town Life.* These notes, culled from the book in notebook VI.B.29: 139–53 and 164–65, are not all in Joyce's hand, and some have been dictated probably by Joyce himself. The litany of "respectable" (three times on VI.B.29: 139), "fairly respectable" (twice on VI.B.29: 140), and then "°as respectable as respectable can be" (VI.B.29: 143) is relatively restrained in the notebook entries, while the word "respectable" and its cognates is repeated twenty-one times, as early as the long typed insertion in BL 47484b fs. 459–60 (JJA 59: 206–7) more or less identical with the final text (FW: 543.22–545.14). The litany climaxes with "and respected and respectable, as respectable as respectable can respectably be" (FW: 545.11–12), creating what Atherton calls a "sardonic refrain" undermining the bland matter-of-factness of these staccato notations on urban poverty in the north of England.[10] It is a Swiftian Joyce who appears here to denounce not only destitution but wooden language of state bureaucracy that sees, indeed, children as vermin: "°children treacly and / verminous [~~illegible~~] have to / be separated" (a note in Joyce's hand in VI.B.29: 145).

This often hilarious prose simply splices and accelerates a few pages from Rowntree. The text reaches surrealist peaks at times, as when we hear about a person who is "mentally strained from reading work on German physics" or about a "decoration from Uganda chief in locked ivory casket"—reality is stranger than fiction, for all the details are indeed provided by Rowntree's text. Or to go back to the analogy with Benjamin's *Passagenwerk,* it looks as if, confronted with the stark reality of urban decay, both Joyce and Benjamin prefer to "remain silent" and act like "bricoleurs" or scavengers who simply salvage trivia. In the theoretical section of his magnum opus Benjamin writes: "Method of this project: literary montage. I need say nothing. Only exhibit. I won't filch anything of value or appropriate any ingenious turns of phrase. Only the trivia, the trash—which I don't want to inventory, but simply allow it to come into its own in the only way possible: by putting it to use."[11] Joyce suggests that the history of Dublin, like that of any "capital" city, confirms that its formation must indeed have been "dirty." Facing such a mixture of concrete accomplishments (as Lacan would say, civilization begins with sewers) and the underside showing the exploitation of the majority, progress appears indissociable from abjection and subjection, the mere act of quoting suffices. Its bittersweet irony exposes how Stephen's "nightmare of history" has left traces in monuments, in its own refuse, and above all in language.

One could compare the rhetoric of multilayered denunciation with Bloom's messianic projections in "Circe." The delirious socialism of Bloom is often undercut by parody, as when he sees the new Bloomusalem of the future in the shape of a gigantic kidney. In "Haveth Childers Everywhere," however, the dominant tense is not the future but the present perfect of proud recapitulation ("Lo, I have looked upon my pumpadears in their easancies and my drummers have tattled tall tales of me in the land" [FW: 545.25–26]) in the name of a strong "I" who is glorified or himself glorifies his accomplishments. As the evolution of the text has shown, the Dublin that originally embodied the love and eternal desire linking HCE and ALP then generates a more fragmented "drama parapolylogic" (FW: 474.05) that stresses contradiction. The community of anonymous sufferers offers a poignant counterpoint to the shrill and inflated egotism of HCE. This is exactly what the textual method of differential accretion produces: the performative gesture of the text becomes one with its meaning, since the endless piling up of textual debris signifies both the erection of a monument and its constant debunking or destruction.

Joyce thus needs the single voice of one speaker in its dialectical interaction with interpolations from the Four one sees in *Finnegans Wake* on pages 534, 535, 540, 546, 547, 550, and 552. This fourfold rhythmical basis not only continues the great dialogical movement begun in III.3A but now and then modulates toward other inflections, undercutting its steady surge forward and upward. The first of these insertions found in the "Haveth Childers Everywhere" text was added relatively late to the typescript—curiously, as a separate sheet glued to the bottom of BL 47484b f. 358. It is not in Joyce's hand and contains:

—Tiktak. Tiktak.
—A wind abuzz awater falling.
—Poor a cowe his jew placator.
—It's the damp damp damp. (BL 47484b f. 358; JJA 59: 88)

In the printed text of "Haveth Childers Everywhere" Joyce ratifies a distortion of the second "Tiktak" as "Tikkak" (he adds "*à maintenir*" for the printer). Why is the allusion to a "jew" hiding a pun on "duplicator," which is itself announced by a French pun on "*pourquoi*"? If the meaning of the third question is "*Pourquoi* his duplicator," what to do with this lost "jew" in the foreground? Does it have anything to do with Benjamin's famous *Reproduzierbarkeit* (technological reproductibility)? Since it would be impossible to answer this question with any certainty without opening a larger theoretical debate between Joyce and Benjamin, let us just note that the text's many "*pourquois*" stand on their own. Whatever the meaning of these impenetrably simple scansions, they imply a puncturing of the speaker's exaggerated confidence.

A relatively long sentence that appears clear enough reflects on the cumulative function occupied by HCE as main speaker:

> Idle were it, repassing from elserground to the elder disposition, to inquire whether I, draggedasunder, be the forced generation of group marriage, holocryptogam, of my essenes, or carried of cloud from land of locust, in ouzel galley borne, I, huddled til summone be the massproduct of teamwork, three surtouts wripped up in itchother's, two twin pritticoaxes lived as one, troubled in trine or dubildin too, for abram nude be I or roberoyed with the faineans, of Feejeean grafted ape on merfish, surrounded by obscurity, by my virtus of creation and by boon of promise, by my natural born freeman's journeymanright and my otherchurch's inher light, in so and such a manner as me it so besitteth, most surely I pretend and reclam to opt for simultaneous. Till daybowbreak and showshadows flee. (FW: 546.11–23)

Earwicker admits here that he sums up in himself if not all of humanity at least his own family. The three soldiers and two tempting girls in the park return as sigla in the Doodles family. Freedom is asserted in such a way that it can connote the *Freeman's Journal*, Fijian mermaids, Sinn Féin inverted, and even *les rois fainéants* (the last Merovingian kings). In this context creativity is confirmed not by the number of children or of satellite plantations but by the simultaneity of a group structure.

Joyce's composite portrait of a man who embodies a city or of a city that turns into a man belongs to an unanimistic technique (one could think of Jules Romains or Dos Passos), although it is more an "Arcimboldo city" that is depicted, made up of all the cities in the world summed up by a few basic names, just as characters keep merging into one another. The link between quotation of the city has never been stronger, as one can still see it in French (*cité/citation*). Quotation implies montage without losing the idea of a general architectonics—and the limit set by the morning and waking up from obscurity. Benjamin uses Proust to define the general outline of his *Passagenwerk* in a paragraph that might be taken as a description of *Finnegans Wake:* "Just as Proust begins his life story with the moment of awakening, so every historical presentation must begin with awakening and, in fact, should deal with nothing else. This one deals with awakening from the nineteenth century."[12]

Since we are kept waiting for the forthcoming moment of awakening from the dream of universal history conjured by the book we are even now reading, the effect is a dynamic portrayal of the universal city as universal family. The city in III.3 is an expanding linguistic site that never bypasses real history but that "re-pairs" it by a system of grafts, duplications, and additions, while the discourse produced by Yawn turning into his own father boasting about his past is presented to our sagacity like an analysand's discourse. The fourfold insertions remind us readers that this is a text to be punctured by "paper wounds, four in type [. . .] gradually and correctly understood to mean stop, please stop, do please stop, and O do please stop" (FW: 124.03–5). Here, as in psychoanalysis, genesis is a never totally arbitrary reconstruction of something that may never have taken place at all but that holds the narrative pattern by which our subjectivity is defined.

This is why the last stage in our story is the final round of revisions performed by Joyce after he inserted all the remaining items from the notebooks. The pages sent to Miss Weaver in July 1934 all concern Book III and are labeled Λa, b, c, or d. They comprise roughly twenty-five dense pages (BL: 47486a fs. 39–54, 67–68, 220–221v; JJA 61: 163–82, 195–200) as well as more irregular notes (BL 47486a fs. 201–23; JJA 61: 275–98). These notes are by definition random and generally add more dialogue (often in the echolalic form of distorted answers to idiomatic questions) than description or theoretical considerations. But these should not be confused with the very late insertions prepared when the book had reached its final shape and Joyce was putting together all the *transition* pages and some galley proofs. From this complex corpus I will focus on four key entries.

First, in 1937 Joyce inserted a series of longhand notes for III.3 (and not Λd any longer) in which he wrote the famous "his producers are also his consumers" (BL 47487 f. 134; JJA 62: 243), then added to the galley proofs (BL 47487 f. 65; JJA 62: 125; FW: 497.01–2). This occurs in a passage in which it is clear that the object of the examination by the Four is not just Yawn or the Earwicker family but *Finnegans Wake* itself, already commented on in advance of its publication by the *transition* disciples: "*Quis est qui non novit quinnigan* and *Qui quae quot at Quinnigan's Quake!*" (FW: 496.36–497.01).

Second, once more in 1937 Joyce added in longhand to the continuous galleys for the *Wake*: "His dream monologue was over, ~~true~~ ^[1]of cause,[1]^ but his drama parapolylogic had yet to be, affact" (BL 47487 f. 185v; JJA 62: 340)—a remark that could be paired with another late insertion: "as question time drew nighing, and the map of the souls' groupography rose in relief within their quarterings" (BL 47487 f. 187v; JJA 62: 344). This shows the degree of reflexivity the text has reached after more than a hundred rereadings and revisions. It keeps describing itself, suggesting as well that recurrent rhythms or numerological calculations can provide a substitute "reason."

Third, Joyce added quite late, as an insertion, "I scent eggoarchicism" (BL 47487 f. 221v; JJA 62: 412), which provides the most effective diagnosis about the central character—both hidden beneath all the figures of history and shrilly overassertive, Yawn betrays all the weaknesses and faults of the Freudian ego when it identifies itself with a dreamer who has regressed to a childish *his majesty the baby.* The subject of all the dreams is more "anarch" and "egoarch" (FW: 188.16) than what Ibsen was supposed to be, just like Joyce, in fact.

Finally, in the same series Joyce added "—The aurthor, in fact, was mordred" (BL 47487 f. 216v; JJA 62: 402), a sentence that could be set rhyming with "Arise, sir Ghostus! As long as you've lived there'll be no other" (BL 47487 f. 225v; JJA 62: 420). This would be the last missing corner of the gnomon described by the text in its fourfold root. Here, the author becomes a ghost, he has been murdered, or he is possibly mad, leaving the task of sense production to the reader/critics who stand in for him and are responsible for the presence of any coherent meaning in the general chaos. In this confusion all the characters appear like oneiric projections of an "egoarchy" without a subject.

I could multiply examples but choose only these four statements: they tend to prove that the meanings we want to use for our interpretative approaches tend to be given not earlier with the first-draft elements but very late, when Joyce reread once more an almost completed text and became his first reader, this time just a little ahead of us. But Yawn should be allowed to sign this chapter, even in its reconstructed genesis, since his "Y" deserves to figure as its ad hoc siglum.

Notes

1. "It may be possible, with considerable effort, to disengage from the text identities and qualities for each of the four. They do after all draw upon the qualities associated with the gospelers (gossipelers?) and the provinces of Ireland. . . . However, the reader is hard-put, in the absence of the clear but clearly artificial markers in their interactive discourse to distinguish among them. Joyce has made them into paradigmatic elders and comic types rather than individuals" (David Hayman, "Substantial Time: The Temporalities of Mamalujo," *"Finnegans Wake": "teems of times,"* ed. Andrew Treip [Amsterdam: Rodopi, 1994], 95–105, 104 n. 8).

2. Jacques Derrida, *Ulysse gramophone* (Paris: Galilée, 1987), 84.

3. Marcel Proust, *The Guermantes Way, Remembrance of Things Past,* trans. C. K. Scott Moncrieff and Terence Kilmartin (New York: Random House, 1982), 2:134.

4. See BL 47484a fs. 179, 262, and 194 (JJA 58: 415, 423, and 430).

5. Stuart Gilbert, *Reflections on James Joyce: Stuart Gilbert's Paris Journal,* ed. T. Staley and R. Lewis (Austin: University of Texas Press, 1993), 20–21. Hereafter abbreviated as PJ.

6. A similar hand added to the left margin of BL 47484b f. 401 (JJA 59: 124) this vertical insertion: "and the Poe's Toffee's Directory." Having been missed by the typist when "Haveth Childers Everywhere" was retyped, this was re-added by hand on BL 47484b f. 429 (JJA 59: 168) without any modification. This confirms how closely Joyce checked his different typescripts and also that, in this conflation of *Thom's Directory* with the post office and Edgar Allan Poe, the fatefully polyglottic orangutan mentioned in JJA 59: 119 must owe something to Dupin's solution to the mystery of the murders in the rue Morgue.

7. I develop this point in *James Joyce and the Politics of Egoism* (Cambridge: Cambridge University Press, 2001).

8. Ada Peter, *Dublin Fragments: Social and Historic* (Dublin: Hodges, Figgis and Co., 1925); Dillon Cosgrave, *North Dublin—City and Environs* (Dublin: Catholic Truth Society of Ireland, 1909); David Alfred Chart, *The Story of Dublin* (London: Dent, 1907).

9. B. S. Rowntree, *Poverty: A Study of Town Life* (London: Macmillan, 1902); see James S. Atherton, *The Books at the Wake* (Carbondale: Southern Illinois University Press, 1959), 75–79.

10. Atherton 1959, 76.

11. Walter Benjamin, "N. re the Theory of Knowledge, Theory of Progress,"

trans. Leigh Hafrey and Richard Sieburth, *Benjamin, Philosophy, Aesthetics, History,* ed. Gary Smith (Chicago: University of Chicago Press, 1989), 47. The original is to be found in Walter Benjamin, *Das Passagenwerk* (Frankfurt: Suhrkamp, 1983), 1:574.

12. Benjamin 1989, 52; Benjamin 1983, 580.

Wondrous Devices in the Dark

Chapter III.4

DANIEL FERRER

According to a letter addressed to Harriet Shaw Weaver, what is now chapter III.4 of *Finnegans Wake* was started in the last days of September or early October 1925 (in close association, let us note, with the revision of chapter I.8—"Δ"):

> I began ∧d (otherwise the last watch of Shaun) a few days ago and have produced about three foolscapes of hammer and tongs stratifications lit up by a fervent prayer to the divinity which shapes our roads in favour of my ponderous protagonist and his minuscule consort.
>
> Shall I send you the corrected typescript of Δ there or wait till you return? I composed some wondrous devices for ∧d during the night and wrote them out in the dark only to discover that I had made a mosaic on top of other notes so I am now going to bring my astronomical telescope into play. (LI: 234–35, 10 October 1925)

It is striking to see that most of the major themes of the chapter (superposition, discontinuity, night, [pro]creation as an act of darkness, astronomical projection of earthly matters) surface in this liminal genetic narrative, this primal scene sketched for the benefit of Miss Weaver's curiosity. It is even more significant that Joyce should shift, within a few lines, from the position of a demiurgic blacksmith illuminated by the fervor of his own creative work to that of a perplexed decipherer of unknown constellations in a dark sky. Joyce's characteristic emphasis on control over his creation is balanced by the description of a *nocturnal accident.* The Joyce of the day has forgotten what the Joyce of the night wanted to write, and he can only hope to recover something of the original intention by a laborious and hazardous process of interpretative reading. He seems, however, confident that he will find, with the help of celestial bearings, the pattern—or rather *a* pattern—in his own mosaic.

In the Dark, Stumbling along the Roads

A close succession of moments of illumination and perplexity characterizes the whole period of the conception of this chapter—and more generally of the Book of Shaun.[1] At that stage Joyce definitely knew that he was going somewhere with his work in progress, but the direction was still rather vague. He was reassured by what he had already composed, aware that it included some of his finest writing and at the same time he knew that it implied a limitation of freedom, a constraint upon what remained to be written.

If we look at the chapter in its present place in the published work, the structural constraints look very strong: it is the fourth chapter in a Book, the third, which entertains subtle relations of balance and symmetry with Book I; in the Vichian cyclical pattern it is a *ricorso* chapter and the end of a pre-*ricorso* Book. But much of what now looks like structural determinations is the result of a later rearrangement. When the chapter was being written, Book I was far from being what it is now, and Joyce was only just beginning to imagine that he could turn his book into a Vichian wheel. It remains true, however, that Book III was, from the start, from its most embryonic form, conceived as a structural counterpart to Book I. It was, at first, supposed to be another chapter in Book I (just as *Ulysses* developed out of the idea of a story for *Dubliners*), but this chapter, devoted to Shaun as previous chapters had been devoted to Shem and to Anna Livia, was to be a kind of Circean mirror image of the earlier chapters, or a retrograde imitation in the musical sense. This is suggested by several cryptic notations in notebook VI.B.1 and made clearer in a subsequent letter to Harriet Shaw Weaver: "I am sorry I could not face the copying out of Shawn which is a description of a postman travelling backwards in the night through the events already narrated. It is written in the form of a *via crucis* of 14 stations but in reality it is only a barrel rolling down the river Liffey" (LI: 214, 24 May 1924).

What was planned as the concluding chapter of Book I soon split in two and turned into a part of its own, with three chapters. For several months Joyce does not seem to have contemplated a fourth chapter at all. Then he mentions four "watches of Shawn," but the fourth, which he calls Λ4 or Λd, is little more than an empty structural slot. Its content is not specified, except, again, as a kind of recapitulation of earlier material: it is to be a dream of the first three Shaun chapters (VI.B.9: 19).

At last, in a letter written to Miss Weaver on 27 July 1925, while he was on holiday in Normandy, Joyce reports a moment of illumination: "While I was returning from an excursion to S. Valéry the idea for the last watch of Shaun came into my head" (LI: 229). It is difficult to know exactly what Joyce had in mind at this point. It has been suggested that the idea was the one expressed in a letter written a month later (29 August 1925) to Weaver: "I know that Λd ought to be all about roads, all about dawn and roads" (LI: 232),[2] but this can hardly be considered as a decisive breakthrough, since Joyce had been collecting a great quantity of notes about roads for more than a year, presumably to describe the *via (crucis)* on which the postman was supposed to be traveling.[3] As for dawn, it could hardly fail to be the conclusion of the last watch of the night. Whatever the idea was, it did not prove decisive, and perplexity soon returned, as the rest of the sentence shows: "I know that Λd ought to be all about roads, all about dawn and roads, and go along repeating to myself all day long as I stumble along the roads hoping it will dawn on me how to show them roads so as everybody'll know as how roads etc."

In fact, neither roads nor dawn occupy a central place in the first drafts or in the finished chapter.[4] Roads are almost absent, except for the "fervent prayer to the divinity which shapes our roads" (LI: 234) mentioned in the 10 October letter, a brilliant piece that sounds a little forced in the context in which it appears (BL 47482a fs. 6–8; JJA 60: 9–13; FDV: 259–60; FW: 576.18–577.35). If Joyce had planned, at one point, that the last chapter of the book of Shaun, for structural reasons, "was to be *about roads* in an analogous manner to the way in which the [then] final chapter of Book I, (I.8, 'ALP') was *about rivers*,"[5] we have only to compare the two texts to see that roads do not occupy anything like the kind of place occupied by rivers in ALP.

In the same way, if "Dawn" is, as Danis Rose has suggested, the logical sequel to the first three chapters, "Shaun," "Jaun," and "Yawn" (such verbal games do play an important part in the logic of *Finnegans Wake*), the heading remains as formal and almost devoid of substance as some of the Homeric parallels or some of the pseudodeterminants in the Linati and Gorman *Ulysses* schemata (TDJJ: 44 n.). Dawn finally breaks, toward the end of the chapter, but its principal manifestation is the triumphant singing of the rooster at the conclusion of the coitus that is the culmination of the chapter. Locally, the cockcrow is interpreted as a rather predictable sexual metaphor, but genetically it seems likely that the coitus was suggested by the cockcrow—or rather that the morning song of the cock is one of several generators of the sexual scene. In this respect it can be considered as a trace of the superseded or rather displaced project, but something more must be brought in to explain the displacement, the radical change of nature or at least of proportions that took place between the chapter as Joyce planned it as late as the end of August 1925 and what was actually written a few weeks later.

In this short span of time not only was the theme altered beyond recognition (instead of being about roads and dawn it turned out to be ostensibly about a parental couple having sex after they have been disturbed by their son, who is crying because he has had a nightmare about a terrifying father figure) but Joyce's faltering quest for inspiration was replaced by note taking so feverish that, as we have seen, the work of the day was supplemented and overlaid by the results of nocturnal activity and by an intensive session of drafting, during which Joyce wrote and revised at great speed, almost without pausing.[6] Such discontinuities and leaps of inspiration, big or small, are familiar to genetic criticism, which concerns itself with *invention,* that is to say, the irruption of the new. When invention is analyzed there is always, by definition, a remainder that cannot be explained away, reduced to existing elements or circumstances—but it is the business of genetic criticism to propose schemes of explanation that will account as far as possible for those moments of invention, that will narrow the gap between preexisting factors and the radically new elements.

Case Studies: The Freudian Deferred Effect

As often with *Finnegans Wake,* we must look at the notebooks for clues, not with the hope to trace the chapter back to self-explanatory atomic constituent elements but, in this case, because they help us to trace a major source and influence unrecorded elsewhere.

In 1925 Joyce was using several notebooks: VI.B.8, VI.B.9, VI.B.19, VI.D.1, and VI.D.3. The chronology of usage is not easy to establish, for he did not fill them one after the other, as was his general habit, but shifted from one to the other to a considerable extent. One source, Sigmund Freud's then recently published *Collected Papers,* volume 3, appears in no less than four different notebooks.[7]

The ubiquity of this source is not, of course, its sole claim to prominence. This is not the place to insist on the importance of this reading for the history of ideas (it is the only documented extended contact of Joyce with the text of Freud),[8] but we must look in some detail at the inscription of these notes to understand the crucial part they have played in the development of Shaun d. Joyce seems to have started reading the book sometime in the beginning of 1925, taking notes from "Little Hans" ("Analysis of a Phobia in a Five-Year-Old Boy"), the second case history in the book, first in VI.D.3 for a few pages (as far as we can tell from VI.C.2: 142–43, corresponding to CP: 151–58), then more extensively in VI.B.19, probably during the second quarter of 1925, starting again at the beginning of the case and going to the end (VI.B.19: 17–48, corresponding to CP: 150–278). He then started taking notes in the same notebook from the fifth case, "The Wolfman" (VI.B.19: 68 [or 57]–84, corresponding to CP: 477–566). For some reason he then changed notebooks, using VI.B.9, and went back to the fourth case study that he had skipped, "President Schreber" ("Psychoanalytic Notes on an Autobiographic Account of a Case of Paranoia [Dementia Paranoides]"), taking notes from it (VI.B.9: 22–25, corresponding to CP: 391–418) before returning to "The Wolfman" for two pages, stopping with the note "X look for Λ / in sky" (VI.B.9: 39, corresponding to the words "When he died he looked for him in the sky" [CP: 566]). At an undetermined time he took a few notes from the same case study in notebook VI.D.1 (as far as we can judge from VI.C.3: 178–79, retracing his steps to CP: 562).

Altogether, the notes derived from Freud are few and apparently random.[9] Some of them would be crossed out later and used in the drafts, in the strange manner Joyce used his notes, while others are simply abandoned. Some of this material may have been immediately useful for Shaun c, which was in the process of being written. For instance, on VI.B.19: 45 he noted the phrase "to lay a ghost," which derives from CP: 264: "In an analysis, however, a thing which has not been understood inevitably reappears; it is an unlaid ghost, it cannot rest until the mystery has been solved and the spell broken." On CP: 153 Joyce found a crucial idea for the future chapter II.2: "Thirst for knowledge seems to be inseparable from sexual curiosity." Although he did not take notes from that sentence, he noted other words from the same page.

One note, on VI.B.19: 70, would prove particularly important for our chapter: "Δ Il a pleuré / m Quoi. Il a ple[uré]." Deriving from the *Collected Papers* and already assimilated in the Joycean system of sigla, this exchange in French introduces the idea or even the scene of the parental couple disturbed by the child's cry. The implementation of that idea in Shaun d would not, however, take place for a few months.[10] Joyce probably left behind in Paris both notebooks, VI.B.9 and VI.B.19, as well as the Freud volume when he went for a period of summer holidays in Normandy. It is there that the Saint-Valéry-en-Caux episode of inspiration (or pseudo-inspiration) took place, followed by a relapse into perplexity. Sometime in September, still looking for inspiration, Joyce returned to the Freud volume, using VI.B.19 again, and resumed the reading exactly where he had left it in VI.B.9. On VI.B.19: 90 we find the note "look for me in / sky," which derives from the same material ("When he died he looked for him in the sky" [CP: 566]) as the item in VI.B.9 on which the note taking had stopped. This reiteration is immediately followed by another entry, "coitus between / heavenly bodies," deriving from Freud's footnote to the same sentence: "These dreams represented the coitus scene as an event taking place between heavenly bodies" (CP: 556 n.). This is clearly the origin of the passage, at the end of our chapter (FW: 583), where the parental coitus is projected first on the window blind, to the view of the passersby, and then assumes cosmic dimensions. But although this afforded a neat transition to the expected dawn, it was probably not the turning point yet. After all, the very same passage had been read a few months before without triggering the inspiration for the chapter. Two notes on the same page of VI.B.19 were probably more decisive.

The first of them, "sympathy / pen in war! / —out peace" (VI.B.19: 90), derives from CP: 567:

> Then suddenly, in connection with a dream, the analysis plunged back into the prehistoric period, and led him to assert that during the coitus in the primal scene he had observed the penis disappear, that he had felt sympathy with his father on that account, and had rejoiced at the reappearance of what he thought had been lost. So here was a fresh emotional trend, starting once again from the primal scene. Moreover, the narcissistic origin of sympathy (which is confirmed by the word itself) is here quite unmistakably revealed.

This is not simply a voyeuristic scene, somewhat reminiscent of a passage in "Circe,"[11] a powerful dramatization of the sexual congress in which the spectator is compellingly implied; it brings together the ancient idea of dreams as a vehicle of revelation and a new notion of the parental coitus as a point of universal origin, not only biological but psychological.

The next note on the page, "Roman V / V oclock her legs" (VI.B.19: 90), derives from CP: 569: "[T]he butterfly wings [. . .] had looked, so he said, like a woman opening her legs, and the legs then made the shape of a roman V, which, as we know, is the hour at which . . . he used to fall into a depressed state of mind." This is developed in another note on the next notebook page: "$^{g}\wedge$ turned a Roman" (VI.B.19: 91). We witness here Joyce, who was at the time exploring the visual aspect of his sigla,[12] discovering new potentialities for his Shaun symbol. It suddenly absorbs the Wolfman's pregnant V shape, with its various meanings: a Roman numeral, marking an hour, and the open legs of a woman during coitus.[13] A new structural pseudodeterminant, a new rationale for the chapter's belonging to the book of Shaun emerges, based on an inversion, or rather a (clockwise?) rotation of the siglum: if Shaun is walking backward along the road, it is only natural that he will trip and fall on his head, feet up. He will then become a (Roman) V, indicating the time, the time of the coitus, "kicksolock in the morm" (FW: 584.03),[14] the time of open legs, the time when the feet are in the air, the time when one gets one's kicks.

The continuity of the book of Shaun, "logical," literal, and temporal, being thus assured, the content of the chapter could be supplied to a large extent by the case study that was being read: the parental intercourse, the child's Oedipal nightmare, the bed-wetting and/or soiling, and something more subtle, the visual setup and narrative organization of the chapter (perhaps also the very peculiar ambience of Freud's case studies, blending levelheaded, sometimes sordid matter-of-factness with an oneiric atmosphere). The sequence of events, however, is distorted almost beyond recognition by the process of assimilation to *Finnegans Wake,* comparable to the displacement and "secondary elaboration" characteristic of the dream work,[15] but also similar to Freud's own hermeneutics, which involve, in this particular case, a very drastic rearrangement of the chronology and causality presented by the manifest material.

Our Forced Payrents: Primal Motives

The parental intercourse, so central in the final version of Shaun d and in Freud's interpretation, does not come in early at the draft stage. On the other hand, the child's nightmare is more prominent in the early phase. This, together with the bed-wetting, is already announced at notebook stage, on VI.B.19: 91, by the words "pyroneira / micturates," inspired by Freud's discussion of the relation between enuresis and the symbolism of fire. The note is inserted in between the two crucial "V" phrases, so it really belongs to the moment of discovery. It is remarkable that Freud does not mention *dreaming* of fire in this case study,[16] so the note is already a step toward an assimilation to the *Wake*'s night language and to the earlier dream-related project for Shaun d.

The first manifestation of the dream—in the draft and in the finished chapter—is indirect: a noise is heard in the night, a noise that turns out to be the crying of a child. The first words written in the first draft ("What was thass? Fog ^[1]what[1]^ wars? Too mult sleepth. Less me sleepl" [BL 47482a f. 4; JJA 60: 5; FDV: 247) are very close to the final text: "What was thaas? Fog was whaas? Too mult sleepth. Let sleepth" (FW: 555.01–2). The stertorous breathing of a sleeper is perhaps more audible in the last version, some multilingual puns have been added, others have been lost, but what remains unchanged is the idea of a sound encroaching on a deep slumber. The sleepers, protesting against the interruption with their tongues made thick from sleep in a language that is indeed a night language, are not identified, although two abandoned insertions offer ambiguous clues.[17]

In the chapter as it is published the origin of the interruption does not appear before a long delay caused by a series of interpolations, but in the first draft the crying of the child follows immediately, without even the pause of a paragraph break. We can hear him directly, complaining that he is abandoned by his family and calling to his soothing mother to protect him from his terrifying father: "All gone. ~~Missed~~ ^[1]Mistold[1]^ and ~~Misses~~ ^[1]Mistrams[1]^ Gonakong ^[1]Ah ho![1]^ And old Dudud Deadenman. Anna living one. Pour the winds and waters on. ~~The~~ ^[1]~~o'er~~[1]^ whelming waters on. Tears! Ah tears! Ah tears! Mamma! ~~Big~~ ^[1]Goat[1]^ ~~Dad~~ ^[1]Fawdla[1]^ ~~crush~~ tuns ~~on me~~ ^[1]me belong[1]^! Fawtrick! Save me!" (BL 47482a f. 4; JJA 60: 5; FDV: 254).[18] The invocation to Anna Livia is quite melodious, certainly influenced by chapter 8, which Joyce was revising simultaneously.[19] This kind of lyricism is not very childlike and was probably inappropriate for the tone of the new chapter: it does not survive beyond the first draft, like this whole passage of direct expression.[20] Keeping the dream out of the book altogether and offering only indirect access to it has several advantages: it remains more vague and appealingly mysterious, it is able to carry greater symbolical weight, it recalls the panther dream in *Ulysses,* and it mischievously reverses Freud's text, in which the child's dream is part of the manifest material, while the parental coitus is only indirectly (and somewhat laboriously) inferred.

The mother's answer, however, makes the Oedipal content of the dream quite explicit in the first draft as well as in the final version:

> Shoo! Shool aroon! Were you dreaming, dear! The Fawdra! The fall! Shoo! There is no father in the room at all. You dear one. No bad big father, dear one. Only in your imagination? your little magnnation. Shoo, my dear one! (BL 47482a f. 4, first layer; JJA 60: 5; FDV: 254)

> You were dreamend, dear. The pawdrag? The fawthrig? Shoe! Hear are no phanthares in the room at all, avikkeen. No bad bold faathern, dear one. Opop opop capallo, muy malinchily malchick! Gothgorod father godown followay tomollow the lucky load to Lublin for make his thoroughbass grossman's bigness. Take that two piece big slap slap bold honty bottomsside pap pap pappa.
> [. . .]
> Sonly all in your imagination, dim. Poor little brittle magic nation, dim of mind! Shoe to me now, dear! Shoom of me! (FW: 565.18–30)

The main difference is that in the final text the mother's consolation is separated from the liminal "What was thaas?" by ten pages (but Joyce takes care to sustain the connection by frequent reminders).[21] This is the result of a narrative strategy that progressively establishes itself as the first draft develops, systematically generating a series of interpolations. Before this process was under way, however, a few additions were made to the mother's speech, and an important passage of a quite different nature was inserted on the preceding verso page: "Li ne dormis? S! ~~Dormas~~ Malbone dormas. Kial li krias nokte? Parolas infanetes. S!" (BL 47482a f. 3v; JJA 60: 4). We recognize here, its French turned into Esperanto, the Freud-inspired parental dialogue from VI.B.19: 70 that I discussed above: "Δ Il a pleuré / ᗰ Quoi. Il a ple[uré]."[22] The Freudian elements noted a few months before are now falling into place within the new framework. They also generate (or contribute to the generation of) complex passages that are less direct transpositions of the notes.

In the first draft four passages follow directly the mother's soothing words. We will soon come back to the first of these, corresponding to FW: 565.33–566.06.

The second takes the form of a dialogue:

> —He is quieter now. ^[1]Sh![1]^ Let us ~~listen~~ ^[1]wait a min[1]^.
> —Legalentitled ^[1]non[1]^accesstopartnzz. Byrightofcaptzz. Asiftwerewildebeestzz. ^[1]Bsurd![1]^ Haveandtoholdpp. Twainbeonefleshz.
> —Sis? ^[1]Let us go.[1]^ Make a noise! Slee . . .

—Obstructrightofwayz^[1]surd[1]^. Beauty of unionzz. Claimtopossesskk.
—Quiet! Put out the li! ~~Pu!~~ ^[1]Pout![1]^
—Hues of the richunfoldmm. Waken and uprising proveff. <I^[1]E[1]^>nnoinsiholymatrimonnn (BL 47482a f. 5; JJA 60: 7; FDV: 256–57)

We can recognize the parents' voices by the bedside and another voice that is probably the voice of the dreaming child, but what he is saying remains quite mysterious at this stage.

The third passage, corresponding to FW: 571.35–572.06, is a description of a foul underground universe: "For in unclean spirits which are working. In earthpits deathmines & saltclosets underfed nagging nibbling knocking us up out of ? afternoon. Down with their tools! youngdammers are pocking on the dournoggers. The yungfries will be frisking over their underlayers. Spick & spade troweling a gravetrench for their forebear Fortinbrace. Up with his club!" (BL 47482a fs. 5–6, first layer; JJA 60: 7–9; FDV: 257). We soon realize that this festering subterranean world, peopled with "unclean spirits" or "netherworld bosomfoes" "working tooth and nail" at an unspecified task, is a purely interior universe of gnawing remorse, an Oedipal/Hamletian world where much energy is spent on the endless task of digging a grave for the primeval father ("Spick & spade troweling a gravetrench for their ^first^ forebear Fortinbrace") whose phallic potency inhibits his successors ("Down with their tools! [. . .] Up with his club!") and attracts the young females ("youngdammers are pocking on the ^old gammer's^ dournoggers").

In later versions, as a part of a general strategy of extroversion that characterizes the further development of the chapter, this shadowy inner world will be exteriorized in two long and deliberately abstruse passages, "Honuphrius" (FW: 572.21–573.32) and "Tango-Pango" (FW: 573.33–576.09). The involved depravities revealed in the confessional box or listed in the casuist's manual and the legal jungle of the business world are adequate transpositions of the intricate perversions and obscure debtorships that, according to Freud's case studies, lurk beneath the surface of the consciousness of all of us, including innocent maidens and sweet little children. Those difficult passages are easier to understand when they are juxtaposed with the "netherworld" paragraph—and in their turn they help us retrospectively to understand the mysterious words uttered by the sleeping child: here too, the labyrinth of the unconscious, as revealed by the dream, is expressed in terms of a jumbled mixture of (among others) legal jargon and ecclesiastical views on matrimony and sexual conduct ("—Legalentitled accesstopartnzz. Byrightofcaptzz. Asiftwerewildebeestzz. Haveandtoholdpp. Twainbeonefleshz. [. . .] / —Obstructrightofwayz. Beauty of unionzz. Claimtopossesskk. [. . .] Injoinsinholymatrimonnn").

Then comes at last the "prayer to the divinity which shapes our roads" mentioned in the letter to Miss Weaver.

> Projector & ~~sole tracer~~ ^[1]giant builder[1]^ of ^[1]all[1]^ causeways ^[1]~~wheresoever~~ wheresoeven[1]^, hoppingoffpoint and terminus of ^[1]straf[1]^straightcuts and corkscrewn perambuloops, zeal whence ~~&~~ ^[1]~~for~~ to[1]^ goal whither wonderlust ^[1]whereas[1]^ ~~on account~~ ^[1]in sequence[1]^ of which every ~~might~~ ^[1]mortal mucker[1]^ ~~must make~~ ^[1]makes[1]^ a ^[1]partial[1]^ mickle, as different as York from Leeds ~~as~~ ^[1]being[1]^ the only way ~~of~~ ^[1]in[1]^ the world, to look after itself beforehand; mirrorminded curiosity and would-to-the-large which brings hill ^[1]up[1]^to ^[1]mole[1]^hunter, home ~~to~~ ^[1]through 1st[1]^ husband, perils before swine, & ~~horse upon~~ ^[1]horsepower down to[1]^ hungerford, prick this man and ~~bob~~ ^[1]twot[1]^ this woman ^[1]our ~~first~~ ^[2]forced[2]^ payrents[1]^, [. . .] and guide them [. . .] through the labyrinth of their ~~similars and~~ ^[1]semilikes[1]^ & the ~~devious trials~~ ^[1]~~alterations~~ ^[2]~~vapulations~~ alteregoases[2]^[1]^ of their ~~own~~ ^[1]pseudo[1]^selves [. . .] baron and feme: that he may ~~discover~~ ^[1]dichcover[1]^ her: that she may ~~uncover~~ ^[1]uncouple[1]^ him. (BL 47482a fs. 6–7; JJA 60: 9, 11; FDV: 259)

As was said earlier, the presence of this prayer in the context seems a little forced, insofar as it is an archaeological remnant of a superseded project (roads as the main theme of the chapter), but if we look closely, we will find that it is fully integrated with the Oedipal tenor of the chapter. This prayer is a hymn to the father, who is both, in the terms of the letter to Miss Weaver, the "ponderous protagonist" and the "divinity which shapes our roads": HCE/Mr Porter, the all-too-human genitor as well as the mythical figure that stands for the key position in the symbolical structure, the polar star of the Oedipal constellation. The same superior force guides our conduct in all circumstances, preserves our identity against the "alteregoases" of our "pseudoselves,"[23] and makes copulation between man and woman possible.[24] An addition in the margin makes it clear that the couple in question is "our ~~first~~ ^[1]forced[1]^ payrents" (BL 47482a f. 7; JJA 60: 11)—our first parents, the *first forebear(s)* mentioned above, the primeval couple but also the original inescapable debt that we will never finish paying.

Contrary to what we might think, this praise of Oedipal normality is not ironic. The paternal function remains central in *Finnegans Wake,* comparable to the Central Post Office in Dublin (Oedipal triangulation and geographical localization have the same function). It is the universal goal and point of departure in spite of all the vagaries ("hoppingoffpoint and terminus of ^1straf1^straightcuts and corkscrewn perambuloops, zeal whence ~~&~~ ^1~~for~~ to1^ goal whither wonderlust"), or, to be more accurate, it is the stable underlying structure that allows for linguistic and narrative freedom.[25] One can afford to wander and stumble in the dark if there is a main road that can be reached ultimately.

Seequeerscenes: The Elaboration of Perspective

More important perhaps than all this thematic material is the contribution of "The Wolfman" to the visual setup and narrative organization of the chapter.

In *Ulysses* Joyce had carried very far the experimentation with perspective: the shot/reverse shot of "Nausicaa," the stereoscopy of "Wandering Rocks," the parallax engendered by the juxtaposition of monocular perspectives in "Cyclops," the invasion of a scenic viewpoint by a hallucinatory subjectivity in "Circe," the diabolically involved play of gazes and mirrors in "Sirens." In Shaun d the optical setup, associated, as in the case of "Sirens," with a dense vocal polyphony, is even more complex.

Although (or perhaps because) we never find out what the child's dream *looks like*,[26] although (or perhaps because) the boy actually sees very little during the short time when he is awake (at most, he catches sight of the father's erection, as we can guess from the mother's objurgations to her husband),[27] the chapter is infused with an intense visual curiosity—Freud's term, as noted in VI.B.19: 37, is "scoptophilia."[28] This does not take the form of the *simple* voyeurism referred to earlier. The inspiration here is probably the Wolfman's nightmare, with its strange displacement and multiplication of the gaze: according to Freud, the seven wolves staring through the window represent the dreamer's own fascination with the primal scene. In the same way, the perspective on the very banal events of our chapter is extraordinarily diverse and made palpable through the use of several optical devices.

This dimension, however, is only gradually introduced as the chapter develops. On the first page of the first draft there is absolutely no visual element. We simply hear a succession of voices in the deep of the night: the sleepers, the crying child, the consoling mother. Then, abruptly, a very different voice intrudes: a travel guide, a kind of Baedeker, describing the amenities of Chapelizod/Lucan: “When you ~~move~~ ^1travel1^ through ~~Chapelizod~~ ^1Lucalizod1^. ~~On~~ ^1At1^ the ~~Lucan~~ ^1sulphur1^ spas to visit. It’s safer to hit than to miss it. Stop at the inn!” (BL 47482a f. 4; JJA 60: 5; FDV: 255).[29] This introduces the idea of visiting and, indirectly, of *sightseeing*. The following pages, however, are still entirely devoid of any visual sensation, except for a brief mention of “silvery ~~streams~~ ^1moonbeams1^” (BL 47482a f. 5; JJA 60: 7; FDV: 256), which are ambiguous in this respect, since their function is to keep the child “~~safely~~ ^1softly1^ dreaming,” that is to say, to keep his eyes shut. More voices are heard,[30] sensations of warmth and clamminess are felt, odors emanate from “earthpits” and “cheeseganglions,” food is tasted or nibbled, but there is nothing to be seen in this obscure cavity, this gloomy and foul “underground” (the recesses of the soul).

It remains so in the next pages of the draft until the last part of the “prayer,” when we encounter the words “baron and feme: that he may discover her: that she may uncover him: that he may close over: that they recover themselves” (BL 47482a fs. 7–8, first layer; JJA 60: 11, 13). The sexual sense of covering and the erotic dimension of discovery are here closely entangled with their etymological meaning of hiding and showing. The formulation revives the optical and even the voyeuristic dimension implicit in the phrase, currently used to denote a purely animal copulation: to speak of covering a female implies an external point of view, a witness of the copulation. From there on the externality of the perspective will become increasingly affirmed, and the fascinated gaze on the sex act (the primal scene) will be made increasingly concrete.

What is immediately noticeable is the progressive expansion and hypertrophy of the optic dimension. On the draft pages immediately following there is a proliferation of the words “see,” “look,” “watch,” “leer,” and all the visual vocabulary that was conspicuously absent from the early pages. Sometimes the concentration is intense:

> Leary, leary Twentytonleary, he’s working ~~steady~~ ^~~hard~~^ ^Kingsdown^ for his ~~own~~ ^1orb’s1^ extension. Look at him now ^1a momentum1^ ~~Now~~ ^1that1^ his bridges are blown to babyrags ~~and~~ by the ~~lie~~ ^1lee1^ of his ~~juniper~~ hulk ~~in riding her~~ ^1upright on her orbit1^ & the heave of his ^1juniper1^ arks in action, he’s naval I see. (BL 47482a fs. 22–23; JJA 60: 41–43; FDV: 263)

> The other twin, you see, has been crying in his sleep, the little devil. That is Jerry but you cannot see what he had in his hand because I have not told

> you. He is quite one of the blake tribe already. Blake? Whatever do you mean with blake? With blake I mean ink. O, I see. You will never know all that you did not see that you saw. (BL 47482a fs. 34v–35v, first layer; JJA 60: 66–68; FDV: 253)

> At what do you leer? I leer because I must see a buntingcap so pinky on the ponks. (BL 47482a f. 38v; JJA 60: 74; FDV: 255)

> They are from her springwell of our park which makes the blind to see the blind? How it is clear? (BL 47482a f. 39v, first layer; JJA 60: 76; FDV: 256)

> Let's see. See you. All seeing, together. Sirs? Where saw him? (BL 47482a f. 8v, first layer; JJA 60: 14; FDV: 267)

When we look at the final text we find that more of these concentrations have been added.

> Gauze off heaven! Vision. Then. O, pluxty suddly, the sight entrancing! Hummels! That crag! Those hullocks! O Sire! So be accident occur is not going to commence! What have you therefore? Fear you the donkers? Of roovers? I fear lest we have lost ours [. . .] respecting these wildy parts. How is hit finister! How shagsome all and beastful! What do you show on? I show because I must see before my misfortune so a stark pointing pole. Lord of ladders, what for lungitube! Can you read the verst legend hereon? (FW: 566.28–36)

> I saw. I'm sorry! I'm sorry to say I saw! (FW: 581.25)

And it could have been worse: when he sorted the notes copied by Mme Raphaël in VI.C.1, organizing them for use in the four chapters of Book III,[31] Joyce automatically assigned the words "saw see shall see" to Shaun d (BL 47486a f. 59; JJA 61: 186), but they somehow landed in III.3 (FW: 508.27).

Even more important than this lexical concentration is its negative counterpart. As Joyce copied his first draft, immediately after the two first sleepy lines ("What was thass? [. . .] Less me sleepl"), he left space for a new passage that eventually became the series of paragraphs beginning with "So, nat by night by naught by naket" (FW: 555.05–24), "night by silentsailing night" (FW: 556.01–22), "nowth upon nacht" (FW: 556.23–30), "wan fine night and the next fine night and last find night" (FW: 556.31–557.12), "each and every juridical sessions night" (FW: 557.13–558.20), and "niece by nice by neat by natty" (FW: 558.21–25).

This superlative piling up of nocturnal layers, this "scotographia,"[32] is very different from the gloom that prevailed in the first draft: the relentless insistence on *darkness visible* is quite another matter than the mere absence of anything to see. It has the effect of multiplying the visual curiosity and the intensity of the gaze. Indeed, the same character (Sickersen) is called "Watchman Havelook Seequeersense" (BL 47482a f. 27v; JJA 60: 52), and, a few pages later, "patrolman Seekasun" (BL 47482a f. 16v; JJA 60: 30), suggesting wandering in darkness in search of light and implying the same visual eagerness.

The impression of *sightseeing,* fugitively and implicitly introduced in the early passage describing Lucalizod in guidebook tones, is prevalent in these paragraphs and in the other interpolations that make up the bulk of the text between FW: 555.05 and 578.03: we are visiting the house and its surroundings, examining the cast of characters as if they were exhibits. The dreaming, sleepy, or "semiwakened" atmosphere that pervaded the early part of the draft is no longer relevant (see JJA 60: ix). Although some of the characters are actually asleep, the narration is quite alert and wakeful; it expresses wide-eyed fascination rather than slumber.

One of the most memorable features of the finished chapter is the clear succession of four distinct perspectives, explicitly identified with the Four Old Men, on the parental couple, each view being graphically described in terms of erotic, theatrical, and cinematographic performances. But it is only quite late in the development of the chapter that this setup was progressively established and that the Four became a major narrative focus.

A substantial part of the second draft had already been written when Joyce added on a verso (BL 47482a f. 30v; JJA 60: 58) the passage beginning with "A cry off. Where are we at all?" (FW: 558.32–33). It opens with a description of a suburban dwelling, its master bedroom, and its furniture. The description is detailed and matter-of-fact; it sounds like some sort of naturalist novel or perhaps rather like a survey or a police report: "Interior of house on the outskirts of city. Ordinary bedroom set. Bed for two. Chair for one. Woman's clothes on chair. Man's trousers, collar with tie on bed-knob. Linen man's coat on nail, well right. Woman's gown on ditto, ditto left. Small table near bed, front. Lamp without globe, newspaper, Saint Andrew's tie, glass etc on table. Time: about four a.m." (BL 47482a f. 30v; JJA 60: 58). But the interlinear addition of one word ("^^{1}practicable^{1}^ Lamp without globe") suddenly transforms the objects into props and radically changes the status of the setting. What is being described is a stage scenery or a cinema set—or perhaps, we come to suspect, it is not described but prescribed: we may be reading a didascalia or a film scenario, or perhaps we are hearing the voice of the continuity man, reading the script to the crew.[33]

Then we find a note in the margin that, judging by the indentation of the text, seems to have been written before the remainder of the paragraph:

HCE
CEH
Sidomy[34] EHC
HCE (BL 47482a f. 30v; JJA 60: 58)

As is often the case, Joycean invention closely associates here the visual with the literal and the musical. Joyce realizes that his hero's name is a chord in German musical notation: HCE = si do mi.[35] He is, of course, aware of the punning opportunities (*sodomy;* the homonymy between the notes C, si, and the verb "to see"), but he resists using them immediately in favor of an important structural decision. Each of the literal (and musical) permutations of the initials will be associated with a numbered position, referring not to the Terpsichorean classification but to a repertoire of erotic postures. The result, however, is less a kind of Kama-sutra than a voyeur's handbook: the emphasis is not on the sexual experience of the participants but on the visual opportunities offered by each position (corresponding to Freud's remarks on the coitus *a tergo* as the only posture affording the child an opportunity to fully observe his parents).

This is what Joyce wrote next to the marginal note: "Man with nightcap in bed, fore, Woman with curlpins, discovered. First position. Man looking round, beastly expression, exhibits rage. ruddy blond, large build, any age. Woman, sitting up, looks at ceiling: haggish expression, beaky nose, exhibits fear: sallow tint, undersized, any age" (BL 47482a f. 30v; JJA 60: 58). He then made the following additions: "Woman with curlpins, discovered. ^[1]~~Aside~~ ^[2]Sidelong[2]^ Point of view[1]^ First position. ^[1]Man partly masking female Domicy[1]^" (BL 47482a f. 30v; JJA 60: 58), introducing the musical theme and emphasizing the optical dimension (the couple's bodies are like heavenly bodies, eclipsing and revealing each other in turn to the observing astronomer). The point of view thus determined is, however, left completely impersonal at this stage.

The same is true of the second permutation: "What is the view which now takes up second position, tell it, please? You notice that way because the male imposition masks the female. It is called meseedo" (BL 47482a f. 35v, first layer; JJA 60: 68; FDV: 253). Drafted sometime after the first passage, it already integrates in its basic layer the optical and the musical elements. Additions here simply reinforce the obscene allusions, mixing them with legal jargon ("way" is replaced by "rereway," "imposition" is replaced by "entail," "female" is replaced by "famcovert").

The third and fourth permutations appear in two additions in the margin of the second draft, too similar in appearance and structure not to have been inserted at the same time, although they are twenty pages distant:

> Third position. ^[1]Excellent view from front[1]^ Sidomy. Female partly masking male. (BL 47482a f. 39; JJA 60: 75)

> Fourth position ^[1]View from horizon[1]^ Twomesee. male and female unmask we them. (BL 47482a f. 59; JJA 60: 115)

They include in the same order the catalog number for the position, a punning interpretation of the chord, and a description of the posture of the participants in its relation to an external observer. This last essential feature is duplicated by an addition, identically situated in both cases, defining the perspective with greater precision.

The first passage was then modified again in the process of fair-copying it.

> Interior of dwelling on outskirts of city. Ordinary bedroom set. Salmonpapered walls. Back, empty Irish grate. North, wall with window, practicable. No curtain. Blind down. South, party wall. Bed for two, chair for one. Woman's garments on chair. Man's trousers, collar on bedknob. Man's corduroy coat on nail. Woman's gown on ditto. Over mantlepiece picture of Michael, lance, slaying Satan, dragon with smoke. Small table near bed, front. Lighted lamp, practicable, scarf, gazette; tumbler etc.
>
> Time: about four a.m.
>
> Man with nightcap in bed, fore, Woman with curlpins. Discovered. Side point of view. First position of harmony. Male partly masking female. Man looking round, beastly expression, fishy eyes, exhibits rage. Ruddy blond, gross build, any age. Woman, sitting, looks at ceiling: haggish expression, peaky nose, exhibits fear. Welshrabbit tint, undersized, no age. Play! (BL 47485 fs. 7, 30; JJA 60: 256, 258)

The crucial word "practicable" (which at the same time affirms the solidity of the object and its function as a part of a decoy) is used a second time. The "First position" is described as a position of "harmony" (to be understood, like its counterparts "consonance," "dissonance," and "resolution" in the other parallel passages, both in a musical and a sexual sense). The passage now closes with an imperative "Play!"—a director's injunction reminiscent of the conductor's "Begin!" at the end of the "Sirens" overture. New additions were then added in a different ink that make it absolutely clear that the scenery is artificial and belongs to the performing arts ("Scene and property plot"), the world of pantomime, Elizabethan plays, or brothel tableaux ("Act. dumbshow"), and that the action is accompanied with recorded music ("Groove 2") and is being filmed ("Closeup"). At last, the name of the first old man is introduced in this connection ("Check action. Matt!").

The second passage has undergone only two modifications in the process of fair-copying: "What is the view which now takes up a second position, tell it, please? You notice it in that rereway because the male entail partially eclipses the famcovert. It is so called for its discord the meseedo" (BL 47485 f. 32; JJA 60: 260). The substitution of the word "eclipses" has made more explicit the identification of the couple with heavenly bodies. A "discord" has also been introduced in the position to balance the "harmony" of the first passage, but an interlinear addition makes the symmetry more specific: "takes up a second position ^1of discordance.1^" Probably at the same time the name of Mark is similarly introduced: "[T]ell it, please? ^1Mark!1^" (BL 47485 f. 32; JJA 60: 260).

By the time the third passage was fair-copied the definition of the position was already integrated in the text, but the name of Luke is also a late addition: "Third position of concord. ^1Luk!1^ Excellent view from front. Sidome. Female imperfectly masking male" (BL 47485 f. 21; JJA 60: 272). In the fourth passage both the definition and the name of John are included in the same addition: "Fourth position ^1of solution. How Johnny! Finest view1^. ~~View~~ from horizon. Two me see. Male and female unmask we them" (BL 47485 f. 41; JJA 60: 279). In the second fair copy only the first passage was further modified, with one significant addition: "Say! Eh? Ha! [CEH]," to complete the symmetry and the range of literal puns.

What does all this suggest? It is clear that the near perfect parallelism of the four passages and the symmetry of the four perspectives are not the result of thorough planning but something that emerged in the course of writing. The starting points are the discovery or rediscovery of the musical significance of the initials HCE and a purely formal principle of permutation of the three letters/notes, allowing the return to the original position. Hence four chords, four lovemaking postures, and, in the environment of the chapter as it was developing at that moment with great emphasis on the visual dimension, four distinctively marked points of view. That the four perspectives were necessarily associated with the Four seems evident to the reader of the earlier chapters of Book III, but we have seen that in fact the Old Men appeared quite late in the evolution of the text.

Now, when we look at VI.B.19 we find, on page 87, crossed out in green pencil: "^{g}X 4 poster bed^{g} /—master." This means that very early, probably before the chapter was begun, Joyce had already had the idea of identifying the Four with a four-poster. Obviously, if they are identified with the four posts, they have a privileged view of what is happening in the bed, and the rest seems to follow as a matter of course. However, this is again a case of retrospective reading, authorial as well as critical: Joyce himself interpreted his own note, when he crossed it out to use it in the chapter in progress, in function of his current needs. We can remark that the second part of the note, apparently equally promising, identifying the four Masters with a four-master ship, never gave rise to as important a structural development and was not even crossed out.

A Retroussy from Her Point of View: The Impossible Archaeology of Motivation

Another striking example of this process can be found in the chapter, although it occurs in a passage (corresponding to FW: 587.03–588.34) genetically so complex that it would require a full-length paper to properly explicate.[36] The parental coitus has been completed, and the narrative seems to move on to other matters, but an introductory paragraph shows that the visual avidity is as great as ever:

> Let's see. See you. All seeing, together. Sirs? Who d saw him? So and so. Buzz, cease to cease. Begin you. Spake truth to sooth none other? Were you there? Were we where? Were you there, holly and ivy, where you were when he? Did you climb the creeper's wall, cling to it, remember now the Yule remember me. O. Why were you in the prickly hedges, redcoat robin, roundface chumberries? Answer by your numbers. Were you then, in the eyeful hollow? (BL 47482a f. 8v, first layer; JJA 60: 14; FDV: 267)

Scoptophilia now reverts to its usual object in *Finnegans Wake:* what happened exactly that time in the park. In other words, the events in the park reveal themselves retrospectively to be a version of the primal scene. We can remark that here there are not four perspectives and four numbered positions but three witnesses (the three soldiers, representing, with their marked gender ambiguity, a parodic version of the Oedipal triangle).[37] Those witnesses are explicitly requested to identify themselves by their number. An addition to the first draft insists on this count: "Answer by your numbers. ^^{1}1 to 3^{1}^." By the time this passage reaches the third draft (BL 47482a f. 52; JJA 60: 101), the succession of three perspectives on the scene seems clearly announced: "Answer by your numbers, one to three. ^^{1}Number one ~~from~~ ^^{2}in^{2}^ our point of view^{1}^."

And yet other interpretations are also possible and even necessary. If we take the sentence literally, the numbers are the answer to the previous question: "O. Why were you in the prickly hedges?" In this passage curiosity is focused not only on HCE's doings but also on the activities of the witnesses themselves. Like war prisoners, the soldiers are instructed to answer enemy inquiries only by giving their role number. The numbers can also be understood as a relevant answer, describing the nature of the activity of the soldiers in the hedge: this is elucidated by a note in VI.B.19: 18: "do no 1" (which derives from CP: 160: "Hans: 'Oh, I'll come up again in the morning to have breakfast and do number one'"). Number one and number two are nursery euphemisms for urinating and defecating.[38] The phrase is taken up again on page 168 of the same notebook in a mildly scatological context ("no 1 or no 2"), crossed out this time in green crayon, indicating usage, probably in our passage. This sense is further developed in a marginal addition to the third draft (BL 47482a f. 54; JJA 60: 105), which introduces "number one in deep humidity," and in the fifth draft (BL 47482a f. 51v; JJA 60: 100) with "in umber hue, his fulmenbomb? Number two coming!"

The trend is clear enough in the final text: "Mr Black Atkins and you tanapanny troopertwos, were you there? Was truce of snow, moonmounded snow? Or did wolken hang o'er earth in umber hue his fulmenbomb? Number two coming! Full inside! Was glimpsed the mean amount of cloud? Or did pitter rain fall in a sprinkling? If the waters could speak as they flow! Timgle Tom, pall the bell! Izzy's busy down the dell! Mizpah low, youyou, number one, in deep humidity!" (FW: 588.18–25). It is all the more so that the whole introductory passage, with the questioning of the soldiers and the request to "answer by your numbers," has disappeared (the introductory paragraph never made it into the fair copy). With the advent of the Four and their numbered positions, the "one to three" numbering has receded into the background, the status of the three witnesses assumes less importance, and only the scatological motif remains prominent, associated more with HCE's deeds than with his onlookers. A whole rearrangement has occurred, internal to the passage but also closely connected with the evolution of the rest of the chapter, throwing a different light on the same elements.

The same can be said of this chapter as a whole in relation to the rest of the book. It will have an important influence on the composition of some of the chapters that were not yet written when this one was drafted, in particular I.7 and II.2, but since those chapters precede it in the order of the book, they influence our reading of it—and of course influenced Joyce's revisions.

Several different accounts of the genesis of a chapter such as this one are therefore possible. Because its original impetus is necessarily overdetermined by causes of a different and sometimes contradictory nature but also because the evolution of the whole continually imposes new frames of interpretation on its various elements. Our reading of Shaun d has privileged one strand, perhaps arbitrarily, but it is important to note that "The Wolfman" remains deeply embedded in the final text, at the same time concealed and paraded. Freud's corpse is smuggled through the chapter in the beer "barrel rolling down the river Liffey,"[39] perfectly camouflaged behind the numerous *porter* references, unknown to everyone who has not seen on VI.B.19: 122 the surprising equation: "flow = unconscious / = beer." But it is important enough for Joyce still to be planting clues several years after the initial drafting of the chapter, inserting, for instance, just after the Oedipal evocation of "our forced payrents" the phrase "Bogy Bobow with his cunnyngest couchmare," bringing back pointedly the Wolfman's nightmare/*cauchemar*, his fear of female genitals, his father as bogey and as God (*Bog* in Russian, the Wolfman's language),[40] as well as Freud's couch.

Notes

1. Compare the letters to Harriet Shaw Weaver of 9 November 1924 and 16 November 1924. See also the letter of 16 August 1924 (LI: 220). On the early history of Book III see the introduction to this volume and Wim Van Mierlo's essay.

2. Danis Rose (TDJJ: 83) remarks that the place of the excursion is mentioned in VI.B.8, the notebook that Joyce was using in Normandy, "S. Valéry en Caux /— sur Somme" (VI.B.8: 5), and that we find very near "Λ_4 Dawn /roadmaker" (VI.B.8: 3). However, the deduction is weakened by the fact that the potential idea appears two pages *before* the mention of the place where it is supposed to have been conceived.

3. A more fundamental significance of this theme is suggested by Jacques Derrida in one of his famous asides: "Il faudrait méditer d'ensemble la possibilité de la route et de la différence comme écriture, l'histoire de l'écriture et l'histoire de la route, de la rupture, de la via rupta, de la voie rompue, frayée, fracta, de l'espace de réversibilité et de répétition tracé par l'ouverture, l'écart et l'espacement violent de la nature, de la forêt naturelle, sauvage, salvage. La silva est sauvage, la via rupta s'écrit, se discerne, s'inscrit violemment comme différence, comme forme imposée dans la hylé, dans la forêt, dans le bois comme matière; il est difficile d'imaginer que l'accès à la possibilité des tracés routiers ne soit pas en même temps accès à l'écriture" (*De la grammatologie* [Paris: Éditions de Minuit, 1967], 58).

4. This is not to say that they disappear. Hardly anything disappears in *Finnegans Wake.* One of the most striking examples of this is the near absence of Shaun from this chapter, which remains, nevertheless, Λd, the fourth watch of Shaun.

5. Luca Crispi, "The Mechanics of Creativity: A Genetic Study of *Finnegans Wake* II.2," Ph.D. dissertation, SUNY–Buffalo, 2001.

6. We are able to follow this process in great detail because Joyce drafted the chapter in one single copybook (FDV: 37–40; JJA 60: vii–xv). Thirty-seven years later David Hayman's hypothetical reconstruction of the composition of this chapter still seems entirely valid.

7. Sigmund Freud, *Collected Papers,* vol. 3, trans. Alix and James Strachey (London: Hogarth Press, 1925). Hereafter abbreviated as CP.

8. See Daniel Ferrer, "La scène primitive de l'écriture: une lecture joycienne de Freud," *Genèse de Babel: James Joyce et la création de Finnegans Wake,* ed. Claude Jacquet (Paris: CNRS, 1985), 15–35; Daniel Ferrer, "The Freudful Couchmare of Shaun d: Joyce's Notes on Freud and the Composition of Chapter XVI of *Finnegans Wake*" *JJQ* 22.4 (Summer 1985): 367–82; and Wim Van Mierlo's excellent article, "The Freudful Couchmare Revisited: Contextualizing Joyce and the New Psychology," *JSA* 8 (1997): 115–53, which brings out important new facts (although I sometimes disagree with their interpretation).

9. Several of them are immediately assimilated by Joyce to his own universe. For instance, on VI.B.19: 36 "Sheml" is an appropriation of the Austrian boys' nicknames encountered in "Little Hans" ("Franzl and Fritzl" [CP: 235]). On VI.B.9: 39 "his little babes (lice) K" applies to Kevin an interpretation from "The Wolfman" ("The analysis showed that all small animals, such as caterpillars and insects, that he had been so enraged with, had had the meaning of babies to him" [CP: 560]). See Van Mierlo 1997, 132, 152. The interlinear addition "toto" that

puzzled Van Mierlo here is simply French children's slang for "lice" and also a boy's name: another form of translation/assimilation.

10. As Wim Van Mierlo has shown convincingly in "The Freudful Couchmare Revisited," my hypothesis, according to which the reading of this passage was the turning point of the conception of Shaun d, is difficult to sustain for chronological reasons. This is clearly a case of deferred action.

> 11. BOYLAN: (*to Bloom, over his shoulder*) You can apply your eye to the keyhole and play with yourself while I just go through her a few times.
> [. . .]
> BOYLAN'S VOICE: (*sweetly, hoarsely, in the pit of his stomach*) Ah! Godblazegrukbrukarchkhrasht!
> MARION'S VOICE: (*hoarsely, sweetly, rising to her throat*) O! Weeshwashtkissinapooisthnapoohuck!
> BLOOM: (*his eyes wildly dilated, clasps himself*) Show! Hide! Show! Plough her! More! Shoot! (U: 15.3787–3816)

12. For example, see the many instances in VI.B.8.

13. This may also be the source of the phrase "we had seen all we desired only our jimmy, he's a roman," in a passage rife with sexual ambiguities and homosexual overtones (BL 47482a f. 8v; JJA 60: 14). Apparently, Joyce does not make much of the third meaning of the shape: butterfly wings (although he does note on the same page the Russian word for butterfly, *babushka*, given by Freud).

14. In the first draft it is "kick^^{1}s^1^oclock" (BL 47482a f. 25; JJA 60: 47). The final text may be the result of an uncorrected error of transmission. The hour is also specified as "half past ~~kick~~ ^^{1}quick^1^ in the morning" (BL 47482a fs. 24–25; JJA 60: 45, 47).

15. The distortions occasioned by the dream work are, Freud tells us, the allies of censorship. Joyce will not acknowledge his debt to Freud but at the same time plants a series of ironical and ambiguous clues.

16. But this question is treated at length in "Fragments of an Analysis of a Case of Hysteria"—"Dora" (CP: 15–16).

17. One of them is identified by the Issy siglum, the other is simply signaled with an *empty* caret, which could also be the Shaun siglum. See Daniel Ferrer and Jean-Michel Rabaté, "Paragraphs in Expansion (James Joyce)," *Genetic Criticism: Texts and Avant-Texts,* ed. Jed Deppman, Daniel Ferrer, and Michael Groden (Philadelphia: University of Pennsylvania Press, 2004), 132–51.

18. His brother and sister, Tristram and Isolde, his parents, identified as old Dudud Deadenman and Anna Living One. These names show clearly that the child is, like Little Hans, "a little Oedipus who wanted to have his father 'out of the way'" (CP: 253).

19. But it is also remarkable that on VI.B.8: 206 the words "thass? / ^^{1}Too^1^

mult sleepth," obviously the source of the beginning of the chapter, are immediately followed by the entry "Tears O tears."

20. Something of the diction of chapter 8 remains at the end of the mother's consoling answer: "While elvery stream wends ealing on. For to keep this barrel of bounty rolling" (BL 47482a f. 5; JJA 60: 7; FDV: 255; FW: 565.30–32). This is clearly a transition passage, endeavoring to recycle into the chapter the motif of the "barrel rolling down the river Liffey."

21. "A cry off" (FW: 558.32); "Cry off" (FW: 559.30); "The other, twined on codliverside, has been crying in his sleep" (FW: 563.01–2).

22. In the final text the disposition reverts to the dialogue form, as in the notebook:

—*Li ne dormis?*
—*S! Malbone dormas.*
—*Kia li krias nikte?*
—*Parolas infanetes. S!* (FW: 565.25–28)

23. Conversely, this severely limits the possibility of radical transformations and the subversive power of literature, "[f]or there is scant hope to escape his or her semperidentity by subsisting upon variables" (BL 47482a f. 21; JJA 60: 39; FDV: 263). The second passage of Oedipal thanksgiving (FW: 582.02–27) has more ironical overtones than the first.

24. Similarly, on FW: 579 (BL 47482a f. 16; JJA 60: 29; FDV: 261) the *Law* is called upon to preside over the *meeting* and *mating* of the parents.

25. Interestingly, Jacques Lacan hits on the same road metaphor when he discusses the psychotic structure of President Schreber, one of the cases studied by Freud in CP: "Le signifiant être père est ce qui fait la grand-route entre les relations sexuelles avec une femme. Si la grand-route n'existe pas, on se trouve devant un certain nombre de petits chemins élémentaires, copuler et ensuite la grossesse d'une femme. Le président Schreber manque selon toute apparence de ce signifiant fondamental qui s'appelle être père. . . . Comment font-ils, ceux qu'on appelle les usagers de la route, quand il n'y a pas la grand-route, et qu'il s'agit de passer par de petites routes pour aller d'un point à un autre? Ils suivent les écriteaux mis au bord de la route. C'est-à-dire que, là où le signifiant ne fonctionne pas, ça se met à parler tout seul au bord de la grand route. Là où il n'y a pas la route, des mots écrits apparaissent sur des écriteaux. C'est peut-être cela, la fonction des hallucinations auditives verbales . . . —elles sont les écriteaux au bord des petits chemins. Si nous supposons que le signifiant poursuit son chemin tout seul, que nous y fassions attention ou non, nous devons admettre qu'il y a en nous, plus ou moins éludé par le maintien de significations qui nous intéressent, une espèce de bourdonnement, un véritable tohu-bohu, dont nous avons été abasourdis depuis l'enfance. Pourquoi ne pas concevoir qu'au moment précis où sautent, où se

révèlent déficients les accrochages de ce que Saussure appelle la masse amorphe du signifiant avec la masse amorphe des significations et des intérêts, le courant continu du signifiant reprend alors son indépendance? Et alors, dans ce bourdonnement que si souvent vous dépeignent les hallucinés en cette occasion, dans ce murmure continu de ces phrases, de ces commentaires, qui ne sont rien d'autre que l'infinité de ces petits chemins, les signifiants se mettent à parler, à chanter tout seuls" (*Le Séminaire III: les psychoses* [Paris: Éditions du Seuil, 1981], 330). It seems that *Finnegans Wake* combines the two modes, a superficially psychotic language covering a deep-rooted Oedipal structure, which prevents it from dissolving into the monotonous babble of verbal hallucination.

26. For all we know, the child's dream might be an "auditory dream," like Little Hans's dream described by Freud ("there was no visual content whatever in this dream, and it was of the purely auditory type" [CP: 162]) and annotated by Joyce on VI.B.19: 19, for we only overhear some words and cries uttered by the child in his sleep.

27. The boy cannot witness the parents' coitus, since he does not sleep in their room. But an addition introduced at fair copy stage takes the trouble of informing us that the sleeping arrangements have changed: "This once was the other but this is the other now" (BL 47485 f. 30; JJA 60: 258). Once upon a time, then, the child may have been exposed to the traumatic, nightmare-generating spectacle. The mother says: "*—Vidu, porkego! Ili vi rigardas. Returnu, porkego! Maldelikato!*" (FW: 566.26–27), which was introduced at fair copy stage (BL 47485 f. 33; JJA 60: 261).

28. The term derives from CP: 248: "scoptophilia (or sexual pleasure in looking) in its active and passive forms."

29. "Lucan" was crossed out and replaced by "sulphur," while the first part of the word "Chapelizod" was deleted and replaced by "Luca." Later on (on a lost typescript) this compound became "Lucalized"—it is indeed what Joyce calls in II.2 "THE LOCALISATION OF LEGEND" (FW: 264.R6–8), for until that point the voices have no spatial or temporal bearings, the scene has the universality of the night world (cf. Freud's "timelessness of the unconscious" [CP: 477], noted on VI.B: 19–68).

30. But probably not the voice of the four here. Rose and O'Hanlon's interpretation (UFW: 277–78), which is supposed to rely on the drafts, is here surprising. It is, however, a good example of the process of retrospective reinterpretation induced by the final text.

31. See Dirk Van Hulle, "Économie textuelle: recyclage chez Proust, Mann et Joyce," *Genesis* 18 (2002): 91–104.

32. See VI.B.19: 124: "⊏ scotographia /—scribia."

33. This change and the resulting ambiguous status are reminiscent of what happened in the case of Circe in the first pages of the early draft. See Daniel Ferrer, "Archéologie du regard dans les avant-textes de 'Circé,'" *James Joyce: "Scribble" 1, genèse des textes,* ed. Claude Jacquet (Paris: Lettres modernes, 1988), 95–106.

34. FDV: 252 reads "Sodomy" (as well as UFW: 282—without acknowledging the use of Hayman), but the manuscript has "Sidomy."

35. See Jack Dalton, "Music Lesson," *AWN* o.s. 16 (September 1963): 1–5.

36. It is the only passage in this chapter that was drafted five times before being fair-copied.

37. But we must keep in mind that this passage was drafted *before* the four positions were introduced.

38. One question remains: What does number three represent in this context? Presumably, ejaculation?

39. See the letter to Weaver of 24 May 1924 quoted above (LI: 214); see also "For to keep this barrel ~~of~~ ^[1]in[1]^ bounty rolling" in the first draft of the chapter (BL 47482a f. 4v; JJA 60: 6; FDV: 255; FW: 565.27–28).

40. See VI.B.19: 76, "bogy," which derives from CP: 510. This was insistently reinforced by the introduction, at the same late level, of "Boggey Godde" (FW: 560.14–15) and "I leer ^[1](O my big, O my bog, O my bigbabone !)[1]^ because I must see a buntingcap of so a pinky on the point" (BL 47486b fs. 354v and 498; JJA 61: 522 and 655; FW: 567.06).

The Lost Word

Book IV

DIRK VAN HULLE

The last part of *Finnegans Wake,* marking the Viconian period of renewal, is divided into five sections that correspond to the following narrative sequences. In section 1 the sleeping giant slowly wakes up, "feeling aslip and wauking up, so on, so forth" (BL 47488 f. 5; JJA 63: 5; FDV: 271; FW: 597.12). The twenty-nine leap-year girls divert the attention to Saint Kevin (section 2), who was born on the island of Ireland in the Irish ocean and goes to Lough Glendalough to live on an isle; on this isle is a pond in which is an islet; on this islet he builds a hut and digs a cavity, which he fills with water; in the center of this pool he places a tub, filled with water, in which he seats himself and meditates on the sacrament of baptism. In section 3 the archdruid, "Barkeley," explains to Saint Patrick the "illusiones of the colourful world" (BL 47488 f. 99; JJA 63: 146a; FDV 279). Throughout the *Wake* ALP's letter has been referred to numerous times; in section 4 it is finally quoted in full. In section 5 ALP also has the last word.

As early as 21 May 1926 Joyce had informed Harriet Weaver about his plans for the last part: "I have the book now fairly well planned out in my head. I am as yet uncertain whether I shall start on the twilight games of ⊏, ∧ and ⊣ which will follow immediately after Δ or on K's orisons, to follow ∧d" (LI: 240). If he had decided to start with the final part at that moment, the writing process might have taken a completely different course. Joyce eventually did not start writing Book IV until February 1938, but apparently his original 1926 plan did not undergo many changes. Although no mention is made of "K" or "Kevin" in the first draft of the first section, the additions to the second and third drafts suggest that Joyce still had "K's orisons" in mind.

The first draft of the first section is only a few pages long (level IV§1; FW: 593–604.26). It opens with the words "Calling all dawns" (BL 47488 f. 4; JJA 63: 3; FDV: 270; FW 593.02). This entry in notebook VI.B.45: 51 marks the original opening of Book IV. Joyce wrote this prelude in February 1938,[1] shortly after his fifty-sixth birthday, while he was staying at the Carlton Elite Hotel in Zürich to consult Dr. Vogt about his eyes. When the first draft was typed out Joyce made some changes to the opening. The "dawns" became "downs," and from this moment on they were preceded by the triple repetition of the Sanskrit word "Sandhyas!" referring to the twilight before dawn (BL 47488 fs. 8v–9; JJA 63: 8–9; FW: 593.01). The text of this second-draft stage was also extended by a few extra paragraphs, in which more "regenerations" are announced and the twenty-nine leap-year girls "all setton voicies about Keavn," alias Kevin (BL 47488 f. 13; JJA 63: 17; FW: 601.18). At the third-draft stage the old stories of HCE's indiscretion are unearthed again, and the meeting in the park is echoed: "~~Have~~ Have you the ~~timas~~ time, Hans ahike? Heard you the crime, senny boy?" (BL 47488 f. 21; JJA 63: 31, simplified; FDV: 273; FW: 603.15–16). Nevertheless, the question "What does Coemhghen [Kevin], the fostard?" (BL 47488 f. 21; JJA 63: 31; FDV: 273; FW: 603.34) becomes pressing; thus, the story of Saint Kevin is introduced.

In July 1938 Joyce searched through his papers and called on Miss Weaver's help to find the sketches he had made in 1923.[2] One of these was the "Saint Kevin" sketch, drafted during the summer of 1923 and written in relatively plain English. This episode is first-drafted in one of the earliest VI.B notebooks (VI.B.3: 42–45), which is exceptional, for these notebooks rarely contain any syntagmatic narrative entities. The nine concentric circles of water and land surrounding Saint Kevin were numbered by Joyce in the next draft (BL 47488 f. 24; JJA 63: 38a). From this draft stage on Joyce started to complicate Kevin's short hagiography. He did so "by incorporating models of flawed and hypocritical piety," as Christopher Bjork has demonstrated.[3] The first addition to the second draft specifies that Kevin has "^[1]been granted privilege of a portable altar[1]^" (BL 47488 f. 24; JJA 63: 38a; FDV: 273; FW: 605.08). This addition is based on a note in VI.B.10: 13 referring to "[br]Fr. Bern[ard] Vaughan," who, according to Bjork, served as a model for Saint Kevin, "the worldly cleric, who is both pious and pompous."[4] Bjork also draws attention to some of the Bywaters notes in VI.B.10, such as "[br]He simply had no / time for girls. He used / to say his sisters / were good enough for him" (VI.B.10: 73; *Buffalo VI.B.10,* 89–90).[5] These were the basis for a short account of Kevin's youth:

> As an infant ^1~~The little Stranger~~1^ ^1Shortly after his coming into this world1^ Kevineen delighted himself by playing with the sponge on tubbing night ~~wh~~ As a growing boy ^1under the influence of holy religion which had been instilled into him across his grandmother's knee1^ he grew more & more pious and abstracted like the time God knows he sat down on the plate of mutton broth. He simply had no time for girls and often used to say ^1to his dearest mother & dear sister1^ that his dearest mother & dear sisters were good enough for him. At the age of six ^1years and six months1^ he wrote a prize essay on kindness to fishes. (BL 47488 f. 24v; JJA 63: 38b; FDV: 276)

This hagiography of a haloed murderer was written on the back of the rest of the second draft, which may explain why this passage did not make it into the published text of *Finnegans Wake.* But even though this passage is not part of the final version, its combination of extremes perfectly illustrates how Joyce made Giordano Bruno's *coincidentia oppositorum* into a writing method and how this system of applied ambiguity characterizes the work's progress from the beginning to the very end.

To the first typescript of the first section (IV§1.1) Joyce had added a few paragraphs, including a list of thirty-two saints/churches, reduced to the number of rainbow girls in the next typescript (IV§1.2). The "Kevin" sketch became the second section of Book IV (IV§2; FW: 604.27–607.22) and was added to section 1 when an integrated version of both sections was typed out, probably in the summer of 1938.[6] In this integrated version three of the twenty-nine churches ("S. Innocycora's, S. Aungiel Calzata's, S. Clovinturta's") were accidentally skipped by the typist, as Robbert-Jan Henkes discovered.[7] As a result, the published version of *Finnegans Wake* only mentions twenty-six of the intended twenty-nine, matching the number of rainbow girls.

Since the "Kevin" episode was copied from a sixteen-year-old document, the transition between the "mature" *Wakean* language of section 1 and the pre-*Wakean* language of section 2 is very sudden. Joyce therefore immediately added some "distorted" passages. Nevertheless, apart from a few instances (such as the distortion of "privilege" into "praviloge"), the original text was left remarkably intact. In the case of an accidental distortion by the typist the original text was even restored so that "most blessed kevin" is not "nenthly" but again "ninthly enthroned in the interconcentric centre of the translated water" (BL 47488 f. 38; JJA 63: 63; FW: 606.03). On the other hand, Joyce did add a separate sheet with four numbered additions, notably, a short summary of Saint Kevin's childhood miracles: "4, shearing aside the four wethers and passing and passing over the dainty daily dairy and dropping by the way the lapful of live coals and smoothing out Nelly Nettle and her lad of mettle, full of stings, ~~full~~ fond of stones, friend of ~~deadmen~~ gnewgnawn sbones and leaving all that messy messy to look after our douche douche" (BL 47488 f. 36v; JJA 63: 60, simplified; FW: 605.01). R. J. Schork discovered that this catalog is based on the Reverend John Canon O'Hanlon's nine-volume work, the *Lives of the Irish Saints*.[8] By means of these miracles Joyce reshaped the old "Kevin" sketch so that it links up almost seamlessly with the first section.

To this first part of the integrated version of the first two sections Joyce added several passages based on entries in notebook VI.B.46 derived from Fritz Mauthner's *Beiträge zu einer Kritik der Sprache*.[9] The three volumes of this "critique of language" were published between 1901 and 1903. The main idea behind the philosophical and linguistic skepticism elaborated in this work is that thought and language are identical and that they do not bear any reliable relationship with reality. Since language, according to Mauthner, is based on the memory of past sensory experiences, it is only an approximation, a mere metaphor, often more of an obstacle than a bridge between man and reality.[10] Therefore, language is unsuitable to discover the essence of reality or to acquire knowledge, for every word is accompanied by the overtones of its history. Moreover, since words are based on the memory of past experiences and since every human being has different memories, language is even unsuited for communication.[11]

Joyce's notes in VI.B.46 are divided quite systematically into different sections or "indexes," as Danis Rose has called them in his transcription and edition of the index manuscript.[12] Each index is preceded by a subject heading, such as Hebrew, East Vikings, Chinese, or Buddha, showing an explicit interest in (often exotic) languages.[13] But not all indexes were equally extensive, and some pages were left blank. The Mauthner notes are probably of a later date than the indexes, since they were jotted down wherever Joyce found some blank space, starting on pages 60 and continuing in retrograde direction on pages 54–55, 50, 49, 48, and 46.[14] Most probably, these notes were taken more or less simultaneously with the Mauthner notes in notebook VI.B.41: 235–74, which are derived from the first and second volumes of Mauthner's *Kritik*.[15] At first sight, Joyce's notes give the impression that he only scanned the text, for instance, by means of the marginal glosses such as "Staunen, Weinen, Lachen" (KS 2: 439; VI.B.41: 252), or that his reading only focused on linguistic oddities such as VI.B.41: 249(g) ("[g]papa / wowow"; FW: 378.33: "Pawpaw, wowow!"), which refer to Mauthner's discussion of what Max Müller called "the Wauwau theory," the hypothesis that the origins of language are onomatopoeic.[16] But in spite of the impression that Joyce was only looking for exotic verbal expressions, the notes do betray an interest in the content of Mauthner's work as well. Many notes are derived from chapter X in volume II, concerning the origins of language, in which Mauthner discusses—among other things—the hypothesis that an individual's ontogenetic linguistic development reflects the phylogenetic development of language. Joyce's interest in this hypothesis is evidenced by several notes on children's language. The entry "relle relle—chocolate" (VI.B.41: 252[g]), for instance, refers to a passage under the heading "Spracherfindung der Kinder" (Children's invention of language), where Mauthner discusses the case of a child who links a coincidental sound ("Rellerelle") to a particular object but gradually discovers that most adults call this object "chocolate." As a consequence, the child will adapt itself in order to speak like anyone else in order to improve communication (KS 2: 391).

Another instance that shows that Joyce was not only looking for exotic linguistic oddities is the material evidence of Joyce's focused search for Mauthner's opinion on Vico. Apparently, Joyce looked up the entry "Vico" in the index at the back of the *Kritik,* where he found two page numbers (KS 2: 455 and 479).[17] In notebook VI.B.41: 269 he took down these two page numbers, referring to passages where Mauthner argues that Vico came close to writing a language critique. Joyce wrote down the note "speech lit by facts," which refers to this passage in Mauthner's *Kritik:* "Wäre Vico imstande gewesen, seine beiden genialen Einfälle, daß die Sprachen erst durch die Sachen erhellen und daß der Ursprung der Sprache in poetischen Personifikationen zu suchen sei, zu Ende zu denken, so hätte er mit den Kenntnissen seiner Zeit eine Sprachkritik geliefert" (KS 2: 483). This detail is significant because it illustrates again how Joyce raised ambiguity to a system by applying Vico's scheme as a mold for his work and at the same time filling it with Mauthner's linguistic skepticism to shape the *Wake's ricorso.*

A number of abstract notions among the notes also indicate a more profound interest in Mauthner's discussion of the linguistic expression of time and space, especially the fact that time is often qualified by means of spatial concepts. One of Joyce's main interests was the development of language. Thus, for example, the complicated way to denote the number of leap-year girls calling for Kevin is based on two different clusters of Mauthner notes: "^^{1}Fiftines and ^^{2}but^{2}^ fortines by nov<e^a^>nas and ^^{2}or^{2}^ vantads by octettes ^[2]ay[2]^ and decadendecads by a lunary ~~and~~ ^[2]with[2]^ last a lone[1]^" (BL 47488 f. 33v; JJA 63: 54; FW: 601.13–15). The composite conjunctions "andbut" and "andor" are derived from Mauthner's suggestion that "originally the conjunctions and, but, or . . . were only poor aids to pursue one's thoughts. . . . In Hebrew, for instance, there is only one particle for and, but and or" (KS 3: 196; cf. VI.B.46: 48). The circumscription of the number twenty-nine (15 + 14 = 29 and 8 + 21 = 29) is inspired by a table in Mauthner's *Kritik,* illustrating the diversity of numerical systems, listing nine languages in which the number 18 is composed in ten different ways, such as "decem et octo" (10 + 8) or "duodeviginti" (20-2) in Latin (KS 3: 151; cf. VI.B.46: 49). Mauthner also argues that "there have always been sentences in prehistoric times, never separate words"; that "the first cry already expressed a sentence" (KS 3: 47). It is not surprising that such a statement attracted Joyce's attention.[18]

The theme of linguistic development keeps recurring throughout the writing history of *Finnegans Wake.* Notebook VI.B.46 also contains notes on Otto Jespersen's book *An International Language.*[19] As early as August or September 1923, during the composition of both the "Saint Kevin" and the "Saint Patrick" sketches, Joyce had already taken notes on another book by Jespersen, *Language: Its Nature, Development and Origin.*[20] He may have reread the book in 1938 while composing the last part of *Finnegans Wake.* A few units on page 64 of notebook VI.B.46 seem to be derived from Jespersen's *Language,* more specifically from the last part, "The Development of Language." One of these entries, "[r]n(oxe)" (VI.B.46: 64), was used in an addition to the same typescript as the crossed-out Mauthner notes: "But why pit the cur afore the noxe?" (BL 47488 f. 29v; JJA 63: 44; FW: 594.29).[21] A few pages farther on the issue of whether the day comes "afore"—before or after—the night and the changeability of temporal concepts in general, today being tomorrow's yesterday, are touched upon in other additions to the same typescript, based on a few clusters of Mauthner notes:[22] "Then's now with now's then in tense continuant. Heard. Who having has he shall have had. Hear!" (BL 47488 f. 32v; JJA 63: 52, simplified; FW: 598.28–29) and "The has goning at gone, the is coming to come. Greets to ghastern, hie to morgning. Dormidy, destady. Doom is the faste. Well dawn, good other!" (BL 47488 f. 49v; JJA 63: 50, simplified; FW: 598.09–11).

The typist seems to have misread the latter addition, for in the next typescript (BL 47488 f. 50; JJA 63: 79) "dawn" has become "down," whereupon the variant was either "passively authorized" by Joyce or simply escaped his notice. Both hypotheses are equally plausible: at the first section's second-draft stage (IV§1.1) Joyce had already changed the opening "Calling all dawns" into "Calling all downs" (BL 47488 f. 9; JJA 63: 9; FW: 593.02); on the other hand, this would not be the only error that escaped Joyce's notice. Jack P. Dalton has pointed out several mistakes that occurred during the textual development of the Kevin sketch, most notably, the line "lustral domination contained within his most portable" (BL 47488 f. 25; JJA 63: 38c), which was accidentally left out by Joyce himself when he fair-copied it (BL 47488 f. 26; JJA 63: 38d).[23] The author, however, was certainly not unaware of the danger of transmissional errors, and in order to follow the production process, given his bad eyesight, he occasionally made a remark to the typist, such as this note in the margin of IV§1.3/2.6: "This typescript is too faint. Can't read it" (BL 47488 f. 37; JJA 63: 61). Joyce clearly indicated the metatextual nature of this kind of note by marking it with a large "N.B." in red crayon.[24]

At the back of the last 1923 fair copy of the "Kevin" sketch sent to Miss Weaver on 20 July 1923 Joyce wrote the following notice: "Dear Miss Weaver: May I trouble you to make three copies of this at your leisure? Please keep one yourself for in moving today I have lost one of your typed sheets and I should like to have a complete set of these scattered passages when needed" (BL 47488 f. 27v; JJA 63: 38f). He needed them sixteen years later, when the rediscovered Kevin sketch reminded him of the piece on "Saint Patrick and the Druid," which would become section 3 (IV§3; FW: 607.23–614.18). Miss Weaver, however, did not send all of the documents she had kept for such a long time. Richard Brown has described a number of typescripts that were discovered (after the publication of *The James Joyce Archive*) in a brown paper package among Miss Weaver's papers.[25] Apart from typescripts of the "Roderick O'Conor" and "Mamalujo" sketches, the package contained two typescripts of the "Kevin" episode and two typescripts of the "Saint Patrick and the Druid" sketch, in both cases a top copy and a carbon. On the top copy of both sketches Joyce had already made a few revisions in 1923, but because these documents fell out of the direct line of textual descent the early revisions were lost in this blind alley of the work's progress.

The "Saint Patrick and the Druid" sketch was written immediately after the Kevin episode and sent to Weaver on 2 August 1923: "I send you this as promised—a piece describing the conversion of S. Patrick by Ireland" (LIII: 79). It is significant that Joyce judged it necessary to explain to Miss Weaver what the episode was about, for it was the first piece to be written in *Wakean* language. From the start Miss Weaver expressed her worries concerning the opaque nature of this linguistic experiment, and Joyce replied that he was "sorry that Patrick and [?] Berkeley are unsuccessful in explaining themselves" (LI: 204, 9 October 1923). Possibly, the mysticism of the archdruid's theory may have prompted Joyce to find a mystic way to express it and thus influenced the first *Wakean* linguistic distortions. In the first overlay on the first draft (July 1923), for instance, Joyce Latinized several words:

> The archdruid ^1Barkeley ^2in his heptachromatic sevenhued roranyellowgreeblandigo [. . .]2^1^ then explained ^1to silent ^2whiterobed2^1^ ^1Patrick1^ the illusion^1es1^ of the colourful world [. . .] appearing to fallen men under but one reflect<ed^ion^>^1em1^ of the several iridal gradations of solar light, that one which it had been unable to absorb^1ere1^ while for the seer beholding reality, the thing as in itself it is, all objects showed themselves in their true ~~colours~~ ^1coloribus1^ (BL 47488 f. 99; JJA 63: 146a; FDV: 279; FW: 611.04–23)[26]

The archdruid's ideas are based on George Berkeley's theory of perception and reality, according to which objects have no knowable existence outside of the mind that perceives them. When the archdruid tries to explain his theory "^1in other words1^" (BL 47488 f. 9; JJA 63: 146a; FDV: 279), he seems to contradict his own thesis, for instead of showing themselves in their true colors, all the objects he enumerates appear green.

In the summer of 1938, as soon as Miss Weaver had sent a version (IV§3.3) of the old "Saint Patrick and the Druid" sketch, Joyce extended it with an introduction on the deceptive nature of "this vague of visibilities" (BL 47488 f. 88; JJA 63: 149; FW: 608.01), especially in the twilight of dawn, when "Daysgreening gains in schimninging" (BL 47488 f. 88; JJA 63: 149; FW: 607.24). The cry of Stena (stone/Shaun) disturbs the draper's (HCE's) half-sleep, but the voice of Alma (elm/Shaun or "Alma Luvia, Pollabella"/ALP) reassures him. From a distance Muta and Juva (variants of Mutt and Jute/Shem and Shaun) are watching the encounter of Saint Patrick and the druid. This encounter is followed by another addition. Although this addition deals with the growing daylight, it is a rather obscure passage, unless one knows where the words are derived from. In the third volume of Mauthner's *Kritik* Joyce read and made notes on a passage about Linnaeus (KS 3: 506–9).[27] According to Mauthner, the famous botanist was "probably the greatest language creator ever" (KS 3: 508), which made him one of Joyce's greatest competitors. Therefore, notebook VI.B.41: 140–42 contains more notes not only on Mauthner (discovered by Vincent Deane) but also on Linnaeus.[28] The heading "Linnaeus" is followed by three pages of notes on the Swedish botanist's sexual system of classification, an incomplete list of plant groups, as well as Linnaeus's analysis of the principal parts of a flower: the calyx, the corolla (consisting of the tubus, the limbus, and the nectarium), the stamen, the pistillus, the pericarpum, and the semen. The six variants of the calyx or cup (involucrum, spatha, perianthum, amentus, gluma, and calyptra) were the basis for the following paragraph: "A spathe of calyptrous glume involucrumines the perinanthean Amenta: fungoalguceous muscafilicial graminapalmular planteon: of increasing, ~~livavi<d^e^>~~ ^[1]livivorous,[1]^ feelful thinkamalinks: chlorid cup" (BL 47488 f. 95; JJA 63: 161; FDV: 280; FW: 613.17–26). At this draft stage (IV§3.3) the above paragraph follows immediately after a typescript of the last 1923 version of the "Patrick" sketch.

According to Joyce, "[m]uch more is intended in the colloquy between Berkeley the arch druid and his pidgin speech, and Patrick the arch priest and his Nippon English. It is also the defence and indictment of the book itself, B's theory of colours and Patrick's practical solution of the problem" (LI: 406, 20 August 1939). This is also suggested by the text itself when Muta clearly alludes to Joyce's own work: "An I could peerceeve amonkst the gatherings who so ever they wolk in process?" (BL 47488 f. 93; JJA 63: 157; FW: 609.30–31). Most of the "gatherings" for this last stage in the work's progress were written down in notebooks VI.B.46, VI.B.45, a missing notebook (X.5), and VI.B.41/C.18. The bulk of the notes in notebook VI.B.45 deal with either language (76–82) or founders of religions such as Muhammed (103 ff.) and Confucius (119 ff.).[29] This combination of interests, together with the references to the "language creator" Linnaeus, supports James Atherton's thesis that "the artist is God-like in his task of creation" as the fundamental assumption underlying *Finnegans Wake*.[30]

The last clearly identifiable index in VI.B.46: 122–25 is preceded by the title "Buddha" and is derived from a book called *La Vie du Bouddha*, written by A.-Ferdinand Herold.[31] Danis Rose has retraced the passages excerpted by Joyce in notebook VI.B.46, among which the name of Maya recurs twice.[32] Maya, denoting "the power of a god or demon to produce illusory effects" or simply "the production of an illusion" in Indian philosophy,[33] is also the title of a book by Heinrich Zimmer, from which Joyce took two pages of notes in VI.B.47: 75–76 and two in VI.B.41: 188–89.

Many of the notes in notebooks VI.B.46, B.45, and B.41 were not used for the composition of Book IV but for the revision of the galley proofs of Books I and III. This also applies to the notes on Herold's and Zimmer's books, most of which were added to episodes where the park scene is investigated or recalled, such as the interview concerning HCE's crime (FW: 58–61), the discussion of his indiscretion (FW: 492–99), and Treacle Tom's version of the encounter in the park (FW: 523–26). All of these passages are meant to unveil the truth but lead instead to even greater confusion. This confusion is to a large extent due to Joyce's accretive writing method, which is the essence of his own "production of an illusion." The incident in the park—which possibly never took place at all—and by extension the whole *Wake* only exist by the grace of rumors. Joyce deliberately covered the facts with an obscuring "veil of Maya."

The Mauthnerian awareness that words are only metaphors has not "parolysed" (VI.B.41: 241) Joyce's creativity; on the contrary, it was a challenge to apply language as "Kunstmittel" (KS 1: 94) and (re)create a textual *Erscheinung:* "[B]e in our scheining!" (FW: 613.10). Whatever "essence" one tries to unveil or discover, the very attempt to do so wraps it up again in a cloud of words.[34] "^[1]Cumulonubulocirrhonimbant heaven electing[1]^" (BL 47488 f. 203v; JJA 63: 292; FW: 599.30–31), for instance, is the opening of a paragraph regarding the "the fog of the cloud in which we toil and the cloud of the fog under which we labour," which Joyce added to Book IV at one of the very last draft stages in order "^[1]to remind us how ^[2], in this drury world of ours,[2]^ Father Times and Mother Spacies boil their kettle with their crutch[1]^" (BL 47488 f. 203v; JJA 63: 292; FW: 600.02–3). In this context it is significant that Joyce refers to his own work by means of the Dutch word for cloud, *wolk.*[35]

It is only appropriate that the leitmotif of the veil, which recurs under different appearances in *Finnegans Wake,*[36] is added to the archdruid's explanations about the "all too many much illusiones through photoprismic velamina of hueful panepiphanal world" (FW: 611.12–13): "through photoprismic velamina" was inserted at level IV§3.4 in the same green ink as the Mauthner and Zimmer notes (BL 47488 f. 112v; JJA 63: 170). Only one of the numerous other additions on page 112v is also in green ink, "puradduxed," which is a perfect portmanteau to characterize the paradox of *Finnegans Wake* as a textual veil (purdah), woven in order to be able to unveil "the secret workings of nature" (BL 47473 f. 18; JJA 46: 286). Thanks to an addition on the same page (BL 47488 f. 112v; JJA 63: 170), Saint Patrick finally gets the chance to react against the archdruid and calls him a "pore blackinwhitepaddynger" who reasons "paralogically." Patrick wipes his nose in "a handcaughtsheaf of shammyrag ~~as~~ ^[1]to himshers seemingsuch[1]^ the sound sense sympol ^[1]in a weedwayedwold[1]^ of the fire ^[1]there[1]^ ~~that~~ the sun in his halo cast. ^[1]Onman[1]^" (BL 47488 f. 112v; JJA 63: 170, simplified; FDV: 280; FW: 612.25–30). Whether this *Amen* marks the conversion of the snot green island or rather—as Joyce explained to Miss Weaver—the conversion of Saint Patrick by Ireland does not seem to make much difference: "Yet is no body present ^[1]here[1]^ which was not there before. Only is ~~the~~ order other^[1]ed. Nought is nulled. *Fuitfiat!*[1]^" (BL 47488 f. 113v; JJA 63: 172).

In order to explain the incorporation of the two old sketches about saints in Book IV, Joyce suggested to his friends the image of a stained-glass triptych in the church of Chapelizod. It was not clear who was the third saint in this triptych next to Saint Kevin and Saint Patrick. Frank Budgen apparently asked Joyce for some explanation about the third panel, for Joyce suggested to him on 20 August 1939: "Reread the second paragraph in the hagiographic triptych in Part IV (S. L. O'Toole is only adumbrated)" (LI: 406). Saint Laurence O'Toole, bishop of Dublin at the time of the English invasion of Ireland in 1171 by King Henry II, has a more prominent role in the fable of "The Mookse and the Gripes." In Book IV only one sentence is devoted to this third saint, added at a very late stage to the galley proofs, dated by the printer 29 November 1938: "^[1]Lo, the laud of laurens ^[2]now[2]^ orielising benedictively when saint and sage have said their say[1]^" (BL 47488 f. 212v; JJA 63: 308; FW: 613.15–16).

Although Saint Patrick has a more prominent place in Book IV, he only needs a few lines to make his point. In his opinion it is impossible to perceive any *Ding an sich* "aposterioprismically" (BL 47488 f. 108v; JJA 63: 176; FW: 612.19). In the same typescript the archdruid's and Saint Patrick's arguments are respectively preceded by the words "Tunc" and "Punc" (BL 47488 fs. 107v, 108v; JJA 63: 174, 176; FW: 611.04, 612.16). "Tunc" refers to the so-called Tunc page of *The Book of Kells* and its analysis by Sir Edward Sullivan (see chapter I.5), parodied by Joyce with reference to the "Revered Letter" with which ALP tries to defend her husband against the accusations.[37] The actual letter was withdrawn from chapter I.5 early in 1924, and instead the focus shifted to para- and metatextual aspects such as the envelope. The archdruid seems to be put in the right when the *Ding an sich,* the Revered Letter itself, finally (re)appeared in Book IV§4 after more than six hundred pages or sixteen years of hidden existence. The original letter, however, underwent such a thorough metamorphosis after its rediscovery that it is hardly recognizable and consequently rather proves Saint Patrick's point. Punc.

Section 4 (IV§4; FW: 614.19–619.19) starts with the question "What has gone?" On a narrative level, this may apply to the end of the dream (fading as the dreamer awakes), but it also refers to the work itself: "How it ends? Begin to forget it. It will remember itself from every sides, with all gestures, in each our word. Forget, remember" (BL 47488 f. 117; JJA 63: 183; FW: 614.19–22). Fourteen years after ALP's letter had been removed from chapter I.5, it remembered itself.

Flashback

Joyce's plan to write a letter dates from the first stages of the writing process. Laurent Milesi has drawn attention to the fact that "the earliest seminal trace of a letter project appears in the *Exiles I* subsection of the 'Scribbledehobble' notebook, compiled when Joyce was sorting out unused material left over from previous work."[38] These notes on VI.A: 753–55 mention not only "Boston (Mass.)" but also an addressee, who is referred to as "Maggdsty" (VI.A: 753), "dear Maggy" (VI.A: 754), and "Maggesty" (VI.A: 755). Milesi has drawn up a list of thematic and lexical echoes to these notes in the first draft of the letter.[39] At the time Joyce wrote this first draft of the Letter (December 1923) he had written about twenty-nine pages in the so-called red-backed notebook (BL 47471b). The last section preceding the Letter is I.4§2, which ends in the middle of BL 47471b f. 29. Immediately after having finished the first draft of this section Joyce apparently decided that he would write a letter, but instead of starting with the beginning he left open two blank pages and only wrote the closing formula and the signature of ALP, with a short postscript.[40]

> For it was she who still ~~hoped~~ ^1believed1^ that her face was the best part of her & hoped for
> ^1Her mark & seal1^ Dame Lara Prudence Earwicker
> (valued wife of ——)
> It was this last alone that at last gave HCE the raspberry. Groaning of spirit, he lifted his hands & many who did not dare it, heard him say: I will give £10 ^1tomorrow & gladly1^ to the 1st fellow who will put that W in the royal canal. (BL 47471b f. 30, simplified; JJA 46: 233)

It is remarkable that the first draft of ALP's Letter (BL 47471b f. 31; JJA 46: 255; FDV: 81) is preceded by this protodraft of its signature and the conclusion. The fact that Joyce wrote the conclusion before the rest of the letter suggests a special interest in the signature and the question of authorship. As a possible source for the Revered Letter, Adeline Glasheen has suggested Morton Prince's *Dissociation of a Personality*, more specifically, the letters received by Prince's patient ("Miss B") from her second self ("Sally").[41] The nature of these letters "selfpenned to one's other" (FW: 489.33–34) may be important "in establishing the identities in the [Letter's] writer complexus (for if the hand was one, the minds of active and agitated were more than so)" (FW: 114.33–35). In the first draft of I.5§1, written on the back of (and probably also chronologically after) the first draft of the Letter, the "multiplicity of personalities inflicted on the provoking document" is discussed. According to a remark following the postscript of the letter (second draft) the letter is "written by the joint author" (BL 47471b f. 42; JJA 46: 272).

The letter is signed differently in each of the versions contained in the red-backed notebook: the first draft only says it is "(signed)," which might be a reference to the "predraft" of the Letter's closure on the bottom of BL 47471b f. 30 (JJA 46: 56), immediately preceding the first draft of the Letter, signed by "Dame Lara Prudence Earwicker"; the second draft is signed by "Dame Bessy Plurabelle Earwicker" (BL 47471b f. 42; JJA 46: 272); the third is signed by "Dame ^[1]Anna[1]^ Plurabelle—Earwicker" (BL 47471b f. 23v; JJA 46: 280). In the fair copy it is finally signed by "Dame Anna ^[1]Livia[1]^ Plurabelle" (BL 47473 f. 19; JJA 46: 287), to be changed to "Alma Luvia ~~Poolabella~~ Pollabella" (BL 47488 f. 118; JJA 63: 189; FDV: 284; FW: 619.16) much later, at the very end of the writing process, when the letter was finally incorporated in Book IV. In the published version the signature is not followed by Xs, representing kisses, although reference is made to these "crosskisses" (FW: 111.17) throughout the book.[42] In the last section of Book IV (a few pages after the Letter) ALP mentions a "Jermyn cousin who signs hers with exes" (FW: 625.02), which again seems to imply that the text of the letter that is discussed throughout the book is not the same as the one printed in Book IV. Patrick A. McCarthy has pointed out several phrases from the account of the Letter in chapter I.5 that do not recur in the published version of the Letter.[43]

In notebook VI.B.10: 109 there is an even earlier version of ALP, "[r]Dame Alice Barbara Esmonde" (see also *Buffalo VI.B.10*, 129; WiT: 168–70). The moment the name Livia is introduced (connecting ALP with the tea-colored river Liffey)[44] almost coincides with the first draft of I.5§4, which starts with a paragraph discussing the tea stain on the letter and the "identity of the writer complexus," but it also contains the assurance that "[w]hile we may have our irremovable doubts as to the whole sense of the text, the meaning of any phrase in it, the meaning of every word deciphered and interpreted we ~~can~~ must not have any doubts as to its authorship and authoritativeness" (BL 47471b f. 40v, simplified; JJA 46: 299; FDV: 87; FW: 117.35–118.04). If an author writes these words, the effect is the same as ALP's suspicion-arousing letter, assuring that none of the rumors about HCE's alleged crime are true. The signature that is thematized by means of the tea stain is the sum total of all the characteristic features and stylistic idiosyncrasies that mark ALP's letter as well as Joyce's own artifact, for "why, pray, sign anything as long as every word, letter, penstroke, paper-space is a perfect signature of its own?" (FW: 115.06–7). Although ALP calls her own writing an "erronymous letter" (an addition to the second draft of the letter on BL 47471b f. 38v [JJA 46: 266]), this pun on the words "anonymous" and "erroneous" is one of the earliest samples of the typically *Wakean* "signature."[45]

The sequence of the passages in the red-backed notebook corresponds rather well with their final sequence in the published version of *Finnegans Wake.* In comparison with other modernists' writing methods (e.g., Proust's) the movability of textual units in Joyce's *Work in Progress* is rather limited. Nevertheless, there are some "vagabond" or peregrinating sections, and the Letter is by far the most ambulant one: it covered the longest distance both on a narrative level (from Book I to Book IV) and in time (from 1923 to 1938).

Sections I.4§2 and I.5§2 (the Letter) belonged together for a long time. The first and especially the second drafts of both sections merged almost seamlessly.[46] When Joyce made a third draft of the letter he did not redraft the first and second pages of the second draft (because they did not contain many corrections). Since the more substantial changes in the second draft start on page 38, Joyce began to write his third draft with the same words as the first words on page 38 ("Mr Earwicker") where he happened to find some blank space (on page 14v). Because he foresaw that this unsystematic filling-up of blank versos could cause some confusion later on, Joyce indicated the new sequence of pages by numbering them in pencil:

1–3 = BL 47471b fs. 34–36 (= section I.4§2.*1)
3–12 = BL 47471b fs. 36, 37, 14v, 15v, 16v, 18v, 19v, 20v, 22v, 23v (= section I.5§2.*2)

Early in January 1924 Joyce made a fair copy of the already drafted chapters and sent it to Harriet Shaw Weaver. Around this time Joyce decided to shift the Letter backward, and he renumbered the already written passages. First, he renumbered the same pages in the sequence mentioned above (this time in the left margin and in red crayon); he subsequently seems to have changed his mind and numbered I.5§1.*1 and I.5§4.*0 in such a way that these two sections follow I.4§2.*1.[47] The red crayon numbering of the Letter (5–12, on pages 14v–23v) was then changed into 15–22 (by placing a digit [1] in front of the numbers 5, 6, 7, 8, and 9 and overwriting the first digit in the sequence 10–12 with the digit 2). The second page of I.5§2.*1 (which Joyce had not recopied because it was "fair" enough to serve as a third draft) was renumbered "4" instead of "14"—most probably by mistake. This results in the following sequence of sections:

1–3 = BL 47471b fs. 34–36 (= section I.4§2.*1)
4–10 = BL 47471b fs. 43, 44, 45, 46, 47, 48, 49 (= section I.5§1.*1)
11–13 = BL 47471b fs. 41v, 42v, 43v (= section I.5§4.*0)
[1]4–22 = BL 47471b fs. 37, 14v, 15v, 16v, 18v, 19v, 20v, 22v, 23v (= section I.5§2.*2)

At this stage the Letter was not yet withdrawn from chapter I.5. At the beginning of January 1924 it was meant to follow I.5§4.[48] After having redrafted I.5§4 (I.5§4.*1 [BL 47471b fs. 44v, 45v, 46v, 47v, 48v, 49v]), Joyce made a fair copy of the Letter. This fair copy was typed out, but only one page and a carbon of the same typescript page are preserved. On this typescript page the opening of the Letter is preceded by (the last lines of) I.5§1. The sections are divided by a red line. Joyce explained the meaning of this red line in a letter to Miss Weaver (7 January 1924): "Dear Miss Weaver: Here is what I managed to get done. The pieces divided by a red line are not consecutive. There are three longish pieces in between. The first one is nearly finished" (BL 57437 f. 132). About a week later he wrote her again, asking her: "Did you get the MS and typescript sent you a week or so ago? I am sending you more enclosed, also the pages to replace the faulty ones. The passage 'Let us now . . . Shem the penman' [I.5§4.*2] follows the words 'the hen saw' [end of I.5§1.*2]. Between the words 'penman' and 'Revered' are three further passages, a description of Shem-Ham-Cain-Esau etc and his penmanship, Anna Livia's visits and collaboration and delivery of the memorial by Shawn the post" (LI: 208, 16 January 1924).

Joyce's plans for the insertion of these three passages would eventually lead to a much more radical shift of the letter to the very end of the book in 1938. The letter, however, was not simply pasted into Book IV, as in the case of the sketches. Apparently, the letter was originally meant to be much shorter. The first 1938 draft (BL 47488 f. 117; JJA 63: 183; FDV: 281; FW: 615.13–14) is an elaboration of only the last quarter of the final 1923–24 version of the Revered Letter, starting from "we frankly enjoyed more than anything the secret workings of nature" (BL 47473 f. 18; JJA 46: 286). Joyce immediately translated the early version into late *Wakean* style. Thus, HCE, "dearest of husbands who I'll be true to you unto life's end as long as he has a barrel full of Bass" (BL 47473 f. 19; JJA 46: 287), becomes "that direst of housebonds, whool wheel be true unto loves end so long as we has a pockle full of brass" (BL 47488 f. 188; JJA 63: 189; FDV: 282; FW: 617.07). In this short version of the letter ALP denounces the slander in general and announces the death and funeral of the slanderers (at least in her imagination).

Joyce gave this letter its own signature by adding some idiosyncrasies of ALP, such as the interjection "well," which is inserted in at least five places. Joyce also added several passages that only seemingly echo the original letter; in reality, they recall other parts of the work's long history. Between 1923 and 1938 the Letter changed because of the commentaries it had provoked in the meantime. McCarthy has shown that, for instance, "the scholar's phrase 'About that original hen' (FW: 110.22), used in I.5 as part of the introduction to the text of the letter, becomes in Book IV an integral part of the letter itself":[49] "About that erogenal hun" (BL 47488 f. 122; JJA 63: 187; FDV: 282; FW: 616.20). Again, Joyce immediately translated this and other passages into late *Wakean* style. In 1923 it was "forbidden by the 10 commandments thou shalt not bear false witness against thy neighbour's wife," (BL 47473 f. 13; JJA 46: 281), whereas in 1938 it was "[s]tringstly [. . .] forbidden by the honorary tenth commendmant to shall not bare full sweetness against a neighboor's wiles" (BL 47488 f. 121; JJA 63: 185; FDV: 282; FW: 615.33). The letter was already signed when Joyce decided to extend it with another three-page addition, echoing the 1923 version of the letter. After having defended HCE, ALP now tries to denounce the accusations against herself, such as the alleged relationship with clerical friends: "Well, here's lettering you erronymously anent other clerical fands alleged herewith" (BL 47488 f. 123; JJA 63: 191; FDV: 283; FW: 617.30). She concludes with an affirmation of her faith in regeneration, for "herewaker" will live on in his "namesame" Shaun, who in turn, "young as of old," will woo a "wee one" (BL 47488 f. 125; JJA 63:

195; FDV: 284; FW: 619.14–15). When this recomposed letter was typed out it was signed again by "Alma Luvia, Pollabella" (BL 47488 f. 134; JJA 63: 203; FW: 619.16), the nourishing Alma Mater, the river Liffey with its alluvial material, and the *polla,* or hen.

The association of the hen with ALP is reinforced by the last variation on the Quinet theme (in an addition to the first typescript of section 4, IV§4.2), which ends as follows: "as sure as herself puts hen to paper" (BL 47488 f. 196; JJA 63: 206; FW: 615.10).[50] By adding this Quinet variation just before the opening of the letter Joyce emphasizes the letter's self-referential function and focuses on its textual evolution, which is an inherent part of its content. Here, textual and literary criticism merge, as both the letter and the Quinet variations exemplify the inevitability of transmissional variants, which—by extension—applies to the book as a whole.

The original letter had served as a scaffolding to build chapter I.5. By treating this text in Book IV to some extent in a similar way as he treats other external source texts Joyce parodies his own intertextual method of writing, which is "a clappercoupling smeltingworks exprogressive process" (BL 47488 f. 195; JJA 63: 205; FW: 614.31). The incorporation of external elements inevitably raises the question of authorship.[51] With reference to the Revered Letter, ALP's authorship was questioned from the start in an addition to the first draft (on the top of BL 47471b f. 31, above "Revered") that was left out in later versions: "^[1]Alone she cannot have indited it for the hand was fair. We can suppose it that of Shemus the penman, a village soak[1]^" (BL 47471b f. 31; JJA 46: 255; FDV: 81). Nevertheless, it is reasonable to assume—as it is being argued in chapter I.5—that "somebody somewhere sometime wrote it" (BL 47471b f. 38v; JJA 46: 266; FW: 118.11–14), and indeed, in the last section of Book IV (IV§5; FW: 619.20–628.16) Anna Livia explicitly claims the authorship of the letter: "Sometime then somewhere there, I wrote me hopes and buried the page" (BL 47488 f. 146v; JJA 63: 228, simplified; FW: 624.03–4).

Against the background of Mauthner's and Jespersen's views on language ALP seems to become the personification of language itself, "the langua of flows" (BL 47488 f. 145; JJA 63: 227; FW: 621.22). In notebook VI.B.46: 15 Joyce wrote: "[r]not bathe twice in / same R," which is possibly derived from the introduction to the *Kritik,* where Mauthner argues that "the old Greek aphorism saying that 'one cannot bathe twice in the same river' also applies to language. Its words and forms have changed continuously" (KS 1: 7). In notebook VI.B.46: 50 Joyce wrote: "[r]Δ name for Poddle / name of bed."[52] These entries correspond with a passage where Mauthner compares the name of the river "Donau" to the river bed, the way the name "Peter Müller" only stands for a collection of vessels and organs through which a continuously changing, daily regenerated mass of blood is flowing, "a poddlebridges in a passabed" (BL 47488 f. 33, simplified; JJA 63: 53; FW: 600.08).[53] The comparison of language with a river "whereinn once we lave 'tis alve and vale" (BL 47488 f. 18v; JJA 63: 26; FW: 600.07) offers a plausible explanation why Joyce used his Mauthner notes for the composition of Book IV. Joyce realized that it is an illusion to try and undo Babel, but he also saw the irony of Mauthner's critique, for even skepticism of language can only be expressed by means of language. Joyce pushed the irony one step further by recycling the very words from Mauthner's critique and adding them to the opening of Book IV, marking the hopeful "and ^[1]or[1]^" (BL 47488 f. 33v; JJA 63: 54; discussed above) desperate renewal of an inevitably vicious circle.

The name of the work that had been in progress for sixteen years was guessed by Eugene Jolas in the summer of 1938 (JJII: 708). At that moment, however, ALP's final monologue still had to be written. Its first words remained the same from the first draft up until the published version: "Soft morning, city!" (BL 47488 f. 120; JJA 63: 209; FDV: 284; FW: 619.20). The word "soft" recurs several times in the final monologue; ALP speaks softly because the children are still fast asleep. At the second draft stage ALP complains that her "boys are so contrairy." Joyce added: "Unless they changes by mistake. I seen the likes in the twinngling of an aye. So oft. Time after time. The sehm asnuh" (BL 47488 f. 134v; JJA 63: 212, simplified; FW: 620.14). This addition is based on a few entries on one of the last pages of notebook VI.B.41, "[bl]in the twingling of an / aye / so oft / soft" (VI.B.41: 290), immediately following the notes on Zimmer's *Maya*—which implies that these entries and hence the additions to the second draft of section 5 were not written before 8 October 1938.[54] In order to compose the final monologue Joyce compiled a rather small notebook, VI.B.47. As Daniel Ferrer points out, gathering lexical material was no longer the main priority for Joyce at this stage of the work's progress. Whereas most of the VI.B notebooks serve as a filter between reading and drafting, VI.B.47 is atypical in that it contains a high amount of syntactic passages or short drafts. Even in the instances where the notes are paratactic, the entries in VI.B.47 are remarkable because their usage in the drafts was so immediate that it is possible to divide the notebook into segments according to the corresponding draft levels. Levels 0 to 3 contain elements derived from VI.B.47 up to page 22. Level 4 contains phrases based on notes up to page 30. The writing of the subsequent draft stages proceeded analogously, following the gradual compilation of notes in VI.B.47: level 5, up to page 46; level 6, up to page 51; level 7, up to page 87. According to Ferrer, this remarkable stage of composition was between early October 1938 and early January 1939 (see *Buffalo VI.B.47,* 4–12).

Apparently, Joyce had a fairly precise idea of ALP's last words. The notebook entry "[bl]alast alost / aloved along the" already appears on VI.B.47: 10. In the first three versions of section 5 the last words had been "A bit beside the bush and then a walk along the / Paris 1922–1938" (BL 47488 f. 126; JJA 63: 210; FDV: 285).[55] According to Louis Gillet, Joyce's comment on the last word of *Finnegans Wake* was that he deliberately chose the definite article because it is the most furtive word in the English language, not more than a breath.[56]

It is remarkable that at every draft stage the final "the" is followed by the indication of the place and time of composition.[57] The most striking example of this paratextual curiosity appears on a separate page, where it is an integral part of an addition to the carbon of the second typescript, the same draft stage as the one to which Joyce added the passage where ALP claims the letter's authorship, "Sometime then somewhere there" (BL 47488 f. 146v; JJA 63: 228): "^[1]So soft this morning ours. First. We pass through grass behush the bush. So. But I'm taller now. And there. As then. Softhee, mememormee! Lps. Take. The keys to. Given! A way a lone a lost a last a loved a long the / Paris / 1922–1938[1]^" (IV§5.3; BL 47488 f. 148v; JJA 63: 231).

Luca Crispi discovered a remarkable textual curiosity. After having written the last word, Joyce added full stops after definite articles at other places in the text in similar contexts, since each time a door is being closed: "who oped it closeth thereof the. Dor" (FW: 020.17–18).[58] The full stop between "the" and "Dor" was added in 1936, when Joyce revised the *transition* 1 pages for the printer (BL 47475 f. 184; JJA 44: 274). Geert Lernout has shown that this sentence was inspired by J.-C. Mardrus's translation of the essential suras of the Koran (which ends in the form of a triangle) and that its first version ("Daleth, who opened it, closes the ^[1]reof the[1]^ door" [BL 47482a f. 78v; JJA 44: 87]) was followed by a triangular version of ALP's "signature":

p \ / p
l l
a

(BL 47482a 78v; JJA 44:87)[59]

As early as November 1926 Joyce apparently planned a literal visualization of a "delta at end" (VI.B.12: 137). He more or less stuck to his initial plan, but eventually ALP chose to close the. Door softly by taking her time (ten pages) to sign the text with her delta.

Even after the first edition had appeared Joyce added a full stop on FW: 257.27 before one of the thunder words (a combination of the phrase "Shut the door" in several languages),[60] marking the fall and at the same time the beginning of everything, the closing of the door in order to enable its opening. In the *Wake* the full stop is never used only to mark an end but to indicate the possibility to start a new sentence. Although this extra full stop is camouflaged and disguised as one of the "Corrections of Misprints" on the errata lists, it is not just an "accidental" but one of the most subtle substantive variants in modern literature, Giordano Bruno's *coincidentia oppositorum* summarized in the smallest of textual marks. It is significant that this change was made after the work was "finished" and presented to the public, emphasizing the fact that even as *Wake* the work continued to be in progress: a full stop indicating the unfinishedness of a sentence, as a textual counterpoint to the full-stopless closing of the book.

By means of a minor grammatical change ("along the" becomes "a long the") the last definite article became a substantive, just as the sixteen years "along the" *Continuation of a Work in Progress* became "a long the" when Joyce decided that the book was finished, ready to be published and lead a life of its own. But in the twilight zone between revision and publication some words mysteriously disappeared. The additions to level III were included in the next typescript: "Given! A way a lone a lost a last a loved a long the" (IV§5.4; BL 47488 f. 160; JJA 63: 243). As if to illustrate the inevitability of transmissional variants, thematized in connection with the letter, the words "a lost" were lost during the transmission from level IV to level V and never reinstated. When the book was finally published on 4 May 1939 it ended the way it still does(n't): "A way a lone a last a loved a long the" (IV§5.5; BL 47488 f. 178; JJA 63: 262). Again, the question whether Joyce passively authorized this loss or simply did not notice it can lead to endless discussions. In the end, the final version always has the last word, but the lost ones will only be discovered "along the."

Notes

1. See the letter to Paul Léon, 16 February 1938 (JJ/PL: 38), mentioned in TDJJ: 132.

2. On 20 July Miss Weaver wrote a letter to Paul Léon, thanking him and

Joyce for the first corrections of the *transatlantic review* piece of *Work in Progress* ("Mamalujo"). A week later she informed them she had "found the bit on St Patrick that she typed for Mr Joyce when he was at Bognor," mentioning that "there were four bits" (JJ/PL: 71–72). Three weeks later, on 17 August, she received a message from Léon saying that Joyce had "the O'Connor [*sic*], Kevin and St Patrick parts" but did not remember the fourth piece, copied while he was in Bognor. This was the "Tristan and Isolde" vignette, which Miss Weaver sent two days later (JJ/PL: 72–73). According to Danis Rose, Joyce searched for the very first piece of the work in progress (the "Roderick O'Conor" sketch), with which he planned to round off Book II, and found three other pieces, "Saint Kevin," the "Revered Letter," which he had withdrawn from chapter I.5, and the "Mamalujo" sketch (TDJJ: 130–31). Since Joyce had already been working on the first section of Book IV in February 1938, and for at least more than twelve years he had had "K's orisons" in mind for the last part, it seems equally plausible that the old sketch he was looking for was not (only) the "O'Conor" but the "Saint Kevin" sketch.

3. Christopher Bjork, "'Sinted Sageness': Some Sources for Kevin in *Finnegans Wake*," *Probes,* 85–100, 86.

4. Ibid., 87.

5. See also Vincent Deane, "Bywaters and the Original Crime," *"Finnegans Wake": "teems of times,"* ed. Andrew Treip (Amsterdam: Rodopi, 1994), 165–204.

6. The possibility that Joyce had already been working on the Kevin piece in the spring (probably early 1938, according to the JJA) cannot be ruled out. But as the additions to this typescript (based on books by John A. O'Hanlon and Fritz Mauthner) date from late 1938 (see below), this does contradict the JJA dating (mid-1938) of the next draft stage, in which these additions are already incorporated.

7. Robbert-Jan Henkes, "Lost and Found, textual note 601.25," *Genetic Joyce Studies,* online, April 2001, http:www.antwerpjamesjoycecenter.com. Accessed March 2006.

8. R. J. Schork, "Sheep, Bones, and Nettles: St. Kevin's Childhood Miracles," *Writing Its Own Wrunes For Ever: essais de génétique joycienne,* ed. Daniel Ferrer and Claude Jacquet (Tusson: Du Lérot, 1998), 151–62, 155–56. Schork notes that the page numbers of the relevant passages on Kevin's childhood miracles in the *Lives of the Irish Saints* are mentioned in notebook VI.B.47: 57, compiled in November and December 1938, according to Danis Rose (TDJJ: 35). Since the four numbered additions are already incorporated in the next draft, this implies that the additions to typescript IV§1.3/2.6 are probably older than mid-1938 (JJA 63: 41).

9. Fritz Mauthner, *Beiträge zu einer Kritik der Sprache,* 3 vols. (Leipzig: Felix Meiner, 1923 [1901–3]). Hereafter cited as KS, followed by the volume and page number(s). The last part of the Mauthner notes in VI.B.41 precedes the Zimmer notes (VI.B.41: 288–89) by a mere fifteen pages, which may be an indication that they were written not much earlier than 8 October 1938 (the date of Heinrich Zimmer Jr.'s dedication to Joyce in the copy of *Maya* in Joyce's personal library).

10. "Jedes einzelne Wort ist geschwängert von seiner eigenen Geschichte, jedes einzelne Wort trägt in sich eine endlose Entwicklung von Metapher zu Metapher" (KS 1: 115); "Sprache ist immer Erinnerung" (KS 1: 212).

11. "Die Worte dieser Sprache sind wenig geeignet zur Mitteilung, weil Worte Erinnerungen sind und niemals zwei Menschen die gleichen Erinnerungen haben" (KS 3: 641).

12. Danis Rose, *James Joyce's Index Manuscript: "Finnegans Wake" Holograph Notebook VI.B.46* (Colchester: A Wake Newslitter Press, 1978).

13. One of the miscellaneous pages at the back of the last JJA volume (BL 47488 f. 180; JJA 63: 343) is a list of forty languages, several of which (such as Romansch, Basque, Burmese, Hebrew, Russian, Chinese, Malay, Ruthenian, Polish, Czech, Albanian, Kissuaheli, etc.) are indexed in notebook VI.B.46.

14. The notes on page 48 seem to indicate that Joyce probably started to skim through the volume more quickly at a certain moment but only after having read at least some 250 pages (roughly corresponding to part 1 of the third volume of *Kritik*) rather closely. (Volume 3 of Mauthner's *Kritik* is divided into two parts, "Sprache und Grammatik" [1–258] and "Sprache und Logik" [259–642].)

15. Vincent Deane discovered that the notes under the heading "Mauthner" on VI.B.41: 235 ff. correspond to the first volume of Mauthner's *Kritik*.

16. "die Wauwau-Theorie . . . ist die älteste Lehre über Entstehung der Sprache, und zu ihr ist man seit Platon immer wieder zurückgekehrt. Onomatopöie hieß bei den Griechen—wie schon das Wort besagt—eben gar nichts anderes als Wortbildung. Auch wir glauben, daß in Urzeiten die Menschen sehr häufig Dinge dadurch zu bezeichnen suchten, daß sie ihre eigentümlichen Geräusche mit der Menschenstimme nachzuahmen glaubten" (KS 2: 434).

17. See VI.B.41: 269: "p. 455 / [. . .] / p. 479"; "Auch die Geschichte der Sprache, um deren willen Vico uns hier interessiert, zerfällt ihm in drei Abschnitte: in die Götterzeit, wo die Sprache hieroglyphisch war oder eine Zeichensprache, in die Heroenzeit, wo die Sprache poetisch oder metaphorisch war, und in die Menschenzeit, in der sich unsere Sprachen ausbildeten. Aus seiner Geistesentwicklung, die Vico selbst beschrieben hat, ist in meinen Augen dies der wichtigste Punkt, daß Vico zuerst die Philosophie bei einem Nominalisten kennen lernte, bevor er in die orthodoxe Schule des mittelalterlichen Wortrealismus geriet" (KS 2: 481–82).

18. See VI.B.46: 55: "in beginning was / the sentence."

19. Otto Jespersen, *An International Language* (London: Allen & Unwin, 1928); cf. Rose 1978, 312 f., 325 f.

20. Otto Jespersen, *Language: Its Nature, Development and Origin* (London: Allen & Unwin, 1922); cf. notes in VI.B.2, retraced by Roland McHugh, "Jespersen's *Language* in Notebooks VI.B.2 and VI.C.2," *AFWC* 2.4 (1987): 61–71; and Erika Rosiers, "Jespersen at the *Wake*," unpublished paper.

21. This entry probably derived from Jespersen: "Another instance of secretion

is *-en* as a plural ending in E. *oexn,* G. *ochsen,* etc. Here originally *n* belonged to the word in all cases and all numbers" (Jespersen 1922, 385).

22. VI.B.46: 55: "[r]he shall have / not tense enough"; cf. KS 3: 42. Also VI.B.46: 50: "[r]he is coming to come / morning (tomorrow) / yesterday other day"; cf. KS 3: 120–22.

23. Jack P. Dalton, "Advertisement for the Restoration," *Twelve and a Tilly: Essays on the Occasion of the 25th Anniversary of "Finnegans Wake,"* ed. Jack P. Dalton and Clive Hart (London: Faber and Faber, 1966), 119–37.

24. The other N.B.'s on this page (BL 47488 f. 37; JJA 63: 61) stipulate: "N.B. Please first change all initial 'i's to 'y's: e.g. ysle not isle"; "NB Kevin ^[1]and Glendalough[1]^ have a capital initial all through the piece. Also the piece should be punctuated properly." The latter remark is significant since it indicates the importance Joyce attached to this infinitesimal textual aspect, which already prefigures the very last finishing touch: the "nonpresence" of a last full stop.

25. Richard Brown, "The Missing Typescripts of *Finnegans Wake,*" *AFWC* 4.1 (Autumn 1988): 1–18.

26. Danis Rose and John O'Hanlon refer to an early note in VI.B.3 ("[r]Culter of the thing in / itself see the grass // (r+o+y+b+i+v)" [VI.B.3: 64–65]), which may be regarded as the germ for this sketch (UFW: 303 n.).

27. See VI.B.46: 46: "Linnaeus / better—[names]."

28. These notes are discussed in John O'Hanlon, "In the Language of Flowers," *AWN* 16.1 (February 1979): 9–12.

29. VI.B.45: 76–81, under the heading "Rabelais," contains notes from Lazar Sainéan, *La Langue de Rabelais* (Paris: Éditions de Boccard, 1922). See Claude Jacquet, *Joyce et Rabelais: aspects de la création verbale dans "Finnegans Wake"* (Paris: Didier, 1972); also Danis Rose, "Corrections to Jacquet's *Joyce et Rabelais,*" *AWN* 13.6 (December 1976): 106–8. For the notes on Uralic see Laurent Milesi, "From the Notebooks to the Text," *AFWC* 1.4 (Summer 1986): 79–84. Another source for these pages is A. Meillet and Marcel Cohen, *Les langues du monde* (Paris: Edouard Champion, 1924); see Vincent Deane, "*Les Langues du monde* in VI.B.45," *AFWC* 3.4 (Summer 1988): 61–74.

30. James S. Atherton, *The Books at the Wake* (London: Faber and Faber, 1959), 27.

31. A.-Ferdinand Herold, *La Vie du Bouddha* (Paris: Édition d'Art, 1922).

32. Rose 1978, 297–308. According to Rose, VI.B.46 was composed between December 1937 and February 1938 (cf. TDJJ: 34).

33. This is how Joseph Campbell, coauthor of *A Skeleton Key to "Finnegans Wake,"* defines the notion of Maya in his edition of Heinrich Zimmer, *Philosophies of India,* ed. Joseph Campbell (Princeton: Princeton University Press, 1974), 19.

34. Trying to scrape away the phenomena may reveal nothing but a void: "In the buginning is the woid, in the muddle is the sounddance and thereinofter you're

in the unbewised again, vund vulsyvolsy. You talker dunsker's brogue men we our souls speech obstruct hostery. Silence in thought! Spreach!" (FW: 378.29–32). Therefore, Joyce's answer to Mauthner's linguistic skepticism is "Wear anartful of outer nocense!" (FW 378.33). This passage is also based on Joyce's Mauthner notes (KS 1: 73–96; VI.B.41: 236[a–d]). An excellent illustration of Joyce's method of reveiling is the description of the cloud Nuvoletta (FW: 157.08–158.20) in "The Mookse and the Gripes" episode, just after the Gripes's mention of "the Veiled Horror" (FW: 156.32–33). The motif of the veil is mostly associated with the character amalgam of Nuvoletta/Issy. No matter how hard Nuvoletta tries to uncover herself, she fails to draw the attention of the Mookse and the Gripes. Instead, she is veiled by a dense curtain of always more and hazier words.

35. See above: "wolk in process" (BL 47488 f. 93; JJA 63: 157; FW: 609.30–31).

36. "Maye faye, she's la gaye [. . .] Veil, volantine, valentine eyes" (BL 47476a f. 146; JJA 49: 315; FW: 020.34); "Listeneath to me, veils of Mina!" (BL 47479 f. 172v; JJA 54: 266; FW: 318.18), possibly based on the entry "°vale of Mina" (VI.B.45: 107). In other notebooks the veil and its Indian equivalent, purdah, recur several times, for example, in VI.B.26: 80: "purdah (veil)"; VI.B.4: 17: "purdah"; VI.B.27: 134: "purdah (veil)"; and VI.B.20: 50: "ʳtake the veil."

37. The Tunc page contains the crucifixion text from the Gospel according to Matthew: "Tunc crucifixerant XRI cum eo duos latrines." The shape of this text (a cross) not only reflects its content but in *Finnegans Wake* it also symbolizes the artist's situation, "the cross of [his] own cruelfiction!" (FW: 192.18–19).

38. Laurent Milesi, "Metaphors of the Quest in *Finnegans Wake,*" *"Finnegans Wake": Fifty Years,* ed. Geert Lernout (Amsterdam: Rodopi, 1990), 79–107, 90.

39. Milesi 1990, 96.

40. At that moment the rest of pages 30r and 29v was still blank. This would mean Joyce had foreseen only one or two pages for the Letter (depending on whether he chose to write only on the recto pages or not). Possibly, he immediately saw that this would not be enough and therefore decided to start the letter on page 31r, that is, both topographically and chronologically after its conclusion at the bottom of page 30r.

41. Morton Prince, *The Dissociation of a Personality* (New York: Longmans, Green, 1905); Adeline Glasheen, "*Finnegans Wake* and the Girls from Boston, Mass.," *Hudson Review* 7.1 (Spring 1954): 89–96.

42. "With Kiss. Kiss Criss. Cross Criss. Kiss Cross." (FW: 011.27); "must now close it [. . .] with four crosskisses" (FW: 111.16–17); "Such crossing is antechristian of course" (FW: 114.11); "kissists my exits" (FW: 280.27); "Ex. Ex. Ex. Ex." (FW: 424.13); "X.X.X.X." (FW: 458.03).

43. Patrick A. McCarthy, "The Last Epistle of *Finnegans Wake,*" *Critical Essays on James Joyce's "Finnegans Wake,"* ed. Patrick A. McCarthy (New York: G. K. Hall, 1992), 96–103, 97–98.

44. According to Ellmann, Joyce insisted that the Crosby Gaige deluxe edition

of *Anna Livia Plurabelle* be published in a tea-colored cover because the Liffey was the color of tea (JJII: 603).

45. "We can also look on the word as the beginning of the later style, for it is very much like words in the book Joyce eventually produced" (Fred Higginson, "Two Letters from Dame Anna Earwicker," *Critique* 1 [1957]: 3–14, 11).

46. On page 36 of the red-backed notebook (BL 47471a f. 36; JJA 46: 261) the second draft of section I.4§2 ends in the middle of the page and is immediately followed by the second draft of the Letter.

47. At the "Genetic Networks" conference in Antwerp (December 1998) Bill Cadbury and I discovered that we have come to quite similar conclusions about the implications of the page numbering in the red-backed notebook. I am grateful to him for the helpful discussions we have had about them, both at the time and since.

48. See BL 47473 fs. 20–21 (JJA 46: 288–89). On this (incomplete) typescript the end of I.5§4 ("to see as much as the hen saw") is immediately followed by the letter.

49. McCarthy 1992, 101.

50. "[S]ince the days of Plooney and Columcellas when Giacinta, Pervenche and Margaret swayed over the all-too-ghoulish and illyrical and innumantic in our mutter nation, all, anastomosically assimilated and preteridentified paraidiotically, in fact, the sameold gamebold adomic structure of our Finnius the old One" (FW: 615.02–7). This is the "sameold" Quinet sentence as the one quoted in Book II.2 (FW: 281.04–13). See also Geert Lernout's, Sam Slote's, and Wim Van Mierlo's essays in this volume.

51. The notes on Zimmer's *Maya* serve as an excellent illustration of how almost anything could be absorbed in the *Wake*. The Zimmer connection originally had nothing to do with Indian philosophy. A student in Paris had drawn Joyce's attention to the works of Heinrich Zimmer senior, a linguist and professor of Celtology at the University of Berlin who lived from 1851 to 1910. Joyce was interested in his "Keltische Beiträge" (see VI.B.41: 102: "Keltische Beiträge [Zimmer]") because they confirmed his own theories about Finn MacCool's Scandinavian origin. Joyce's respect for Heinrich Zimmer junior, a professor of Sanskrit at the University of Heidelberg, was mainly due to the latter's summary of his father's works (see the letter to Louis Gillet, 8 September 1938; LI: 401) rather than to his own writings.

52. The Poddle is a tributary of the Liffey.

53. "Names of rivers are proper names. . . . In this sense, 'Danube' is a notion like 'Peter Müller.' And the comparison does not stop because of the fact that 'Danube' only denotes the river bed; for after all, 'Peter Müller' too is only the bed, the sum of . . . vessels and organs through which a continuously changing, daily regenerated mass of blood is flowing. . . . it is a coincidence that the main river was called the Inn, the tributary the Donau. But because the part downstream

of the confluence was called . . . Donau, the whole course of the river was given the name of the tributary" (KS 3: 90–91).

54. Joyce received his copy of *Maya* early in October 1938, but not before 8 October, because Zimmer wrote a dedication ("James Joyce in Bewunderung") dated "8.10.38." The dedication is transcribed by Thomas E. Connolly in *The Personal Library of James Joyce* (Buffalo: Norwood Editions, 1978), 42. On 11 October Joyce wrote to his German translator, Georg Goyert: "Professor H. Zimmer (son of the famous Celtic philogiest and presently Professor of Sanskrit at Heidelberg) has lately been of great help to me" (LIII: 432). In the same letter Joyce writes: "*Work in Progress*—pfui!—is almost finished. So am I. Since last October I have been working like a mule at it all day long and almost all night long too."

55. See also BL 47488 f. 150 (JJA 63: 233).

56. "Dans *Ulysses*, me disait-il, pour peindre le balbutiement d'une femme qui s'endort, j'avais cherché à finir par le mot le moins fort qu'il m'était possible de découvrir. J'avais trouvé le mot '*yes*,' qui se prononce à peine, qui signifie l'acquiescement, l'abandon, la détente, la fin de toute résistance. Dans le *Work in Progress*, j'ai cherché mieux, si je pouvais. Cette fois, j'ai trouvé le mot le plus glissant, le moins accentué, le plus faible de la langue anglaise, un mot qui n'est même pas un mot, qui sonne à peine entre les dents, un souffle, un rien, l'article '*the*'" (Louis Gillet, *Stèle pour James Joyce* [Marseille: Sagittaire, 1941], 164–65).

57. Joyce attached great importance to this paratextual element. On the last page of the galley proofs he specified that the place and date had to be "(small)" and printed in italics (BL 47488 f. 223; JJA 63: 329). Even in the corrections for the page proofs Joyce specified: "Please print the Place and Date much lower approximately where I indicated or lower" (BL 47488 f. 240; JJA 63: 340).

58. See also "that henchwench what hopped it dunneth there duft the. Duras" (FW: 334.29–30).

59. See Lernout's essay in this volume.

60. "the. Lukkedoerendunandurraskewdylooshoofermoyportertooryzooysphalnabortansporthaokansakroidverjkapakkapuk" (FW: 257.27–28).

"~~The~~ End"; "Zee End"

Chapter I.1

FINN FORDHAM

As we have seen in Geert Lernout's essay, once Joyce had begun writing the Overture he revealed to his patron that the book "really has no beginning or end. (Trade secret, registered at Stationers Hall.) It ends in the middle of a sentence and begins in the middle of the same sentence" (LI: 246). This essay traces how Joyce worked through this structural strategy by reading the first and last chapters together and interpreting some of the many ways they echo each other. Through these echoes I show how Joyce developed the thematic consequences across both chapters, for though written in different ways over different periods, the Epilogue (Book IV) and the Overture (I.1) are in large part conceived, composed, and recomposed as a unit. In terms of theme, motif, and structure they have a tight and reflective relation to each other that is unique compared to the way they relate to other chapters or the way other chapters relate to each other. They are like distorted reflections, readings of each other made, as it were, through a glass darkly.

I cover the interrelated composition through five stages:

1. late 1926: the early drafts of chapter I.1, where the form of the "open" ending joined to the "open" beginning is anticipated
2. by 1936: as he neared the final stages Joyce revised *Work in Progress* as it had appeared in *transition* and there are more references to "the end," especially toward the end of chapter I.1
3. late 1937: first galleys of Book I, running up to the first sketches for Book IV; revisions emphasize imagery that prefigures the end (like the phoenix and the archipelago)

4. early to mid-1938: the early drafts for Book IV and the second set of galleys for Book I; the timing is tricky here: Joyce inserts structural and motival correspondences in both the Epilogue and the Overture
5. mid- to late 1938: Leafy's monologue, which responds to many revisions in the second galleys, especially toward the end of the Overture; finally, last-minute revisions to the Overture reflect and recall the Epilogue

While moving sequentially through these stages at times, in tracing the "destiny" of an image or motif, I move to and fro between them.

"In my beginning is my end": The Overture as Prolepsis

Beginning and ending halfway through a sentence was a fantastic discovery for Joyce, resolving the problem of how to avoid "denouement," that convention of narrative whereby loose ends are tied up or snarled knots undone. The problem of resolution was resolved by avoiding resolution. Joyce thus undermines certain readers' expectations of finality. As Geert Lernout and Dirk Van Hulle pointed out, it would end with a delta—the point not just where the river meets the sea but also where the river's channel divides into multiple passages. Rather than a plot climax there would be a proliferation and dissolution of finality. This was consistent with both Vichian *ricorsi*—since their joining indicated one of Vico's cycles of history—and Brunian *coincidentia oppositorum*, for these chapters were both the farthest apart and also the closest together. It was a formal solution, providing an end that was not an end. Paradox would reign forever over interpretations of the *Wake*, since we could never finally disentangle what follows and/or precedes what. Narratological analyses would flounder as they tried to separate flashback from anticipation, analepsis from prolepsis. For whatever is to come has already happened. Narrative would be undone though maintained at the same time. The beginning would be an end (of a sentence), and the end would be a beginning (of a sentence). It is so simple an idea that it seems extraordinary no one thought of it before.

Being without an end is a bid for the eternal, the extreme version of the artist's hope for "ars longa, vita brevis." As a hope, and twinned with a hope for life's resurrectability, this is expressed in the first draft of the first section in 1926: "Till nevernever may our pharce be phoenished!" (BL 47482a f. 85; JJA 44: 5; FW: 004.17). While reiterating the name of the park where Earwicker meets the Cad, it also introduces proleptically the link between the regenerative bird and the "finish," where, indeed, the Phoenix, as a "Phoenican," will rise again. It is also a hope—and a plea to the reader—never to have the pleasure finished by being punished. This sentence would change considerably for the first fair copy, so a finish of sorts is asserted, though guardedly deferred: "[N]one so soon either shall the pharce for the nunce come to a setdown secular phoenish" (BL 47472 f. 5; JJA 44: 106: FW: 004.17). Though confidently predicted, the time for the phoenix's resurrection is "none so soon"—an understatement for "a long way off."

The return of the phoenix's life reflects the circularity of the resurrection myth that informs the structure of the novel. Hinting at his "trade secret" ending, Joyce acknowledges this structure in several ways. One is through the snake with its tail in its mouth or the worm that seems to regenerate when cut in two. Joyce evokes a time prior to the arrival of Patrick after which, so the legend goes, he banished snakes from Ireland: "Sss! See the snake worms everywhere our durl bin is sworming with sneaks! Subdivide and sumdolot but the tale comes out the same. [. . .] What a tale to unfurl & with what an end in view!" (BL 47482 f. 83v, simplified; JJA 44: 85; FW: 019.12).

Worms are supposed to survive if you cut them in two: they develop another similar end to replace the lost one. Whether you "subdivide" it (sever its tail from its mouth, separate one end from the other) or "sumdolot" (bring its ends together and consider it as one), the same old story proliferates. The "end in view"—as projected purpose—is to tell and retell this tale of exposure and to watch how the same old tale "comes out," how it appears when published. This tale of revelation, where an "end" (a tail or rear end) is in view, is to be "unfurled." However final or singular this end may seem, it will simply lead into multiple repetitions of it. In proliferating, they are letters too—S, s, s!—and are to be banished/censored as troublemakers. The snaky ends/beginnings evoke also the first and last letters of *Ulysses*—"Stately" and "Yes"—or its end—"yes . . . yes . . . Yes." Tails and tales, ends and rear ends (and HCE's rear ends) are repeated and proliferate. Putting an end to both is a challenge, for written squiggly letters are irrepressible, and eventually—through being reset—they will become solid type/s, repeatable through the printing press. Readings will, in the end, multiply, as this early draft of the Overture shows: "Till we finally (though not yet for all) meet with Mr Typ, Mrs Top and all the little typtoppies—Fillstap. So you need hardly spell me that every word will carry

3 score and ten readings through the book of ~~life~~ duble ends” (BL 47482a f. 78v; JJA 44: 87; FW: 020.11–15).

The “book of Life,” that is of *Liffey*, while the whole is ALP’s letter, or *Finnegans Wake* itself, is revised at once to become “the book of duble ends,” that is, Dublin, but also the “double ends” of the book’s edges—one at the close (FW: 628), the other at the opening (FW: 003). Joyce sharpens this self-reference in the fair copy, where he expands it to “Doublends Jined” (FW: 020.15), sounding like “Dublin’s Giant.” He has joined the “duble” to the “ends,” glancing forward and backward to the empty space at both ends, which have been variously *joined* in our consecutive readings.

The Overture begins by evoking an end, the mortal fall of Finnegan and the wake that is held over his corpse. Joyce had already decided that the Epilogue would be a dawning and an awakening, so the chapter is the obvious punning response to it—not “awake” but “a Wake.” In the song “Finnigan’s Wake,” of course, Finnegan wakes. In *Finnegans Wake* he rises but is lulled back to sleep—or passivity. Part of soothing him is to say, “Everything’s going on the same” (FW: 026.25), life continues its repeated rounds, reassuring him that his wife and children are okay: “[H]erself is fine too” (FW: 028.02).

Whether already planned to do so or not, the description of “herself”—or ALP—will attract, as Geert Lernout pointed out, many many more words. It began with just 29 and, by the last draft, increasing by a factor of more than 12, has 366: “And herself is fine too and fond of the concertina of an evening. Her hair’s as brown as ever it was. And wivvy and wavy” (BL 47472 f. 41; JJA 44: 138; FW: 028.02–3). Because these words tell us how ALP is since her man’s gone, they will develop strongly into an echo (and pre-echo) of the Epilogue, which also presents ALP when her man is going.

Transforming *transition*

In 1936 Joyce had still not begun the Epilogue but was revising all the work that had appeared in *transition*. Just one revision need concern us. When he came to the passage above describing ALP, the end, now nearer in sight, could feature more explicitly. She is reading something, and the saltiness—perhaps bitterness—of it is inserted: “She’s seeking her way in and out of their serial story Les Loves of Selskar and Pervenche, freely adapted. There’ll be bluebells blowing in salty sepulchres the night she signs her final tear. The End. But that’s a world of ways away” (BL 47475 f. 269;

JJA 44: 285, simplified; FW: 028.29). The present is emphasized—"She's seeking"—but also followed by the prophecy of a future—"There'll be bluebells blowing." Just as she moves in and out of the story she reads, ALP moves in and out of the book we read, she and her letter/s appearing and disappearing. The "in and out" is also the entrance and exit of the book that she, the river, circles. She flows into the sea and evaporates out of it to fall as rain and renew the river. The sea is a grave, containing "salty sepulchres," or salt tears drowning her blue eyes as she finishes reading her sentimental serialized love story blabbing through its final pages. But "The End" is on the other side of the text, through which, on the way to that end, we may move in a great number of ways, a "world of ways," so many indeed and of such labyrinthine forms that we may never really get there. The end is a world away, like the "other world," that heaven we may never reach, especially if, like the book's end, it doesn't really exist. Anticipation is aroused but then infinitely deferred, keeping anticipation, paradoxically, alive.

As we shall see again, Joyce would return to this passage, this mini-proto-end, and what he added would be fertile material for the end of the book as a whole. It became a place to develop initial sketches of Anna Livia's closing monologue.

Book I Galleys: The First Set

The revisions on the *transition* pages were typed up and transferred to the galleys. Joyce worked on one set before beginning the Epilogue, but with it in mind. Since the Epilogue would be an awakening and *ricorso,* Joyce in the winter of 1937 examined the "ur-awakening" of the tyrant Finn and inserted a sentence that has recourse to Phoenix imagery—crucially, just before he rises. I'm inserting an X to show the point of expansion:

> he made louse for us and delivered us to boll weevils amain [. . .] And would again could whispering grassies wake him. X *Usqueadbaugham.*
>
> Anam much an dhoul! Did ye drink me dead? (BL 47476a f. 16; JJA 49: 27; FW: 024.12–15)

Joyce inserts just before "*Usqueadbaugham*" (the spilled toast of whiskey) "X And may again when the fiery bird disembers. And will again if sooth the elder to his youngers shall be said." When the phoenix rises the dead man may rise to repeat all he's done. Speaking rationally, this is never—but if the superstitious retrogressive old men are to be believed, he will. The insertion stretches the crescendo, deferring the immediate climax, but invokes the ultimate climax of the Phoenix rising from his embers (disembering). The Phoenix image is stressed in another revision made at this level (though not necessarily on the same day or even week) "in Healiopolis now," which evokes the Egyptian city of the sun, where the phoenix was supposed to resurrect once every five hundred years.[1] It is also there in a prophecy made to reassure the waked Finn about his good Catholic daughter, Hetty Jane: "She'll be coming (for they're sure to choose her) in her white of gold with a tourch of ivy to rekindle the flame on Felix Day" (BL 47476a f. 16v; JJA 49: 28; FW: 027.11–14). "Felix Day" is the happy day (the marriage day?) and the Phoenix Day, as her torch and flame point out. Perhaps the end of the book is this happy-phoenix day.

Other "proleptic" self-references at this level are subtler than the phoenix imagery. The mourner who attempts to reassure the now-risen corpse tries boosting his ego: "[W]here was your like to lay the cable [. . .]?" Laying the cable could easily refer to the attempts at establishing telegraphic communication lines between America and Europe in the nineteenth century, especially as this involved a connection that joined specifically Ireland to America. Under the waves, joining separate parts of the world, they produce an instance of "Doublends Jined." The mourner admires Joyce's own technique and formal concept of joined endings and diverts him from his own fading reputation.

Laying the cable links places that are isolated from each other. Communities on continents are more easily linked than communities on an island system or archipelago. Joyce exploits this geographical image as an emblem of isolation and the challenge of unifying disparate parts: Joyce's own composition process engaged in this practice of linking up the disparate. So at this level and at the end of chapter 1 Joyce introduces the phrase "this archipelago's first visiting schooner" to describe the boat that brought the "rody lad," the Viking trader/invader and substitute for the warrior Finn. The only other use of "archipelago" in the text up to this point had been in the Kevin sketch from July 1923. Joyce had turned the phrase "Procreated on the ultimate island in the encyclical Irish ocean" (BL 47488 f. 27; JJA 63: 38d) into "Procreated on the ultimate island in the encyclical Irish *archipelago*" (BL 47488 f. 27; JJA 63: 38e; FW: 605.05, emphasis added). This suggests that Joyce turned to the Kevin sketch as he revised the galleys for Book I. And this pairing of the image may well have spurred Joyce to take notes about the Bismarck Archipelago on the other side of the world, which includes New Ireland (see TDJJ: 132). As we shall see, these notes would be inserted on the other side of the book. The imagery itself travels through the book, linking one archipelago to another, laying the cable between their disparate parts.

Another revision that is made at this level, though tiny, is a highly significant and beautiful adjustment. In the sentence quoted above, where Anna is described reading her "serial story," Joyce crossed out "The" and placed "Zee" so it reads: "There'll be bluebells blowing in salty sepulchres the night she signs her final tear. Zee End. But that's a world of ways away" (BL 47476a f. 17, simplified; JJA 49: 63). "Zee," being the last letter of the alphabet (at least to Americans), is an end—of an alphabet, of all the letters, of letters themselves. "The" had been there as a prolepsis of the end where "the" would mark the end, at the point where the river flows into the sea. But since "Zee" means "Sea" in Dutch the sea has the last word, as it were. It also suggests "*See* end," no longer a statement of finality—as we find at the end of novels or films—but a suggestion that we cross-refer—such as we might find in academic books.

The timing at this stage is difficult. It is the winter of 1937–38, and it is unclear whether Joyce began Book IV while still working on the first set of galleys for Book I. A clue may appear in the revisions themselves. The mourner lulling the corpse describes his twin sons, Kevin and Jerry, the good and the bad: "Kevin's just a doat with hs cherub cheek but the devil does be in that knirps of a Jerry sometimes. T" (BL 47476a f. 17; JJA 49: 31). Joyce further characterized Jerry: "T, the tarandtan plaidboy, making encostive inkum out of the last of his lavings and writing a blue streak over his bourseday shirt" (BL 47476a f. 16v; JJA 49: 28). Jerry is a caricature of how some critics presented Joyce during the *Ulysses* scandal (as disruptive and indecent), so this refers back to Shaun's description of Shem's method of writing, where he uses shit and piss (hence en-*costive*) as ink and his naked flesh (hence the *birthday suit*) as paper. Being the "*last* of his lavings" specifies the last stages of the book, when little more (conceptually and from the notebooks) needed to be accessed. The blue streak not only is a mess on his smart shirt but could be the night sky lightening with the dawn—about which Shem/Joyce has just begun to write.

The Beginning of the End

The image of "lavings" as the water left over after a wash (part of the whole "washerwoman" theme in which, as Bloom thinks "dirty cleans" [U: 4.490], whereby writing cleanses by soiling) reemerges in a minidialogue in the first sketch for Book IV, just as the sun rises. A Pears Soap advertisement provides the melody: “Guld modning, have yous viewsed Piers’ aube? Thane yaars agon we have used yoors up since when we have fused now orther” (BL 47488 f. 4; JJA 63: 3). The original advert was “Good morning, have you used Pears Soap?” A cartoon in *Punch* had a filthy tramp sardonically replying: “Three years ago I used your soap since when I have used no other.” Joyce reworks a reworked advertisement to describe how he has reworked his own work. Did you foresee a “dawning” for Piers O’Reilly (“Piers’ aube”)? *Ten years ago we used that up*—that is, in 1928, having exhausted his original creative vision, Joyce hit a writer’s block. His “agon” began, and since then he fused another, managed to *author* and bring in different elements.[2] As we have seen in Van Hulle’s essay, this is essentially how Joyce composed Book IV: he took elements that he had already written and laid aside elsewhere; then, with some choice revisions, he *fused* them in amongst more material, devising the current structure. The “active elements” he used in Book IV were “Kevin,” “Patrick,” and the “Letter.”

Embedding these early sketches, enfolding them with material, Joyce does partly by looking back and commenting on his writings as an extraordinary experience: “It was a long, very long, a dark, very dark, an allburt unend, scarce endurable [. . .] night” (FW: 598.06–09). What has passed is the night of the book and the demanding composition process that has *produced* that night. Morning is a time of conscious and unconscious remembering—a struggle to remember the dreams passed in the night and quickly receiving messages from our environment reminding us what we had become by the previous night. The frame of the Epilogue was already there: the just-risen sun and then the river delta and a thematic of *ricorso*—recapitulating what had gone before. In the recapitulation the journey seems to have come full circle, but the beginning no longer looks like it did when it was first quitted. The metaphor of the writing as a quest comes to an end that transforms the points of departure. The silence of Humfrey and Livia in the Overture, for instance (a secret that binds them as manandwife), is recalled in the first section of Book IV. Here is the “source” and its “echo”:

Overture (first draft: 1926)	Epilogue (1938)
They will not speak the secret of their silentness. Quarry silex, Homfrie Noanswa? Undy festiknees, Livia Noanswa? (BL 47482a f. 36; JJA 44: 99; FW: 023.17–20)	Not a sallutary sellable sound is since [. . .] Nuctumbulumbumus wanderwards the Nil. Victorias neanzas. Alberths neantas. (BL 47488 f. 17v; JJA 63: 24; FW: 598.04–7)

Our initial quarry has taken us only toward "nothing." Another journey from start to finish leads to this transformed ending:

Overture (first draft: 1926)	Epilogue (1938)
the best plan is to tour [. . .] and review the two mounds (BL 47482a f. 99; JJA 44: 30)	hence we've lived in two worlds (BL 47488 f. 216v; JJA 63: 316)

The "two mounds" are the buttocks of HCE but also the influential and respectable periodical *La Revue des Deux Mondes:* two quite different worlds that reappear in translation at the end as "two worlds": the world of the prose work that Joyce has created and the world outside that he hasn't. The world of the book has only become a world once it's completed, once the world of its end is as complete as the world of its beginning. Only "hence" can it be claimed that we've "lived in two worlds."

The equaled and opposed ends of these two worlds produce other conventional—if not opposed—pairings, like bread and wine. Here in images that evoke such a pairing are precise echoes, though separated by 594 (or just 32) pages of both "yesterday" and Swift's "The Tale of a Tub." Both linked by yeast, there is drink in the beginning and bread at the end:

Overture (onto *transition* by 1936)	Epilogue (1938)
One yeastyday he sternely struxk his tete in a tub. . . . (BL 47475 f. 92v; JJA 44: 254; FW: 004.21–22)	Old yeasterloaves may be a stale as a stube. . . . (BL 47488 f. 17v; JJA 63: 24; FW: 598.20–21)

These are just a few small examples of self-echoing at the beginning of the end. There are many more, but, to get an idea of how bridges were being constructed right through to the last minute, we should move on.

As the composition of Book IV went ahead it wasn't just imagery but structure that became echoic, by chance and by design ("as hophazards can effective it"). In its episodic structure, its swerves from scene settings to set pieces, from narrative to dialogue, "interior dialogues" to closing monologues, IV came to resemble I.1. These shifts may sound like any chapter in the *Wake,* and of course all of *Finnegans Wake* reflects, repeats, and reworks itself. Like any other chapter, IV and I.1 are dense in their motival construction. But these chapters as extremities overlap, melt into each other, and are welded together—like some textual version of the metamorphosis of Hermaphrodite; indeed, the feminine river "brings us back" to the masculine earth of Howth. Because of their symbolically coordinated positions they set up echoes of each other that can be identified as either distant or extremely close. The Overture, drafted in 1926, was in part a condensed version of themes that Joyce had up to that point written. The Epilogue is a similar re-collection, bringing essences from all over the book and condensing them. A table of their structure, placing them in parallel rather than in series, helps illustrate this point.[3]

Intro (invoking the shape of things to come)	Dawn (recalling the shape of the past)
The buried giant (FW: 003.20–21)	the "macrolith" (FW: 594.22)
Set piece: Waterloo (FW: 008.09–010.23) annals of history—Quinet (FW: 014.35–015.11)	Set piece: St Kevin
Mutt and Jute (FW: 016.10–018.16)	Muta and Juva (FW: 609.24–611.32)
Patrick banishing snakes/letters of the alphabet (multiple readings) (FW: 019.10–27)	Set piece: Berkeley and Patrick debate color (multiple readings)
Set piece: Prankquean (FW: 021.05–023.15)	Quinet ALP's Letter
Mourner's monologue (addressing HCE) (FW: 024.16–029.36)	ALP's monologue (addressing HCE) (FW: 619.20–628.16)

Some correspondences are less "local," less striking, more inevitably coincidental than others. In general, most motifs have a bookwide proliferation determined by the reticular composition technique over the whole text. Yet some echoic correspondences we might expect are *not* there—we hear no thunder word in the Epilogue. However, this has an inverse correspondence, for we *see* lightning instead: "Lok! a shaft of shivery" (FW: 597.24). There are other such inversions of parallel imagery. In the Overture the letter is *found;* in the Epilogue it is *written out.* In the first chapter the Quinet passage follows the letter's discovery; in the last it precedes its inscription. Meanwhile, several direct correspondences stand out. The "Mutt and Jute" dialogue morphs into *Muta* and *Juva.* There are "pluralistic" theories of interpretation, of textual hermeneutics ("three score and ten toptypsical readings" [FW: 020.15]) and visual perception ("all objects [. . .] showed themselves in trues coloribus resplendent with sextuple gloria" [FW: 611.24]). In both, Patrick is the adversary of these positions. Finally, especially, the monologues at each end both address some form of HCE.

Examining the Overture galleys and the Epilogue drafts allows us to trace how Joyce moved back and forth between them and to illustrate the sense of reflective correspondence most strongly. As Van Hulle says, Joyce redrafted the "Kevin" sketch for inclusion probably in the summer of 1938, and the color debate came a little later. The revisions to the second set of galleys for Book I were finished before then, and yet certain additions strongly suggest Joyce was aware of these sketches. After all, Joyce had his own copies and had already used them in other parts of the Wake, especially III.3.

Prefiguring the Irish Legends

The original "Kevin" sketch of 1923 had a curious string of words based on "create," and this string is echoed when Joyce returned to revise the Overture in a paragraph introducing Finn's "substitute," the "rody lad":

Epilogue (1923/1938) (FW: 604.27–606.07)	Overture (1938) (FW: 029.14–15)
of increate God the servant, of the Lord Creator [. . .] was procreated [. . .] precreated [. . .] postcreate [. . .] concreate [. . .] recreated (BL 47488 f. 25; JJA 63: 38c)	Creator he has created for his creatured ones a creation (BL 47476a fs. 150, 152; JJA 49: 323, 325)

The material in Book IV perhaps mockingly illustrates Kevin's servile relation to the originator God as creative artist. The Overture places the act of creation as something completed, an appraisal that reflects Joyce's own sense of completion—though it is also pompous praise of the "rody lad." In Book IV we find Kevin, isolated, setting up a life that will meditate God's creation—especially in its form as water. In chapter 1 we encounter HCE, who has made a creation of his own. The "Kevin" sketch, drafted near the time of the work's inception but included near its close, takes us back to the early moves, when Joyce began creating his own language ("postcreate" and "precreated" are neologisms, "concreate" and "increate" are obsolete). The Overture sentence, drafted near the time of the work's completion but included near the opening, shows Joyce returning to the language of daylight though looking back at what has been made: the language of the night.

Similarly, the Berkeley and Patrick contest originally dates from 1923 and was revised in 1938. Its elements of pidgin echo in revisions made once again to chapter 1—near its end.

Epilogue (1923/1938) (FW: 611.04–28)	Overture (second set of galleys: 1938) (FW: 028.02–25)
Bymby topside joss pidgin fella [. . .] chinchinjoss [. . .] the his mister guest belongahim [. . .] savvying [. . .] Patrick fella no catch all that preachybook bymby topside joss pidgin fella say him (BL 47488 f. 100; JJA 63: 146c)	Shirksends? You storyan Harry ~~fella~~ chap longa me Harry ~~fella~~ chap storyan grass woman ~~plenty~~ plealthy good trout. Shakeshands [. . .] Ding Tams he noise about all same Harry chap (BL 47476a fs. 150, 152; JJA 49: 323, 325; FW: 028.02–25)

What most strongly indicates the intention of an internal echo is the use of "fella" in the Overture. The revision to "chap" makes this echo less obvious. Added to the first pidgin sentence were two words, one at each end: "Shirksends? [. . .] Shakeshands." The question and answer indicate a meeting, an exchange, a deal being struck: one asks, "Does she (ALP) shirk ends? Avoid finishing things off?" and one answers, "She's 'good' quality and 'grass' (or fat) into the bargain"—like the thick book itself. With this understood there is agreement when they "shake hands." By contrast, in the Book IV inversion there is misunderstanding and disagreement. Indeed, Joyce developed an image not of hand shaking but of what looks like Patrick abusing Berkeley in an act of male rape: "As he shuck his thumping fore features apt the hoyhop of His Ards" (FW: 612.34–35).

At one stage Joyce himself did shirk ends, unwilling and unable to put an end to his work. But now the "storyan" he has produced is packed with stuff and nearing completion. Shaking hands marks the linking of opposites in agreement (like the deals struck in II.3, where a young ALP is sold into marriage and Butt and Taff come together to admire the shooting of the Russian general). In the sense of his structure Joyce *does* avoid (shirk) ends as closure by linking the extremes together.

What these two examples show is the way Joyce recomposed chapter 1, however lightly, in the light of Book IV—it was not simply always the other way round.

Embedding the Sketches

Joyce had to embed these self-contained passages in other material, to link them in to the Epilogue as a whole. To do so he wrote passages that look back over the writing process as a whole. They also draw on imagery that had just been emphasized in the Overture. Here are three examples.

The Archipelago

As mentioned earlier, Joyce had used "archipelago" in 1923 and in the first set of Book I galleys. Now he took notes about the Bismarck Archipelago, which includes the island New Ireland. In a passage designed to "embed" the "Kevin" sketch, where advice is given before his departure, many units find their way in. They appear in advice given to Kevin. His condition, after all, is to be isolated, insular. As a missionary he explores islands for a secluded place to set up his "mission": "You must be extra acquarate to inter irrigate all the arkypelicans. Milenesia waits. Be smark" (BL 47488 f. 20; JJA 63: 29; FW: 601.36). The Bismarck Archipelago is part of Melanesia. The real Saint Kevin set up his mission in Ireland—now on the other side of the world/book, a mission in "Milenesia." But the exchange of *e* for *i* is a way of indicating Ireland, since the "Milesians" were early inhabitants of Ireland. This identification allows us to picture a movement from the "NW European archipelago" (Britain and Ireland) to an archipelago on the opposite side of the world. The Irish Free State is metaphorically a "New Ireland," so Joyce incorporates this "New Ireland" as an analogy and a diametrically opposite alternative.

Joyce also inserts New Ireland references when he finds a reference to the giant hidden in the landscape: "Hill of Hafid, knock and knock, nachasach, gives relief to the langscape X and the bride of the bryne is" (BL 47488 fs. 45–46; JJA 63: 70–71; FW: 595.03–5), to which he added an X: "as he strauches his lamusong untoupon gazelle channel." Adjacent sentences had many other references to New Ireland, such as "Lambel on the up! [. . .] Newiregland's premier." Lamusong is a town on the Gazelle Channel, a stretch of water—both part of New Ireland. So the giant stretched under the northern bank of the Liffey is now a giant stretched under New Ireland on the other side of the world, giving relief to the "langscape." If the former giant is taken as a symbol of national/ist revival, and if that giant has risen, a global perspective reminds us of the number of other sleeping giants around the world in other more recently colonized archipelagos. This is stressed by one of those tiny revisions that benefit from being annotated just as much as Joyce's arcane allusions. Joyce wrote originally "Newireland" but crossed out the *e* to make "Newirgland's," thus verbally combining Ireland and England (not unlike "Benelux") into some political unit, imaginable perhaps only in a parallel universe, or when the moon turns blue—or at the end of the world. But this is where Joyce's imaginary language often takes us—to an imaginary world of a dreamed future, to situations that are beyond our world—beyond its own ends, its own last day.

The archipelago image does not stop here. One more revision seems to speak of it. On the second set of galleys for Book I Joyce added the words "a toll, a toll" (BL 47476a f. 133; JJA 49: 290; FW: 004.08). At all, at all; a bell tolling; a tollgate to regulate your passing; and "atoll"—a tiny island, little more than a sandbank, just poking up through the ocean, the smallest of land masses, a geographical image of isolation, perilous to ships.

The archipelago is a subtle image for the opening/closing of the novel. It conjures up the idea of discrete fragments that may still be connected according to some criterion.

What separates and joins the end and the beginning is a stretch of estuary/sea. Moving from the shore to the bay and back to Howth Castle is a movement similar to possible moves between the units of an archipelago. Joyce takes this image further by his reference to the archipelago on the other side of the world: it creates a global vision where the world itself is one large archipelago of solitary disparate units that have to struggle to be a unity. If *Finnegans Wake* is like this, it serves as an analogy of the self and society—conceptual units whose make-up may consist of separate contradictory parts. Readers sail between these discrete parts, either linking them up or questioning their mutual isolation. The archipelago is also part of the "geographical" structure of the *Wake* that gives spatial dimensions to temporality (so we could move backward and forward through it). The sphere has no beginning or end.

The Phoenix

The phoenix is a more obvious image for a climax and echo: it is introduced in a passage smoothing the way between Kevin and the color debate: appearing now it seems like the fulfillment of the proleptic image of the Phoenix that had appeared in chapter 1. It finally wakes in a stunning passage that blurs the Phoenix with Finnegan and with a Phoenician (like T. S. Eliot's sailor) and even a *funny can*—the lamp out of which a genii, like a flame, rises. "In the wake of the blackshape, *Nattenden Sorte;* whenat, hindled firth and hundled furth, the week of wakes is out and over; as a wick weak woking from ennemberable Ashias unto fierce force fuming, temtem tamtam, the Phoenican wakes" (FW: 608.28–32).

If we link this waking "Phoenican" with the forecast "fiery bird" and the "Felix Day" of the Overture we find a narrative that links the hopes in the beginning with a resurrection at the end. Of course, it's not a fulfillment of *exactly* that prediction—it's something slightly different from what is expected. But it is a reference to the underlying image of the phoenix that points to both resurrection and the eternal. The archive, where we can see the specific network being worked on, emphasizes this link. The dense, complex distance of the novel separates these two ends, the prediction and the awakening (like the five hundred years of a Phoenix's life), signaling a journey between one end and the other. But the five hundred years mark the transition of life to death: the speedy transition of death to life is marked in the journey backward through the end to the beginning.

Cyclical Processes

The linking passages between Kevin and the color debate included a dialogue between *Juva* and *Muta,* an echo of Mutt and Jute from chapter 1. In chapter 1 Mutt tells Jute about the history of now-dead peoples, their migrations, their mortality: "Mearmerge two races, swete and brack. [. . .] Hither, craching eastuards, they are in surgence: hence, cool at ebb, they requiesce. Countlessness of livestories have netherfallen by this plage, flick as flowflakes [. . .] Now are all tombed" (FW: 017.24–29). In Book IV Juva helps Muta understand a lesson about historical cycles. It is a late addition to Book IV at the sixth level and corresponds with a late addition to chapter 1 that appears just after the Mutt and Jute dialogue.

Overture (by May 1938)	Epilogue (by November 1938)
In the ignorance that implies impression that knits knowledge that finds the nameform that whets the wits that convey contacts that sweeten sensation that drives desire that adheres to attachment that does death that bitches birth that entails the ensuance of existentiality. (BL 47476a f. 143v; JJA 49: 310; FW: 018.24–28)	*Muta:* So that when we shall have acquired unification we shall pass on to diversity and when we shall have passed on to diversity we shall have acquired the instinct of combat and when we shall have acquired the instinct of combat we shall pass back to the spirit of appeasement? *Juva:* By the light of the bright reason which daysends to us from the high. (BL 47488 f. 211v; JJA 63: 306; FW: 610.23–29)

In both the language is lucid; the sense, though complex, is not compromised by a vast range of allusions or the usual interference of *Wakese.* They share senses of circular processes, on the one hand, of the Buddhistic twelvefold chain of dependent origination and, on the other, of Vichian/Hegelian cycles of history. The former chain is authorized by the night (begins and ends in dark ignorance), the latter by the day ("by the light of reason"). The first happens just after Mutt and Jute stop speaking, the latter just before they stop. They both appear as questionably succinct distillations of the way sequences in *Finnegans Wake* operate.

"Leafy speafing"

Joyce is thought to have begun Leafy's monologue in mid- or late 1938, once the structure of Book IV was well in place. It went through nine levels, the first draft—two pages—sounding like a nurse addressing an invalid—"You know where I am bringing you? You remember? [. . .] How well you'll feel"—or a lonely old woman addressing an imaginary companion—"You will always call me Leafy, won't you? Queer grand old Finn, if I knew who you are!" In either case it's an *address* that, like the end of chapter 1, attempts to *reassure* the addressee. On the other hand, the Epilogue wants to raise up the addressee, while the Overture wants to lull him back to rest. "It's Phoenix, dear," a holiday, at last, the day of rebirth from the flames, fulfilling the prophecies of the phoenix in chapter 1.

While material for Leafy's monologue echo with many parts of the book, I wish here to point out correspondences to revisions specifically to the end of chapter 1. The passages thus call across nearly the considerable length of the whole book, or of just the first chapter.

On the second set of galleys Joyce wrote one longish revision. Being handwritten postdates it from the rest of the revisions to these galleys. Here is the bulk of it: "If only you were there to explain the meaning, best of men, and talk to her nice of goldensilver [. . .] her lips would moisten again. As when you drove with her to Findrinny Fair. What with reins here and ribbons there all your hands were employed so she never knew was she on land or at sea or swooped through the blue like Airwinger's bride" (BL 47476a f. 151; JJA 49: 323; FW: 028.10–15). This is, in effect, a first sketch of the book's close. Phrases and ideas from this worked their way directly into Leafy's monologue as Joyce reread/recalled his own work at analogous moments of closure.

In the phrase "To explain the meaning" Joyce, with mock self-conceit, playfully predicts readers' mourning his absence and preventing meaning being authorized (something he patently never did anyway). This is inverted in Book IV, where ALP asks, "Is there one who understands me?" If we are to identify Joyce apropos his difficult text here, he moves from being the addressee—"If only you were there"—to being the subject—"Is there one who understands me?" (FW: 627.15). Of course, this is a common enough shift in the *Wake,* which seems to address itself and its reader interchangeably, but the two contrary audiences—self and other—are getting mixed and joined as an analogy to the mixing of the opposing end and beginning.

The narrator/mourner of the Overture thinks ALP was charmed by HCE's flattery "talk to her nice." But at the end Leafy replies, as it were, to these comments and has seen through them. She dismisses all his talk of "gold and silver" as "exaggeration." There is plenty of depreciation of HCE in Leafy's monologue, an inversion of the adulation that Mr Finnimore receives in the Overture: "I thought you all glittering with the noblest of carriage. You're only a bumpkin" (FW: 627.21–23). This carriage echoes the drive to "Findrinny Fair," setting up the possibility that it's the same carriage, though we are not supposed to know for sure. A similar suggestion and doubt come with the line "Carry me along, taddy, like you done in the toy fair" (FW: 628.08–09) in its link to Findrinny Fair. Both recollections share the fact of being taken to a fair. The remembered confusion of the child's excitement—when "she never knew was she on land or at sea or swooped through the blue like Airwinger's bride"—generates rhythms that will recur in the monologue and also prefigures the confusion of the end—"Or is it me is? I'm getting mixed" (FW: 626.36)—and the elemental features of land, sea, and air at the end.

Joyce picks up phrases in the mourner's address from before the second galleys too. Not surprisingly, one such phrase is the proleptic sentence "serial story, *Les Loves of Selskar et Pervenche,* freely adapted. There'll be bluebells blowing in salty sepulchres the night she signs her final tear. Zee End. But that's" (BL 47478a f. 16; JJA 49: 31, simplified). Leafy voices a strong echo of this: "But I read in Tobecontinued's tale that while blubles blows there'll still be sealskers" (FW: 626.18–19). The echoes, in reverse order, mirror each other: ALP reproduces the earlier sentences in a morphed and backward form (1-2-3-4-5: 5-4-3-2-1). "Selskar" has become "Sealskers," "there'll be" has become "there'll still be," "bluebells blowing" have become "blubles blows," and "Zee End" has become "Tobecontinued." Finally, "But" ends one passage and begins the other. "Tobecontinued" is a continuous word in a novel that, since it is endless, is always *to be continued,* forming its own perpetual serial story. The book ALP reads is a romantic love story, so the Overture contains its romantic vision of death, when the sea floods the flowers. The Epilogue contains a romantic vision of love: as long as bubbles are blowing there'll be "lovers" (Danish *elskere*, "lovers"). Bluebells, bugles, but also the 1919 music hall song "I'm Forever Blowing Bubbles," forever because they are evoked at both beginning and end. The earlier sentence predicts the bluebells/bubbles blowing. This prediction is not fulfilled but has become the condition of another situation: the existence of "lovers."

The Overture and Epilogue look forward to and back over each other. They contain both prolepses and analepses of each other. Moving from page 628 to page 3, with ALP just faded out, allows us to perceive that it is "A way [. . .] a long the" "riverrun" that "brings us [. . .] back to Howth Castle." Narratologically speaking, she moves along in the same "duration" as the narrator on FW: 003. Within this duration, technically, her words precede those of the voice (a tourist guide/historian) that begins the Overture. She is past, dead and gone. But the voice that rounds off the Overture describes her as alive ("I seen your missus in the hall [. . .] it's herself is fine too"), and it predicts a "Felix Day" that seems to have arrived in Leafy's monologue as "Phoenix day." So she is still to come. Either a slip back to the time before her monologue has occurred or we assume, as readers have always done, that *Finnegans Wake* undoes such sequential linearity and asks us to hold in mind temporally separated events (like those of two generations) as happening simultaneously: in parallel rather than in sequence. In which case the narratological analysis is undone. Nonetheless, there is another sequential and linear narrative that can be apprehended, and that is the narrative of writing. Over a single day Joyce might of course have written in several different parts of his text, jumping grasshopper-like over his small dense and complicated world, but still Joyce was only ever writing one thing at a time: in sequence rather than in parallel. What *The James Joyce Archive* allows us to do is retell the story, the stories, the ways along the stream of writing. But that's a world of ways . . .

Coda: SOS

To return. So, small and subtle revisions to chapter 1 have responses in Leafy's monologue. It happens the other way round too, especially in one last striking instance. Lernout mentioned the phrase from the very first line of *Finnegans Wake:* "from swerve of shore to bend of bay" (FW: 003.01) was added on the page proofs. In a sense it had appeared before, since it echoes lines in Leafy's monologue, where she has been coaxing her man to walk and then rest by the sea: "Ourselves alone at the site of salvocean. And watch would the letter you're wanting be coming maybe. [. . .] After rounding his world of ancient days. Carried in a caddy or screwed and corked. On his mugisstosst surface. Blob. With a bob, bob, bottledby bob" (BL 47488 f. 127; JJA 63: 211; FW: 623.34–624.02).

By the sea they will watch for a letter, sent, perhaps, in a bottle "screwed and corked," *plop,* bobbing on the surface. In the first typescript of this passage "Blob" is shifted to the end, so it reads "bottled by bob. Blob." A blob, some stain of ink or other, blots out the name, or is it a fat person, a "blob"? (HCE and Shaun both being "stout.") What's in the message, should it ever arrive? The "sight of Salvocean" gives us a clue: an SOS, a plea for salvation, a final flourish (or "salvo") that is brought back by the water's currents onto the shores of Howth, where the beginning asks us, initially, to read the message contained. For the initials spelled out in this minute last-minute addition help us to read that message: "from swerve of shore [SOS] to bend of bay [BOB]." From the writing to the casting of it onto the waters, from the seventeen years of its conceptualization to its publication, set adrift in the outside world.

As a late image it is tempting to view this as Joyce's description of what his book had become for him—a message sent from a position of isolation to anybody who might happen to come across it, with a strong likelihood that it may never even arrive, and a plea to be rescued from the isolation of death. This melodrama may seem like a pose (the reception of *Finnegans Wake* would be a disappointment for Joyce), but the image of it even potentially sinking without trace is excessive. On the other hand, have we got the message? Will we ever? How much language is obscured by the blobs of Joyce's inky revisions? Every word is a bottled message. How many of them have arrived and been understood? If we are to continue picking out and understanding the stories and the meanings of the *Wake,* one of the best ways is to take the container—the bottle or magic lamp—of *The James Joyce Archive* and, attending to it, watch the genii grow.

Notes

1. However, the spelling points more precisely to the name given to the viceregal lodge in Phoenix Park when Tim Healy, first governor-general of the Irish Free State, moved in: a substitute, now that the British have gone.

2. What he has fused may well be the early Irish sketches of "Kevin" and "Berkeley"—but the timing here is difficult. This minidialogue comes from early 1938, while the "Kevin" and "Berkeley" passages are thought to have been rediscovered in July 1938. But an addition to the first set of galleys may witness the rediscovery or uncovering or retrieval of "Kevin." To chapter I.2 Joyce adds "Saint Kevin's bed in the" to a description of "Hosspittles" (BL 47476a f. 27; JJA 49: 51; FW: 040.36). Kevin is put into Book I, as Joyce plans to place Kevin as a climax in Book IV. The hosspittle of Book I looks like his destiny.

3. One chapter is an exception: II.3—it shares the fact of *two* set pieces and an address to HCE toward the end (FW: 373.13–380.05). Butt and Taff also feature in the form of a dramatic dialogue. Setting off from the midpoint of the book, it is of course implicated in another symmetrical structure.

APPENDIXES

CONTRIBUTORS

INDEX

Appendix 1

Draft Sections and Subsections

This table lists all the sections and subsections of *Finnegans Wake.* The logic of these divisions follows from the composition of the *Wake.* Instances where this list departs from Danis Rose's organization in *The James Joyce Archive* are noted. This table only gives the earliest draft date for each section.

Chapter, Section, Subsection	*Finnegans Wake* pages	Name	Earliest Draft Date
I.1§1	003.01–018.16		10/1926
§1.A	003.01–010.23		
§1.B	010.24–013.29		
§1.C	013.30–014.27		
§1.D	014.28–015.28		
§1.E	015.29–018.16	"Mutt and Jute"	
I.1§2	018.17–029		11/1926
§2.A	018.17–021.04		
§2.B	021.05–029		
I.2§1	030.01–034.29	"Here Comes Everybody"	8–9/1923
I.2§2	034.30–044.21		10/1923
I.2§3	044.22–047	"Ballad of Persse O'Reilly"	10–11/1923
I.3§1	048.01–061.27		11/1923
I.3§2	061.28–074		11/1923
I.3§3	067.28–074		11/1923
I.4§1	075.01–096.25		11/1923
§1.A	075.10–092.05		
§1.B	092.06–096.25		
I.4§2	096.26–103		11–12/1923

Chapter, Section, Subsection	*Finnegans Wake* pages	Name	Earliest Draft Date
I.5§1	104.01–113.22		12/1923
I.5§2[1]		"The Revered Letter"	12/1923
I.5§3[2]		"The Delivery of the Letter"	12/1923–1/1924
I.5§4	113.23–125		12/1923–1/1924
I.6§1	126.01–150.14		Summer 1927
§1.A	126.01–149.10		
§1.B	149.11–150.14		
I.6§2	150.15–152.03		6–8/1927
I.6§3	152.04–159.23	"The Mookse and the Gripes"	7–8/1927
I.6§4	159.24–168		8/1927
I.7§1	169.01–187.23		1/1924
I.7§2	187.24–195		2/1924
I.8§1	196.01–216	"Anna Livia Plurabelle"	/1924
§1.A	196.01–208.26		
§1.B	208.27–216		
II.1§1	219.01–222.21		Mid-1932
II.1§2	222.22–236.32		10–11/1930
II.1§3	236.33–240.04		12/1930
II.1§4	240.05–244.12		1/1931
II.1§5	244.13–246.36		1/1931
II.1§6	246.36–257.02		Early 1932
§6.A[3]	246.36–248.12, 252.14–32		
§6.B	248.11–249.05		
§6.C	252.33–253.36, 255.12–256.10		
§6.D	249.06–252.13		
§6.E	254.01–255.11		
§6.F	256.11–257.02		
II.1§7	257.03–259		Mid-1932
II.2§1	260–263		1934
II.2§2	264–266.19		1934
II.2§3	266.20–275.02		1934
§3.A	266.20–274.13		
§3.B	274.13–274.27		
§3.C	274.27–275.02		
II.2§5[4]	275.03–279.09	"Scribbledehobbles"	1932
II.2§6	279 (footnote)		1934
II.2§7	280.01–282.04		1934

Chapter, Section, Subsection	*Finnegans Wake* pages	Name	Earliest Draft Date
II.2§8	282.05–304.04	"The Triangle"	7/1926
§8.A	282.05–288.13		
§8.B	288.13–292.32		
§8.C	293.01–304.04		
II.2§9	304.05–308		1934
II.3§1	309.01–331.36	"The Norwegian Captain"	Early 1935
§1.A	309.01–309.10		
§1.B	309.11–310.21		
§1.C	310.22–331.36		
II.3§2	332.01–337.03		1936
II.3§3	337.04–338.08		12/1936
II.3§4	338.04–354.06	"Butt and Taff"	1936–37
II.3§5	354.07–355.07	"Butt and Taff"	Early 1938
II.3§6	355.08–370.29	"Butt and Taff"	1936–37
§6.A	355.08–355.13		
§6.B	355.14–370.29		
II.3§7	370.30–382		
§7.A	370.30–380.06		1938
§7.B[5]	380.07–382	"Roderick O'Conor"	3/1923
II.4§1[6]		"Tristan and Isolde"	/1923
II.4§2	383.01–398.30	"Mamalujo"	3–10/1923
II.4§3	398.31–399.34		11/1923
§3.A	398.29–398.30		
§3.B	398.31–399.34		
III.1	403.01–428		
§A	403.01–414.13		3/1924
§B	414.14–414.21		2/1928
§C	414.22–419.10	"The Ondt and the Gracehoper"	2/1928
§D	419.11–428		3/1924
III.2	429.01–473		
§A	429.01–461.32		3/1924
§B	461.33–468.19	"Dave the Dancekerl"	11/1925
§C	468.20–463		3/1924
III.3	474.01–532.05		
§A	474.01–532.05		11–12/1924
§B	532.06–554	"Haveth Childers Everywhere"	11–12/1924
III.4	555.01–590		10/1925
§A	555.01–556.22		

Chapter, Section, Subsection	*Finnegans Wake* pages	Name	Earliest Draft Date
§B	556.23–556.30		
§C	556.31–557.12		
§D	557.13–558.20		
§E	558.21–558.31		
§F	558.32–565.16		
§G	565.17–566.06		
§H	566.07–571.34		
§J[7]	571.27–571.34		
§K	571.35–572.06		
§L	572.07–576.09		
§M	576.10–577.35		
§N	577.36–578.02		
§P[8]	578.03–585.21		
§Q	585.22–587.02		
§R	587.03–588.34		
§S	588.35–589.11		
§T	589.12–590		
IV[9]	593.01–628		
§1	593.01–604.26		1937
§2	604.27–607.22	"St Kevin"	Summer 1923
§3	607.23–614,18	"St Patrick and the Druid"	7/1923
§4	614.19–619.19	"The Revered Letter"	12/1923
§5	619.20–628	"Soft Morning City"	1938

Notes

1. In January 1924 Joyce removed I.5§2, "The Revered Letter," from Book I and set it aside until 1938, when he incorporated it into Book IV. See the introduction as well as the essays by Mikio Fuse and Dirk Van Hulle in this volume.

2. Also in January 1924 Joyce used I.5§3, "The Delivery of the Letter," as the foundation of what became Book III. See the introduction and Wim Van Mierlo's essay in this volume.

3. The subsections here do not correspond to Rose's arrangement in the JJA. See Sam Slote's essay in this volume.

4. Joyce wrote the fragmentary first drafts of II.2§4, "Scribbledehobbles," in 1932. Then, after two fair copies and three typescripts, he abandoned the piece as such in 1934. He cannibalized the same third typescript II.2§4.5' to create a new piece, also known as "Scribbledehobbles." See Luca Crispi's essay in this volume.

5. Danis Rose does not designate the "Roderick O'Conor" sketch as a distinct subsection.

6. Joyce did not use II.4§1, "Tristan and Isolde," as such in *Finnegans Wake*. Rather, he merged this section into the revision of the next section in a complex fashion. See Jed Deppman's essay in this volume.

7. There is no section III.4§I.

8. There is no section III.4§O.

9. Because Book IV consists of only one chapter, units in it are considered subunits.

Appendix 2

Publication History of Work in Progress/Finnegans Wake

This list is not meant to be comprehensive but rather indicates the most significant and interesting installments of *Work in Progress* during its various serial incarnations from 1924 to 1938 as well as the most important variations of the text of *Finnegans Wake* since its first publication in 1939.

"From Work in Progress," *transatlantic review* 1.4 (April 1924): 215–23. ["Mamalujo," II.4§2 (FW: 383.01–398.30).]

"From Work in Progress," *Contact Collection of Contemporary Writers,* ed. Robert McAlmon (Paris: Contact Editions, 1925), 133–36. ["Here Comes Everybody," I.2§1 (FW: 030.01–034.29).]

"Fragment of an Unpublished Work," *Criterion* 3.12 (July 1925): 498–510. [I.5 (FW: 104–125).]

"A New Unnamed Work," *Two Worlds* 1.1 (September 1925): 45–54. [I.5 (FW: 104–125), reprinted from *Criterion* 3.12.][1]

"From Work in Progress," *Le Navire d'Argent* 1 (October 1925): 59–74. [I.8 (FW: 196–216).]

"Extract from Work in Progress," *This Quarter* 1.2 (Autumn–Winter 1925): 108–23. [I.7 (FW: 169–195).]

"A New Unnamed Work," *Two Worlds* 1.2 (December 1925): 111–14. [I.2§1 (FW: 030.01–034.29), reprinted from *Contact Collection.*]

"A New Unnamed Work," *Two Worlds* 1.3 (March 1926): 347–60. [I.8 (FW: 196–216), reprinted from *Le Navire d'Argent* 1.]

"A New Unnamed Work," *Two Worlds* 1.4 (June 1926): 545–60. [I.7 (FW: 169–195), reprinted from *This Quarter* 1.2.]

"A New Unnamed Work," *Two Worlds* 2.5 (September 1925): 35–40. [II.4§2 (FW: 383.01–398.30), reprinted from *transatlantic review* 1.4.]

"Opening Pages of a Work in Progress," *transition* 1 (April 1927): 9–30. [I.1 (FW: 003–029).]

"Continuation of a Work in Progress," *transition* 2 (May 1927): 94–107 [I.2 (FW: 030–047).]

"Continuation of a Work in Progress," *transition* 3 (June 1927): 32–50. [I.3 (FW: 048–074).]

"Continuation of a Work in Progress," *transition* 4 (July 1927): 46–65. [I.4 (FW: 075–103).]

"Continuation of a Work in Progress," *transition* 5 (August 1927): 15–31. [I.5 (FW: 104–125).]

"Continuation of a Work in Progress," *transition* 6 (September 1927): 87–106f.[2] [I.6 (FW: 126–168).]

"Continuation of a Work in Progress," *transition* 7 (October 1927): 34–56. [I.7 (FW: 169–195).]

"Continuation of a Work in Progress," *transition* 8 (November 1927): 17–35. [I.8 (FW: 196–216).]

Work in Progress Volume I (New York: Donald Friede, 1927). [I.1–8 (FW: 003–216), reprinted from *transition* 1–8.][3]

"Continuation of a Work in Progress," *transition* 11 (February 1928): 7–18. ["The Triangle," II.2§8 (FW: 282.05–304.04).]

"Continuation of a Work in Progress," *transition* 12 (March 1928): 7–27. [III.1 (FW: 403–428).]

Work in Progress Parts 11 and 12 (July 1928). ["The Triangle," II.2§8 (FW: 282.05–304.04) and III.1 (FW: 403–428), reprinted from *transition* 11–12.][4]

"Continuation of a Work in Progress," *transition* 13 (Summer 1928): 5–32. [III.2 (FW: 429–473).]

Work in Progress Part 13 (August 1928). [III.2 (FW: 429–473), reprinted from *transition* 13.]

Anna Livia Plurabelle (New York: Crosby Gaige, 1928). [I.8 (FW: 196–216).]

"Continuation of a Work in Progress," *transition* 15 (February 1929): 195–238. [III.3 (FW: 474–554).]

Work in Progress Part 15 (February 1929). [III.3 (FW: 474–554), reprinted from *transition* 15.]

Tales Told of Shem and Shaun (Paris: Black Sun Press, 1929). ["The Mookse and the Gripes," I.6§3 (FW: 152.04–159.23); "The Triangle," II.2§8 (FW: 282.05–304.04); and "The Ondt and the Gracehoper," III.1§C (FW: 414.22–419.10).]

"A Muster from *Work in Progress,*" *transition stories,* ed. Eugene Jolas and Robert Sage (New York: Walter V. McKee, 1929), 177–91. [Brief excerpts from I.1, I.3–4, and III.1–2 (FW: 023.16–26, 030.01–034.29, 065.05–24, 074.13–19, 076.33–078.06, 413.03–26, and 454.26–455.29), reprinted from *transition* 1, 3–4, and 12–13.]

"Continuation of a Work in Progress," *transition* 18 (November 1929): 211–36. [III.4 (FW: 555–590).]

Work in Progress Part 18 (January 1930). [III.4 (FW: 555–590), reprinted from *transition* 18.]

Haveth Childers Everywhere (Paris: Fountain Press, 1930). [III.3§B (FW: 532.06–554).]

Anna Livia Plurabelle (London: Faber and Faber, 1930). [I.8 (FW: 196–216).]

"Three Fragments from Work in Progress," *Imagist Anthology 1930,* ed. Richard Aldington (London: Chatto and Windus, 1930), 121–22, and (New York: Covici, Friede, 1930), 177–79. [Excerpts from "The Ondt and the Gracehoper," III.1§C (FW: 417.24–419.10), reprinted from *Tales Told of Shem and Shaun.*]

Haveth Childers Everywhere (London: Faber and Faber, 1931). [III.3§B (FW: 532.06–554).]

Two Tales of Shem and Shaun (London: Faber and Faber, 1932). ["The Mookse and the Gripes," I.6§3 (FW: 152.04–159.23), and "The Ondt and the Gracehoper," III.1§C (FW: 414.22–419.10).]

"Continuation of a Work in Progress," *transition* 22 (February 1933): 49–76. [II.1 (FW: 219–259).]

"The Mime of Mick, Nick and the Maggies," *Les Amis de 1914* 2.40 (23 February 1934): 1. [Excerpt from II.1 (FW: 258.25–259.10), reprinted from *transition* 22.]

The Mime of Mick, Nick and the Maggies (The Hague: Servire Press, 1934). [II.1 (FW: 219–259).]

"Work in Progress," *transition* 23 (July 1935): 109–29. [II.1§§1–3 and §9 (FW: 260.01–275.02 and 304.05–308).]

"Work in Progress," *transition* 26 (February 1937): 35–52. ["The Norwegian Captain," II.3§1 (FW: 309.01–331.36).]

Storiella as She Is Syung (London: Corvinus Press, 1937). [II.2§§1–3 and §9 (FW: 260.01–275.02 and 304.05–308).]

"A Phoenix Park Nocturne," *Verve* 1.2 (March–June 1938). [Excerpt from II.1 (FW: 244.13–246.02), reprinted from *The Mime of Mick, Nick and the Maggies.*]

"Fragment from Work in Progress," *transition* 27 (April–May 1938): 59–78. ["Butt and Taff," II.3§§4–5 (FW: 338.04–355.07).]

Finnegans Wake (London: Faber and Faber, 1939; New York: Viking Press, 1939).

"Corrections of Misprints in *Finnegans Wake*" (London: Faber and Faber, 1945; New York: Viking Press, 1945).[5]

Finnegans Wake (London: Faber and Faber, 1946). [Errata list included as an appendix.][6]

Finnegans Wake (New York: Viking Press, 1947). [Errata list included as an appendix.]

Finnegans Wake (London: Faber and Faber, 1950). [Corrections from the errata list incorporated into the text with a shortened errata list included as an appendix.]

Finnegans Wake (New York: Viking Press, 1957). [Corrections from the errata list incorporated into the text.]

Finnegans Wake (London: Faber and Faber, 1964). [Correction of errors inherited from the "Corrections of Misprints."]

Finnegans Wake (London: Faber and Faber, 1975). [Correction of the alignment of margin notes in II.2.][7]

Notes

1. The five installments of *Work in Progress* published in *Two Worlds* were not directly authorized by Joyce and are corrupt reprints of earlier publications. Joyce did briefly consider publishing portions of Book III in *Two Worlds* (LI: 240; LIII: 139; see also Adelaide Kugel, "'Wroth Wrackt Joyce': Samuel Roth and the 'Not Quite Unauthorized' Edition of *Ulysses*," *JSA* 3 [1992]: 242–48).

2. The unusual pagination was the result of the late inclusion of the fable "The Mookse and the Gripes"; see the introduction.

3. The title page states 1927, whereas the copyright page states 1928. This was published on 9 January 1928. Only twenty copies were printed, solely for the purpose of establishing copyright in the United States. The text was reset, and chapter divisions are not indicated.

4. No publication information is supplied. Only five copies were printed, solely for copyright purposes. The text is directly reprinted from *transition.* Three further installments, again of five copies each, were later published for the same reason. Donald Friede, who published *Work in Progress Volume I* (also for establishing copyright), denies having published these later installments (see John J. Slocum and Herbert Cahoon, *A Bibliography of James Joyce* [New Haven: Yale University Press, 1953], 43–44).

5. Printed separately as a pamphlet for purchasers of the first edition. The

incorporation of the corrections into subsequent printings was handled differently by Faber and Faber and by Viking.

6. The text of II.2 was reset in this edition, resulting in errors of alignment between the marginal notes and the main text. See the following note.

7. The original "Corrections of Misprints" was made from a typescript prepared from the unbound copy in which Joyce and Paul Léon recorded corrections to the text (the unbound copy is Buffalo VI.J.4.a, and the typescript is VI.J.4.b). This typescript contains several errors that were then transferred to the text in subsequent printings. The 1964 Faber and Faber edition redresses these corruptions and attempts to correct the misalignment of the marginal notes in II.2 that was caused in the 1946 reset text; however, the alignment was not perfectly restored. The alignment of these notes was again corrected in the 1975 Faber and Faber edition, which thus represents the most accurate instantiation of the text of *Finnegans Wake.* See Finn Fordham, "The Corrections to *Finnegans Wake*," *James Joyce: The Study of Languages,* ed. Dirk Van Hulle (Brussels: Peter Lang, 2002), 37–52.

Contributors

BILL CADBURY is professor emeritus of English at the University of Oregon. Publication of his book with Nathan Tenny, *The March of a Maker: A Genetic Representation of "Finnegans Wake" Chapters 2–4*, has been prevented by the Estate of James Joyce.

LUCA CRISPI is lecturer in Joyce and modernism at the Research Centre for James Joyce Studies, School of English and Drama, University College Dublin.

JED DEPPMAN teaches English at Oberlin College. He has published articles on nineteenth- and twentieth-century literature in *European Joyce Studies,* the *Emily Dickinson Journal, Style, Qui Parle, Symploké,* and other journals. He recently co-edited and co-translated *Genetic Criticism: Texts and Avant-textes* (2004).

DANIEL FERRER is director of research at the Institut des textes et manuscrits modernes (ITEM-CNRS) in Paris. He has published books on Joyce, Virginia Woolf, literary theory, and genetic criticism. He is editor of the journal *Genesis.* With Vincent Deane and Geert Lernout he is currently editing the *Finnegans Wake* notebooks.

FINN FORDHAM is a lecturer in twentieth century literature at the University of Nottingham. His book about *Finnegans Wake* will come out in 2007. He has published widely in journals and collections chiefly on Joyce but also on contemporary American fiction and poetry in English.

MIKIO FUSE is associate professor in Irish literature at University of the Sacred Heart, Tokyo.

MICHAEL GRODEN is professor of English at the University of Western Ontario. He is the author of *"Ulysses" in Progress* (1977), general editor of *The James Joyce Archive* (1977–79), compiler of *James Joyce's Manuscripts: An Index* (1980), co-editor of *The Johns Hopkins Guide to Literary Theory and Criticism* (1994, second edition, 2005), and co-editor and co-translator of *Genetic Criticism: Texts and Avant-textes* (2004).

DAVID HAYMAN, emeritus professor of comparative literature at the University of Wisconsin, began writing genetic criticism of *Finnegans Wake* in 1958. He has since published, along with *A First-Draft Version of "Finnegans Wake,"* numerous essays and *The "Wake" in Transit.* (Parallel Press at the University of Wisconsin Libraries has reprinted his *First-Draft Version.*) He was coeditor of the *Finnegans Wake* volumes of *The James Joyce Archive.* He is currently working on a book analyzing the draft development of Samuel Beckett's transitional novel *Watt.* Also in progress is a *Samuel Beckett Manuscript Archive.*

INGEBORG LANDUYT wrote her PhD dissertation, "'Words in Distress': A Genetic Investigation into James Joyce's Early Work in Progress," on Joyce's early notebooks. She has published on Joyce and the *Finnegans Wake* notebooks in *European Joyce Studies,* the *Joyce Studies Annual, Papers on Joyce,* and *Genetic Joyce Studies.* She currently teaches at Hogeschool Antwerpen.

GEERT LERNOUT teaches comparative literature at the University of Antwerp. He has published books on James Joyce, Friedrich Hölderlin, and Johann Sebastian Bach. With Vincent Deane and Daniel Ferrer he is currently editing the *Finnegans Wake* notebooks.

PATRICK A. MCCARTHY, professor and chair of the English department at the University of Miami, is the author or editor of ten books, including *The Riddles of "Finnegans Wake," "Ulysses": Portals of Discovery, Critical Essays on James Joyce's "Finnegans Wake," and Joyce/Lowry: Critical Perspectives,* as well as volumes on Samuel Beckett, Malcolm Lowry, and Olaf Stapledon. He contributed a pamphlet, *Joyce, Family, "Finnegans Wake,"* to the National Library of Ireland's Joyce Studies 2004 series.

JEAN-MICHEL RABATÉ, professor of English and comparative literature at the University of Pennsylvania, has authored or edited twenty books on modernism, psychoanalysis, and literary theory. Recent titles include *James Joyce and the Politics of Egoism* (2001), *The Future of Theory* (2002), *The Cambridge Companion to Lacan* (2003), *Palgrave Advances in James Joyce Studies* (2004), *Tout Dire ou Ne Rien dire: Logique du mensonge* (2005), and *Given: 1° Art, 2° Crime. Modernity, Murder and Mass Culture* (2006).

R. J. SCHORK is a professor emeritus of classics at the University of Massachusetts–Boston, with a special research interest in Roman Egypt. His primary Joycean publications (most with a genetic slant) involve ancient languages and culture and Christian saints. Several times a year he lectures on cruises in the Mediterranean and from Singapore to Mumbai to Alexandria and Istanbul.

SAM SLOTE is Lecturer in James Joyce Studies and Critical Theory at Trinity College, Dublin, and is the author of *The Silence in Progress of Dante, Mallarmé, and Joyce* (1999) and has co-edited *Probes: Genetic Studies on Joyce* (with David Hayman, 1995) and *Genitricksling Joyce* (with Wim Van Mierlo, 1999). He has written on Joyce, Beckett, Woolf, Queneau, modernism, literary theory, and genetic criticism. He is presently editing a volume of essays on Joyce and Derrida.

DIRK VAN HULLE teaches English literature at the University of Antwerp. He is editor of the online journal *Genetic Joyce Studies* and author of *Textual Awareness, a Genetic Study of Late Manuscripts by James Joyce, Marcel Proust, and Thomas Mann* (University of Michigan Press, 2004). He works at the Antwerp James Joyce Centre and recently edited the collection of essays *Beckett the European* (Journal of Beckett Studies, 2005).

WIM VAN MIERLO (Institute of English Studies, University of London) has co-edited *Genitricksling Joyce* (with Sam Slote, 1999), *The Reception of James Joyce in Europe* (with Geert Lernout, 2004), and *Reading Notes* (with Dirk Van Hulle, 2004). His work on modern manuscripts, textual scholarship, and marginalia has appeared in *Joyce Studies Annual, Yeats Annual, Variants,* and various essay collections.

Index

Irish Studies in Literature and Culture

Joyce's Critics: Transitions in Reading and Culture
Joseph Brooker

Wild Colonial Girl: Essays on Edna O'Brien
Edited by Lisa Colletta and Maureen O'Connor

Locked in the Family Cell: Gender, Sexuality, and Political Agency in Irish National Discourse
Kathryn A. Conrad

How Joyce Wrote Finnegans Wake: *A Chapter-by-chapter Genetic Guide*
Edited by Luca Crispi and Sam Slote

Riot and Great Anger: Stage Censorship in Twentieth-Century Ireland
Joan FitzPatrick Dean

The Wee Wild One: Stories of Belfast and Beyond
Ruth Schwertfeger

www.ingramcontent.com/pod-product-compliance
Lightning Source LLC
Chambersburg PA
CBHW031700230426
43668CB00006B/56
9780299218645